About This Book

This book starts where you are likely to start—at the beginning. Its design ensures that you learn concepts as you need them, as you start your exploration of Windows NT Server 4.0.

By following the book, with its orientation and examples, you will learn simple tasks that build on each other until you have mastered the basics of Windows NT Server. If you faithfully follow the book, you can administer a simple Windows NT Server and network.

Anyone with a working knowledge of DOS or Windows can learn how to back up servers, add and delete users, create logon scripts, and maintain security.

Who Should Read This Book

Anyone interested in learning to use Windows NT Server 4.0 will find something of value in this book. The thrust of the book is, however, toward those people who will administer a Windows NT Server network and must grasp the key tasks.

For both, this book covers NT Server from the basics to tasks and ideas that we know you will find interesting and useful as you progress beyond the basics.

This book is for you if one or more of the following statements applies to you:

- ☐ You are interested in becoming a Microsoft Certified Professional.
- ☐ You just found out that you'll take over administration of an existing Windows NT Server LAN.
- ☐ You were told that your organization will install Windows NT next month.
- ☐ You applied for a job at an organization that uses Windows NT LANs exclusively, and you want to get the job.
- ☐ You just want to learn about a widely used network operating system.

Teach
Yourself
WINDOWS NT®
SERVER 4
in 14 Days

Teach Yourself
WINDOWS NT ®
SERVER 4
in 14 Days

Peter T. Davis
Barry D. Lewis

SAMS
PUBLISHING

201 West 103rd Street
Indianapolis, Indiana 46290

For Clement Beecher King and Janet Marie Davis. One for helping make me what I am today, and the other for helping make me what I'll be tomorrow.

—Peter T. Davis

For my wife, Elizabeth, and my son, Derek Lewis. And to all those who encouraged and supported me during the last few months.

—Barry D. Lewis

Copyright © 1997 by Sams Publishing

Trademarks

Publisher and President   Richard K. Swadley
Publishing Manager   Dean Miller
Director of Editorial Services   Cindy Morrow
Assistant Marketing Managers   Kristina Perry, Rachel Wolfe

Acquisitions Editor
Cari Skaggs

Development Editor
Brian-Kent Proffitt

Production Editor
Cheri Clark

Copy Editors
Chuck Hutchinson
Kris Simmons

Indexer
Ben Slen

Technical Reviewer
Matt Butler

Editorial Coordinator
Katie Wise

Technical Edit Coordinator
Lynette Quinn

Resource Coordinator
Deborah Frisby

Editorial Assistants
Carol Ackerman
Andi Richter
Rhonda Tinch-Mize

Cover Designer
Tim Amrhein

Book Designer
Gary Adair

Copy Writer
Peter Fuller

Production Team Supervisors
Brad Chinn
Charlotte Clapp

Production
Sonja Hart
Polly Lavrick
Dana Rhodes
Mary Ellen Stephenson

Overview

Contents

Appendixes

Acknowledgments

Writing and publishing a book requires a great deal of dedication and hard work by many people. This book is no different. For their part, the authors would like to thank:

Mark Taber for suggesting that we talk to Cari.

Cari Skaggs for going to bat for us in the beginning, and for her patience in the end.

Brian Proffitt and Cheri Clark, whose excellent editing is evident in the final product.

Matt Butler, who kept us honest, for his valuable insight and technical advice.

Everyone at Sams who worked on this book that we didn't mention.

Everyone who contributes to CompuServe and Internet user forums. We found some useful utilities and helpful information about Windows NT.

Everybody who encouraged us to write the book.

Barry thanks Elizabeth and Derek for putting up with his endless disappearance into his office.

And Peter would like to thank Janet, Kelly, and Ruth for their encouragement.

About the Authors

Peter T. Davis

During 22 years in information systems, Peter Davis worked in data processing in large-scale installations in the financial and government sectors, where he was involved in the development and implementation of applications and specification of requirements. Most recently, he worked as the director of information systems audit for the Office of the Provincial Auditor (Ontario). In addition, Peter was a principal in an international public accounting firm's information systems audit practice, and he has acted as the Canadian representative for a U.S. company specializing in the manufacture and integration of communications products.

He is now principal of Peter Davis & Associates, a training and consulting firm specializing in the security, audit, and control of information systems.

Peter is the author or co-author of five other books, including *Teach Yourself NetWare in 14 Days* (Sams Publishing) and *Computer Security for Dummies* (IDG Books Worldwide). He also is an internationally known speaker on quality, security, audit, and control, frequently speaking at user and professional conferences and meetings.

He received his Bachelor of Commerce (B. Comm) degree from Carleton University. He also is a Certified Management Accountant (CMA), Certified Information Systems Auditor (CISA), Certified Computing Professional (CCP), Information Systems Professional (ISP), Certified Information Systems Security Professional (CISSP), and Certified Novell Administrator v3.11 (CNA).

Peter currently lives in Toronto, Ontario, with his wife and daughter.

Barry D. Lewis

Barry Lewis has more than 17 years of experience in the field of computer security. He is president of Cerberus ISC Inc. and is a Certified Information Systems Security Professional (CISSP). He has worked in the information technology field for more than 25 years, obtaining experience in most major computing and data communications environments. In addition, he has spent years as a volunteer on the board of directors with the organization that is helping to set qualifications within the information security field, the International Information Systems Security Certification Consortium, (ISC)².

He is an author of many articles on information security and is a frequent speaker at a number of major conferences. He is co-author of *Computer Security for Dummies* (IDG Books Worldwide).

Barry is a frequent speaker and seminar leader and travels extensively. You can reach him at (416) 777-6768, or via e-mail at `lewisb@Cerberus.com`. You can also visit his Web page at `www.cerberus.com`.

Barry lives in the Toronto area with his wife and son, three cats, and a dog. It's a busy house.

Tell Us What You Think!

As a reader, you are the most important critic and commentator of our books. We value your opinion and want to know what we're doing right, what we could do better, what areas you'd like to see us publish in, and any other words of wisdom you're willing to pass our way. You can help us make strong books that meet your needs and give you the computer guidance you require.

Do you have access to CompuServe or the World Wide Web? Then check out our CompuServe forum by typing GO SAMS at any prompt. If you prefer the World Wide Web, check out our site at http://www.mcp.com.

NOTE

> If you have a technical question about this book, call the technical support line at 317-581-3833.

As the publishing manager of the group that created this book, I welcome your comments. You can fax, e-mail, or write me directly to let me know what you did or didn't like about this book—as well as what we can do to make our books stronger. Here's the information:

Fax: 317-581-4669

E-mail: opsys_mgr@sams.mcp.com

Mail: Dean Miller
           Sams Publishing
           201 W. 103rd Street
           Indianapolis, IN 46290

Introduction

If you are reading this Introduction, you certainly want to learn about Windows NT Server. You recognize that Microsoft will capture a very large share of the LAN market, and that knowledge of the product makes you more valuable to your present and future employers.

Regardless of your purpose for wanting to learn Windows NT Server, this book is for you. For the next 14 days, you will find out things you need to know to operate NT efficiently, effectively, and economically. Completing the 14-day curriculum will provide you with a solid base for embarking on the Microsoft Certified Professional (MCP) accreditation programs.

You will build on tasks in each lesson and progressively move to more complex tasks. At the end of the 14 days, you should have a firm grounding in Windows NT Server. Let's look at how we have organized the rest of the book.

Organizing the Job of Learning Windows NT Server

As the title of the book suggests, you can learn NT Server concepts in a short period of time—two weeks. Material in this book has been organized to lead you through a logical step-by-step approach to learning Windows NT Server easily and quickly. Obviously, your speed of progression depends on your skills and background knowledge. Even though this is the case, we encourage you to read the book in sequential day and chapter order. Days and chapters tend to build on each other. For instance, we introduce the concept of networking early in the book so that you will think about it throughout the book.

The following sections give you an idea of what you can expect to cover each day.

Day 1: Introducing Windows NT Server

On Day 1, you'll explore introductory networking concepts. Included in the day's lessons are descriptions of network components and options. You also will learn basic Windows NT Server components and features.

Day 2: Installing Windows NT Server

On this day, you'll actually install Windows NT Server on file servers and at client workstations.

You will also see how to install Windows NT Workstation, Windows 95, Windows for Workgroups, DOS/Windows 3.*x*, and Macintosh clients.

Day 3: Understanding Windows NT Server

The morning of Day 3 provides you with the tools to navigate your way through the files and directories in NT.

During the afternoon, you'll learn to explore NT and find out about the new tools and accessories NT offers. You'll also learn about sharing and using Explorer.

Day 4: Understanding Windows NT Server Registry

Day 4 introduces the NT Registry, and you'll learn what this important aspect of the system does and why it is so important. You'll also learn to manipulate the entries within the registry in a safe, effective manner.

Day 5: Introduction to System Management

On this day, you'll learn all about domains: what they do, how they work, and why they are important to using NT Server in a network.

In the afternoon, you'll learn the nuances and controls involved in securing your NT Server from prying eyes, and you'll learn to properly set up your user accounts.

Day 6: Managing User Accounts

By Day 6, you will have a basic knowledge of Windows NT system administration. You then will be able to log on and add users. On this day, you will learn about account management, security equivalence, restricting users, changing defaults, and detecting and locking out intruders from your system.

Day 7: Windows NT Server Files and Directories

Day 7 sees the pace quicken. First, you'll learn how to manipulate your way through the different file structures NT offers. You'll find out about the new file system called NTFS and learn what makes this important.

Then you will learn about how Windows NT Server protects access to files and directories through access rights, and you'll see how trustees can be set up. Then you'll explore how to grant and remove these rights.

Day 8: Managing Windows NT Server Servers

Day 8 demonstrates how to manage your file server and use the various server tasks that are necessary for effective server operation.

You also will see how to set up and run Windows NT print servers so that users can print output at different places on the network using different forms.

Day 9: Understanding Communication Gateways

Day 9 introduces Remote Access Services, or RAS. You'll learn how to set up and manage a RAS environment, allowing users to dial in and access NT resources.

This day also gets you into the world of network communication protocols—a world that is often misunderstood. You'll also learn how other network protocols are supported at the same time and even on the same network cable.

Day 10: Understanding Windows NT Server Communication Protocols

On Day 10, you will find out about important network functions and what TCP/IP is and how it works. You'll learn to implement the protocol on your server.

In the afternoon, you'll discover NT naming facilities such as the HOSTS file, LMHOSTS file, Windows Internet Name Service (WINS), Domain Name Service (DNS), and Dynamic Host Configuration Protocol (DHCP).

Day 11: Backing Up and Recovering

On Day 11, you will learn to protect your files and sensitive data from loss, and you'll learn to set up and run an effective backup and recovery program.

You'll also learn about ways to protect your Windows NT Server system against loss of data through good backup and recovery planning and procedures. We'll cover ways to configure your system so that it keeps processing even when there is a hardware failure.

Day 12: Tracking Users and Resources

Day 12 shows you how to manage the audit and tracking of important actions within your NT system. You'll see how to set audit and security objectives and use the audit Event Viewer program.

You also will learn more details about using audit trails to detect when someone has been trying to bypass your security measures.

Day 13: Implementing Windows NT Services

On this day you'll discover what comprises the BackOffice product and see how to set up and run the various components.

You also will learn about the Internet Information Server, Gopher, and FTP service. Configuring IIS securely is an important administrative task.

Day 14: Windows NT Server Performance Monitoring and Tuning

Day 14 shows you the tools you can use to get the best performance, both from your file servers and from the network itself. You'll learn about the Performance Monitor and Network Monitor, and about tuning Windows NT.

You also will find out about tools such as ARP, IPCONFIG, PING, NBTSTAT, NETSTAT, ROUTE, and TRACERT, and you'll learn how they can be used to monitor traffic on the network cable.

Appendix A: Microsoft Windows NT Server Certification Programs

Appendix A provides a useful starting point for the Microsoft Certified Professional (MCP) and other programs.

Appendix B: Windows NT Server Command Reference

Appendix B lists the NET commands used by Windows NT in an easy-to-use format.

Appendix C: Migrating to NT from Novell

Appendix C provides useful information for those who are migrating onto NT from a Novell network.

Glossary

The Glossary contains definitions of the major networking and information processing terms used throughout the book.

Conventions

The presentation of Windows NT Server is best accomplished by providing menus and screens as you will see them. You will make choices by working through these menus and screens. Because "a picture is worth a thousand words," we will supplement the visual aids with detailed descriptions of everything you need in order to use or understand the menu or screen. For that reason, as you develop new skills, you'll see screen shots of Windows NT to help in your understanding and to help you judge your progress.

Icons in this book will draw your attention to information considered interesting or important. The icons are used as explained here:

☐ The Tip icon offers advice, teaches an easier way to do something, or explains an undocumented feature.

☐ The Note icon presents interesting tidbits of information related to the surrounding discussion.

☐ The Warning icon helps steer you clear of disaster, alerts you to potential problems, or warns you when you should not skip a task.

Each lesson contains many different tasks. We present most tasks in the following format:

Description—This section provides you with the basic concepts and terminology for Windows NT relating to the task.

Action—This section's step-by-step instructions demonstrate the topic you are working on. Usually, the exercises are strung together to realistically represent the working environment.

Review—This section reviews what you should know after going through the preceding two sections. This becomes the reference to remind you about the learned skill.

In addition, each lesson ends with a Workshop, which includes a review of key terms, a list of the tasks you should have learned, and questions and answers for the day's tasks.

In the text, terms are treated in the following manner:

☐ Menu names are separated from menu options by a vertical bar (|). For example, "Select File|Close" indicates that you should select the File menu and choose the Close option.

☐ User-typed entries appear in `computer font`.

☐ Information that appears on-screen also appears in `computer font`.

☐ Windows NT commands appear in `computer font`.

☐ Windows NT command placeholders appear in *`italic computer font`*.

☐ New terms introduced to the reader appear in *regular italics*.

Mark up the book. Make notes in the margin. Highlight significant sections. Tear out the commands and use them. Last of all, please enjoy using this book as much as we enjoyed writing it for you.

If you have questions or comments about the book, you can send e-mail to Peter T. Davis at either `ptdavis@istar.ca` or `ptdavis@compuserve.com` and to Barry D. Lewis at `lewisb@cerberus.com`.

DAY 1

Chapter 1

Introducing Networking

Over the past few years, the term "network" has expanded from an arcane technological expression for big mainframe computers that fill up rooms in a data center to an everyday term. Do people understand the term and the technology it represents? In the olden, golden days of the mainframe, you had to be a network specialist to build and maintain the terminals and their connection to the mainframe. This specialized knowledge was necessary because mainframes are extremely complex, which means the network staff had some level of job security.

These days of old changed into the networks of today and things called local area networks, or LANs. Previously, specialized technical expertise was necessary to set up a company network, but the job is a little easier today, although vastly different. Confused? Never fear; we explain it all. LANs today are far more flexible and often larger than the network you once used. Whereas once your network consisted of the terminals in your building and perhaps the adjoining building, today's networks span the country with ease.

The mainframe network consisted of a large computer, some wiring, and a bunch of terminals. The Windows NT Server's network consists of servers, clients, wiring topologies, and protocols.

By the time you finish this chapter, you will know these key concepts, terms, acronyms, and structure well enough to bluff with the best of them. Best of all, that understanding will help guide you through the intricacies of putting together your Windows NT Server network.

What Is a Network?

Network is such a common term, yet it can mean so many different things. In a social sense, networking relates to the gathering of various persons of similar interest for purposes of communicating those interests. Computer users, on the other hand, tend to think of the network as the components involved in connecting various computers that allow users to share information or resources such as printers or CD-ROM drives. Once that connection exists, other sharing occurs, such as electronic mail or file transfers. Regardless of how you use the network, any connection of two or more computers qualifies as a network.

 NOTE

> Most networks connect using some form of physical wire usually referred to as the cabling. Network staff also commonly refer to these physical cables as *bounded media*. Larger, more complex networks use *unbounded media*. This media type consists of radio frequencies, microwave transmissions, and infrared technologies. This type of media is typically used to transmit over great distances or in places where cables are hard to place. Although this definition sounds exacting, it's all you really need to know to set up your own server. You can do more research by purchasing a book on networking.

A typical Windows NT Server network consists of one or more NT servers, connected through coax, fiber, or twisted-pair cables to some personal computers set up to act as clients. Coax and twisted pair? Servers and clients? Aren't they all just wires and computers? Perhaps it's time to delve deeper.

 TIP

> If you think you know all about networks, you can skip to the next chapter and install your copy of NT Server. A good understanding of how networks work is essential to installing and maintaining NT Server, so be certain.

The major components of a good network include various pieces:

- ☐ Cabling
- ☐ Network interfaces
- ☐ Nodes
- ☐ Protocols

You will examine these in more detail in the following sections. You are introduced to various other items such as the standards that help make networks more consistent by applying a form of order to the cables, protocols, and other network devices. After you become more comfortable with NT Server, we'll introduce more specific details on how to use the various network components. Finally, remember that this book provides details on Microsoft NT Server, not networks. To fully understand all the components, you need to reference some of the good networks books that are available, such as *Understanding Local Area Networks* (Sams Publishing, 1995).

Network Cabling

What's a network cable and how do you use it? This section introduces you to the physical world of cabling. What are all the types of cables you can use to connect computers? Earlier, we mentioned several types, including coax and twisted pair. Before going too far, you need to realize that *coax cable* is a shortened version of the actual name, coaxial cable. You can use this longer name if you want, but to belong to the secret world of network installers, you should use *coax*.

The objective of cabling is to connect two or more computers by plugging some type of cable into each computer. For instance, you might use a parallel port or serial cable and the Windows 95 software called TranXit, which provides a simple connectivity solution for connecting your Windows 95 computers together. Although very rudimentary, this does constitute a network.

A more typical set of cables are twisted pair and coax, so we'll review them in a little more detail.

Coaxial Cable

Coaxial cable, or coax, is a popular means for connecting computers, and some of the earliest LANs were built using it. The cable consists of an inner wire typically made from some form of copper alloy and another wire that surrounds this main one but is separated from it by an insulating layer (or shield).

Anyone with cable television can see a typical example of coax by looking no further than the back of your television set. The cable that connects your TV to the cable provider is coax. If you look closely at one end of the connector, you can see the small piece of copper sticking out. This is the inner cable. You cannot see the shield because it is hidden by a layer of outer insulation. (You hold this layer as you peek at the small piece of copper.)

The shielded cable surrounding the common axis of copper alloy gives us the term coaxial (for common axis) cable (see Figure 1.1). Coax comes in various types, so don't rush out to use your television cable in your network! Each type relates to the way it handles the electrical impulses sent along it. One type you can use in your network consists of RG58/U coaxial cable.

Figure 1.1.

A picture of coax cable.

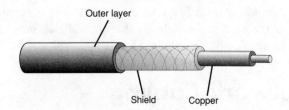

The shield shown in Figure 1.1 provides a good layer of insulation against external electrical noise while also providing good bandwidth. (Bandwidth is a term used to denote the amount of data that can be sent across a line. For example, an Ethernet implementation typically provides a bandwidth of 10Mbps. Mbps is a term used in place of megabytes per second.)

To connect the wires to your computer or television, you need a connector. You buy the cable in preset lengths, complete with a connector attached, such as the cable and connectors used for your television. Large companies may simply buy rolls of plain cable so they can cut each piece to a desired length. They need to manually add a connector to each end. Typical connectors are called British Naval Connectors or BNC. Coax is commonly available at most computer shops.

Finally, the terms thin and thick coax are used a lot. Basically, the term applies to the size (thickness) of the cable. The original engineering specification for thick coax consisted of cable that was about a half an inch thick in diameter. The proliferation of microcomputer networks provided a cheaper solution called thin coax (RG-58). If you purchase computer coax from your local store, it is usually thin coax and easy to use. The coax you find at the back of your television is an example of thick coax and is less pliable and therefore a little harder to install. Most small networks today use thin coax rather than thick.

Twisted Pair

Twisted-pair cable consists of two wires twisted together and covered by a plastic sheath of some kind. Household telephone wiring is an example.

Twisted-pair cable comes in both shielded and unshielded varieties with differing numbers of connecting wires. The inner wires are twisted around each other to reduce radiation and electrical interference (see Figure 1.2). Electrical standards refer to these as Shielded Twisted Pair (STP) and Unshielded Twisted Pair (UTP).

Figure 1.2.

A twisted-pair cable.

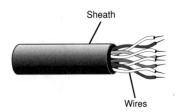

One wire sends a signal and the other wire obtains the return signal. In a small office, it probably does not matter which type you use because electrical interference is minimal. Larger offices have more places where the cable might rub against an electrical field (such as a large appliance), where the signal can get distorted. Using the shielded variety in these cases can minimize the interference.

Twisted pair has the advantage of being cheaper than other types of cable, such as coax. It is also easy to work with during installation and maintenance and is readily available. Many buildings remain pre-wired with this type of cable. The connectors for this cable look very similar to your telephone jack. Some, in fact, use that jack, called the RJ11, whereas others use a larger connector called the RJ45.

Some of the drawbacks to using this cable are its susceptibility to interference from electromagnetic energy and the limited distance resulting from this interference potential. Improvements in this field are legion, however, so expect these limits to be reduced over the coming years.

Fiber-Optic Cable

Fiber-optic cable is science's latest creation and uses light to transmit its signal. You have probably seen it in use at high tech fairs because it can spread light around corners, into designs, or into small places.

Fiber-optic cable consists of a strand of material (usually glass) inside a protective covering (see Figure 1.3). Instead of sending electrical energy down a wire, this medium uses a burst of light. It can carry huge amounts of data for tremendous distances. It is far more complex to set up and run than conventional wiring, so it is still reserved for sophisticated networks.

Figure 1.3.
A fiber-optic cable.

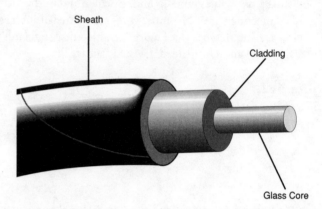

Sheath

Cladding

Glass Core

Of all the cables, fiber-optic cable is the most immune to noise and is far less susceptible to surveillance from wire-tapping techniques. As you see in the figure, connecting these cables to your network has special requirements. A special transceiver and signal amplifier turn the signal into something legible for your network, and these items are costlier than the simple connectors used in coax and twisted-pair cables.

Network Interfaces

Now that you understand the wiring needed to connect computers, you need to understand how they connect to each computer. Between the wire and the computer, you need a *network interface card*, or NIC as it's commonly referred to by network staff. This card provides the interface between the cable and the internal components of your computer.

There are many varieties of these cards. Some fit inside the computer and attach directly to the computer's internal bus, giving it fast access to the memory and computer processor. These cards typically show at the back of your computer and include a special connector or two that allow the network wires to attach.

Other types consist of small external devices that attach to the parallel port of your computer, removing any necessity to take the cover off the machine and poke around inside. The parallel port already attaches inside your computer (the one where you find your printer). Even though the external NIC is not an actual card, it is still called a network interface card because that's easier than coming up with another name—and it does provide the same function. This card has various names:

☐ Network card

☐ Network adapter

☐ Intelligent network interface card (NIC)

You can use any of these terms, although the more common terms are network card and NIC.

These cards perform three major functions: send, receive, and format data in a way that is acceptable to the network. They must obey certain rules generated by the computer and set out by the type of network in use. These rules are well-defined. For example, the IEEE 802.*x* standards set out the different criteria for designing local area networks. (IEEE stands for the Institute of Electrical and Electronics Engineers.)

The card responds to directions given by software running on the computer and sends information across the network. It also responds to messages sent to it. (Each card has an address provided by the vendor and set according to another set of standards.) There is a reasonably complex method to all this sending and receiving that is described in advanced networking manuals.

Network Nodes

A network node is the point where a cable ends and a computer begins. How these nodes connect to each other depends on the type of network you are using. We discussed types of wiring and network interface cards in the earlier section; now, we'll show how those wires and NICs form part of the network as they connect to either a server or a client computer.

Computers provide two primary types of service when they are attached in a network: *server* or *client*. Each type is defined here:

☐ A server computer is one that provides services to the network. These services are typically such things as printing, storing files, or providing a connection to other computers and networks.

☐ A client computer acts as an interface to the network, allowing you to use the services provided by the servers.

In Windows NT Server, one computer can act as both the client and the server. Other network operating systems such as Novell need both a server and client computer before you can use the services provided.

These terms are widely used today to describe a particular type of computing, as in client/ server technology. To form an effective network, of course, you need more than just one server and one client. You will often find one server with 50 or 100 clients attached, providing a company or department with centralized services. If this sounds a lot like mainframe processing, then guess what: It is similar. The mainframe (server) connects a bunch of work-stations (clients) and lets each person access various services such as printing and storing files.

Before all the purists jump all over us, note that this is merely an example to show that the underlying structure really hasn't changed all that much. What changed, of course, was the size, speed, and complexity. Client/server networks are far easier to set up, manage, and maintain than the older mainframes. In addition, the workstation changed from a passive, dumb terminal to an interactive microcomputer.

At the heart of it all, you are connecting a bunch of terminals (clients) to a central processor (server). Finally, a major difference includes the ease with which you can connect a whole bunch of servers across the country or across your organization, without the need for expensive cooling and the large rooms that mainframes need. Today's organizations have more processing power in their servers and workstations than they ever had with their mainframes.

The following sections describe what the terms client and server mean in more detail.

Servers

As discussed earlier, the server consists of a computer that provides certain services to other computers—the clients. A typical server waits for a client program to request something, such as a file or printer. Servers spend a lot of time just waiting for someone to ask them for something. They must be prepared to manage any mad rush that might occasionally ensue, such as when everyone signs on in the morning. The server listens for a request and performs some action.

Many organizations use a number of servers to spread the load by having each server perform a specific task. For example, one server might be set up to handle all print requests, whereas another server manages file access. In this manner, each server can be tuned to provide the most effective level of service.

Server computers can be grouped into two primary categories:

☐ Special-purpose computers designed to provide a particular service

☐ General-purpose computers that provide a wide range of services

In the following sections, you'll learn that each category provides some unique capabilities.

General-Purpose Servers

Most of the computers you might already know can be used in a network—from mainframe computers to your desktop microcomputer and everything in between. Attached to a network, these computers supply you with the files, processes, and features you need. Of course, the operating system also helps makes this possible. MVS, UNIX, VMS, OS/400, NetWare, and Windows NT Server are some of the more common operating systems. These

host machines have been in use for many years, offering functions similar to the new client/server technologies.

To access these systems, you usually need to log in (or log on and sign on) and supply a special name (account) and password.

TIP

In spite of the need to standardize how you perform tasks, the industry cannot yet agree on what to call things. For example, do you sign on or log in? Are you using a username, an account name, or a logon ID? Which term you hear depends mainly on the operating system the speaker is most familiar with using. For example, a person with a UNIX background refers to the personal identifier as the account. NT uses the term username to identify the individual.

Once signed on, the user can type commands and instruct the computer to perform some action such as printing a report or reading a file. What actions each person can take depends on the level of authority that is granted to the person by the system administrator.

Some of the more common uses for host machines include

- [ ] *Sending and receiving electronic mail.* The host usually acts as the central focus for all the mail entering and leaving the LAN. The mail program typically resides on the server with a small client program running on the client workstation. The mail program might also know how to communicate with the Internet or with other organizations' mail programs.

- [ ] *Moving files from one computer to another.* You can send files to another department in your organization with its own host computer. Perhaps you use the host as a backup for your workstation by backing up all your local files onto the host machine's hard drive. The host typically provides you with the programs and commands that let you perform these transfers.

- [ ] *Allowing other computers on the network to access server files.* In this instance, the host acts as a part of your computer, allowing you to see certain files as if they are just another disk drive. This can make data sharing simple for the end user, who might not even know the files he uses are not on his machine.

The hosts mentioned can consist of large mainframe computers running MVS or VM, UNIX machines, or AS/400 minicomputers. They all support users signing on and using their services. Servers also often contain applications such as word processors and databases, enabling users to use these services without the need for a copy on their own machines.

Special-Purpose Servers

Now that you have a smattering of understanding about servers, we need to further muddy the water. There are servers and then there are servers! The client/server architecture evolves daily to provide for the needs of the user. Because microcomputers are inexpensive compared to yesterday's behemoths, diversity and specialization are welcome. Special-purpose servers have evolved to provide a specific service in the fastest, most efficient manner. This diversity helps you manage your computing needs by upgrading only those areas that need it, adding a larger hard drive on the file server or more memory on a database server.

Organizations pick and choose the specialty machines that are best suited for their present needs. Some of these might consist of the following servers:

☐ *Authentication server.* A computer that contains special security software that authenticates all users before permitting them into the network. Usually only larger firms use this type of server, although it is starting to gain acceptance in the general business world.

☐ *File server.* The most common type of server on a LAN, a file server works in the same manner as the host computers mentioned previously. The remote machine establishes a network connection with the server, which allows it to view the server files it is authorized to see as if they were physically on the remote machine The software on the client machine then evaluates each request for data and decides which request it needs to send to the server. The file server takes each request for data and, if the requester is authorized, supplies the data.

☐ *Database server.* A database is an improvement over files. Instead of providing a requester with an entire file when he might desire only a portion of the information, the database server enables you to retrieve only those specific records that are needed. (Records are just portions or pieces of a file.) Such an approach speeds up delivery of information, allowing the server to be tuned and optimized to provide this type of service. The database server acts to provide only the data you need, removing redundant network traffic, and to specialize in that task, further reducing the time needed to provide you with the information you need.

☐ *Mail server.* The mail server specializes in managing your electronic mail. Larger organizations with many employees use this type of server to provide the overall level of service that is necessary when communicating electronically.

☐ *Other servers.* The nature of the client/server architecture responds well to diversification, and the number and granularity of services available for specialization is almost endless. There are servers that provide gateways to other types of networks, servers that manage document printing, and communication servers that provide access between host mainframe computers and the LAN.

1

The diversity and classification of server types continues to expand as we witness new or improved technology such as the Internet or video communications. Look for new, fresh uses of this technology over the coming years.

Clients

When we write about client computers, we mean those machines that take advantage of a network and the services provided by the servers on those networks. There is nothing arcane or mysterious about these machines. Many consist of your typical microcomputer running DOS, Windows, or Windows 95. Others are Macintosh computers or UNIX workstations.

In a typical Windows-based or UNIX-based machine, the microcomputer does all the things it usually does. Perhaps it runs your word-processing software or spreadsheet. It might (and should!) run specific virus-protection software to guard against viruses.

What makes these machines clients is the network connection and some special software that lets you use that network. Almost any computer can be a client, even large mainframes. Although they typically act as the hosts or servers, they can become clients to another server.

The special software knows how to talk to the network and server and manages client requests. Once it receives the requested data or service, it carries on as a normal microcomputer and continues its processing.

To summarize, it's not the machine that makes a client; it is the connection to the network and the software that's running that defines the computer as a client machine.

LAN Wiring Topologies

Earlier sections in this chapter discuss wiring, interfaces, and nodes. Now we need to talk about how these things are physically connected. The physical, or geometrical, arrangement of the cables in a LAN is called the *topology*. Which particular topology you use is dictated by the standards you plan to use in your network. For example, IBM's Token Ring standard uses a ring topology and must be cabled in this manner.

There are many types of topology in use today. The more common ones include the ring, the bus, and the star. Other topologies exist, but we do not have space to discuss them all.

Ring Topology

You might think that the ring topology involves a circle or ring, and of course, you are right. The network nodes each connect in concatenation to form a circle. The path in use across these cables passes through each client machine that is attached to the ring in a circular fashion. A complete circuit involves passing through all the clients on that ring. Figure 1.4 illustrates a ring topology. As implied by its name, a token (a 24-bit piece of information) is continuously passed around the network. All data is transmitted in one direction, called a unidirectional broadcast.

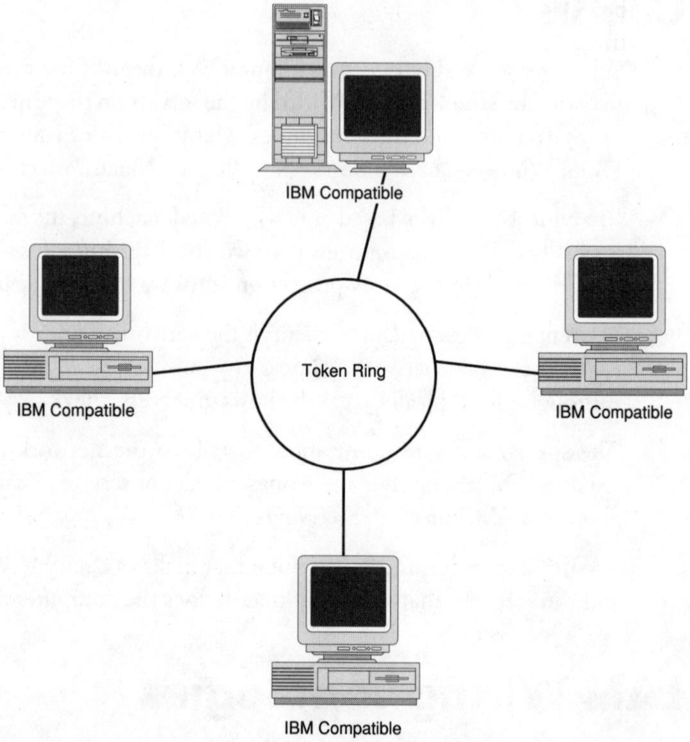

Figure 1.4.
A ring—specifically,
Token Ring—topology.

To connect a new machine to the ring, you must break the ring, insert the new machine, and reconnect the ring. In a small network, you might actually manage it in this manner. Larger networks usually cannot afford to disconnect the ring every time a new client station is added, so they use a special connection device. Each machine then connects to this device. To operate, all stations must remain connected. If one is disconnected or broken, the data flow stops.

This type of network can run at speeds from a low of 4Mbps to the more usual 16Mbps. A 16Mbps network is fast enough for most types of business LANs. You can use almost any type of wiring—coax, fiber optic, or twisted pair—on a ring network, although twisted pair is the most common. IEEE standards for this type of network are set in the IEEE802.5 specification.

Bus Topology

The bus topology runs in a straight line with each computer attaching one after the other. An advantage of this arrangement is the ease with which you can add new computers. The cable needs a special terminator at each end to tell the network where it starts and ends. In between sit all the computers that are attached in a T-shaped pattern. Signals in this network travel in both directions and every transmission is available to every attached computer. Figure 1.5 shows an example of a bus network.

Figure 1.5.

Bus topology.

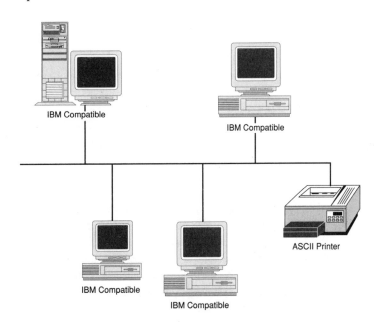

This type of network is simple and fast to configure, making it popular with small office networks. The network is fairly vulnerable, however. Should a break occur anywhere in the line, it usually disrupts the entire network. The classic example of bus technology is Ethernet using 10BaseT wiring.

Star Topology

In a star network, all communication between nodes is routed through a central device. The attached computers span out from that device, forming the *star* (see Figure 1.6). This type of network predominates in the mainframe arena, with the mainframe forming the device and all the terminals connecting from there. (Note that this is a greatly simplified example.)

Figure 1.6.

Star topology.

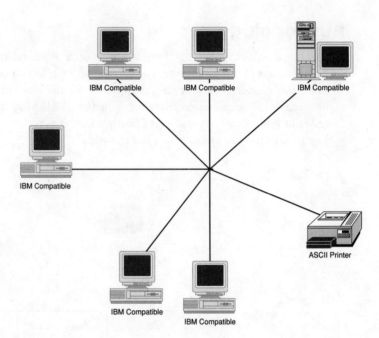

Although this type of design is prone to a single point of failure—the central device—in practice, it is extremely stable and reliable and provides for easy addition and removal of client machines. Additionally, any failure of one machine does not generally cause an impact to the network because the central device handles such failures. One disadvantage of the design concerns the additional cable lengths needed as each machine must be wired from the central device, even if they sit next to each other.

Logical Versus Physical

In the examples used, the various topologies appear to be straightforward. In reality, however, things are not so simple. Physical describes the manner in which the cables are connected. Logical refers to the way the network signal is managed, or behaves. You can touch the physical topology; you need software to manage the logical topology.

For example, Token Ring is described as a ring because the signal travels one way around the network from station to station until it returns to its starting point. Not all terminals see the signal depending on where they sit on that ring. Ethernet, or bus technology, sends the signal from the starting point in both directions and all terminals see every signal.

If you view a Token Ring network, you find that it looks suspiciously like a star topology. Confusing? It surely can be. What you need to know is that the device each machine connects

to is called a MAU, or Multistation Access Unit. Although each machine connects to a port on the MAU, inside the MAU is a ring that connects all the ports! It is this technique that allows you to add or drop machines from the ring without affecting the entire network.

On the Ethernet side, the network can be implemented physically using a star and 10BaseT wiring standards, but it still uses the bus topology for its internal signals.

Routers and Bridges

A major reason for the growth of LANs is the ease with which you can connect them together. After a while, however, your LAN reaches its potential in terms of the number of clients and servers attached, or you want to connect more than one LAN together. For example, your NT Server in the Graphics department might want a connection with the network used by Marketing to facilitate the flow of messages and files. How do you accomplish such a connection?

You need to use some type of device to provide this connection. There are three typical devices you can use:

☐ Routers allow you to connect different topologies together such as a Token Ring and Ethernet LAN, which are typically the most intelligent of this type of device.

☐ Bridges allow your LAN to connect between similar LAN technologies and also to split a busy LAN into separate segments.

☐ Repeaters are simple devices that allow your network to overcome some of its physical restrictions.

The following sections examine each of these devices in more detail.

Routers

The key benefit of a router is its capability to span the different cabling technologies. For example, if the Marketing department uses an Ethernet LAN, a router is needed to connect to the Graphics NT Server running on a Token Ring network. (Note that our example presumes the need for some level of intelligence. If the intelligence is not needed, a gateway computer with an Ethernet and Token Ring card could do the job.)

What do you use the intelligence in these machines for? They offer features such as filters, which enable you to block certain protocols or IP addresses to increase security and minimize network traffic. Newer routers such as the CISCO 7000 offer the capability to handle more than one protocol, such as IPX and IP. This is useful in organizations with mixed technologies.

The advantages of routers include flexibility, the capability to perform load balancing and sharing, and the capability to reduce broadcast storms. The cons of using routers include that they are difficult to set up and that some protocols cannot be routed.

Bridges

A bridge is less sophisticated than a router, but it does provide some capabilities for manipulating traffic. It can also span cabling technologies. If set up with both a Token Ring card and an Ethernet card, the bridge routes traffic between these two networks. A bridge performs most of its work using the Media Access Control (MAC) header of each data packet. This address corresponds to the physical station address or hardware address of the network board.

Using these devices, you can manage the flow of data, restricting it within each LAN by setting up a bridge. This provides network traffic control (by reducing the amount of data one portion of your network sees) as well as an extra level of security. Because these devices do not have access to the routing layer of the data packets, they cannot perform the high level of routing needed in larger LANs and are more applicable in the smaller network.

The advantages of using bridges include their simplicity to install and configure and their capability to be used with protocols that cannot be routed. Cons include the lack of load-balancing capability and their inability to prevent broadcast traffic storms.

Repeaters

You use the repeater as a simple device to extend the physical range of your network cabling. Most cabling has maximum lengths that it can be run before the signal deteriorates too much for reliable use. Each network segment cannot pass this range or it might not work.

A repeater can extend the range by amplifying the signal and passing it on to the next segment of the LAN. It has no knowledge of the data passing through and it cannot be addressed itself. It follows a basic function: Detect the signal, amplify it, and send it on. Repeaters are typically used only on Ethernet LANs because each station in a Token Ring acts as a repeater, so no separate device is needed.

Repeaters have an advantage in their simplicity and their capability to forward any protocol. Their disadvantage is that same simplicity and inability to route between cabling systems.

Media Access Control

Once a group of computers is set up to talk to each other, you need to be concerned with some code of conduct that ensures that everyone doesn't talk at the same time or interrupt each other without some form of control.

You can liken this to the CB radio. If everyone starts talking at once, all you hear are pieces of conversation with the rest of the conversation getting lost. No effective communication takes place. For a computer network, losing data is disastrous and needs to be avoided.

To avoid data loss, computer networks use two types of approaches: deterministic and contention. The following sections review these in more detail.

Deterministic Approach

The deterministic approach adds certainty to when each party can speak and how often. This is accomplished through the use of a *token* that is passed around the network from node to node. When a computer is in possession of the token, it can send messages. You can use this token-grabbing technique to determine the worst-case time for a computer to get access to the cable to send data.

Under a token-passing, deterministic approach, each node on the ring must wait for a token before transmitting any data. Once it has the token, the node can send the data to another node on the network. The receiving node can only acknowledge that it has the data; it cannot send any data. Once the sender obtains the acknowledgment, it must give up the token, even if it has more data to send. Another node then gets to pick up the token and perform its send function. In this manner, each node gets a chance to use the token.

These systems tend to be more complex than contention approaches because they must deal with the addition or deletion of nodes and lost tokens, as well as other problems. On the other hand, these methods make this approach quite reliable. Finally, the token approach gives a deterministic performance even under heavy network loads and thus can be counted on to perform in a consistent manner regardless of network load. As mentioned earlier, the IBM Token Ring (described in the IEEE 802.5 standard) uses this approach.

Contention Approach

The contention approach of media access control is geared toward determining whether too many stations are talking at once, or colliding. This collision approach uses the Carrier Sense Multiple Access (CSMA) technique to determine whether collisions are occurring. There are two type of CSMA: collision detection (CSMA/CD) and collision avoidance (CSMA/CA).

Using collision detection (CSMA/CD), a node waits until it hears no traffic on the network and then sends its data in that moment of silence. It continues to listen, however, as it sends the data and if the node hears another piece of traffic, it assumes that a collision occurred with the data it sent. The node then waits a randomly specified period of time and sends the data again. The random time period helps ensure that the two nodes do not retransmit at the same time again. After the elapsed wait time, the node tries again.

With collision avoidance (CSMA/CA), each node sends in the same fashion, waiting for silence before sending. However, the node doesn't wait to see whether others are also transmitting. Instead, it waits for an acknowledgment from the receiving node. After waiting a set period, if it has not received that acknowledgment, it assumes that something happened to the data and it is lost. It then waits for the next silence and sends the data once again.

Contention approaches are usually used on bus and tree topologies, such as the Ethernet. These methods are typically referred to as probabilistic because you cannot precisely determine when each node gets to talk on the network. This is primarily because of the randomness that is built into each access.

Summary

This chapter discussed many of the elements involved in building a network. However, the information provided is only a guide to assist in the installation and management of your NT Server operating system and therefore is far from detailed. Understanding and building a network is an involved and technical task, so we recommend additional study beyond that supplied in this chapter.

In this chapter, you discovered the following points:

- [ ] LANs consist of several items, including cables, network cards, and nodes such as servers and clients.
- [ ] Servers manage the requests of client machines, allowing specialization and optimization.
- [ ] Network standards allow some consistency in how each system operates. Standards such as Token Ring and Ethernet allow you to use standardized hardware and software.
- [ ] Devices such as routers and bridges allow several networks to connect and exchange data.

Workshop

To wrap up the day, you can review terms and tasks from the chapter, and see the answers to some commonly asked questions.

Terminology Review

bridge—A device used to connect separate sections of a network.

bus—A network topology where each node is connected in parallel to a single cable and terminated at each end by resistors.

cabling system—The wiring used to connect networked computers together.

client—The computer used in a client/server network that makes service requests.

coax—Also known as coaxial, a cable that consists of two wires running inside a plastic sheath, insulated from each other.

fiber-optic cable—A cable constructed using a thin glass core that conducts light rather than electrical signals.

hub—The central connector that comprises the core of a star-wired network.

log in—A popular term for identifying oneself to a computer usually through an identifier and password. Also referred to as sign on or log on.

mainframe—The term used for very large computers that support thousands of users and huge databases.

node—An interconnection point on a network.

repeater—A device that extends the range of a network cable segment.

ring—A network topology that connects each workstation in a circular fashion and sends the network signal in a unidirectional manner through the circle.

router—A device that connects separate network segments and passes data across each segment based on implemented criteria within the device.

server—A network computer that provides services to client computers. Can also be called a gateway server, mail server, database server, and file server.

star—A topology where each node is connected to a central hub.

topology—The physical configuration showing how network nodes are connected.

twisted pair—A common type of wiring that uses two wires twisted together yet insulated from each other. Can be purchased shielded and unshielded.

unbounded media—A medium that uses radio frequencies, microwaves, or other medium to transmit data.

workstation—Another name for the computer that performs local processing and acts as a client on a network.

Q&A

Q What wiring topology should be used with Microsoft NT Server?

A You can use the wiring that best suits your purpose. Generally, organizations tend to standardize on one type of topology for ease of use. One of the more common configurations in a large office consists of the star-wired configuration. As you might recall, both Token Ring and Ethernet use this configuration.

NT Server runs whether you use Token Ring or Ethernet. Ethernet tends to be less expensive (at the 10Mbps range) but is slower than the 16Mbps Token Ring.

Q When the NT Server fails, does the access to the network become unavailable?

A On a Microsoft NT Server network, access to the server is necessary for most of the things you might do in your day-to-day work. Access to files, programs, and mail, for example, might become unavailable. If your network consists of only one server, you will be unable to log in. However, many networks contain more than one server, and NT allows you to set these up in such a way that if one fails, another takes over, minimizing your loss. You can read more about this in Chapter 22, "Configuring Fault-Tolerant Computing Systems."

Q Can I connect NT Server LANs together?

A You can connect multiple NT servers to one LAN. You might also use an NT Server as a router between two LANs using different topologies. For example, you might set up an NT machine with both a Token Ring card and an Ethernet card and use it to manage traffic between a Novell Ethernet LAN and an NT LAN.

Chapter **2**

What Is Windows NT Server?

What is Windows NT? What is NT? Does it stand for Not There? Network This? Not in Time? Many connotations have been attached to the acronym NT; some are not too flattering. Actually, NT stands for the code name for the Intel chip (i860) used by Microsoft to develop the operating system and not New Technology as most think, although Microsoft has since adopted the New Technology meaning. This explanation doesn't tell us much either. What is Windows NT Server? This chapter provides an answer to that question and an overview of Windows NT.

Before answering that question, we'll look quickly at Microsoft networking and NT's history. Early on, Bill Gates knew that networking was the key to capturing the computer business. Microsoft has been working on networking for quite a while. Microsoft introduced MS-NET on April 15, 1985 (along with its companion operating system, DOS 3.10). IBM, which repackaged it as PC Network Support Program, and 3Com, which heavily reworked MS-NET to improve its performance, sold MS-NET. It was a DOS-based, peer-to-peer network providing print and file sharing for PCs. It was remarkably like today's Windows for Workgroups. In truth, the DOS-based NET menu system from MS-NET remains nearly unchanged in Windows for Workgroups.

From 1985 to 1988, Microsoft worked on the next generation of networking software. Basing the new software on its OS/2 software, it partnered with 3Com to develop LAN Manager. 3Com sold it as 3+Open before getting out of the software business. LAN Manager's success was limited because it was tied to the Intel 286 architecture. Microsoft decided that rather than climb the processor ladder with Intel, it would develop networking software that was hardware independent.

In the mid-1980s, Digital Equipment Corporation (DEC) tried to develop an operating system to replace its popular and successful VMS operating system. Even though the DEC project failed, Microsoft recognized an opportunity and hired the designers and program-mers (for example, Dave Cutler, the team leader) to staff the new operating system project. In 1988, Microsoft earnestly started work on Windows NT. It did this at a time when it was still supporting the LAN Manager product. However, despite supporting LAN Manager into the early 1990s, Microsoft put all its eggs in the NT basket as the future of the company.

This simple story points out that Microsoft carefully and thoroughly designed and developed NT. The good and bad features of MS-NET, LAN Manager, OS/2 (at one time, Microsoft partnered with IBM on OS/2), Windows, and even Novell's NetWare were evaluated when developing NT.

In August 1993, in a stroke of marketing genius, Microsoft released Windows NT Advanced Server Version 3.1. The genius was in assigning a version number that made NT look like it was a release of LAN Manager, even though they have little in common (but the wallpaper that NT Server displays when no one is logged in is LANMANNT.BMP!). The version number also coincided with the version of the desktop version of Windows. Brilliance!

September 1994 brought a new version and name—Windows NT Server Version 3.5. Thirteen months later, Microsoft brought out version 3.51. In 1996, it released version 4.0.

Microsoft's Windows NT Server (NTS) network operating system (NOS) is not simply another program running on a PC. It is a sophisticated operating system that is purpose-built to deliver high-performance services to clients connected through a network. Its features and performance allow it to play a major role in the downsizing of information systems from traditional mainframe computers to distributed processors connected by local area networks (LANs). That's one of the reasons Windows NT Server is beginning to gain a foothold in so many organizations throughout the world.

Windows NT Design Goals

Before starting NT development, the designers constructed the goals for its design. Ostensibly, Microsoft's design goals were

- [ ] Compatibility
- [ ] Reliability
- [ ] Portability
- [ ] Extensibility
- [ ] Scalability
- [ ] Distributability
- [ ] Certifiability

Compatibility

Compatibility refers to an operating system's capability to execute programs written for other operating systems or for earlier versions of the same system. Microsoft didn't want to abandon the millions of DOS and Windows users. Windows NT had to be compatible with file structures used by those systems. Therefore, Windows NT supports

- [ ] AFP (Apple Filing Protocol) used by MacOS
- [ ] CDFS (Compact Disc File System) used by CD-ROMs
- [ ] FAT (File Allocation Table) used by MS-DOS
- [ ] HPFS (High Performance File System) used by OS/2
- [ ] NTFS (New Technology File System) used by Windows NT

Windows NT also supports binary-level compatibility; that is, you can take an executable and run it successfully on a different operating system. Through use of protected subsystems, Windows NT provides execution environments for applications other than its primary programming interface. Generally, binary compatibility is available for MS-DOS, 16-bit Windows, OS/2, and LAN Manager. Windows NT supports MS-DOS, Windows 3.1*x* (Win16), Windows 95, Windows NT (Win32), POSIX, and OS/2 1.*x* character-mode applications.

Windows NT provides a Windows-On-Windows (WOW) subsystem—a way to emulate a Windows 3.1*x* environment. You can run Win16 in a shared or separate memory space. Thus, you can use interprocess communication (IPC) capabilities such as Dynamic Data Exchange (DDE) and Object Linking and Embedding (OLE).

Another compatibility feature with Version 4.0 of NT is the use of the Windows Explorer interface introduced with Windows 95.

Finally, Windows NT supports NetWare clients by including IPX/SPX and Client Services for NetWare (CSNW), UNIX clients by including the TCP/IP protocol suite, and Macintosh clients by providing AppleTalk aid.

Reliability

Generally, a system should protect itself from internal and external malfunction and tampering. It also should be robust and behave predictably in response to error conditions, even hardware errors. Under Windows NT, a program cannot interfere with the operation of another program. Also, Windows NT does not allow a program to modify the behavior of the operating system itself. These goals are met by managing the operation of the system itself and by trapping and messaging errors.

The operating system uses structured exception handling for capturing error conditions and responding uniformly. Either the operating system or the processor issues an exception whenever an abnormal event occurs; exception handling code, which exists throughout the system, is automatically invoked in response to the condition, ensuring that no undetected error wreaks havoc on user programs or on the system itself.

Windows NT also provides reliability by providing redundant systems that protect the computer when a single component fails. This feature, fault tolerance, guards against failure of critical systems. For example, NT supports, in software, RAID (Redundant Array of Inexpensive Disks), using technologies such as disk mirroring and striping, to offer redundancy for hard drives. Also, NT Server has built-in support for uninterruptible power supply (UPS) devices, which provide backup power and automatically shut down the system in the case of power problems. In addition, NT Server supports multiple network cards in a server, directory replication, and hot fixes for the NTFS file system. Hot fix is a feature in which the file system constantly monitors the disk area it is using and, when it finds a damaged area, marks the area as bad and takes it out of service.

In addition, the NT File System (NTFS) can recover from all types of disk errors, including errors occurring in critical disk errors. It does this through the use of redundant storage and a transaction-based scheme for storing data.

All this protection had to be accomplished while not reducing resource availability.

Portability

Traditionally, vendors designed operating systems for a single hardware platform, such as Intel's *x*86 family of processors. Strategically, this is an unsound practice because it doesn't allow the operating system to take advantage of newer, more powerful hardware. As you know, the computer industry changes rapidly, so Microsoft wanted to develop an operating system easily portable to other computing platforms. This would prevent it from being trapped into one hardware platform.

The designers included other features to ensure the portability of Windows NT:

☐ *Portable C:* Windows NT was written almost entirely in C, a portable language, with only a few routines written in Assembler (for those routines that must communicate directly with the hardware—for example, the trap handler). The C language is standardized and C compilers are widely available. Nonportable code is isolated within the components that use it.

☐ *Processor Isolation:* Certain low-level portions of the operating system must access processor-dependent data structures and registers. The code doing this is contained in small modules that can be replaced by analogous modules for other processors.

☐ *Platform Isolation:* Windows NT encapsulates platform-dependent code inside a dynamic-link library known as the *hardware abstraction layer* (HAL). HAL abstracts hardware, such as caches and I/O interrupt controllers, with a layer of low-level software so that higher-level code need not change when moving from one platform to another. In the future, vendors can create additional HALs for new processors.

Extensibility

A valued feature of mature operating systems is extensibility. You can adapt an extensible operating system to your various needs. As hardware, software, or your needs change, you easily can modify the operating system. For example, vendors can independently develop device drivers without affecting the secure operation of Windows NT.

In addition, Windows NT allows command-processing subsystems—or in other words, servers—to emulate other operating systems. This means you can run DOS, Windows 3.*x*, character-based OS/2, and POSIX.

Windows consists of a privileged executive and a set of nonprivileged servers, called protected subsystems. The term *privileged* refers to a processor's mode of operation. Most operating systems have at least one privileged mode, where all machine instructions are allowed and system memory is accessible, and nonprivileged mode, where certain instructions are disallowed and system memory is inaccessible. With Windows NT, the privileged processor mode is called *kernel mode,* and the nonprivileged processor mode is called *user mode.*

Usually, an operating system executes only in kernel mode and application programs only in user mode, except when they call operating system services. Windows NT is unique in design because its protected subsystems execute in user mode just as applications do. This structure allows protected subsystems to be modified or added without affecting the integrity of the executive.

In addition to protected subsystems, the designers included other features to ensure the extensibility of Windows NT:

☐ *Object Oriented:* Windows NT uses objects to represent system resources. Objects are abstract data types managed uniformly by object services. Adding new objects does not undermine existing objects or require existing code to change.

☐ *Modularity:* The executive comprises a discrete set of individual components interacting with each other through functional interfaces. You can add new modules to the executive as needed using interfaces.

☐ *Loadable Drivers:* The input/output system supports drivers you can add to the system dynamically (in real time). You can support most new file systems, devices, and networks by writing a file system driver, device driver, or transport driver and loading it into the system.

☐ *Remote Procedure Calls:* Remote procedure calls (RPC) allow applications to call remote services without regard to their location on the network—this is known as data location transparency (DLT). You can add new services to any machine on the network so they are immediately available to applications on the network.

There is a relationship between extensibility and portability. Extensibility allows you to enhance easily an operating system, whereas portability enables the entire operating system to move to a machine based on a different processor or configuration, with as little re-coding as possible.

Scalability

A scalable system is one that will run in many hardware environments. Applications should take advantage of the broad range of computers available today. Windows NT is adaptable to many processing environments and will take advantage of multiprocessing capabilities of a computer. You can run Windows NT on anything from a 80486 CISC-based system, to a RISC-based system, to a symmetrical multiprocessor (SMP).

Windows NT provides multiplatform support through its layered, microkernel architecture and use of the HAL.

Windows NT supports two different security models—the workgroup and domain models—so you can support small networks of two or three PCs or ones with as many as 20,000 workstations.

Distributability

With the increasing availability of personal computers in the 1980s, the nature of computing was irrevocably changed. Everybody was a hammer looking for a nail; they wanted to communicate and share data. Microsoft designed Windows NT to support peer-to-peer and client/server networking. In addition, it supports distributed computing, so that means the operating system can distribute tasks across a network to improve performance. For instance, NT supports the domain name system, directory replication, RIP routing, dynamic host configuration program (DHCP) services, and network printers.

Certifiability

In the late 1980s, the Institute of Electrical and Electronic Engineers developed a portable operating system interface for UNIX called POSIX (IEEE 1003.1-1988). Using POSIX, programmers can write applications to run on many UNIX platforms. The U.S. Government saw the benefit of POSIX and issued a procurement standard pronouncing that software developed for the Government must be POSIX-compliant. Windows NT conforms to POSIX through a command subsystem.

In addition, the U.S. Department of Defense (DOD) defined a trusted computing base in its Rainbow series. In the Orange Book, the DOD defines a discretionary access level called C2. This level specifies capabilities for protecting one user's resources from another's, and establishing resource quotas to prevent one user from using all the resources such as memory. Windows NT conforms to C2, and indeed the government has certified a standalone Windows NT system as C2.

The adoption of these design goals ensures that Windows NT Server will be very successful in the world of information systems. Teaching yourself about Windows NT Server is definitely a good idea; it allows you to be a part of Windows NT Server's success.

In the preceding chapter, you learned about network concepts and terminology. You can now apply what you've learned as we introduce you to Windows NT Server: its structure, how it communicates with others, and how it stores files and makes them available to a variety of systems. By the end of this chapter, you should have a strong foundation in Windows NT Server, preparing you to begin using and understanding its many facilities as you follow through subsequent chapters.

Getting to Know Windows NT Server

At first blush, Windows NT resembles the familiar Windows 3.1x interface, its poor relative. However, Windows NT Server is not Windows 3.1x. For some of you, that fact might be a revelation; for others, it is simply cause for relief or even celebration. What you see is only the tip of the iceberg; many powerful features lie under that friendly graphical user interface. Because the most popular method of using Windows NT Server, by far, is running on IBM-compatible personal computers (PCs), many people believe that Windows NT Server has some ties to Windows 3.1x. In fact, the main relationship between Windows NT Server and Windows 3.1x is that they are both operating systems that can run on the Intel 80x86 series of microprocessors.

Windows NT comes in two flavors: Windows NT Workstation (formerly Windows NT in Version 3.1) and Windows NT Server (formerly Windows NT Advanced Server in Version 3.1). You can use Windows NT Workstation in any situation in which you use any other client operating system, such as Windows 3.1x or Windows 95. Consider Windows NT Workstation for high-performance processing, such as CAD/CAM, graphics, or computational work. Windows NT Server, on the other hand, runs the disks, controls memory, schedules programs to run, takes commands from the keyboard, and talks to its clients across the network.

Table 2.1 provides recommended configurations for both Windows 95 and Windows NT for your comparison.

Table 2.1. Windows hardware configurations.

Operating System	Microsoft Recommended Minimums
Windows 95	Any 80386-based system with 4MB RAM, VGA display, 65MB free disk space
Windows NT	Any 80486-based system with 12MB RAM, VGA display, CD-ROM drive, 100MB free disk space

Windows NT Server was designed to do one main function and do it well: manage resources for clients. By managing, we mean storing and retrieving client files quickly but also safely. Windows NT Server includes many features for high performance, as well as features to protect files against damage due to hardware problems (for example, bad disk areas). It is not a general-purpose operating system like DOS or UNIX or OS/2. Windows NT Server was purpose-built for service.

2

Microsoft developed Windows NT with the following objectives in mind:

☐ Allow full exploitation of the 32-bit microprocessors for which NT was designed.

☐ Improve on the graphical user interface introduced with Windows by becoming more object-oriented.

☐ Provide simple, transparent access to network services.

☐ Maintain investment in DOS and Windows products on the market.

☐ Allow for future growth.

In Chapter 1, "Introducing Networking," you learned about the various types of networks. In the remainder of this chapter, you'll pick up information on planning your NTS network.

Planning Your Network

Earlier today in Chapter 1, you saw many possibilities that open up to you when you install a network—possibilities such as sharing documents, e-mail, and printers, as well as sharing applications such as word processors and spreadsheets. This section will help you develop a network plan so that you can take advantages of these services.

Before planning your network, gather information about how people physically move and interact to get their work done and the physical layout of your building. Talking with the people in your company about the network is a good way to get valuable feedback for your network plan.

Understanding the work flow within your company will help you decide what applications you need, determine the potential workload for the network, and identify the best layout for your network (that is, where to place printers, the topology that makes the most sense, and other layout issues). In general, you'll find that Pareto's Law applies to networking as well. (You remember Pareto; he was the philosopher who believed in the 80/20 rule. For instance, 80 percent of the wealth is held by 20 percent of the population.) Eighty percent of network traffic is usually local to a workgroup. Setting up the network involves identifying employees whom you can cluster in groups, making network administration easier. The best way to group people together for network administration purposes comes from identifying how employees fit naturally.

Knowing your building layout will help you identify potential problems that might crop up when you start putting the network in place. Although it is probably wise, in most buildings, to let the building maintenance staff or a professional install your network cable for you, it's helpful to have a few bits of information you can round up in advance. When using a professional installer, get the phone number of the maintenance person in charge of the building where you have your offices. You'll need to let him or her know that you're installing the cable for your network, and the installer will probably need permission to start or might have questions about the best way to route the cable. The maintenance person can provide access to engineering or architectural drawings of the conduits, electrical systems, or other building systems and features that might affect where the cable goes. Maintenance staff also might know about local ordinances that might come into play (although your installer should also know about them).

Get some sense of the best location for the server. You'll want to locate it in a reasonably secure area with restricted access. Most vendors state you must physically protect the server should you want to logically protect it. Also, protect it as much as possible from any potential disaster. For example, don't place it directly under a sprinkler or a washroom. You also should locate the server so that it's easy to put tapes in the tape backup system or to provide an uninterruptible power supply so your server continues to work, even during a power failure.

The key to your planning is figuring out how much of a load your network will bear. This includes the number of dial-in users and how often users will concurrently need certain types of network-related tasks such as access to a database. Once you've completed these calculations, you need to buy the right hardware to accommodate that load. The primary hardware that is affected by the load includes

- ☐ Your server's CPU
- ☐ The system's random access memory (RAM)
- ☐ The hard disk
- ☐ The network adapter cards (also sometimes called network interface cards, or NICs)
- ☐ The backup devices (such as a tape drive)
- ☐ The modems

In the following sections, you'll see some key metrics to use when you start planning your network. Just keep in mind that you should over-purchase when in doubt. It's easier to grow into your hardware than the other way around.

Choosing the Right Hardware

Microsoft Windows NT Server can run on an abundance of hardware, as long as the processor is

- ☐ A system with 386, 486, or Pentium-compatible chips
- ☐ Digital Alpha AXP
- ☐ Motorola or IBM PowerPC

Version 4 ships with MIPS, Intel, PowerPC, and Alpha code.

This range of hardware options means that you can find a server to meet virtually any network needs you're likely to encounter. In general, you can start with a 486/66 processor. However, in most cases, a Pentium-based computer will cost only a few more dollars and provide better performance. Once you have a Pentium-based machine, as a general rule, buying additional RAM, such as 32MB rather than 24MB, provides more benefits than simply purchasing a faster processor.

Windows NT Server is capable of taking advantage of even more powerful hardware. When you move to a multiprocessor machine, such as a Compaq or ProLiant, Windows NT Server can take immediate advantage of the new hardware without requiring any modifications.

There are two other ways to take immediate advantage of hardware. First, buy equipment on Microsoft's Hardware Compatibility List (HCL). Second, buy equipment that supports PCI 2.1. This standard will help you virtually eliminate hardware interrupt conflicts among network components from the various manufacturers. Make PCI 2.1 your benchmark for the server, video cards, network interface cards, and any other hardware for your server.

Do yourself a favor and make sure that the following network hardware is on the HCL and conforms to the PCI 2.1 standard:

- ☐ Server
- ☐ CD-ROM drive
- ☐ SCSI adapter
- ☐ Video
- ☐ Network adapter cards
- ☐ Uninterruptible power supply
- ☐ Tape backup system

CD-ROM Drive

Check the HCL for a CD-ROM drive. You need a CD-ROM drive to install Windows NT Server and third-party software and to share CD-ROM programs with users who don't have CD-ROM drives on their own computers.

WARNING

If you have an ATAPI IDE CD-ROM drive, you should attach it to the primary IDE port when installing Windows NT. When you attach the CD-ROM to the secondary port, NT loads the ATDISK.SYS driver rather than the ATAPI.SYS driver that the drive requires. After NT loads and recognizes the ATAPI device, you can put the CD drive on either port.

SCSI Adapters

Windows NT supports the Small Computer System Interface, or SCSI (pronounced "scuzzy"). SCSI is an input/output parallel-type interface that can support several external devices or computer peripherals, such as hard disks, tape drives, CD-ROM drives, printers, and scanners, through a host adapter. SCSI adapters compatible with Windows NT Server are listed in the HCL.

As of mid-1996, Windows NT supports

- ☐ 60 SCSI host adapters
- ☐ 30 SCSI CD-ROM drives
- ☐ 40 SCSI tape drives
- ☐ 10 SCSI removable media systems
- ☐ Several SCSI scanners

There are many reasons you might want to use SCSI devices. Here are four notable ones:

- ☐ SCSI supports multitasking to provide better performance over other technologies.
- ☐ A SCSI device has built-in controllers that free up the CPU to perform other tasks, making the server more efficient.
- ☐ You can attach SCSI devices to different types of computers because they are independent of the system bus.
- ☐ Classes of SCSI devices, such as CD-ROM, are easily upgraded because of the similarities at the interface level.

Video

When choosing a monitor for your system, make sure you get Super VGA (SVGA) technology and check the monitor against the HCL.

Surprisingly, you require at least a VGA board to load NT Server. This runs counter to the days when you used a low-quality video display because nobody needed it for any extended period.

Network Adapter Cards

While you are planning your network adapter card selection, do yourself a huge favor: Purchase and install the same type of card in all your PCs. If you don't, you'll kick yourself the first time you must troubleshoot your network. Keep in mind that a 32-bit version of a network interface card will result in substantial performance increases over a 16-bit network adapter card.

Unfortunately, network adapter cards open up a world of arcane problems during installation. Two of the most common and most easily prevented causes of network installation problems occur with network adapter cards: hardware compatibility problems and interrupt alerts caused by duplicate usage of special hardware numbers. With patience and a little pre-installation checking, you'll avoid these issues. The most important item to remember is that the card you choose should be listed on the HCL.

If you're not running MS-DOS or Windows on your client PCs, make sure that you check with your operating system manufacturer and cross-reference its list against the HCL before you begin your installation.

Uninterruptible Power Supply

Uninterruptible power supplies come in many forms, but generally, they are battery packs that kick in when the power goes off. Trade off the expense of the more elaborate ones against the cost of having the server down when the power goes off.

Tape Backup System

There are two components to a tape backup system: the physical tape drive and tapes, and the software that controls the backup. Again, check the HCL for a tape drive.

There are a number of things you can do should you underestimate the hardware you need to keep your network running at an acceptable level, and they all hinge on how well you plan. First, make certain that the server hardware you select has the capability of accepting substantial RAM upgrades and a Single Large Expensive Disk (SLED) (or has extra slots available for attaching external disk drives or RAID packs) and has slots (or ports) available for installing additional modems and fax modems when they are required. Also, select a tape subsystem that is SCSI based.

Choosing the Right Amount of Memory

The amount of random access memory you have in your server is a key factor in your server's performance. The law of networking is that *more is better*. This definitely is true for Windows NT Server because it holds as many active files as possible in RAM so it doesn't have to keep accessing the hard disk to get information. You can use Table 2.2 to calculate the amount of RAM that's adequate for your current needs (and make sure that you buy a server that will let you keep upgrading RAM as your network grows).

Table 2.2. Computing memory requirements.

Element	Factors	Total RAM
System Memory	1. Minimum requirement	1. 16MB
Applications	2. Average size of executables run off the server	2.
	3. Number of applications run off the server	3.
	4. Multiply answer 2 by answer 3	4.
User Data	5. Average size of data files open per user	5.
	6. Number of users	6.
	7. Multiply answer 5 by answer 6	7.
	8. Total required memory (1+4+7)	8.

Let us offer a few points of explanation before you tackle an example using Table 2.2:

☐ To calculate the average size of data files open per user, go to several computers within your company and use Windows Explorer (should you have Windows 95 or Windows NT Workstation 4.0), File Manager (should you have Windows 3.1*x*), or the MS-DOS prompt DIR command to find out the number of bytes for typical database files, spreadsheets, presentations, and word processing documents. Select templates or files that people typically share over the network. Then, average the number of bytes found in those files.

☐ The number of users is the number of people who would simultaneously access a file.

☐ To find the average size of executables run off the server, look in a couple of the directories for the applications on the desktop machines, such as the Microsoft Excel directory, and search for all the files ending with the .EXE or .DLL extension. Find out how many bytes they contain and use that the number as the average number of bytes.

Sound a little confusing? Well, it's not. Perhaps a simple example would clarify things. Let's say you recently purchased Microsoft Office, so your business uses four applications regularly whose file sizes are as listed here:

Microsoft Excel	4.72MB
Microsoft PowerPoint	4.26MB
Microsoft Schedule+	.92MB
Microsoft Word for Windows	3.76MB

Add them up and average them, which gives you 3.41 for answer 2. When you multiply the number of applications (answer 3 is 4) by the average size of the executables (4×3.41), you get 13.64MB for answer 4.

Next, look at the size of the various data files created by these applications. You might see this:

Microsoft Excel	60KB
Microsoft PowerPoint	300KB
Microsoft Schedule+	60KB
Microsoft Word for Windows	150KB

Add them up and average them, which gives you 142.5 for answer 5. When you multiply this by the number of network users (suppose it's 25 for answer 6), you get 3,562.5KB. Divide by 1024 (to convert from kilobytes to megabytes to use the same units all around), and you get 3.48MB for answer 7.

Therefore, the total system memory requirement is 16MB (answer 1) + 13.64MB (answer 4) + 3.48MB (answer 7), or 33.12MB. This means you should probably configure your system with 36MB of RAM.

As a rule of thumb, if you intend to use SQL Server on an NT Server, you need at least 32MB of RAM.

Choosing the Right Amount of Hard Disk Space

When you plan your hard disk requirements, consider partitioning your hard disk into three logical drives: C, D, and E. Using these partitions, you can designate certain parts of the disk for certain functions, as shown here:

☐ C partition, or drive C for the Windows NT Server operating system

☐ D partition, or drive D for network applications

☐ E partition, or drive E for user data

Again, there is a fairly simple formula to help you calculate how much hard disk space to specify when you buy your server. For drive D, you can find out the size of the applications by looking at the installation requirements for that application and the amount of hard disk space required. For drive E, in the factor "Budgeted disk space per user," you should have a corporate policy on how much space you will provide (see Table 2.3). If not, check with a representative sample of your users and see how much data (excluding the applications themselves) they have on their desktop machines. As a rough guideline for your calculations, one page of text equals approximately one kilobyte (KB).

Table 2.3. Computing hard drive requirements.

Element	Factors	Total RAM
System Disk Drive (C Drive)	1. Greater of 250MB or 150MB + server memory + 12MB	1.
Applications (D Drive)	2. Average size of installed applications	2.
	3. Number of applications run off the server	3.
	4. Multiply answer 2 by answer 3	4.
User Data (E Drive)	5. Budgeted disk space per user	5.
	6. Number of users	6.
	7. Margin of error (10 percent)	7. 1.1
	8. Multiply answer 5 by answer 6 by answer 7	8.
	9. Total hard disk space (1+4+8)	9.

As you did for system memory, you can calculate hard disk requirements. Continuing the preceding example, the sizes of the applications are as listed here:

Microsoft Excel	10.20MB
Microsoft PowerPoint	11.40MB
Microsoft Schedule+	3.18MB
Microsoft Word for Windows	7.55MB

Add them up and average them, which gives you 8.08 for answer 2. When you multiply the number of applications (answer 3 is 4) by the average size of the executables (4×8.08), you get 32.32MB for answer 4.

Next, assume you allow users 40MB of budgeted disk space (answer 5). When you multiply this by the number of network users (suppose it's 25 for answer 6), you get 1GB. Gross this number up by the 10 percent fudge factor (answer 7), and you get 1.1GB for answer 8.

You must also select the lesser of

☐ 250MB

☐ 150MB + 33.12MB (from the previous calculation) + 12MB, or 195.12MB

Therefore, the total hard disk space requirement is 250.00MB (answer 1) + 32.32MB (answer 4) + 1.10GB (answer 8), or 1.38GB. This means you should probably configure your system with at least 1.38GB of disk space.

Selecting a File System

Before you install Windows NT Server, you should decide which file systems you need. Windows NT Server supports the following file systems:

- ☐ Windows NT File System (NTFS)
- ☐ File Allocation Table (FAT)
- ☐ High Performance File System (HPFS)

Planning for NTFS

Windows NT Server supports NTFS. If you are not familiar with NTFS, you can jump to Chapter 12, "Managing User Access," in Day 6 right now. Other operating systems, such as Windows 3.*x*, cannot access NTFS partitions. If you will use only Windows NT Server on the computer, choose NTFS. You also should choose NTFS when

- ☐ You use Services for Macintosh (NTFS must be used where the Macintosh files are located).
- ☐ You require file-level security.
- ☐ You will migrate directories and files from a NetWare server, and you want to save permissions.
- ☐ You want to use Windows NT file compression.
- ☐ You want file or directory names of up to 255 characters.

Planning for FAT

FAT is the lowest common denominator among PC file systems. The FAT file system allows access by either MS-DOS (with or without Windows) or OS/2 operating system clients. To switch or boot between Windows NT Server and MS-DOS, you must format one partition on the computer with the FAT file system so that MS-DOS can run.

With FAT, you cannot use the security features of Windows NT and you cannot support extremely large files.

Also, because FAT uses 16 bits to record the allocation status of any volume, it can support 2^{16}, or 65,536 clusters per volume. So the FAT volume is limited to 65,518 files, regardless of the size of the disk. Compare this to the 32 bits used by HPFS and the 64 bits used by NTFS.

Planning for HPFS

HPFS is available with OS/2 versions 1.2 and later. It ensures file compatibility if you want to switch between Windows NT and OS/2 on your hard disk. It supports long filenames and provides better error correction than the FAT file system.

However, HPFS files are not protected by the security features of Windows NT, and you lose compatibility with MS-DOS and Windows 3.1*x* when you use long file or directory names.

Other File System Considerations

In addition to the preceding considerations, you should consider the following points when selecting file systems:

☐ If you want to dual boot between Windows NT Server and MS-DOS, drive C must be FAT.

☐ RISC hardware specifications require that drive C be FAT.

☐ NTFS is the only file system that provides local security.

With any hardware you buy for your system, consult the Hardware Compatibility List (HCL) for Windows NT Server to ensure that the components are compatible with the operating system. Again, HCL compatible means that Microsoft tested the hardware to ensure that it works with its desktop operating systems as well as with the Windows NT Server operating system. Microsoft has tested thousands of machines and other peripheral devices (such as CPUs, printers, and network interface and video cards). This means you can choose from a wide range of compatible equipment. Selecting HCL-approved components helps reduce the number of problems you might encounter.

Selecting a Network Protocol

You should decide which network protocol you will support. Protocols are part of the network operating system. For a client and server to communicate, you need the same client/server software and protocol. If networks are an information highway, protocols are the rules of the road.

When you select a protocol, some considerations will make your decision easier. If you have an existing Novell NetWare network and you want to add a Windows NT Server, you can use Windows NT's IPX support.

Maybe you want to convert an existing LAN Manager network, so you'll continue to use NetBEUI.

You may select TCP/IP when you want to connect to the Internet. Because the TCP/IP protocol suite is in the public domain, it provides more flexibility, no matter how large your network.

Table 2.4 provides a simplistic view of some of the decisions involved in the selection process. Selecting an enterprise is an important decision in your organization.

Table 2.4. Protocol characteristics.

Application	NetBEUI	IPX/SPX	TCP/IP
Small network	X	X	X
Large network			X
Integrate with NetWare		X	
Integrate with UNIX			X
Support wide area networks (for example, a routable protocol)			X
Connect to Internet			X

Selecting the Server's Role

You should decide the role the server will serve on the network. An NT Server can assume one of the following three roles in the network:

- [ ] A primary domain controller in a new domain
- [ ] A backup domain controller in an existing domain
- [ ] A file or application server

It is important to decide the server's role early because once you make the decision and install, you cannot change the role unless you re-install the system.

You should install a server as a primary domain controller only when you are creating a new domain. Because no other machines are members of this domain, there are no security considerations.

Planning for Administration

There are a number of administrative tasks you must perform to keep your network operating efficiently and securely. These activities include creating accounts for new network users (see Chapter 9, "Understanding Domains"), giving users a password so that they can get onto the network (see Chapter 10, "Understanding Security"), and backing up the network so that your data is safe (see Chapter 21, "File Backup and Recovery"). Closely tied to administration of your network is the need to think about and plan for how you want to handle network security. Understandably, you want to keep unauthorized people from gaining access to the network or to specific information, such as confidential customer data. In this section, you'll start thinking about administration activities.

Naming Your Computers

The best way to keep track of client PCs and other computers or printers on your network is to name them uniquely. Doing this helps you diagram and troubleshoot the system, and it also provides a point of reference for someone who might succeed you in administering the network. As part of your network plan, create a diagram that displays the location of each server and client and includes the names you choose for your computers and printers.

Naming computers is important. Should you select an inflexible naming system, you might find yourself making changes later on. Select a system that is flexible, makes sense, and will grow with your organization. When it comes to naming network components, here are some suggestions for naming servers:

☐ Keep the names short. You must remember the name and enter it in systems from time to time. Therefore, select a name that is easy to remember and type. *PeterDavisMacintosh* is not a good computer name. Use something like *Pdavis* instead.

☐ Choose a name that people can remember and pronounce.

☐ Don't use locations to name computers because locations often change. *ComputerOnNorthSide* is also a bad computer name.

☐ Don't use spaces in computer names. *Marketing System* is a bad name, whereas *MarkSys* is a good name.

☐ Choose a name that represents how the client uses the server or the name of the group that uses it; for example, *Sales1* is a good name for the first server in the Sales department.

☐ Use a consistent scheme; for example, you can use mythological characters, such as Kerberos, or Greek letters, such as Alpha.

For workstations, consider the previous suggestions, as well as the following ones:

☐ Choose a name associated with the person who uses the system.

☐ Use the owner's first name and the first initial of his or her last name; for example, *PeterD* is a good name.

☐ Use the owner's first initial and last name; for example, *Blewis* is also a good name.

☐ If you use e-mail, use the owner's e-mail name.

Creating a good naming scheme can save you time in the future. Make sure your naming scheme can carry you into the future. After you create an account naming scheme, you can create some accounts.

2

Creating Accounts

Clients of the network must have an account set up. The system uses the account to identify clients. After the owner of the client account enters a valid password to authenticate himself, the system gives that user certain rights and privileges—that is, authorities. A user account gives that customer certain privileges, such as changing the configuration of the machine, adding new devices, and accessing data.

As part of your plan, write down the rights and privileges you want to give your clients. You'll use this information later when you actually set up the server. Table 2.5 offers a brief description of accounts and the circumstances where you might assign the rights.

Table 2.5. NTS accounts.

Account	Description and When to Use
Administrator	Manages the overall computer configuration. A most powerful account because as an administrator, you can perform almost all tasks, including setting security, defining accounts, adding devices, and troubleshooting. One trusted person in the organization should have the privilege associated with this account. This may be the person in your office who will administer the server.
Users	Provides privileges most users need to perform normal tasks. They can log on and use the server but cannot make any changes to the server itself. Obviously, this is the account to give the majority of your users.
Guests	Allows occasional or one-time users to log on and provides limited privileges on the server.

Planning for Security

Windows NT Server includes full security for both the network and the resources stored on the server. As an administrator, you can control server resources your clients can access. Following are some of the major features that make Windows NT Server a secure system:

☐ Mandatory logon to access resources on the server

☐ Controlled access (and the method of access) to shared resources (for example, files and directories)

☐ Customized user account security

☐ Capability to define who can perform specific tasks

☐ Tracked access to resources and tasks

☐ Security on network resources such as CD-ROM drives, printers, directories, and files

All these features represent areas where you have control and areas where you need to plan how you will exercise that control. As you plan and install your network, you should think about using these features to control your system.

A key to Windows NT Server security is the requirement that users log onto the server with a password each time. In planning, you should decide on an account policy for your network, including the maximum password age, the minimum and maximum password length, and the password composition.

Using Domains

In Windows NT Server, a *domain* is a linked set of workstations and servers sharing a Security Account Manager (SAM) database that you can administer as a group. Users with an account in a network domain can log onto and access their accounts from any system in the domain. The server that authenticates domain logins and maintains the security policy and the master database for a domain is called the *domain controller*. A *domain name* simply is the name of a domain within the network. With a single server, there is usually a single domain. Obviously, creating domains and selecting adequate names is key to a successful NTS implementation.

Using Groups

Usually, the user rights for access to data such as sales contract templates, current pricing lists, and customer information is the same for a number of clients of your network. Groups let you grant privileges to a set of users so that your clients with the same job function have the correct privileges to do their jobs. You also can group users to ensure that people who perform a variety of functions or who are part of several groups can easily be assigned the correct privileges. As a member of two groups, an individual can have the rights and privileges of both. Start planning how you will group your users. Once you know the various groups you need to create, you can develop templates to save you time, instead of creating a new, individual account profile for each person in a group.

For your expedience, Windows NT Server has built in the following groups:

☐ Administrators

☐ Server Operators

☐ Print Operators

☐ Account Operators

☐ Backup Operators

☐ Guests

☐ Replicators

☐ Power Users

☐ Users

By default, each of these groups is granted a particular set of tasks or user rights. For example, the administrative group has the user rights of an administrative account, but rather than set up each person you want to be an administrator with a unique set of rights, you can simply add their accounts to the administrative group and they will obtain all the rights and privileges of that group.

User rights allow individual users or groups to perform specific tasks on a computer running Windows NT Server. User rights provide the capability both to log in locally to a network based on Windows NT Server and to access a server across the network.

As mentioned, using groups is an easier method of granting or restricting access to resources than trying to control access on a user-by-user basis. Depending on your needs, you might also want to create customized groups with special rights and privileges. Groups you create usually depend on the structure of your organization and the needs of your users.

For example, an administrator might create groups containing users with the same job, access requirements and restrictions, or location. Again, start planning how to group people in your organization according to the groups to which they naturally belong so that later during setup, it will be easy to create the accounts you'll need.

You will learn about the Security Reference Model in greater detail starting with Chapter 8, "Managing the Registry."

Managing Your Licenses

To access a Windows NT Server network and to meet licensing requirements, you need licenses for the server and for each client connected to the network. This section reviews your licensing options so you can pick the one that best suits your needs.

When you have only one server in your environment, license planning is simple. Just count the number of client workstations that will access the server and purchase client access licenses equal to that number.

When you have more than one server, a better understanding of how your users will access those servers is important because Windows NT Server has two licensing options—Per Server and Per Seat. With the Per Server option, you assign each client access license you buy to a particular server, which lets you make one connection to that server. You need as many client access licenses for the server as the maximum number of dedicated clients that will connect to it. This is the most economical option for networks where clients tend to connect to only one server, connect infrequently, or connect to special purpose servers.

With the Per Seat option, a client access license is given to a client. The license gives that client the right to access any Windows NT Server in the network. This option is the most economical in a network where clients tend to connect to more than one server.

When you are unsure of which option is optimal for your organization, select the Per Server option because as part of that option you get a one-time, no-charge opportunity to convert your licensing option to Per Seat.

Licensing is complex and causes problems, so Microsoft came up with a tool called the License Manager. Using it is simple.

Task 2.1. Using the License Manager.

Step 1: Description

This task describes how to use the License Manager to see purchase history and product information.

Step 2: Action

1. Log onto the Windows NT Server as Administrator.

2. From the Start menu, select Programs|Administrative Tools (Common)|License Manager. This opens the dialog shown in Figure 2.1.

Figure 2.1.

The License Manager dialog.

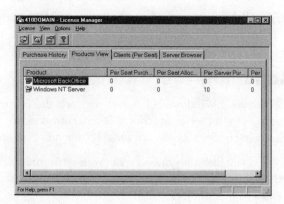

3. Click the Purchase History tab to see a record of all the software licenses you've purchased and entered into the database. The database knows only what you tell it.

4. Click the Products View tab to see product information for either the entire network or a selected domain.

5. Click the Clients (Per Seat) tab to see information about clients who have accessed a particular product throughout the network or for a selected domain.

6. Click the Server Browser tab to see information for other domains. You also can add and delete Per Server client licenses for servers and products and add new Per Seat licenses for the entire enterprise.

Step 3: Review

Use the License Manager to help you make sure that you are in compliance with your licensing agreements.

Summary

In this chapter, you learned about the following points:

- [ ] The sophistication of the Windows NT Server network operating system.
- [ ] The differences and advantages of Windows NT–supported file systems.
- [ ] The differences and advantages of Windows NT–supported protocols.
- [ ] The planning activities necessary for setting up Windows NT Server.

Workshop

To wrap up the day, you can review terms and tasks from the chapter, and see the answers to some commonly asked questions.

Terminology Review

AppleTalk—Macintosh native protocol.

board—Chiefly, a term used for the flat circuit board holding chip sets and other electronic components and printed conductive paths between the components.

boot—(v) To start a computer or initial program load. (n) The process of starting or resetting a computer.

card—Another name for board.

client—A computer that accesses shared network resources provided by another computer (a server).

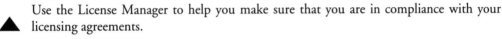

device—A generic term for a computer subsystem such as a printer, serial port, or disk drive. A device frequently requires its own controlling software called a device driver. (See following entry.)

device driver—A software component permitting a computer system to communicate with a device. For example, a print driver is a device driver that translates computer data into a form understood by the intended printer. In most cases, the driver also manipulates the hardware in order to transmit the data to the device.

disk drive—An electromechanical device that reads from and writes to disks. The two types of disk drives in common use are floppy disk drives and hard disk drives.

disk partition—A logical compartment on a physical disk drive. A single disk might have two or more logical disk partitions, each referenced with a different disk drive name.

domain—A collection of computers that share a common domain database and security policy. Each domain has a unique name.

file server—A computer sharing files with other computers.

file size—The length of a file, typically given in bytes.

file system—In an operating system, the overall structure where files are named, stored, and organized. The native file system for Windows NT Server is NTFS.

hardware abstraction layer (HAL)—A dynamic-link library that encapsulates platform-dependent code.

icon—As used here, a small graphics image displayed on the screen to represent an object that can be manipulated by the user; for example, a recycle bin can represent a command for deleting unwanted text or files.

interrupt request lines (IRQ)—Hardware lines over which devices can send signals to get the attention of the processor when the device is ready to accept or send information. Typically, each device connected to the computer uses a separate IRQ.

kernel—The core of an operating system; the portion of the system that manages memory, files, and peripheral devices, maintains the time and date, launches applications, and allocates system resources.

login—The process of identifying oneself to a computer after connecting to it over a communications line. During a login procedure, the computer usually requests the user's name and a password. Also called logon. Opposite of logoff or logout.

network adapter—A circuit board that plugs into a slot in a workstation with one or more sockets to attach cables. Provides the physical link between the workstation and the network cable. Also called network adapter card, network board, network card, and network interface card (NIC).

2

server—A computer sharing its resources, such as files and printers, with other computers on a network.

small computer system interface (SCSI)—A standard used for connecting microcomputers to peripheral devices, such as hard disks and printers, and to other computers and local area networks.

workstation—In general, a powerful computer with considerable calculating and graphics capability. For Windows NT, computers running the Windows NT Workstation operating system are called workstations, as distinguished from computers running Windows NT Server, which are called servers.

Task List

In this chapter, you learned how to perform the following task:

☐ Use the License Manager

Q&A

Q I want to purchase some hardware and need to know whether my hardware is compatible with Windows NT Server. Where can I get a copy of the Hardware Compatibility List?

A The Hardware Compatibility List or HCL ships with every package of Windows NT Server software. You also can obtain it from Microsoft Sales Fax Services at 800-727-3551. The order numbers for the Hardware Compatibility List can be found in the Windows NT Server section of the catalog. In addition, you can find the HCL online at `ftp://ftp.microsoft.com/advsys/winnt/winnt-docs/hcl` or `http://www.microsoft.com/ntserver//hcl/hclintro.htm`.

Q What workstation operating systems work with Windows NT Server?

A NTS can support workstation computers running MacOS System 7, MS-DOS, OS/2, Windows 3.1*x*, Windows for Workgroups 3.11, Windows 95, and Windows NT Workstation.

DAY 2

Chapter 3

Installing Windows NT Server on the File Server

Unlike some other network operating systems (NOS), NT 4.0 can be simple to install. Like everything in life, however, there are plenty of caveats. NT is a big, complex piece of software, but handled properly, it is downright wonderful to install.

Now you might be asking, "If it's so easy to install, does that mean I don't need a Microsoft Certified Expert to help?" Well, as the song goes, the answer depends on you (or something like that, anyway). If you follow the instructions outlined in this chapter with particular zeal, you might never need additional assistance. Miss a step or two, however, and get out the checkbook.

First Things First

NT is very, very particular about the hardware base it resides on. Under DOS, it really didn't matter what hardware you ran as long as it was Intel based. Because DOS is kind of dumb concerning hardware, it doesn't monitor it. Programs under DOS just fail, often mysteriously, when there is a problem. You cannot afford to have this happen in your LAN; therefore, you must ensure that the hardware you use is fully prepared and compatible with NT Server.

Microsoft offers a number of ways for you to check your hardware configuration before you load NT. It publishes a Hardware Compatibility List (HCL) that contains every device that manufacturers have paid Microsoft to test and add to the list. (Nice work if you can get it, isn't it? Create a NOS and have companies pay you to tell us that their hardware will work on that NOS.) If you don't find particular vendors on the list, don't despair! Call them and see whether they are NT compatible. They might not have paid the Microsoft fee, or their software might be in the test phase. You can find the HCL on the Internet at the following address:

```
http://www.microsoft.com/ntserver/hcl/hclintro.htm
```

NT runs on a number of different platforms, including Intel, MIPS, PowerPC, and Alpha. Make sure you have the correct version of NT for your platform. Microsoft recommends at least a 486-class processor to run NT. A Pentium—or better yet, a Pentium Pro—is desirable.

In general, the memory rule to remember with NT is more is better. Although NT Server runs in 12MB, if you actually want to do something, use at least 16MB. I (Barry) run NT Server on my laptop with 24MB of RAM, and it runs well, but I don't really make any true use of it. (I use it mostly for writing this book and doing seminars.) Of course, as you add services such as RAS and SQL Server, the need for memory increases, and 64MB or 128MB servers are more common.

NT has changed the architecture in version 4, and one impact of this is in the video card needed for your monitor. The change moved video services into the *kernel mode* and out of the *user mode* to speed up NT Workstation. When programs running in user mode crash, they generally just impact themselves and not other programs that might be running. Kernel-mode failures take down the entire server. Placing the video drivers into the kernel means that vendors must carefully test their drivers or risk severe impact to your server. You know how well video manufacturers handle that, don't you?

Regardless, the drivers are there now, and that brings us to a new requirement in NT. You must use a VGA video card on the server. Well, Microsoft strongly recommends it, anyway. Those who are accustomed to throwing in some old driver (who uses the server as a workstation anyway?) need to make sure Microsoft supports this requirement before proceeding. Be sure that the card you choose is on the HCL. The NT VGA driver is reputed to be one of the best in the business; we recommend using it. Installing your own might bring you a lot of pain and hassle. To summarize, use a VGA card and the NT driver. Do not use older cards or SVGA cards unless it's really necessary.

NT supports most types of hard drives, although its SCSI host adapter support is very good and worth considering for several reasons. First, SCSI is faster than EIDE, and second, disk mirroring and RAID need SCSI to work well.

Check the hard disk for errors. NT loads data to disk heavily in a process it calls *paging*. This allows NT to use disk space as additional memory. When NT recovers that paged data, it doesn't check to see whether what it saved is what it gets in return. It expects the data to be reliable and safe. Make sure that your disk drive is fully tested for errors before you begin to load NT.

A good CD-ROM drive is a must when installing NT Server. Unless you train a monkey to flip disks for you (does that violate animal rights?), using the CD-ROM drive simplifies installation immensely. Most machines come with a CD-ROM drive these days, so this generally isn't a problem. If you are using an older machine, pick up a SCSI-II drive. You'll never regret it.

The type of network interface card (NIC) you use is entirely up to you—as long as it is listed in the HCL, that is. Whether you plan to use an Ethernet or Token Ring network, make sure that you write down any settings you use when installing the card. You might need them later when things go bump in the night. Test the card before continuing with the NT installation.

You do this in a couple of ways. Perform the onboard diagnostic. Perform a loopback test. If you have a network already set up, you might also try a live test. These tests are usually found on the diagnostics disk that ships with your network card. The first test verifies the card settings such as the IRQ and I/O address. The loopback test sends a piece of data out and back to the card, verifying basic functioning. You need a specific connector for this that you purchase at your local network dealer. The network test does the same thing as the loopback, except by passing the data through the network using another machine.

After you've verified all your hardware, you are ready to install NT. One last message: Check the Hardware Compatibility List. We cannot stress this enough. If all your equipment is listed, your install has a great chance of going so smoothly that you'll be amazed.

Preparing for the Install

Now that you have all the hardware verified, you move to the next step. If you are moving to NT 4.0 from another server, now is the time to back up your data. If you are setting up a brand new server, there really isn't anything to do in the way of data backup.

Use Another Machine for Backup

If you have the luxury of more than one server on your network, you might use one of the other servers, provided it has sufficient disk storage. Do an XCOPY /S command from the server you are upgrading to the other machine. After you have NT 4.0 set up and running, do an XCOPY to get the data back.

Use a Tape Drive to Back Up

You can use a tape drive to back up all your data. There are some problems with this approach, however. If you move from a DOS FAT-based file system server such as Windows for Workgroups to the New Technology File System (NTFS), the files you previously backed up become unavailable.

NOTE
To obtain the security features of NT Server, you must use the NTFS file system. If you decide to stay with a FAT-based server for some business reason, be sure to weigh the lack of security in the decision-making process. All file-level controls in NT are dependent on the newer NTFS structure.

The reason for losing access to your data comes from the manner in which tape backup devices work. When recovering files, most tape drives depend on the operating system that was used to back up the files. Using a DOS-based backup program and running it under NT to recover the files just won't work. In the book *Mastering Windows NT Server 4* (Network Press, 1996), the authors suggest that one sound method consists of backing up to a FAT volume and initially setting up Windows NT Server 4 with a FAT volume. After it's set up, you restore the backups and then convert the new NT volume to NTFS. This is a tried-and-true method of ensuring that your data remains available to you after the conversion.

Backing Up and Then Converting FAT to NTFS

To convert to NTFS from your FAT volume, follow these steps:

1. Perform your DOS-based backup.
2. Install NT Server with a FAT volume. Do not format under NTFS!
3. Reboot the NT machine under DOS using a floppy.
4. Run your restore program.

5. Boot the server under NT and immediately run the conversion program:

```
CONVERT drive: /FS:NTFS
```

6. Run an NTFS-based backup program immediately to begin saving your files under the new file system.

Finally, be sure to take the time (great amounts of it as necessary) to perform these steps. After all, losing your data causes you a lot more pain than this initial work.

Final Thoughts Before Installation

Now you are almost ready to insert the CD-ROM. Before you do, think of these questions and provide the answers:

Do you know how you want to partition the hard drive?

Do you have all the hardware settings documented?

If you plan to use TCP/IP, what are all the protocol addresses?

What type of server do you want?

What kind of product license do you want to use?

Thinking about these questions and providing the answers before inserting that CD-ROM will make your install perform as smoothly as a baby's bottom. (Not that babies' bottoms perform smoothly—oh, heck. You know what we mean.)

As you remember from earlier, using the NTFS file system has its strengths; it allows file-level security. It also has its weakness; you cannot use DOS-based, low-level utilities to read or manipulate the drive. Additionally, you might have to create it as a FAT system so you are able to recover old data from a backup. Determining which direction you will take helps ensure that you stay on track and don't lose anything.

As you go through your new machine setup, documenting all the settings for the NIC, modem, sound card, and so on will make life a lot easier when conflicts occur. Setting up TCP/IP requires a copious number of addresses: IP addresses, subnet masks, default gateways, and DNS servers. Make sure you know them all before beginning. That way, you will not get stuck in the middle of an install, unable to continue without a particular address.

The type of server you want is a little more complicated. The NT install program wants to know whether you plan on creating a standalone server, a primary domain server, or a backup domain server. It won't let you complete the install without that data.

Primary domain? Backup domain? What are these terms and what do they mean? An NT Server is only one of three things:

- [ ] A primary domain controller in a new network
- [ ] A backup domain controller in an existing network
- [ ] A standalone server with no domain authorities

The decision to make your machine one of these types is not to be taken lightly because after you've committed, you cannot change your mind without completely re-installing!

What's this *domain* thing? The word is used in many ways, but within the Microsoft NT Server world, it means groups of NT machines that delegate security tasks to one or more of their machines. They call these machines domain controllers. Note that only NT servers can perform this function; you cannot add Windows 95 or DOS machines to a domain because they remain clients. Within this collection of NT machines, you designate one of them as the boss—the primary domain controller. This machine then manages all user accounts, passwords, file accesses, and other security features. It becomes a *centralized* security storage and management facility. In fact, you cannot have a domain without specifying one server as a primary domain controller. Only one machine can be the primary, although all your servers can be domain controllers.

After you create a domain, you add other servers to it and designate them as backup domain controllers. These are machines that share the workload by verifying user authentication (login) requests.

Finally, you add NT servers as, well, as servers. These are machines that provide services to clients but require login and authentication before allowing any access. What? Does this mean the other servers don't require login and authentication? Of course they do. What is different is how the machines act and what a user needs to accomplish in order to use the services on these servers.

In a domain, NT decided that users might not want to log onto each and every server they encounter before getting access to files and services—hence, the centralized approach of a primary domain controller. This machine controls all user logins and authentication. With this approach, a user needs to log onto the network only once, and each time he needs the services of a different server, NT manages the login—a single sign-on with one user account name and one password. Cool! The backup machines are used to help out and manage the workload. They get all their data from the primary domain controller, which replicates its security database onto each backup domain controller at regular intervals.

If you are creating a new domain, you want to make the first server you add the primary domain. Additional servers become backup domain controllers as needed. The size of your network determines how many of your servers become backups or ordinary servers.

Typically, you need only one backup domain controller for every 2000 users. (NT does not allow creation of a backup domain controller unless a primary already exists, so create the primary first.)

Finally, during this phase of the install, NT creates an Administrator account for you. This account has authority over all servers in the domain in a primary domain controller, so do not forget the password! If you do, you must re-install the server. When you set up a backup domain, NT again asks for an administrative account and password. This time, however, you must use the primary domain controller's Administrator account. (Remember, the primary controls all the servers in the domain.) If you set up a server without domain responsibility, you create an account that is used only for that server.

The install also wants you to tell it whether you are joining a domain or a workgroup. All domains contain a workgroup, and any computer can join this workgroup—not just NT machines. The basic difference is in the view of the network you end up having, depending on which you join. Workgroup access needs separate logins for each machine; they cannot use the primary machine's login. Joining the domain means you need set up each user only once.

Chapter 9, "Understanding Domains," discusses domain management in more depth.

Finally, the type of server license you use is determined by a complex, arcane algorithm created by Microsoft to make life as difficult as possible. Okay, we're kidding. Don't tell Mr. Gates, please.

Microsoft allows two types of client licenses for its NT Server software, *per seat* and *per server*. What's a client license? After buying the server software, you need to license each person who uses that server. This license is figurative. It doesn't actually *do* anything; it merely allows you to use the server.

It is easier to understand if you consider the per seat as a per-person approach. You must decide which approach you'll use before you install the product because the installation asks for your decision and does not continue until you enter your choice. After you decide, it allows you to change your mind only once without re-installing the server.

A per-seat approach to licensing means you need to buy a license from Microsoft for each user. If you have 100 users who will log in and use the domain, you need 100 licenses. Each of these users can access all your NT servers using this license. It gets complicated to decide depending on how many users will access the domain at any one time. For example, if your organization employs temporary workers, how many licenses do you buy? In a fluid employee situation, you can easily have licenses but no people to use them.

The per-server license works differently. It suggests that one person access the server at a time. Buy 100 per-server licenses, and you can have 100 people on the domain at any one time.

In a shift worker situation, you could buy enough licenses for any one shift because each shift never (theoretically) signs on at the same time. In the per-seat approach, you need enough licenses for all the workers, regardless of shift. You buy additional licenses for each server you add. Generally, if you have two or more servers, the per-server option is the way to go.

Outfitted with this information, you are ready to continue and start installing NT Server.

Installing the NT Server Program

You have two ways to start the installation program. Either way works just fine. If you have only floppies—save yourself! Buy a CD-ROM drive before continuing.

1. Use the WINNT or WINNT32 program on your CD-ROM.
2. Insert the CD-ROM and the first startup floppy and reboot.

The following sections discuss these methods.

NOTE   If you are installing on an existing machine, consider running a virus protection program before you begin. To be really efficient, run it on brand-new machines as well, because you can never tell nowadays. The NT install process gets really annoyed if it finds a virus, and it does not allow the install to conclude properly.

Using the WINNT or WINNT32 Program

The CD-ROM that Microsoft supplies with NT Server comes complete with several versions of NT. Intel users will choose the folder called I386 whereas RISC-based machines will use a different directory.

You install NT from the CD-ROM, from a network drive, or from a hard disk on the local machine. To do either of the latter, copy the appropriate directory, such as I386, onto the desired location and run the WINNT or WINNT32 command from there. You use the WINNT command if you're installing from DOS or Windows, and you use the WINNT32 command if you are upgrading from an older version of NT. On a Windows 95 machine, the installation CD-ROM automatically starts after you insert the CD-ROM. Finally, use the /b and /s switches following the WINNT or WINNT32 command to install solely from the CD-ROM.

Using the Floppies and CD-ROM

Using the floppies and CD-ROM is only slightly different in execution. Insert the floppy called "Setup Boot Disk" into drive A and reboot your machine. Not all the NT software is on these floppies, only the bare minimum needed to start up the install program. The first thing NT install does is run a machine configuration program called NTDETECT.COM that determines what kind of hardware and software you have on the system. A message from the program tells you that it is inspecting your hardware configuration.

Tip

> If NTDETECT.COM hangs and doesn't appear to want to continue with the setup, reboot the machine under DOS and run the debug version. This version tells you everything it does (in painful detail, so don't use it indiscriminately) and allows you to see where the problem lies. Follow these steps:
>
> 1. Rename the existing NTDETECT.COM or copy it to a safe location.
> 2. Copy the file called NTDETECT.CHK from the CD-ROM. (It's located in a directory called support/debug/i386/ntdetect.chk.)
> 3. Rename this file to NTDETECT.COM and execute the program.
> 4. Remember to replace everything at the finish so you don't run the debug version later inadvertently.

Next, you see a blue screen and the words "Windows NT Setup" as the install continues. After NT asks for the second floppy, a few messages appear that indicate that NT config data, fonts, PCMCIA (or PC card as it's now known), and other items are being loaded. Finally, the NT kernel loads and tells you the version and build number and sets up the "Welcome to Setup" message with options to continue, repair, or exit. Because this is a fresh install, you ignore the repair option. You use that option to fix NT when things go wrong. That option is discussed more in the section called "Creating the Emergency Repair Disk."

Replying to the prompt by pressing Enter (to continue) and loading disk 3 continues the setup.

Windows NT Setup

Now that setup is underway, NT continues finding out what hardware is on your system. If you followed the earlier instructions when setting up the machine for this installation, this phase will probably surprise you as it continues with few, if any, problems.

If you are upgrading from another version of NT, you see a message indicating that the install realizes you are upgrading an older version and providing you with two options. Your response to this option is important. The two options are

To upgrade, press Enter.
To cancel upgrade and install a fresh copy, press N.

Choosing the latter response removes all prior directory share and user account information in the SAM (Security Account Manager) database, forcing you to start all over. (We'll tell you all about the SAM database on Day 4 and Day 5, when we discuss security and the Registry.) This might be okay if you decide that the old version needs cleaning up anyway. If your previous version was well used and you do not want to re-enter all your users, choose the upgrade option. The upgrade option keeps the existing SAM database, preserving all your user account data.

To gain up-to-date information and details concerning special considerations such as upgrading from beta versions of NT, read the setup.txt file in your specific installation directory.

When you pass this step, NT Setup tells you what it believes you have on the system. This includes the following components:

- ☐ The type of PC
- ☐ Video card
- ☐ Keyboard
- ☐ Mouse

By now, you should be getting accurate information. The only interesting part here concerns the video driver. You notice that the NT Setup program wants to set your video card to VGA mode. This might be disconcerting if you know that you have super VGA capabilities on your card.

NT does this for a very good reason. The good people at Microsoft figured that if they let administrators pick a video card, they might mess it up and pick the wrong one, making the install unable to boot. Knowing that current VGA drivers work on almost every card available today, they decided that using this mode helps ensure a smooth install. You change the mode later after NT is set up. Finally, to make sure you can always boot NT regardless of whether you mess up a video card change, the NT Setup program includes an option in the OS Picker called NT4 [VGA Mode]. No matter what you do, you can always use this command to load NT because changes you make to video card drivers modify the other command line, the default startup command, always leaving you with the NT4 [VGA Mode] command to fall back on.

Disk Partitions

Now that you have progressed smoothly, NT Setup wants to know what disk partition you want to install NT on. It starts by showing you the available partitions. If you have only one, choose that partition and press Enter. If you have multiple disk partitions, select the specific partition NT will reside on and press Enter.

The setup program gives you a number of options concerning this partition, and it is at this stage of the setup that you decide whether to use a FAT-based file system or move to NT's NTFS file system.

If you are dual-booting NT, make sure you do not choose to format or convert the existing partition to NTFS, or your Windows, NT, or other operating system will be gone.

FAT or NTFS?

Which system should you use? It depends. Take a look at some of the considerations. First, unless there is a compelling reason, you should use NTFS. Why? NT security is largely dependent on the newer NTFS file system. Using a FAT-based partition leaves your server vulnerable to unauthorized access and low-level, DOS-based utilities.

If you maintain old DOS-based programs or files, this is a reason to stay with the FAT-based system. Perhaps you might maintain a small FAT-based partition for this reason. You probably do not need the entire system to be FAT based. Having a FAT-based partition also leaves some of the DOS-based utilities available for use in case you have server problems. This leaves that partition vulnerable but ensures that your server files and programs are protected with available NTFS security options.

TIP

> Until recently, moving to NTFS prevented you from booting from a DOS floppy and reading the hard disk. This is no longer the case because several tools are available on the Internet that allow you to read an NTFS file after booting from a DOS floppy. Try this site for further information:
>
> `http://www.ntinternals.com/ntfsdos.htm`

Using NTFS offers the ultimate protection for your server. Among these benefits are sorted directories, access permissions for each file and directory, faster access, file names of up to 254 characters (if that doesn't move you from a DOS, FAT-based system, nothing will!), and improved space utilization.

After you decide, the setup program asks you what directory you want to install the files in. Use the default of \winnt or create your own if you have a corporate naming standard. After checking your hard disks for corruption, NT Setup copies more files and finally (after about 10–15 minutes using the CD-ROM) asks you to reboot the system.

Continuing Setup

After your computer reboots and finishes running the NTDETECT program (we told you to replace the debug version), you get a short message indicating that you can return to the "Last Known Good Menu." NTDETECT and this message appear each time you boot NT. You cannot make use of the message at this time because there isn't a previous menu, but in the future, it allows you to recover from some of your boo-boos.

Because it's Microsoft, the first thing you now see is the End User Licensing Agreement. If you are in the habit of ignoring these, don't. You cannot continue without pressing Yes. The next thing you see is a list of several installation options:

☐ Typical
☐ Portable
☐ Compact
☐ Custom

If you are new to NT, choose Typical. Otherwise, choose the appropriate setting. You can read more about each setting in your installation manual if you need to. NT next asks you to personalize your copy by entering your name and company name. I suggest leaving your name blank, unless you really want the recognition in perpetuity. Use the correct product number because if you leave it blank or create a random number, you cannot communicate with any other server using the identical number. Press Continue when you are finished and again to verify.

Now you need to enter what type of licensing option you are using, per seat or per server. The per-seat option is considered per user, whereas per server means each person must have a license for each server they connect and log onto. Specify the proper number of licenses you own in the box provided, or printer and file services, among others, will not start.

WARNING

You use the Licensing icon in the Control Panel to change from per server to per seat only once before needing to re-install. You cannot legally change from per seat at all without re-installing.

3

Now you need to specify what type of server you are creating. Remember that we discussed the pros and cons of each type earlier. Now you must decide. If this is the first server on the network, it must be set up as a primary domain controller. If not, you need to choose between backup and just plain server. Create one backup and consider whether the remaining servers need to be additional backup machines or ordinary servers. Remember to carefully account for any administrator passwords you create. Not only must you guard against unauthorized persons discovering the password, but you also must guard against losing or forgetting the password. They cannot be re-created on primary domain controllers and servers without re-installing NT.

Creating the Emergency Repair Disk

What is an emergency repair disk and why do you need one? Recall earlier during the installation that the system asked about your next step. One of the options provided is to perform an emergency repair. This is where you use the emergency repair disk. This disk provides NT with just enough information to bring up your system based on the last time you updated this disk.

When something goes wrong, you first attempt to recover using the "Last Known Good" option provided when NT first loads. This option supplies you with the last time NT started successfully and at least one user signed on. If this fails to recover, you use the emergency repair disk.

The emergency repair disk stores the critical system configuration files needed to recover NT. The first time you run the disk, it creates the system with a Guest and Administrator account only. All your user data is lost. (We tell you how to update the disk a little later in this chapter.) To use the disk, run the WINNT program, insert the disk when requested, and reply R for repair when asked. It then asks for your setup disks; follow the instructions presented to finalize the repair and reboot the system.

TIP

> If you cannot find your repair disk or didn't create one despite our warning, NT 4.0 helps by keeping a version of it in your main NT directory in a subdirectory called repair. You can just copy this to a floppy or point the repair process to that directory.

Because it is unlikely that you'll want to restore your NT system back to the original setup parameters (after you use NT for a while), you need to update this repair disk regularly. To do this, run the program called RDISK.EXE, which is in the system32 directory, and follow the instructions until it finishes.

An undocumented feature of this program is its capability to also back up the SAM for you using the /s switch while creating a new emergency repair disk. Figure 3.1 shows the command for creating a new repair disk and including a copy of your Security Account Manager (SAM) database.

Figure 3.1.
Running RDISK to
back up the SAM.

One thing you need to be aware of is that over time, your Registry might become too large to be created on a disk. RDISK actually updates the directory called \winnt\repair (assuming you installed NT in the winnt directory).

Following this process helps ensure that the final option, re-installing NT, is rarely needed. You find more detailed information on backup and recovery techniques in Chapters 21, "File Backup and Recovery," and 22, "Configuring Fault-Tolerant Computing Systems."

How often do you run the RDISK program? We recommend that you run it each time you make major changes to your system, such as adding a multitude of users or programs. You can also run it at least on a monthly or weekly basis, depending on the amount of change to your system. This way, the next time you need to repair NT, your Registry and SAM will be up-to-date, and you will not need to re-enter too much information.

Continuing Setup

As you continue the setup program, you encounter the section that requires you to tell NT what software components to install. These include items such as Microsoft Messaging and Remote Access Services. Include those you need and follow the instructions as presented. Don't worry about it if you are unsure of what you want to use. You can add them later.

The NT installation then moves to the next phase, installing networking components.

Network Setup

The NT installation moves into the network phase by asking how you will connect. If you are setting up NT to be a domain controller, you need to be connected to a network. An NT domain controller, whether primary or backup, cannot be created in standalone mode.

Install informs you that Windows NT needs to know how this computer should participate in a network.

The install process shows you the following message and asks for your input:

Do not connect this computer to a network at this time.

This computer will participate on a network

☐ Wired to the network

☐ Remote access to the network

Reply by selecting "This computer will participate in a network—Wired to the network" to cause the NT installation to continue. After you reply, you are asked whether you want to install Microsoft Internet Server (IIS). For these purposes, reply no at this time. You will review the install and setup of IIS in several days when you review Chapter 26, "Using NT with the Internet Information Server."

Setup now asks you to select and install your network card. NT 4.0 does a very good job of finding and auto-detecting your card, especially if you use only approved hardware. If not, you might find out now why it is a good idea when NT cannot automatically find and configure your network card.

If your card is not automatically detected, you might find it by manually reviewing the choices provided. If it is not there, rerun setup and choose the "Do not detect" option and use the NT driver software supplied with your card. Software? With the card? Now, you are really in deep. Take our advice. If you cannot find an NT driver for your card, save yourself oodles of trouble and go buy a new card that is on the approved list. You won't regret it! To really play it safe, many Microsoft administrators use the Intel EtherExpress 16 LAN card. You probably won't go wrong by following the trend.

Now that your card is set up, you need to tell the install the IRQ, I/O, and RAM addresses your card uses. Because you wrote those down when you installed the card, just insert them now. Next, you need to tell the install process what protocols you are using. The install automatically assumes you want NetBEUI and IPX/SPX. Unless you plan on using Novell with this server, de-select IPX/SPX. NetBEUI, on the other hand, is necessary, so continue the install using that option.

Setup then asks whether you want to install services. It installs the RPC configuration and NetBIOS interface by default. You can install a whole pile of other services, but we suggest you bring up a fairly light version first to become used to NT. Add services later as you become more accustomed to the product.

3

NOTE

> Some of the services you can add include
>
> Internet Information Server
>
> Gateway Services for Novell
>
> DNS and DHCP Servers
>
> Remote Access Service (RAS)
>
> TCP/IP and SNMP

The NT Setup continues and installs those services selected. This might take a while, depending on how many services you select. Remember, though, for the purposes of this book, don't go hog wild and add everything; it will just be confusing.

If you are installing in an already designed domain, setup wants some more information about the role of security on your machine. Recall that you decided earlier what type of machine to install—domain, backup, or standalone server. Now the setup program wants you tell it more. Why it doesn't do this when asking earlier is beyond us. You need to tell NT whether this machine is joining a workgroup or domain. (Remember, if this is your only server in a new domain, you won't see this message.) This is because all NT servers and workstations must be granted access to join a domain; they cannot just add themselves.

NT Server is a very secure system and needs to validate all other machines in the network with one caveat: They are validated only if they are NT servers or NT workstations. A DOS, Windows, or OS/2 machine is not validated. As long as you have a valid account and password, you can use these machines on the network. Within NT, however, there is a fair amount of internal security that provides for a more robust security environment if your network consists only of NT machines. If you are adding a new NT machine to an existing domain, you need to use Server Manager and tell the existing machine to expect to hear from a new one.

Chapters 9, "Understanding Domains," and 10, "Understanding Security," tell you how to add a new NT machine to your domain and provide additional security information.

Finally, initial setup is nearly complete. NT provides you with an opportunity to modify the video screen setup. Remember my earlier advice about using the VGA driver that comes with NT. However, if you really want prettier colors, set them up now in the screens provided. Make sure you test your choices before continuing because it saves you headaches later. If you really mess it up, remember that NT knew you might do this and gave you the VGA driver default option to use when you boot the system, which allows you to recover.

The NT Setup program will reboot (possibly more than once depending on the options selected earlier, such as using the NTFS conversion program), and you have the basic operating system up and running. You now see a desktop that looks as shown in Figure 3.2.

Figure 3.2.
The NT Server desktop.

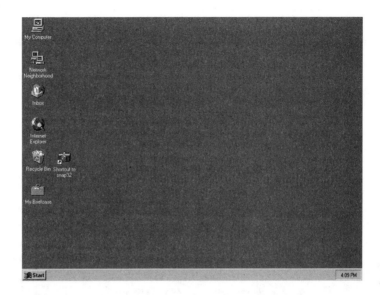

Does this mean you're finished? Well, yes and no. Use the present system for the next couple of chapters and get a feel for what NT 4.0 looks like and see how similar it is to the Windows 95 interface. You might decide later to add additional printers or some application programs to see how they run.

Migrating from Other Systems

If you are currently using another product such as Windows, NetWare, or Windows 95, there a few issues you want to review prior to your install of NT 4.0.

Dual Boot

Dual boot means retaining an existing operating system such as Windows 95 and choosing which system to use at boot time. Most people do not use this system because NT is rather expensive for occasional users. However, there are times when you might choose such an option. For example, I installed NT Server in dual boot mode on my laptop. This allows me the option of using my existing system for consulting work while retaining the capability to boot NT Server for client seminars and, of course, for writing this book.

The good news with NT 4.0 is that it automatically installs itself in dual boot mode if it finds another system on the install drive. This applies to DOS, Windows 95, and older versions of NT.

When you boot your system after installing NT in addition to another operating system, you see a message like this:

1. Windows NT Server Version 4.0

2. Windows NT Server Version 4.0 [VGA Mode]

3. Microsoft Windows

4. Using default version in 30 seconds

The boot process will automatically bring up NT after a default time period of 30 seconds if you do nothing. Otherwise, you select the system you plan to use and continue with the boot process.

The only major caveat to dual booting concerns the hard drive and security. Some of you might be under the illusion that NT security is so strong, physical control over the server is unnecessary. Get this straight right now: If anyone has physical access to your server, you do not have any security! The chapters on security discuss this in more detail, but it's important enough to mention here. Regardless of whether you use a FAT-based or NTFS-based file system, if someone gets access to the server, he can break any level of file security used by the operating system and can gain access to your data. The only way you change this is by using an encryption tool to fully encrypt your data files. There are several new tools available that allow a person to read an NTFS file system using a DOS boot disk, so access to the NT operating system is no longer necessary (or providing security) to have access to the data residing on the server hard drive.

For the hard drive, the caveat concerns the space and type of file system you use in a dual boot scenario. For DOS or Windows, you need to remain FAT based, leaving you without the advantages of the NTFS file system. NTFS provides greater speed and more effective use of the space than FAT based file systems. Unless there is a real business need, you might want to remove the older system from your server and fully convert to NT instead.

Migrating from NetWare

In case you currently use Novell's NetWare and decide to change from that environment to NT Server 4.0, Appendix C, "Migrating to NT from Novell," details the necessary steps. You can also find information about using NetWare and NT together in the same network in Appendix C.

Migrating Applications from Windows

The good news is that moving from a DOS-based or Windows 95 system to NT Server poses no real problems. The bad news is you have to re-install your applications. NT provides an install that recognizes other systems, allowing you to dual boot these systems, but does not let you use the applications you might already have loaded that are NT compatible.

A number of programs just will not work, including most system-level utilities such as data recovery programs like Undelete and fax programs that aren't specifically designed for Windows 95 or NT. Other programs such as Norton Utilities or Rescue Data Recovery Software will not operate unless you purchase a specific NT version.

Some software will operate under NT if you choose the executable and double-click it under Explorer. We tried this on some shareware packages that are made for Windows 95, and they ran just fine. After determining that the program runs, add the icon to the desktop or to the Start menu under Programs. Strangely enough, Microsoft Office seems to rely too heavily on the Registry and needs to be re-installed. You'd think that its own software…

Finally, you can try to copy the application's .INI files to your main NT directory and see whether that helps before resorting to a full re-install.

Migrating from NT 3.51

Microsoft does a good job handling a migration from NT 3.51. During install, the NT 4.0 Setup program detects the older version and allows you to choose between updating it to the new version (effectively removing 3.51 from your system) or adding the new version in a separate directory and setting up a dual boot mode automatically.

If you are upgrading a server that is widely used and has been extensively modified to include numerous user accounts, choose the upgrade option. NT 4.0 keeps all the data from your SAM and includes it in the new version, enabling your users to access the system without needing to be re-created.

If you are updating a test system or a system you'd rather start from scratch, choosing the Refresh option wipes out all prior NT information from the SAM and leaves you with a disabled Guest account and one Administrator account. You then add all your users and their access levels as needed by your organization.

Licensing Those Users

You've installed a few services and added a number of clients. Everyone seems happy getting used to the new Windows 95 look and feel and using the services. Did you license all those users? You want to remain legal, don't you?

Microsoft provides a tool called License Manager to manage adding and removing users and services. You find it in the Administrative Tools group (see Figure 3.3).

Figure 3.3.

License Manager.

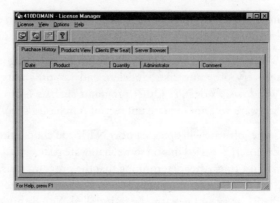

This tool provides a number of neat methods and processes for managing your licenses. It includes an area that allows you to update a small database with all the software licenses you've purchased. You need to manually add this information, but using it will save you time and hassle later as you find a need for the information.

In addition, License Manager shows you the products for your domain or network, depending on your selection. This section shows you which products are licensed and which are not and whether each product is at its license limit. You add and delete per-seat licenses using this section of License Manager.

A server browser gives you access to the license information of other servers that are available to you. In this section, you add or delete per-seat and per-server licenses, allowing you to perform all your license maintenance from a central location.

Task 3.1. Modifying the number of licenses in use on NT Server.

Step 1: Description

This task enables you to modify the number of licenses in use on NT Server. You should perform this each time you add or remove licensed users or software.

Step 2: Action

1. Log in using the Administrator account.
2. Under the Start menu, find the submenu called License Manager. Your screen looks as shown in Figure 3.4.

Figure 3.4.

Finding License Manager.

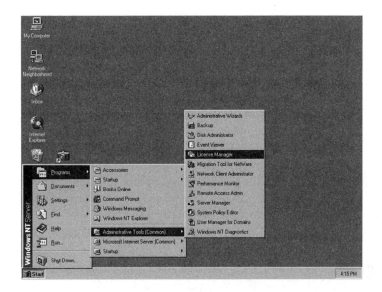

3. Click License Manager to start the program. You see a screen like the one shown earlier in Figure 3.3.

4. Click the Purchase History tab, and you see a list of all the products you entered in to the database. It is empty at this time because you have not entered any information. As you install products, it's a good idea to update this section because it makes managing all the product licenses a lot easier.

5. Click Clients (Per Seat) to see your license information. If you used the per-server option during the install, click that instead. You see the number of licenses you are allowed on the server. Keep this up-to-date according to your license agreement with Microsoft.

6. Click the Help file to obtain detailed information on how to use License Manager. This Help file is extensive and answers most of your questions. When you are finished, click License|Exit to leave the program.

Step 3: Review

In this task you learned to manage your software licenses by using Microsoft's License Manager tool. By updating this information regularly, you can enhance your ability to quickly ascertain what products you have and how they are licensed.

Installation Problems

As you have progressed through this chapter, you might have encountered various problems and difficulties. Here are some of the more common ones:

System freeze-ups—When encountering a system freeze while installing NT 4.0, remember that this chapter warns you to stick to regulation equipment. Verify that all the hardware in use is on the Microsoft Hardware Compatibility List (HCL). Remember that NT is fanatical about proper IRQ and I/O settings and will have a huge hissy fit if these settings are incorrect. Use the debug version of NTDETECT to find the general area where NT is failing and correct the problem. Also, don't forget to run an anti-virus program before starting because virus infections often result in system freeze-ups.

To find this program, load your NT CD-ROM and look in the directory called \support for the program NTDETECT.CHK. Copy this program and rename it (after carefully renaming the original so you don't override it) to the .EXE extension onto the original setup disk.

`Boot cannot find NTLDR. Please insert another disk.`—NT will never load without the loader program NTLDR, and it must find it in the root directory. On some larger systems with FAT-based hard drives, the root directory can fill, causing NT to be unable to find the loader program. This is because FAT-based file systems can have only 512 files in the root directory. Remove some files and start the install again.

`Cannot read drive a:`—During the install, you cannot read one of the floppy disks. This error can result from many causes such as spilling your drink all over it first or accidentally sitting it on the magnet in your office. Seriously, sometimes the disk is unreadable, so what do you do? Insert the CD-ROM and run the WINNT32 program. Other causes include a hardware error or problem with the actual drive. If you followed the earlier install criteria and checked all your hardware before starting, you might be able to eliminate this as a cause. Otherwise, correct the problem and begin the install again. Don't forget that you can add the /b and /s switches after the WINNT or WINNT32 commands to eliminate the need for a floppy and run solely from the CD-ROM.

Summary

In this chapter, you learned the following points:

☐ Avoid installation problems by carefully following the Hardware Compatibility List.

☐ The best protection is proactive. Making backups of important data before beginning is essential to your well-being and peace of mind.

☐ Licensing your software on a per-server or per-seat method is critical to understand because you are offered only one chance to change before needing to re-install NT.

☐ You choose which type of hard disk format to use during install, either FAT-based or NTFS. Using a FAT-based system allows you to dual boot your machine but is less efficient than NTFS. You must use NTFS if you plan to use file- and directory-level security.

Workshop

To wrap up the day, you can review terms and tasks from the chapter, and see the answers to some commonly asked questions.

Terminology Review

boot—The process of starting up your computer by loading the operating system.

DNS (Domain Name Server)—A method of allocating a recognizable name for the IP address, letting you use something like www.microsoft.com rather than 207.68.137.8 to find a Web page.

FAT (File Allocation Table)—The particular style of tracking the location of each disk file on a DOS-based machine.

HCL (Microsoft's Hardware Compatibility List)—This is a list of all hardware that is certified to run with NT. You can find the list on the Internet at the following address:

http://www.microsoft.com/ntserver/hcl/hclintro.htm

I/O (Input/Output)—The process of transferring data between the computer's memory and its keyboard, printer, disks, and other devices.

kernel—Windows NT services run in two modes, kernel and user. Kernel mode is the inner guts of NT and provides system stability through its minimalist approach. In version 3.51 and earlier, the kernel was very robust and added to the strength of NT because little was placed in there that might impact the system in a negative fashion. In 4.0, more has been added to this layer, such as the video card drivers, resulting in the possibility that NT will not remain as stable as prior versions. Time will tell.

NTFS (New Technology File System)—The file system used by NT. It is more efficient than FAT-based systems and allows for file- and directory-level security.

partition—Specifying which sections of a hard drive that another operating system can use. Also used to break up a large disk into several smaller *logical* disks.

server—A network computer that provides services to client computers. Can also be called a gateway server, mail server, database server, and file server.

TCP/IP (Transmission Control Protocol/Internet Protocol)—A collection of software that allows connectivity between LANs and WANs.

workstation—Another name for the computer that performs local processing and acts as a client on a network.

Task List

With the information provided in this chapter, you installed NT Server and learned the pitfalls to avoid during installation. In most of the chapter you learned to install NT Server. You also learned how to carry out the following task:

☐ Modify the number of licenses in use on NT Server

Q&A

Q What do I need before starting the install?

A You can use any equipment you like to run NT, but if you do not want a million headaches, start by using the HCL and buying equipment that is on the list. Clones might save you money initially, but if they do not work with NT, you have a major problem. In addition, getting up-to-date NT drivers can be next to impossible.

Q How can I find out what NTDETECT is actually doing?

A NTDETECT determines the hardware in use on your machine. If a conflict occurs, the program might just stop running, leaving you puzzled. You find out all the steps that this program is taking by using the debug version. We outline exactly how to do this in the section titled "Using the Floppies and CD-ROM."

Q What can I do to help ensure an easy install?

A Use approved equipment. Test all components before trying to install NT Server. In this manner, you can be more assured that a problem lies with the install and not with some hardware malfunction. Write down all relevant information such as all I/O and IRQ settings of PC cards (formerly known as PCMCIA), sound cards, and so on.

3

Think carefully about the following queries and decide on the answers. Make sure you decide how you intend to license your software. Will you use a per-server or per-seat approach? Is the machine being added to an existing domain? If so, will it be a backup controller or ordinary server? Doing some homework prior to laying your hands on the software helps ensure that your install is relatively painless.

Q Should I use a FAT-based or NTFS file system?

A If you plan on using NT as your primary server with no other operating system, using NTFS provides sound, effective security and more efficient use of disk space. Use a FAT-based system if you need to boot different operating systems or have application needs that depend on FAT-based files.

3

Chapter 4

Installing Primary Clients

As a Windows NT Server administrator, you will spend a great deal of your time dealing with the file server. Naturally, the file server is the focus of your attention because it provides the resources your users need.

Having resources is not much use, however, when clients cannot get to them. You must spend some of your time setting up your client's computers—adding new workstations, changing network interface cards, and updating client software versions.

In this chapter, you'll get details about installing the proper software and configuring it so that your clients can get to your server. You'll see how Windows NT Server works with MS-DOS, Windows 3.*x*, Windows for Workgroups, Windows 95, Windows NT Workstation, and MacOS.

Compared to the complexities of Windows NT Server, adding and running a few files on a client computer must be a snap, right? Well, like many other areas of computers, installing and configuring workstations can go very smoothly. It also can be one of your worst nightmares. With that admonition, take a look at configuring the various clients that Windows NT Server supports.

What Is Client Software?

Client software lets desktop computers connect to your network. The software is designed to interact with a specific operating system on the client PC. Table 4.1 shows you what resources are available to the various clients. If you want to use the available resources, you need different client software for each operating system where you want to connect. Windows 95, Windows NT Workstation, and MacOS have this software built in. The rest are available on the Windows NT Server installation CD; you just have to install it on your various clients.

Table 4.1. Clients sharing resources.

Operating System Clients	Resources
MacOS	Can share with MacOS or NT network clients. Macs can use NT resources directly while also using MacOS-based network resources.
Microsoft DOS based	Basic redirector can only use network resources. Enhanced redirector can share and use network resources.
Windows 3.x	Can share and use resources.
Windows for Workgroups	Can share and use resources.
Windows 95	Can share and use resources.
Windows NT	Can share and use resources.

Before starting your installation, you should make sure that you have all the required information.

Pre-Installation Checklist

When you are ready to install software on a client, you need to gather the following information:

☐ *Software:* The Windows NT Server installation CD, this book, and the Microsoft documentation.

☐ *Hardware:* A client workstation, which is listed in the Windows NT Hardware Compatibility List (HCL).

☐ *Network interface card:* A network interface card (or adapter) for the client (listed in the HCL) and the manual. If you have a card not listed in the HCL, you need a Windows NT–compatible driver for the card.

☐ *CD-ROM drive:* You need a CD-ROM drive for your Windows NT Server to copy the software for all the clients you want to support. You also need the manual for your CD-ROM drive (just in case).

NOTE

NT does not recognize a CD-ROM connected to a third IDE port (for example, hard drives on primary and secondary ports, and a CD-ROM—for instance, Creative Labs SoundBlaster—on the third port).

☐ *Floppy disks:* During the installation process, you might need to create client installation disks for MS-DOS/Windows, Remote Access Service (RAS), and Windows for Workgroups clients.

☐ *Network configuration information:* You need the hardware interrupt (IRQ) number and the base Input/Output (I/O) address (300h, 320h, 340h, 360h, and so on) for the network interface card.

TIP

You can run WINMSD, the Windows NT diagnostics tool, to see and print the IRQ and base I/O address.

Installing the Client's Network Interface Card

Other than the workstation itself, the only other hardware you need to access the network is a network interface card (NIC) or network adapter board. As you learned in Chapter 1, "Introducing Networking," there are several popular types of networks—for example, Ethernet, Token Ring, and *ARCnet.* (Developed by Datapoint Corporation, ARCnet, or Attached Resource Computer Network, is a token-passing bus architecture with 2.5Mbps capacity. ARCnetplus has 20Mbps capacity.) Even within these types of networks, different types of media exist. For example, one Ethernet variety, known as 10Base2, uses coaxial cable, whereas another, known as 10BaseT, uses unshielded twisted-pair cable.

Physically installing the card is relatively straightforward. Just follow the manufacturer's instructions. Getting the card to work, on the other hand, might not be as easy, even with good instructions.

Task 4.1. Installing a network interface card.

Step 1: Description

This task describes how to install a network interface card (NIC) in a workstation.

Step 2: Action

1. Install the network interface card in an open slot in your workstation. Due to the varied cards and options, follow the recommendations from your card manufacturer.

2. Using your manuals, set the card to an IRQ number and a base I/O address that doesn't conflict with other workstation devices (such as the CD-ROM, video card, fax card, and so on).

> **TIP**
> Regardless of the settings you select for your card, write down the IRQ and I/O address.

3. Connect the NIC to the network cable.

Step 3: Review

Use your manufacturer's manual to learn how to install your client's NIC. You might want to simplify things by trying to use the same type of NIC for every machine. You'll gain experience with the product and its various configurations as you install and configure subsequent cards.

> **TIP**
> Don't close the workstation's cover yet because you might have to adjust the card and its settings. Fortunately, most network adapters come with configuration programs that can help determine the correct settings or at least diagnose conflicts. In addition, later versions of DOS and Windows come with the Microsoft Diagnostics program (MSD.EXE and WINMSD.EXE). This program, and others like it, examines the hardware and software on your system and reports details such as the in-use hardware interrupts. These programs are very valuable in assisting in your determination of conflicts.

Software Installation Overview

In this section, you will learn to configure Windows NT Workstation and Windows 95 clients and communicate with a Windows NT Server.

When installing a client of any ilk, you need

☐ *Software:* An operating system, such as Windows 95, pre-installed.

☐ *Hardware:* A workstation with a NIC.

☐ *Protocol:* You must know whether you're going to connect using NetBEUI, IPX/SPX, or TCP/IP.

☐ *User's name and password:* You should set up a valid account for your new users, so you can test the connection after installation.

Installing and Configuring Windows NT Workstations

In this section, you'll learn how to configure a Windows NT Workstation to use Windows NT Server and how to add a workstation client to the domain.

Task 4.2. Configuring Windows NT Workstation.

Step 1: Description

This task describes how to install and configure a Windows NT Workstation client.

Step 2: Action

1. Double-click the Control Panel icon and then double-click the Network icon. Your Network settings dialog box should look like the one shown in Figure 4.1.

Figure 4.1.

Network settings panel.

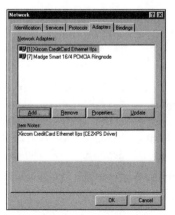

2. Select the Adapter tab and click the Add button. This opens the Select Network Adapter list as shown in Figure 4.2. Scroll through the list until you see your NIC.

Figure 4.2.
The Select Network Adapter dialog.

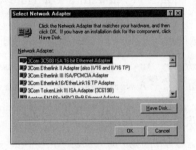

>
> **TIP**   If you do not see your network interface card listed, select Other and use the appropriate Windows NT Server adapter driver disk from the card manufacturer.

3. Choose the name of the card and then click OK. Setup displays a screen similar to the one shown in Figure 4.3.

Figure 4.3.
Network card setup screen.

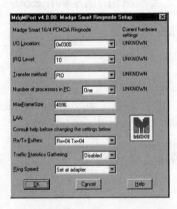

4. Complete your NIC's configuration information and click OK. The system prompts you for the location of the Windows NT distribution files. Obviously, the location of these files depends on where you originally installed Windows NT Workstation. Enter the location of the disk from which you want to load the drivers, and click OK.

5. From the Network settings panel, select the NetBEUI protocol and click OK.

6. Click OK to lock in changes.

7. Click Restart Now to restart your workstation.

8. Log in to the Windows NT Workstation as Administrator.

9. In the Main window, double-click the Control Panel icon and then double-click the Network icon.

Step 3: Review

After you install and configure a Windows NT Workstation client, you must configure your workstation so that it knows about your NIC and the protocol you selected for your network.

Task 4.3. Adding a workstation client to the domain.

Step 1: Description

This task describes how to add a Windows NT Workstation to a Windows NT domain.

Step 2: Action

1. Log in to the Windows NT Server as Administrator.

2. From the Start menu, select Programs|Administrative Tools (Common)|Server Manager.

3. Select Add to Domain from the Computer menu. This opens the Add Computer To Domain dialog as shown in Figure 4.4.

Figure 4.4.
Add Computer To
Domain dialog.

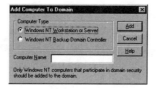

4. Select Windows NT Workstation or Server.

5. Enter the computer name of the workstation (not the user's login ID) you want to add to the domain and click Add.

6. Repeat step 5 and add all the Windows NT Workstations you are setting up, and then click Close.

Step 3: Review

Configuring the workstation is half the battle—you still need to add the workstation to a Windows NT domain. Remember that you are defining the workstation, not the individual who may use the workstation.

Task 4.4. Joining the domain as a workstation client.

Step 1: Description

This task describes how to join a Windows NT Server domain as a Windows NT Workstation.

Step 2: Action

1. Press Ctrl+Alt+Delete, and log in to the Windows NT Workstation as Administrator. Click OK.
2. From the Start menu, select Settings | Control Panel and double-click Network.
3. From the Network panel, click Change under Workgroup to display the Identification Changes panel.
4. Click Domain and enter the name of your Windows NT domain.
5. Click OK to lock in the settings.
6. Restart your workstation and log in to the workstation again.

Step 3: Review

After logging into your workstation, you joined a Windows NT Server domain by selecting Network from Settings|Control Panel under the Start menu.

Configuring a Windows 95 Workstation

If you already have Windows 95 installed, connecting to a Windows NT Server is relatively easy. If the PC already connects to a peer-to-peer network, you just have to select the domain. If the PC is currently a standalone workstation, you need to install a NIC (see Task 4.1) and select a network adapter and protocol for the workstation.

Task 4.5. Configuring Windows 95.

Step 1: Description

This task describes how to install and configure a Windows 95 client.

Step 2: Action

1. From the Start menu, select Settings|Control Panel and double-click the Network icon.
2. On the Configuration tab, click Add to open the Select Network Component Type dialog shown in Figure 4.5.

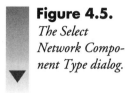

Figure 4.5.

The Select Network Component Type dialog.

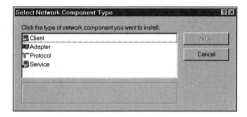

3. Highlight Adapter and click Add to open the Select Network adapters list shown in Figure 4.6.

Figure 4.6.

Select Network adapters dialog.

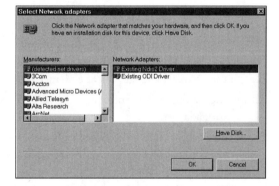

4. Choose the appropriate network adapter card manufacturer from the Manufacturers list. Select the appropriate card in the Network Adapters list. Click OK to return to the Select Network Component Type panel.

NOTE

If your card is not on the list, it probably isn't on the HCL. You have to click the Have Disk button on the Select Network adapter panel. You need a Windows 95 driver from your card manufacturer.

5. From the Configuration tab, double-click your network adapter card in the installed network component list to open the Properties dialog box for your card. You should see a screen that looks as shown in Figure 4.7.

Figure 4.7.

*The Adapter
Properties dialog.*

6. On the Driver Type tab, select Enhanced mode (32-bit and 16-bit) NDIS driver.

7. On the Resources tab, make any corrections you need to make for your particular network adapter.

8. At this point, you need to select a protocol to bind to the network adapter. (If you already connect to a network, double-click the Network icon after selecting Settings|Control Panel from the Start menu.) Select the Bindings tab and select the protocol you want to install. Click OK to return to the Network dialog box.

9. On the Configuration tab, click Add to open the Select Network Component Type screen shown previously in Figure 4.5.

10. Highlight Protocol and click Add to open the Select Network Protocol list shown in Figure 4.8.

Figure 4.8.

*The Select
Network Protocol
dialog.*

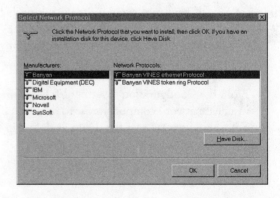

11. Choose Microsoft from the Manufacturers list. Select NetBEUI in the Network Protocols list. Click OK to return to the Select Network Component Type panel.

12. Click OK to approve all your changes.

Step 3: Review

You learned how to configure the network adapter card and protocol for a Windows 95 client. After you get this far, you can connect the Windows 95 workstation to the server.

Task 4.6. Connecting the Windows 95 workstation.

Step 1: Description

This task describes how to connect a Windows 95 client to the network.

Step 2: Action

1. From the Start menu, select Settings|Control Panel and double-click the Network icon.

2. On the Configuration tab, click Add to open the Select Network Component Type panel previously shown in Figure 4.5.

3. Highlight Client for Microsoft Networks and click Properties to open the Client for Microsoft Networks Properties dialog shown in Figure 4.9.

Figure 4.9.

The Client for Microsoft Networks Properties dialog.

4. In the Logon Validation box, select Log on to Windows NT domain. Enter the name of your Windows NT domain and click OK, which returns you to the Network dialog box.

TIP
When entering the domain name in the Logon Validation box, use uppercase. If you or someone else sets up the domain using capital letters for the name, Windows 95 will not see the server when you enter the name in lowercase.

5. On the Identification tab, you should see information you provided during setup. Change this information when it is incorrect. In either case, click OK once, and click OK twice to lock in your choices.

6. Restart your computer when prompted.

Step 3: Review

In this task, you learned how to connect a Windows 95 client. Select Client for Microsoft Networks and make sure that you have selected Log on to Windows NT domain. Now, you can test your network connection.

Task 4.7. Testing your network connection for a Windows 95 workstation.

Step 1: Description

This task describes how to verify that you have successfully connected a Windows 95 client to the network.

Step 2: Action

1. From the desktop, double-click the Network Neighborhood icon. You see a display of the network devices your workstation can see.

2. Double-click the icon for your Windows NT Server to display the shares available for this workstation. If you see share resources, you are connected and viewing files on the hard disk.

Step 3: Review

This simple task described how to test your Windows 95 connection. Select the Network Neighborhood icon to see what you can access. Now, you have configured a Windows 95 workstation as a client running on your Windows NT Server.

Configuring an MS-DOS/Windows 3.1x Workstation

In this section, you'll learn how to copy needed software from the CD-ROM to the server and to configure MS-DOS and Windows 3.1x clients.

Task 4.8. Copying client software onto your server.

Step 1: Description

This task describes how to copy client software to your server. You'll learn how to make an installation disk for MS-DOS/Windows 3.1x clients.

Step 2: Action

1. Press Ctrl+Alt+Delete and log in as the Administrator.
2. From the Start menu, select Network Client Administrator from the Programs| Administrative Tools (Common) menu. You should see a dialog like the one in Figure 4.10.

Figure 4.10.

The Network Client Administrator dialog.

3. Select Make Installation Disk Set. This option will copy all the client software and client-based network administration tools onto the server's hard disk. You should see the Share Network Client Installation Files dialog shown in Figure 4.11.

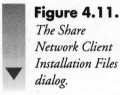

Figure 4.11.
*The Share
Network Client
Installation Files
dialog.*

NOTE

You need approximately 64MB of disk space on the server to copy the files. The first time you do this, the system copies 254 directories and 1141 files.

4. Select Copy Files to a New Directory, and then Share. You can use the default (C:\clients and Clients).

NOTE

Every time you run this option, your system changes the Destination Path and Share Name. For subsequent installations, the system changes the name of the client's subdirectory on the server where it installs the client software, starting with 0 and automatically incrementing the counter by 1. The Share Name also increments by 1.

5. Click OK. When the installation completes, click OK again, which should result in the Make Installation Disk Set dialog box.

6. Select Network Client v3.0 for MS-DOS and Windows and the appropriate Destination Drive, and click OK.

7. Insert two floppy disks when prompted, and click OK when the copying is complete.

8. Click Exit on the Network Client Administrator panel.

Step 3: Review

To create installation disks for MS-DOS and Windows clients, you use the Network Client Administrator from the Programs|Administrative Tools (Common) menu. You need two disks. Now, you can install and configure your MS-DOS and Windows 3.1x clients.

Task 4.9. Configuring MS-DOS/Windows 3.1x.

Step 1: Description

This task describes how to configure an MS-DOS workstation. You'll also use the information here as the first part of configuring a Windows 3.1x workstation.

Step 2: Action

1. At the workstation where you want to install the client software, insert Network Client v3.0 for MS-DOS and Windows Disk 1 into drive A.

2. At a DOS prompt, type a:setup. You should see the Setup for Microsoft Network Client v3.0 for MS-DOS screen. Press the Enter key to continue.

3. Setup suggests C:\NET as the location to store the networking files. Press Enter to accept, or change the path and then press Enter.

4. After you enter a user name, press Enter to continue.

5. Highlight Change Names and press Enter to continue.

6. Highlight Change Computer Name and press Enter.

7. Enter a new 15-character computer name on the screen that appears. Press Enter to continue.

8. Highlight either Change Workgroup Name or Change Domain Name (depends on how you configured your network) and press Enter.

9. Enter a new 15-character workgroup or domain name on the screen that appears. Press Enter to continue.

10. Highlight The listed names are correct and press Enter to continue.

11. After setup modifies files and archives system files, you return to the setup screen. After removing all disks, press Enter to restart the machine.

12. When prompted, type your password and press Enter.

13. Next, enter the domain you want.

14. At the prompt There is no password-list for PDAVIS. Do you want to create one? (Y/N), press Y and press Enter.

15. You are prompted for a password and then you are asked to re-enter the password to confirm you entered it correctly.

16. You are prompted for your domain password. Then you should see The command completed successfully.

17. If you are configuring a Windows 3.1x workstation, jump to Task 4.10. Otherwise, type NET USE G:\\XXXX\CLIENTS at the DOS prompt, where *XXXX* is the name of your Windows NT Server.

TIP

> When you get the error message Bad command or filename, check that C:\NET is in the path statement in the AUTOEXEC.BAT file. Use the command TYPE AUTOEXEC.BAT ¦ MORE to display the contents of the file to your screen.

Step 3: Review

With this task, you learned how to create an MS-DOS/Windows 3.1x installation disk and how to install a DOS client. In the next task, you'll use these steps to configure your Windows client. However, your DOS clients now can log in and use resources.

Task 4.10. Finishing Windows 3.1x installation.

Step 1: Description

This task describes how to complete the installation and configuration of a Windows 3.1x workstation.

Step 2: Action

1. In the Program Manager, double-click the Main icon.

NOTE

> When doing this installation, you might need the MSNET.DRV file found on Disk 6 of the Windows 3.1x installation disks.

2. Double-click the Windows Setup icon.

3. Under the Options menu, select Change System Settings.

4. Click in the Network list box, select Microsoft LAN Manager Version 2.1 Enhanced, and click OK.

5. When prompted, insert Disk 6 of the Windows 3.1x installation disks so that Windows Setup can copy the driver. When it finds the driver, or when Setup finishes, you've finished everything except connecting to the drive.

6. When prompted, restart Windows by pressing Enter.

7. Go into File Manager, and look for drive G. If you see it and didn't receive any error messages upon restart, you're finished.

Step 3: Review

With this task, you learned how to finish installing a Windows 3.1*x* client. You saw you must cut an installation disk and install some software using DOS. Then, you used Windows Setup to select the Network list box to finish configuring your client.

Configuring a Windows for Workgroups 3.11 Workstation

If you have Windows for Workgroup clients, they probably are ready for networking with your NT Server. You might have used the workstation in a peer-to-peer network. After making sure you have configured the adapter and selected the NetBEUI protocol, you can log onto a Windows NT domain.

Task 4.11. Logging a Windows for Workgroups 3.11 client onto a Windows NT domain.

Step 1: Description

With this task, you'll attach a Windows for Workgroups client to the Windows NT domain.

Step 2: Action

1. In the Program Manager, double-click the Main icon.

2. From the Main window, double-click the Control Panel icon and then double-click the Network icon. Click Startup.

3. In the Startup Settings box, check the Log On To Windows NT or LAN Manager Domain box.

4. In the Domain Name text box, type the name of the server's Windows NT domain. Click OK twice.

5. Open File Manager.

6. From the Disk menu, select Connect Network Drive.

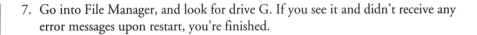

7. Pick an available drive; suppose it's G. This drive represents your connection to the network. You can use any letter of the alphabet you want, as long as the letter is not already in use. By convention, drives A through E are in use, so you might want to select a letter from F to Z.

TIP   It is a good idea to make sure that the `lastdrive=` statement in config.sys is not set to Z. By doing this, you will avoid having too few drives available to map to the network.

8. Select the server where you want to connect under Show Shared Directories on.
9. Select the shared directory you want, and click OK.

TIP   If you want to connect to this shared directory each time you start this client, check Reconnect at Startup on the Connect Network Drive window. Otherwise, your client must go through this procedure each and every time it logs on.

Step 3: Review

Adding a Windows for Workgroups client to a Windows NT domain is easy. Just select Main | Control Panel | Network | Startup and enter the name of the domain in the Domain text box and check Log On To Windows NT or LAN Manager Domain. Then, use File Manager to map the shared directories to your machine.

Activating Services for a Macintosh Workstation

In addition to Microsoft clients, you may have Macintosh clients. Installing services for MacOS clients is fairly complicated; you should read pages 1-5 of the Services for Macintosh Help File on the Windows NT CD under the support/docs subdirectory. Macintosh clients must have version 6.07 or higher of the operating system, must support LocalTalk, Ethernet, Token Ring, or Fiber Distribution Data Interface (FDDI), must support AppleTalk Phase 2, and must be capable of using AppleShare.

Task 4.12. Configuring the AppleTalk Macintosh client.

Step 1: Description

This task describes how to configure Macintosh (MacOS) clients.

Step 2: Action

1. Under the Apple menu, select Control Panels.
2. Double-click the Network icon.
3. In the Network control panel, highlight either LocalTalk or EtherTalk and close the panel.
4. Under the Apple menu, select Chooser.
5. Click the AppleShare icon. In the right-hand scroll window, select Windows NT Server and click OK.
6. When prompted, select Microsoft Authentication and click OK.
7. When prompted, connect to the server in the zone you want.
8. Click registered user, enter your login name and password, and click OK.
9. When prompted, select Microsoft UAM Volume and click OK. The Microsoft UAM Volume icon pops up on the desktop.
10. Close Chooser.
11. Double-click the Microsoft UAM Volume icon.
12. Inside the window, double-click the AppleShare folder. Click the left arrow symbol on the menu bar and then select the System folder.
13. When you have the AppleShare and System folders open on the screen, drag the Microsoft UAM Volume icon from the AppleShare folder to the System folder.
14. Restart the client and perform steps 5 through 11 to remount the Microsoft UAM Volume.

Step 3: Review

You used the control panels to configure network information and the Chooser to select the Windows NT Server. Acquiring a Windows NT Server volume is equivalent to acquiring a shared volume on an AppleTalk network.

Summary

In this chapter, you learned to

- [ ] Configure MS-DOS, Windows 3.1*x*, Windows for Workgroups 3.11, Windows 95, Windows NT Workstation, and MacOS clients.
- [ ] Create an installation disk for MS-DOS and Windows 3.1*x* clients.
- [ ] Log onto Windows NT Server from various clients.

Clients are obviously an important component of your network, for without them there wouldn't be much call for services. Take time to install your clients correctly. Test and make sure they can connect. Tomorrow, the pace quickens as you begin making your way around the system.

Workshop

To wrap up the day, you can review terms and tasks from the chapter, and see the answers to some commonly asked questions.

Terminology Review

attach—To log a workstation into a server. Also, to log a workstation onto another file server while the workstation remains logged onto the first.

directory—Pictorial, alphabetical, or chronological representation of the contents of a disk. A directory is sometimes called a catalog. The operating system uses the directory to keep track of the contents of the disk.

map—(v) To assign a workstation drive letter to a server directory.

server—A computer providing network stations with controlled access to shareable resources.

Task List

The emphasis of this chapter is on installing and configuring the various clients you might have on your network. These are the tasks you should grasp from this chapter:

- [ ] Installing a network interface card or adapter
- [ ] Installing and configuring Windows NT Workstation, Windows 95, Windows for Workgroups 3.11, MS-DOS/Windows 3.1*x*, and AppleTalk Macintosh clients

☐ Adding a workstation client to the domain

☐ Joining the domain as a workstation client

☐ Copying client software onto the server

Q&A

Q Do I have to activate services for Macintosh clients or can they use resources directly?

A Yes, you must activate services for your Macintosh clients. Read pages 1-5 of the Services for Macintosh Help File included on the Windows NT Server CD in the support/docs subdirectory.

Q Can I make my C drive available to other users?

A Not through Windows NT Server, but you can provide file service to your local drives through a peer-to-peer network operating system, such as AppleTalk, Windows 95, or Windows for Workgroups. Suppose you have Windows NT Server client programs and Windows for Workgroups client and service programs. You make your C drive available to the other users and provide them with any passwords they need. They then use Windows for Workgroups client programs to access your drive.

Q Can I use protocols other than NetBEUI?

A Yes, you can use IPX/SPX and TCP/IP. In fact, you might want to use one of these protocols because NetBEUI is not a routable protocol. You will learn about TCP/IP on Day 9, in Chapter 18, "Understanding TCP/IP."

4

DAY 3

Chapter 5

Navigating Through Windows NT Server

Now that you have learned about networks and installed a basic NT Server environment, you can begin to explore your NT Server network. The easiest method of learning something is to actually try it, so in this chapter, you'll learn how to log on and log off, how to manipulate your way through the Windows 95–type menu system, and how to use various NT tools.

Logging Onto NT Server

You can log onto NT Server from a client workstation only after you complete a number of steps. You learned how to set up the various client workstations in Chapter 4, "Installing Primary Clients." Now that you have installed NT Server 4.0, you can log on. First, though, you must log on at the server console because only two accounts are created during installation. An NT installation automatically sets up a Guest account and an Administrator account. No other accounts exist.

NOTE

> If you're upgrading to NT Server 4.0 from a prior version and choose to retain your SAM directory during the installation by selecting the Upgrade option and not the Fresh Copy option, then your old user accounts are available to you and you can use them at this time. In Chapter 10, "Understanding Security," you'll learn that the SAM (Security Account Manager) database is the place where NT maintains all security information, such as your username, password, and resource access.

The Guest Account

NT automatically sets up an account called Guest but leaves it disabled so that it cannot be used. The Guest account is typically used by staff or visitors to your business who want to perform some rudimentary actions such as typing letters or printing documents. Many organizations leave this account disabled because of the potential security risks involved.

A Guest account is often the first used by interlopers to gain access to your system. So what, you might ask? If it cannot do anything and is limited in its capability to see and modify data, what kind of risk does the Guest account pose? First, anyone can try to access your system by typing Guest at the account prompt and then typing a blank password. If you allow the Guest account to be active, the user then has access to a number of items, including anything placed into the Everyone group. Many organizations put information and resource access into this group because doing so is easy and the information applies to everyone in the organization. The organization might get sloppy over time and include items that are not for public or non-staff access. Now when someone uses the Guest account, who knows what data and resources that person can gain.

Second, if you enable the Guest account, NT decides that you want people to access the resources available to this account and therefore allows such access even without their using the account. How does this work? When you use your workstation, no sign-on is needed for a DOS-based or Mac machine. You might have a local account on your NT Workstation and so can use that machine's resources. As you work away at your workstation, you forget that you're not signed onto the network and request a domain resource. If the domain resource is one that is permitted to the Guest account, NT allows access even though you have not logged onto the server.

5

Finally, you cannot delete this account, but you can rename it. We recommend that you rename the account to something less obvious and leave the Guest account disabled.

The Administrator Account

This account is the Big Cheese, the numero uno on NT Server. It is all-powerful, which makes it a huge target for external, unauthorized access. Naturally, the account is enabled and ready for use at completion of the installation. (Not having it enabled would be kind of silly—no one could sign on!) Remember that you should have secured the password you used to create the account during the installation process. You need that password now. If you have forgotten what it is and where you placed the written backup, you are in deep trouble and need to go back to Chapter 3, "Installing Windows NT Server on the File Server." (Ugh. We really don't like suggesting that you write down passwords, but people are prone to error and forgetfulness, so what can we do? Make sure that you keep the copy somewhere really safe, however.)

Because the account is always available from the time you complete the installation, you need to think of ways to protect it. NT does not let you delete the account, so that's not an option. Deleting it would be pretty silly at this stage anyway—you wouldn't have any other accounts to use and you'd end up with the most secure NT system in the world. NT protects you from yourself, however, by making this option unavailable. So if the account is available, how can you protect it from unauthorized access attempts?

One good way to protect the account is by creating and using an effective password. Consider using a long password composed of a couple of words strung together. You must use some common sense, so avoid the rather vulgar, common terms, and use terms similar to these:

> itsalovelydaytoday
> byethebyehesaid
> wheregoeththou

Silly, but effective. Stringing words together is one of the most effective ways of creating long passwords that remain reasonably undetectable. So how long a password can you use? NT allows a maximum length of 14 characters. You determine the minimum length of a password in the Security Policies. You'll learn how to adjust this setting in Chapter 10. You should select at least six characters as the minimum length for any password. You increase the protection of any given password by remembering that this field is case-sensitive, so you can mix upper- and lowercase letters.

As you do with the Guest account, rename the Administrator account something less obvious. It remains a target for hackers, so make it as hard as possible to crack by using an account name that doesn't stick out like a sore thumb. We recall hearing of one administrator who called his account God, because it was so powerful. This type of name makes the account an easy target.

5

Log On Using the Administrator Account

Now the NT Server system is set up and ready to use. The installation process is finished, and you are eager to check out the system. If you have not installed any workstations yet, can you log on at this time? On a Novell NetWare system, you cannot use the server as a workstation and must connect from another machine. NT enables you to use the server as both a workstation and a server.

We installed NT on our laptops, for example, and used those machines to log on, run programs, and create the screen shots for this book. No workstation was attached or needed. We understand that you will probably make better use of the machine than this example, but being able to use NT in this manner is handy.

Your first task is to log onto NT and see what happens. When NT Server boots, you see a screen that indicates someone must log on. As part of NT's security, you must press the Ctrl, Alt, and Delete keys simultaneously to begin the logon process. This security helps ensure that a Trojan horse does not capture your logon keystrokes. Although this process is not entirely secure, it certainly helps. After you press this key sequence, NT loads its logo screen, as shown in Figure 5.1, with a logon screen on top of it.

Figure 5.1.

The NT Server Logo screen.

The logon screen asks for your username and, if required, your password. Remember that NT, like most systems, allows the use of blank password fields. We don't recommend setting up an account with no password because it does not provide any user accountability and presents a security exposure. Also, when you're using a workstation, NT needs to know what domain you want to use. In Chapter 9, "Understanding Domains," you'll learn about this field in detail. For now, use the default you created when you first set up NT Server.

The username you use is Administrator. As you create and set up new users, they sign on with the names assigned to them. A username in NT Server can be 20 characters long and consist of upper- or lowercase characters. It cannot include special characters such as ", /, [,], ;, :, !, and others. Ideally, you should set up usernames with a consistent standard across your organization, regardless of platform. Many organizations use an individual's last name and initial to create accounts. In this manner, you can track the person across the organization and multiple platforms, and you help give the person a sense of ownership. As a result, he or she might take better care of protecting his or her account and password.

After you enter the username and password, NT Server authenticates that information using the SAM database it created during the installation. If the information is correct, NT logs you on. If you made it this far, you should see a screen that looks like a Windows 95 desktop.

Figure 5.2 shows your NT Server desktop with its new look. Whether you love it or hate it, you're stuck with it, so you might as well enjoy it. Microsoft seems determined to move Windows 95 and NT into a symbiosis that likely will see Windows 95 eventually disappear.

Figure 5.2.

NT Server desktop.

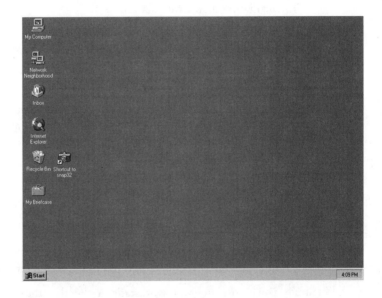

WARNING

After you sign on, remember that the username you're using has total control over this system. Do not leave it logged on and wander off to lunch or coffee. You might not have access when you return because someone has changed the password, or others might have provided themselves with all kinds of privileges while you were away. Always log off before leaving your workstation. If you do not want to log off, consider pressing Ctrl+Alt+Delete and clicking on Lock Workstation to lock the machine. This way, your programs continue to run and other people cannot gain access to your machine. You need to enter your password to regain machine access.

Task 5.1. Logging onto NT Server.

Step 1: Description

This task enables you to log onto NT Server. You perform this task each time you want to use the server.

Step 2: Action

1. Boot your workstation or server. Be aware that most times you use a workstation to log on, and an administrator boots the server first. Here, you use the server you just installed rather than a workstation.

2. Press Ctrl+Alt+Delete to start the logon process.

3. Type in your username in the User name field.

4. Press the Tab key or use the mouse to move to the Password field and enter your assigned password.

5. In the Domain area, select the domain you want to sign onto. If this installation is the first NT Server you installed, only one domain is available. If you installed in an existing domain structure, select the appropriate domain. If you're unsure, ask your help desk staff or technicians.

6. Click OK to continue the logon process.

Step 3: Review

By using the Ctrl+Alt+Delete key sequence, you executed your first command on the NT network in this task. You included your username to identify yourself to the network and included your password (if required) to verify you're accountable for the use of that username.

Typically, you log on using your workstation rather than the server console. The process does differ depending on the operating system in use on your workstation. You need to install the proper client software before NT will allow the access. You learned how to set up workstations and log on using those workstations yesterday afternoon in Chapter 4. Only the administrator should have access to the server console as this poses a certain risk. You'll learn about these risks two days from now when you begin working with Chapter 10.

If you need to log off from a session to go to lunch, leave for the day, or for any other reason, go to the "Logging Off from NT Server" section.

Using NT Server Utilities

Several utilities are available in NT 4.0. These tools are typically divided up into the following groups:

☐ Command prompt utilities

☐ Administrator Graphical User Interface tools

Command prompt utilities such as NET START and NET SEND operate from the Run command or from a Command Prompt window. These commands are often ignored, yet they serve a quick and useful function. They work on NT workstations and NT Server; however, some commands run only from the server. These commands are listed in Appendix B, "Windows NT Server Command Reference."

Administrator Graphical User Interface (GUI) tools are specially designed for a supervisor's use. They are extremely powerful and must be used judiciously. Examples of these utilities include User Manager and Server Manager.

Using the Command Prompt Utilities

Some of the command prompt commands are available only to administrators; however, the remaining commands are available to users. See Appendix B for details as to what commands can be used by each type of account.

To begin using these utilities, you open a window that allows connectivity from the command prompt. You can find it by choosing Start|Programs, as you can see in Figure 5.3. You also can run the commands from the Run line in the Start menu; however, this way the commands execute by opening and then promptly closing the window, leaving no trace of what happened. This method might be all right for a quick command that you're sure will produce the desired result, but most of the time you want to see what happens and the ensuing results of your command. If this is the case, stick with the command prompt window.

Figure 5.3.

Opening the Command Prompt window.

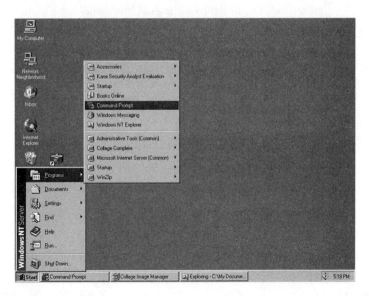

The commands you use in the Command Prompt window include being able to start and stop services, manipulate user accounts, view and change domain members, and send and receive messages. You can get Help from NT Server if you need to explore the commands in more detail.

Using NET HELP

If you're a new user of NT Server 4.0, you will probably use the NET HELP command the most until you become familiar with each NET command. This command shows you all the variables available in the help database and the syntax for obtaining the appropriate help information. Figure 5.4 shows an example of the NET HELP command in use. Note that the reply shows a list of available commands but not the specific options each command has available to it. That information comes later.

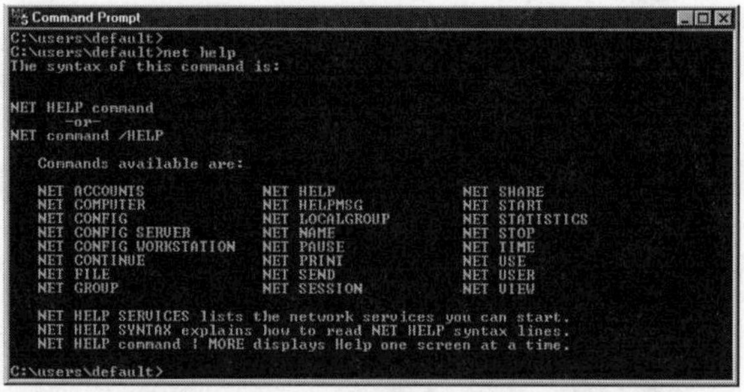

Figure 5.4.

Using the NET HELP *command.*

As you begin to learn the available commands, you might need specific help on a particular command. You find it by adding the command name to the end of your NET HELP command. To get help on the VIEW command, for example, type NET HELP VIEW in the Command Prompt window.

Don't forget to use the ¦more switch for commands that offer more than one screen of information. For example,

NET HELP USER ¦MORE

Using this command provides you with the information shown in Figure 5.5.

5

Figure 5.5.

Using specific Help options.

As you saw in Figure 5.4, the help command does not provide any assistance for a number of services available in NT. As you come across these services and require additional understanding, you need to reference the NT documentation or some of the excellent books currently available. For example, consider acquiring the excellent book *Windows NT Server 4 Unleashed*, Sams Publishing, by Jason Garms, et al, 1996.

If you use the NET HELP SERVICES command, you find that no help is available for the following services:

> DHCP Client or Server
> Gateway Service for NetWare
> OLE
> Remote Access Server (RAS)
> Remote Procedure Call Service (RPC)
> Remoteboot
> Spooler
> TCP/IP
> Windows Internet Name Service (WINS)

This list is not complete, but it should give you the general idea that the existing help, although useful, is not a panacea. You have to use other books and information sources when manipulating NT.

If you're unsure of some of the conventions used in the help area of NT, use the command NET HELP SYNTAX, as shown in Figure 5.6, to familiarize yourself with the particulars.

5

Figure 5.6.

Help command syntax.

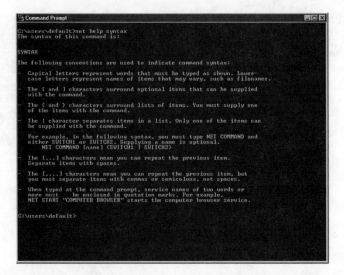

Task 5.2. Using the NET HELP command.

Step 1: Description

This task shows you how to obtain help within NT Server. You perform this task each time you need additional information on a particular command.

Step 2: Action

1. Make sure that you are signed on with an Administrator account.

2. Choose Start|Programs|Command Prompt. The Command Prompt window then opens.

3. At the prompt, type NET HELP SYNTAX and press the Enter key. (Remember to add ¦More after the word SYNTAX if too much information is available to fit on one screen.)

4. After reviewing any command syntax you might need, type CLS and press Enter to clear the screen. (Remember that case of the letters doesn't matter.) Although clearing the screen isn't entirely necessary, doing so makes it easier for you to read the information presented from each command.

5. Type in the help command you need. For this example, to get more information on how to use the SEND command, type NET HELP SEND. You can enter any valid command after the word HELP to get specific help on that topic.

6. After you're finished, type EXIT to close the Command Prompt window.

Step 3: Review

By using the command prompt and various help commands in this task, you obtained the information necessary for you to understand how the NT commands work. You'll use this

 task repeatedly as you learn to manage Windows NT Server.

Using Other NET Commands

A number of commands are available from the command prompt. They are handy if you prefer keying commands to using the GUI interface. In the following sections, you'll read about some of the more useful commands. If you remain unconvinced of the benefits, use the GUI interface. After all, our intent is to introduce you to NT, not change your particular keying preference.

NET STATISTICS

The NET STATISTICS command provides statistics for the computer on which you run it. The list includes all the services you're running that provide statistics. You can run this command for either the server or the workstation. The command does not travel the network, though; it applies only to the machine on which you execute it. As you can see in Figures 5.7 and 5.8, the command provides you with the number of password and permission violations as well as the number of files accessed and other information. To run the command, select either workstation or server, and append that word to show either NET STATISTICS WORKSTATION or NET STATISTICS SERVER.

Figure 5.7.

Running the NET STATISTICS WORKSTA-TION *command.*

5

Figure 5.8.

Running the NET STATISTICS SERVER *command.*

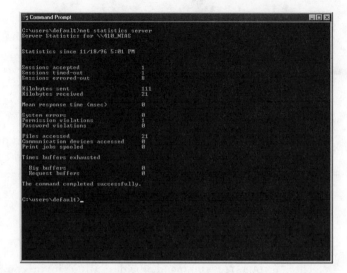

NET SEND

The NET SEND command enables you to send messages to the servers and workstations on your network. You use it to send a message to an individual user, the users within your domain, or all the users connected to the server.

This command works only when you add parameters that tell it who and what to send. This command is a useful alternative to electronic mail, but if your organization is already functioning well with an electronic mail package, you likely will use the send message infrequently. Typically, you use the send command to tell everyone that the network will be unavailable at a certain time and to log off. The major advantage to using this command is its prominence on the user's screen. When a person on an NT workstation receives a send message, the message pops up on the screen immediately and doesn't disappear until he or she clicks OK. Electronic mail messages are easily buried within a user's mailbox, never to reappear until it's too late.

In older versions of NT, you could use this command to send files across the network. This capability is no longer supported in NT 4.0.

The typical parameters you use at the command prompt look like

```
NET SEND name message
```

where *name* is the field used to identify the person or persons you want to receive the message, and *message* is the text you want to tell everyone. You don't need to use quotation marks, and you can send fairly long messages. A typical message can be as long as a dozen lines or so, more than enough for day-to-day messaging needs.

You can get help on this command using the NET HELP SEND command, as shown in Figure 5.9.

Figure 5.9.

Getting help with the
SEND *command.*

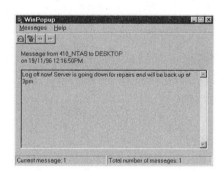

The NET SEND command provides you with a relatively simple method of reaching your user community. As long as each user is logged on and running a messenger service on his or her machine, he or she gets any message sent. NT machines, specifically, need to run the messenger service. Windows and Windows 95 machines should run the WinPopup program, as shown in Figure 5.10. WinPopup can be run minimized but must be running all the time for the user to receive messages. Place this program in the user's startup box so that it runs each time the user starts Windows.

Figure 5.10.

Receiving a message with
WinPopup.

After receiving the message, the user might want to reply to the sender. Figure 5.11 shows a message being returned using the WinPopup Send command and specifying the server as the receiver. Figure 5.12 shows how the message appears on the server.

Figure 5.11.

Replying to a message.

Figure 5.12.

The reply on the server.

You can use the following sample commands over the next few days to send surprise messages to any users you might have installed in your NT 4.0 system.

To send a simple message telling everyone on the domain to log off, type this:

```
net send * Log off now, please
```

To send a message to a computer named Desktop on your system, type this:

```
net send desktop Hi machine user, How are you?
```

To send a message to Bill who is part of another domain, such as Accounting, type this:

```
net send bill \accounting This is a test of the send command
```

Experiment with other commands until you're familiar with the send message and know some of its quirks.

NET CONFIG

The NET CONFIG command enables you to see the current configuration information for any NT 4.0 server or workstation. Although you also can change some of the information, we discuss viewing data only. It's better for new users to use the GUI interface when changing data until you fully understand the ramifications.

Remember that your server can also act as a workstation (mine does), and this capability is one advantage over a Novell system in which you would need a second machine to get to this part of your two-week journey. Using the NET CONFIG command, you can specify either server or workstation as a variable. The command gives you the following information:

☐ The computer's name

☐ The software version in use (Note that it does not differentiate between NT Server and NT Workstation.)

☐ The network card and its address

☐ Whether the server is visible to the network, how many users can log on, and how many files each user can open

☐ The current idle time

Using this command, you can quickly determine some basic configuration information. Figure 5.13 shows an example of a workstation command.

Figure 5.13.

Using the NET CONFIG WORKSTATION *command.*

NET VIEW

The NET VIEW command provides a quick overview of the resources being shared on a computer. When used without any other options, it displays a list of computers in the current domain or network.

To see what resources are available to the computer you're using, type

```
net view
```

Figure 5.14 shows the output from this command on a server with one connected desktop workstation.

Figure 5.14.

Using the NET VIEW *command.*

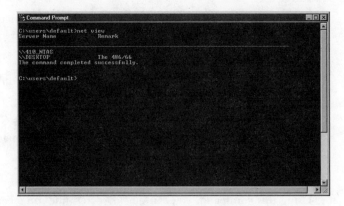

To see what resources the server is sharing with the network, type

```
net view \\servername
```

where *servername* is the server you want to select. Figure 5.15 shows the output from this command on a server called \\410_NTAS.

Figure 5.15.

Using the NET VIEW *servername command.*

A number of other commands are available within NT. The commands listed in this chapter are primarily information-gathering commands and as such can be relatively harmless. Other commands enable you to set up new users, change domain memberships, and set the time across the network. You'll see some of these other commands demonstrated in the following sections using the GUI interface that NT provides.

Using Administrator GUI Tools

As an administrator on an NT server, you have a lot of powerful tools available to you for managing the server accounts and restricting access in an appropriate manner. You'll learn more details about security in Chapter 10. In that chapter, we take you on a tour of the tools and show you around the city, so to speak.

You can find the Administrator GUI tools by choosing Start|Programs|Administrative Tools (Common) on your desktop machine, as shown in Figure 5.16. These tools are available on a workstation running NT or on the server itself.

Figure 5.16.

Finding the NT Server Administrative tools.

NT Server 4.0 provides a number of tools for the administrator, as you can see in Figure 5.16. The key tools are Server Manager, User Manager for Domains, Performance Monitor, and Diagnostics tools. Each tool has a valid use, but as the administrator, you'll use some more than others in the day-to-day operation of your network.

During the 14 days of working through this book, you'll use these tools as you perform the tasks assigned to each day. Here, you get an overview so that you understand what is available and gain an understanding of the purpose of each tool. This way, you are prepared if problems occur and you need to resolve them using the tools available to you.

Administrative Wizards

One of the new items NT 4.0 brings you is the Administrative Wizard. When you use this tool, NT guides you through the steps necessary to perform various administrative tasks. This feature is a real boon for new administrators, although it quickly pales as you begin to understand the various processes and use the tools designed for each specific task.

The Administrative Wizard takes you step by step through the tasks necessary to complete the objective. As you see in Figure 5.17, you can add new user accounts, perform group management tasks, set file and folder permissions, and add printers and modems.

Figure 5.17.

Using the Administrative Wizard.

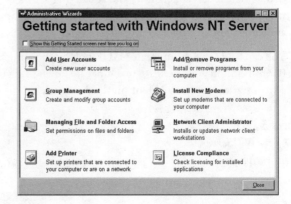

Use this tool early to gain understanding of NT or to get new administrators active quickly in supporting the user community.

Backup

The Backup tool provides you with a method for performing backup and recovery of server data. The first time you start the program, it runs awhile collecting all the relevant data on your file structure and discovering what tape backup device you're using. Sometimes NT does not find your tape device even though it exists on the HCL, or it tries to install the wrong one. In these cases, you need to install the device manually.

Many organizations use more robust products to back up their systems, such as Seagate's Desktop Management Suite with the new Backup Exec program for both NetWare and NT. If you have a smaller site and don't need these more expensive tools, the Backup tool performs just fine. Figure 5.18 shows the Backup window.

Using the Operations drop-down menu in the Backup window, you can back up, restore your data, and manage your backup tapes. You can find more detailed information on using Backup in the extensive Help menus.

Figure 5.18.

The NT Backup window.

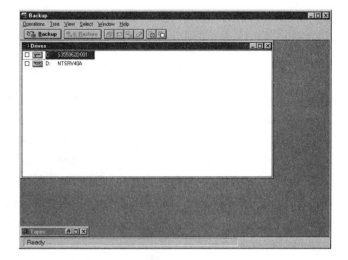

Disk Administrator

The Disk Administrator tool enables you to manage your disk drives. It includes and adds to such operations as formatting a drive and performing fault tolerance functions. Using this tool, you can create and delete partitions on new disk drives, find out what free space is available for use, change drive letter assignments, and establish or remove disk-mirror sets. (You use this tool in Chapter 13, "Exploring Windows NT Server Files and Directories," on Day 7.)

Event Viewer

You use the Event Viewer tool to monitor events occurring within NT. Events consist of any significant occurrence in the operating system, such as an interrupted power supply or a server hard drive that has run out of free space.

These are the three main event logs:

- [ ] System
- [ ] Security
- [ ] Application

The System log records all events logged by the NT system components such as the failure of tape and modem drivers or other components during startup.

The Security log provides details about attempted logons and file and object accesses. The events shown in the Security log are a result of using the Audit Policy in User Manager for Domains. By starting User Manager for Domains and choosing Options|Audit, you are presented with a screen in which you can select events, as shown in Figure 5.19.

Figure 5.19.

Audit Policy events.

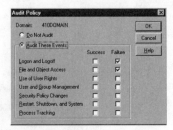

Select the events that will help you ensure the security of your system. At the least, consider tracking failed logons and logoffs, and file and object accesses. Consider recording successful changes such as User and Group Management, Security Policy Changes, and Restart, Shutdown, and System events by selecting these check boxes. In this manner, you can review what happened if something goes wrong. The application log is used primarily for tracking events issued by your system applications. Microsoft BackOffice products make good use of these logs. The good thing about these logs is their capability to provide event data in one location instead of having each application create its own log.

Event logging starts automatically when you run NT. It can be stopped by using the Services tool in the Control Panel. You might want to ensure occasionally that it is still running to prevent another administrator from accidentally shutting it down and removing your audit capabilities. You examine this audit process further on Day 13.

License Manager

You learned about the License Manager tool in Chapter 3. You'll learn how to set up licenses and track them across the domain using this tool in Chapter 24, "Using the Windows NT Server Audit System."

Note that License Manager does not enforce licensing requirements. Compliance must still come from within each organization. Remember to observe all legal requirements to save your organization from the embarrassment and cost of a lawsuit.

Migration Tool for NetWare

If you're planning to use your NT LAN with Novell's NetWare, the Migration Tool for NetWare will be invaluable. Although far from perfect, it does provide a useful function if you plan to eliminate NetWare and move all your users to NT. As you move your NetWare users to NT, you need to re-create all their accounts on the NT machine, resulting in a lot of duplication and overhead. The migration tool helps ameliorate this process.

The Migration Tool for NetWare moves user accounts to the NT server with options for providing the new NT accounts with different passwords. It has to set up new passwords because NetWare does not provide you with the current ones (and rightly so). It also moves all the current server files from the NetWare file system onto your selected NT server. You use this tool at the end of your 14 days, in Appendix C, "Migrating to NT from Novell."

Network Client Administrator

You use the Network Client Administrator tool to install or update your network client workstations. We found it easier to simply copy the disk sets from our NT CD-ROM onto floppy disks and perform a standard setup command on the workstation. The Network Client Administrator tool doesn't enable you to tell it what card settings are being used when you install, for example, a Xircom Ethernet adapter. You need to modify a file manually to change the IRQ and I/O addresses.

The Network Client Administrator requires a DOS-formatted floppy disk but doesn't provide any way of making one. You need to go to a DOS machine, format a disk, and bring it back to your server. Too many extra steps, in our opinion. Stick to the client machine setup steps outlined yesterday in Chapter 4.

Performance Monitor

The Performance Monitor is a graphical tool that measures the performance of your computers. It provides detailed information on the behavior of processors, memory, cache, threads, and processes. This tool gives you valuable information about queue lengths, delays, and throughput or congestion information.

The Performance Monitor, shown in Figure 5.20, provides a number of different options that enable you to tell it to provide ongoing charting, alerts, or logging. You can select these activities for different computers on your network. Use this tool regularly on your network to ensure that no bottlenecks or problems have an impact on the user community.

Figure 5.20.

The Performance Monitor.

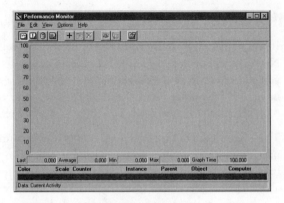

You'll learn how to use this tool effectively when you reach Day 14.

Remote Access Administration

Version 3.5*x* of NT offered a service called Remote Access Service (RAS). In NT 4.0, Microsoft begins to rename this facility Dial-up Networking (DUN), just as in Windows 95. (See, we told you that the secret plan is to eliminate Windows 95 eventually and have NT take over the world.) Basically, DUN sets up your dial-in modem access to run and look just as if you were on the local area network. However, throughout NT documentation you find both terms used, so a complete name change is still a ways off. We stick to RAS in this chapter because this term is currently the one best-known by those using NT.

This service works a lot like Carbon Copy or pcANYWHERE, two products that enable a user to connect to another machine and gain LAN access. NT makes your modem act like a network card, connecting you to the network just as though you were physically connected via a NIC, rather than dialing in from some remote location.

An advantage of using this tool over third-party tools is cost. DUN comes with NT and is therefore essentially free. The other tools get expensive as you increase the number of users who need remote access.

Dial-up Networking enables you to use your computer as an Internet gateway, an Internet service provider, and for remote dial-in to NT or other servers. This tool is really flexible and reasonably robust. You'll learn how to set up and use DUN (or RAS) in Chapter 19, "Understanding DHCP."

Server Manager

Server Manager, which enables you to manage domains and computers, is arguably one of the tools you'll use the most within your NT network. It allows access to both the machine you're signed onto as well as remote computers, whereas the Services and Server tools in the Control Panel allow access only to the local computer. Using Server Manager, you can view a list of connected users, view the open and shared resources, and manage a number of functions such as replicating directories, adding and removing computers from the domain, and synchronizing servers with the Primary Domain Controller.

To use this tool to administer a domain, you must be signed on with membership in either an Administrator, Domain Administrator, or Server Operators group. A member of the Account Operators group can use it, but only to add or remove computers. Some of the functions within Server Manager are further restricted to only Administrator and Domain administrators, and this tool issues an error message if others try to use those functions.

On Day 8, you examine the use of Server Manager in detail, looking at each function and learning effective management of your network.

System Policy Editor

The System Policy Editor, a powerful new tool in version 4.0, enables you to control any user's machine entirely, allowing the user to execute only the applications you specify. Both Windows NT and Windows 95 use a System Policy Editor (SPE), and both modify the Registry of a workstation to restrict a user's access.

You must be careful when using this tool because you can easily lock out all users, including the administrator. Be extra careful when you're setting up a policy for either Default User or Default Computer to ensure that you do not apply the wrong settings and lock everyone out of the system.

We know clients who install this tool to manage their user workstations and enforce company-wide policies. Properly used and managed, it is a powerful compliance tool. We suggest that you test all changes on a test network before applying them to a production environment.

User Manager for Domains

User Manager for Domains is the most heavily used facility for NT administrators. With it, you can manage security for domains, servers, and workstations. It enables you to add and modify user accounts, create or change groups, and implement trust relationships.

As an administrator, you will become very familiar with this tool and use it on a day-to-day basis. You'll learn how to use the various functions on Day 6 as you proceed through the chapters on account management and managing user access. For now, you can catch your first look in Figure 5.21, where you see the basic screen using a 410DOMAIN server.

Figure 5.21.

*User Manager for
Domains.*

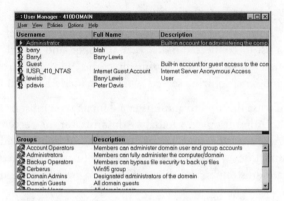

As you see in Figure 5.21, User Manager allows access to User, View, Policies, and Options menus, in addition to the standard NT Help menu. You choose the User menu to create new groups or view the properties of selected users and groups. The View menu enables you to sort the list either by full name or username. This capability is especially handy when you're hunting for a particular user and know only his or her name.

By using the Policies menu, you can set up the basic standards you want user accounts to adhere to, such as minimum password age and length and account lockout options. You also can set individual rights for users here, such as the ability to add workstations to a domain or shut down the system. This menu provides a great degree of detail and flexibility in who is permitted to perform what functions within NT. You also can set the audit of events in this menu by selecting the events on which you want to report. The Options menu provides standard functions such as Fonts and Save Settings on Exit.

Windows NT Diagnostics

The final tool available in the Administrative Tools menu is the NT Diagnostics monitor. This tool shows information about your machine in a number of different windows. It includes what version of NT you're running, what system is in use, the current display options, and the current drives attached to the system.

In addition, the NT Diagnostics monitor provides separate views for Memory, Services, Resources, Environment, and Network. Each one provides you with detailed information that helps you resolve problems and troubleshoot the system. Figure 5.22 shows the amount of detail available in the Memory panel. As you can see, this small server runs with one processor and 24MB of physical memory.

Figure 5.22.
Windows NT Diagnostics showing memory usage.

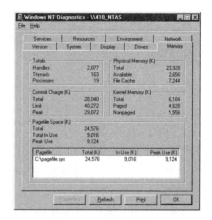

Understanding and Using NT 4.0 Books Online

In the Windows NT Programs menu, Microsoft provides NT manuals online. You can find three primary books, although the third concerns copyright information and as such is not really applicable to day-to-day administration of the server. We don't want to diminish the need for understanding the issues involved in protecting software from copyright abuse, but we are merely pointing out that this section of the book is a copyright notice, not a learning tool.

The two main books available are *Concepts and Planning* and *Networking Supplement*. Within these books is a plethora of useful information. In the first book, *Concepts and Planning*, you find the following chapters:

- ☐ Welcome
- ☐ Managing Windows NT Server Domains
- ☐ Working with User and Group Accounts
- ☐ Managing User Work Environments
- ☐ Managing Shared Resources and Resource Security
- ☐ Setting up Print Servers
- ☐ Backing Up and Restoring Network Files
- ☐ Protecting Data
- ☐ Monitoring Performance
- ☐ Monitoring Events
- ☐ Monitoring Your Network

5

☐ Managing Client Administration

☐ Licensing and License Manager

☐ Windows NT Registry

☐ Other Application Environments

The other main book contains valuable information about networking. In this book, *Networking Supplement*, you find the following chapters:

☐ Welcome

☐ Microsoft TCP/IP and Related Services for Windows NT

☐ Microsoft TCP/IP Architecture

☐ Implementation Considerations

☐ Routing in Windows NT

☐ Understanding Remote Access Service

☐ Installing and Configuring Remote Access Service

☐ RAS Security

☐ Maintenance and Troubleshooting

☐ X.25 PAD Support

☐ Logging onto Remote Computers Using RAS Terminal and Scripts

☐ Point-to-Point Tunneling Protocol (PPTP)

☐ Overview of NetWare Compatibility Features

☐ Gateway Service for NetWare

☐ Migration Tool for NetWare

☐ Introduction to Services for Macintosh

☐ How Services for Macintosh Work

☐ Planning Your AppleTalk Network

☐ Setting Up Services for Macintosh

☐ Configuring Services for Macintosh

☐ Setting Up Printers

☐ Working with Macintosh-Accessible Volumes

☐ Managing the File Server

☐ Troubleshooting

☐ RAS Registry Values

☐ RAS Cabling

☐ Understanding Modem.inf

☐ Services for Macintosh Registry Values

☐ How Macintosh Filenames are Translated

These books can be placed on the server or left on the NT CD-ROM. If space is an option, leave them on the CD-ROM and make them available when needed. To use the books, follow the steps outlined in Task 5.3.

Task 5.3. Using the Microsoft Windows NT Server Books Online.

Step 1: Description

This task shows you how to obtain additional help within NT Server using the Online Books. This task demonstrates using the books from an NT workstation.

Step 2: Action

1. Sign onto your workstation in the normal fashion. You don't need Administrative privileges to view the books.

2. Choose Start|Programs|Books Online. You should see a window similar to the one shown in Figure 5.23.

Figure 5.23.

Help Topics: Windows NT 4.0 Books Online.

3. Select the main topic shown in the window under Contents. Then press Enter or double-click. You see the three books under the main entry.

4. Select one of the books. For this example, select Concepts and Planning. Then press Enter or double-click your selection. You then are shown a series of chapters.

5. Choose a chapter that interests you, and take a look at it. At any time, you can exit by clicking the close button.

Step 3: Review

By using the Books Online function in this task, you obtained the information necessary for you to understand how to manage NT networks. You'll use this task as needed as you learn all about Windows NT Server.

Logging Off from NT Server

You have now finished exploring the wonders of NT Server. It's time to log off from the network. Logging off disconnects you from the network properly. Never disconnect from the network by turning off your computer or rebooting your workstation because these methods can cause problems with the files and programs you're using. In a similar vein, as mentioned yesterday, never walk away and leave your workstation logged on because an unauthorized person could gain access to the network and your files and programs. As mentioned earlier, you might use the Lock Machine option or consider setting up a password-protected screen saver instead of logging off.

Logging Off NT 4.0 Workstations

To log off an NT workstation, choose Start|Shut Down and then select the appropriate option. If you're finished for the day, for example, choose Shut down the computer? Then click the Yes icon. If you're rebooting the machine, choose Restart the computer. If you want to log on as a different user, choose Close all programs and log on as a different user.

Logging Off Windows 95 Workstations

To log off from a Windows 95 workstation, follow the steps in the preceding section. You choose Start|Shut Down and then select the appropriate option. If you're finished for the day, for example, choose Shut down the computer? Then click the Yes icon. If you're rebooting the machine, choose Restart the computer. If you want to log on as a different user, choose Close all programs and log on as a different user.

Logging Off Windows and DOS Workstations

To log off from a Windows or DOS workstation, get to a DOS prompt and type net logoff. Then press Enter.

You now know that you can log off using various commands depending on the workstation you use to attach to the network.

Summary

In this chapter, you learned the following points:

- [ ] How to log onto NT Server using an Administrator account or a User account
- [ ] All about the Help function available in NT and how to migrate through the various panels
- [ ] How to use the command prompt and access the NET utilities available to you as an administrator
- [ ] What the various Administrator tools are and how they assist you in the day-to-day administration of NT networks
- [ ] How to access and use the Microsoft Books Online to get help in understanding Windows NT
- [ ] How to properly log off the network

Workshop

To wrap up the day, you can review terms and tasks from the chapter, and see the answers to some commonly asked questions.

Terminology Review

command line—The DOS prompt or area within the Run command on the Start menu in a Windows operating system.

command prompt—The window in NT that provides DOS-like capabilities, enabling you to enter commands that execute within that window.

guest—The name provided to a type of account usually used by people who do not normally have an account on the system. The account is typically restricted in capabilities. NT 4.0 automatically provides this account but leaves it disabled for safety.

GUI—Graphical User Interface.

log off—To disconnect from the network or server.

log on—To identify yourself to a server or network after a connection has been established.

5

SAM—Security Account Manager. The database that NT uses to maintain user account information and other security-related data. It resides in the Registry of the Primary Domain Controller.

Task List

With the information gained in this chapter, you can begin to explore the facets of NT Server. You now know how to log on and use Help and how to get additional detailed information using the Microsoft Books available online. You learned to do the following tasks:

- ☐ Log onto NT Server
- ☐ Use a number of NET commands to get information about the network
- ☐ Obtain additional information using Microsoft Books

Q&A

Q Is a Help menu still available?

A As you learned in this chapter, you can get help from a number of locations. Each window usually offers a Help menu specific to that particular function. Additional help is available in both the Microsoft Books and when you use the NET command through a Command Prompt window.

Q Should I use the command prompt or GUI interface?

A NT provides both options for a number of tasks. If you're more comfortable issuing command-line options, then by all means utilize this tool. For beginners and those more familiar with pointing and clicking, use the GUI interface. There is no right or wrong way here; your choice is primarily a personal preference.

Q Can I use my server machine as a workstation?

A One of the major differences between NT and NetWare is the capability to run a one-machine network. In most cases, running such a network is hardly a valid reason for having a server because it defeats the purpose of building a network. Being able to use the server in this manner occasionally is handy, especially in small organizations, so that you don't have to buy a dedicated server machine. We find it useful for doing training seminars because we don't always have to bring a second machine to demonstrate NT server facilities.

Chapter 6

Exploring Windows NT Server

In the preceding chapter, you spent the morning learning how to navigate Windows NT Server. In this chapter, you expand on that knowledge and gain a more in-depth understanding of the nuances involved in exploring all the facets of NT. You start with the simple task of finding out who you are when connected to the server. This task is easier than finding out who you are in the metaphysical sense.

Discovering Who You Are

Discovering who you are is such a common challenge. You go through life attempting to refine this process. Or perhaps you're comfortable in the knowledge of who you are and you're no longer searching. In NT, the process is a little different.

Typically, you know how you signed on and what username you're using, but you might be unsure of which groups you belong to or what file and directory access you have. You can find this information while logged into a workstation by submitting the NET CONFIG command in a command prompt window. Figure 6.1 shows a Windows 95 workstation example of this type of window.

Figure 6.1.

Using the command NET
CONFIG.

In this figure, you can find various pieces of information. This information includes the name of the computer and the username you're using. The workgroup you are part of is also shown. (You'll learn about workgroups in more detail on Day 5 in the chapters about domains and security within NT 4.0.) Finally, you'll see information concerning the version numbers of the software in use.

When you use a Windows NT workstation, the command looks a little different, as you saw in this morning's chapter on navigating.

Manipulating the Command Prompt Window

You probably use the command prompt a lot, but perhaps by now you want to change how the window appears on the desktop. When we first used the command prompt on our laptop computers, the box was too small, so we made it appear larger and then made that size the default.

How do you manipulate the window? You see in NT that this window cannot be enlarged using the standard drag-and-drop windows formatting. You can make the window smaller, but not any larger. That's strange, don't you think?

How do you manage this chore in NT? One method is to begin by opening a command prompt window. Next, place the mouse cursor somewhere on the blue top section of the open

6

dialog box (the title bar), and click the right mouse button. (If you place the mouse cursor actually in the open box, the left button does not work.) A Properties dialog box similar to the example shown in Figure 6.2 then appears.

Figure 6.2.

The Command Prompt Properties dialog box.

Within this properties dialog box are four main tabs:

☐ Options

☐ Font

☐ Layout

☐ Colors

You explore each of these tabs in the following paragraphs. Because you use the command prompt so often, you might as well ensure that the open window suits your personal preferences.

On the *Options* tab, you can perform various changes. The first change is modifying the size of the cursor. If you're like me, and small items are getting a little harder to see, then select the large cursor option. Instead of seeing a small blinking box, you then see one about three times larger. A medium selection gives you a cursor about twice as large as the standard one. When you select the different size, NT asks if you want the selection to apply to the current window or if you want it to become the one used each time you open the command prompt. NT doesn't make this decision awfully clear, however, as the prompt asks the following two questions:

☐ Apply properties to current window only

☐ Modify shortcut which started this window

The second option makes your changes more permanent by telling the system to add this change each time it opens the command prompt window. The first (and default) option applies the changes to the open window but does not save the changes, so you need to add them each time you open the window.

In the Display Options field, you can select whether the window opens in Full Screen or Window mode. The typical setting is Window mode, which is the default on an $x86$-based machine. With this option, you can use the command prompt and still see other parts of the desktop. Full Screen does just that—it makes the open window fit across the entire screen, hiding all other parts of the desktop. Choose the option you want to use. Press Alt+Enter to toggle between the two settings while a command prompt window is open.

Command history works in a similar fashion to the old Doskey command that enabled you to reuse previously keyed commands. In an NT command prompt window, you need to hold the Shift key and press on the up or down arrow to scroll through the previous commands you typed.

 TIP

> You don't need to add Doskey anywhere in an NT Server or workstation. Command reuse is always available in the command prompt window.

How many commands are available for scrolling depends on the Buffer Size you use. NT defaults to save commands automatically using four buffers, each with a size of 50. This number affords many keystrokes—more than you'll probably need. You can discard duplicate entries by selecting the Discard Old Duplicates check box.

If you like using the mouse to select text, select the QuickEdit Mode check box. Insert mode allows text to be inserted at the cursor instead of being replaced.

On the *Font* tab, you can modify how the text appears in the window. You select the size and particular font you want to see by clicking in the appropriate Size and Font option boxes.

On the *Layout* tab, you modify how and where the screen appears on the desktop. You select the Screen Buffer size, which sets the amount of data the buffers hold, and you select a Window Size by increasing or decreasing the Width and Height as needed. Finally, you either let the system place the window on the screen or set specific placement options.

You can play with the colors of the command prompt window on the *Colors* tab until the cows come home. NT enables you to set a color for the text and the background.

TIP
You need to restart the command prompt window to see the changes made using the Font, Layout, and Colors options. Changes made in the Options component take effect in the current window.

Task 6.1. Resizing the command prompt.

Step 1: Description

This task enables you to change the default size of the command prompt window. You perform this task any time you want to use a different size window.

Step 2: Action

1. Log onto the workstation. You learned this process in this morning's session on navigating NT Server.

2. Open a command prompt window. Choose Start|Programs|Command Prompt.

3. Place you cursor on the line where you see the words Command Prompt and right-click. Then select Properties.

4. In the Properties dialog box, click the Layout tab. You then see three selection boxes called Screen Buffer Size, Window Size, and Window Position.

5. Move the cursor to the area called Window Size and change the settings. You see the effects of your change in the small preview window on the left. Try different settings until you're comfortable with what you see.

6. Click OK when you're ready to continue. NT asks whether you want the change to apply to the current window only or to all future command prompt windows. The message isn't very clear. When it asks whether you want to modify the shortcut that started this window, NT really is asking whether you want to make the change permanent.

7. Select the Apply properties to current window button and click OK. You then see the new window size.

8. Repeat these steps as needed. If you like a certain size, choose the option to make those changes permanent. You can change other options at the same time such as the background and text colors or font type and size.

Step 3: Review

By using the Properties dialog box, you manipulated the command prompt window to suit your particular idiosyncrasies. We changed ours, for example, to appear with a blue background and black text.

Understanding and Using UNCs

UNC is the acronym given to the *Universal Naming Convention* in Microsoft products. When you want to access a machine or a share on another drive, you need some way to tell NT where that machine or library is contained. To understand this convention properly, you need to review the system for sharing data in NT. (This sharing might be familiar to you if you use other Microsoft products such as Windows 95.)

To allow access to a particular directory on a machine, you can set up a share name and allow people to have access as long as they know the password. NT provides many more detailed ways of protecting and allowing access, but this common method helps you understand the UNC standard.

How do you set up a share? First, you decide what directory to share and then need to tell NT to allow access to the directory and call it by a particular share name. To allow access to my Desktop directory called Data, for example, I need to tell the network software that I want to allow access to C:\Data and reference it by the share name called Barry_Data. Barry_Data, then, is the share name for the Data directory and the name that people on the network will use to access that directory. You can call this share name anything, as shown in the example. It doesn't have to equal the actual directory name being shared.

You can name machines using up to 15 characters; you can set up share names using up to 12 characters. Finally, the desktop needs to be told to allow the share. You do so using the following command:

```
NET SHARE Barry_Data=c:\data command
```

In Windows 95, you need to use the Control Panel options to perform the same function. You can find sharing under the Network|Properties|Access Control settings in the Control Panel. By choosing an option here, you set up the machine to allow sharing to occur. Figure 6.3 shows an example.

After you're set up to allow sharing, you just left-click in Explorer to add sharing to any directory you want.

Now that you have a shared directory, you need to tell other people it is available and give them the name they should use to access it. To access the example, another user needs to use the following command:

```
NET USE d: \\desktop\Barry_Data
```

Figure 6.3.

Setting up sharing in
Windows 95.

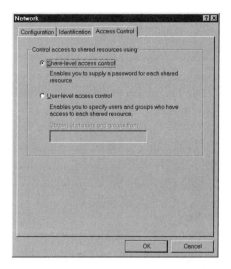

At this point, the Universal Naming Convention, or UNC, is needed. You can break down the command in the following manner. First, the two backslashes tell the network that what follows is a *machine name,* and the backslash that follows is the *share name* Barry_Data, not an actual directory name. The command is not case sensitive. The network software on the other user's machine now understands that it has a drive letter of D with a directory called Barry_Data available to it.

Task 6.2. Creating and removing shares with NT's GUI interface.

Step 1: Description

This task enables you to create new shares in NT.

Step 2: Action

1. Log onto your server. You must be an Administrator, a Server Operator, or a Power User to manage shares.

2. Double-click the My Computer icon on the desktop. You then see the list of drives available on your computer.

3. Double-click on the drive you want shared to display a list of file folders. Select the folder you want to share, and right-click to display the context-sensitive menu.

4. Click the Sharing tab to display the available options. By default, the folder is shown as Not Shared. Click the Shared As button to activate the remaining controls in the dialog box.

5. Type a descriptive name for your share in the Share Name box. This is the name your users see when looking for available shares on the network.

6. If desired, specify the User Limit information. By default, any number of users can use the share at the same time. Use the Allow button to select a limited number of users, and then fill in the specific number of users in the space provided.

7. You can remove shares by following the first four steps of this task, and selecting the Not Shared option and clicking the Apply button.

8. You can modify the share name by following these steps and changing the name in the Share Name box. This changes the name your users see when looking for available shares on the network.

Step 3: Review

By using the NT GUI interface, you created and managed shares on your NT Server. You use this technique any time you add or change a file folder and want to let other users access the folder.

The negative side to this operation concerns not knowing what the machine and share names are unless you are told by someone. In a small office, this situation is fine because you can call across the room and ask for the information. This situation is not as simple in larger businesses where you might be separated from other people by offices, floors, or even buildings. So how do you find out what machines and shares are available?

The solution used by Microsoft is called *Browse Services*. What other networks call *name servers*, Microsoft decided to call *browse masters* or *master browsers*. (Either name is correct.) In a Microsoft network, each machine broadcasts a request for a browse master until it finds one. Yoo hoo! Is there a browse master in the network?

The first browse master to hear the request returns a call telling the machine to direct all future name service requests to it. After a server finds a browse master, it tells the browse master to add its shares to the list the browse master is maintaining. You see this list, called a *browse list*, when you open a Windows 95 or NT 4.0 Network Neighborhood folder. You can see an example in Figure 6.4.

By clicking the particular machine icon in the browse list, you can see the actual list of shares that machine has to offer. In DOS, you type the NET VIEW command to get the list of servers and then add the machine name of the server you want by using the UNC as described earlier.

For the example, you use net view \\desktop\barry_data. This command provides the same general information as clicking Network Neighborhood does in Windows NT.

Figure 6.4.

A sample browse list in Windows 95.

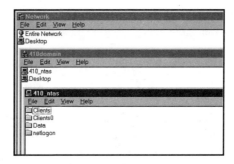

This method works fine in small networks, as we mentioned earlier. But what about using this browser when you have hundreds or thousands of servers? Scrolling through long lists to find the particular server you need becomes awfully hard. At this point, Microsoft *workgroups* come into play.

Task 6.3. Opening a browse list in NT.

Step 1: Description
This task enables you to see what resources are available to you on the network.

Step 2: Action
1. Log onto the workstation.
2. Double-click the Network Neighborhood icon on the desktop. You then see a list of servers you can access.
3. Select a server and double-click that server's name.
4. Select the data folder you need, and double-click again to see what files are available. You can see the printers available for you to use.
5. After you're finished, choose File|Close to return to the desktop.

Step 3: Review
By using the Network Neighborhood icon, you executed a command to list what resources are available to you on the network. Remember that the list can change from time to time as servers are added or removed from the network.

You can use some of the shortcuts available to both Windows 95 and NT 4.0 machines when browsing. To browse a server quickly, for example, use the Start|Run|*servername* command. Using the Run option in the Start menu, you can type in a server name and go directly to the shared directory of that server, as shown in Figure 6.5.

Figure 6.5.

A sample run command
to access a server.

Using this command can be a fast way to go directly to servers you commonly use without waiting for NT to search through the entire network and build a complete list of available resources. You can create shortcuts for these server shares by dragging the particular data folder from the open window onto the desktop. Then you can access the data on that server by merely clicking the desktop icon you just created.

Workgroups

All a workgroup really consists of is a subdivided browse list. Using it is like using a DOS directory structure. If you place all the files in the C: root directory (as some new users do), when you list the root directory, the listing scrolls forever. Hard to see what's in the machine and find anything of value, isn't it? In large networks, the browse list can look just like the DOS root directory. A mess. Hard to read. Even harder to find anything.

Workgroups come to the rescue by placing all the servers into useful groupings so that a particular machine sees only the servers it needs to see. Workgroups are often set up in a manner similar to a corporate structure, with Accounting, Finance, Executive, Sales, and Manufacturing. Now when a user browses for available resources, he or she sees only the resources in his or her workgroup.

NOTE

Workgroups should consist of a group of people who mostly share data among themselves and rarely share that data outside the workgroup. Workgroup names in NT can be 15 characters long, like machine names.

You join a workgroup in NT 4.0 or Windows 95 by updating the Control Panel|Network| Identification options. You have little security or control over adding a machine to a workgroup. On a DOS machine, you set the workgroup using the network Client Setup program or by manually updating the [network]|workgroup= parameter in the SYSTEM.INI file.

Although we said that no real security is involved with workgroups, Microsoft does enable you to hide the share or add a password to it. Hiding the share in NT 4.0 is as easy as naming it with a $ at the end. If you want to hide Barry_Data, for example, you add the $, making the share name equal Barry_Data$. NT 4.0, however, still shows you these hidden shares if you use the command net localgroup users rather than the usual net users command.

You add a password to control access. In Windows 95, a password applies to all users of that share. It's a generic password that applies to the resource, not the person. Not bad, but could be better. The problem with this approach is that once you give out the password you have no idea who is using it. Worse, if you want to remove access from one person, you must implement a new password and tell everyone else what it is except that person. Cumbersome process, isn't it?

NT 4.0 goes one step further, enabling you to set a password for each person who wants to use the share. On an NT workstation, you do not put passwords on the share; you create user accounts for all the people using the machine and then tell NT which people can access which shares. Before access is granted, you need to identify yourself to NT, whether you're signing on from a DOS machine or an NT workstation.

When you get to Day 5, you examine security and domains, so some of this information might begin to make more sense to you.

New Programs and Accessories in Windows NT

For those of you not aware of Windows 95, Microsoft added a new look to the way you manipulate through the NT file system. First, you no longer see the familiar Program Manager and File Manager. You start programs by choosing Start|Programs|*program name*. All the programs are placed within the Programs menu in groups, similar to earlier versions of Windows, or in NT 3.51.

NT 4.0 sets up some basic groups that you add to as you install products on the server. The basic groups include

☐ Accessories

☐ Startup

☐ Books Online

☐ Command Prompt

☐ Windows Messaging

☐ Windows NT Explorer

A couple of these groups are dependent on the options you replied to during NT installation. Books Online and Messaging are optional components added during the installation. The

6

Accessories folder continues to provide groups that include Games, Multimedia, and System tools, as well as objects such as the Clipboard Viewer, Clock, and Notepad.

Using Explorer

The familiar File Manager is replaced with Explorer, which offers the added benefit of displaying all the drive connections you have available to you in one window. If you're looking for the familiar MS-DOS prompt, it is now called *command prompt* and is found under the Programs group as you learned earlier.

The process of copying files becomes a little different in this new Explorer. You essentially copy and paste just like you've always done for text, except now the procedure applies to files also.

First, open Windows NT Explorer and select a file. From the Edit menu, choose Copy. Select and open the folder where you want to place the file; then choose Edit|Paste. Presto, file copied.

The Explorer looks different, as you can see in Figure 6.6, but still provides the basic functions you have in the NT 3.51 and Windows systems.

Figure 6.6.

The new Explorer.

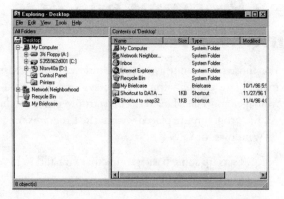

You can print a file by dragging the file from an Explorer window onto a printer icon. Using Explorer, you also can drag and drop files to new locations. Make sure that you can see the place where you want to drop a file before starting to drag it. If you drag a file to another location on the same disk, it is moved. If you drag the file to a folder on another disk, the file is copied. Also, if you copy .exe files, holding the Shift key while dragging the file moves it, and if you press the Ctrl key, the .exe file gets copied. Dragging an .exe file to anywhere other than a floppy disk drive creates a shortcut.

Learning to manipulate files this way takes a little additional effort until you're comfortable with the process. After you become comfortable, however, the process becomes an essential part of your day-to-day work. You'll use Explorer frequently in the coming days, so take some time now and practice until you're familiar with the process.

Using Scraps

If you write a lot of policies and procedures or other material on an NT machine, one handy hint makes life a great deal easier. You might be familiar with the cut and paste operations of Windows. This feature goes one step further by letting you throw scraps onto the desktop, making them readily available for pasting into documents. It's faster than cut and paste, and it enables you to store a bunch of separate items rather than the one item that Clipboard allows. This feature works only for applications such as MS Word or WordPerfect that support the drag-and-drop features of OLE. It doesn't work for WordPad, unfortunately.

To use the feature, select the text or graphic you want to copy and drag it onto the desktop. NT creates an item called a *scrap* that you can then drag and drop into another program or use later in a document. After you finish with the item, delete it from the desktop.

Internet Information Server for Windows NT Server

One of the new accessories is the Internet Information Server (IIS) program bundled with NT 4.0. Web server programs enable you to publish home pages and documents on the Internet using your own machine rather than an external Internet service provider, or ISP.

IIS, which is Microsoft's answer to Netscape, is being given away free to generate market share. (At least, that's what we think; Bill Gates might disagree.) This extremely powerful new program is far too detailed to go into here.

Setting Up and Managing Printers in NT Server

Back in 1988, one of this book's authors, Barry, wrote an article on the paperless office and the expected decrease in the use of paper. In the article, he postulated that computers were increasing rather than decreasing the amount of paper. He certainly doesn't think he's wrong today! An office without a printer is cast adrift, lost forever in the need to put screen to paper.

6

Printers, however, cost money. They can cost big money—especially if everyone needs one and needs it close by or even on his or her desk. The client/server revolution provided the answer to the need for printers. Place printers strategically around the organization, and network everyone so that they can reach a printer close to their workspaces.

The NT printer sharing services seem easier to use than most other systems, and therefore the process is fairly straightforward. You do need to understand the following buzzwords, however, before you get started:

- [ ] *Printing device:* The actual printer. It typically is the big machine that spews out paper when you least expect it.

- [ ] *Printer:* Nope. You might like to think that this word represents the physical device, but as you see, it doesn't. It is the logical printer—what NT Server sees. You typically use this printer in combination with the printing device, as you'll learn later in this section.

- [ ] *Network-interface printers:* Most printers in use on the server connect to the network using a print server that is the device actually connected to the network. Network-interface printers have built-in network cards that allow them to connect directly to the network just like a workstation.

- [ ] *Print server:* The machine that stores the printer drivers and allows printers to connect directly to it. You can consider a normal desktop with a printer attached to the Lpt1 port to be a print server if you allow that computer to let other machines use the printer.

- [ ] *Queue:* A place you spend way too much time, lining up for just about everything. Actually, on NT Server, the queue represents the group of documents that are sent to a printer and are waiting to print.

These terms provide you with an understanding of how NT considers the facets of printing. Understanding them is important because they differ somewhat from other operating system terms.

Almost any system on the network can become a print server. It doesn't have to be NT Server or workstation machines. In addition to NT, you can use Windows for Workgroups, Windows 95, and even good old MS-DOS with Windows, although this machine needs a special package called MS Workgroup DOS Add-On. So the advantage of using a print server appears obvious. Rather than purchase a printer for each person, you can purchase one printer for each group of persons, with proximity to each other being the criteria for the group.

NT Printer Features

We mentioned earlier that adding and using printers in NT is simpler than what you might be used to. Why? Because NT usually doesn't require you to obtain special printer drivers. Connecting the workstation to a new printer is therefore as easy as starting the Add New Printer Wizard and following the prompts. These prompts guide you to what printers are available on the network, so all you need to do then is double-click to connect. If NT cannot find a suitable driver on the machine that the printer is connected to, or if you are connecting to a network interface printer, NT requests the install CD so that it can load the necessary driver.

NT provides support for printers with an internal network interface card. This card enables you to connect the printer directly to the network just like connecting a workstation. These printers do not have to be attached to a print server. You find an appropriate connector on the network card at the back of the printer and plug in the network cable. They work with both Token Ring and Ethernet topologies. Using these special types of printers enables you to place them anywhere you have a network connection instead of limiting the connection to a serial or parallel port on a server. This capability provides you more flexibility.

One downside to a directly connected printer that is attached to the network without using a print server is the single data path. Because it is a connected device with only one network card, when the printer receives a print job, it must make all other print jobs wait until that job finishes because no queue is available. For this reason, connecting these printers to a print server is best. To do so, you need to load the Data Link Control protocol on the server. Then the printer can queue jobs because they are sent through the multiple data paths of the print server.

Adding a Printer

Adding a printer in NT 4.0 is different from adding one in NT 3.51 primarily because Print Manager is retired and is no longer used. Now you use the Control Panel|Printers window for all your print needs. (You can also use Start|Settings|Printers.)

To add a printer, now you go to the Printers window in the Control Panel and click the Add Printer icon. As we mentioned earlier, a Printer Wizard guides you through all the necessary steps of adding the printer to the network. You see this dialog box in Figure 6.7.

Figure 6.7.

Add Printer Wizard's
opening dialog box.

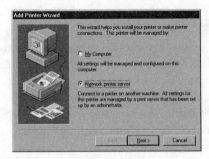

Select My Computer to set up a printer for the server to manage, or select Network printer server to connect the machine to an existing printer on another server somewhere in the network. As a user, you would most likely choose the Network printer option because you want to connect to existing printers. You use the My Computer option if you're physically adding a new printer either directly onto the network or onto the computer.

Because you just installed NT yesterday, add a printer to this server now. Click My Computer and then click Next. You see a dialog box asking which printer port the printer is connected to, as shown in Figure 6.8.

Figure 6.8.

The Choose a Printer
Port screen.

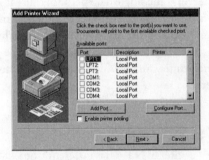

Select the appropriate port, and click Next when you're ready. NT provides you with a new window, shown in Figure 6.9, wanting to know what manufacturer made your printer.

Figure 6.9.

Choosing a printer
manufacturer.

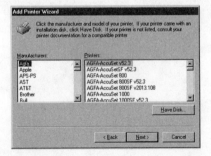

Choose the manufacturer from the left side of the screen, and a list of its printers shows on the right side. Choose the printer you're installing from that list, and click Next when ready. You can use the drivers from the vendor or use NT drivers. Generally, you use NT drivers because they are up-to-date for the moment. Choose the vendor drivers for newer printers as time goes on and these newer printers are added to the marketplace, because Microsoft drivers might not be as up-to-date. If you choose a printer that NT already knows about, the Wizard asks if you want to use the existing drivers or replace them, as shown in Figure 6.10.

Figure 6.10.

Replacing printer drivers options.

Select the option you want; then click Next to continue. A dialog box like the one shown in Figure 6.11 appears. Here, type in a meaningful name for the printer and click Next.

Figure 6.11.

Naming the printer.

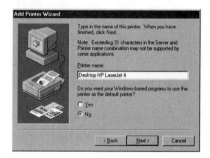

NT then asks whether this printer is going to be shared with other users. If you're planning to share it, you need to assign a share name first. Figure 6.12 shows the options you use to decide whether the printer is shared.

Figure 6.12.

Sharing the printer.

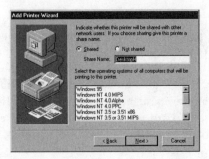

If you plan to share the printer, create a name that makes sense to others on the network, and then select all the operating systems that will be using the printer. You need to have the drivers for the systems you select. Finally, click Next and the last wizard window asks whether you want to print a test sheet, as shown in Figure 6.13. After you select Yes or No, click the Finish button and you're done. Now everyone can use the printer.

Figure 6.13.

Choosing to print a test page.

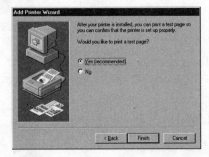

Now you know all there is to adding a printer in NT. Pretty straightforward process, isn't it?

Task 6.4. Adding an existing printer.

Step 1: Description

This task enables you to add an existing printer to the NT workstation. You then can print jobs across the network onto that printer. You perform this task each time you want to use a new printer.

Step 2: Action

1. Make sure that you are logged into the workstation.
2. Click the Printer window in the Control Panel.
3. Double-click the Add Printer icon.

4. Select the Network printer server option on the opening screen of the Add Printer Wizard.

5. Find an existing printer in the list. You might need to drill down some of the machine names to finally see a printer icon.

6. Select the printer. You see the Printer field with a machine name and the printer name. For example, mine looks like \\DESKTOP\HP4. Click OK. Windows NT workstations use the printer drivers stored on the printer server, so you don't need to add any.

7. Click Finish. The printer is added and available. You can try it by sending a small print job and watching for the output to show.

Step 3: Review

By using the Add Printer icon, you added your first network printer. You perform this task each time a printer is added or changed on the network and you want to use it.

Changing Printer Properties

After a printer is set up, you might want to change the setup and specify additional information such as the printer's location and when it is available for printing. You can set up printers to print only at certain hours of the day, print separator pages between jobs, or manage who can use the printer.

You change properties for a printer by choosing Start|Settings|Control Panel and then selecting Printers. After the Printers window opens, select the printer you want to change, and left-click the icon to go to the Properties dialog box like the one shown in Figure 6.14.

Figure 6.14.

Printer properties.

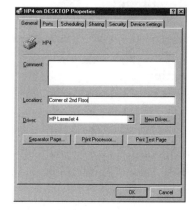

In the Properties dialog box, you can select and change various items. In a large office, for example, the Location text box is useful for guiding staff to where the printer actually resides in the building. You should use this text box unless you work in a small office with only one printer.

You can set up the printer to print special separator pages between each job. Using separators is a good practice because it clearly identifies each job and provides a useful way of separating the various stacks of output. By selecting the Separator Page option, you can designate a particular page as your job separator. Create a unique page by manipulating the sample pages provided by Microsoft as \winnt\system32*.sep files.

In a large organization, you might want to create a printer area and have all output routed to this print department, which then handles all distribution. To do so, you need to use *Printer Pooling*. Using a number of identical printers, you set up the ports where each printer is located. NT then automatically spools output to the printers on a predetermined priority basis.

In addition to these options, NT enables you to set up the hours when a printer can produce output. This way, printers cannot produce paper when they are unattended.

You also can set the permissions to decide who is allowed to control these options and who can use the printer. By default, NT allows Administrators, Print Operators, and Server Operators to modify settings and allows the Everyone group to use the printer.

We have touched on some of the available functions in the printer properties. On the afternoon of Day 8, you go through these tasks in detail in the chapter on managing the print server.

Task 6.5. Changing a printer to print only during the day.

Step 1: Description
This task enables you to ensure that the printer prints only when staff are on hand to manage the paper trays or clear sensitive documents quickly before unauthorized people see them.

Step 2: Action
1. Make sure that you are logged into the workstation with an Administrator, Print Operator, or Server Operator account.
2. Click the Printer window in the Control Panel.
3. Left-click the Printer icon you want. Then select Properties.
4. Click the Scheduling tab. In the From list box, select the hours you want to have the printer available. The printer still queues jobs regardless of this setting. It does not physically print anything outside the hours you select.
5. Change the From time to show 8:00AM. Change the To time to show 7:00PM.

You change the hours by using the scroll keys. To show PM, however, you need to select AM and then type PM. You'd think Microsoft would know how to change the time, wouldn't you?

6. Click OK to finish. The printer then prints only during the specified hours.

Step 3: Review

By using the Printer properties, you made the printer more secure. Now output is printed only during the times staff are on hand to pick up the output.

Summary

You learned many of the methods you use to explore Windows NT and discover the vast richness this product offers. The information provided, however, is an overview designed to quickly assist in your day-to-day operation of the new server. As you progress, you will become more familiar with the richness and depth of NT.

In this chapter, you discovered the following points:

- [ ] That the NET CONFIG command provides information about you and the machine you're using
- [ ] What the command prompt window is used for and how to change how its looks to suit your personal preferences
- [ ] That UNC is an acronym for Universal Naming Convention
- [ ] That Microsoft calls its name server either browse master or master browser
- [ ] What a workgroup consists of and how it is used
- [ ] What's new in programs and utilities in NT 4.0
- [ ] How to set up and modify printers

Workshop

Terminology Review

command prompt—The old familiar DOS prompt.

Explorer—The new name for what you know as File Manager in older versions of NT and Windows.

Messaging—Microsoft's new name for its electronic mail system. It used to be called Microsoft Exchange. Now Exchange is the server and Messaging the client.

network-interface printer—Printers with built-in network cards that allow them to connect directly to the network just like a workstation.

print server—The machine that stores the printer drivers and allows printers to connect directly to it.

printer—The *logical printer*—what NT Server sees. It doesn't represent the physical device.

scraps—No, not what you feed your dog. Pieces of text you cut and paste and place on the desktop for reuse.

share—The capability of other users to access a resource in NT or Windows 95.

Task List

The information provided in this chapter takes you deeper into the tools and techniques necessary in using NT Server 4.0. Now you can attach printers, use Explorer, and change the properties of windows to suit your personal preferences. You learned to perform the following tasks:

☐ Resize the command prompt window and change other facets of the window such as color and font type

☐ Create and remove shares with NT's GUI interface

☐ Open a browse list to discover what machines and printers are on the network

☐ Add a printer to the network and make it available for use

☐ Change printer options, control when the printer produces output, and control who can change the printer properties

Q&A

Q Can I still use the command prompt and not bother with the GUI interface?

A You can use the command prompt to perform most tasks in NT 4.0. You should find it easier, however, to add and maintain users with the User Manager interface. Most administrators find that they use both facilities depending on the task and their comfort level with direct command input.

Q I don't like the type of text used in the command prompt because it's too small for me to see clearly. Can I change the size?

A Yes, you can modify most of the parameters used by the command prompt window. You can change the size of the text and also change the background colors to create a combination that is more pleasing to your eye.

Q **I have a printer that is used by our executives. They do not want anyone using the printer or having a reason to approach the area because they often print sensitive documents. Can I restrict who can use that printer?**

A You can set a number of variables to manage printers. You learned how to change these properties in a task in this chapter. You can select Start|Settings|Printers and left-click to select properties. In the Properties dialog box, choose the Security tab and change the options as needed.

Q **I often use the same text numerous times when creating procedure manuals. Clipboard allows only one selection, but I need to reuse more than that. Is there a better way than constantly moving back and forth, cutting and pasting?**

A NT 4.0 provides a technique called *scraps* to help with just this problem. You can select the text you want and drag it onto the desktop. Do so for each of the pieces you need to reuse. Then just drag a copy into the document as needed. When you're finished, delete the scraps from the desktop.

6

DAY

4

Chapter **7**

Understanding the Registry

To this juncture, you have been creating, looking at, or talking to *Registry* objects. Before you learn how to create Registry objects, you need to learn about the Registry. What is a Registry? Why a Registry? To support the services on a Windows NT Server network, including accounting and security, the system must have a place to define and maintain objects. The Registry is that place, and it is critical to the operation of NTS because it is the place where you define all system objects, such as users, groups, and computers. When an object is requested, the system can retrieve and use information about the object before carrying out the request. The Registry, therefore, is the heart and soul of the NTS security system.

As you learned in Chapter 2, "What Is Windows NT Server?" Windows NT was designed as an extensible and scaleable operating system—one that could evolve in a consistent, modular way over time. The *configuration manager,* for example, represents the demise of the AUTOEXEC.BAT file, the

CONFIG.SYS file, and all the INI files you are most likely accustomed to seeing, fiddling with, and sometimes breaking. The configuration manager consists of several components, the most important being the Registry. The Registry is a repository for all information about the computer hardware on which the operating system is running, the software installed on the system, and the person or persons using the system.

The purpose of the Registry and its associated software is, first and foremost, to make the system easier for you to manage. It does so by examining the hardware and learning what it can at boot time, by configuring automatically as much of the system as possible, by asking you a minimum number of questions when the operating system is installed, and by storing all the information it gleans in the Registry so that you never have to be bothered twice for the same information. Device drivers, applications, and users also can place information in the Registry, and they can query the Registry to retrieve the information they need. You can view, update, or modify configuration information by using the graphical Registry Editor. Information in the configuration registry is stored in *key objects,* which are subject to the security mechanisms and other semantics applied to NT executive objects. This design allows Windows NT to maintain a unified storage facility for this seemingly random information and, at the same time, to make it available in a distributed but secure manner on networked systems.

As a system administrator, you face an enormous challenge in managing hardware, operating systems, and applications. In Windows NT, the Registry helps simplify the burden by providing a secure, unified database that stores configuration data in a hierarchical form, enabling you to use the administrative tools in Windows NT to provide local or remote support easily. This chapter covers the inner workings of the Registry and its use. The Registry is integral to using NTS, and it is so complex that you will spend a whole day focusing on it. In this chapter, you'll learn the fundamentals of the Registry and start using the Registry Editor.

Registry Overview

Does anybody remember Windows 3.1? If you're familiar with earlier versions of Windows, you probably remember all those INI, SYS, and BAT configuration files. But where did Windows keep its color settings? Let's see, they could be in SYSTEM.INI or WIN.INI. But wait, that kind of stuff is set by the Control Panel, and you also have a CONTROL.INI. Or maybe these settings are in AUTOEXEC.BAT? And this is just the color settings. What about all the other components and software? Obviously, something needed to change.

NT tries to improve on this configuration mess with the Registry. The Registry works in conjunction with these INI files and even makes the old MS-DOS stalwarts (AUTOEXEC.BAT and CONFIG.SYS) more or less unnecessary. The Registry is remarkable in that it's one big, central, secure database containing all the NT configuration information about the server, its applications, and its users. Everything's here, from color settings to users' passwords. (In case you're wondering, you can't directly access the part containing the passwords.) The Windows NT Registry describes the hardware configuration, installed system and application software, user and group account security, desktop settings and profiles, file associations, and applications supporting Object Linking and Embedding (OLE). When you make a configuration change on the server, the system usually records it in the Registry database. Even better, the Registry uses a fault-tolerant approach to writing data to ensure that the Registry remains intact even when a failure occurs in the middle of a Registry update.

Starting at boot time, the Registry is populated by a variety of Windows NT or NTS system modules and is added to or modified by the configuration tools in Control Panel, the Windows NT Setup applet, User Manager or User Manager for Domains, third-party configuration tools, and software installation procedures.

Some NT Server configuration information isn't available in menu format. Instead, you must manually edit the Registry to make changes. Editing can be extremely dangerous when you don't know what you're doing—you can render the system inoperable with the wrong changes. Don't edit the Registry unless you absolutely have to and have investigated the changes thoroughly. Furthermore, make a backup of the Registry when you plan to make changes so that you can get back to where you started if anything goes wrong. This afternoon you'll learn about Registry backup.

Every server maintains its own Registry containing the information for that server. The Registry is a database containing configuration data for applications, hardware, and device drivers, as well as data on network protocols and adapter card settings. Each record in the database represents an object. (If you want to add a new user before you learn about the Registry, skip to Chapter 12, "Managing User Access.") It is an object-oriented database containing definitions for users, groups, and other objects on the network.

Changes to the Registry can be made through applications in the Administrative Tools directory, applications within Control Panel, or by opening up Registry Editor and manually changing field values. To edit the Registry, you must run the Registry Editor utility. You can launch the Registry Editor by choosing Start|Run and then typing regedt32. Doing so pulls up a window with five embedded windows called *subtrees*. You'll learn about these and other important Registry components next. Because the Registry has no cautionary messages for entering incorrect values in fields, users should refrain from directly changing field values.

7

In summary, the Registry provides several benefits to an administrator:

☐ It collects all configuration information while accommodating the data and storage needs of system components. The Registry replaces the complex and fragmented collection of batch, initialization, and configuration files used in Windows 3.1x and provides all the data required to describe and operate a specific workstation or server.

☐ It allows discretionary access control to local and remote configuration data. Each key in the Registry can be protected by an Access Control List (ACL), which allows some users to modify Registry contents and grants other users read-only access to the same data.

☐ It records and preserves security and desktop information on an individual basis. Although Windows NT currently supports only one interactive user, it is common for workstations and servers to have multiple concurrent network connections. In the Registry, you can find a permanent record of per-user, per-application, and per-machine configuration information.

☐ You can use the Registry to determine all the hardware components installed on a local or remote system, the BIOS revision levels for motherboards and video adapters, the numbers and types of SCSI adapters, the devices installed on each adapter, and IRQ and base address and DMA channel assignments for specific components. On the software side, you can see installed applications and system configuration data set by various Windows NT applets.

So you've just got to like NT's Registry—except, of course, for the annoying things about the Registry, including its cryptic organization and excessively complex structure. But read on, and it will become clearer.

What Is the Registry?

As just mentioned, the Registry is a hierarchical database of settings, much like INI files, that describe your user account, the server's hardware, and your applications. Knowing how to work with the Registry is an important key to tuning and controlling NT Servers and NT Workstations. You might be relieved or saddened to know that it is not, by the way, the same as the Registry that is part of Windows 95, although it is similar. Windows 95 experts will know, for example, that you can do some very powerful things under Windows 95 by exporting a Registry to an external file, modifying that file, and re-importing it to a Windows 95 Registry. You cannot do anything like that with NTS.

Simply, the Registry is a database you view and manipulate through a program called the Registry Editor. The Registry Editor uses a hierarchical structure to display *subtrees* that allow access to the contents of the database. At first glance, the hierarchical structure displayed in the Registry Editor looks similar to Explorer's hierarchical directory structures. The difference lies in the kinds of information contained in the Registry and the impact that manipulating the Registry has on the system.

Under Windows 3.1*x*, whenever you started the system, connected to a network, or ran an application, the system hunted for and read several configuration files to set up its operating environment. In contrast, Windows NT stores and checks the configuration information in only one location—the Registry. The Registry contains the following types of configuration information:

☐ AUTOEXEC.BAT, CONFIG.SYS, WIN.INI, SYSTEM.INI, CONTROL.INI, LANMAN.INI, PROTOCOL.INI, and miscellaneous INI files

☐ Device driver data

☐ Network protocols and network adapter settings

The following Windows NT components and applications use the Registry:

☐ *Setup.* Whenever you run the Windows NT Setup program or other setup programs for applications or hardware, the Setup program adds new configuration data to the Registry.

☐ *Hardware Detector.* Each time you boot a Windows NT machine, the Hardware Detector places hardware configuration data in the Registry. This information includes a list of hardware detected in the system at startup.

☐ *Windows NT Kernel.* During system startup, the Windows NT Kernel extracts information from the Registry, such as the device drivers to load and the order in which to load them. The NTOSKRNL.EXE program also passes information about itself to the Registry, such as its version number.

☐ *Device drivers.* Device drivers send and receive load parameters and configuration data from the Registry. This data is similar to what you might find on the DEVICE= lines in the CONFIG.SYS file under MS-DOS. A device driver must report system resources it uses, such as hardware interrupts and DMA channels, so that the system can add this information to the Registry. Applications and device drivers can read this Registry information to provide users with smart installation and configuration programs.

☐ *Administrative tools.* The administrative tools in Windows NT, such as those provided in the Control Panel and in the Administrative Tools program group, can be used to modify configuration data. The Registry Editor is helpful for viewing and occasionally making detailed changes to the system configuration. You also can use the Windows NT Diagnostics program (WINMSD.EXE) to view configuration information stored in the Registry.

7

Now, editing the Registry is likely the part you won't like about NT. The Registry is not documented well in the pile of manuals you get from Microsoft.

Understanding the Registry will make you a better administrator, should you understand it. The goal for this chapter, then, is to give you a feel for the Registry, how to edit it, and when to leave it alone.

Understanding Registry Terminology

To get a first insight into the Registry, look at the Registry Editor. You can see it by running the program REGEDT32.EXE (it's in the C:*SystemRoot*\SYSTEM32 directory, where *SystemRoot* might be winnt) or by accessing it through WINMSD.EXE (choose File|Run and a list of programs to run appears, one of which is "Registry Editor [Please use caution]"). Run it and click the HKEY_CURRENT_USER window. You see a screen like the one in Figure 7.1.

Figure 7.1.

The Registry Editor.

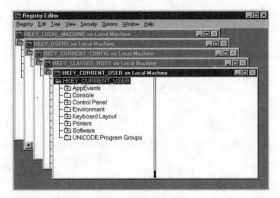

The terms to know so that you understand the Registry are *subtree, key, value, data type,* and *hive.* The following text covers these terms.

WARNING

Accidentally blowing away important data is easy with the Registry Editor. You might be wise at this point to put the Editor in *read-only* mode by choosing Options|Read Only Mode.

You always can reverse the read-only state whenever necessary in the same way. You simply can render a server completely unusable with a few unthinking Registry edits, so be careful.

The first step in mastering the Registry is understanding the design and layout of the database. Learning how to interpret the database, relate keys and values to specific hardware or software components, and modify and add keys and values is an essential survival skill for system and network administrators. Because the Registry contains data critical to system operation, such as data accessed by loaded device drivers and client or server processes, be careful when performing modifications.

The Registry is composed of thousands of individual data items that describe every aspect of a specific operating system installation, from the hardware to valid users to customized logon messages and performance monitoring profiles. These data items are organized into *keys* and optional values. Keys are grouped so that related information can be accessed and cross-referenced.

Each area of the Registry has a standard set of keys that are common across all Windows NT installations. Within these keys, system-specific values describe hardware components, operating system components, and bootable configurations. Then the variations begin. If a network card is installed, for example, several entries describe the hardware type (such as NE2000 and EtherExpress), the IRQ and base address, loaded driver, and related network services. Additional entries indicate the protocols that have been bound to the network driver for the card. Another common variation is the type of graphics adapter installed or the type and mode of a sound card or SCSI adapter.

Standard Keys

If you compare one key with another, you find standard keys with a significant variation in value entries. Each hardware component causes multiple subkeys to be placed in the hardware, software, and ControlSet keys. When one system has several applications and another has only a couple, the system with many understandably has more keys in the software section. Similarly, when one system is a domain server, many entries appear in the users' area, as compared to only one or two entries for a standalone workstation with a single dedicated user and only two network connections.

The Registry is one database, structured like a hierarchical file system. If you ever supported Windows 3.1*x*, you know that it had two essential INI files, WIN.INI and SYSTEM.INI. Generally, WIN.INI contained user-specific settings and SYSTEM.INI contained machine-specific settings. NT's Registry is divided up as well. It is presented in five major views called *subtrees*. Each Registry subtree contains keys holding configuration data about a specific computer and each of its users. These subtrees describe hardware and software configuration, security data, all connected-user operating environments (profiles), the currently logged on

7

user, and file associations used for Object Linking and Embedding. Each view has a name that begins with HKEY, which stands for Handle to a Key. A *handle* is a programming construct used to access Windows NT objects. These are the subtrees shown in Figure 7.1:

```
HKEY_LOCAL_MACHINE
HKEY_CLASSES_ROOT
HKEY_USERS
HKEY_CURRENT_USER
HKEY_CURRENT_CONFIG
```

HKEY_LOCAL_MACHINE

The most important subtree is HKEY_LOCAL_MACHINE, because in it the system stores hardware, software, and security information. It contains information about the local computer system, including hardware and operating system data such as bus type, system memory, device drivers, and startup control data. In this subtree, you most often make changes to the Registry. It contains five main keys—HARDWARE, SAM, SECURITY, SOFTWARE, and SYSTEM—described in detail in the following subsections.

The HKEY_LOCAL_MACHINE\HARDWARE Subtree

This HKEY_LOCAL_MACHINE\HARDWARE database describes the physical hardware in the computer, the way that device drivers use the hardware, and mappings and related data that link kernel mode drivers with various user mode code. All data in this subtree is volatile and is re-created whenever the system is started. The Description key describes the actual computer hardware—the make of the motherboard, type of video adapter, SCSI adapters, serial ports, parallel ports, sound cards, network adapters, and so on. The DeviceMap key contains miscellaneous data in formats specific to particular classes of drivers. The ResourceMap key describes what device drivers claim what hardware resources. The Windows NT Diagnostics program (WINMSD.EXE) can report on this database's contents in an easy-to-read form.

All information in HKEY_LOCAL_MACHINE\HARDWARE is disposable (or more correctly, volatile), meaning that the settings are recomputed each time the system is started and then discarded when the system is shut down—they are not saved. Hardware configuration changes are reflected in the HARDWARE key at the next boot. Applications and device drivers use this subtree to read information about the system components.

Do not try to view or edit the data in HKEY_LOCAL_MACHINE\HARDWARE because much of the information appears in binary format, making it difficult to decipher. Instead, use Windows NT Diagnostics to view hardware data in an easy-to-read format for troubleshooting.

The HKEY_LOCAL_MACHINE\SAM **and** HKEY_LOCAL_MACHINE\SECURITY **Subtrees**

The Security Account Manager (SAM) and SECURITY keys have no visible information, as they point to site security policies such as specific user rights, as well as information for user and group accounts and for the domains in Windows NT Server. This information is in User Manager, and it also appears in the lists of users and groups when you use the Security menu commands in Explorer. You create, modify, and remove keys and values in these two keys with either User Manager or User Manager for Domains.

WARNING

> The information in the SAM database is in binary format. You should not use Registry Editor to change it. Errors in this database might prevent users from logging onto the computer—another reason that system administrators should not allow typical users to log on as members of the Administrator group.

The HKEY_LOCAL_MACHINE\SOFTWARE **Subtree**

HKEY_LOCAL_MACHINE\SOFTWARE is the per-computer software database. Remember that you learned about this database in Chapter 2. This key contains data about software installed on the local computer, along with miscellaneous configuration data. The entries under this handle, which apply for anyone using this particular computer, show what software is installed on the computer and also define file associations and OLE information.

The HKEY_LOCAL_MACHINE\SYSTEM **Subtree**

The HKEY_LOCAL_MACHINE\SYSTEM database controls system startup, device driver loading, Windows NT services, and operating system behavior. The SYSTEM key describes bootable and nonbootable configurations in a group of ControlSets, where each ControlSet represents a unique configuration. Within each ControlSet, two keys describe operating system components and service data for that configuration. This key also records the configuration used to boot the running system (CurrentControlSet), along with failed configurations and the LastKnownGood configuration.

HKEY_CLASSES_ROOT

The HKEY_CLASSES_ROOT subtree contains information on file associations (equivalent to the Registry in Windows for MS-DOS) and data required to support Microsoft's Object Linking and Embedding technology. This subtree is a clone of data contained in the HKEY_LOCAL_MACHINE view and is separated primarily for usability reasons, because the machine subtree is so large and complex.

The `Classes` subkey provides information on filename-extension associations and OLE that can be used by Windows shell applications and OLE applications.

The OLE information must be created by the specific application, so you should not use Registry Editor to change this information. When you want to change filename-extension associations, use Explorer. Under View|Options, use the File Types tab and associate extensions.

HKEY_USERS

A third subtree, `HKEY_USERS`, describes a default operating environment and contains one top-level key for each user logged on either interactively or via a network connection. It contains all actively loaded user profiles, including `HKEY_CURRENT_USER`, which always refers to a child of `HKEY_USERS`, and the default profile. Users who are accessing a server remotely do not have profiles under this key on the server; their profiles are loaded into the Registry on their own computers.

HKEY_CURRENT_USER

The `HKEY_CURRENT_USER` subtree contains the user profile for the user who is currently logged on, including environment variables, personal program groups, desktop settings, network connections, printers, and application preferences.

HKEY_CURRENT_CONFIG

The last subtree, `HKEY_CURRENT_CONFIG`, contains the volatile information for the present hardware configuration. Because the `HKEY_LOCAL_MACHINE` subtree is so large, the system duplicates some information in this subtree.

To summarize, the Registry stores all information about a computer and its users, as shown in Table 7.1.

Table 7.1. Current subtrees.

Subtree	Description
HKEY_LOCAL_MACHINE	Contains information about the hardware currently installed in the machine and about programs and systems running on the machine. You do most of your work in this subtree. The information includes, but is not limited to, startup control, data, memory, and devices and drivers. Applications, device drivers, and the Windows NT system also use the information in this database to establish configuration data for the local computer, regardless of who's logged on and what software is in use.

Subtree	Description
HKEY_CLASSES_ROOT	Holds the file associations, information that tells the system, for example, "whenever the user double-clicks a file with the extension .BMP in the File Manager, start up PBRUSH.EXE to view this file." It also contains the OLE registration database, the old REG.DAT from Windows 3.1*x.* This subtree contains information about the file-class associations and Object Linking and Embedding (OLE). This subtree is actually redundant, as you can find all its information in the HKEY_LOCAL_MACHINE subtree.
HKEY_USERS	This subtree contains information about active users. It also includes profiles on any user who has local access to the system. It contains two user profiles: a DEFAULT profile used for someone logging in who hasn't logged in before, and a profile with a name like S-227362152... (the Security ID of the user), which is the profile of a user already known to the system.
HKEY_CURRENT_USER	This subtree contains the user profile for the person currently logged onto the NT Server machine. This information includes the user's profile groups, desktop settings, printers, application preferences, and network connections.
HKEY_CURRENT_CONFIG	This subtree contains configuration information for the particular hardware configuration you booted with.

Sometimes these subtrees contain conflicting information. Data in HKEY_CURRENT_USER, for example, might include some of the same parameters as HKEY_LOCAL_MACHINE; in this case, HKEY_CURRENT_USER takes precedence.

Where the Registry Lives: Hives

Mostly, the Registry is contained in a set of files called the *hives.* Some of the Registry is built automatically every time you boot up the system. The system doesn't know devices on a SCSI chain, for example, until you boot. Hives are binary files, so you can't look at them without a special editor of some kind, like the Registry Editor. Using hives is, however, an easy way to load or back up a sizable part of the Registry.

Most, although not all, of the Registry is stored in hive files. They're not hidden, system, or read-only but are always open, so you're somewhat limited in what you can do with them.

Below each subtree is a collection of hives and files. You're probably wondering why Microsoft picked the name *hives;* they did so because the structure resembles a beehive. Below the HKEY_LOCAL_MACHINE subtree, for example, you typically find the following important hives:

- ☐ HARDWARE: Contains information about the system's hardware and configuration.
- ☐ SAM: Contains information about the Security Account Manager (SAM) that houses domain, user, and group security information.
- ☐ SECURITY: Contains information about the local security information that this machine's security subsystem uses.
- ☐ SOFTWARE: Contains information about the local software and its configuration.
- ☐ SYSTEM: Contains information about the operating system and related information.

By default, all hives are stored in the *SystemRoot*\SYSTEM32\CONFIG subdirectory, which also includes SYSTEM.ALT and the .LOG files, which are backup hive files. Whenever a new user logs onto a computer, the system creates a new hive for that user. Because each user profile is a separate hive, each profile is also a separate file. (If you prefer, you can store profile hives in other directories.) You can copy a user profile as a file and view, repair, or copy entries using Registry Editor on another computer.

A Look at the Hive Files

The hive files are in the *SystemRoot*\SYSTEM32\CONFIG directory. As they're listed in Table 7.2, you can see the hive files corresponding to parts of the subtree.

Table 7.2 needs a few explanatory notes. First, about the HKEY_CLASSES_ROOT subtree: It is copied from HKEY_LOCAL_MACHINE\SOFTWARE\Classes at boot time. The file exists for use by 16-bit Windows applications. While you're logged onto NT, however, the two keys are linked; if you make a change to one, the change is reflected in the other.

Table 7.2. Subtrees and hives.

Subtree/Key	Filename
HKEY_LOCAL_MACHINE\SAM	SAM (primary) and SAM.LOG (backup)
HKEY_LOCAL_MACHINE\SECURITY	SECURITY (primary) and SECURITY.LOG (backup)
HKEY_LOCAL_MACHINE\SOFTWARE	SOFTWARE (primary) and SOFTWARE.LOG (backup)
HKEY_LOCAL_MACHINE\SYSTEM	SYSTEM (primary) and SYSTEM.ALT (backup)

Subtree/Key	Filename
HKEY_USERS\DEFAULT	DEFAULT (primary) and DEFAULT.LOG (backup)
HKEY_USERS\Security ID	*xxxxxnnn, xxxxxnnn*.LOG
HKEY_CURRENT_USER	USE### or ADMIN###(primary); USER###.LOG or ADMIN###.LOG(backups); ###=system ID for user
HKEY_CLASSES_ROOT	(Created from current control set at boot time)

The user profiles now live in *SystemRoot*\PROFILES*username*, where each user gets a directory named *username*. I've got a user account named "peter," for example, so I have a directory named d:\winnt\profiles\peter on my computer. If I look in it, I find the files ntuser.dat and ntuser.dat.log.

One question remains about the user profiles, however. Why do all the files have a paired file with the extension .LOG? You'll learn about these LOG files in the next chapter.

Values

Progressing down the Registry tree, below the hives you'll find Registry keys, which contain items called *value* entries. This is typically the place where you edit, add, or delete values. Be sure you know what you're doing (and have a backup)!

Registry Keys

Figure 7.1 shows the Registry Editor displaying five cascaded windows, one for each subtree. HKEY_LOCAL_MACHINE is on top; you can see the other four subtrees' windows, too. The HKEY_CURRENT_USER window has right and left panes. The pane on the left looks like a screen from the Explorer or the old Windows 3.1 File Manager.

In the File Manager, the folders represented subdirectories. Here, however, they separate information into sections, in the same way that old Windows INI files had sections whose names were surrounded by square brackets, names like [386enh], [network], [boot], and the like. Compare the HKEY_LOCAL_MACHINE window in Figure 7.1 to an INI file. If it were an INI file, the name of its sections would be [hardware], [sam], [security], [software], and [system]. Each of these folders or sections is actually called a key in the Registry.

But at this point the analogy to INI files fails: you can have keys within keys, called *subkeys* (and sub-subkeys, and sub-sub-subkeys, and so on). Opening the SYSTEM key, you find that it contains subkeys named Clone ControlSet001, ControlSet002, CurrentControlSet, Select, and Setup; and CurrentControlSet is further sub-keyed into Control and Services.

Notice, by the way, the key called `CurrentControlSet`. It's very important. Almost every time you modify the system's configuration, you do so with a subkey within the `CurrentControlSet` subkey.

Key-Naming Conventions

The tree of keys gets pretty big as you drill down through the many layers. `CurrentControlSet`, for example, has dozens of subkeys, each of which can have subkeys. Identifying a given subkey is important, so Microsoft has adopted a naming convention that looks just like directory trees. `CurrentControlSet`'s fully specified name would be, then, `HKEY_LOCAL_MACHINE\SYSTEM\CurrentControlSet`. In this book, however, you'll see it just called `CurrentControlSet` for space and simplicity's sake.

Value Entries, Names, Values, and Data Types

If you drill down through `CurrentControlSet`, you can find the subkey `Services`, and within `Services` are many subkeys. In Figure 7.2, you can see some of the subkeys of `CurrentControlSet\Services`.

Figure 7.2.

Subkeys of
`CurrentControlSet\`
`Services.`

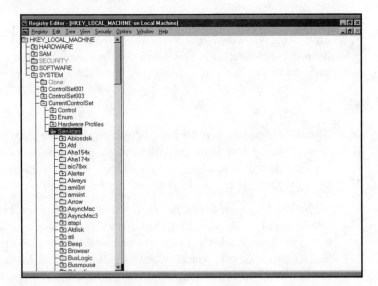

One of these keys, `Browser`, contains subkeys named `Linkage`, `Parameters`, and `Security`. After you get to `Parameters`, however, you can see that it's the end of the line—no subkeys from there. Just to review Registry navigation quickly, the key you're looking at now is in `HKEY_LOCAL_MACHINE\SYSTEM\CurrentControlSet\Services\Browser\Parameters`.

In the right-hand pane, you see two lines:

```
IsDomainMasterBrowser:REG_SZ:False
MaintainServerList:REG_SZ:Yes
```

In this way, the Registry says what would be, in the old INI-type files, something like this:

```
IsDomainMasterBrowser=Yes
MaintainServerList=Yes
```

Each line like `IsDomainMasterBrowser:REG_SZ:False` is called a *value entry*. The three parts are called *name, data type,* and *value,* respectively. In this example, `IsDomainMasterBrowser` is the name, `REG_SZ` is the data type, and `False` is the value.

Most of this explanation is fairly straightforward, but what is `REG_SZ`? It's an *identifier* to the Registry of the kind of data to expect: numbers, messages, yes/no values, and the like. The Registry Editor currently contains five data types (although others could be defined later). A value entry has three components, which always appear in the following order: the name of the value; the data type of the value; and the value itself, which can be data of any length. Microsoft notes that each value entry cannot exceed about lMB in size. Imagining one that size is difficult, but it's worth mentioning.

Table 7.3 lists the data types currently defined and used by the system.

Table 7.3. Data type descriptions.

Data Type	Description
REG_BINARY	Raw binary data. Most hardware component information is stored as binary data. Data of this type usually doesn't make sense when you look at it with the Registry Editor (unless you're a robot). Binary data shows up in hardware setup information. It can be displayed with the Registry Editor in hexadecimal format or via the Windows NT Diagnostics program (WINMSD.EXE) in an easy-to-read format. The data is usually represented in hexadecimal for simplicity's sake. Editing binary data can get you in trouble when you don't know what you're doing.
REG_DWORD	More binary data represented by a number that is 4 bytes long. Many parameters for device drivers and services are this data type and can be displayed by the Registry Editor in binary, hexadecimal, or decimal format. For example, entries for service error control: `ErrorControl:REG_DWORD:0x1`.

continues

7

Table 7.3. continued

Data Type	Description
REG_EXPAND_SZ	An expandable data string, which is text that contains a variable to be replaced when called by an application. It's often information understandable by humans, like path statements or messages. It is "expandable" in that it might contain information that will change at runtime, like %username%—a system batch variable that is of different sizes for different people's names. For the following value, for example, the string %SystemRoot% is replaced by the actual location of the directory containing the Windows NT system files: File:REG_EXPAND_SZ:%SystemRoot%\file.exe.
REG_MULTI_SZ	Another string type (a multiple string) that enables you to enter a number of parameters on this one value entry. The parameters are separated by binary zeros (nulls). Values that contain lists or multiple values in human-readable text are usually this type. The following value entry, for example, specifies the binding rules for a network transport: bindable:REG_MULTI_SZ:dlcDriver dlcDriver non non 50.
REG_SZ	A simple string of characters representing human-readable text. For example, a component's description: DisplayName:REG-SZ:Messenger.

If you first met a Registry with Windows 95, you might notice a few differences here. Windows 95 has six subtrees but only three data types: string, which is like REG_SZ, REG_MULTI_SZ, and REG_EXPAND_SZ; dword, which is like REG_DWORD; and binary, which is like REG_BINARY.

And should you be wondering how on earth you'll figure out what data type to assign to a new Registry value, don't worry about it; if you read somewhere to use a particular new value entry, you'll be told what data type to use.

Working with the Registry: An Example

Now, probably you want to get in the Registry and try it out despite the numerous warnings, so here's an innocuous example. Remember: It's innocuous only if you follow the example to the letter; otherwise, it will soon be time to get out your installation disks.

We're not just whistling Dixie. Don't get mad if you blow away the server because you didn't pay attention to the warnings. Actually, you can avoid a reinstallation if the thing you modified was in the CurrentControlSet key; NT knows that you often mess around in there, so it keeps a spare. In that case, you can reboot the server and wait for the message that says, Press Spacebar now to restore Last Known Good menu. Again, pressing the Spacebar doesn't restore the entire Registry; it just restores the control set. Fortunately, the current control set is a lot of the Registry.

Now that you know what the Registry is, how it works, and what it contains, you might want to know how to manipulate its entries. In any case, you can try out something, something relatively harmless. For this example, change the name of the organization that you gave NT when you installed it. The Registry Editor enables you to change organization names without reinstalling.

Task 7.1. Changing the Registry.

Step 1: Description

This task enables the Administrator to change the Registry.

Step 2: Action

1. To open the Registry Editor, choose Start|Run.

2. In the command line, type REGEDT32 and press Enter.

3. Click Window and choose HKEY_LOCAL_MACHINE. Maximize that window, and you see a screen somewhat like the one in Figure 7.3.

Figure 7.3.

The Registry Editor local machine box.

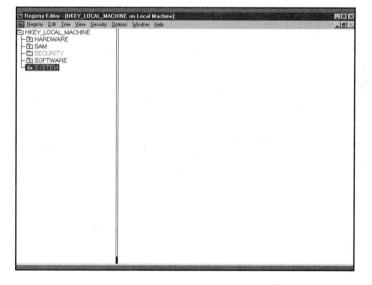

4. Modify the value entry in HKEY_LOCAL_MACHINE\Software\Microsoft\Windows NT\CurrentVersion. To do so, double-click the Software key and then double-click the Microsoft key. Next, double-click the Windows NT key, and finally, double-click the CurrentVersion key. You see a screen like the one in Figure 7.4. On the left pane, you still see the Registry structure. On the right, you see the value entries in the RegisteredOrganization subkey.

Figure 7.4.

The
CurrentVersion
window.

5. Double-click RegisteredOrganization, and you see a screen like the one in Figure 7.5.

Figure 7.5.

Updating the
CurrentVersion
window.

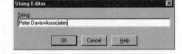

6. Highlight the old value and replace it with Peter Davis+Associates. Click OK and then close the Registry Editor.

7. Click Help and About for any program (even the Registry Editor will do), and you'll see that your organization is now Peter Davis+Associates.

Step 3: Review

In this task, you learned how to use the Registry to change the name of your organization.

WARNING

> Click all you like, but you will not find a Save button or an Undo button. When you edit the Registry, it's real-time and it's forever. So, again, be careful when you mess with the Registry.

Using the Registry Editor

When you install Windows NTS, the system sets appropriate Registry values for the local hardware and software configuration. Although the standard tools do a good job of maintaining configuration information, for many entries no graphical user interface exists. In this case, to make adjustments to system configuration or operation, you must directly edit the configuration database.

WARNING

> The full pathname for the Registry Editor is *SystemRoot*\system32\ regedt32.exe, where *SystemRoot* normally is the directory where you installed Windows NT (most probably, winnt). The system does not load the Registry Editor as an icon at installation. Note that another file in the *SystemRoot* directory, called REGEDIT.EXE, exists for compatibility with Windows applications. Do not use the older version to access the Registry—it might trash the system.

With the Registry Editor, you can load either the local or a remote Registry, when you have a valid username and necessary rights and permissions on the target system. When the database is in place, you can display, add, modify, and delete keys and values in the database, protect keys with an ACL, modify user profiles, and audit the success or failure of access to selected keys.

If all you need is to examine information stored in the Registry, use the Windows NT Diagnostics tool, called WINMSD.EXE. Windows NT Diagnostics installs in the *SystemRoot*\SYSTEM32 directory when you set up Windows NT. NTS places a program icon for the diagnostic tool under Administrative Tools (Common). You run this program like any program in Windows NT. It's a handy tool and a whole lot safer than mucking about with the Registry Editor.

With Windows NT Diagnostics, you can display specific data from the Registry in an easily readable format. You cannot edit value entries using Windows NT Diagnostics, so the Registry contents are protected while you browse for information. You can, however, select and copy any value if you want to paste information in a Registry Editor edit box or text editor.

7

Before going on to perform what could very well amount to open-heart surgery on the system, you should acquaint yourself with two very important tools used for Registry management:

- [ ] *Backup:* Backs up Registry hives as part of a tape backup routine.
- [ ] *Emergency repair disk:* Restores default hives to the system.

The processes of backing up and restoring the Registry are covered this afternoon in Chapter 8, "Managing the Registry." As a precautionary measure, back up the Registry and critical system files. Also, make sure that you have an emergency repair disk on hand to rescue the system from any Registry-tweaking mishaps. If you have a good set of backup files, you can restore damaged or missing Registry hives.

Running the Registry Editor Program

The Registry Editor program does not appear on the Start menu after you install Windows NT, but it is installed automatically.

Run the REGEDT32.EXE file from the Explorer or by using Run on the Start menu. Or type `start regedt32` at the command prompt and press Enter. You should see a Registry Editor window similar to the one in Figure 7.1. The four local windows appear, each of which bears the name of a predefined key:

- [ ] `HKEY_CURRENT_USER`. The `HKEY_CURRENT_USER` window is the root of the configuration information for the user who is currently logged on. Information such as the user's program groups, screen colors, and Control Panel settings are stored here. This information is referred to as a user's *profile*.
- [ ] `HKEY_USERS`. The `HKEY_USERS` window is the root of all user profiles on the computer. `HKEY_CURRENT_USER` is a subkey of `HKEY_USERS`.
- [ ] `HKEY_LOCAL_MACHINE`. The `HKEY_LOCAL_MACHINE` window contains configuration information particular to the computer (for any user).
- [ ] `HKEY_CLASSES_ROOT`. The `HKEY_CLASSES_ROOT` window is a subkey of `HKEY_LOCAL_MACHINE\SOFTWARE`. The information stored here is used to perform operations such as opening the right application when a file is opened from File Manager (file association) and for Object Linking and Embedding (OLE).
- [ ] `HKEY_CURRENT_CONFIG`. The `HKEY_CURRENT_CONFIG` contains information similar to `HKEY_LOCAL_MACHINE`; that is, information about the local computer.

Each subtree contains multiple keys, and each key contains a plus sign if it can be expanded with a double-click of the mouse. The display is normally divided into two; keys appear on the left, and values, if any, appear on the right. You can display keys (tree) only, values only (data), or both (tree and data) by making the appropriate selection from the View menu.

If the currently highlighted key has a value or series of values, they appear to the right of the key in the data portion of the window. Some keys have a single value; others have 20 or more, depending on how the Registry entry is used. A value consists of three parts separated by colons: a field name, data type, and the actual data. There are six standard data types: REG_BINARY, REG_DWORD, REG_EXPAND_SZ, REG_MULTI_SZ, and REG_SZ. Many Registry entries are written in one of the three string formats—REG_SZ, REG_EXPAND, REG_MULTI_SZ—which represent a single string, a string that contains variables such as SystemRoot as well as text, and a string consisting of multiple strings, respectively.

NOTE

> Your ability to make changes to the Registry using Registry Editor depends on your access privileges. In general, you can make the same kinds of changes in Registry Editor as your privileges allow for Control Panel or other administrative tools. Choose Options|Read Only Mode to protect the Registry contents while you explore its structure and become familiar with the entries. This afternoon you'll get a closer look at the Registry Editor.

Summary

The Registry is a convenient and powerful component of the Windows NT Server operating system. As stressed throughout this chapter, you should exercise caution when working with the Registry. In this chapter, you learned about the following topics:

- ☐ The Registry
- ☐ Subtrees, hives, and values
- ☐ Using the Registry Editor to change the Registry

You will learn more about the Registry in the next chapter. Now, however, you can review what you learned today.

Workshop

Terminology Review

access control list (ACL)—The part of a security descriptor that enumerates the protection (that is, permission) given to an object.

choose—As used in this book, to select or pick an item that begins an action in Windows NT. Often, you choose a command on a menu to perform a task, and you choose (or select) an icon to start an application.

click—As used in this book, to quickly press and release the mouse button.

double-click—As used in this book, to quickly press and release the mouse button twice without moving the mouse. Double-clicking is a means of rapidly selecting and activating a program or program feature.

key—In the Registry, one of five subtrees. Each key can contain value entries and additional subkeys. A key is analogous to a directory, and a value entry is analogous to a file.

object—1. A single runtime instance of a Windows NT–defined object type containing data that can be manipulated only by using a set of services provided for objects of its type. 2. Any piece of information, created by a Windows-based application with Object Linking and Embedding capabilities, that can be linked or embedded into another document.

object handle—Includes access control information and a pointer to the object itself. Before a process can manipulate a Windows NT object, it first must acquire a handle to the object through the Object Manager.

Registry—As used here, the database repository for information about the computer's configuration, including the hardware, installed software, environment settings, and other information.

Task List

With the information provided in this chapter, you now can begin your understanding of NTS objects. You learned how to carry out the following tasks:

☐ View the Registry

☐ Change the Registry

Q&A

Q How do I look at the Registry?

A You can view the Registry through applications in the Administrative Tools directory, applications within the Control Panel, or using the Registry Editor.

Chapter 8

Managing the Registry

In the preceding chapter, you changed the organization name in the Registry. When you want to change that value, how do you know to go to `HKEY_LOCAL_MACHINE\Software\Microsoft\Windows NT\CurrentVersion`? Well, you can find it by poking around in the Registry. But, at this point, you still might feel nervous around the Registry. This nervousness is understandable considering the ramifications of a false move. So, in this chapter, you'll learn how to perform the following tasks:

- ☐ Use the Registry Editor and Windows NT Diagnostics
- ☐ Manage the Registry for a remote computer
- ☐ Edit Registry value entries
- ☐ Maintain the Registry

Now, you can get started.

Altering Registry Data

Poking around is not a desirable action or a time-saver, and this points out a glaring weakness of the Registry Editor: it has no effective search routine. Suppose you know that you have something called RegisteredOrganization, but you have no idea where it lives in the Registry. You're just out of luck. REGEDT32 includes a View/Find Key, but you can use it to search only the names of keys, not value entries. Because RegisteredOrganization is a value name within the key CurrentVersion, you can search for it only when you know that the key's name is CurrentVersion, which isn't very likely.

 TIP

> You can use REGEDIT.EXE to search both key names and values. But weren't you told this morning not to use this program because it might damage the Registry? Well, yes, you were. But you can use REGEDIT to view, but not edit, the Registry. This application displays the Registry as one tree and makes finding particular values easy, because it searches for partial matches.

Within the Registry, you can alter the value entries for a selected key or assign new value entries to keys. This section covers how to find keys and edit, add, or delete keys and value entries.

When possible, use the graphical administrative tools such as Control Panel and User Manager to make configuration changes, instead of using the Registry Editor. Using the administrative tools is safer because these applications know how to store values properly in the Registry. If you make errors while changing values with the Registry Editor, you get no warning because the Registry Editor does not understand or recognize errors in syntax or other semantics.

The location of a Registry key in the tree structure might be different from what is described here, depending on whether a computer is running Windows NT as a workstation or as a server, and other factors (such as your version). You can search for a specific key name in the Registry tree. Key names appear in the left pane of the Registry Editor windows. The search begins from the currently selected key and includes all its descendant keys.

Each search is local to the tree where the search begins; that is, when you're searching in the windows for HKEY_LOCAL_MACHINE, the search does not include keys under HKEY_CURRENT_USER.

Task 8.1. Searching for a key in the Registry Editor.

TASK

Step 1: Description
This task enables the Administrator to find a key in the Registry.

Step 2: Action
1. Log onto the Windows NT Server as Administrator.
2. Choose Start|Run and type regedt32. You should see a Registry Editor similar to the one shown in Figure 8.1.

Figure 8.1.

Registry Editor windows.

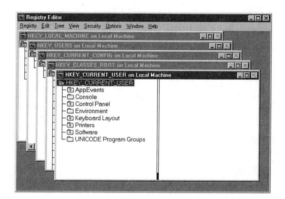

3. Choose View|Find Key.
4. In the Find box of the Find Key dialog box, type the name of the key you want to find.

    If you want to restrict the scope of the search or define the search direction, select the Match Whole Word Only box, the Match Case option, or Up or Down in the Direction box.

    To see the next occurrence of the key name you specified, click Find Next.

5. Click Find. Because key names are not unique, searching for additional occurrences of a specific key name is a good idea, to ensure that you find the key you want.

TIP

Some key names include spaces (such as Session Manager); others use underscores (such as Ntfs_rec) or a continuous string (such as EventLog). To ensure that you find the key you want, search for a portion of the name, and make sure that the Match Whole Word Only check box is unchecked in the Find dialog box.

Step 3: Review

 Working with the Registry is a key system administration responsibility. Before you can alter any entry, you need to find the entry. This task showed you how to find a key.

Now that you have found the key, you can edit the value using the Registry Editor.

More Cautions About Editing the Registry

If you're just learning about the Registry, you're probably eager to wade right in and modify a value entry. Before you do, however, let me just talk about using caution when manipulating the Registry.

The vast majority of Registry items correspond to some setting in the Control Panel, Server Manager, User Manager for Domains, or the like. For example, you saw earlier today in Chapter 7, "Understanding the Registry," that you could change the value of RegisteredOrganization directly via the Registry Editor. That example, however, is fairly illustrative and simple to understand. In general, don't use the Registry to modify a value that can be modified otherwise.

Suppose, for example, you choose to set a background color on the screen to medium gray. That color is represented as a number triplet: 128 128 128. How do you know what these color values mean? Because they're the same as Windows 3.1x color values. Color values in Windows are expressed as number triplets. Each number is an integer between 0 and 255. When you input a value greater than 255, the Registry Editor neither knows nor cares that you're putting in an illegal color value. Now, in the case of colors, that probably wouldn't crash the system. In the case of other items, however, the system could easily be rendered unusable. Suppose you're running NT Server on a system with a single 486 processor; the Registry would reflect that, noting in one of the Hardware keys that NT is running in "uniprocessor" mode. Altering that to a multiprocessor mode wouldn't be a very good idea.

Why, then, learn about the Registry Editor? Here are three reasons:

☐ Some settings—important ones—can be altered only with the Registry Editor, so there's no getting around the fact that an NT administrator has to be proficient with the Registry Editor.

☐ You can use the Registry Editor to change system value entries on remote computers. Here's a simple example: You're in New York, and you want to change the background color on a server in Atlanta. One way to do so would be to get on a plane and travel to Atlanta to run the Control Panel on the NT machine at that location. A better way, however, would be to start up the Registry Editor, choose Registry|Select Computer, and edit the Registry of the remote computer. (This way assumes that you're running NT Server, and you have the security access to change the Registry of the remote computer; that is, you're a member of the Administrators group on that computer.)

☐ A program called REGINI.EXE that comes with the *Resource Kit* enables you to write scripts to modify the Registry. Such a tool is quite powerful. You could write a REGINI script, for example, to reconfigure an NT setup completely. Again, however, before you start messing with that program, be sure that you have become proficient with the Registry. As explained earlier, you can get into all kinds of trouble when working with the Registry Editor. Imagine what kinds of automated disasters you could start at 100MHz with a bad REGINI script!

Task 8.2. Editing a key with the Registry Editor.

Step 1: Description

This task enables the Administrator to edit a key in the Registry.

Step 2: Action

1. In the right pane of the Registry Editor window, double-click the value entry, or from the Edit menu, choose the String, Binary, Dword, or Multi String command as appropriate for the selected value.

2. Edit the value that appears in the related Editor dialog box and then click OK.

TIP

To view numbers in decimal format, double-click the value entry and select the Decimal format option. Cancel the dialog box when you finish checking the value.

Step 3: Review

Working with the Registry is a key system administration responsibility. This task showed you how to edit a value.

The Binary and Dword editors give you the flexibility to select the base of a number system in which you want to edit the data. In the Binary editor, you can edit the data as binary (base 2) or hexadecimal (base 16) format. In the Dword editor, you can edit the data in binary, hexadecimal, or decimal (base 10) format. Hex is the default base for both editors. The Registry Editor always displays these types of data in hex format in the right pane.

Information stored in a nonvolatile key remains in the Registry until you delete it. Information stored in a volatile key is discarded when you shut down the system. Everything under a volatile key also is volatile. Everything stored under the HKEY_LOCAL_MACHINE\HARDWARE key, for example, is volatile.

You can add a key to store data in the Registry. You might, for example, add a subkey under `CurrentControlSet\Services` to start a service process you have written or to install a device driver that doesn't have an installation program.

Task 8.3. Adding a key to the Registry Editor.

Step 1: Description
This task enables the Administrator to add a key to the Registry.

Step 2: Action

1. Select the key or subkey under which you want the new key to appear. Then choose Edit|Add Key, or press the Ins key.

2. In the Key Name box of the Add Key dialog box, type the name you want to assign your key. The key name cannot contain a backslash (\). It must be unique in relation to other subkeys at the same level in the hierarchy; that is, Keyl and Key2 can each have a subkey named Key3, but Keyl cannot have two subkeys named Key3.

3. Leave the Class box blank, as this entry is reserved for future use.

4. Click OK to display the new key in the Registry Editor window.

Step 3: Review
This task showed you how to add a key to the Registry using the Registry Editor.

Saving Registry Data

Using the Save Key command, you can save the information in a key and all its subkeys in a hive file. Then you can use this hive file with the Restore and Load Key commands.

Changes in the Registry are saved automatically, whether you make changes by using Registry Editor or by changing settings in applications. The Save Key command specifically is used to save portions of the Registry as a file on disk. To use the Save Key command, you need Backup privileges, which you have when you're logged on as a member of the Administrators group.

You can use the Save Key command on any key. This command, however, does not save volatile keys, which are destroyed when you shut down the system. For example, the `HKEY_LOCAL_MACHINE\HARDWARE` key is volatile, so it is not saved as a hive file.

TASK

8

8

TIP

If you want to view the Hardware hive for debugging, you can save it in a text file by choosing Registry|Save Subtree As.

Task 8.4. Saving a Registry key.

Step 1: Description

This task enables the Administrator to save a Registry key.

Step 2: Action

1. Select the key you want to save as a hive file on a disk.

2. Choose Registry|Save Key and then complete the filename information in the Save Key dialog box. Under the FAT file system, this filename cannot have an extension. When the key you're saving is in the Registry of a remote computer, the drive and path you specify for the filename are relative to the remote computer.

Step 3: Review

This task showed you how to save a Registry key using the Registry Editor.

The selected key is now saved as a file. When you use the Load Hive command, you can select the filename for any files saved using the Save Key command. As part of system maintenance, for example, you might use the Save Key command to save a key as a file. When the key you saved is ready to be returned to the system, you use the Restore command.

You can use the Restore or Restore Volatile command to make a hive file a part of the system configuration. The Restore and Restore Volatile commands enable you to copy information in a hive file over a specified key. This copied information overwrites the contents of the specified key, except for the key name.

To use the Restore or Restore Volatile commands, you need Restore privileges, which you have when you're logged on as a member of the Administrators group.

Task 8.5. Restoring a Registry key.

Step 1: Description

This task enables the Administrator to restore a Registry key.

Step 2: Action

1. Select the key where you want to restore the hive.

2. Choose Registry|Restore and then complete the filename information in the Restore Key dialog box to specify the hive you want to restore. If you're running the FAT file system, this filename cannot have an extension. Also, when you're restoring a key on a remote computer, the drive and path of the filename are relative to the remote computer.

TIP

> If you want to add a key temporarily to a system, use the Restore Volatile command. When you use this command, the Registry makes a volatile copy, which disappears when the system is restarted.

Step 3: Review

This task showed you how to restore a Registry. You cannot restore keys or subkeys that have open handles. For this reason, you cannot restore the SAM or SECURITY subtrees (Windows NT always has handles open in these keys). You use the Restore command only for special conditions, such as restoration of user profiles on a damaged system.

Compacting Registry Data

The memory the system uses for the Registry approximately equals the size of a hive when loaded into memory. Hives vary in size on disk from 20KB to over 500KB. The space used depends primarily on how many local user profiles you keep and how much information is stored with each user profile.

You should remove unused or out-of-date user profiles from a computer by choosing the Delete User Profiles command in Windows NT Setup. (Use the Setup program because it protects you from deleting the profile for a currently logged-on user.)

You can use the Save Key command to save a user hive and then use the Restore command so that you can use this smaller hive. Using Save Key after deleting unused entries compacts the key. How much space you gain depends on how much was stored in various user profiles. You will want to repeat this procedure whenever you have many unused or out-of-date user profiles. Set up a procedure to monitor routinely used profiles with the aim of compacting the key. This procedure is useful only for user profiles, not for the SAM, SECURITY, SOFTWARE, or SYSTEM hives.

You might want to examine the contents of a Registry key as text for troubleshooting. You can save a key as a text file, and you can print data from the Registry Editor, including a key, its subkeys, and all the value entries of all its subkeys.

The Save Subtree As command also works for the HKEY_LOCAL_MACHINE\HARDWARE subtree, which you cannot otherwise save as a hive file.

To save a Registry key as a text file, in a Registry window, select the key you want to save as a text file. Then choose Registry|Save Subtree As and specify a filename.

To print a Registry key, in a Registry window, select the key you want and then choose Registry|Print Subtree.

Limiting Registry Size

The total amount of Registry space that the Registry data (the hives) can consume is restricted by the Registry size limit, which prevents an application from filling the paged pool with Registry data. Registry size limits affect both the amount of paged pool that the Registry can use and the amount of available disk space.

You can view or set the value for RegistrySizeLimit under the following subkey:

HKEY_LOCAL_MACHINE\SYSTEM\CurrentControlSet\Control

RegistrySizeLimit must have a type of REG_DWORD and a data length of 4 bytes; otherwise, the system ignores it. By default, the Registry size limit is 25 percent of the size of the paged pool, which is 32MB, so the default RegistrySizeLimit is 8MB (which is enough to support about 5,000 user accounts). Setting the PagedPoolSize value under the CurrentControlSet\ Control\Session Manager\Memory Management subkey also affects the Registry size limit. The system ensures that the value for RegistrySizeLimit is at least 4MB and no greater than about 80 percent of the size of PagedPoolSize.

 TIP

Incidentally, you also can adjust the PagedPoolSize (and hence the RegistrySizeLimit) by using the System icon within the Start|Settings|Control Panel. Select the Performance tab and click Change. Highlight the volume, change the page size values, and then click OK. You will need to click OK again to exit the System applet.

The RegistrySizeLimit limitations are approximate. You can set the PagedPoolSize to a maximum of 128MB, so RegistrySizeLimit can be no larger than about 102MB, which supports about 80,000 users (although other limits prevent a Registry this large from being very useful). Also, RegistrySizeLimit sets a maximum, not an allocation (unlike some similar limits in the system). Setting a large value for RegistrySizeLimit does not cause the system to use that much space, unless it is actually needed by the Registry. A large value also does not guarantee that the maximum space actually is available for use by the Registry.

The space controlled by RegistrySizeLimit includes the hive space, as well as some of the Registry's runtime structures. Other Registry runtime structures are protected by their own size limits or other means.

To ensure that you always can at least start the system and edit the Registry when the RegistrySizeLimit is set wrong, quota checking is not turned on until after the first successful loading of a hive (that is, the loading of a user profile).

As you learned this morning in Chapter 7, by convention, when similar data exists under both HKEY_CURRENT_USER and HKEY_LOCAL_MACHINE, the data in HKEY_CURRENT_USER takes precedence. Values in this key, however, also might extend (rather than replace) data in HKEY_LOCAL_MACHINE. Also, some items (such as device driver loading entries) are meaningless if they occur outside HKEY_LOCAL_MACHINE.

Fault Tolerance in the Registry

As you learned previously, every hive file has another file named the same but with the extension .LOG. This convention is really useful because NT Server and NT Workstations for that matter use it to protect the Registry during updates.

Whenever you or the system changes a hive file, the change is first written into its LOG file. The LOG file isn't actually a backup file; it's more a journal of changes to the primary file. After the description of the change to the hive file is complete, the journal file is written to disk. Often, a disk write ends up hanging around in the disk cache for a while, but this write is flushed to disk. Then the system makes the changes to the hive file based on the information in the journal file. If the system crashes during the hive write operation, enough information is present in the journal file to roll back the hive to its previous position.

The exception to this procedure comes with the SYSTEM hive. The SYSTEM hive is really important because it contains the CurrentControlSet. For that reason, the backup file for SYSTEM, SYSTEM.ALT, is a complete backup of SYSTEM. When one file is damaged, the system can use the other to boot.

Notice that HKEY_LOCAL_MACHINE\HARDWARE does not have a hive. That's because the key is rebuilt each time you boot, so NT can adapt itself to changes in computer hardware. The program NTDETECT.COM, which runs at boot time, gathers the information that NT needs to create HKEY_LOCAL_MACHINE\HARDWARE.

Confused about where all the keys come from? You can find a recap in Table 8.1. It's similar to the table you saw in Chapter 7 (refer to Table 7.2), but it's more specific about how the keys are built at boot time.

Table 8.1. Key construction.

Key	How Constructed at Boot Time
`HKEY_LOCAL_MACHINE:`	
`HARDWARE`	NTDETECT.COM
`SAM`	SAM hive file
`SECURITY`	SECURITY hive file
`SOFTWARE`	SOFTWARE hive file
`SYSTEM`	SYSTEM hive file
`HKEY_CLASSES_ROOT`	SYSTEM hive file, Classes subkey
`HKEY_USERS_DEFAULT`	DEFAULT hive file
`HKEY_USERS\Sxxx`	*username*OOO hive file
`HKEY_CURRENT_USER`	*username*OOO hive file

Remote Registry Modification

As you just learned, you can modify another computer's Registry, perhaps to repair it or to do some simple kind of remote maintenance, by loading that computer's hive. You do so with the Registry Editor by using the Load Hive or Unload Hive command.

You can load or unload the hives only for `HKEY_USERS` and `HKEY_LOCAL_MACHINE`. The Load Hive option appears only after you select one of these two subtrees. Unload Hive is available only after you select a subkey of one of those two subtrees.

Why might you load a hive or a remote Registry? First, you might load a hive to get to a client's profile. Suppose that a user has set up all the colors as black or navy blue on black and made reading the screen impossible. (Believe it or not, this happens! At least one consultant has made money troubleshooting this one!) You could load the hive corresponding to that user, modify it, and then unload it.

Second, you can use the remote feature to view basically anything on a remote system. Suppose you want to do something as simple as changing screen colors. You would do so on a local system by running the Control Panel, but the Control Panel doesn't work for remote systems. Answer: Load the Registry remotely.

You could load and save hive files to a floppy disk, walk the floppy over to a malfunctioning machine, and load the hive onto the machine's hard disk, potentially repairing a system problem. This solution isn't possible when you're using NTFS, unless you have multiple copies of NT on the system—something most people don't have. But if you have an NT workstation running a FAT file system, you can always boot from DOS, replace the hive files under DOS, and then reboot under NT.

When you boot under NT, you see the reference to a "known good menu." That's because NT keeps track not only of the current control set, but also the previous control set. This way, when you mess up the system, you always can roll back to the previous good configuration. These control sets are kept in the same key as the `CurrentControlSet`. Within `HKEY_LOCAL_MACHINE\SYSTEM\Select\Current`, `\Default`, `\Failed`, and `\LastKnownGood` are numbers indicating which of the two kept control sets are current, good, failed, and so on.

In the same way that you can use Event Viewer or User Manager to view details on another computer, you can use the Registry Editor to view and change the contents of another computer's Registry when the server services on the remote computer are running. This capacity to view a computer's configuration remotely enables you, as a system administrator, to examine a user's startup parameters, desktop configuration, and other parameters. You therefore can provide troubleshooting or other support assistance over the telephone while you view settings on the other computer from your workstation.

NOTE

> Auto Refresh is not available when you're viewing the Registry from a remote computer. When Auto Refresh is turned on, manual refresh is disabled. Therefore, when you open a remote Registry, Registry Editor checks to see whether Auto Refresh mode is on. When it is, the Registry Editor displays the following message: `Auto Refresh is not available for remote registries; Registry Editor disables Auto Refresh mode`.

To view the Registry for a remote computer, do either of the following procedures:

- ☐ Choose Registry|Select Computer and then select or type the name of the computer whose Registry you want to access.
- ☐ Double-click the name of a computer in the Select Computer list. Under Windows NT Server, the first name in this list represents the name of a domain. When no computer name appears after this domain name, double-click the domain name to view a list of the computers in that domain.

Two Registry windows appear for the remote computer: one for `HKEY_USERS` and one for `HKEY_LOCAL_MACHINE`. You can view or modify the information on keys for the remote computer when the access controls defined for the keys allow you to perform such operations. If you are logged on as a member of the Administrators group, you can perform actions on all keys.

You can use the Load Hive and Unload Hive commands in the Registry Editor to display and maintain another computer's Registry without viewing it remotely. As mentioned previously, you can load and save files to a floppy and walk them over to a machine that isn't working, so you can do the reverse. You can load and save the hive files from a malfunctioning machine, and then look at them on your machine. You might want to use this method to view specific values or to repair certain entries for a computer that is not configured properly or cannot connect to the network.

The hives that make up the computer's Registry are loaded automatically when you start the computer, and you can view the contents of these hives in the Registry Editor. If you want to view or change the contents of other hive files, you must use the Load Hive command to display their contents in the Registry Editor.

The Load Hive and Unload Hive commands affect only the Registry windows that display HKEY_USERS and HKEY_LOCAL_MACHINE. To use these commands, you must have Restore and Backup privileges, which you have when you are logged on as a member of the Administrators group. The Load Hive command is available only when HKEY_USERS or HKEY_LOCAL_MACHINE is selected. The Unload Hive command is available only when a subkey of one of these handles is selected.

Task 8.6. Loading a hive into the Registry Editor.

Step 1: Description
This task enables the Administrator to load a hive in the Registry Editor so that you can view or change the contents of a hive.

Step 2: Action
1. Select the HKEY_LOCAL_MACHINE or HKEY_USERS root.
2. Choose Registry|Load Hive.
3. Use the File Name, Drives, and Directories boxes and the Network button of the Load Hive dialog box to select the file containing the hive you want to load, and then click OK. (If you're loading a hive on a remote computer, the drive and path in the filename are relative to the remote computer.)

 TIP
> You can find the directory location and names of hives on a computer in HKEY_LOCAL_MACHINE\SYSTEM\CurrentControlSet\Control\Hive list.

This file must have been created with the Save Key command (as described earlier in this chapter), or it must be one of the default hives. Under the NT file system, the filename cannot have an extension.

If you're unable to connect to another computer over the network, you can load a hive file that you copied to a floppy disk.

4. In the second Load Hive dialog box, type the name you want to use for the key where the hive is loaded, and then click OK. This name creates a new subkey in the Registry. You can specify any name using any characters including blank spaces. You cannot load an existing key. Data from the loaded hive appears as a new subkey under HKEY_USERS or HKEY_LOCAL_MACHINE (whichever handle you selected before loading the hive). A loaded hive remains in the system until it is unloaded.

Step 3: Review

The Load Hive command creates a new hive in the memory space of the Registry and uses the specified file as the backup hive file (filename.LOG) for the hive. The specified file is held open, but nothing is copied to the file unless the information in a key or value entry is changed. Likewise, the Unload Hive command does not copy or create anything; it merely unloads the loaded hive.

To unload a hive from the Registry Editor, select the key that represents a hive you previously loaded, and then choose Registry|Unload Hive. The selected key is removed from the window and is no longer actively available to the system or for editing in the Registry Editor. You cannot unload a hive that was loaded by the system. Also, you cannot unload a hive that contains an open key.

Backing Up and Restoring a Registry

Mark this section, because you'll no doubt want to come back to it when you need to perform maintenance on the Registry. You might need to restore backed-up versions of Registry hives, for example, when you replace your current Windows NT computer, when a disk controller or hard disk goes bad, or when an electrical failure zaps large parts of a disk.

By now, you should understand that the Registry is important and should be protected. It protects itself pretty well with its LOG files, but how can you back it up?

Unfortunately, the fact that Registry hive files are always open makes it tough for you to back up the Registry, because most backup utilities are stymied by open files. The NTBackup program that comes with NT works well, but it backs up to tape only. Nevertheless, if you use NTBackup—which is pretty good, particularly for its price—then you should tell it to back up the Registry every night.

Outside NTBackup are a couple of other protection possibilities. A program named RDISK creates emergency repair disks. And the *Resource Kit* includes two useful utilities: the REGBACK.EXE program enables you to back up a Registry file, and the REGREST.EXE restores it.

Backing Up Registry Hives

You can back up Registry hives using one of four methods:

☐ Using a tape drive and the Windows NT backup program (NTBackup), select the Backup Local Registry option in the Backup Information dialog box to include automatically a copy of the local Registry files in the backup set.

☐ If you don't have a tape drive, run the REGBACK.EXE or REPAIR.EXE program from the Windows NT Resource Tool Kit, or use another tool that uses the same techniques to back up Registry files.

☐ Start the computer under a different operating system. Then copy all files in the *SystemRoot*\SYSTEM32\CONFIG directory to a safe backup location.

☐ Use the Save Key command in the Registry Editor. This command essentially performs the RegBack procedure manually.

For each direct subkey of HKEY_LOCAL_MACHINE and HKEY_USERS, you must choose Registry|Save Key and then specify filenames that match the key names. For example, save the SYSTEM key to \BACKDIR\SYSTEM. On the FAT file system, the filename should not have an extension.

Don't use Save Key with the HARDWARE hive, which contains volatile data. You don't get any data because Save Key cannot save volatile keys to disk.

Restoring Hives from Backup Files

To restore a damaged Windows NT system, you must first restore the basic operating system installation. You have two options for restoring the operating system:

☐ You can use the Emergency Repair disk to restore the system to the same state it was in just after installation.

☐ You can run Windows NT Setup again. You end up with a system that starts the computer but lacks changes made since you first set it up. You can recover most of those changes by copying files from backups by using the Windows NT backup program for tape backups or by copying from disk backups.

Restoring the basic operating system is only half the battle. Registry hive files are protected while Windows NT is running, so you cannot simply copy these files back onto the system. So, after the system and all the additional files such as device drivers are restored, you must restore the Registry. Just how you restore the Registry depends on which backup mechanism you used:

☐ For tape backups, you can use the Windows NT Restore program to restore the Registry. Then restart the computer.

☐ Start the computer using an alternate instance of the operating system (or using MS-DOS when the system files are on a FAT partition). Copy back the files to the *SystemRoot*\SYSTEM32\CONFIG directory. Then restart the computer using the regular operating system.

☐ Use the REPAIR.EXE program from the Windows NT Resource Tool Kit.

☐ Use the REGREST.EXE program from the Windows NT Resource Tool Kit. The RegRest program performs a ReplaceKey operation, which swaps backup files for the default files that the Emergency Repair or Windows NT Setup programs installed, and saves the default files under other filenames. Restart the computer after running the RegRest program to see the restored Registry.

Securing the Registry

You have seen the importance of the Registry in this chapter and the preceding chapter. Obviously, you need to protect the Registry. One way to restrict access to the Registry Editor and its subtree is to place the Registry files on an NTFS system partition and restrict access to the directory through the file directory permissions. This method is easier to administer than changing the default security permissions for each of the subtrees.

The Registry contains data that should not be accessed by all users. Even when the Registry resides on a FAT system partition, security permissions and auditing can be implemented through the Registry Editor. The default security permissions for files within the Registry Editor vary by subtree.

By now, you understand how the Registry affects the Windows NT system and how important it is to keep the Registry intact. As you begin to set up more Windows NT installations in your enterprise, you need to plan strategies for protecting the Registry for each of the new installations. Following are some suggestions for protecting Registry files under most conditions:

☐ Do not allow anyone to log on as a member of the Administrators group unless that individual has administrative duties.

☐ Because you can administer any workstation from a remote computer, you can remove REGEDT32.EXE from workstations. If, for some reason, you need the ability to administrate each workstation locally, you can place access controls using Explorer on REGEDT32.EXE, thereby limiting the rights of users to start this program. Day 7 introduces you to file access rights.

NOTE

Windows NT enforces access control on Registry files, so it is difficult for users accidentally or intentionally to damage or delete hives on a running system. While the system is running, it keeps hive files open for exclusive access on all file systems. If the Windows NT *SystemRoot* is not on an NTFS volume, the Registry files can be tampered with; specifically, users can remove hives for user profiles that currently aren't loaded. With NTFS, you can prevent such tampering.

One of the most common Registry mistakes occurs when a user inadvertently deletes the Registry. You can protect the Registry from accidental deletions in one of two ways:

- ☐ *Read-only mode.* Choose Options|Read Only. When this command is checked, Registry Editor does not save any changes.

- ☐ *Confirmation.* Choose Options|Confirm On Delete. When this command is checked, the Registry Editor asks you to confirm deletion of any key or value.

Protecting Registry Files for User Profiles

You can protect the Registry hive files for user profiles in the same way that you protect other files in Windows NT—by restricting access through File Manager. If the files are stored on an NTFS volume, you can use Explorer to assign permissions. You should change permissions only for user profile hives. The permissions for other hives are maintained automatically by the system and should not be changed.

Assigning Access Rights to Registry Keys

You can assign access rights to Registry keys regardless of the type of file system on the partition where the Windows NT files are stored. To determine the users and groups with access to specific Registry data, set permissions on the Registry keys. This process is sometimes called *changing ACLs*, in reference to the Access Control Lists governing who has access to data. You also can add or remove names from the list of users or groups authorized to access the Registry keys.

WARNING

Changing the permissions to limit access to a Registry key can have severe consequences. Be careful not to set No Access permissions on a key that the Network Control Panel application needs for configuration; doing so causes the application to fail.

At a minimum, ensure that Administrators and the System have full access to the key so that the system starts and the Registry key can be repaired by an administrator.

Because assigning permissions on specific keys can have drastic consequences, you should reserve this action for keys you add to accommodate custom applications or other custom settings. After you change permissions on a Registry key, be sure to turn on auditing in User Manager, and then test the system extensively through a variety of activities while logged on under different user and administrative accounts. You also should audit the key for failed access attempts.

Task 8.7. Assigning a permission to a key.

Step 1: Description

This task enables the Administrator to assign permissions on a key. In the Registry Editor, the commands on the Security menu for assigning permission and ownership of keys work the same as similar commands in File Manager for assigning access rights for files and directories.

Step 2: Action

1. Make a backup copy of the Registry key before making changes.
2. Select the key for which you want to assign access permission. Choose Security|Permissions.
3. In the Registry Key Permissions dialog box, assign an access level to the selected key by selecting an option in the Type of Access box as described in Table 8.2, and then click OK.

Table 8.2. Registry key permissions.

Type of Access	Meaning
Read	Allows users on the Permissions list to read the key's contents but prevents changes from being saved
Full Control	Allows users on the Permissions list to access, edit, or take ownership of the selected key
Special Access	Allows users on the Permissions list some custom combination of access and edit rights for the selected key

4. Turn on auditing in User Manager, and then test the system extensively to ensure that the new access control does not interfere with system or application operations.

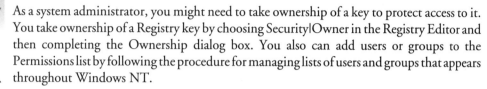

Step 3: Review

Changing the permissions to limit access to a Registry key can have severe consequences, so be careful how you use this task to set permissions.

As a system administrator, you might need to take ownership of a key to protect access to it. You take ownership of a Registry key by choosing Security|Owner in the Registry Editor and then completing the Ownership dialog box. You also can add users or groups to the Permissions list by following the procedure for managing lists of users and groups that appears throughout Windows NT.

You (or any user) can take ownership of any Registry key by logging onto the system as a member of the Administrator group. When an Administrator takes ownership of a key without being assigned full control by its owner, however, the key cannot be given back to its original owner, and the event is audited.

Learning More About Managing the Registry

In addition to the Registry Editor, NTS includes a program called the Policy Editor. To open it, choose Start|Programs|Administrative Tools|System Policy Editor. After the program starts, choose Files|Open Registry to see some of the icons that NT provides. This utility enables you to change Registry settings on a limited basis for only HKEY_CURRENT_USER and HKEY_LOCAL_MACHINE. (NT changed the icon names to confuse you a little.)

If you want to stay on the safe side and only view information, use the Windows NT Diagnostics program, WINMSD.EXE (choose Programs|Administrative Tools|Windows NT Diagnostics). Think of this program as a way to inspect the Registry's configuration information in read-only mode.

You've learned only the basic concepts of the NT Registry. Before you make any changes manually, read Microsoft's in-depth discussion of the Registry in Appendix A of its *Concepts and Planning Guide.*

If you have the *Windows NT Resource Kit* from Microsoft—and if you don't, then get it—you'll find 150 pages detailing each and every key. Additionally, the Registry keys are documented in an online help file. Unfortunately, some keys aren't documented anywhere except in bits and pieces on Microsoft TechNet or another support group.

If you don't have the *Resource Kit,* you can download the Registry key help file from the WINNT forum on CompuServe. You also can find some tools that make it easier to search for things in the Registry.

Summary

The Registry is a convenient and powerful component of the Windows NT Server operating system. As we stressed, you should exercise caution when working with the Registry. In this chapter, you learned about the following points:

☐ Remote management of the Registry

☐ Saving and compacting Registry data

☐ Backing up the Registry

☐ Protecting the Registry

The Registry is an important database. You will use it in a couple of days, in Chapter 12, "Managing User Access," to create users. The system stores this information in Security Account Manager (SAM) in the Windows NT Registry. Now, however, you can review what you learned today.

Workshop

To wrap up the day, you can review terms and tasks from the chapter, and see the answers to some commonly asked questions.

Terminology Review

configuration registry—A database repository for information about a computer's configuration; for example, the computer hardware, the software installed on the system, and environment settings and other information entered by the person or persons using the system.

control set—A complete set of parameters for devices and services in the HKEY_LOCAL_MACHINE\SYSTEM key in the Registry.

fault tolerance—A computer and operating system's ability to respond gracefully to catastrophic events such as a power outage or hardware failure. Usually, fault tolerance implies the ability either to continue the system's operation without loss of data or to shut down the system and restart it, recovering all processing in progress when the fault occurred.

permission—A rule associated with an object (usually a directory, file, or printer) to regulate which users can access the object and in what manner.

read-only—A term used to describe information stored in such a way that it can be played back (read) but not changed (written).

8

Registry Editor—An application provided with Windows NT that enables users to view and edit entries in the Registry.

remote administration—Administration of one computer by an administrator located at another computer and connected to the first computer across the network.

Task List

With the information provided in this chapter, you now can begin your understanding of NTS objects. You learned how to carry out the following tasks:

- ☐ Search for a Registry key
- ☐ Edit a Registry key
- ☐ Add a key to the Registry
- ☐ Save a Registry key
- ☐ Restore a Registry key
- ☐ Back up and restore the Registry
- ☐ Load a hive
- ☐ Secure the Registry

Q&A

Q What happens if the Registry is not available?

A Well, for one thing, users can't log in because system software consults the Registry to determine whether the username is a valid account and then matches the password supplied to the one stored in the Registry. You can't create new objects, such as new users. Also, you can't use any NTS process or device. So, the short answer is, not very much.

DAY

5

Chapter **9**

Understanding Domains

In the preceding days, you learned about installing and exploring NT and managing the Registry. Today you'll learn all about domains and security. First, in this chapter, you'll review, update, and manage domains, and later today, in the following chapter, you'll learn the nuances of security within NT Server.

Discovering Domains

Domains are merely groups of NT machines. The machines must be either NT workstations or servers. No other client operating systems such as Windows 95 or Windows for Workgroups can join the domain.

Why do you use domains in NT? Typically, they provide you with a single entity to manage and to use for signing in, regardless of the number of machines you're using. You will discover other reasons, but this one is probably the best reason for the user community.

In a one-server environment, you don't use domains. Doing so would be a redundant exercise because you have only one machine. With two servers or more in your network, however, using domains begins to make sense. In a two-server environment, you obtain one account from server1 and a second account from server2. They might actually be called the same name—lewisb, for example—but an administrator logs onto each machine and sets up the account. As a user, you sign onto server1 with your username and password to be validated. Perhaps you retrieve your mail or do other work. After a while, you decide you need a file from server2 and go to retrieve it. Before you can gain access to server2, that machine says, "Who are you? Give me a name and password, please." (The machines are very polite.) You need to enter this information again using the username and password set up on the second machine.

With more servers, the process becomes cumbersome and time-consuming. We know a client with over 100 NetWare 3.x servers. The administrators must sign onto each server individually to perform their work. They spend most of their time just signing on!

Most people in this situation try to make all their passwords and accounts the same, regardless of the machines. Therefore, they actually have to remember only the one account and one password. If your administrator or administrators use the same name for your account on all the machines you access, which we strongly agree with, then signing on is less of a problem. You need to remember only what your username is and what password you use on each machine.

Unfortunately, every 30 days or so you need to change the password according to your company's policy. This task is time-consuming because you need to sign onto each server and tell it what your new password is without making any mistakes or forgetting the first password change you perform. Believe me, it's a hassle finding out your password is expired on one machine, changing the password, and continuing your work only to remember later that you need to change all the other server passwords and cannot remember the earlier change.

In this scenario, every server handles its own security with its own database of usernames and passwords. Administrators must deal with access on an individual machine basis. You learned earlier about name servers and print servers; perhaps you need a security server as well. Figure 9.1 shows a simple diagram of user access without the benefit of a domain structure.

NT helps by enabling you to set up domains, or groups of machines. After a domain is registered, users sign on once to obtain the services of any machine on the domain that they are authorized to use. The domain relegates certain functions to certain servers, telling the other servers when it's okay to allow users access.

A domain really takes on that function within NT only when one or more of the machines in the domain are delegated to be in control. NT calls these machines *domain controllers.* On each network, you need one machine that is called the *Primary Domain Controller,* or *PDC.*

Figure 9.1.
Simple network authentication process.

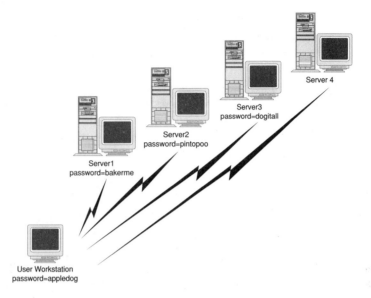

This machine maintains the central database containing all the accounts, passwords, and access control lists that are part of NT security. You'll learn about each of these database components this afternoon, in the chapter on security.

Microsoft would be remiss if it suggested the use of only one domain controller, wouldn't it? What about backup? Redundancy? Contingency planning? *Backup Domain Controllers,* or *BDCs,* take on this role. These Backup Domain Controllers assist the primary controller and help share the workload of authenticating users.

You don't need Backup Domain Controllers to have a domain, but you must have a Primary Domain Controller. As mentioned earlier, only NT Servers can be controllers. Microsoft does not allow other types of operating systems to have this level of control in an NT network.

One of the controlling factors in deciding how many domains you need is the size of the organization and the size of the Security Account Manager (SAM) database server. The SAM can be only so large, and if your organization is larger than that size, you need to split up your network into multiple domains. You'll learn more details about this issue later in this chapter.

The Security Access Manager Database

How does NT control all the users and their access levels? Recall that NT maintains a database called the Security Account Manager database, or SAM, which is the crux of NT security. For this reason, you must install and use one NT machine as a domain controller. Only domain controllers can read and use the SAM database in an NT domain. Don't go looking for a file called SAM. NT has hidden it within the NT Registry because you don't ever need to access it directly. That access is a job for NT Server itself.

NOTE

> Only NT can use the SAM database. This is true only in the sense that NT is designed to read and maintain the SAM. You can get to the data in the database in other ways, but that isn't what we mean in this instance.

Entry in the Primary Domain Controller's SAM database generally means that a user needs to sign on only once. After that initial sign-on, NT validates access to other resources on the network and allows access if authorized without additional user identification and authentication. One NT Server talks to another, discussing the needed access, ensuring that the person asking is permitted to access the resource, and then allowing that access—all without the user needing to sign onto the second machine.

Use of this database can be a problem, though. If all the users are located in one file on the Primary Domain Controller, what happens if that machine fails? At this point, the BDC comes in. Each backup controller carries a complete copy of the SAM, backed up every five minutes by default. (You can change the backup parameter. You'll learn how later in the chapter.)

In a small organization, using one backup controller with the primary controller might be sufficient. Of course, if you're really paranoid about recovery, you can add other backup machines. Remember the rule: One primary, many backups.

The SAM database can get very large if your organization is large; thus the whole idea of domains comes into play. You use domains to split up the organization into manageable chunks.

Microsoft recommends that the SAM not be too large, however; otherwise, bootup time increases enormously because of NT's processing of this database at startup. You can figure 1KB per user and 0.5KB per machine to see how large your SAM will become. Anything over 40MB or so will cost you big time. On a 486/66MHz machine, for example, NT will take about 15 minutes to boot using a 40MB SAM database.

As you can see from these figures, you need to factor the size of your organization alongside the speed of your servers to decide how large a domain you can create. Remember that you can have only one Primary Domain Controller and that the SAM database on that controller needs to be smaller than 40MB. The best method for determining the number of domains is to take the size of your server into consideration (a 486/66 being less effective than a Pentium Pro 200MHz) along with the number of staff multiplied by 1KB, the anticipated number of machines multiplied by 0.5KB, and the result divided into the suggested size limits of the SAM database.

With 5,000 staff using 1,000 NT workstations and 10 NT servers, for example, you need a SAM database of around 5.5MB. If you plan to run it on a small 486/66, the machine will likely choke. Breaking down the database into a few domains allows you the flexibility to manage the server response speed. Because we don't know what type of machines you're running, figuring out the specific entitlements and optimal SAM sizes is too difficult. You need to decide the type of server and then try different size SAM databases, incrementing each size by a consistent number so that you can see the point at which your machine chokes.

 TIP

> NT keeps the SAM database in memory when it loads. The amount of physical memory on your servers therefore must be at least the same as the size of the SAM database. Although you might run servers with 128MB of memory, using a smaller size SAM database is advisable because NT reads and parses the SAM each time it loads. This process is very slow. Microsoft says it takes a 486/66 PDC 15 minutes to load a 40MB SAM database. If your machine is slow to start, this might be the reason.

On a final note, the memory of your server must equal the size of the SAM database.

Task 9.1. Reviewing domain and SAM database sizes.

Step 1: Description

This task enables you to decide the default size of your domains. You usually perform this task once to decide on the initial number of domains and size of your SAM database.

Step 2: Action

1. Note how many staff expect to be using the NT network, and estimate what that number will be in the near future. You might use an existing business plan for introducing NT to get these figures.

2. Decide on the size and speed of your NT servers. The bigger the CPU, the more you can handle.

3. Learn how many NT workstations will connect to the network.

4. Set up a PDC with a small SAM and load about 100 or 1,000 user accounts. (The number depends on the size of your machines and organization.) See how long NT takes to load that database. Increase the SAM size by another 100 or 1,000 user accounts, and then try again. Track these start times carefully, and after three or four attempts, you should get a feel for the load factor of your particular environment. Don't forget to ensure that the physical memory of the machine remains equal to or higher than the size of your SAM database.

5. Decide on the optimal SAM size for your organization. Using this number, figure out how many users and machines will fit in that SAM. Use the rough calculations of 1KB per user and 0.5KB per machine.

6. To calculate the number of domains needed, divide the number of users and machines into the size of the organization that expects to use the NT network. The number of SAM databases needed equals the number of domains needed. Be careful not to use too many domains as a simple solution. Setting up 100 domains in NT and managing the trust relationships are onerous tasks. They are discussed later in this chapter.

Step 3: Review

By using the rough calculations outlined here, you can size the NT domain structure and ensure that your organization's access needs are efficiently managed.

Understanding Domain Models

In this part of the chapter, you'll read about how different domain structures are created, and you'll learn some of the pros and cons of each model. Microsoft allows four basic methods for combining servers and workstations: the single domain, a master domain, multiple master domains, and the complete trust model.

A small organization usually chooses to set up a network using a single domain. This form of domain is the simplest, with only a small number of users and a few servers. If you have a large number of users or servers, one domain might be insufficient, as you discovered earlier in this chapter.

A master domain sets out a domain for controlling all the user accounts (the master) and any number of resource domains. The *resource* domains contain only server and NT workstation machine accounts—no users. These resource domains can contain print servers, file servers, and applications servers, for example. Trust relationships between the master and all the resource domains are set up, completing the arrangement. No trust relationships are needed between the resource domains themselves.

Some organizations are too large even for this type of domain structure, so Microsoft created the multiple master domain model for them. This model creates any number of master domains needed, as in the master domain model discussed earlier. Then the master domains are set up to trust each other. Each resource domain is also set up to trust all the masters.

As the size of the network grows, so does the complexity, but Microsoft offers no relief for all this "trusting." Maintenance and creation of trust relationships are time-consuming, and trying to figure out all the permutations can be frustrating. It's all you have though, folks. We do hear rumors, however, that this is one of the issues being looked at very carefully in the next version (Cairo), and in all likelihood, it will be significantly enhanced.

The trust model suggests that, as the number of domains grows, you need to manage users who have valid business needs across several domains. User Barry in domain A, for example, needs constant access to a server in domain B, so you set up a trust relationship between the two domains.

What's a trust relationship? In NT, security is a major component of the system, and one domain cannot talk to another domain, in any fashion, unless the two domains are told that doing so is okay. This relationship extends to the workstation level. If Barry tries to use an NT workstation on domain B where he does not have an account, he gets nowhere. The manner in which a domain is told to acknowledge another domain is called the *trust relationship*.

Trust Relationships

When two people get together and form a relationship, it usually relies on some level of trust. At least, successful relationships rely on trust. You trust the other person to do what is expected of him or her. You trust that person not to spend all your money or buy things you don't need, and so on. You normally build this trust because of your understanding of the other person and the impression he or she gives that he or she can be trusted. In NT domains, you need to establish the same idea.

As you create domains in your organization, they become standalone units. They cannot trust the other domains because Microsoft built in an enhanced level of security and control in the network. They are like a couple at the beginning of a relationship. Before they can get anywhere, the couple must be introduced to each other. Before one domain recognizes another, the domains need to be introduced also. Well-mannered little devils, aren't they?

So what happens next? First, explore what happens when you create a second domain in your office. You populate each domain with the necessary machines and users. Next, users in one domain find a need to access the other domain. This need could be something simple, like users in the Marketing domain needing information from the Accounting domain. They perhaps begin using the informal sneakernet—you know the one—sending someone in sneakers down the hall to pick up a disk with the required data.

The user in Marketing cannot just sit down at an Accounting workstation, log in, and gather data. Without any level of trust, the Accounting domain doesn't acknowledge that any workers exist in a thing called the Marketing domain. The user gets nowhere. You cannot set up access permissions to allow the access either. The Marketing person doesn't exist in Accounting.

So what do you do? You can set up the user on both domains. That user then needs to make sure that his or her passwords are identical on both machines. The sign-on process asks for the first sign-on account and password. When the user asks to connect with the next machine, NT just asks the workstation for the account and password; the workstation then sends the one it first used that day. In an NT environment, this setup works okay (except when it's time to change all the passwords). On some workstations—DOS, for example—the client software doesn't know how to use this relationship, so the process just fails. This is not very user-friendly. In this case, you need to set up the trust relationship. Figure 9.2 shows an example of two separate domains with no trust relationship.

Figure 9.2.

Separated domains.

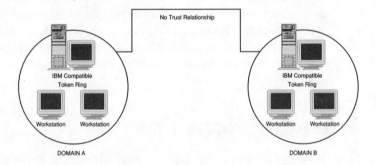

In a trust relationship, the administrator of one domain establishes a link to another domain. We're not talking about a network connection here, although, of course, that is needed; otherwise, the entire exercise is redundant. We are talking about telling the one domain that it can recognize the global users and groups from the other domain.

Trust relationships can be one way or two way. Domain A might trust domain B in a one-way relationship. Users in domain B therefore can access resources in domain A using the accounts and passwords originally set up for them in their home domain (in this example, B). Users in domain A cannot use the resources of domain B, however, because the relationship goes in only one direction.

This type of one-way relationship is useful for the example in which the staff in the Marketing domain needs data from the Accounting domain. Because we never mentioned the reverse—Accounting needing anything from Marketing—no trust is set up, and those users cannot access the Marketing domain. An example of a one-way trust relationship is shown in Figure 9.3.

Figure 9.3.

A one-way trust.

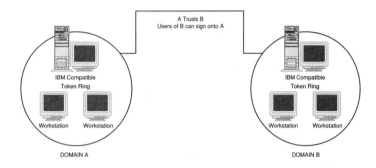

With a one-way trust, users from the trusted domain can sign onto the other domain and access any resources for which permissions have been set up for them. The trusted users don't need accounts set up for them on the new domain. That is the whole purpose of trust relationships. Continuing the example, the Marketing users obtain access to the Accounting domain because the Accounting domain asks the Primary Domain Controller in the Marketing domain to authenticate the users and trusts that server when it says that the users are authorized in the Marketing domain. As you can see, a one-way trust is just that—one way. If you want the Accounting people to also be able to use Marketing resources, you must establish another trust (making it a two-way trust).

As you create trusts, they become very complex and possibly confusing. In the original example, Accounting trusts Marketing. Assume that Accounting already has another trust relationship with the Finance domain. Does this mean that Marketing can get access to the Finance domain after an Accounting trust is set up? In a word, no. Trusts are not cumulative. Just because one trust is set up with a particular domain, that does not mean that the new relationship enjoys all the benefits of existing trust relationships. Figure 9.4 shows this more complex trust relationship assignment.

Figure 9.4.

Trusts do not transfer.

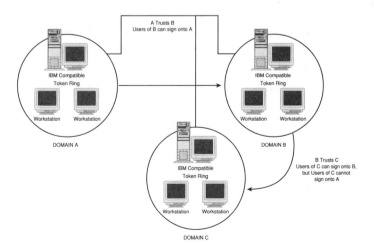

The concept of trusts might sound a little confusing—it certainly is at first glance—but as you get accustomed to it, it all starts to make sense. You need to remember that this type of trust applies only to NT Server domains.

Creating Trust Relationships

You know that security is an integral part of the NT operating system, so you should not be surprised to learn that before a trust can be established, the domain that is to become trusted must allow this trust to occur. Yup! If we administer domain A and you administer domain B, for you to set up a trust with my domain, we must tell domain A that it is okay to be trusted. You need to perform an action in both domains. The actions do not have to occur in any order for them to work. Both of them need to happen. Performing these actions in order, however, is best, as you'll see later.

The domain that is to be trusted must approve the possibility; then the domain that wants to trust it must perform an action to validate the trust of the other domain. These actions still say only that domain A is trusted by domain B. They don't suggest that B trusts A. That's another relationship.

Managing all the associated trust relationships can become onerous. It's one of the weaknesses of the NT architecture.

In the following sections, you'll learn how to create these relationships in NT Server.

Setting Up One Domain to Trust Another

To begin the trust relationship, you need to allow Accounting to trust Marketing. To do so, perform Task 9.2.

Task 9.2. Allowing the trust relationship to occur.

Step 1: Description

This task enables you to set up one domain to allow another to trust it. You perform this task each time you want to establish any trust relationship. In this task, you'll use the example of Marketing needing access to the Accounting domain. This task is only the first of two, telling the Marketing domain to let itself be trusted. In Task 9.3, you'll set up the Accounting domain trust.

Step 2: Action
  1. Log onto the Marketing domain using an account with Administrator privileges.

2. Open the User Manager for Domains by choosing Start|Programs|Administrative Tools (Common)|User Manager for Domains.

3. Choose Policies|Trust Relationships. Figure 9.5 shows the dialog box that appears.

   This dialog box shows all domains currently trusted or permitted to be trusted. None are presently shown because you have not created them yet. The two main windows are called Trusted Domains and Trusting Domains.

Figure 9.5.

The Trust Relationships dialog box.

4. Click the Add button beside the Trusting Domains window.

5. In the box that appears, type the name of the domain in which you want to allow trusts to occur. For the example, type Accounting. Remember, you're not setting up a trust; you're just allowing Accounting to trust Marketing.

6. You can use a password by entering one in the place provided. Using a password really isn't necessary as long as you continue the trust process and finish it. The password applies to the time between allowing a trust with Accounting and the time Accounting sets up and completes the relationship.

7. Click OK when you're ready to continue. You then see that Accounting appears in the Trusting Domains window.

8. Click the Close button in the upper-right corner of the dialog box to complete the task.

Step 3: Review

By setting up the trusting piece of the relationship, you are halfway to establishing a one-way trust relationship. After you complete the next task, the trust relationship between Marketing and Accounting will be complete.

Completing the Accounting Trust Relationship

To complete the trust relationship, you need to create the trust in Accounting. The combination of these two tasks finalizes the trust relationship process and permits easier access from one domain to the other.

Task 9.3. Completing the trust relationship.

Step 1: Description

This task enables you to set up one domain to trust another. You perform this task each time you want to establish any trust relationship. In this task, you'll use the example of Marketing needing access to the Accounting domain. In the second of the two tasks, you'll tell the Accounting domain that Marketing is to be trusted.

Step 2: Action

1. Log onto the Accounting domain using an account with Administrator privileges. Obtain the password from the Marketing administrator if one is in use.

2. Open the User Manager for Domains by choosing Start|Programs|Administrative Tools (Common)|User Manager for Domains.

3. Choose Policies|Trust Relationships. In the dialog box that appears, you see the two main windows called Trusted Domains and Trusting Domains.

4. Click the Add button beside the Trusted Domains window.

5. In the Add Trusted Domain dialog box, type the name of the domain you want to be trusted. For this example, type Accounting. Then enter the password supplied by the Marketing administrator. If no password is used, leave the password field blank.

6. Click OK when you're ready to continue. You then see that Marketing appears in the Trusted Domains window. Accounting now trusts Marketing. Users in Marketing can access resources in the Accounting domain.

7. Click the Close button in upper-right corner of the dialog box to complete the task.

Step 3: Review

You have finished setting up the trust relationship. Users can log on at Accounting NT workstations. The logon prompt on these workstations shows an option for logging users from Marketing onto the trusted domain. Network connections can be set up for shared directories on the Accounting domain to allow Marketing users to access information easily. You'll learn more information about how to allow and restrict access to files and directories in a couple of days, in Chapter 14, "Managing Windows NT Server File and Directory Access Rights."

You now know how to set up a one-way trust relationship. If you want to allow the reverse (allow Accounting users access to the Marketing domain), you simply perform the two tasks again, changing the domain names where appropriate. By performing the tasks both ways, you establish a two-way trust.

You can see that creating trust relationships becomes time-consuming and difficult to manage. Imagine setting up trusts between 30, 40, or even hundreds of domains. With two tasks for each trust, the number of overall tasks begins to rise exponentially as the number of domains rises. With 40 domains, you have 80 tasks. Each time you add a domain, you need to perform another 40 tasks allowing the relationship with an additional 40 tasks to complete the trust between them all. Wow! No wonder that Novell is chuckling in the background.

Removing a Trust Relationship

After all the work you did in the preceding sections, you might decide that a particular trust is no longer necessary and decide to remove it. Removing trust relationships also requires two steps. First, you need to stop one domain from trusting the other; then you need to remove the permission to trust so that it cannot be reestablished.

This task follows the same general path as the two previous tasks, Task 9.2 and Task 9.3. Instead of selecting the Add option, though, you select the Remove option. You need to follow both steps completely to remove the relationship properly. You perform them in reverse order this time, removing the trust and then the permission.

Task 9.4. Removing a trust relationship.

Step 1: Description

This task enables you to remove a trust relationship. You perform this task each time you no longer need one domain accessing another or when a domain is removed from the network. You'll continue using the Marketing and Accounting example.

Step 2: Action

1. Log onto the Accounting domain using an account with Administrator privileges.
2. Open the User Manager for Domains by choosing Start|Programs|Administrative Tools (Common)|User Manager for Domains.
3. Choose Policies|Trust Relationships. You then see the two main windows called Trusted Domains and Trusting Domains.
4. Select the Marketing domain from the Trusted Domains window, and then click Remove. A dialog box that asks whether you want to continue this action appears.
5. Click the Yes button to continue.
6. Double-click the Close button in the upper-right corner of the dialog box to complete the task.
7. Log onto the Marketing domain using an account with Administrator privileges.

8. Open the User Manager for Domains by choosing Start|Programs|Administrative Tools (Common)|User Manager for Domains.

9. Choose Policies|Trust Relationships.

10. Select the Accounting domain from the Trusting Domains window. Then click the Remove button beside the Trusting Domains window. A window appears asking whether you really want to remove the relationship. Click Yes to continue.

11. Click the Close button in the upper-right corner of the dialog box to complete the task.

Step 3: Review

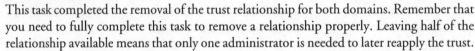

This task completed the removal of the trust relationship for both domains. Remember that you need to fully complete this task to remove a relationship properly. Leaving half of the relationship available means that only one administrator is needed to later reapply the trust.

Next, you'll learn about the different domain structures and how to manage trust relationships. You also need to perform other tasks during the management of your NT domains. You'll learn about allowing users to access files and directories and use printers on other domains in the following sections. Finally, you'll learn about the difference between local groups and domain groups.

Allowing Access to Files Across Domains

Earlier, you set up a trust relationship so that users in the Marketing domain could access resources within the Accounting domain. This capability allowed the users to log on. Now you need to let them get access to the files they need. (If you removed the trust in Task 9.4, you need to reinstate it by following the earlier tasks. Alternatively, you can follow the next section using the users and files on your NT Server rather than a trusted one.)

First, be sure that users do not already have the access. How is this possible? Well, through the anomalies of the Everyone group. As you'll learn tomorrow afternoon, whenever you create a share, NT automatically sets the permissions for that share to Everyone/Full Control as the default. (A well-designed security software package should limit default access, not give it away.) All users belong to the Everyone group, and Full Control means just that. Therefore, as a user, you can do as you please with the information in this share.

Users get this access automatically because of their automatic membership in the Everyone group. By default, because you set up a trust relationship earlier, the users in Marketing automatically get full control over the existing shares on the new server because they join that server's Everyone group. You need to change this relationship by modifying the access provided to the Everyone group, removing Full Control and substituting a more appropriate level of access. You need to perform this action each time a share is added. You therefore need to monitor the Everyone group's access rights regularly.

In general, we think that the Everyone group should be very limited in the number of resources it can access. A sound, effective security program needs to assign access to resources on a job-function basis, not as a default. You might allow access to globally accessible printers or internal telephone lists here, but little else (and maybe not even that much). You'll learn more about access to files and directories tomorrow, when you begin Chapter 12, "Managing User Access."

As you'll see tomorrow, on Day 6, when you're requesting access for members of another domain, a List Names From field in the Permissions dialog box or File and Permissions dialog box provides lists of users and groups from the domains that are available to the network. Using this drop-down dialog box, you can choose the domain containing those users for whom you want to provide access and select individual users from the list provided after you have selected their domain. You then grant these users access as needed.

Understanding Local and Global Groups

In NT Server, you have local groups and global groups. What are these different groups, and why are they necessary? The use of groups adds a level of sophistication and allows for a security approach based on business function, not people, even across multiple domains.

By using a security approach, you can set up a group called Accounting Users, for example, and assign certain levels of access that users from Accounting need to perform their day-to-day jobs. Then, to add a new user to the system, you can place that user in this group. He or she then automatically gains access to all the resources associated with the job function. This approach is much easier than manually adding user after user and allowing each user access on an individual basis. Unfortunately, regardless of the software in use, many organizations have not yet converted to business function access permissions. Perhaps the administrators see this lack of conversion as job security? Anyway, NT attempts to allow the same functionality, as you'll see in the following paragraphs.

To allow a user to access a share on another domain, you first need to understand the difference between a local group and a global group. You'll learn the details concerning groups in the next chapter on security. Here, you'll learn the highlights as they pertain to the management of domain structures.

A group consists of a collection of permissions and rights that can be assigned to a bunch of users, using the business function analogy we started earlier. For example, you might create an Accounting group, a Finance group, a Sales group, and so on. You then can assign the resources these folks need to perform their jobs to the group. As staff are added to the group, these new users gain the access to the resources automatically. "It's a good thing," to paraphrase Martha Stewart. You can assign resources to individuals, but doing so quickly becomes time-consuming and inefficient as the number of users you're managing escalates.

A *local group* exists on each machine and consists of user accounts and global groups as members. They must be from the domain the group belongs to and from trusted domains. Permissions and rights for this group apply only to the servers within the domain to which the local group belongs.

A *global group* can contain only user accounts from within the domain that owns it and that are defined at the domain level. You grant rights and permissions to the group, and the user accounts that are part of the group gain these rights by virtue of belonging to the group. The global group can be used only within the servers and NT workstations of its own domain and in trusting domains. Global groups cannot be created on NT workstations.

NT Server supplies several default groups. They include Server Operator, Account Operator, Print Operator, Administrators, Users, Guests, and Everyone. This list is not exhaustive as it is explained in more detail in the next chapter. You already know that you must belong to the Administrators group to perform NT Server administration functions such as adding user accounts and setting up resource permissions and file and directory rights.

In a multidomain network, you use both sets of groups to manage your network access needs. The nitty-gritty of these two sets of groups revolves around the fact that NT allows local groups to contain global groups, but global groups cannot contain any other groups. Microsoft designed the group structure in this manner to avoid the possibility of administrators accidentally creating *circular* groups, or groups that never end and just keep referring to each other in an endless cycle.

Suppose that the user group of machine A is added to machine B's user group, and machine B's group is added to a user group for machine C. If machine C then adds its group to machine A, a circular reference is formed, with NT never finding a solution. NT needs to go to machine B to verify a user, then to machine A, and then back to machine C, which sends it back to machine B. You get the picture, I'm sure. This process should become more clear this afternoon in the next chapter, where you'll learn about security in more detail.

Planning the Network

Now that you understand some of the logic behind the various types of domains and the trust relationship process, you need to learn about planning your NT Server network. Perhaps you're thinking that you can just set up a single large domain and forgo all this master domain and multiple master stuff.

In general, minimizing the number of domains in your network is not a bad idea. It's less work. You need to balance the degree of security afforded by separating your network into a number of domains by the amount of administration you're willing to put up with on a daily basis. Of course, you might decide that Microsoft will fix this dilemma in the next version (Cairo) and provide an easier "tree" structure similar to NetWare's NetWare Directory Services (NDS), which we understand Microsoft is considering. You must place your faith where you're comfortable.

Keep in mind that Microsoft might take a long time to bring out this new version. It was originally scheduled for 1995, but it currently looks as though you will see it this fall or in the spring of 1998. It also might not perform as expected. With any major operating system, the number of changes that appear in a new release fluctuates according to the effort, difficulty, and cost associated with each change. Finally, as just mentioned, the release date has already been changed. In defense of Microsoft, however, we don't believe that the date was ever officially set. Our personal belief is that Microsoft will make major changes to the domain handling in the next release. This issue is just too important to leave as it is and currently provides Novell with additional marketing clout, because its structure is simpler to use.

Nevertheless, in many large organizations, each division or department is almost an entity unto itself, and, therefore, you could set up the network with each entity having its own domain. For one of my clients, for example, the Treasury department considers itself an upstart and does its own thing, allowing very little access between other departments and itself. It runs its own domain.

In other organizations, the separation between various departments is less concise, so they might want a more connected structure. If size of the organization is not a problem, the departments can use a single master domain structure.

Part of the problem with each solution is that NT likes to chatter. Maintaining the browser means that each server needs to announce itself every 12 minutes so that the browser can be up-to-date. Other "I'm alive" messages also originate and cause network traffic. You might need to draw up your network boundaries with this traffic in mind, restricting the domains over some form of geographical area to minimize the WAN traffic.

As stated earlier in the discussion of the SAM database, you might have too many users for one or even two domains, or you might use small server machines, further restricting your options. You need to define the expected size of the organization, the types of machines in use, the geographical nature of the organization, the expected traffic patterns, and a whole load of other items before committing to any one solution. Consider testing your network and machine load using incrementing numbers of user accounts to find a setup that works for you.

Summary

You learned many of the surrounding infrastructure issues and design considerations when looking at domains in this chapter. In addition, you learned the various domain types and how to add and remove trust relationships.

In this chapter, you learned the following points:

- ☐ The network authentication process that NT performs when users sign on
- ☐ The various type of domains that are available and how each one differs
- ☐ That NT domains offer Primary Domain Controllers (PDC) and Backup Domain Controllers (BDC)
- ☐ How PDCs and BDCs differ and the function of each server type
- ☐ What function the Security Access Manager database performs
- ☐ That the SAM database doesn't really exist as an actual database in the usual sense (it is part of the Registry)
- ☐ How local groups and global groups differ and the function of each group

Workshop

Terminology Review

domain—A collection of computers sharing a common database and security policy.

domain controller—The server that is used to authenticate domain logons and maintain the master security database.

domain name—The name that a domain uses to identify itself to the network.

global group—An NT group that can be used in servers and workstations of a particular domain and in trusted domains. This group is used to assign permissions and rights to a set of user accounts.

group—An account that contains other accounts called *members*. It is used to help assign rights and permissions to resources for a collection of users.

local group—An NT group that can be granted rights and permissions only for servers within its own domain.

SAM—The Security Account Manager. This NT subsystem maintains the security database and provides for API access to that database.

SAM database—The Security Account Manager database. NT Server stores user accounts and permissions here. It is located in the Registry. You can actually find it in the directory \winnt\system32\config.

security policies—The set of security rules that operate and control functions such as password expiration, auditing, and access rights. NT Server uses User Manager for Domains to manage these policies and allows the administrator to set up policies for Account, Audit, and User Rights.

trust relationship—A special relationship that can be used to allow pass-through validation between domains. This relationship allows user accounts access to an entire network after sign-on at only one server.

Task List

The information provided in this chapter shows you how to manage the various domains that NT makes available. In this chapter, you learned how to set up trust relationships and later remove those relationships. You learned to perform the following tasks:

- ☐ Verify the optimal size of your SAM database
- ☐ Set up a domain to allow others to have a trust relationship with that domain
- ☐ Complete the trust relationship by implementing a trusted relationship between the domain allowing trust and one needing that trust
- ☐ Remove a trust relationship completely

Q&A

Q Where do I find the SAM database in an NT domain?

A You normally never need to look directly at the SAM database with utilities or other programs. Access is facilitated through the NT command-line commands or GUI interface. You can find part of the SAM database in the NT Registry under the directory \winnt\system32\config in a file called SAM (assuming that you installed NT in the default directory). Most of the data, however, is hidden within the Registry.

Q Can I find out the optimal size of the SAM database?

A Yes, although the process is not entirely straightforward because it depends on the number of user accounts, size of server hardware, and amount of anticipated network traffic. You learned how to find the size in Task 9.1 in this chapter.

Q Do I have to use this trust relationship model?

A You don't have to set up trust relationships between domains. On a small network, you might have only one domain, and therefore use of a trust is not needed. On larger networks, it is primarily dependent on whether you expect users to cross the domains as part of their job functions. Unless you have users needing access to another domain, a trust relationship is not necessary.

Q We set up a trust relationship some time ago, but that domain is no longer used. Do we need to do anything?

A NT 4.0 continues a trust relationship until you take action to remove it. Removing it requires an action on both domains. Removing only one side of the trust leaves you exposed to unauthorized trust setup. As you learned in this chapter, to complete a trust, you must tell one domain to allow the action and another domain to actually trust the allowing domain. Removing the relationship also requires the two actions—one to remove the actual trust relationship and the other to disallow the trust to occur.

9

Chapter 10

Understanding Security

From the beginning, you should have noticed a major difference between Windows NT and other operating systems, such as Windows 3.1*x*, MS-DOS, or OS/2. As you learned in Chapter 2, "What Is Windows NT Server?" Microsoft included security in Windows NT as part of the initial design specifications. Security is pervasive throughout the entire operating system. Figure 10.1 shows how the Windows NT security subsystem fits into the overall Windows NT architecture.

The Windows NT security subsystem is an integral subsystem rather than an environmental subsystem because it affects the entire Windows NT operating system. Security is an important part of any network operation, necessary for protecting one user's data from being accessed by other users, an organization's records from being tampered with by outsiders, and so on. Security, however, has some administration associated with it.

Figure 10.1.

The Windows NT architecture.

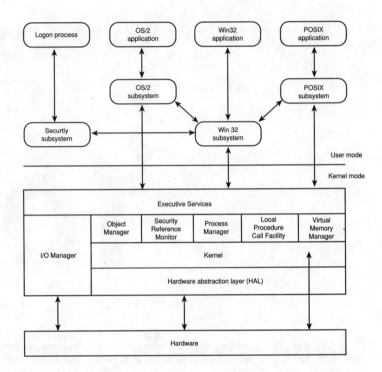

Before you can access any of the resources on a Windows NT system, you must first log on and get authenticated by the Windows NT system. Authentication is required at both the workstation and the server level; that is, the system authenticates you even when you access a standalone Windows NT computer not connected to a file server or host computer. A connection to a Windows NT server is not required to achieve initial resource protection. Windows NT can provide this local security because each machine has an Account and a Security Policy database coupled to the Windows NT server. The security model includes components that control who accesses objects (such as files and shared printers), what actions a user can take on an object, and what events you can audit.

When a user logs onto Windows NT, the system creates a special data structure called a *token object* to represent that user. Windows NT associates this token—or a copy of it—with every process that the user runs. This process-token combination is called a *subject*. Subjects operate on Windows NT objects by calling system services. When the system accesses protected objects, such as files and directories, it compares the contents of the subject's token with the Access Control List (ACL) using a standard access validation routine. The access validation routine determines whether to grant the subject the right to perform the requested operation. The access authentication routine also can generate audit messages as a result of a security mismatch.

10

Microsoft and Certification

Microsoft designed the Windows NT security model to meet national and international security criteria. In the United States, the security criteria Microsoft met are the C2-level criteria defined by the U.S. Department of Defense's *Trusted Computer System Evaluation Criteria* document (DOD 5200.28-STD, December 1985). This document commonly is called the *Orange Book*. The following are important C2 requirements:

- ☐ The system must identify and authenticate each user using a unique name and password, and track all the user's activities using this identification.
- ☐ Resources must have owners who can control access to those resources.
- ☐ The system must protect objects so that other processes do not use them without permission. This protection applies to memory locations, files, and other objects.
- ☐ The system must audit all security-related events, and it must restrict the audit data to all but authorized users.
- ☐ The system must protect itself from external interference or tampering, such as modifications to the running system or to system files stored on disk.

The Windows NT Server C2 implementation is entirely software-based and does not require additional hardware. Windows NT Server and Windows NT Workstation were designed from the ground up to be C2 secure. Some Windows NT Server features are so secure (identification and authentication, and the capability to separate users from their functions) that they meet higher-level B2 security requirements.

Windows NT achieves high levels of security by never letting programs access objects directly. Any action on an object is authorized and performed by the operating system. Windows NT can perform these checks on objects relatively easily because individual objects hold much of the information needed to do a security validation.

The Windows NT Security Subsystem

As mentioned earlier, the Windows NT security subsystem affects the entire Windows NT operating system. It provides a single system in which all access to objects, including files on disk, processes in memory, or ports to external devices, are checked so that no application or user gets access without proper authorization.

The security subsystem components described here are shown in Figure 10.2. So that you understand how Windows NT protects objects, seeing all the major security data structures at work is useful. The security subsystem consists of the following components:

- ☐ *Local Security Authority* (LSA), which ensures that the user has permission to access the system.

    ☐ *Security Account Manager* (SAM), which maintains the user and groups accounts database and validates users for LSA.

    ☐ *Security Reference Monitor* (SRM), which is the kernel-level process that checks access permissions and enforces access validations and audit policies defined by LSA.

    ☐ *Logon processes,* which provide the initial interactive logon and display the Logon dialog box.

Figure 10.2.

Security subsystems.

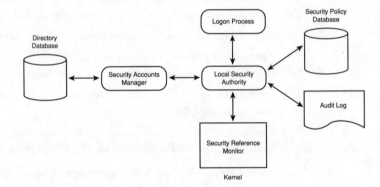

The User Interface (UI) utilities, which are a part of the operating system, also play an important role in the security model of Windows NT. The UI is the only hint to most users of the underlying security mechanisms. As the system administrator, you typically use the UI to perform administrative functions such as adding or removing users from the system and looking at the audit logs.

In addition to the preceding, Windows NT offers the following security components:

    ☐ Discretionary access controls

    ☐ Access tokens

    ☐ Access Control Lists

    ☐ Event auditing

These elements, combined with the logon process, Security Account Manager, the Local Security Authority, and the Security Reference Monitor, provide a number of integrated features that form the backbone of security in Windows NT. In the remainder of this chapter, we further describe the security subsystems and components and how they're integrated.

Local Security Authority

The *Local Security Authority* (LSA), also called the security subsystem, is the heart of the Windows NT Server security system and provides many services. LSA ensures that the user has permission to access the system. It generates access tokens, manages the local security policy, and provides interactive user validation services. The Local Security Authority also controls the Audit policy and logs the audit messages generated by the Security Reference Monitor. Specifically, it performs the following tasks:

- [ ] Creates access tokens during the logon process
- [ ] Allows Windows NT Server to connect with third-party validation packages
- [ ] Manages the security policy
- [ ] Controls the Audit policy
- [ ] Logs audit messages to the Event Log

Security Account Manager

The *Security Account Manager* (SAM) maintains the security account database, called the SAM database. This database contains information for all user and group accounts. SAM provides user validation services, which are used by the Local Security Authority. SAM is invisible to the user. It is responsible for comparing user input in the Welcome dialog box (at logon) with the SAM database and providing a security identifier (SID) for the user and the SID of any groups in which the user is a member.

SIDs are retired when an account is deleted. After you delete a user account, you cannot re-create it because the SID for that account no longer exists. You can create a new account with the same name, but the system assigns a different SID. Fortunately, the new account does not retain previous privileges.

Depending on the configuration of the network, different SAM databases can exist on one or more Windows NT systems. Which SAM database is accessed at logon depends on whether the user logs onto a user account on a workstation or on the network. The directory database is interesting, because in a network environment it might exist on a number of machines. When a user logs onto a local machine, the SAM on that machine retrieves user IDs from the database. In a Windows NT domain network environment, user account information can be stored in a directory database on one or more servers called domain controllers, which share and update account information. This shared database allows users to log on once to access resources throughout the network.

10

The system maintains a database of users who are authorized to access the system and verifies users during the logon process. Windows NT stores account names and passwords in the SAM database. The SAM database can store two passwords for each user where a LAN Manager server is present on the network. One of the passwords is a LAN Manager–compatible password, and one is a Windows NT password:

☐ *LAN Manager password:* This password is compatible with passwords used by LAN Manager. It is based on the standard OEM character set, is not case sensitive, and can be up to 14 characters long.

☐ *Windows NT password:* This password is based on the Unicode character set, is case sensitive, and can be up to 128 characters long.

The Security Account Manager stores information about users in the user account database. The actual database is part of the Registry and is stored in the *SystemRoot*\System32\CONFIG directory. Each password is double-encrypted in the SAM database. The first encryption is a one-way function (OWF) version of the clear text password. The system then encrypts the password again to make it even more obscure. One-way encrypted passwords are generally considered indecipherable. The trick to validating a client is to compare this encrypted password with the encrypted password in the SAM database. You don't need to decrypt (to expose the original passwords) to make this validation. In addition, when a user logs on, the system encrypts the passwords typed in the Logon dialog box before transmitting them across the line to prevent eavesdroppers from capturing passwords.

The encrypted password sent from the client is received by the LSA and sent to the SAM for validation. The SAM compares the encrypted user password with the encrypted password in the user account database. The real password is never exposed in this process. In fact, the password is sent in a double-encrypted form, as described, which virtually ensures that no one can crack (that is, break) it.

Security Reference Monitor

The *Security Reference Monitor* (SRM) is a kernel mode Windows NT Server component responsible for enforcing the access validation and audit generation policy held by the Local Security Authority subsystem. SRM is not visible to the user. It protects resources or objects from unauthorized access or modification by preventing direct access to objects by any user or process. The SRM provides services for validating access to objects (files, directories, and others), testing subjects (user accounts) for privileges, and generating the necessary audit messages. The Security Reference Monitor contains the only copy of the access validation code in the system. This component ensures that object protection is provided uniformly throughout Windows NT regardless of the type of object accessed.

Windows NT prevents direct access to objects; instead, requests by users for access to objects must first be validated by the Security Reference Monitor. When a user opens a file to edit, for example, Windows NT first compares the security descriptor for the file with the security information that is stored in a user's token, and a decision is made whether to allow the user to edit the file. The security descriptor for the file includes all the access control entries (ACEs) that make up the file's ACL. A file without an ACL indicates that any user can access the file for any type of access.

A file with an ACL indicates that the Security Reference Monitor must check each ACE in the ACL and determine whether the user can access the file for the requested type of access. After the Security Reference Monitor grants access to the file, no further access validation check is necessary to access the file with the granted access. Further attempts to access the file are then made through a handle that was created to refer to the file.

The Logon Process

NOTE For the most part, this section describes logon procedures for Windows NT Server and Windows NT Workstation computers. You might find some variation in the background procedure when you log onto a Windows NT domain from Windows 95 and Windows for Workgroups computers.

Be aware that two types of logon exist: interactive and remote. An *interactive logon* occurs when you first log onto a computer. A process verifies that you are who you say you are based on the credentials (that is, username and password) you typed in the Logon dialog box. After they are validated, your credentials are kept on hand because the system might require them again for a remote logon authentication.

The interactive logon process is Windows NT Server's first line of defense against unauthorized access. The process begins with a Welcome box that requests a user to press the Ctrl+Alt+Delete keys simultaneously. (To enhance security in your organization, you should precede this dialog box with a legal notice.) Pressing Ctrl+Alt+Delete offers a strong defense against any application running in the background, such as a Trojan horse, that attempts to capture a user's logon information.

NOTE Windows 95 computers and other non-Windows NT computers do not have the Ctrl+Alt+Delete logon protection feature. Thus, they are susceptible to a Trojan horse acting as the logon process.

The Ctrl+Alt+Delete key sequence assures you that a valid Windows NT logon sequence will initiate. This key sequence should always be pressed when logging onto a machine that is already running.

The Windows NT logon process is outlined here and illustrated in Figure 10.3:

1. When the logon screen appears, you enter your username and password, and the name of the computer or domain where you want to log on. The username is used for identification, and the password is used for validation.

2. The LSA runs an authentication package to validate you. The authentication package can be the built-in Windows NT authentication package or a custom package from another vendor.

3. If you specify a log onto your local machine, the authentication package has the local Security Account Manager verify that your username and password are in the directory database. If domain logon is specified, the authentication package forwards the credentials to a domain controller for authentication via the Netlogon service.

4. The local or domain Security Account Manager returns appropriate security IDs when the account is valid. The SAM also provides other information such as account privileges, home directory location, and logon scripts.

5. The LSA creates an access token that contains your security ID, the security IDs of groups to which you belong, and the rights you have in the local system.

   Windows NT uses subjects to track and manage permissions for the programs you run. A subject is the combination of your access token and a program that acts on your behalf. Programs or processes running on your behalf are running in a security context for you; the security context controls what access the subject has to objects or system services.

6. The last step is to create a subject and run programs.

   At this point, you are identified to the system and can begin accessing objects based on the discretionary access controls on those objects.

The logon process is mandatory and cannot be disabled.

The logon process also enables you to have your own personal desktop configurations on your desktop systems. When you log on, the settings you had in a previous session are fetched from a profile and restored.

The service called Netlogon provides a single access point for you to log onto a domain network. Netlogon is responsible for replicating changes in the security database to all domain controllers so that you can log on from any of the controllers. The Netlogon service runs on any Windows NT computer that is a member of a domain.

Figure 10.3.

The logon process.

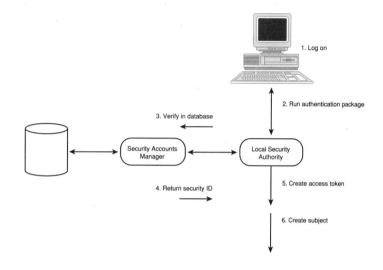

You can either log onto a local computer using an account on that computer, or log on by being validated by another computer. In domain networks, you are validated by a primary or backup domain controller that holds a copy of the directory database. The outcome depends on what you type into the Domain field of the Logon dialog box.

☐ When you type the local computer name in the Domain field, the local computer logs you onto the local system.

☐ When you type a domain name in the Domain field, a Remote logon takes place. The logon request is sent to a local domain controller for verification. If the domain specified is not the local domain, the domain controller forwards the request to a domain controller in the trusted domain specified.

NOTE

> You learned about primary and backup domain controllers this morning in Chapter 9, "Understanding Domains."

Domain controllers authenticate your account name and password by comparing them to entries in the directory database. If the entries are valid, account identification information is sent back to the logon computer through the domain controller that originally tried to verify the user account. When a normal logon fails, you are logged into the Guest account, but only when the Guest account is enabled and passwords are not required.

Assume that you are already logged on and attempt to access resources on other computers. In this case, the credentials that were used to verify the original logon are passed through to the new server and used to authenticate you for access to those resources. This process, called *passthrough authentication,* frees users from having to log onto every new resource they access.

NOTE

> In the next paragraph, the local computer is the computer on which you're working (that is, the one you logged onto), and the remote computer is a computer in the local domain or a trusted domain with a shared resource such as a folder or printer you want to access.

A remote logon occurs when you attempt to access some shared resources such as a folder or printer after you logged on using the interactive logon process. Remote logon really is the process of re-verifying that you are an authentic user. When the remote computer is satisfied that you are authentic, it returns a user ID that you can use for any future requests for service.

Now, assume that you attempt to access a computer in another domain that cannot authenticate you. The remote computer must send your credentials to a domain controller in its domain, and that domain controller asks a domain controller in your domain to authenticate you. This process is like getting cash from an ATM of a foreign bank. The issuing bank checks with your bank to verify that you are a customer and that you have funds.

Local and Domain Logon

You need to understand where the user account database that allows users to log onto a computer or network is stored. The database is stored either on a local computer (that is, the computer at which you are physically sitting when you log on) or on a domain controller. Once again, in the following discussion, we assume that you're logging on at a Windows NT computer rather than a Windows 95 computer, and that you're using domain networking rather than workgroup networking.

When you log on, you can choose to log onto an account on the local computer, log onto an account on the local domain, or log onto an account on some remote domain. The latter is usually called "logging onto a trusted domain." Ideally, all these accounts should be the same, but that often is not the case when different networks have been joined together.

When you log onto the local computer, your credentials are verified against a user account database stored on that computer. A problem occurs if you then try to access a resource on the network because you might need to log on again and have your credentials verified against the user account database on a domain controller.

Assume that you log onto the workstation and then try to open a shared resource on a server. Also assume that you have an account on the local computer and an account in the domain

10

with the same name but a different password. In this case, your original username and password are passed through to the server, but an `Access is denied` message appears because the passwords are different. Although the passwords could be synchronized, it is better to have one account on the domain controller and always log onto the domain rather than have separate accounts on different machines.

The same principle also applies when your network consists of multiple domains. Assume that you need to access resources in other domains. One way to do so is to have a separate user account in each domain; then you can log onto each account when you need to access the domain. However, having separate accounts can cause confusion and problems. Better is to have one account in one domain and then set up a trust relationship that allows your account to access resources in a trusting domain. Then you can log on once with one password.

NOTE   A service called Netlogon handles network logons. To access another computer using this service, your computer must be running the Workstation service, and you must have the "Access This Computer from Network" right on the target server.

Logon Sequence Details

When you press Ctrl+Alt+Delete at a Windows NT computer, the Logon dialog box appears with the Username, Password, and Domain text entry fields.

What you put in the Domain field makes a big difference to what happens during the logon process, as pictured in Figure 10.4.

NOTE   If you originally set up the user's machine as a member of a workgroup and not a domain, you will not see the Domain field in the Logon dialog box.

The user's logon information can be authenticated in a user account database on the local computer, on the home domain controller, or on a domain controller in a trusted domain. To reiterate:

1. If you type a local Windows NT Workstation name to log on locally, the local user account database is used to validate you.

2. If you type a home domain name, the SAM on a home domain controller validates you in its user account database.

3. If you type a remote domain name to log onto another trusted domain, the logon request is passed through to a domain controller on the trusted domain, where you can be authenticated.

Figure 10.4.

Logon types.

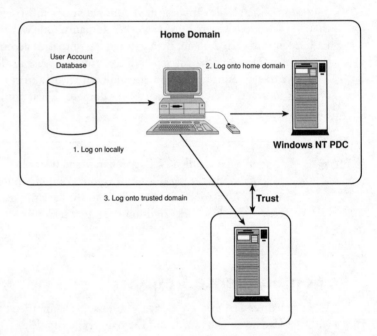

The steps in the initial logon process are to take the credentials (username, password, and domain name) you typed in the Logon dialog box and authenticate you. The security system on the computer (remember, it's called the Local Security Authority) calls up an *authentication package* (technically, the MSV1_0). The authentication package checks your credentials in the user account database by interacting with the Security Account Manager. If you specify a domain logon, this last step takes place over the network at a domain controller.

If your credentials are authentic, they are cached for later use, and an *access token* is created to identify you for all subsequent requests for resources. The access token contains your security identifier, group IDs, and user rights.

The security system determines the access to a resource by matching the user's requested access with the access permissions stored in the ACL for the resource. The user ID determines which access token is used to compare against the ACL for the resource. If a match is found and you (or the group) have not been specifically denied access, then the requested access is granted.

Remote Logon and Access

When you need to access a resource on a remote server, the server must authenticate you or have some other computer authenticate you for it. This process that a computer uses to authenticate a remote user is pictured in Figure 10.5.

Figure 10.5.

Remote logon and authentication processes.

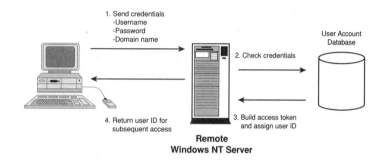

The remote logon process assumes that you already have logged onto a local Windows NT Workstation computer. It then follows this sequence of events:

1. The credentials that are cached in your computer are passed to the remote server.

2. On the remote server, the LSA requests that the SAM authenticate you. The SAM compares the credentials with your information in the user account database.

3. If the logon information is valid, the remote server's LSA builds an access token and passes it to the Server service. The Server service then creates a user ID for the client; this user ID is used to identify all subsequent communication between the client and the server.

4. The user ID is returned to the client so that the client can put the ID in any subsequent requests that it sends to the server.

The Server service allows a computer to entertain requests from a client computer on the network. The user ID is referenced in all requests made by the client to the remote server, and it is packaged into every Server Message Block (SMB) message communicated between the two computers. SMB is the application-level file sharing protocol used by Windows computers. In the Windows graphical user interface, SMB setup commands are initiated when you select remote resources in the Network Neighborhood. At the DOS level, SMB commands are executed with the NET command. SMB messages are embedded in transport-level network protocols like NetBEUI or TCP/IP.

Looking at the session setup process in more detail, assume that a Windows NT client executes the command

```
NET USE x:\\servername\sharename
```

where *x* is a drive letter to map, *servername* is the name of the server to use, and *sharename* is the name of a shared folder on that server. The NET USE command initiates a Session Setup SMB that contains the username, password, and logon domain name for the user. The following might occur:

☐ If the specified domain is the same as the home domain, the logon process pictured in Figure 10.6 takes place.

Figure 10.6.
Remote authentication components.

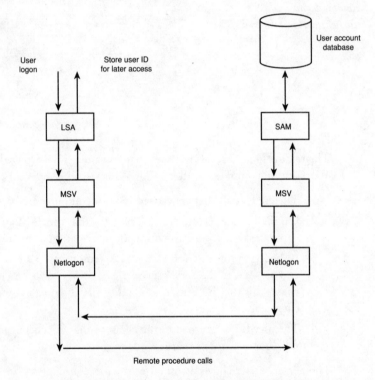

☐ If the user specifies a different domain that is trusted, the server does a pass-through authentication and sends the user's logon request information to a domain controller in the trusted domain. In this case, a logon process similar to that pictured in Figure 10.7 is performed. However, some slight differences occur. If the account is found in the local database and it is a local account, then the Guest account must also be enabled; otherwise, the logon fails. If the account is a global account, the specified password must match. If an account is not found, Guest permissions are tested on the user's home domain controller (not the domain controller remote to the user). If Guest is enabled, the user gets the same guest privileges in the remote domain.

☐ Another logon scenario is that the domain specified by the user is unknown. In other words, the user's local domain controller does not recognize the domain specified by the user as a trusted domain. In this case, the user's account is checked in the local user account database following the procedures pictured in Figure 10.7.

Figure 10.7.

Logon process flowchart.

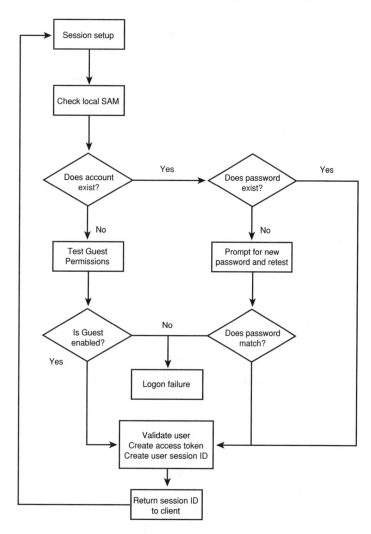

Still another scenario is similar to the preceding one, except that the user does not specify any domain (the Domain field in the Logon box is left blank). In this case, the server treats the logon as a local network logon following the procedure pictured in Figure 10.7. However, if an account is not found in the local user account database, the server asks servers in each of the domains that it trusts whether they have an account for the user. The first trusted server to reply is sent a request to perform passthrough authentication for the client. In addition, the Guest account must be enabled for local accounts, and a global account requires a password.

Authentication Procedure

When a user attempts to log onto a server, the LSA handles user authentication by calling the *MSV1_0 authentication package*. The MSV packages can log a user onto the local machine (assuming Windows NT), to the home domain, or to another trusted domain. You read about these types of logons previously in the "Remote Logon and Access" section; now, however, you look at the actual authentication process.

NOTE   In this discussion, passwords are encrypted to either a LAN Manager OWF or a Windows NT OWF, depending on the local environment.

When users log onto a machine that can directly authenticate them, the clear text password typed at the keyboard is converted into a LAN Manager OWF password or Windows NT OWF password. This OWF password then is compared to the OWF password stored in the local SAM database.

If the user logs onto a server in the domain, a different procedure is used to challenge the user and hide the password as it traverses the network. For example:

1. The user attempts to log on.
2. The server issues a 16-byte challenge (or *nonce*).
3. The nonce is encrypted with the user's password, which has already been encrypted as a one-way function password. This double-encryption further protects the password from snooping.
4. This information is returned to the server as a response.
5. In a separate process, the server gets a copy of the nonce that was sent to the user and the user's OWF password from the SAM database. It then encrypts these two items using a process similar to what took place at the client's workstation in step 3.
6. The server compares its calculated Challenge-Response with the Challenge-Response received from the client.

   If the two agree, the user is authenticated, and the associated account security IDs are retrieved, along with the SIDs of the global groups to which the user belongs.

10

When a user is successfully validated on a system, a new process is created in which the user can run the Program Manager or the Explorer shell (in Windows NT 4.0). The user's token is attached to the process, just as it is attached to every other process that the user runs. When the user opens a file or accesses a network resource, the token is given to the file system that manages that resource. When the file system is NTFS, for example, it can compare the security IDs in the token with the security IDs in the Access Control List for the file that the user wants to open. When appropriate matches are found between the lists, the user is granted access.

WARNING

All these logon procedures go a long way to ensure that the user is valid, but after the user is logged on, information is sent in clear text between clients and servers. You must use encryption to protect data transmissions. For remote users, using the PPTP protocol is a good idea.

10

Discretionary Access Controls

Discretionary access controls enable resource owners to specify who can access their resources and what they can do. Access controls specified through ACLs identify resource access permissions granted to users and groups. System resources include the system itself, files and directories, printers, network shares, and other objects.

Windows NT Server provides tools for controlling access entry to resources. Table 10.1 lists some of these tools.

Table 10.1. Tools for controlling access.

Tool	Allows You To
Explorer	Share files and directories on the network.
Printers in Control Panel	Share printers on the network.
User Manager for Domains	Manage user accounts and group member rights; define security policies.
Network in Control Panel	Define limits for sharing a computer's resources with other users on the network.
Services in Control Panel	Start and stop network services.

You also can use the Administrative Wizards under the Start|Programs|Administrative Tools (Common) to perform most of these functions.

The following examples describe the use of these tools to set discretionary access controls.

Example of discretionary access control through User Manager for Domains for a user account:

☐ Peter is the administrator of a Windows NT server. Peter specifies through User Manager for Domains that user Janet's account be disabled. When Janet attempts to log onto the workstation, access is denied.

Example of discretionary access control through File Manager for a file:

☐ User Peter is the owner of *Pfile*. Peter specifies through permissions and special access in File Manager or Explorer that user Janet can read *Pfile.doc*, but user Barry can both read and write *Pfile.doc*. If Janet attempts to write to the file, her request is denied. The permission settings for files and directories include No Access, List, Read, Add, Add & Read, Change, Full Control, Execute, Delete, Change Permissions, and Take Ownership.

Example of discretionary access controls using Print Manager for a printer:

☐ The administrator is the owner of *printer1*. The administrator specifies through Print Manager that user Janet can print to *printer1,* but user Barry cannot. When Barry tries to print to *printer1,* his request is denied. Permission settings for printers include No Access, Print, Manage Documents, and Full Control.

Discretionary access controls over resources can be applied to specific users, multiple users, groups of users, no one, or everyone who can connect to the Windows NT network. They can be set by a resource owner, the user who has access to the Administrator account, or any user who is granted authorization to control resources on the system.

As mentioned previously, objects in Windows NT include everything from files to communication ports to threads of execution. Every object can be secured individually or as a group. Objects have different types of permissions that are used to grant or deny access to themselves. Directory and file objects, for example, can have Read, Write, and Execute permissions, whereas print queues have permissions such as Manage Documents and Print. Also, note that directories are container objects that hold files, so permissions granted to the container are inherited by the file objects in it.

Keep in mind that access controls and user account rights are two different aspects of the Windows NT security system. User account security identifies and validates users, whereas access controls restrict what users can do with objects.

10

All objects have a security descriptor describing their security attributes. The security descriptor includes the following components:

- [ ] The security ID of the user who owns the object, usually the one who created the object
- [ ] The Access Control List, which holds information about what users and groups can access the object
- [ ] A system ACL, which is related to the auditing system
- [ ] A group security ID that is used by the POSIX subsystem, which is a UNIX-like environment

An ACL basically is a list of users and groups with permissions to access an object. Every object has its own ACL. Owners of objects can make entries in the ACL using tools such as the File Manager or by setting properties for files and folders (in Windows NT 4.0). Other utilities for setting permissions include the Network and Services utilities in the Control Panel.

Users might have multiple entries in an object's ACL that provide them different levels of access. A user might have Read permission to a file based on the user account, for example, and Read/Write permission based on a group membership. Each of these permissions is listed in a separate entry in the Access Control List.

When you attempt to access an object, you usually have a certain desired access such as Read or Read/Write. To grant (or deny) access, the Security Reference Monitor compares information in the user's access token with entries in the ACL. Remember that the access token contains security IDs and the list of groups that the user belongs to. The SRM compares this information with one or more entries in the ACL until it finds sufficient permissions to grant the desired access. If it does not find sufficient permissions, access is denied.

When the SRM finds several entries for the user, it looks at each entry to see whether that entry or a combination of the entries can grant the user the desired permission to use the object.

Access Tokens

As you learned in the section "The Logon Process," security access tokens are objects that contain information about a particular user. When the user initiates a process, a copy of the access token is permanently attached to the process.

During the logon process, the creation and use of the access token are critical. When a user or a process associated with the user attempts to access an object, the SID and the list of groups to which the user belongs that is stored in the user's access token are compared to the ACL for the object. If the object's ACL includes permissions for the user or one of the groups to which the user belongs, the user can access the object.

Table 10.2 describes the objects common to all access tokens.

Table 10.2. Access tokens.

Token Object	Description
User Security ID (SID)	Uniquely identifies the authenticated user on whose behalf the token was created.
Group Security ID(s)	Group SID(s) in which the user is a member.
Privileges	Privileges assigned to the user.
Owner	SID that is assigned as the owner of any objects created on behalf of the user represented by the token. This SID must be one of the user or group SIDs already in the token.
Primary Group	SID that is assigned as the primary group of any object created on behalf of the user represented by the token. It is specific to the POSIX subsystem.
Default ACL	ACL that is assigned by default to any objects created by the user SID.

Access Control Lists

Access Control Lists (ACLs) allow flexibility in controlling access to objects and are a form of discretionary access control. They work in conjunction with the file system to protect files from unauthorized access. They enable users to specify and control the sharing of objects or the denial of access to objects. Each object's ACL contains ACEs, which define access permissions to the object. ACEs contain security identifications and specific access permissions and are inserted into an ACL when the owner sets discretionary access controls for the object. If the object owner does not set discretionary access controls for the object, a default ACL is created. Table 10.3 lists how ACLs for several types of resources can be administered.

Table 10.3. Administration of ACLs.

Resources	Source of ACL
Files	Explorer
Printers	Printers in Control Panel
Users	User Manager (Windows NT Workstation)
	User Manager for Domains (Windows NT Server)

10

When users attempt to access an object, their personal security IDs, or the security ID of one of the groups to which they belong, are matched to the list of ACEs, and their desired activities are compared to the access permission defined in the ACE. If a user's security ID and access request match an ACE's security ID and permission, the user ID is granted access.

ACEs are prioritized by type of access: deny access and grant access. Windows NT first checks ACEs with a deny access, and then it checks ACEs with a grant access. Deny access always overrides a grant access.

If any group to which a user belongs is denied access, that user is denied access regardless of any access rights he or she is granted in either a personal user account or the accounts of other groups to which that user belongs. Therefore, if the No Access permission is given to the Everyone group, all users are denied access including the owner. No Access, however, does not prevent the owner from changing permissions on the file and restoring access.

Using Domains

For each Windows NT computer in your organization, you can choose whether to have it participate in a domain or a workgroup. In most cases, you want each Windows NT computer to participate in a domain. This way, you have more control over what a user can and cannot do at the computer in the configuration.

A Windows NT workstation participating in a domain does not actually get a copy of the domain's user account database. The workstation, however, still receives all the benefits of the domain's user and group database.

A Windows NT computer participating in a workgroup has its own database of users and processes logon requests by itself. Computers in a workgroup do not share account information. On a workgroup computer, Windows NT logs on or gives rights only to those user accounts created at that computer.

In a Windows NT Server environment, a domain is the basic unit of security and centralized administration. A domain consists of one or more servers running Windows NT Server, and all the servers in a domain function as a single system. Optionally, a domain can also include LAN Manager 2.x servers, Windows NT workstations, and other workstations such as those running Windows for Workgroups and MS-DOS.

Using the Windows NT Auditing System

Remember that the Windows NT security subsystem performs two primary tasks: It restricts access to objects and provides an auditing service that keeps track of operations on objects. The auditing system collects information about how objects are used, stores the information in log files, and enables you to monitor events to identify security breaches. If you discover a security breach, the audit logs help you determine the extent of damage so that you can restore your system and lock out future intrusions.

You control the extent to which the auditing system tracks events on your systems. Too much auditing can slow down a system and use tremendous amounts of disk space. You need to evaluate carefully how much auditing you need. When you suspect unauthorized activities, probably the best approach is to audit the following events:

☐ Changes to security settings

☐ Failed logon attempts

☐ Attempts to access sensitive data

You can use the Event Viewer to view the following security events:

☐ User and group management events, such as creating a new user or changing the membership of a group

☐ Subject tracking, which tracks the activities of users, such as when they start a program or access objects

☐ Logon and logoff events on the local system or for the network

☐ Object access, both successful and unsuccessful

☐ Changes to security policies, such as changes to privileges and logon policies

☐ Attempts to use privileges

☐ System events that affect the security of the entire system or audit log

Task 10.1. Using the Event Viewer to view the audit log.

Step 1: Description

In this task, you'll use the Event Viewer to view the audit log.

Step 2: Action

1. Log onto the Windows NT Server as Administrator.

2. Choose Start|Programs|Administrative Tools (Common)|Event Viewer. You then should see an Event Viewer.

3. Choose Log|Security.

4. By double-clicking any event in the log, you can get detailed information about that event.

Step 3: Review

In this example, you opened the Event Viewer to view the security log. You can imagine that tracking these types of events requires quite of bit of the system's time and disk space when many clients are using your system.

The auditing system tracks security events by two IDs: the user ID and the impersonation ID. This setup helps identify users who might otherwise be impersonated by certain processes in the system. A process-tracking mechanism also is used to track new processes as they are created and provide information about both the user account that is performing an action and the program that was used to perform the action.

You probably want to know how to use the auditing system right now. But that's enough for today. Look forward to Day 12 for security monitoring and audit trails.

Summary

Windows NT has several security options you can apply to software and physical security. This chapter covered many of these security options. In this chapter, you learned about the following topics:

☐ The Local Security Authority

☐ The Security Account Manager

☐ The Security Reference Monitor

☐ The logon processes

You will learn more about security administration in subsequent chapters. Now, however, you can review what you learned today.

Workshop

To wrap up the day, you can review terms and tasks from the chapter, and see the answers to some commonly asked questions.

Terminology Review

access control entry (ACE)—An entry in an Access Control List (ACL). The entry contains a security ID (SID) and a set of access rights. A process with a matching security ID is either allowed access rights, denied rights, or allowed rights with auditing.

access token—An object that uniquely identifies a user who has logged on. An access token is attached to all the user's processes and contains the user's security ID (SID), the names of any groups to which the user belongs, any privileges the user owns, the default owner of any objects that the user's processes create, and the default Access Control List (ACL) to be applied to any objects the user's processes create.

10

access validation—The process of checking a user's account information to determine when the subject should be granted the right to perform the requested operation.

event—Any significant occurrence in the system or in an application that requires users to be notified, or an entry to be added to a log.

Local Security Authority (LSA)—A Windows NT security subsystem component that creates a security access token for each user accessing the system.

nonce—A 16-byte challenge issued by the authentication service.

Security Account Manager (SAM)—A Windows NT protected subsystem that maintains the SAM database and provides an application programming interface (API) for accessing the database.

security ID (SID)—A unique name that identifies a logged-on user to the security system. Security IDs (SIDs) can identify one user or a group of users.

Security Reference Manager (SRM)—A Windows NT Server security subsystem that authenticates user logons and protects system resources.

subject—The combination of the user's access token and the program acting on the user's behalf. Windows NT uses subjects to track and manage permissions for the programs each user runs.

Task List

With the information provided in this chapter, you now can begin your understanding of NTS security. You learned how to carry out the following task:

☐ View the Event Log

Q&A

Q No security events show up in the security portion of the event log. How can I fix this?

A You must turn on the Security log by choosing Start|Programs|User Manager for Domains|Policies|Audit. From the Audit Policy page, select Audit These Events. Select the security events you want to monitor.

Q Does the C2 certification apply to networked versions of Windows NT Server?

A Well, the *Orange Book* criteria are for a standalone system (a node on a network). The National Computer Security Center is evaluating the Windows NT operating system for networking functions.

10

DAY

6

Chapter **11**

Account Management

At this time, you should have a good grounding in Windows NT Server basics. You have studied network topologies, cabling, filing systems, domains, the desktop, the Start menu, the toolbar, and the Registry. Today, you look at managing your clients. In this chapter, you take your first look at NTS commands for managing users and groups.

Introduction to Accounts

On Day 5, you were introduced to user accounts. User accounts are the foundation of NT Server's security. Using usernames is simply a method for referring to those user accounts. You assign user accounts and passwords for each domain (over 25,000 per domain and literally hundreds of thousands of users for an enterprise). In addition, you can specify the times that a user can log on, and you control where the logon comes from. You also can set a minimum character limit for the password length and a limit to the time the password can be kept. These controls reduce the chances that an unauthorized user can guess the password. User accounts and passwords are the basis for logon security. User account information, such as the username and password, resides in the SAM of the Primary Domain Controller's *SystemRoot*\system32\config directory.

As you learned yesterday in Chapter 10, "Understanding Security," logon security is an important layer of the NTS security model. These are the other security layers that you'll learn about in this book:

- [ ] Rights security (Chapters 13, "Exploring Windows NT Server Files and Directories," and 14, "Managing Windows NT Server File and Directory Access Rights")
- [ ] File and print server security (Chapters 15, "Managing the File Server," and 16, "Managing the Print Server")

Logon security controls access at the *portal*—the entrance to the network. Logon security is effective because it requires an authorized username for identification and a valid password for verification. The username and password must match exactly the information kept by the system. Because you enter your account's username first, you look at accounts and usernames first in this chapter.

Understanding User Accounts

User accounts provide the first point of access. They identify the user of an account; the username is the identification. Usernames can be anywhere from 1 to 20 characters in length. You can use any upper- or lowercase characters, except the space and tab (DOS command-line delimiters), the 32 control characters, and the characters shown in Table 11.1.

Table 11.1. Invalid characters for usernames.

Character	Description
=	Equal sign
>	Greater-than sign
<	Less-than sign
¦	Vertical bar
+	Plus sign
[	Left square bracket
]	Right square bracket
\	Backslash
/	Slash
*	Asterisk
;	Semicolon
:	Colon

Character	Description
.	Period
,	Comma
?	Question mark
"	Quotation mark

As you learned in Chapter 7, "Understanding the Registry," user accounts are automatically assigned a *security identifier* (SID) when they are first created. A SID is a unique number for identifying an account in the NT Server security system. The system never reuses SIDs; when an account is deleted, its SID is deleted with it. SIDs look like

S-1-5-D1-D2-D3-RID

where S-1-5 is a standard prefix; 1 is a version number, which hasn't changed since NT 3.1; 5 signifies that the SID was assigned by NT; and D1, D2, and D3 are 32-bit numbers specific to a domain. When you create a domain, the NT sets D1 through D3, and all SIDs in that domain henceforth have the same three values. The RID stands for relative ID. The RID is the unique part of any given SID.

Every new account always has a unique RID number, even when the username and other information are the same as an old account. The new account therefore does not acquire any of the rights and permissions of the old account, and security is preserved. Four billion RIDs are possible, so you aren't likely to run out of them for a while.

When you create a new Windows NT domain, the system creates the following two user accounts:

☐ Administrator
☐ Guest

In the following sections, you look at these special accounts.

Administrator Account

When you create a Windows NT Server Primary Domain Controller, the Administrator account is created automatically. The purpose of the Administrator account is to manage accounts on the file server. Generally, the administrator can do the following:

☐ Access any file or directory
☐ Create and delete users and groups
☐ Establish trust relationships

- ☐ Manage printers and print sharing
- ☐ Assign operators
- ☐ Create and modify logon scripts
- ☐ Set default account policies
- ☐ Set and change passwords
- ☐ Manage auditing and security logs
- ☐ Not be deleted

The Administrator account is omnipotent—with complete power over a domain. You need to control its use tightly.

You might want to create some accounts—Account Operators—with responsibility for a group or groups. Distributing responsibility to a few people is a good control—separation of duties—and gives the administrator time to concentrate on system-management functions, as opposed to user-management functions. Logging on as a member of the Account Operators group prevents you from using some of the User Manager for Domain's capabilities, but you can manage most user accounts.

Guest Account

Guest is another account that is created automatically on your file server when you create a Windows NT Server domain. Guest means "anyone the domain doesn't recognize." By default, the Guest account is disabled and should remain that way. With most other operating systems, you might get access to the operating system by logging on with the username Guest and a blank password. In other operating systems, such as NetWare, the Guest account has a simple raison d'être. A Guest account enables users to access the server's print queues when they don't have accounts on the server. With NetWare, they can use NPRINT and CAPTURE to do so. Usually, the Guest account is restricted in what it can do. That's true with NT, as well, although remember that the Everyone group includes the guests.

The Guest account in Windows NT does work differently! Suppose someone tries to log onto an NT network with the Guest account enabled. She logs on as KELLY with the password grade1. If this domain does not have a KELLY account, it rejects the logon. On a DOS, Windows for Workgroups, or Windows 95 workstation, KELLY still can do work because these operating systems don't require users to log onto a domain to access the local workstation. On an NT workstation, KELLY might log onto an account on the local machine. Now she's working at a computer and tries to access a domain resource. And guess what? KELLY gets in!

Even though an explicit domain logon requires that you use a username of Guest, you needn't explicitly log onto a domain to use Guest privileges. If your network is attached to my network and you enable the Guest account, then I can browse through your network and attach to resources that the Guest can access. I needn't log on as Guest because enabling the Guest account leaves the back door open. You therefore should take care when enabling the Guest account.

Now look at how to create some user accounts of your own by using different tools.

Creating User Accounts

You can divide user account administration into two phases: creating user accounts and maintaining user accounts. You can create user accounts in several ways. The most popular way is using the User Manager for Domains program because it is easy to work with. Most Windows NT administrators are familiar with its use. You can use User Manager when you need to create one or two user accounts. In addition, you can use the Administrative Wizards program or NET commands.

First, you look at User Manager because you might select it as your tool of choice.

Using User Manager for Domains

The administrator uses User Manager for Domains to perform the following tasks:

- [ ] Create, modify, and delete user accounts
- [ ] Assign logon scripts to user accounts
- [ ] Create and manage groups
- [ ] Manage the domain's security policies
- [ ] Establish trust relationships

Existing accounts always need managing, whether modifying account properties, disabling accounts, or deleting accounts. Here you'll learn about creating, copying, and deleting user accounts.

Task 11.1. Creating user accounts using User Manager for Domains.

Step 1: Description
In this task, you'll use the User Manager for Domains program to create new users.

Step 2: Action
1. Log onto the Windows NT Server as Administrator.
2. Choose Start|Programs|Administrative Tools (Common)|User Manager for Domains. You should see a window similar to the one in Figure 11.1.

Figure 11.1.
The User Manager window.

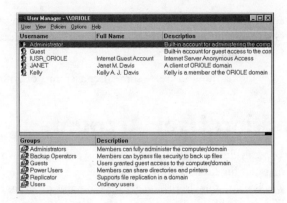

3. Choose User|New User. The New User dialog box appears, as shown in Figure 11.2.

4. Type the new user account name KELLY in the Username box. The username is a unique name the user enters when logging on. Press Tab to move to the next field.

5. Type the user's full name, such as Kelly A. J. Davis in the Full Name box. Press Tab to move to the next field.

6. Enter a comment for the user in the Description box. Press Tab to move to the next field.

7. Enter a password from 1 to 14 characters for the user. Press Tab to move to the next field. If you need help on creating good passwords, jump ahead to this afternoon for help.

NOTE

Windows NT Server displays the password as asterisks to protect its confidentiality as you enter it.

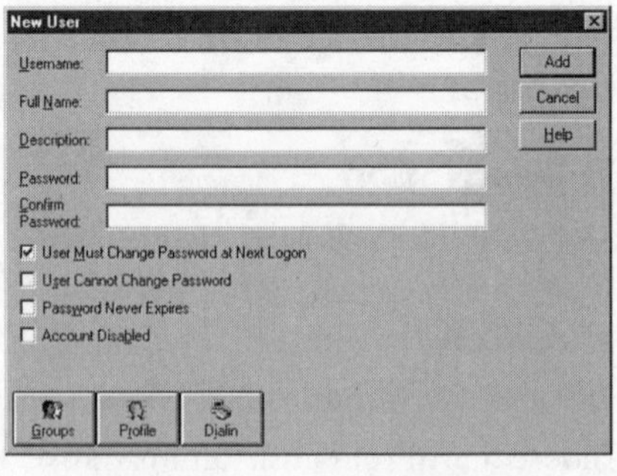

Figure 11.2.
The New User dialog box.

11

8. Confirm the password by retyping the password you entered in step 7.

9. Select the appropriate options for the following additional user properties listed in Table 11.2.

Table 11.2. New User options.

Option	Default	Description
User Must Change Password at Next Logon	ON	Selecting this option forces the users to change the password when they log on the first time. Selecting this option is a good idea so that the administrator doesn't know the password.
User Cannot Change Password	OFF	Selecting this option prevents the users from changing the password. Selecting it is not a good idea, especially when the users have access to confidential or critical data.
Password Never Expires	OFF	Selecting this option bypasses the Maximum Password account policy. Again, selecting it is not a good idea because the password will not change and will become easier to guess with time.
Account Disabled	OFF	Selecting this option creates an inactive account. You can use this feature when you're creating accounts for future use or when you think the account is being used by system intruders.

TIP

You also can select Account Disabled to suspend an account before you delete it. If you immediately delete the account, you might create orphan files. (On Day 7, you will look at ownership.) The administrator needs to take ownership of orphaned files so that others can access the files.

10. Click the Add button. The New User panel reverts to its original default settings.

11. To add another account, repeat steps 4 through 10.

12. Click the close button after you finish creating new accounts.

Tip

Sometimes, you might find copying an existing user account quicker and easier than creating a new account. This procedure is useful because you copy group memberships as well. To copy a user account, select a user account from the window (such as the one in Figure 11.1) and choose User|Copy (or press the F8 key). As you can see, you need to complete steps 4 through 10 of Task 11.1. After you finish creating all the accounts you need, click the close button.

Step 3: Review

With this task, you created your first user account. You'll place some restrictions on this account this afternoon in Chapter 12, "Managing User Access."

To delete a user's account, you perform basically the same steps as you do for copying a user account. First, you select the user's name by choosing Start|Programs|Administrative Tools (Common)|User Manager for Domains, and then you choose User|Delete. You need to confirm your intention to delete this account.

Using Administrative Wizards

As mentioned previously, you can manage user accounts in other ways. If you're just starting out with Windows NT, you might want to use the Administrative Wizards. As the administrator, you can use the Administrative Wizards to carry out the following actions:

☐ Add user accounts

☐ Manage groups

☐ Manage file and folder access

☐ Add printers

☐ Add and remove programs

☐ Install a new modem

☐ Install or update network clients

☐ Check licenses

Task 11.2. Creating user accounts using the Administrative Wizards.

Step 1: Description

In this task, you'll use the Administrative Wizards to create new users.

Step 2: Action

1. Log onto the Windows NT Server as Administrator.

2. Choose Start|Programs|Administrative Tools (Common)|Administrative Wizards. You should see a window similar to the one in Figure 11.3.

Figure 11.3.

The Administra-tive Wizards window.

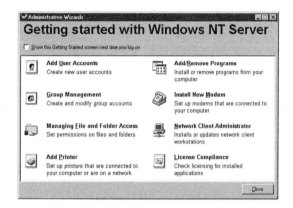

3. Click Add User Accounts. The Add User Account Wizard panel appears, as shown in Figure 11.4.

Figure 11.4.

The Add User Account Wizard panel.

4. Ensure that the domain is correct; then click the Next button.

5. Type the user's full name, such as Max Davis in response to the question "What is the user's full name?" Press Tab to move to the next field.

6. Type the new user account name MAX under "Type a unique name to identify the user. This username will be used for logging on and using resources." Press Tab to move to the next field.

7. Enter a comment for the user in the Type a description for this user (optional) box. Press Tab to move to the next field.

8. Enter a password from 1 to 14 characters for the user. Press Tab to move to the next field.

9. Confirm the password by retyping the password you entered in step 8.

10. Select whether you want to enable these options: User Must Change Password at Next Logon, User Cannot Change Password, Password Never Expires, and Account Disabled.

11. Select the groups to which you want the account to belong. You then should see a panel for configuring options. You'll learn about this panel in Chapter 12.

12. Click the Finish button.

Step 3: Review

With this task, you used the Administrative Wizards to create a user account. Just use the Add User Account Wizard and walk through the steps.

If you like command lines, you can manage user accounts another way. If you don't want to use the User Manager for Domains or the Administrative Wizards, you can use the NET USER command-line option. With this command, you can add, change, or delete a user account from the domain database. The command works with the parameters shown in Table 11.3 as shown here:

To add a new user account, enter this:

```
NET USER username [Password *] [/ADD] [Options] [/DOMAIN]
```

To modify an existing account, enter this:

```
NET USER username [Password *] [Options] [/DOMAIN]
```

To delete an existing account, enter this:

```
NET USER username {Password *] [/DELETE] [/DOMAIN]
```

Table 11.3. The NET USER **parameters.**

Parameter	Description
Username	Specifies the name of the account you want to create, change, or delete.
Password	Specifies the password for the username. Alternatively, you can use *, and the system prompts you for the password and masks the characters you enter.
/DOMAIN	Specifies that the action applies to the Primary Domain Controller.
Options	Specifies one or more options as shown in Table 11.4. You must separate your options with at least one space.

Table 11.4. The NET USER **command options.**

Option	Description
/ACTIVE:{NO YES}	Enables or disables the account. The default is to enable the account.
/COMMENT:"*User Description*"	Provides a maximum length 48-character descriptive account about the user.
/COUNTRYCODE:*NNN*	Specifies the user account country code. A value of 0 specifies the default system country code.
/EXPIRES:{*Date* NEVER}	Specifies that the account expires on the date shown or never. The date is either MM/DD/YY or DD/MM/YY depending on the country code.
/FULLNAME:"*Username*"	Specifies the user's full name.
/HOMEDIR:"*pathname*"	Specifies the path for the user's home directory. The specified path must exist; otherwise, you get an error message.
/HOMEDIRREQ:{YES NO}	Specifies whether a home directory is required.
/PASSWORDCHG:{YES NO}	Specifies whether the user can change the password.
/PASSWORDREQ:{YES NO}	Specifies whether the account requires a password. The default is to require a password.
/PROFILEPATH:"*Pathname*"	Specifies the pathname for the user profile.
/SCRIPTPATH:"*Pathname*"	Specifies the pathname for the user's logon script. The pathname is relative to the logon server's logon script path.

continues

Table 11.4. continued

Option	Description
/TIMES:{*Times* ALL}	Specifies the valid logon times for the user in the format *Day* [-*Day*], *Time* [-*Time*], where the day can be spelled out or abbreviated, and the time can be in either 12- or 24-hour notation. For example, M-F, 0600-1800 specifies 6:00 a.m. to 6:00 p.m. Monday to Friday.
/USERCOMMENT:"*User Description*"	Changes the user comment field.
/WORKSTATION:{*Computername* *}	Specifies up to eight workstations (separated by commas) where the user can log on. The * specifies that there are no restrictions.

Figure 11.5 shows a sample of using the command line in practice. By using the command line, you learned a third way to create, modify, or delete user accounts. In Chapter 12, you'll learn about account restrictions.

Figure 11.5.

Using NET USER *to create an account.*

Creating Groups

After creating user accounts, you might want to create group accounts and add users to them. Groups simplify administration because you can assign rights at the group level. To simplify administration of user accounts that have similar resource needs, you can categorize the user accounts into groups. A *group* is a name, similar to the username of a user account, that you can use to refer to one or more users. Using groups provides a convenient way to give and control access to users performing similar tasks. Without groups, you would have to modify each user's account so that it has the same capabilities or restrictions as another user's account. By placing users within a group, you give all the users in that group the same capabilities or restrictions in a single action. If you need to change the permissions or rights assigned to the users within the group, you have to modify only one account—the group account.

Tip

> To find out the user accounts belonging to a group, open the User Manager for Domains and double-click the name of the group. You then see a dialog box describing the group and a list of its current members.

Two types of groups exist in the Windows NT environment: *local groups* and *global groups.* The terms *local group* and *global group* do not refer to the contents of the group, but to the scope of the group's accessibility. Local groups are local to the security system where they were created. Domain local groups have rights and permissions in a single domain. Member servers (Windows NT Servers that are not domain controllers) and Windows NT Workstation computers have their local groups with rights and permissions on those computers only. With a Windows NT Workgroup workstation, the operating system uses the group only on the workstation itself. Think of local groups in terms of tasks that need to get done or resources that users need to access.

With a server domain group, the operating system uses the group only on the servers in the domain. A local group is available only on the domain controllers within the domain where you create the group, whereas a global group is available within its own domain and in any trusting domain. Thus, global groups extend the network without increasing the administrative burden. A trusting domain can use a global group to control rights and permissions given members of a trusted domain.

Think of global groups as a logical grouping of people. You can add a global group (and thus its members) to a local group to give the former the rights and permissions of the latter. Windows NT has default local and global groups, as you'll learn in the following sections.

New Windows NT users are often confused by global groups because the name seems to imply a group that contains accounts from all over the network, or possibly a group of users who can be assigned rights for the entire network, not just a computer or domain. In fact, a global group contains only members from a single domain, and you add the group to a local group or a local group in another domain. Microsoft likes to call global groups "export" groups and local groups "import" groups. Global groups are imported into local groups.

The procedure for setting up global groups is to add a user's account to a global group in the user's domain and then add the global group to a local group, either in the same domain or in another domain where a trust relationship has been established. This procedure is illustrated in Figure 11.6. In step 1, you create a new user account. In step 2, you add the user account to the appropriate global groups. In step 3, you add the global group to local groups in the same domain or other domains. Global groups already may belong to local groups when you add a new user to the group. The new user then gets all the rights and permissions already assigned to the global group.

11

Figure 11.6.

*Managing users and
group relationships.*

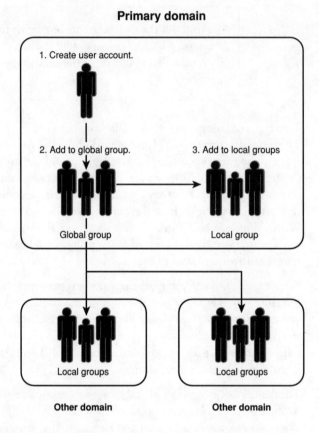

These are some other points to keep in mind:

☐ Local groups on domain controllers have rights only on the domain on which they were created.

☐ Local groups on Windows NT Workstation computers and member servers (non-Primary Domain Controllers) have rights on the computer on which they were created.

☐ Local groups cannot contain other local groups from the same domain. They can contain only user accounts or global groups from the same domain or other domains.

☐ Groups on NT Workstation computers and member servers aren't applicable to domain groups.

☐ Trust relationships must exist before you can add a global group from a different domain to a local group in another domain.

☐ Global groups contain user accounts from only one domain. They cannot contain local groups or other global groups.

11

So how do you take advantage of these groups and use them to promote security? You can start by creating very precise global groups for users with specific job titles and tasks. Then you can easily set rights and permissions.

For security reasons, the members of global groups must be reviewed on a regular basis. Because you can add global groups to local groups, thereby obtaining the rights and privileges of the local groups, some members of those groups might obtain inappropriate access rights. Suppose a former member of your team, for example, moves to another department in another domain. If that person is a member of a global group that is added to your local Administrators group, that person gains administrative rights that might be inappropriate in the new job, especially because the person knows a lot about your department.

You might consider some users in other domains as untrustworthy. One approach is to remove the user from the global group in the other domain where you have permissions to do so. You also can create a new global group with only appropriate users, or remove the global group from the local group and add only the accounts of users who should have access to the local group.

Keeping on top of global groups available on the network and the members for those global groups is a good idea. You should fully document the rights and permissions available to both local and global groups.

Using Local Groups

Local groups define permissions to resources only within the domain where the local group exists. Hence, the term *local* defines the scope of the resource permissions granted to users within the group.

Not only is using local groups an effective way of collectively assigning user rights and permissions for a set of users within the home domain, but you also can use them to gather together numerous global groups and users from other domains. Thus, you can change access to domain resources globally with a single modification to the local group permissions.

Using a local group is a good way to import a group of users and global groups from other domains into a single unit for use in the local domain. A local group can contain user accounts or global groups from one or more domains. You can assign the group privileges and rights only within its own domain. Local groups created on a Windows NT Workstation computer or a Windows NT Server computer in a workgroup are available only on that computer.

Local groups can contain users and global groups from the local domain (but not other local groups), as well as users and global groups from trusted domains. However, you can assign a local group permissions and rights only in its home domain. Table 11.5 summarizes the possible contents of local and global groups.

Table 11.5. Local and global groups.

Local Groups	Global Groups
Can contain local users, global groups, and other domain accounts (trusted)	Can contain local users
Cannot contain other local groups	Cannot contain local groups

Predefined Local Groups

Windows NT automatically creates default local and global groups during installation. Table 11.6 lists the predefined local groups on both Windows NT Server computers and Windows NT Workstation computers.

Table 11.6. Predefined groups.

Name	Description
Administrators	Members can fully administer the local computer and any domain resources. This group is the most powerful. Within the Administrators group is a built-in account you cannot delete. Because you cannot disable the Administrator account, you might want to create a backup Administrator account for emergencies.
Account Operators	Members can use User Manager for Domains to manage domain user and group accounts. An Account Operator cannot change or delete the Domain Admins, Account Operators, Backup Operators, Print Operators, or Server Operators groups. Also, an Account Operator cannot change or delete administrator user accounts or administer security policies.
Backup Operators	Members can perform backups and restores, and bypass the security restrictions on directories and files to back them up.
Guests	Members can access the server from the network but cannot log on locally. In other words, Guests have limited access to the domain. In effect, these users can log on, if they know the Guest account and password, but they cannot change any settings on the local computer. This group is for the occasional or a one-time user to log on. The built-in Guest account is automatically a member of the Guests group.

11

Name	Description
Print Operators	Members can administer the domain printers. They can create, manage, and delete printer shares for an NTS server.
Power Users	Members can do everything that members of the Users group can. In addition, these members can create user accounts, modify the user accounts they created, put any user accounts on the computer into the Power Users, Users, and Guests built-in groups, share and stop sharing files and directories and printers located at the computer, and set the computer's internal clock.
Replicator	Members can manage replication services. They are granted the appropriate privileges to replicate files in the domain. You use this group only to support the Directory Replication service.
Server Operators	Members can manage the servers in the domain. Tasks include logging on locally, restarting the server, or shutting down the server.
Users	Members can access the server from the network but cannot log on locally. They are normal users of the domain and have limited access to the domain and their computers. They can make some configuration changes to their environment but have limited functionality. They cannot create new shared directories, for example, or stop and start services.

NOTE

> Account Operators, Print Operators, and Server Operators local groups are available only on Windows NT Server computers acting as Primary Domain Controllers (PDCs) or Backup Domain Controllers (BDCs). The Power Users group is available only on Windows NT Workstation computers or on Windows NT Server computers not acting as domain controllers.

Using Global Groups

A global group, available only on Windows NT Server domains, contains only individual user accounts (no groups) from the domain where it was created. After you create a global group, you can assign it permissions and rights, either in its own domain or in any trusting domain. In fact, because they have no user rights associated with them, global groups are powerless until you assign them to a local group or to a user right.

Using a global group is a good way to export a group of users as a single unit to another domain. In a trusting domain, for example, you can grant identical permissions to a particular file to a global group, which then pertain to all individual members of that group. Also, global groups defined in a domain can be "exported" to Windows NT workstations because domain Windows NT workstations support local groups and can, therefore, make use of global groups defined in either the workstation's own domain or from other domains.

By using trust relationships, users within a global group can access resources outside their locally defined domain. Global groups are therefore quite suitable for large, multi-domain networks. Global groups can provide an inclusive list of all user accounts within a domain that require a particular type of access to resources that exist within another domain.

A local group and a global group sharing the same name are two separate entities each with its own distinct security identifier. Permissions assigned to one group do not apply to the other group sharing the same name.

When Windows NT Server is installed on a computer, it is configured with three predefined global groups, as shown in Table 11.7.

Table 11.7. Default global groups on Windows NT Server.

Group	Description
Domain Admins	Members can fully administer the home domain, the workstations of the domain, and any other trusted domains that added this group to the local Administrators group. These members are added automatically to the local Administrators group.
Domain Guests	Members can access the Guest account and potentially access resources across domains. Members are added automatically to the Guests group.
Domain Users	Members have normal access to the domain and any NT workstation in the domain. The group contains all domain users, and its members are added automatically to the local Users group.

Special Groups

Besides the predefined local and global groups, Windows NT has a few special groups with no members. These special groups do not refer to the privilege level of users, but rather access to computer resources. These groups have no members because they apply to any account using the computer in a specified way. You do not see these groups listed in the User Manager for Domains window; however, they might appear when you're assigning permissions to directories, files, shared directories, or printers.

Windows NT uses special groups to organize users according to how they access different resources. You cannot assign users as members of a special group; users are either members of these groups by default, or they become members by virtue of their network activity. Table 11.8 lists the special groups created under Windows NT Server.

Table 11.8. Special groups.

Group	Description
Interactive users	Users who log onto the local computer. Interactive users access resources on the machine at which they are sitting.
Network users	Users who log onto a network or remote computer using their account or an enabled Guest account.
Everyone	All users who access a computer, whether locally or remotely. This group includes both interactive and network users.
Creator Owner	A user who creates or takes ownership of a resource, such as subdirectories, files, and print jobs.
System	The operating system.

NOTE

The System account and the Administrator account (Administrators group) have the same file privileges, but they have different functions under Windows NT. The System account is used by the operating system and by services running under Windows NT. Many services and processes within Windows NT need to log on internally (for example, during a Windows NT installation). System is an internal account, does not show up in User Manager, cannot be added to any groups, and cannot have user rights assigned to it. The System account, however, does show up on an NTFS volume in the Windows NT Explorer in the Permissions portion of the Security menu. By default, the System account is granted full control of all files on an NTFS volume.

The difference between the Network and Interactive groups is an important concept to grasp because it affects permissions. Consider this example: User KELLY logs onto machine BALLIOL and accesses only the resources physically attached to machine BALLIOL. That user is a local or interactive user, and Windows NT assigns the user KELLY to the Interactive group. If user KELLY moves to another machine, say MERTON, and uses the network to access the same resources on BALLIOL, user KELLY then works with permissions assigned to the Network group and becomes a member of that group. The permissions assigned to the Interactive group are no longer valid for user KELLY.

Now that you know about the various types of groups, you can learn how to create group accounts.

Task 11.3. Creating local groups using User Manager for Domains.

Step 1: Description
In this task, you'll use the User Manager for Domains program to create new local groups.

Step 2: Action
1. Log onto the Windows NT Server as Administrator.
2. Choose Start|Programs|Administrative Tools (Common)|User Manager for Domains.
3. Choose User|New Local Group. The New Local Group panel appears, as shown in Figure 11.7.
4. Type the new group name WRITERS in the Group Name box. Press Tab to move to the next field.
5. Enter a comment for the group in the Description box.
6. Click the Add button.
7. From a window similar to the one shown in Figure 11.7, select a member of the group, and click the Add button.
8. After you add all the members of the group, click OK.

Figure 11.7.
*The New Local
Group panel.*

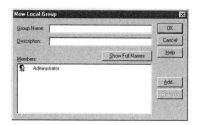

Step 3: Review

With this task, you created your first local group by choosing Start|Administrative Tools (Common)|User Manager for Domains|User|New Local Group.

To delete a group, first choose Start|Programs|Administrative Tools (Common)|User Manager for Domains, select the group's name from the bottom pane, and then choose User|Delete or press the Delete key. You'll have to confirm that you really mean to delete the group.

Using Administrative Wizards

As mentioned earlier, you can manage groups in other ways. Again, when you're just starting out with Windows NT, you might want to use the Administrative Wizards.

Task 11.4. Creating local groups using Administrative Wizards.

Step 1: Description

In this task, you'll use the Administrative Wizards program to create new users.

Step 2: Action

1. Log onto the Windows NT Server as Administrator.
2. Choose Start|Programs|Administrative Tools (Common)|Administrative Wizards. You should see a window similar to the one in Figure 11.3.
3. Click Group Management. The Group Management Wizard panel appears, as shown in Figure 11.8.
4. Select the Create a new group and add members option; then click the Next button.
5. Type the group name WRITERS under "Type the name you want to give this new group." Press Tab to move to the next field.
6. Enter a comment for the user in the Type a description for this group (optional) box. Click the Next button.

Figure 11.8.

The Group Management Wizard opening panel.

7. Select whether you want to create the group on the local or remote computer, as shown in Figure 11.9. Click the Next button.

Figure 11.9.

The Group Management Wizard, panel 2.

8. If you select the On another computer or a domain option, you need to select the computer from the available ones on the next panel. Then click the Next button.

9. Select Local Group, and click the Next button.

10. Click the Finish button.

Step 3: Review

With this task, you created your second local group by choosing Start|Administrative Tools (Common)|Administrative Wizards|Group Management.

Adding global groups using User Manager for Domains and the Administrative Wizards is exactly the same.

If you like command lines, you can manage groups another way. If you don't want to use the User Manager for Domains or the Administrative Wizards, you can use the NET GROUP and NET LOCALGROUP command-line options. With these commands, you can add, change, or delete a global (GROUP) or local (LOCALGROUP) group.

To add a new global group, enter this:

```
NET GROUP "groupname" /ADD
```

To add a user to an existing global group, enter this:

```
NET GROUP "groupname" username /ADD
```

To add a new local group, enter this:

```
NET LOCALGROUP "groupname" /ADD
```

To add a user to an existing local group, enter this:

```
NET LOCALGROUP "groupname" username /ADD
```

To delete a user from an existing local or global group, enter this:

```
NET [LOCAL]GROUP "groupname" username /DELETE
```

If you want to add the account PETER to the WRITERS local group, for example, you type the following command at the DOS prompt:

```
NET LOCALGROUP "WRITERS" PETER /ADD
```

Summary

In this chapter, you learned about these topics:

- ☐ User accounts in general
- ☐ Local, global, and special groups

As you saw, NT allows for different types of users. You should review the different types and review how you can use them in your particular case. Now you should be thoroughly familiar with the User Manager for Domains program. You use it again in subsequent chapters, but you should be comfortable with it now. Finally, you learned about the Administrator account. You must treat this account with respect. The rights and privileges make this account powerful. With privileges comes responsibility. You must learn to use the Administrator account responsibly and only when necessary.

Take time to practice using User Manager for Domains to create and delete users and groups. Practice, as they say, makes perfect. In the next chapter, you study additional ways to control accounts and passwords.

Workshop

To wrap up the day, you can review terms and tasks from the chapter, and see the answers to some commonly asked questions.

Terminology Review

access—The capability and the means necessary to approach, store, or retrieve data, and to communicate with and make use of any resource of a computer system.

accountability—The quality or state that enables violations or attempted violations of a security system to be traced to individuals who then can be held responsible.

administrator—The person responsible for the operation of the network. The administrator maintains the network, reconfiguring and updating it as the need arises.

grant—To authorize.

Task List

The emphasis of this chapter has been to introduce you to accounts and their management. As a system administrator, you will repeatedly use these commands in your daily work. The emphasis of this session has been to set up proper password controls. Following are the tasks you should understand from this chapter:

- [ ] Using User Manager for Domains
- [ ] Using Administrative Wizards
- [ ] Using NET USER, NET GROUP, and NET LOCALGROUP
- [ ] Creating user accounts
- [ ] Creating groups

Q&A

Q Should I keep the Guest account?

A The Guest should remain disabled unless you have a specific, well-researched need for the account. When your organization's policy is to require users to have unique accounts to provide accountability, you can remove the Guest account.

Q Should users share accounts?

A No. The whole reason for having account names is to provide accountability for the actions of the owner of the account. When users share an account, how do you tie the actions of the account to one user? You cannot. As soon as you have problems with a shared account, everybody will be doing a lot of finger pointing.

Q When should I use the Administrator account?

A You should use the Administrator account only for problem resolution and for setting up security restrictions and managers and operators. You should not use the Administrator account for sending electronic mail, accessing network services, or composing documents.

Q What should my usernames look like?

A Your organization should have a standard for the composition of usernames and passwords to which all Windows NT Server usernames should adhere. If you're developing a standard for usernames, use something meaningful—for example, the user's last name and first initial. Remember that usernames are not meant to be security mechanisms: They should be meaningful. You might use them as electronic mail addresses, so they are lot easier to use when they are meaningful.

Q How do I make sure that users are not members of a particular group in a domain?

A To make sure, carry out the following steps:

1. Highlight the users in the User Manager for Domains window.
2. Choose User|Properties.
3. In the User Properties dialog box, choose Groups. Add the particular group from the Not All Are Members Of box to the Members Of box.
4. Click OK to save the change.
5. In the User Properties dialog box, choose Groups again. Select the group in the All Are Members Of box and click Remove.

Or you simply can double-click the group you want to check in the bottom pane of the User Manager for Domains. A box pops up showing the users in the group, as well as those who are not in the group. Then, you can select all the users you don't want in the group and remove them.

Chapter **12**

Managing User Access

On Day 5, you learned that logon security is an important part of the Windows NT Server security model. You also learned that usernames and passwords are integral parts of logon security. At this point, you're ready to learn about another key part of logon security. By first looking closely at passwords, you gain knowledge about the NTS verification system. In this chapter, you also learn about the authentication portion of the NTS security.

What does all this mean? First, look at the generic security process. When you make a request for data, you need to go through the steps illustrated in Figure 12.1.

At the first step, you provide a username to the system for identification. The username identifies you as the administrator or whomever. Associated with a username is a password. You supply the password to prove you are the administrator. The system verifies that you are the administrator by matching the password you supplied with the stored password. If the password match is successful, the system makes assumptions about you.

Figure 12.1.
The security process.

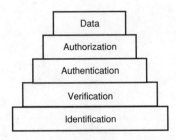

Next, the system authenticates you by checking restrictions, such as workstation access, time of day, and day of week. If this check is successful, you can request data. When you request data, the system checks whether you are authorized to access the data according to the file and directory attributes and your access rights. If you qualify, the system sends the data back over the network to you.

This chapter introduces you to the authentication step of this process. On Day 7, you look at attributes and rights, and you get your first glimpse of the authorization step. Start by quickly looking at passwords and their use.

Managing Passwords

In the preceding chapter, you looked at creating and controlling accounts. This section covers passwords and the parameters associated with them. You probably have direct experience with passwords. Indeed, you might think that passwords are something you know plenty about, but take the time to study this section. Because of the nature of NTS, passwords are the major control mechanism on your system. One poorly administered or derived password can put all your valuable data at risk. Many users consider using passwords a waste of time. The problem is that when one unauthorized individual has access to one account, that individual can compromise the whole network.

The stories about systems broken into owing to poor passwords are too numerous to name in this book. At this time, you should have an appreciation for the need for passwords. Consequently, in the following sections, you'll learn how to manage passwords and ensure that other users understand the need for good passwords.

Understanding User Account Passwords

In Windows NT Server, passwords are optional but highly recommended. They provide an effective strategy for filtering out unwanted users. NTS provides a number of restrictions for passwords. Password protection can be enhanced by making passwords mandatory, setting minimum lengths, or expiring them after a set period of time.

Assigning a password immediately on completion of the creation of a user account is a good idea. Users can then choose and change the passwords you created. In this manner, you are not aware of the users' passwords. This process enhances the users' accountability. The following lesson on how the system uses the password might help your understanding.

Creating Strong Passwords

As you just learned, passwords are an integral part of logon security, so it behooves you to create strong passwords. An NTS password can consist of any ASCII character except the 32 control characters. Passwords are case sensitive.

An NTS password can have from 1 to 14 characters. Thinking of a good password is not easy. A good password is something the user can remember but others won't guess. Some passwords are too obvious or easily guessed. The following are passwords to avoid:

- Words in the dictionary
- First and last names
- Street and city names
- Valid license plate numbers
- Room numbers, Social Security numbers, Social Insurance numbers, and telephone numbers
- Beer and liquor brands
- Athletic teams
- Days of the week and months of the year
- Repetitive characters
- Software default passwords

The temptation for users to create weak passwords is overpowering. Paradoxically, you want to allow users to change their passwords, yet you want strong passwords. Fortunately, Windows NT Server provides several password controls you set. When setting the security policy, you make decisions about password options and parameters for the system and individual users. You learn about the account policy later in this chapter.

Changing passwords is simple. While you're logged on, press Ctrl+Alt+Delete. You then see a Windows NT Security dialog box in which you select Change Password. To prevent people from trying to change a password at a workstation where someone has walked away, enter your old password. Then, in the appropriate boxes, type in your new password and retype it to confirm the new password.

In addition to passwords, you can set other authentication parameters for restricting user access.

12

Managing User Account Properties

You can modify or customize properties associated with a user account by clicking the buttons at the bottom of the New User dialog box, shown in Figure 12.2, or by using the User Properties dialog box, which you access by choosing File|Properties from the User Manager for Domains window. You can set these parameters when creating a new account, or you can modify these parameters for an existing account. Table 12.1 describes each of the buttons in the New User dialog box.

Figure 12.2.

The New User dialog box.

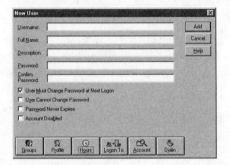

Table 12.1. The New User dialog box buttons.

Button	Description
Groups	Specifies the groups in which the account is a member.
Profile	Specifies a user profile, logon script, or home directory for user accounts.
Hours	Restricts the days and hours during which a user can connect to a server.
Logon To	Restricts the computers where users can log onto domain accounts.
Account	Defines an account expiration date (if any) and the account type for the selected user accounts.
Dialin	Specifies whether the account can use Dial-Up Networking for connecting to the domain.

When you're administering a domain, you see six buttons: Groups, Profile, Hours, Logon To, Account, and Dialin. When you're administering a Windows NT Workstation computer, only the Groups and Profile buttons appear. In the following sections, you look at the account restrictions in more detail.

12

Assigning Profiles

One of the most powerful methods open to administrators for managing user environments is through user profiles for users of Windows NT computers. A profile defines the application settings, Control Panel settings, printer connections, window size and positioning, and screen colors.

Task 12.1. Creating a user's environment by assigning profiles.

Step 1: Description

In this task, you'll learn to create a user's environment.

Step 2: Action

1. Click the Profile button on the New User, Copy Of, or User Properties dialog box. The User Environment Profile dialog box appears, as shown in Figure 12.3.

Figure 12.3.

The User Environment Profile dialog box.

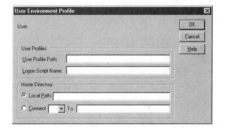

2. To assign a user profile, type its full pathname in the User Profile Path box. The path should be a network path. The filename can be that of a personal user profile (with a .USR filename extension) or a mandatory user profile (with a .MAN filename extension). You might type, for example, \\wnt\profiles\profile.man.

3. To assign a logon script, type the filename in the Logon Script Name box. If the logon script is stored in a subdirectory of the logon script path, precede the filename with that relative path.

4. To specify a home directory, select the Connect box, specify a drive letter, select the To box, and then type a network path. Or select the Local Path box and type a local path (including the drive letter). You might specify drive F:, for example, and type a network path of \\wnt\users\writer. You also might type a local path of c:\users\writer. When you're administering domain user accounts, specify a network path. Optionally, substitute %*username*% for the last subdirectory in the path. You might specify drive Z:, for example, and then type a network path of

\\wnt\users\%*username*%. When no home directory is assigned, the system assigns the user account the default local home directory (\USERS\DEFAULT on the user's local drive where Windows NT is installed).

5. Click OK.

Step 3: Review

This task showed you how to give a user a user profile and home directory. Giving users a home directory is important so that they have somewhere to store their data. Otherwise, they might look for somewhere to store data, and that place might not be where you want it.

Restricting User Access

The primary authentication mechanism for user access is logon restrictions. Logon restrictions include the following types of restrictions:

- ☐ Time restrictions
- ☐ Workstation restrictions
- ☐ Account restrictions
- ☐ Dialin restrictions

You study each one of these restrictions in turn in this chapter.

Permissible Logon Hours

You can restrict user access to a Windows NT server based on the time of day and day of the week. Time restrictions are useful because you can control when users can access the system. You can apply these restrictions as a system default for all users, or you can apply them for individual users.

After carefully studying the requirements of your network, you might decide to set default time restrictions. If you have only one work shift each day, for example, then it is unlikely that anyone logs on at 3:00 a.m. You also might want to set time restrictions to prevent workers from logging on at times when they are tired and more apt to make errors.

You might argue that some users need to log on anytime. Agreed. For that reason, you can change time restrictions on a user-by-user basis. You can set default time restrictions in the same way that you set account restrictions.

NOTE

When you apply time restrictions with a plan or according to a company policy, they provide extra protection. On the flip side, improperly conceived parameters hamper the work of your users.

12

Time restrictions are dynamic; that is, after you come across a blank time period, the system clears your connection. You do, however, have approximately eight minutes to log out. After several minutes in a disallowed period, you receive a message telling you to log out. If you choose to ignore this first message, you receive a second message. If you ignore the NTS message, Windows NT Server clears your connection in another minute.

So how do you use this facility? Suppose you have clients on your system who you know use the system only from 9:00 a.m. to 5:00 p.m. Monday to Friday. If this is the case, for no reason should these clients have access to the system outside these hours. NTS enables you to set permissible hours for all clients.

By choosing the Hours button in the New User dialog box, you can specify the days and hours during which a particular user of your system can access the network. Click the Hours button on the Properties dialog box of any user or group of users, and you see a dialog box similar to the one in Figure 12.4.

Figure 12.4.

The default Logon Hours dialog box.

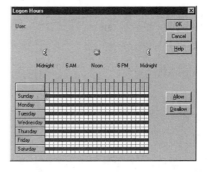

By default, a user can connect to the network all hours of all days of the week. As you can see from Figure 12.4, all times of all days are allowed for this new user. If, for some reason, you don't want a user to get access to the network all hours of the day, you can restrict logon hours by using this dialog box.

To administer the hours when you allow the user account to access the network, select the hours by dragging the cursor over a particular block of hours. Conversely, you can select all the hours of a certain day by clicking that day's button, or you can choose certain hours across all seven days by clicking the button on top of an hour's column. Then click either the Allow or Disallow button to grant or deny access to the network at those selected hours. Filled boxes indicate the hours when the user is authorized to connect to the network; empty ones indicate the time when access is denied. After you finish setting logon times, click OK. In Figure 12.5, you can see that the user is not allowed to log on now on Sundays.

Figure 12.5.

A modified Logon Hours dialog box.

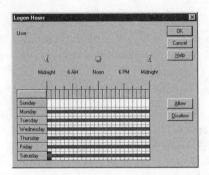

As its title implies, you must understand that the Logon Hours dialog box controls logon hours. Suppose that you've restricted your client to log on between 9:00 a.m. and 5:00 p.m., as mentioned earlier, and the client tries to log on at 8:59 a.m. In this case, your client cannot get on, and will see a message like the following one (if you have an NT workstation):

```
Your account has time restrictions that prevent you from logging on at
this time. Please Try again later.
```

If the client has a Windows 95 workstation, the client sees the following message:

```
You are not allowed to log on at this time.
```

DOS clients see a much wordier message:

```
Error 2241: You do not have the necessary access rights to log on at
this time. To change access rights, contact your network administrator
about changing the logon hours listed in your account.
```

Of course, when your client tries to log on a few minutes later, after 9 a.m., he can get in without a problem. But what happens when your client still is logged on at the end of the logon hours? What happens, for example, when 5:01 p.m. rolls around? Does the system dump the client off?

No, not by default. Later in this chapter, you see the Account Policy dialog box. (If you want to look ahead to it, turn to Figure 12.9 or go to the User Manager for Domains and choose Policies|Account.) Account Policy is a big dialog box, and it would be easy to miss one small check box at the bottom labeled Forcibly disconnect remote users from server when logon hours expire. That's not a very clear statement in the Account Policy dialog box. You tend to think of a "remote user" as someone who's dialing into the network; but to NT, it just means anyone who's accessing the server over the network rather than sitting down at the server itself. By default, the box isn't checked. If you check it, the client in the example gets this message five minutes before the end of the logon hours:

```
Your logon time at ORIOLE ends at 9:00 PM. Please clean up and log off.
```

Three minutes later, the message gets more ominous:

```
WARNING: You have until 9:00 PM to log off. If you have not logged off
at this time, your session will be disconnected, and any open files or devices
you have open may lose data.
```

Finally, at the appointed hour, the client is history:

```
Your logon time at ORIOLE has ended.
```

To get these messages, your client must start a message receiver such as either Winpopup (for Windows for Workgroups or Windows 95 clients) or the Alerter service on a Windows NT workstation. The client is logged off even when the client is not running a message receiver—the client just doesn't know it's going to happen.

After the system boots off your client, whatever network resources the client was using just seem to vanish. A network drive named F:, for example, likely generates this error message or one like it:

```
No files found on directory F:.
```

Trying to browse in a domain server might lead to an error message like this:

```
ORIOLE is not accessible. You are not allowed to log on at this time.
```

WARNING

The system tells you twice to log out when a disallowed time period arises. After the system warns you of an impending time restriction violation, you should log out immediately. If you don't log out, the system clears the connection, which means the system does not save the file you're working on.

12

Remember that changes to a user's account don't take effect until the next time the user logs on, so changing someone's logon hours today probably won't have any effect until tomorrow.

Similar to controlling logon hours is controlling logon locations. By choosing the Logon To button, you can limit from which workstations a user can log on.

Controlling Where Users Can Log On

Making station restrictions is another way to control user access, by restricting the physical workstations where users log on. When you choose the Logon To button in the New User dialog box, the Logon Workstations dialog box appears, as shown in Figure 12.6. In this dialog box, you can restrict from which workstations the user can log on. As with the logon times, the default is no restrictions. A user therefore can log on at any workstation on the network.

Figure 12.6.

*The Logon Workstations
dialog box.*

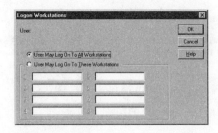

If you want to restrict the user's choice of workstations for logging onto the network, click
the User May Log On To These Workstations button, and type in the computer names
(without preceding backslashes) of the allowed workstations. You can specify up to eight
workstations. If the machines that your client regularly logs onto are WS_1000 and
WS_1001, for example, you can just type those names with no preceding backslashes. This
feature works for all workstation types.

Workstation restrictions, like other authentication mechanisms, can enhance access security.
When you apply workstation restrictions with a plan or according to a company policy, they
provide extra protection. But similar to time restrictions, improperly conceived restrictions
hamper the work of your users. When a user's workstation is broken, perhaps the user cannot
log onto the network. You can handle these contingencies, however, when you create your
users' list.

TIP

This morning in Chapter 11, "Account Management," you learned
about the Account Operators group. Now is a good time to make use
of this group. Because you have users who can administer accounts, you
can restrict the use of the Administrator account to a workstation in a
physically secure location.

Account Duration and Type

When creating or managing a user account, you can set the account to expire after a certain
time period. If you have a consultant or other temporary personnel, you don't want them to
log onto the network beyond the time for which they're authorized (or the contract expires).
An expiration date is a useful tool for temporary employees or students in an academic
institution. It enables you to lock an account after a specific date. A locked account cannot
be used without being reset. The account therefore expires at midnight on the expiration date.
By default, the expiration date is set to Never.

12

Setting an account to expire helps you avoid the problem of employees logging on when they're not supposed to. Click the Account button in the New User dialog box to display the Account Information dialog box shown in Figure 12.7.

Figure 12.7.

The Account Information dialog box.

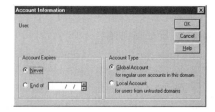

An account with an expiration date becomes disabled (not deleted) on the day specified in the Account Expires section of the dialog box. If the user happens to be logged on when the account expires, the system does not terminate the session, but the user cannot make any new connections. After the user logs off, she can't log back on.

In addition to setting an account expiration date, you also can set whether the user account in question is a *global account* or *local account* (don't confuse these accounts with *global* and *local groups*).

Global accounts, the default setting, are normal user accounts in the user's home domain. These accounts can be used not only in the home domain, but also in any domain that has a trust relationship with the home domain. (You learn more details about trust relationships later in this chapter.)

Local user accounts, on the other hand, are accounts provided in a particular domain for a user whose global user account is not in a trusted domain (that is, an untrusted NT Server domain or a LAN Manager 2.*x* domain). You cannot use a local account to log on interactively at an NT workstation or an NT Server server. Like other accounts, however, a local account can access NT and NT Server computers over the network, can be placed in local and global groups, and can be assigned rights and permissions. When a user from an untrusted domain (either NT Server or LAN Manager 2.*x*) needs access to other NT Server domains, that user needs to have a local account on each of those other domains because local accounts from one domain (the user's home domain) can't be used in other trusting domains.

All user accounts are global by default. You have to click a radio button, as you can see in the dialog box in Figure 12.7, to make a user account a local account. The main difference between a local account and a global account is that you can never get an external domain to recognize a local account. Microsoft had some plan for the use of local user accounts. Presently, there is no good reason to create a local account.

After you select the account options you want, click Add, click Close, and then click OK. Then click OK in the New User dialog box to create the new user account with the properties you've just specified. The new account then appears in the list of users on the current domain shown in the User Manager for Domains window.

Dialin Restrictions

The last button in the New User dialog box is Dialin. Choose this button when you want to grant the user permission to dial into the network from a remote location, that is, to use Dial-Up networking for connecting to the network. Click the Dialin button in the New User dialog box to display the Dialin Information dialog box shown in Figure 12.8.

Figure 12.8.

The Dialin Information dialog box.

If you want to allow the user to dial in, select the Grant dialin permission to user check box. You then need to configure the callback options.

Callback options deal with calling a user back at a predefined number and preventing intruders who have obtained valid logon information from dialing in at an unauthorized location. The options also provide an additional bonus for remote and mobile users by reversing the charges on calls. When a client calls in, the server authenticates the user; then it hangs up the call and calls back. Thus, the call is charged to the server.

These are the three callback options:

☐ *No Call Back:* This option disables callback options.

☐ *Set By Caller:* This option reverses toll charges for users. When a user calls in, the server authenticates him or her, and a dialog box appears asking for the callback telephone number. The server then disconnects the call and calls the client back. Note that this option provides no additional security.

☐ *Preset To:* This callback option does provide security because you can specify in advance the telephone number where a user should be called back.

In the following sections and tasks, you practice setting up an Account Policy.

12

Managing Account Policy

Every network operating system, whether Novell NetWare or Banyan Vines, has certain rules for user accounts that can be used to provide additional security for the network. Windows NT Server is no exception. To establish these rules, choose Policies|Account from the User Manager for Domains window. The Account Policy dialog box then appears, as shown in Figure 12.9. In this dialog box, you can set the options listed in Table 12.2.

Figure 12.9.

The Account Policy dialog box.

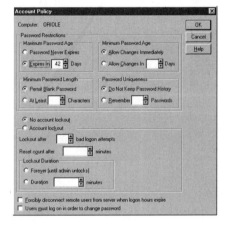

Table 12.2. The Account Policy options.

Option	Description
Maximum Password Age	You can require a user to change the password every so often by specifying a number in the Expires in Days field. Changing the password frequently helps reduce the possibility that someone might guess it. Depending on the type of data on your system, a good value for maximum password age is between 30 and 45 days. The default maximum password age is 42 days.
Minimum Password Age	By specifying a number in the Allow Changes In Days field, you can establish a minimum length of time before the user can change the password. This feature can provide two benefits. Use this field when you enable the Password Uniqueness option because it prevents a user from setting the password back to the password used immediately before the one that just expired. Allow Changes Immediately is the default.

continues

12

Table 12.2. continued

Option	Description
Minimum Password Length	To specify the minimum length of a password, enter a number in the At Least Characters field. When you set this parameter, remember that the shorter the password, the easier it is for the user to remember. Having a short password, however, also makes it easier for someone to gain access by guessing. Long passwords are harder for users to remember. A good minimum password length is six characters. Permit Blank Password is the default.
Password Uniqueness	The number entered in the Remember Passwords field specifies the number of passwords that the system records in the history list. The history list is a record of old passwords. Any password in this record cannot be used by the user when it is time to choose a new password. Do Not Keep Password History is the default.
Account lockout	This option is your best defense against system intruders because it limits the number of times that a user account can be used with the wrong password before the user account is disabled. On the downside, it also can lock out users who forget their passwords during a logon sequence. You specify the number of logon attempts before an account lockout occurs in the Lockout after bad logon attempts field. This number is based on the Reset count after minutes field, which specifies the time frame for determining the number of bad logon attempts. If the number of attempts occurs within the time frame you specify here, the account is locked out. In the Lockout Duration section, you can specify whether the account is locked out for a specific period of time by entering a number in the Duration minutes field, or you can specify that the account is locked out until an administrator reactivates it by selecting the Forever field. No account lockout is the default.

12

The final two options in the Account Policy dialog box enable you to log users off the network forcibly when their permissions to use the network (as specified in their user accounts) expire. You also can use these options to force any connected user off the network and close any shared network files (such as an SQL Server database) so that you can make system backups. The last option requires that the user log on first before changing a password. This way, you can prevent a user from using an expired password to gain access to the network for an idle account. By default, these options are set off.

NOTE

> Default account restrictions work for all accounts only after the parameters are set. New default parameters therefore have no effect on existing accounts. Consequently, you should look at setting the default parameters before you start adding all your users.

Let me add a few words about intruder detection and lockout before moving on. In your travels or reading, you might have heard of intruder detection and lockout. Your first question is probably "What do you mean by intruder?" An *intruder* is someone who attempts unauthorized access to someone else's account. Generally, intruders get this access by guessing passwords. Intruders might be internal to an organization (for example, disgruntled employees) or external (for example, *hackers*). If an intruder succeeds in guessing, or otherwise deriving, a password, the intruder has all the rights and privileges of the account. Unfortunately, the Administrator and Guest accounts become targets of intruders.

Because an intruder normally doesn't know the passwords, the intruder might try a brute-force attack. Hence, the intruder manually or automatically tries random passwords until finding a match. The Account Lockout feature kicks in then.

Account Lockout is not so much a restriction as it is a security feature. This feature tracks invalid logon attempts, that is, users who try to log on with incorrect passwords. It keeps track of invalid password attempts and locks a user account when the user reaches the threshold number of password attempts. Users activate Account Lockout as soon as they enter an invalid password. The system increments the "bad logon attempts" count for invalid passwords. The "Reset count after 'x' minutes" is a complementary parameter describing the period during which you track bad logons. After you reach the threshold within that period— you guessed it—you can lock out the user account.

An example might be appropriate at this juncture. Assume that you set "Lockout after 'x' bad logon attempts" to 3 and "Reset count after 'x' minutes" to 30 minutes. The system tracks all invalid logon attempts and locks the user account when the number of invalid logon attempts exceeds 3 in a 30-minute period.

You don't have to lock out an account that has passed the threshold; however, you can. You arm account lockout by setting the lockout duration. Normally, you would want to activate lockout upon detecting an intruder. You need to decide the appropriate time to lock the account. Then you specify the amount of time that must pass before the account automatically unlocks. If you set this number to a day or two, users need to come to you to get reset.

In the following task, you set up a default security policy for your organization.

Task 12.2. Setting a default security policy using the User Manager for Domains.

Step 1: Description

In this task, you'll use the User Manager for Domains program to set default user account restrictions that apply to any new users created.

Step 2: Action

1. Log onto the Windows NT Server as Administrator.

2. Choose Start|Programs|Administrative Tools (Common)|User Manager for Domains.

3. Choose Policies|Account. The Account Policy dialog box then appears, as shown in Figure 12.9.

4. Press Tab to move to the Expires in Days value field under Maximum Password Age. Type 30 in the box. Thirty days is a good period to keep a password. If you have users who always deal with confidential or critical data, you might want to set this number to fewer than 30 days. The maximum value is 999 days.

5. Press Tab to move to the Minimum Password Age, and select the Allow Changes in Days field. Immediately, a 1 pops up in the Days field. This value is good; it ensures that your users cannot change their password more than once per day, thus preventing them from looping through passwords and returning to their original password. If you don't enter a value here, users can just enter a number of passwords to get around the password uniqueness feature and use the original password. The maximum value is 999 days.

6. Select At Least Characters in the Minimum Password Length section. Immediately, a 6 pops up. This value is good. Picking one of seven characters is even better. Using combinations of seven letters and numbers (exactly 78,364,164,096), you can come up with enough combinations for more than 300 passwords for every person in the United States. The maximum value is 14.

TASK

12

7. Select Remember Passwords in the Password Uniqueness section. Immediately, a 5 pops up. If you force periodic password changes, you might be able to prevent users from repeating passwords. If you don't require unique passwords, users can change the password from alpha to beta and back to alpha. This option was created for exactly this reason. Normally, you want users to change their passwords because you're worried whether the password is still confidential. You don't require a change to improve typing skills. Allowing users to use the original passwords defeats the purpose of forcing password changes. If you decide a user needs unique passwords, NTS maintains a table of the old passwords. A good value is 10, which is similar to what other systems provide. The maximum value is 24.

8. Select Account lockout. Immediately, 5 pops up for bad logon attempts, 30 pops up for the Reset count after minutes value field, and 30 pops up for the Duration minutes value field. These default values are not bad. You might want to try 3, 30, and 99,999. The maximums are 999 bad logon attempts, and 99,999 minutes for reset count and duration. As the administrator, you can unlock the account when the system disables it. Just choose Start|Programs|Administrative Tools (Common)|User Manager for Domains|[*username*] and then deselect Account Disabled.

9. Select the Forcibly disconnect remote users from server when logon hours expire check box. This feature is good, especially if you want everybody off the system so that you can back up the server.

10. Select the Users must log on in order to change password check box.

11. Click OK.

Step 3: Review
In this task, you practiced using User Manager for Domains to set default user account restrictions that apply to all new users created.

Configuring Account Policies from the Command Line

In Chapter 11, you learned that you could create user accounts and groups from the command line. Just as you can create user accounts and local or global groups from the command line with the NET command, you also can specify the domain account policies. This is the NET syntax using options listed in Table 12.3:

```
NET ACCOUNTS [/FORCELOGOFF{Minutes NO}] [/MINPWLEN:Length]
[/MAXPWAGE:{Days UNLIMITED}] [/MINPWAGE:Days] [/UNIQUEPW:Number] [/DOMAIN]
```

Table 12.3. The NET ACCOUNTS **command options.**

Option	Description
/FORCELOGOFF	Specifies that the system should issue a warning message minutes before a user is forcibly logged off. When No is specified, users aren't forced off the system.
/MINPWLEN	Specifies the minimum password length. The default is 6; valid password lengths are 0 to 14.
/MAXPWAGE	Specifies the maximum time that a user's password is valid. The default is 90 days; the valid range is from 1 to 49,710 (same as unlimited when set to 49,710).
/MINPWAGE	Specifies the minimum time before a user can change a password. The default is 0; the valid range is 0 to 49,710 (again, 49,710 is the same as unlimited).
/UNIQUEPW	Specifies that a user cannot reuse the same password for the number of changes defined. The default is 5; the valid range is from 0 to 8.
/DOMAIN	Specifies that the operation should be performed on the Primary Domain Controller when the command is executed on a Windows NT Server operating in server mode or from a Windows NT Workstation.

Summary

In this chapter, you learned all about managing user accounts. First, you learned about user profiles and home directories, time restrictions, workstation restrictions, expiration dates, and dial-in restrictions. Next, you saw how to set an account policy for your server. You also mastered the procedure for changing the account restrictions for individual users. This chapter emphasized controlling users and demonstrated one of Window NT Server's primary security mechanisms. You should study these account restrictions and use them where they are applicable to improve the security of your network.

Workshop

To wrap up the day, you can review terms and tasks from the chapter, and see the answers to some commonly asked questions.

12

Terminology Review

access period—A segment of time, generally expressed on a daily or weekly basis, when access rights prevail.

authentication—The act of identifying or verifying the eligibility of a station, originator, or individual to access specific categories of information.

authorization—The process that grants the necessary and sufficient permissions for the intended purpose.

brute-force attack—A computerized trial-and-error attempt to decode a cipher or password by trying every possible combination. Also known as *exhaustive attack*.

hacker—A computer enthusiast; also, one who seeks to gain unauthorized access to computer systems.

identification—The process that enables recognition of an entity by a system, generally by the use of unique machine-readable usernames.

intruder—A user or other agent attempting to gain unauthorized access to the file server.

Task List

The emphasis of this chapter was to introduce you to accounts and their management. As a system administrator, you will repeatedly use these commands in your daily work. You should understand the following tasks from this chapter:

☐ Setting an account policy

☐ Changing a user's account restrictions

☐ Changing a user's time restrictions

☐ Changing a user's station restrictions

☐ Setting intruder lockout

☐ Unlocking a user's account

☐ Requiring and restricting passwords for users

12

Q&A

Q **How can I boot everyone off the server at 2 a.m. so that a scheduled backup can occur?**

A That's simple. Just write a batch file with these commands:

```
Net pause server
Net send * The server is shutting down in 15 minutes for routine
➥maintenance.
Sleep 900
Net stop server
```

The pause command keeps anyone new from logging on. The send command sends a message to everyone running the messenger service and a network pop-up. The sleep command tells NT to wait for 900 seconds (15 minutes). SLEEP.EXE isn't shipped with NT, but it does come with the NT *Resource Kit.* You should install the SLEEP program for instances like this one. The stop command shuts down the server, disconnecting everyone.

Q **If I use Account Lockout, what should I set my thresholds to?**

A Normally, you would set bad logon attempts to 3. Anymore than three attempts is probably something other than pilot error.

Q **When and where would I use workstation restrictions?**

A Using workstation restrictions is an excellent control for enforcing program pathing. By using program pathing, you can force specific users to execute programs from specific locations. You might want to ensure, for example, that payroll transactions come from workstations only in the human resources area. Also, you should tie the use of the Administrator account to a specific workstation used by the system administrator. Doing so obviates the exposure of an unattended workstation in session to the administrator. You also might want to tie the Guest account to a specific workstation. Any jobs or processes without passwords should also be associated to a workstation.

Q **What is a good password length?**

A The length of a password determines the potential security of your system. A password length of one reduces the potential password space to the number of characters in the composition set—for example, 0 to 9 for numeric and A to Z for alphabetic. Increasing the length of a random password can make it drastically more difficult to discover. With each additional character, both the number of possible combinations and the average time required to find the password increase exponentially. A length of two characters squares the number, and a length of three cubes this number, and so on.

Having said this, the consultant's answer is the length should be such that it cannot be easily guessed during the lifetime of the password. The practical answer is your passwords should be at least six characters long to thwart a brute-force attack.

But this probably doesn't help. So what is a good password length? In this chapter, you saw that the minimum password length is 0 (you can have a blank password), but there is a maximum password length. Practically, the maximum password length is 14 characters. (We say "practically" because User Manager for Domains enables you to create a maximum 14-character password only. The password field itself, however, is 128 characters.) But most of us cannot remember a 128-character password. The practical answer is that your passwords should be at least 6 characters long and no more than 14 to thwart a brute-force attack.

12

DAY

7

Chapter 13

Exploring Windows NT Server Files and Directories

In the preceding days, you learned about installing and exploring NT and managing the Registry. You also learned all about domains and delved deeply into the security that NT offers.

In this morning's session, you'll learn all about how NT manages files and organizes them into directories. This organization is similar to structures you might already understand, such as the DOS file structure.

In this chapter, you learn, however, that NT offers you choices when setting up and managing files. You discover that in addition to the FAT file system, NT uses a new file system called *New Technology File System*, or NTFS. You also discover that file-level security depends on the use of NTFS and that using the older DOS FAT format limits the amount of security available to you.

Reviewing the Basics

First, take a few minutes to review the basics of files and directories. In particular, this information concerns the hardware and how it is set up within the machine and the operating system.

In all systems, you begin with a physical drive that is mounted in the server and attached with screws; it is the actual hard drive. You cannot change the size of the drive without physically removing it and replacing it with a new drive. Someone performs a *low-level,* or *physical,* format so that you can begin using it. This formatting cannot be done from NT; it is done with tools that usually exist within the hard drive controller. Because each drive is different, you need to review the manuals that come with your particular drive for details on how to format. Rarely does an administrator need to perform this function, however.

You might have worked on systems that cannot recognize large hard drives. If so, you will be pleased to know that NT recognizes hard drives that are larger than any in use today.

NT also uses, just as the other operating systems do, logical partitions. Such a partition is the opposite of the physical drive; it's a drive created using software. When you run the DOS FDISK command on a hard drive, for example, it asks whether you want to set up one or more partitions. Be careful using this command, however, because it can destroy all information that already exists on the hard drive.

To run the FDISK command, you must first ensure that all your data is backed up safely onto tape or another disk. FDISK, in its zeal to create the partition, destroys any information that already exists. You see FDISK in action in Figure 13.1.

Figure 13.1.

Using FDISK *to format a hard drive.*

Remember, because this process destroys all the data on the disk, don't play with FDISK indiscriminately. You can create only four partitions on any one physical hard drive. A *primary partition* is the only partition that is bootable, meaning that an operating system uses that partition for starting up. Why would you need more than one primary drive? In most cases,

13

you might not, but if you plan to share your machine with more than one operating system, you do so this way. To run both NT Server and Windows 95, as we do on our laptops, for example, you might create one drive for running NT Server and another for Windows 95.

You can run both NT Server and Windows 95 using only one drive, but doing so limits you to using only the FAT type of drive. NT runs better and more securely if it uses its own NTFS file system. You therefore need to create additional drives to handle this discrepancy. Using Disk Administrator, you see the primary partition indicated through a dark purple stripe across the top as NT shows you a different color for each type of partition, enabling you to quickly see the different partitions. These colors change according to the capabilities of your video card, however, so yours might look slightly different.

NOTE

You must define and use the NTFS format with NT Server to be able to utilize file- and directory-level security and control. In addition, the newer NTFS file system is more efficient, supports better recovery processes, and ultimately offers improved operating efficiencies. The FAT system works just fine in your NT Server, but it does not allow you the granularity of protection and efficiency that you get with the newer NTFS.

The other type of drive is the *extended drive,* which is created using the free space available on a given drive. Extended partitions can be further subdivided into smaller units called *logical drives.* The Disk Administrator does not provide color coding for easy recognition of logical drives, so you need to check the status bar after clicking the free space to see a description.

The logical drives that an extended partition provide act as though they are physical drives for the user. You can use as many logical drives as you need, with these exceptions:

☐ You have only 25 fixed-disk drive letters (assuming one floppy).

☐ Each logical drive must be at least 2MB in size.

☐ A logical drive can extend across only one physical drive.

Royal blue stripes indicate logical disk drives in the Disk Administrator.

Here's some sound advice: You should back up all your data before messing around with partitions. You always need to back up data, regardless of the type of activity you're performing, because sooner or later you're going to lose data and regret not taking a more positive approach to data safety and backup. As any security guru will tell you: back up, back up, back up.

13

One other way of dealing with partitions is to use special software that helps automate the task. As we began this book, both Peter and I had laptops with only one partition with Windows 95 on them. Prior to setting up our network, we installed NT on the laptops with Windows 95. NT 4.0 blithely installed on the FAT drive to coexist with Windows 95. It did prevent us from using the NTFS system, however. At some point, we needed to reinstall NT after setting up more than one partition because we intended to remain with a dual-boot machine.

Rather than go through backups, partition creation, and restores, we used a tool called Partition Magic from Power Quest. This tool manages FAT-based file systems and enables you to create, modify, and maintain partitions without all the steps outlined earlier. Note that we always backed up the machine first, regardless. I mean, would you trust any software to protect all your hard-earned data and clever repartee? After our regular backups, we used Partition Magic and created a new partition for NT to use. This way, we managed to keep our FAT-based Windows 95 systems while changing NT Server to use its newer NTFS system. Partition Magic works only with Windows 95 and DOS-based file systems. After NTFS is installed, you can use NT's Disk Administrator to manage changes.

Task 13.1. Using Disk Administrator to view your current disk drives.

Step 1: Description

This task enables you to see all the colors we keep talking about and to find out what types of disk drives are available on your system. The available drives change as you add new disks, with Disk Administrator automatically finding the new drives.

Step 2: Action

1. Log onto your system using an Administrator account.
2. Choose Start|Programs|Administrative Tools (Common)|Disk Administrator.
3. Click Disk Administrator to open the dialog box. You then see the current disk setup for your server, as shown in Figure 13.2.

   In the example, NT is used on a FAT-based hard drive, with no other partitions. Later you see how to change the partition setup to include NTFS.
4. Choose Partition|Exit or click the Close button on the upper-right corner of the window to close Disk Administrator.

Figure 13.2.

*Using Disk Adminis-
trator.*

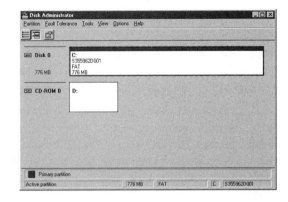

Step 3: Review

By using Disk Administrator, you see how your drives are partitioned and can modify the existing setup. Be careful playing with this tool because serious damage can occur if you execute a command you later regret. You'll examine the use of this tool in more detail later, in the section called "Managing Disk Volumes and Partitions."

Reviewing NT Specifics

You reviewed the basics of NT earlier in this chapter, but now you can delve deeper and discover some of the additional file and directory capabilities in NT.

Along with partitions, extended partitions, and logical drives, NT uses volume sets. A *volume set* is a drive that is combined with other physical drives to make one large volume. (Disk Administrator displays yet another color—yellow—to indicate a volume set.) As you might recall, logical drives apply to only one physical drive. What happens if you need a huge database that cannot fit on one drive? With volume sets, you can create a volume that uses the space available across a number of physical hard drives. This way, you can use your free disk space more efficiently by assigning the needed increments to a volume set. You can enlarge a volume set after it is created, but you can reduce that size only by deleting it and creating a new set.

You might believe that with your data spread over a number of volumes, it is safer. You might think that if one drive fails, the others are still operating. However, this is not the case. Extending volume sets increases your risk because you then have the potential for more drives to fail and affect one set of data. Failure of any one of the drives within a volume set destroys the volume set, leaving you with no data. Follow the earlier advice: back up, back up, back up.

Another concept to learn is mirroring. *Mirroring* is a fairly simple, effective way to provide protection for your data while speeding recovery of any lost data. Disk mirroring copies all your data onto another identically sized area on another disk drive. The original and copied data combined are called a *mirror set*. If anything happens to your original files, you can use the copies stored on the other drive.

Each drive must use the same data size for mirroring to work. This process isn't very efficient because you need to duplicate all your data exactly, meaning you need twice the space. It does provide a backup solution with little or no loss of time because each disk drive can perform its own writing. Disk Administrator shows these drives with yet another color—magenta. It's a shame that this book isn't in color so that you could see all the pretty colors rather than shades of gray.

Another similar method of backing up files and data is called *disk duplexing*. This process is essentially identical to mirroring, except that in duplexing the data is written to drives that run on their own disk controllers. In this way, the possibility of failures is minimized because each drive has its own controller. In mirroring, each drive runs off the same disk controller, leaving this solution more vulnerable. NT doesn't differentiate between terms, so the term *mirroring* is used to refer to either duplexing or mirroring. You can see what we mean in Figure 13.3.

Figure 13.3.

Mirroring versus duplexing.

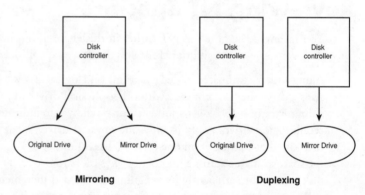

Finally, you need to learn about stripe sets. You use stripe sets to increase security of your data and possibly increase your disk's read time, speeding things up. A *stripe set* consists of two or three selected areas of free space on your disks that are combined to store data. Data in a stripe set is stored in certain sizes, called *stripes*. After you format a new stripe set, it is assigned a drive letter and acts just like a disk drive. It is, of course, only a logical partitioning of data across a number of different drives to provide additional security and speed.

Each time you write to a stripe drive, your data is written in chunks across all members of the set. The concept is not restricted to NT. It is a familiar tool in NetWare and other operating systems. Because the data is written to several drives with the same performance and storage characteristics, operating efficiencies are gained. In other words, your file gets spread across the drives and can be combined and manipulated faster because, as one drive is busy, the system uses the other drives. Typically, you use three drives, two to hold the chunks of data and the third to manage disk parity and re-create lost data. Although you can use striping with only two drives, without the parity portion, all parts of the stripe must be working; otherwise, all the data is lost. Parity allows recovery if one drive is lost, hence the more common use of three-drive stripe sets.

Managing Disk Volumes and Partitions

As an administrator, you need to manage the machines in your domain. Your job includes setting up, removing, and maintaining partitions and logical drives. Using the concepts you learned earlier, look at the steps needed to perform some of these critical tasks.

Task 13.2. Using Disk Administrator to create an extended partition.

TASK

Step 1: Description

This task enables you to set up an extended partition as a first step to creating logical partitions on your system. NT uses the logical drives as if they were disk drives, enabling you to manage your resources more effectively. You use this procedure when you install a new drive or implement an application that you want to segregate onto its own partition.

Step 2: Action

1. Log onto your system using an Administrator account.
2. Choose Start|Programs|Administrative Tools (Common)|Disk Administrator.
3. Click Disk Administrator to open the dialog box. You then see the current disk setup for your server.
4. Choose the drive you want to use, and click the free space indicated for that drive.
5. Choose Partition|Create Extended Partition. The resulting dialog box tells you the amount of space available.
6. Select the size you want the new drive to be by using the arrows. Then click OK after you finish the operation.

Step 3: Review

Using the Disk Administrator, you set up new drives easily and quickly. Be careful using this powerful tool, however. After changes are committed, it's too late to back out.

After creating the extended partition, you need to format it into the logical drives you want. This second step is necessary to finish the task of setting up new partitions for data use.

13

In the following task, you set up a new logical drive using the space provided by the extended partition you just set up.

Task 13.3. Using Disk Administrator to create logical drives.

Step 1: Description

After you set up extended partitions, you can continue by setting up the logical drives. This task enables you to set up a logical drive, picking up where you left off in Task 13.2.

Step 2: Action

1. Log onto your system using an Administrator account.
2. Choose Start|Programs|Administrative Tools (Common)|Disk Administrator.
3. Double-click Disk Administrator to open the dialog box. You then see the current disk setup for your server.
4. Click the area of the newly created extended drive to select it.
5. Choose Partition|Create to open a new dialog box showing the space available.
6. Select the size you want the new logical drive to be by using the arrows. You can press Enter to select all the space. Click OK after you finish this operation.
7. When you leave Disk Administrator, you see a dialog box asking you to confirm that you want to save the changes you just made. Click Yes to save. Disk Administrator then shows you another dialog box indicating that the changes were successfully made and suggesting you update your Emergency Repair disk.

Step 3: Review

Using Disk Administrator, you set up your logical drives and make them ready for use. You must format the drives before you can actually store any data on them.

You'll learn how to format a drive in Task 13.4. You need to decide whether to use the NTFS or FAT file system for your new drive as part of the format task. Using NTFS is best unless you have a compelling reason to do otherwise, because this system provides faster data access and better security options.

Task 13.4. Formatting a new drive.

Step 1: Description

After adding a new drive to your system, you need to format it so that it becomes available to NT. In NT 4.0, you can use the GUI interface and either Explorer or My Computer to perform the formatting. You also can use the Disk Administrator. After you complete the first two steps in Task 13.3, simply open Explorer, choose the new drive, and right-click.

Right-clicking brings up a format command. Use this method or the following Disk Administrator method to format. (The method you choose depends on whether you're still in a Disk Administrator window or want to use Explorer or My Computer. They all do the same job.)

Step 2: Action

1. Log onto your system using an Administrator account.
2. Choose Start|Programs|Administrative Tools (Common)|Disk Administrator.
3. Click Disk Administrator to open the dialog box. You then see the current disk setup for your server.
4. Choose the file system you want to set up. You can set up an NTFS- or FAT-based system. The best choice is to use NTFS because it provides greater security.
5. Choose Quick Format if you want to tell NT not to scan the disk for bad sectors.
6. After you decide on all the options, click OK to start the format. A dialog box appears asking you to confirm your choice. Click OK again to continue and complete the task.

WARNING

Be sure you choose the correct disk to format. As mentioned earlier, this change is irreversible and all data is lost. Although the Format dialog box has a Cancel option, after the operation has started, it's unlikely that canceling the task will restore the partition to its previous condition.

Step 3: Review

You format the drive to make it accessible to your operating system. After formatting is complete, NT uses the drive as you direct, and rights and permissions are assigned as needed. You'll learn about rights and permissions in more detail in the following chapter.

Task 13.5. Creating a volume set.

Step 1: Description

After adding a new drive to the system, you formatted the drive to make it available to NT. In this task, you'll set up a new volume set so that you can create and manage a large file over several disk drives, treating it as if the multiple drives were one drive.

Step 2: Action

1. Log onto your system using an Administrator account.

2. Choose Start|Programs|Administrative Tools (Common)|Disk Administrator.

3. Click Disk Administrator to open the dialog box. You then see the current disk setup for your server.

4. From the available space, choose the areas of free space to be included in the volume set. You can choose as much or as little as necessary. After you do so, however, you must delete the set to make it smaller. You can increase its size without deleting it first.

5. Choose the size of the set you want to create from the assigned free space. You can choose any size within the given parameters by using the arrow keys.

6. After you choose the size, click OK to continue.

7. Exit from the Disk Administrator by clicking the Close button in the upper-right corner of the window. NT prompts you to reboot the system.

   The new volume appears when you reopen Disk Administrator, but it is not yet available for NT to use. It must be formatted.

8. Using the steps outlined in Task 13.4, format the drive to prepare it for NT to use.

   You're now finished preparing the volume set and can begin to use it.

Step 3: Review

You create a volume set when you need a large database that can span more than one disk drive. Like any other drive, it must be formatted prior to use. After the drive is formatted, NT treats the drive like any other, disregarding the fact that it covers more than one physical disk drive.

Examining the NTFS File System

You've learned about using Microsoft's new file system, NTFS, in the preceding chapters and in today's chapter. What is this new system, and how might it have an impact an your decision whether to use NTFS or continue with a FAT-based server?

NTFS is the file system designed as part of the then-new Windows NT operating system. Presently, only Windows NT Server and Workstation use this file system. Note the following major differences between this system and the FAT-based system you might be used to working with:

☐ NTFS uses a file-naming standard of 256 characters. This standard is 248 characters longer than the old DOS system is capable of using. As a result, you can use names that mean something to you when creating a file instead of needing to create cryptic eight-character names.

☐ With NTFS, you see the filenames in glorious upper- and lowercase. Having mixed case means only that the filenames look pretty, though, because NT doesn't enable you to search by case. This system sure seems more civilized, though.

- [ ] NTFS maintains a log of activities so that you can restore the disk in the event of a power failure or other type of interruption.

- [ ] The new file system is designed for security and allows access restrictions at the file level. No such facility exists within the DOS FAT system. Both systems do allow restrictions at the directory level, however.

- [ ] Within the NTFS file system, you can create and use mirror sets, stripe sets, and volume sets, providing a greater degree of efficiency and availability.

- [ ] The new file system enables you to handle huge hard drives. NT enables you to use hard drives to a size in the terabyte range. Nice if you have 'em.

Within the NTFS file-naming structure, you can include spaces and separating periods. Additionally, you can use upper- or lowercase but cannot use certain special characters that are reserved for other functions. NT does not allow the |, :, <, >, /, \, ", or ? characters within filenames.

NT supports these long filenames and also allows compatibility with the older DOS format by converting any long name into the 8.3 DOS format. It accomplishes this by taking the first six characters of the NTFS filename, adding a tilde and a sequence number.

In addition, during the conversion NT ensures that no illegal DOS characters remain, removes all spaces and periods (except the last one because NT assumes that it marks the beginning of an extension), and truncates any extension present to three characters. Therefore, a file called Recipes for Holidays.doc becomes recipe~1.doc. If you start a whole bunch of files with *Recipes for* and use the next characters to differentiate them, NT leaves you with a list that looks like the following:

- [ ] recipe~1.doc
- [ ] recipe~2.doc
- [ ] recipe~3.doc
- [ ] recipe~4.doc

As you see, these filenames are not descriptive enough to read in a DOS program, so you have to spend time trying to figure out which file contains what data. Consider putting the descriptive identifier in the first six characters if you use many DOS-based programs. You see how using a naming convention is important so that you can readily understand what is in a particular file as DOS strips away your nice long filename and replaces it with something that leaves you guessing about what is in the file.

Many administrators might disagree, but we believe that leaving a FAT-based partition on your server is useful. This applies only if you operate within the DOS world in any way. If you're a UNIX guru and are moving to NT, you might choose not to have a FAT-based partition. By leaving a FAT-based partition on your server, though, you can boot the machine

13

from a DOS disk—a capability that is sometimes useful in troubleshooting situations. Additionally, you can run DOS programs on the server or store the NT installation CD directly onto the server for speed. (Copy the I386 directory off your CD and onto the server.)

You'll discover additional advantages of using NTFS as you move through this chapter. Directories in NTFS, for example, are automatically sorted and can consist of upper- and lowercase characters, making them easier to read. Access to files over 0.5MB is faster, as is all access to NT disk files. Finally, for all Macintosh users, NTFS allows compatibility between NT and Mac. Mac users cannot share volumes with NT unless it uses NTFS.

One last important feature that the NTFS file system provides is the capability to constantly monitor the disk area for errors. If the file system finds any damaged sectors, it removes the data to a safe place automatically while taking the affected area out of service.

NT and Floppy Drives

Just when you thought it was safe to go in the water again, Microsoft muddies it up a bit. (Sorry, I'm a fan of the movie *Jaws*.) You cannot format a floppy with NTFS; it just doesn't work. NT offers a useful message indicating that it Cannot lock current drive. Lock? And you thought you were going to format something.

We're not saying that NT doesn't work on floppy drives or that you cannot use long filenames. The system places two names on a floppy for each file—the long name that NT knows about and a DOS-based 8.3 name. This way, both DOS and you get to see and work with files from floppies.

The process is not entirely perfect, however. If you use NT to update and save changes to these files, the names are maintained. If you use a DOS-based program and change one of these files, good old DOS obliterates the NTFS long name, leaving you with only the 8.3 name. The file itself is fine; only the NTFS name disappears. As long as you have some sensible naming convention, you can quickly ascertain what the file contains and reuse it in NT.

 TIP

NT supports a number of file systems. In addition to its new file system called New Technology File System (NTFS), it also supports the DOS FAT-based system and OS/2's High Performance File System (HPFS). The flexibility that comes with using NT is useful when you combine multiple operating systems.

13

File Forks

Mac users are already familiar with the term *file forking*. This capability helps Macs in their ease of use and simplicity. A fork tells NT to do something when the file is opened. For example, Microsoft uses the .DOC extension for its word processor, MS Word. When a user opens Explorer and double-clicks a filename with this extension, NT sees the fork and knows to also start up a copy of the word processor. Bingo, bango—the application you need is automatically started merely by your selecting the file.

NT uses a form of forking by providing an area that keeps track of file extensions and associates a program with each extension. True file forking would place a pointer with each file regardless of the extension used. NT should, in effect, just know that Word creates a particular file even if you save the file with an extension of .dog.

Using Windows NT Explorer

If you used Windows or Windows NT 3.*x*, you surely remember using File Manager to manipulate files and directories. You're used to the click-and-select type of action that File Manager provides and the options and idiosyncrasies of the tool.

In Windows NT 4.0, you use Microsoft Explorer. If you already use Windows 95, little of this section will be new to you, so you might feel comfortable skipping it and moving on to the next section.

You find NT Explorer by choosing Start|Programs|Windows NT Explorer. Choosing this menu item opens a new window for you, like the one shown in Figure 13.4. As with other programs, you can open as many Explorer windows as your system resources allow.

Figure 13.4.

The Explorer window.

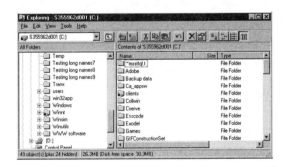

Explorer opens showing a list of your hard drives and floppies and includes any network components you might have.

Actually, we already mentioned one of NT Explorer's main benefits. It shows all the drive connections. In a networked world, seeing these connections is nice. Rather than merely being content to show you your C: and D: drives, though, it shows you all of them, however many you might have, right up to NT's limit of 24.

Explorer is Windows NT Server's File Manager. Take a quick tour around the menus. NT Explorer starts with a File menu. No surprise here. Inside the File drop-down menu are a number of options, including Open With, New, Send To, Delete, Properties, and so on. If you don't see these options, your cursor is selecting a folder name from the left side of the window. Explorer offers fewer options there. (Move the cursor to the right-hand selection box and select any folder.) If you choose File|New, you see a submenu providing several additional options, as shown in Figure 13.5.

Figure 13.5.

Explorer's File|New submenu.

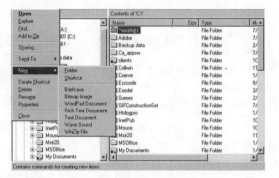

In NT, directories are called *folders*, just as in Windows 95. Note that Folder is the first option on this submenu. If you choose Folder, something surprising happens: A new entry is placed in the currently selected folder. That entry, called New File Folder, appears with a blue color over it and the cursor blinking there as if it expects you to do something.

You, of course, do exactly that—something. If you press the Enter key (Don't! Oh, too late. Read until the end of the paragraph before attempting all these commands, okay?), Explorer creates the file folder called New Folder, unless one already exists. If that is the case, NT Explorer creates another folder called New Folder(2). You can go on for some time until you understand that perhaps you can find another way of managing these folders so that you don't end up with hundreds of folders named New Folder(x).

Before pressing Enter (go back to the start and try again if you pressed Enter earlier), press the Backspace key to remove the words New Folder. Now you can type the name you want to use. Just enter in the characters you want, and when ready, press Enter. Remember, these names can be really long, so enter the name you want here to make the folder easily identifiable. You might call the folder My First Test of Explorer Folder Creation. Notice how NT maintains all the capital letters exactly as you typed them.

13

Explorer does not show you all the name you just typed in, however. What's wrong? Did you miss something? Well, not really. The default setup allows a certain size and uses icons to represent folders. You can modify this size as you want. First, you can size all the sections (Name, Size, Type, Modified, and Attributes) by moving the cursor directly over the connecting lines and dragging the box until it is the size you want. When you're in the correct place, NT places a cursor like that shown in Figure 13.6 between the Name and Size separators. You can also place your cursor between the separators and double-click. This action sets the size to the largest name currently on-screen.

Figure 13.6.

Sizing Explorer columns.

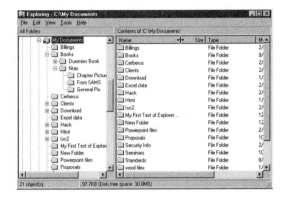

Another new aspect of Explorer is the Send To option on the File drop-down menu. If you choose Send To, you see the following three options:

- ☐ 3½ Floppy (A)
- ☐ Mail Recipient
- ☐ My Briefcase

The first option is easily understood. Choosing it sends the file or folder you selected earlier directly to the floppy drive. This feature is one of the quick and easy tools Explorer offers.

If you install a mail program on NT, you see the icon called Mail Recipient in the menu. (Don't worry if it's not there. In this case, you don't use a recognized mail program.) This icon enables you to send the file to a mail program such as MS Exchange or, as it is now called, Windows Messaging.

My Briefcase is Microsoft's attempt to help the road warriors, enabling them to manage files between the desktop back at the office and a portable computer they use on the road. To use this option, you drag files from shared folders on your desktop computer to the Briefcase icon on your portable computer. After finishing your trip, click Update All in Briefcase, and NT replaces all the files on your desktop computer with your changes from the portable computer. All these changes assume you connect the two machines either through a network or other means.

13

Additional options in the File menu offer you the chance to set up Sharing and to delete and rename files. You can also create a shortcut to a file and place it on your desktop. Because NT uses forks, when you double-click the desktop shortcut, your file opens along with the application that created the file. Using shortcuts is a nice method of quickly accessing something you're working on. Place a shortcut to the policy and standard document you're creating, for example, and you can get to it each day by simply double-clicking.

Task 13.6. Using Explorer to create a new folder.

Step 1: Description

Explorer enables you to add directories (now called folders) in your system quickly and easily. After adding a new folder, you can use Explorer to copy or move files into this folder. In this manner, you organize your desktop and make it more efficient.

Step 2: Action

1. Log onto your system using your user account.

2. Choose Start|Programs|Windows NT Explorer.

3. Place your cursor on the main drive icon, and right-click once to highlight the drive. It is typically the C: drive. Look for the little icon that indicates a disk drive and has C: beside it. You then see the main disk drive with a purple color over it.

4. Choose File|New|Folder. A new folder named New Folder is highlighted under the main drive icon on the right side of the window. The cursor is already in place for you to type in a folder name.

5. Type the words My New Folder for NT Testing and press Enter. You don't need to erase the initial string called New Folder because it is already highlighted and therefore gets overtyped. Explorer now shows a folder called My New Folder for NT Testing, complete with upper- and lowercase. You have created a new folder.

6. After you complete step 5, double-click the folder to open it. Naturally, the folder is empty because it is new. Now move and copy some files from other parts of the system into this folder.

7. Use your cursor to move the scroll bar until you see the folder called winnt. (If you installed NT in another directory, use that name instead.) This time, place the cursor on the small box with a plus sign in it, next to the folder called winnt. Do not click elsewhere in the window. Click once on that small box, and you see the Windows NT folder open, but you remain with the right window open to the new folder you created in step 5. You should see a screen similar to the one in Figure 13.7.

   The winnt folder contains a number of subdirectories or folders within it. Double-click the winnt folder now to see all the files that are in the folder.

Figure 13.7.

Explorer, open to the new folder contents.

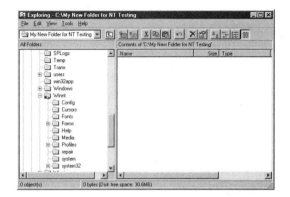

8. Find and select the folder called network.wri by right-clicking the folder once.

9. Move the cursor to the window called All Folders on the left, and using the scroll bar, find your new folder. It's the one called My New Folder For NT Testing. Don't select the folder. Move the cursor back over the network.wri file. Without letting go of the mouse button, hold the Ctrl key and click on the network.wri file and drag it over to the new folder. By using the Ctrl key, you copy the file instead of moving it.

10. Click the new folder, and you see a copy of the file inside. Double-click the filename in your new folder, and NT starts up the Wordpad program to show you the contents of the file. (In the next section, you'll learn some of the tricks to using Explorer effectively.)

11. Now that you are finished creating and copying files in Explorer, remove the new folder (no sense leaving test material lying around the server is there?) by clicking once on the My New Folder for NT Testing folder. Then press the Delete key. NT asks you to verify that you want to remove this folder. Reply Yes to complete the task. Don't forget that NT moves deleted items to the Recycle Bin, and you need to empty the bin occasionally if you want to free up additional space on your hard drive. By default, NT provides for 10 percent of the space on your drive, and this amount becomes significant on larger drives.

Step 3: Review

Using Explorer, you created a file folder, manipulated data using drag and drop, and performed general file and directory tasks. Explorer is easy to use after you're used to the concept.

13

Explorer Hints and Tricks

You now know how to manipulate your files using Explorer. But a number of neat tricks provide you with even more ease of use and speed.

When you're in a folder, use the Backspace key to move up the hierarchy. Explorer moves you up to the next higher folder. If you're in the winnt\forms\Configs folder, for example, using the Backspace key takes you back to winnt\forms. Use it again and you're placed in the \winnt directory. Once more places you back up at the C: drive icon.

You can obtain a quick view of a file by selecting the file, right-clicking it, and choosing Quick View from the menu. This method works only with certain files that are registered to the program, and it doesn't always view the file correctly. For other files, you must use the Open option.

You can set options to either hide or show filename extensions. To do so, choose View|Options and then select the Hide File Extensions for Known File Types check box to either hide the extensions or show them. In this same dialog box, you can set other options such as displaying the full path or using colors to differentiate compressed files.

You can check the disk volume for errors using Explorer. Right-click the volume you want to check, and choose Properties|Tools. Select Check Now to start the error checking. You also can back up files from this dialog box by selecting the Backup Now option and following the directions.

Sort the files within an Explorer window when you're in Detail view by clicking the column heading. To sort in reverse order, click once more. You can sort files by size and by type using this method and selecting either the Size or Type heading.

Quickly copy files to the Briefcase or drive A: by selecting the file, right-clicking, and then selecting the Send To option.

To always copy a file when using drag and drop, also use the Ctrl key. Press Ctrl+Shift while dragging a file to create a shortcut.

You can bypass the automatic starting of CD-ROMs by pressing the Shift key as you insert the CD in your machine. This capability is handy when you want to reference your NT installations CD without having the automatic installation program start.

NT, like Windows 95, places deleted files into the Recycle Bin in case you change your mind and want to recover the file. If you're sure that a file can be deleted and don't want to have it take up disk space, press Shift+Delete while selecting the file. NT deletes the file completely and doesn't keep a copy in the Recovery folder.

To move quickly between frames in Explorer, press the F6 key. Press the F5 key to refresh Explorer after manipulating a bunch of files.

Use the right and left arrows when selecting folders to expand or collapse the folders quickly.

Explorer offers a multitude of shortcuts, hints, and techniques. We offer these more common ones to help speed up your manipulation of files and directories.

Summary

You learned how NT's NTFS file structure is superior to the FAT system and some of the reasons to use NTFS instead of a FAT-based file system. Using files and folders and manipulating them is fairly easy with NT's Explorer.

In this chapter, you discovered the following:

☐ That the FAT file system has a use within NT Server

☐ The advantages that the new NTFS file system offers over other file systems

☐ The different types of partitions and why you use each type

☐ How to format a drive and ensure that data is backed up before starting the format

☐ What forking is and the benefits it provides

☐ The differences between disk mirroring and disk duplexing

☐ How to use Explorer efficiently and effectively to manage your files and folders

Workshop

To wrap up the day, you can review terms and tasks from the chapter, and see the answers to some commonly asked questions.

Terminology Review

duplexing—A method of using two disk drives and two disk controllers to store data. One serves as the primary and the other for backup purposes.

extended partition—A section of free space from a hard disk that allows the disk to be further partitioned into logical partitions or drives.

FAT—The name given to the DOS file system. It stands for File Allocation Table and refers to the method of managing the files and directories on the DOS system.

format—The process of setting up a drive space to allow an operating system to use the space. Each operating system such as Mac, DOS, and NT uses distinct file system formats. A drive must be formatted for the system to be able to use it.

HPFS—The abbreviation for High Performance File System provided by OS/2 operating systems. Files in this format can be read by NT.

13

logical partition—A subpartition of an extended partition on a drive. See *extended partition.*

mirroring—A method of ensuring data replication using two hard drives that are connected to the same disk controller. This method is less robust than duplexing because of the shared controller. Otherwise, duplexing and mirroring can be considered to be essentially the same thing.

NTFS—An NT file system abbreviation for New Technology File System. The particular way data is stored on an NT system if chosen over the FAT or HPFS file systems.

partition—A part of a hard drive that functions as though it were a separate unit.

physical drive—The actual hardware that is set in the computer and used to store information. Often called the hard drive, C: drive, or D: drive after the letter assigned to it by the system.

volume set—A collection of partitions possibly spread over several disk drives that has been formatted for use as if it were a single drive.

Task List

The information provided in this chapter shows you how to manage the files and folders within an NT server. You learned to do the following:

- ☐ Use Disk Administrator to view drives and create partitions
- ☐ Format a new drive to enable the operating system to use the drive
- ☐ Create a volume set
- ☐ Use Explorer to create new folders

Q&A

Q Is the NTFS file system really superior to FAT-based file systems?

A Yes. The NTFS system allows faster data access than FAT-based systems. It also provides greater data recovery options and does not waste as much space when creating files and folders. It also allows for long filenames and enables you to use file-level security controls.

Q Can I run NT Server with only a FAT-based file system?

A Yes, although it isn't recommended because you do not gain any of the advantages that NTFS offers, in particular file-level security. On some occasions, however, such as a recalcitrant mission-critical application, you are forced to use the FAT-based system.

13

Q I cannot find File Manager in my NT system. What happened to it?

A You do not use File Manager in NT Server. It is replaced with Windows NT Explorer. Although each of these tools works differently, the new Explorer offers more functionality and timesaving techniques, such as right-clicking to bring up menus. Using one technique, you can quickly copy a file to the floppy drive by right-clicking while selecting the file to be copied.

13

Chapter 14

Managing Windows NT Server File and Directory Access Rights

In this morning's session, you learned about the file systems NT uses, and you learned about using Disk Administrator and other NT tools. You also learned all about different types of file mechanisms to provide for duplicate copies of your important data and how to use the new Explorer program rather than the old File Manager program.

In this afternoon's session, you'll learn all about setting access controls over files and directories to control who can access what within NT.

As you recall from this morning, NT Server 4.0 allows use of FAT, HPFS, and NTFS file systems. You get security with the NTFS file system, but not with the other two systems. Security is one really sound reason to use NTFS, unless some extenuating circumstances make this impossible. For example, one of our clients runs a mission-critical application that relies on a FAT-based file system. It's a legacy system the client has not had time to convert, so this restricts the client's use of NTFS on the NT Server network.

 NOTE

> We mentioned that NT Server 4.0 supports three files systems: FAT, HPFS, and its own file system, NTFS. You need to be aware that in version 4.0 of NT Server, native support for the HPFS file system was dropped. If you are upgrading from NT 3.51 to 4.0, support continues to be available with the 3.51 drivers.

To control access to files in NT, you use the concept of either *shares* or *file and directory permissions.* You can use both concepts, although this method can be a little confusing. They are actually three separate levels of control. Share-level permissions provide network-level access control over directories. Directory-level controls using NTFS provide a different type of control, and file-level controls are the most granular level of the three types of control. To help separate fact from fiction, we'll start with the controls available to FAT file systems and move on to NTFS controls.

NT Server Share-Level Control Using FAT-Based Files

Let's review the earlier comments about FAT system file security. You read that file and directory permissions are available only with NTFS. Does this mean that there is no control over who accesses files on a FAT-based server? Not at all. It merely means that the level of control available to you is minimal and not nearly as extensive as the control available to NTFS users.

One of the missions of NT is to secure desktop files as effectively as the server files. You can set up NT Workstation to allow multiple people to sign on and use the desktop machine (at different times, of course) but not allow access to any data belonging to one of the other authorized users. But this setup is for NTFS file systems. What do we do for FAT-based controls?

Access to files on a server typically happens only when those directories are *shared.* This designation tells the server that users from the network might need to use or manipulate the shared directories. Note that we say *directories* and not *files.* This is because the user wants to access a specific file, but sharing is performed only at a directory level. When a directory is shared, users have access to all the files in that directory.

14

By default, only those user accounts in the Administrator and Server Operators group can set up shares in NT Server. You can set up sharing in NT Server 4.0 in various ways:

- [ ] With the Administrative Wizard
- [ ] Through the My Computer icon
- [ ] By using Microsoft Explorer
- [ ] By using the command prompt

The easiest method, when you're starting, is to use the Administrative Wizard. This tool provides step-by-step instructions and is fairly easy to follow. It does not provide a great degree of detail, though, and after a while you will use one of the other tools. The command prompt provides access for the "command-line weenies," the old DOS and UNIX types who just love that command line and typically eschew GUI interfaces as a matter of principle. Finally, the more common method is to use Explorer or My Computer.

Using Administrative Wizard to Set Up Shares

If you are new to NT- and Windows-based computing, Microsoft offers Administrative Wizard to guide you through the process of administering NT. It's a good tool for the beginner, but you'll quickly tire of it as you become more knowledgeable.

To set up a share in a FAT-based folder in NT Server 4.0, sign onto your server with an Administrator or Server Operator account, and use Start|Programs|Administrative Tools (Common)|Administrative Wizards. This selection brings up a dialog box offering a multitude of choices. You see an example in Figure 14.1.

Figure 14.1.

Using the Administrative Wizards.

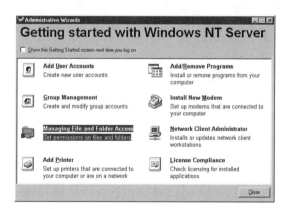

14

Choose the option called Managing File and Folder Access. Although it states that it sets permissions and you know that you are creating shares, this choice still works. The wizard shows a Welcome screen and asks where you want to place the share. Select the On My Computer option to set up a share on your present server.

Select the Next option, and the wizard brings up a screen showing the drives available for sharing. Select drive c:. (Select the drive that remains FAT-based, whichever drive letter it has on your machine.) The NT Wizard shows a list of files and folders. You must select a folder or the wizard will issue a message stating that sharing is not possible for files. Choose a TEMP folder or other innocuous folder, and click the Next button.

Because this is a FAT-based system, the NT Wizard tells you that you can use only sharing on this folder, not permissions. You see an example of this message in Figure 14.2.

Figure 14.2.
*An Administrative
Wizard FAT file system
warning.*

Click the Yes button to continue the sharing setup. You will see a window providing various options, as shown in Figure 14.3. Type a name in the first available field, where you see a duplicate of the directory name. This is the name users will need to use to find your shared directory, so it should be something meaningful. Share names can be 12 characters long, but you might want to use only 8 characters if you have DOS clients accessing the share.

Figure 14.3.
Adding the share name.

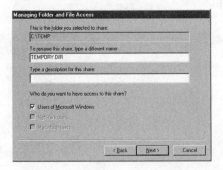

You also have a chance in the next field to add a comment that helps describe the content of this share. When a user browses the server for shares, this comment field shows up as well, offering a chance to make sure that users know more precisely what the directory contains. When you are ready, click the Next button to continue.

14

Now a window appears that shows the current permissions and offers you the chance to modify the default permissions or keep them. Note that the screen offers only three options if you choose the Change Permissions option. You might not find the level of sharing you want. You see an example in Figure 14.4.

Figure 14.4.

Showing the current permissions.

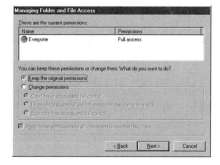

Click the Next button to continue after making any changes you want to make. The Administrative Wizard shows a dialog box that confirms your selection and lets you click the Finish button if you are done. If you think you made a mistake, you can use the Back key to take you back a step in the process to make further changes. This way, you can re-choose one of the available options and change your users' access to full, read, or no access to a share. An example of the final dialog box is shown in Figure 14.5.

Figure 14.5.

Completing the Administrative Wizard.

When you click the Finish button, you get a confirmation from the Wizard indicating that the process completed successfully and asking whether you want to set up more shares. Click the No button to complete the sharing exercise. Clicking the Yes button restarts the Wizard and allows you to set up additional shares.

14

NOTE

> You can remove a share easily by using Explorer. Select the folder you just completed granting access to, and right-click on it. NT provides a drop-down menu with an option called Sharing. Select this option. In the window that opens, click the Permission button for NT to bring up the current share options. Note that you can change the access level by selecting an appropriate level in the lower-right corner of the window in the Type of Access field. You want to select the Remove option here, however, to remove the access. Clicking the OK button finishes the task.

These share rights are applicable only to users who log on from the network. Local signons to the server are not managed through shares, and in a FAT-based system, these users get access regardless of share settings.

Task 14.1. Using Explorer to set up shares.

Step 1: Description

This task enables you to set up share permissions using Microsoft Explorer. Because you often use Explorer to manage the files within NT Server, this is the fastest way to set up shares.

Step 2: Action

1. Log onto your system using an Administrator account.
2. Go to Start|Programs|Windows NT Explorer.
3. Select the folder you want to share, and then right-click on the folder to see the drop-down menu.
4. Select the Sharing option. NT Server shows you the Properties window with Sharing options. The window defaults to Not Shared.
5. Click the Shared as button and fill in the details as needed to set up a share. For example, type the new share name you want users to see, and type a description of the files in the share. Set up the maximum users as needed.
6. Click the Permissions button. You then see the Permissions dialog box. Add and remove access as needed by using the Add and Remove buttons. These allow you to select users and the type of access you want them to have. Double-click on the groups you want, and select the type of access. Click OK. Return to this screen a few times as needed to add any number of groups and access levels. Click OK on the Access Through Share Permissions window when you are finished.
7. Click OK to complete the sharing task.

14

Step 3: Review

By using Explorer to set up shares, you managed the task quickly, easily, and without the need to bring up a special program. You can set up shares for any directory by using this technique.

Hidden Shares

NT allows you to set up shares and hide them so that casual browsers cannot find them. You do this by adding a $ character to the end of the share name. These shares then are not displayed. The reasoning behind this facility is to allow administrators to hide certain shares to minimize the clutter when users browse the server.

Some people on the Internet NTSEC newsgroup appear to think this is a security solution— that you hide sensitive shares (and user accounts) so that attackers cannot find them. There are two problems with this approach:

- ☐ The shares are easily seen through the Net program.
- ☐ You can still access the shares if you know their name.

It is still a good idea to use the capability to hide shares to avoid clutter, but do not depend on this for security through obscurity. It's a false sense of security.

Microsoft uses the hidden share concept for some shares during the installation process. Automatic shares in NT Server include these:

- ☐ ADMIN$. The directory that contains the NT programs.
- ☐ NETLOGON$. Microsoft's Administrative Shares or logon script shares that are hidden on domain controllers.
- ☐ C$ D$. All hard drive partitions and CD-ROM drives are automatically shared at the root.

Microsoft allows only administrators access to these shares; if you remove or modify them, NT automatically rebuilds them the next time you load the system.

Figure 14.6 shows an example of the NET SHARE command.

How Sharing Works with File and Directory Permissions

In the preceding section, we discussed shares and how you use them and hide them. We also, however, need to understand how these shares interact with file and directory permissions.

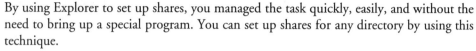

Figure 14.6.

Showing hidden shares using NET SHARE.

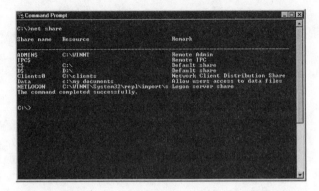

You'll learn all about the file and directory permissions later this afternoon, but for now you need to understand how the two types of controls interact. By default, sharing sets up the Everyone group for Full Control over the selected directory. Does this mean that you obtain this access when using an NTFS partition?

Maybe. Good answer, isn't it? It's just like a consultant to never be specific. Seriously, however, the answer lies in which set of controls overrides the other. These are the base rules:

☐ Sharing never allows more than file and directory permissions.

☐ Sharing can reduce the level of access provided by file and directory permissions.

Remember that shares apply only to user accounts signing on over the network. So they are somewhat limited. If you allow the default share access on a directory (Full Control) and set file and directory permissions that are less restrictive (Read only), the user has read access and can do no more. If you attempt to reduce a user's access by setting up a share with Read only access and then try to provide a new user with full control through file and directory permissions, the user has only read access.

WARNING

> Share restrictions apply even to members of the Administrator group. If you restrict access to a directory to Read only, you will not be able to add or remove any files, even if you are an administrator.

Finally, NT domain controllers create the NETLOGON share with the default access. You should change this share to remove the Everyone group and apply share permissions to Domain Users with Read only access. Next, implement NTFS file restrictions to each user's logon script so that users can see only their own scripts.

14

Setting Up Shares Remotely

The previously described technique works fine when you are attached to the domain that has the folders you want to share. But what if you are in California and the domain you want to set up a share on is in Florida? When you are not physically attached, you cannot use Explorer or My Computer to set up shares.

In this case, you need to use Server Manager. This program allows you to set up shares in the same manner as with Explorer. To use Server Manager, you need to be sitting at the server, or you need to load Server Manager on your NT or Windows 95 Workstation first. The program is found in the CLIENT/SRVTOOLS directory of your NT installation CD-ROM. You can also get a copy from the NT Resource kit.

Task 14.2. Using Server Manager to set up sharing.

Step 1: Description

This task allows you to set up shares remotely. It is handy for administrators who manage large networks that cross buildings, cities, or states. Explorer and My Computer are available only for local access, so Server Manager is necessary if you do not want to manually visit each place where you have domains running. Of course, don't tell the boss that you can manage the domains remotely when one of your sites is Hawaii! It would be a shame to miss out on a trip.

Step 2: Action

1. Log onto your system using an Administrator account. Remember that you need server tools already set up if you are logging in from a machine that is not the server.

2. Go to Start|Programs|Administrative Tools (Common)|Server Manager.

3. Select the server you want to set up shares on by left-clicking once (only once, to select the server but not open it). You might see other machines that are grayed out. These are merely machines that Server Manager has seen before but that are currently inactive.

4. Right-click on the selected server and select the Computer|Shared Directories menu. The dialog box shows all the current shares on the machine.

5. Click on New Share to bring up the familiar sharing dialog box. Choose a share name, enter the path using the full path address (such as D:\Junk), add a comment if appropriate, and set the number of users in the Limit Users box. After you fill in the share information, the Permissions button is enabled, letting you set up the specific permissions you want.

6. Complete the task in the manner you need, and then click OK to finish.

Step 3: Review

By using Server Manager, you saw how easy it is to manage domains across the street or across the country. Use this program whenever you are unable to use the Explorer program.

File and Directory Permissions

If you are not running a server with an NTFS partition, this section is of little use to you. Feel free to skip the rest and return to it later, after you have set up an NTFS partition.

One of the main strengths of the new file system is its capability to provide access-level restrictions down to the file level. What does this mean? Will we set up all our users to have individual file-level access so that they are tightly controlled and the security and audit folks are happy?

Not really. Although it is good to have this level of control, it's important to remember that you need to administer access daily, and therefore restrictive levels of control can cause a lot of work. So how do you mitigate this seeming difference? You learned all about setting up a good security program a couple of days ago, in Chapter 10, "Understanding Security." Here, we need to reiterate the use of job-function or group-level control.

Job-function control suggests that you decide the needs of a particular group of users and then set up file and directory access for them by using the group function of NT Server. In this manner, when you add a user to the specific group, the user automatically obtains all the file access that is appropriate for that user's job.

File- and directory-level access control applies to both NT Server and NT Workstation, providing a level of control over data previously unavailable.

> **NOTE**
>
> This has been said before, but it's important enough to reiterate: File- and directory-level controls are available only on NTFS partitions.

NT is not offering encryption when it uses file and directory permissions. If someone steals your hard drive and places it in another NT machine, that person will eventually gain access to the files stored in it. NT will not allow you to read another machine's hard drive in this manner as a default, but many other ways exist to get the data off a stolen hard drive.

NTFS is not a panacea for lack of physical control over your server. Also, a shareware tool called NTFSDOS will read the hard drive from a floppy, leaving data vulnerable even though it is formatted in the NTFS style. Keep your machine safely locked away in a server room, and limit access.

14

File Ownership

Adding to the complexity of setting permissions and using shares to control access, NT also assigns ownership of a file to the account that creates the file. By default, ownership is granted to the creator of the file, and it cannot be given away. It can be taken away, however, and there is a distinction between the two terms.

Why do we care so much about file ownership? Because the act of creating a file provides the creator with the ability to do anything to the file, even delete it. The creator has Full Control. In an NTFS system, Full Control means the ability to read, modify, and delete the file, as well as change the access to grant someone else Full Control rights. If this file is a production, mission-critical file, ensuring that these rights are properly handled is crucial. You don't want the owner assigning an unauthorized person access to the file.

What the owner cannot do (or anyone else, for that matter, even the administrator) is *give* ownership of the file away to someone. All the owner can do is allow another person Full Control and let him take ownership using the permissions he has been granted. This process can quickly reduce the level of control within an NT environment.

Let's recap. If you create a new file, you own it and gain Full Control access to the file. If you copy a file, you become the owner of the copy with the same rights. As the file owner, you can remove everyone's ability to access the file, even administrators. Needless to say, it would be pretty easy to create havoc if you are the owner of critical files. Ensuring that files are appropriately owned and managed is one of the keys to effective security with NT Server 4.0.

How do you bypass someone trying to cause difficulty in this manner? The administrator can grant someone Full Control access to the file, and then that person can take ownership.

Task 14.3. Taking ownership of a file.

Step 1: Description

In this task, you learn how to take ownership of a file. Note that the current owner or an administrator must grant you Full Control access in order for you to take ownership. You might do this when a file is created for testing purposes and when validated becomes a production file. Ownership will be changed to reflect that status.

Step 2: Action

1. Log onto your system using an Administrator account.
2. Go to Start|Programs|Windows NT Explorer. Open the directory the file resides in.
3. Select the file you want to reassign by left-clicking once on the filename.
4. Using the right mouse key, click on the file to see the drop-down menu.
5. Select Properties.

6. Select the Security frame to see three options:
   - ☐ Permissions
   - ☐ Auditing
   - ☐ Ownership

7. Select Permissions. Grant the user account that needs ownership Full Control over the file by using the Add button. Click OK when finished.

8. Log off and log on with the user account that needs to take over the file ownership.

9. Open Explorer and find the file. Select it; then left-click and select Properties. Select Security. Note that this tab shows only if you are accessing a file on an NTFS partition.

10. Select the Ownership option near the bottom of the screen.

11. You see a small dialog box offering the next option, Take Ownership. Click the button called Take Ownership. Click OK to finish the task.

12. Log off. This user account now owns the file.

Step 3: Review

By using a simple process, you can take control and change ownership of a file. Use this process any time ownership of a file is in question or needs to be changed.

Having ownership of a file does not mean that you have access to the data within the file. Ownership implies the ability to change the permissions on the file, not to access it. Of course, as owner, you can set up permissions so that you do have access, but the reverse is also true—you can set up permissions that deny your account access.

Permissions

You set file permissions by selecting a file using Microsoft Explorer and then selecting Properties|Security|Permissions. You see a dialog similar to the one shown in Figure 14.7.

What are the permissions you can use within an NTFS partition? The following table sets out the various types of security that are available on each file or directory. Note that when you set permissions on a directory, you are asked whether those permissions should also apply to the files within the directory. We'll talk more about this topic later. You can select multiple files when setting permissions and multiple groups and user accounts. The permissions you select are then applied to the collection of groups, users, and files. Table 14.1 shows the types of permissions available for use within NT Server 4.0.

Table 14.1. NT directory permissions.

Description of Action & Type of Access	No Access	Execute	Read	Write	Delete	List	Change	Change Permissions	Add	Add & Read	Full Control
Display attributes	x	A	A			A			A	A	A
Display files within	x		A			A				A	A
Display owner and permissions	x	A	A			A			A	A	A
Go to subdirectories	x	A	A			A			A	A	A
Change attributes	x		x	A					A	A	A
Create subdirectories	x		x	A		x			A	A	A
Add files	x		x	A		x			A	A	A
Change permissions	x		x			x		A			A
Take ownership	x		x			x					A
Delete the directory	x		x		A	x					A

Note: Actions indicated apply to regular permissions, not special, where both are available.

A = Allowed

x = Disallowed

blank = Not applicable

14

Figure 14.7.

The File Permissions dialog box.

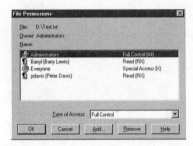

One last thing. For POSIX compliance, there is a hidden permission called DELETE_CHILD that allows someone with Full Control of a directory to also delete any file in the directory, regardless of file settings. This often confuses new administrators who think they have secured file deletion from those with directory access. This permission gets added only with Full Control and can be eliminated by applying RWXDPO directory permissions instead.

During your foray into NT Server 4.0, you'll come across some abbreviations. The following list shows you the current abbreviations in use for each of the permissions used within NT:

> *No Access*
> > Execute (X)
>
> *Read (R)*
> > Write (W)
> > Delete (D)
>
> *Change (RWXD)*
> > Change Permissions (P)
> > Take Ownership (O)
>
> *Full Control (All)*
> > * These are found in the drop-down list within the File Permissions dialog box; the rest are found after the Special Access option at the end of the list has been selected.

You can select and use each of these permissions on your files as needed for excellent security and control. There are some things you should remember when granting access using these permissions. When you grant a user Read access from the primary list, the user automatically obtains Execute access. You need to use Special Access - Read if you don't want the user to be able to execute a program that might be contained in the folder you are granting this access to. Additionally, you can allow a user to run a program but not see what is in it by granting the user Execute only to the program. Be sure to test the access first to ensure that the program will run normally with only this permission set, because some programs require additional permissions.

Read access allows you to see the files displayed in the directory, display the directory's attributes, and display the directory's owner and permissions. Write allows you to add files and subdirectories, as well as change the attributes and display them.

In Table 14.2, you see how each permission applies to some typical actions against files.

You must consider a few additional items when dealing with directories in NT 4.0. You select and update permissions just as you do for files, except that instead of selecting the file and its properties, you select a directory (folder) and its properties. The properties window looks something like the one shown in Figure 14.8.

Figure 14.8.

The Directory Permissions window.

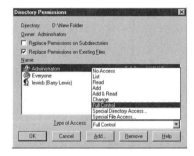

Note that a couple of things have changed. Two additional dialog options are shown at the top of the main window. These options allow you to replace permissions on subdirectories and on files. To make the selected permissions apply to all the subdirectories within your main directory, you must click on the Replace Permissions on Subdirectories box; otherwise, changes affect only the currently selected directory. To replace permissions on the files in the directory, choose the default setting, Replace Permissions on Existing Files.

In addition to the normal permissions, directory permissions include two Special access fields rather than one. The main differences between the types of access offered for files and those offered for directories include the following ones:

- ☐ Special Directory Access
- ☐ Special File Access
- ☐ List
- ☐ Add
- ☐ Add & Read

These combined options allow you to control access to the directory, such as being able to list the directory or add new entries to it. Let's review some of the actions that the additional permissions allow.

14

Table 14.2. Actions of permissions against files.

Description of Action & Type of Access	No Access	Execute	Read	Write	Delete	List	Change	Change Permissions	Add	Add & Read	Full Control
						DIR Permission's Action on Files[1]					
Display file's data	x	A	A			A	A		x	A	A
Display file's attributes	x	A	A			A	A		x	A	A
Display file's owner and permissions	x	A	A			A	A		x	A	A
Run files that are programs	x	A	A			A	A		x	A	A
Change and add data to files	x			A		A	A		x	x	A
Change file attributes	x			A		A	A		x	x	A
Change file permissions	x					x	A	A	x	x	A
Take ownership	x					x	x	x	x	x	A
Delete the file	x				A	A	A	x	x	x	A
Files											
Display file's data	x	x	A	x	x	A	A		x	A	A
Display file's attributes	x	A	A	x	x	A	A		x	A	A
Display file's owner and permissions	x	A	A	A	x	A	A		x	A	A
Run files that are programs	x	A	A	x	x	A	A		x	A	A
Change and add data to files	x	x	x	A	x	A	A		x	A	A
Change file attributes	x	x	x	A	x	A	A		x	A	A
Change permissions	x	x	x	x	x	x	x	A	x	x	A

14

Description of Action & Type of Access	No Access	Execute	Read	Write	Delete	List	Change	Change Permissions	Add	Add & Read	Full Control
Files											
Take ownership	x	x	x	x	x		x				A
Delete the file	x	x	x	A	A		A				A

Note: Actions indicated apply to regular permissions, not special, where both are available.

[1] A permission applied to a directory allows certain actions against the files in that directory.

A = Allowed

x = Disallowed

blank = Not applicable

14

The two Special Access options allow you to set up a custom set of permissions for each of these items. You can set permissions by using the Special Directory Access option and have those permissions apply to all directories, all files in certain directories, or selected files in selected directories. The option window stays the same. What the permissions apply to is a result of which directories you selected before opening the Properties window.

The Special Files Access window allows you to set permissions for files within the selected directories. The option provides another detailed level of control over the files in the selected directories.

The List option allows just that. You can list the directory, any subdirectories, and the files within the directory, but you cannot view files or run any programs.

The Add option permits you to add files to a directory, view the permissions, and change the directory attributes. You also can create new subdirectories. You are not allowed to see any of the files that reside within the directories, however. The Add & Read permission allows you to perform the previous tasks as well as list the files within the selected directories.

As you see, NT offers a wealth of options, and you can quickly get into trouble if you randomly assign permissions without using some forethought. With NT file and directory security, you can gain a level of fine detail in security and control that was previously unavailable. Now you can create the environment that best suits your organization's needs for integrity and control.

NT file and directory security works on the principle of no permission, no access. In other words, it is not necessary to set permissions to deny access for user accounts, because NT treats any access that is not defined as equivalent to No Access.

You do need to look at default permissions, however, when organizing the security of your machine. The Everyone group is especially important because it offers the opportunity for ease of use yet lends itself to becoming a security risk. For example, when creating a new partition and formatting it for NTFS, NT 4.0 puts a default permission of Everyone–Full Control for file access. This might not be appropriate, and you should change the default to something more appropriate for your needs. You might decide to do this and modify the permissions for directories as they are created; but on the other hand, you might be setting up a drive for production use, and letting everyone have access is not necessary.

Some administrators put the general access that they believe all users should get into the Everyone group. This makes life easy yet becomes a problem when inappropriately used because it becomes cluttered with access permissions. Over time, these permissions tend to become inappropriate as access needs change. Set up a well-defined architecture that spells out what and where access should be applied, and put a reporting and auditing mechanism in place to verify that architecture. We'll talk more about auditing on the morning of Day 12.

14

Task 14.4. Assigning file permissions.

Step 1: Description

In this task, you'll see how to restrict access to a file. You can use this task to manage file-level control within your organization by changing the necessary parameters of user account, permissions, and files as needed.

Step 2: Action

1. Log onto your system using an Administrator account.
2. Go to Start|Programs|Windows NT Explorer. Open the directory containing the files.
3. Select the file or files you want to reassign by left-clicking once on the filename. If you hold the Shift key while dragging the cursor over a list of files, you can select a group of files.
4. Using the right mouse key, click on the file(s) to see the drop-down menu.
5. Select Properties.
6. Select the security frame.
7. Select Permissions. If some groups are already showing (the Everyone group is likely), select those groups and click the Remove button. This action clears all unneeded users from the list. Be careful not to leave the list blank or no one will have access. Click the Add button to add new groups or user accounts for which you want to provide access from the list provided, and double-click to select them. Set the desired access at the bottom of the screen, and when you're ready, click OK.
8. Click OK on the File Permissions window to complete the task.

Step 3: Review

By using Explorer, you set up permissions over files as you need them. You'll use this task often in administering user access to files. You can change the access as needed, as long as you are an administrator.

Task 14.5. Assigning file and directory permissions as a user.

Step 1: Description

It is not necessary to be an administrator to set up file permissions. Of course, you must have Full Control over any file you want to change. In this task, you will see how to determine whether you have the necessary access and then perform the changes. You can use this task to give others access to your files within your organization by changing the necessary parameters of user account, permissions, and files as needed.

Step 2: Action

1. Log onto your system using your user account.

2. Go to Start|Programs|Windows NT Explorer. Open the directory containing the file(s) you want to provide access to.

3. Select the file or files you want to reassign by left-clicking once on the filename. If you hold the Shift key while dragging the cursor over a list of files, you can select a group of files.

4. Using the right mouse key, click on the file(s) to see the drop-down menu.

5. Select Properties.

6. Select the security frame.

7. Select Permissions. Verify that you are allowed access by clicking the Permissions. NT shows an error message indicating that access is denied or that you have permission only to view security information if you do not have Full Control, Ownership, or the special permission called Change Ownership.

8. After you get to the permissions window, if groups are already showing that you want to remove, select those groups and click the Remove button. This action clears all unneeded users from the list. Be careful not to leave the list blank or no one will have access. Click the Add button to add new groups or user accounts for which you want to provide access from the list provided, and double-click to select them. Set the desired access at the bottom of the screen, and when you're ready, click OK.

9. Click OK on the File Permissions window to complete the task.

Step 3: Review

Even user accounts can change file and directory permissions if they are authorized to do so. By using Explorer, you allow or refuse access to files as you desire. You'll use this task often in administering user access to files. You can change the access as needed, as long as you are authorized.

Task 14.6. Using the command line to process permissions.

Step 1: Description

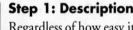

Regardless of how easy it is to use the supplied GUI interfaces, we always run across people who are adamant about using the command line. Sometimes there is good reason, such as wanting to run a bunch of changes at the same time. GUI interfaces are typically ill-equipped to handle multiple requests. Are you listening, Microsoft? So you need to be able to set up batch jobs using command-line operatives. In this task, you'll learn how to restrict access to files by using the command-line interface.

Step 2: Action

1. Log onto your system using an Administrator account.

2. Go to Start|Programs|Command Prompt. Relax—this is as GUI as it gets.

3. Now you need to understand the command syntax for adding and removing permissions. Select the file or files you want to assign, and remember the names, because you'll need them later.

4. The command you use is called CACLS. You can get assistance by typing the command at the prompt and pressing Enter. NT lists the syntax of the command for you. A picture of the command is shown in Figure 14.9.

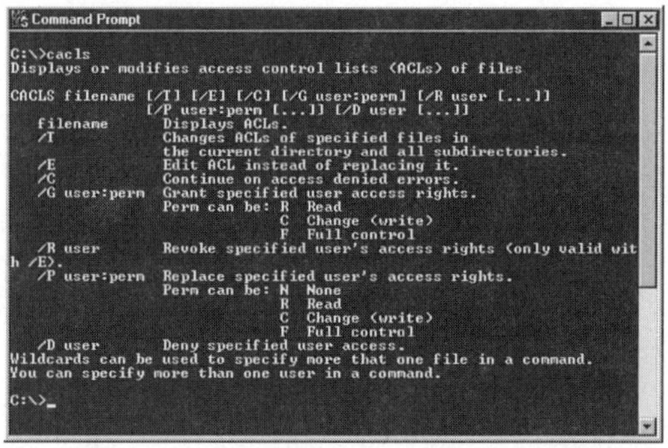

Figure 14.9.

The Help file for the CACLS *command.*

5. Type CACLS and press Enter.

6. Select the file you want to change. Our example uses a file called test.txt.

    We'll add the user called Barry and grant the user Read access in this example.

7. Type the following command to add the Read permission for file test.txt to user Barry and retain the existing permissions:

    ```
    cacls d:\test.txt /e /g barry:r
    ```

    The /e ensures that existing commands are left in the permissions group. If you exclude that, the new command completely replaces existing permissions.

8. Type exit to close the command-prompt window.

Step 3: Review

By using the command line, you can set up multiple access and manage large permission changes more readily. This method is also faster than the GUI interface after you get to know the commands really well. Still, it's just not NT 4.0 to continue using this rather arcane method over the glory of Windows.

14

Let's explain a few of the options you can use with the CACLS command. You can specify the filename only to get a list of current permissions. You see an example in Figure 14.10.

Figure 14.10.

Viewing file permissions from the command line.

The /T option applies the change you are performing to all the files and subdirectories below the directory specified.

Using the /E option is your most common default because it tells NT to add the change you are making to the set of existing permissions. Without this, your changes become the *only* permissions in the ACL. Any other permissions that might have been present are removed.

If you are processing a lot of changes in a batch job, use the /C option because it allows the processing to continue if an error is encountered. This way, most of your changes are completed and you need only fix the one or two that might fail. Without the option, your processing stops at the error.

/G *user:perm* grants users specific permissions. You use this to add rights to your user accounts or groups. The syntax consists of *user*, which is the user account you want to change, and *perm*, which is the rights you want to assign the user. Remember to add the /E to add these changes rather than make them the only ones that apply.

/R *user* revokes a user's permissions and works only in conjunction with the /E option. For example, to revoke the rights of user Barry, type the following command:

```
cacls d:\test.txt /E /R barry
```

The command replies with a rather cryptic message: processed file: d:\Test.txt. What it is saying is that it removed the rights from Barry to the file.

/P *user:perm* also adds permissions for a user. You use this to add rights to your user accounts or groups. The syntax consists of *user*, which is the user account you want to change, and *perm*, which is the rights you want to assign the user. Remember to add the /E option to add these changes rather than make them the only ones that apply. The difference between this and the /G option is that this option only modifies permissions of existing users in the ACL, whereas /G adds a new user to the list.

The /D option denies a user access. There you have it—a complete list of the CACLS command for you to use in batch jobs or if you really, truly love carrying out command-line commands at a DOS prompt.

Moving and Copying Files

In Windows NT, when you copy a file, the security permissions for the file get inherited from the destination directory. This means that security over the file might change. As an administrator or security officer, you need to be aware and manage these copies to ensure that a file with a high level of security isn't copied to a directory that has a lower level of security.

When a file is moved, however, it keeps the specific file permissions and does not get any others, regardless of where it is placed within an NT environment.

After any file copy operation, verify that the level of control remains and is not changed.

Microsoft does provide a way for you to copy files and preserve their access permissions. Of course, it costs. Included in the NT Resource Kit is a program called SCOPY that copies files and retains their permissions after the copy. Naturally, it's available only for NTFS drives because those are the only drives that permissions apply to anyway. Unfortunately, this utility requires the user to have Backup and Restore rights on the machines in use. This might be fine for administrators, but for obvious reasons it does not allow the user community in general to use it. The Backup and Restore rights are powerful and can be used to circumvent your security if used improperly.

Summary

In this chapter, you learned some of the fundamental exercises that are performed in administering files and directories with an NTFS-based NT machine. You learned how to set up and manage shares for those volumes that are FAT or HPFS based and then learned both GUI and command-line options for maintaining security over your files and directories. When you combine this knowledge with the information you'll learn on Days 5, 6, 12, and 13, you should become quite proficient in managing security within NT Server 4.0.

In this chapter, you discovered a lot about using FAT-based and NTFS-based servers. You learned the following points:

☐ File- and directory-level security is possible only on NTFS file-based systems.

☐ This version of NT does not include HPFS support. It's available only if you've upgraded from version 3.51.

14

☐ File and directory control extends to NT Workstations, providing a high degree of security over an NT-based client/server solution.

☐ You can perform file and directory security via four methods: My Computer, Explorer, Administrative Wizard, and the DOS command line.

☐ Share names can be 12 characters long, but you might want to use only 8 characters if you have DOS clients.

☐ You can hide shares and user accounts by appending a $ to the end of the name. Because there are simple ways to find these, however, this should not be used as a security tool.

☐ NT offers an extensive list of file access options, allowing you to provide a degree of control that was previously unavailable.

Workshop

To wrap up the day, you can review terms and tasks from the chapter, and see the answers to some commonly asked questions.

Terminology Review

ACE—The acronym for Access Control Entry. This contains a SID and the associated set of access control permissions for each object.

ACL—The acronym for Access Control List. This is the place where object permissions are kept. ACLs consist of access control entries.

batch program—An unformatted text file that contains NT commands for processing. A batch program typically ends with the extension of BAT or CMD, and when it is run by typing the filename at a command prompt, it executes the commands within it.

CACLS—A command-line program that allows you to modify user permissions by using the DOS command prompt or by placing them within a file and running that file. A handy utility to manage large numbers of changes.

permissions—The authorization to perform certain actions against a specific object. Does not apply to the system as a whole.

rights—The authorization to perform certain actions. Applies to the system as a whole.

14

Task List

The information provided in this chapter showed you how to manage the files and folders within an NT server. You learned to perform the following tasks:

- ☐ Use Explorer to set up sharing
- ☐ Use Server Manager to set up shares
- ☐ Take ownership of a file
- ☐ Assign file permissions
- ☐ Assign file and directory permissions as a user
- ☐ Use the command line for processing permissions

Q&A

Q Can shares be used with NTFS permissions?

A Yes. The NTFS system allows far more detailed levels of security than shares, however, and they apply no matter how you access the system. Sharing applies only to users who sign on remotely and applies to all users rather than individuals.

Q As a new administrator, is there an easy way for me to set up accounts and permissions without having to spend a lot of time learning?

A Yes, although we recommend that you take some courses to become truly proficient in managing your server. The Administrative Wizard guides a new user through the steps for adding new users and setting up permissions. It is designed to be very easy to follow, and you can use this wizard until you are comfortable with the other methods explained in this chapter.

Q I really do not like GUI-based processes, and I like to know exactly what is happening when I manage a server. Is there a command-line interface for setting up permissions?

A You do not have to use the GUI interface in NT. As this chapter explains, a command-line program called CACLS allows you to set up and remove permissions from users and groups. CACLS is also handy when you have a lot of changes to make and want to set them all up in a batch job instead of performing them one at a time.

14

DAY

8

Chapter 15

Managing the File Server

Yesterday, you learned about exploring and managing files and directories. Today, in this chapter, you'll learn to set up and control your NT Server as a file server, and in this afternoon's chapter, you'll learn to manage a print server. This chapter introduces some simple file server commands and utilities to enable you to provide effective use of the server and ensure that those in your user community can obtain the files they need.

You'll learn about setting the time and date across all your servers and how to start and stop the myriad of services that your server might run. Later in the chapter, you'll learn about one of the tools that provides you with desktop shortcuts and domain synchronization.

Let's begin by seeing how to start and stop services within NT.

Starting and Stopping NT Services

What is a service? Services are applications that can be selected to run automatically at startup or that can be run manually. Examples of services include the Alerter program, SQL Server, and Microsoft Exchange.

Finding out what services you have is easy in NT Server. You use Server Manager for this and other tasks. One of the duties you perform as an administrator is stopping and starting services. You'll learn how in this task.

Task 15.1. Starting and stopping services in NT.

Step 1: Description

In this task, you'll learn to start Server Manager and find out about the services that NT is running. You start and stop services using this window. Services are all those programs that make up your server, including Browser, Eventlog, Messenger, and Net Logon, as well as the server itself.

Step 2: Action

1. Begin by signing onto your server as Administrator.

2. Select Start|Programs|Administrative Tools (Common)|Server Manager. This selection starts the Server Manager program as shown in Figure 15.1.

Figure 15.1.

The Server Manager.

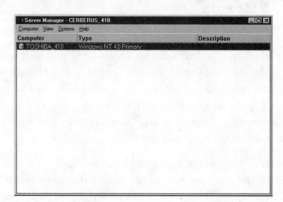

3. Select Computer|Services (or open it through the Control Panel). This starts the Services option in Server Manager and allows you to see which services are running and which are stopped. You see an example in Figure 15.2.

   By scrolling through the list of services, you see what is currently active and what is available but not started.

The viewing box provides three main sections: Service, which tells you the name of each available service; Status, which indicates whether the service is active, paused, or stopped; and Startup, which tells you whether the service starts automatically as part of NT's startup or whether it is a manual process that requires your intervention.

Figure 15.2.

*Viewing services
in NT.*

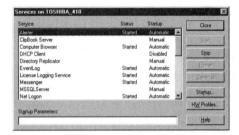

4. Select ClipBook Server using the mouse. You see that the Start button shows now, whereas before it was dim. (If this service is running, choose another service that is set to Manual.) Click the Start button to start the service. NT goes into some disk shuffling, and you then see that the Status is changed to Started. That's all there is to starting a service.

5. To stop the service, select the service using your mouse (continue using the same example) and click the Stop button. NT provides a warning message asking whether you are sure that you want to stop the service. You can see an example in Figure 15.3.

Figure 15.3.

*A service warning
message.*

6. Click the Yes button to continue. You see a dialog box indicating that NT is attempting to stop the service.

   After some processing, you see the Startup return to Manual, indicating that the service is stopped.

7. To pause a running service, select a service from the list and click the Pause button. NT shows you the warning message indicating that it is about to pause the service and asking whether that is what you want. Click the Yes button to continue. Now you see the word Paused in the Status box next to the service you paused.

   Note that the dialog does not provide a Stopped indicator. You know that a service is not running when you see a blank in the Status field.

8. To continue the service you paused, select it again and click the Continue button. After a brief delay, your service resumes.

9. By clicking the Startup button after selecting a service, you see a dialog box like that shown in Figure 15.4. This allows you to decide whether a service should automatically start when the server is booted or whether an administrator needs to take action.

Figure 15.4.

The startup options dialog box.

10. You can also decide what account a service should use to sign onto the system. Services typically sign on when they start using the System account. Only the Replicator Service and Schedule Service log on with other user accounts. You change this if you modify how or what privileges your service needs and have set up special accounts for it to use.

Some services interact with the desktop and provide a user interface. If the service you have selected does this, the Allow Service to Interact with Desktop option is set. Change this option as needed for your services. Generally, you do not modify the default settings because they work fine. Click Cancel to finish, or click the OK button if you made changes.

The hardware profiles button (HW Profiles) is used to modify the services that run at startup when you boot the system using specific hardware profiles. The System tool in the Control Panel creates hardware profiles. You enable or disable configurations using the buttons provided.

11. When finished, click the Close button to return to the Server Manager dialog box. Select Computer|Exit to finish.

Step 3: Review

Starting and stopping services is part of the administration of NT Server. You saw how easy it is to do, and you realized that it is equally easy to pause or stop a service for some reason and then forget to reset the service. You must take care to ensure that you do not impact your clients.

15

As you see, services are those programs NT uses to manage items such the Scheduler and the server itself. You start and stop these services as needed for performing maintenance, introducing new releases, and troubleshooting problems.

This tool allows you to start and stop services across the network, managing all the NT machines in your organization. You do this by selecting the computer you want to manage in the main Server Manager dialog box and then opening the Services menu. This allows for extensive flexibility and operability and lets you centralize this important task.

Adding Computers to Your Domain

As administrator, you will need to add and remove computers from your domain. Before any computer can be a domain member and participate in the domain security, it must be an NT machine and specifically added to the domain.

NT offers three ways to add machines to the domain. First, you add a machine during its installation, whether a workstation or server. To add a machine during installation, you must be an administrator of the domain.

Next, an administrator adds machines by using the Network tool in the workstation's Control Panel. Finally, you add machines by using Server Manager if you are an administrator or Account Operator. First you add the machine by specifying a computer account name in the domain database, and then you let the user add the computer using that name in her Network tool. With this method, a user machine might give away the user's domain name to another machine, creating a security exposure. Although this method allows you to manage machine names across the network, it also poses this potential exposure.

The computer name, as you'll remember from Chapter 3, "Installing Windows NT Server on the File Server," is a 15-character unique name that identifies a machine across the network. This begins the process of establishing a trusted relationship between machines in your network.

Task 15.2. Adding computers to your domain.

Step 1: Description
In this task, you'll learn to start Server Manager and add a new computer name.

Step 2: Action
1. Begin by signing onto your server as Administrator.
2. Select Start|Programs|Administrative Tools (Common)|Server Manager. This starts the Server Manager program.
3. Select Computer|Add to Domain. This starts a dialog box for specifying the computer. You see an example in Figure 15.5.

4. Two options are available. Add a workstation or server, or else add a Backup Domain Controller. You see there is no option for any other type of machine.

Figure 15.5.

Adding a computer dialog box.

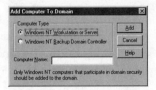

5. The initial selection is to add a workstation or server; this is obviously the most often used option. Type your new computer name in the Computer Name field. For our example, type the name TESTMACHINE. Click Add when you are ready.

6. NT adds the name to the domain database. Repeat step 5 as often as needed to add new computer names to your domain. Click the Close button to finish. Notice that NT adds a machine name even though the machine is not connected to your network. You see that the new machine has been added to this domain in Figure 15.6.

Figure 15.6.

A new machine has been added.

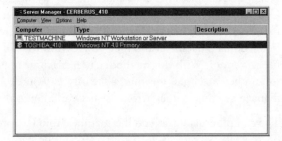

7. Close Server Manager by selecting Computer|Exit.

8. You need to add that computer name to the local machine. If you do not have another machine, skip the remaining parts of this task. If you have a test machine available, sign on and open the Control Panel, and then click Network.

9. Click the Change button. You see a dialog box called Identification Changes. Select the Computer name field and type TESTMACHINE. Be sure that the domain name remains appropriate. Next, click OK to make the change. You see an example in Figure 15.7.

10. When prompted by NT, reboot the machine. After you are reconnected, you'll find that the machine is part of the domain.

Step 3: Review

Adding computer names provides a degree of security because no one except a privileged domain user can add computers. This means that no NT computers can be added without your knowledge. As you saw, the process for adding a computer is not onerous.

Figure 15.7.

The Identification Changes dialog box.

Deleting a machine if you make a mistake or merely want to remove a machine is simple. Open Server Manager, select the machine name you are deleting, and press the Delete key. NT provides a warning message to ensure that you want to perform the delete operation, as shown in Figure 15.8.

Figure 15.8.

Removing a computer from the domain.

Click the Yes button to remove the computer. NT shows you a message indicating that the action was successful.

Using Server Manager allows you to create and manage the machines in your network without needing to provide sensitive privileges to users. As domain Administrator, you add the name that provides control over which names are used, and the user adds her machine by using that name in her Identification section.

When the computer is added to the domain, the Domain Admins group is added to the new computer's local Administrators group, allowing you to administer this machine either locally or remotely.

Adding a computer name creates a unique Security Identifier number (SID). If you accidentally delete an account as Administrator, that machine must rejoin the domain to access the new SID. You cannot just use Server Manager and re-create the computer name. Although this technique will appear to work, NT creates a new SID that does not match the one on the client workstation or server. The client must rejoin the network to establish the new identification.

Managing the Time and Date in NT Server

Setting the time and date used to be so easy. On your DOS machine or Windows client, you just enter the DATE command in a command prompt and set the new date and time. Presto, all done. It can still be done via the command prompt in NT Server.

Just like Windows 95, however, NT offers a GUI-based time and date dialog box. You find it by opening Control Panel and double-clicking the Date/Time icon. You can also select it by double-clicking the clock in the system tray on the task bar. NT shows you a dialog box.

You adjust the date by using the drop-down arrows and selecting the month and year you want the computer to use. You modify the time by selecting the up or down arrows and increasing or decreasing the time as needed.

In the Time Zone tab, NT allows you to set the machine for a particular time zone and choose to allow the time to automatically adjust for daylight savings.

Keeping the time accurate is a difficult task in any computer system, and it is no different for NT. How fast or slow your clock keeps time depends on your particular hardware, and after time, the battery managing the clock does wear down.

One method of managing to keep the time accurate is by using a third-party program that dials out and obtains the time from one of the many atomic clock timekeepers around the world. One such company, Somarsoft, offers a demo version of its product that you can obtain from the company's Web site. The program is called Somar ACTS.

Somar ACTS is a program for Windows NT and Windows 95 that allows you to set your computer clock with an accuracy of around one second, using either the National Institute of Standards and Technology (NIST) or United States Naval Observatory (USNO) time source. The program dials the service you choose, receives the current time, and uses it to set your computer's time. This shareware costs a minimal amount. You'll find the Web site at http://www.somar.com; look under the older products section. You can also find an extensive list of free and shareware time synchronization utilities at the following site:

http://www.enet.it/mirror/WWW/winsock/win95/time.htm

Setting and maintaining the time on a server is a thankless job, but accurate time minimizes problems. Using an automated program frees you from having to worry about this task.

15

Synchronizing the Domain Database

In your network, the master domain database that contains all your user account names and machine accounts resides physically on the PDC. The BDC servers are replicated at specific intervals or manually as you instruct NT. This method provides your network with redundancy and safety. If you lose the PDC, a BDC can be promoted and can take over, allowing minimal interruption to your clients as they use the file server and other servers in the domain.

Occasionally, a replication might fail due to network conditions or other problems, and you'll need to perform the task manually. The task that follows shows how to perform this synchronization.

Task 15.3. Synchronizing the domain database.

TASK

Step 1: Description

In this task, you'll learn to start Server Manager and manually perform a database synchronization.

Step 2: Action

1. Begin by signing onto your server as Administrator.

2. Select Start|Programs|Administrative Tools (Common)|Server Manager. This selection starts the Server Manager program.

3. Select the menu item Synchronize Entire Domain. NT provides a warning that this job might take some time to accomplish. You see an example in Figure 15.9.

Figure 15.9.

A database synchronization warning.

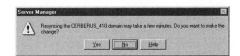

You are shown this warning because the process can impact your network, and therefore you should run it only when the network is not busy. On a small network, it is unlikely to cause major impact. Click the Yes button to continue.

4. NT replies with a message indicating that the PDC has asked all the BDCs to begin and telling you to verify the action using the Event Log. You see an example in Figure 15.10. Click OK to continue.

5. The synchronization might take a while as indicated. After it is complete, check the Event Log to be sure all went well. You'll learn how to use the Event Log in a few days, in Chapter 24, "Using the Windows NT Server Audit System."

If you need to update only one of the BDC servers, select that server after starting Server Manager, and then select the synchronize option.

Figure 15.10.

A Server Manager message during synchronization.

Step 3: Review

Synchronizing domains is necessary to ensure that you are provided with adequate backup in case the Primary Domain Controller should fail. This task showed you how to selectively update one or all of the other machines in the network and ensure that your users are not as impacted by server failure.

We talked about server failure in the preceding task, and this is an important aspect of server management. Ensuring that you are able to manage regardless of machine loss is the result of many things, including data backup, fault tolerance, and domain management.

You'll learn about implementing fault tolerance on Day 11, in Chapter 22, "Configuring Fault-Tolerant Computing Systems," and today you'll learn how to ensure that the Backup Domain Controller is able to manage if the PDC fails. You must keep in mind several considerations when promoting a BDC to take over in the event of a PDC failure.

You need to warn all users to disconnect temporarily so that they do not lose data, because promoting the BDC causes all connections to be lost. When you return the failed PDC to the domain, the prompted BDC remains and you have two PDC servers. NT does not allow this, so you must demote one of the PDC servers to a BDC before continuing.

One method of adding the failed PDC back to the domain is to first demote it and perform a synchronization to ensure that its database is properly refreshed and up-to-date. Do this before you demote the machine that served as a replacement to ensure that the changes you made during the troubleshooting and repair of the broken machine remain available.

Creating Desktop Shortcuts and Start Menu Updates

Modifying your desktop is essential to most people because everyone likes to set up their system using their own ideas of efficiency. In this section, you'll learn how to modify the Start menu using the RDISK utility as an example.

As you learned in Chapter 3, one of the tools available to the administrator for server maintenance is the Repair Disk utility. It creates and maintains your NT Server Emergency Repair Disk.

This utility needs to be run regularly as changes are made to your system. Losing the data in your SAM and Registry is a painful process, as you'll learn if you frequent the NTSEC newsgroup on the Internet. It's also entirely (well, almost) preventable by judicious use of RDISK as you learned earlier.

But running this utility might slip your mind if the icon doesn't appear on the menu to remind you. This quick little task shows you how to add the utility to your Start menu.

Task 15.4. Adding RDISK to the Start menu.

Step 1: Description

In this task, you'll learn to add a program to the Start menu. You can use this information to add any item to the menu.

Step 2: Action

1. Begin by signing onto your server.

2. Move the cursor to the Start menu and right-click once. You are presented with a small menu. Choose Open All Users and click once. NT opens a small window with one item in it called Programs.

3. Double-click the Programs icon to open it. NT opens a window containing various icons. You see an example in Figure 15.11.

Figure 15.11.

The Program folder from the All Users folder.

4. Double-click the Administrative Tools Icon to open it. You see another folder with icons.

5. If this looks familiar, that's because it is the pictorial view of your Start|Programs| Administrative Tools command. Select File|New. Choose Shortcut from the resulting menu list. Type RDISK in the command line that next appears, as shown in Figure 15.12. You will need to type the fully qualified path to the file, or click Browse to find it, if it is not in a directory that is part of the path environment variable.

6. Click the Next button to continue. The program asks you to select a name for the shortcut. Enter RDISK in the field provided, overriding the executable name provided.

Figure 15.12.

The Create Shortcut dialog box.

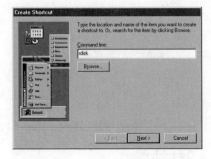

7. Click the Finish button to complete the task.
8. Close any windows that remain open. As you see in Figure 15.13, RDISK is now a part of your Administrative Tools menu.

Figure 15.13.

RDISK as part of Administrative Tools.

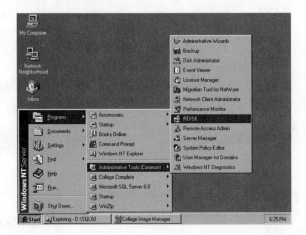

Now the utility is available to you whenever you use the Administrative Tools menu.

Step 3: Review

Adding an item to the menu gives you control over how your system looks and feels, and offers some degree of efficiency as you devise the setup with which you are most comfortable.

You can use this skill to add any program to your menu by changing the various aspects, such as program and location. You can place the same shortcut directly onto the desktop by selecting it in Explorer (RDISK is found in the \winnt\system32 directory) and just dragging it onto your desktop. NT automatically places an icon prefaced with "Shortcut to" on your desktop. To start the program at any time, you double-click on the new shortcut.

NOTE

> NT creates a shortcut during a drag and drop only for an EXE file. To create a shortcut for any other type of file during a drag and drop, hold down Ctrl+Shift during the operation.

Scheduling Jobs in NT Server

As an administrator of the server, you often need to run jobs at odd hours of the day or night. Coming in at 2 a.m. to run a job so that there is little user impact is not always enjoyable.

NT Server provides the AT command for scheduling jobs and automating this task. If you purchase the Resource Kit, you'll find a newer GUI-based product called WinAT that is a lot easier to use.

To use the AT command effectively, you create a new user and place it in the group that provides sufficient authority to run the jobs you plan to automate. This is because by default, the Scheduler Service uses the System account, and this might not provide the access you require. For our example, we created an account called SchedJob, provided a password that never expires, and placed it in the Administrators group. You see this account in the list shown in Figure 15.14.

Figure 15.14.

A new SchedJob user account.

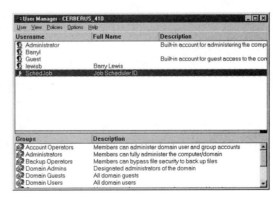

Now you need to configure the Schedule Service to use this account rather than the default user account. You can choose any account you think is appropriate for the exercise as long as it is authorized to do the work that's set out in any jobs you run. Be careful not to expose the service to unauthorized use, because with an Administrator account, it can perform many sensitive tasks.

Task 15.5. Changing a service to log in using a new account.

Step 1: Description

In this task, you'll learn to modify a service, such as Scheduler, to log onto NT with a more powerful user account. You might use this task to add or remove privileges from a service by providing an account that has more or less authority than the current account in use.

Step 2: Action

1. Sign onto your server as Administrator.

2. Select Start|Programs|Administrative Tools (Common)|Server Manager. This starts the Server Manager program. (Or you can open it through the Control Panel.)

3. Select Computer|Services.

4. Locate the Schedule Service, and select it by clicking once on the item. Click the Startup button. You see an options panel with Log On As in the bottom half of the screen.

5. Click the button next to This Account to select a new user account. Next, click the small icon with three periods to select a new user account. NT shows you a list of all current accounts. From the list shown, choose the new account—in our example, SchedJob—and click the Add button. Click OK to complete the selection. You see a dialog box like the one shown in Figure 15.15.

Figure 15.15.

Selecting a new user account for Schedule Service.

6. Enter the user account password in both the Password and the Confirm Password fields. If you forget, NT does not tell you. It merely indicates that the account does not exist. Change the Startup Type back to Manual or Automatic, and then click OK to continue. NT displays a dialog box telling you that the change is successful. Click OK to conclude.

7. To test your change, select the Service and click the Start button to get the service running. Close the Services window.

8. Close Server Manager by selecting Computer|Exit.

Step 3: Review

Adding a new user account to a service provides you with a method for managing these services and permitting or restricting access.

Now that the AT command can be scheduled and is able to perform the necessary tasks, you need to see how to set up jobs that use this command.

Be sure to start the Schedule Service before setting up all your jobs and thinking you are done. Using the AT command consists of typing the command using the following general syntax at a command prompt:

```
at ¦ computer ¦ time ¦ interactive ¦ how often ¦ later ¦ command
```

Note that the example syntax shows the general approach and does not constitute the actual commands. You do not use the separator lines at all; these are shown only to break up the different parameters. These parameters are shown in the following list, followed by some actual commands to clarify their use.

☐ *computer*: Use the syntax *computername* to tell Scheduler which computer the job needs to run on. For example, on our network, you might use \\TOSHIBA_410 as the computer name. Leaving out this parameter makes the command run on the computer on which it is entered.

☐ *time*: Use a 24-hour clock and enter the time with a colon between the hours and minutes; for example, 11:00, 17:30.

☐ interactive: Allows the command to interact with the desktop.

☐ *how often*: You use a particular syntax to make the job run every day or on certain days of every week: /every:*day*, where *day* is the day of the week spelled out or abbreviated to M,T,W,Th,F,S,Su. For example, /every:M,W,F makes the job run every Monday, Wednesday, and Friday.

☐ *later*: You use a particular syntax to make the job run next week or on the next specified day of the week: /next:*day*, where *day* is the day of the week spelled out or abbreviated to M,T,W,Th,F,S,Su. For example, /next:M,F tells Scheduler to run next Monday and Friday. You also use the days of the month to specify a date each month.

☐ *command*: Run any legitimate command or program or batch file. Here you specify what you want done on the schedule created using the earlier parameters. Enter the command in quotation marks for it to be recognized.

Let's look at a series of commands to give you a good idea of how this all works and enable you to get comfortable with using the at command. Use the following examples to practice on your server until you are sure how the commands work and can set your own:

☐ `at 10:30 /interactive dir`

Runs the directory list command at 10:30 a.m. on the local machine.

☐ `at 10:45 /interactive rdisk`

Starts RDISK at 10:45 a.m. on the local machine.

☐ `at \\toshiba_410 16:00 /every:M,W,F "backup.bat"`

Runs a batch job called backup.bat every Monday, Wednesday, and Friday at 4 p.m.

☐ `at \\toshiba_410 01:30 /every:28 "monthbup"`

Runs a job called monthbup every 28th of the month at 1:30 a.m.

☐ `at 21:30 /next:M "copy d:\test.bat D:\tested.bat"`

Runs a copy of one file to another next Monday at 9:30 p.m.

Each time you enter a command, the schedule numbers it, incrementing the number using the last one it recognized. To see which jobs are still waiting in the system, type the at command.

To see which jobs are running on any other machine, add the *computername* to the at command: `at \\toshiba_410`.

If you want to remove a command before its execution, you can delete it with the following syntax. You need to know what number the command is, so list it first using the previous commands.

`at \\toshiba_410 3 /delete`

This example deletes command number 3 on Toshiba_410.

As you see, using this command can be tedious, but it does offer an opportunity for you to avoid that 2 a.m. onsite visit.

Configuring UPS for Your Server

A file server or any mission-critical machine can use an uninterruptible power supply (UPS). You'll learn a little more about these devices in three more days in Chapter 22, but you might need to set up and administer such a device before then.

15

You should consider this one of your more important tasks because without it, your machine is very vulnerable, and customer service is easily impacted by brownouts, power loss, or power spikes. It's better to be able to slowly bring the server down and preserve user data than to lose it instantly due to a power loss.

NT provides software for supporting these devices. As usual, check the HCL to see whether your UPS is supported by NT 4.0 and save yourself a lot of headaches.

Be sure to properly follow the manufacturer's directions concerning a new UPS device, and fully charge the battery before using it. Being impatient can cost you a battery and make the device ineffective. Test the device using a monitor or some other device before using it on your server. This way, you are sure it works before you need it for production use. One quick test is to plug in a monitor and then unplug the UPS from the wall and see what happens. If you have the time and resources, you might do a load test and ensure that the device suits your needs before installing it. Finally, a word of caution. UPS devices generally cannot handle the electrical load of a laser printer; therefore, it's not a good idea to plug one into your UPS.

Task 15.6. Installing a UPS device.

Step 1: Description

In this task, you'll learn to set up NT to handle a UPS device and set the options you want to apply in case the device is needed.

Step 2: Action

1. Test and install the device. Then sign onto your server as Administrator.

2. Open the Control Panel and select UPS.

3. Double-click the UPS icon you selected. You are shown a dialog box like that shown in Figure 15.16.

Figure 15.16.

The UPS dialog box.

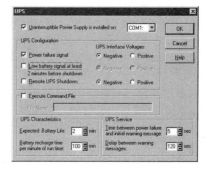

4. Select the serial port your UPS is connected to using the drop-down menu shown on the first line of the dialog box. This lights up a number of options.

Keep your UPS documentation handy because you'll likely need it to select some of the options you're offered. These are the various options in the UPS dialog box:

☐ Power failure signal: Select this box if your device is capable of sending a signal to NT when a power failure is detected. Read your device documentation to see what your device sends, and select either Negative or Positive in the UPS Interface Voltages.

☐ Low battery signal at least 2 minutes before shutdown: This field is used if your device sends a signal to NT when it detects a low battery and plans to shut down. Again, choose either Positive or Negative signal.

☐ Remote UPS Shutdown: Some devices are intelligent enough to act based on a remote command sent to them across the network. If yours is, select this option and specify Positive or Negative.

☐ Execute Command File: NT allows you to run a job or command before shutting down by keying it in this field.

☐ Expected Battery Life: Select an appropriate number based on your device documentation. Be sure to consider all the devices using the UPS and their power load when determining the number. You can select between 2 and 720 minutes.

☐ Battery recharge time per minute of run time: This field is used to determine how long the UPS needs to recharge for each minute of use. For example, if the UPS is used for 5 minutes for a small power loss and then power is recovered, it takes 500 minutes (using the default 100) to recharge the battery. You'll find this drain calculation in your UPS documentation. An incorrect setting provides you with an incorrect calculation of present battery capacity.

☐ Time between power failure and initial warning message: This value determines how long NT waits after a power failure to send an administrative alert letting you know that it is on UPS power. The default of 5 seconds is typical, but you can specify between 0 and 120 seconds.

☐ Delay between warning messages: After sending its first message to you, NT continues to let you know that it is on UPS power. This option determines how often these additional warnings occur. NT will send messages regardless; all you can do is determine the time delay between them. You do not want the messages sent too often or they clutter up the console, yet not often enough might let the situation slip someone's mind in a busy environment.

15

The default of 120 seconds would appear to be adequate. You might set it to 60 seconds if you have full-time administrators monitoring the servers, because they can react quickly.

5. Consider each value carefully and enter it into the appropriate place. Click OK to finish.

6. Close the Control Panel to complete the task.

Step 3: Review

You set up the UPS by reading the documentation and placing the desired values in the appropriate box. After you finish this task, NT takes over and manages UPS use.

After you finish the UPS setup, NT automatically starts the UPS service and sets it so that it starts all the time when the server is started. Although you performed an equipment test earlier, it is useful to know that all is still working, and you can test it again now to verify that NT is sending the proper signals and that all functions work.

One way to test the equipment is to ensure that all users are logged off and unplug the UPS from the wall. See whether NT sends you the proper message telling you that it is using UPS power. Plug it back into the wall outlet. Does NT properly send the message in the number of seconds specified after UPS power was detected? Does NT resend the message in the expected interval?

Finally, it might be prudent to see that NT properly shuts down before UPS battery power fails. Pick a time when no activity is being performed, and unplug the device. See that NT performs properly and shuts down in an orderly fashion. You really do not want to find out there is a problem at some future time because you chose not to conduct this test.

One last thing on power. After all this testing, be sure to let the UPS have sufficient time to recover before it is needed again.

File Server Security

Yesterday, in Chapter 14, "Managing Windows NT Server File and Directory Access Rights," you learned about securing files and directories using the new NTFS file system. You also learned that use of a FAT-based partition offers no security and that even an NTFS partition can be read if someone gets hold of the hard drive.

Physical security is a necessity for any server, but especially for your file server, where all your important data is stored. We often enter a client's organization to see servers sitting under desks or behind doors that are never locked.

There is a saying in the security field that if you get access to the server, you get access to the system. Physical security must be a component of your overall operation, or you run the risk of exposure and data loss.

If you provide this level of control and couple it with the use of NTFS, a sound security policy, and user awareness, your security is vastly improved over what it is if you do not follow all these tasks.

Limit the number of security administrators on your system. Many organizations have far too many staff who have this extensive level of authority, and it typically is unnecessary. If you are not part of day-to-day administration, you should not have administration access.

Keep strict control over all the system logs, and ensure that they are appropriately backed up and placed offsite for safekeeping. These are your guides to what happened, and you might need them some time to retrace the events of a particular day.

Virus Protection

There is a lot of confusion and misunderstanding concerning viruses. You'll find some discussion groups even focusing on whether the plural is viruses or some other term. We choose not to get into those discussions. Whatever the spelling, the basic premise of a virus is a program that can infect other programs by modifying them to include a copy of itself and become self-replicating.

Most virus programs cost organizations in cleanup and system maintenance rather than in data recovery because the viruses usually do not delete files. Although some virus programs certainly can and do delete data and erase hard drives, most create a different kind of havoc. When a virus strikes a firm, the staff are left without workstations until cleanup is performed, and staff are needed to perform a time-consuming, rather tedious cleanup job. This is the true cost of these programs.

What can you do to minimize the chance of virus infection? Start with sound management policy on bringing data from outside the firm into the workstations. You might allow staff to use home machines but require all disks to be reviewed by a virus-check program before being used onsite.

Implement a virus-checking program on the server, and ensure that it always runs. We often see organizations that indicate that they are safe because they use this or that program, yet upon further questioning, we learn that the program is run sporadically.

15

Ensure that users are aware of the risks and the possibility of infection. Also, prepare a response team to quickly discover where an infection occurred and eradicate it both on the machine showing symptoms and any other machines that might possibly have been affected before the virus was noticed.

Finally, ensure that you check all the floppy disks that might have been used during the time frame indicated. Although this is an arduous task, doing it right the first time saves you from returning again and again. Also, be sure to update your virus program definition files continually to ensure that your programs are always aware of the most recent viruses. Contact your vendor to determine how often the vendor makes these updates available.

Summary

In this chapter, you learned about many of the components involved in managing a file server. You learned to manage a file server and control the various components.

You learned to use the Server Manager to start and stop system services. You learned to set up and run scheduled jobs and thus manage your backups or other programs without needing to be onsite.

In this chapter, you discovered a lot about running the server. You learned the following points:

- [ ] How to start and stop NT services
- [ ] How to add computers to your domain
- [ ] How computers are removed from the domain
- [ ] How to set the time and date using either the old DOS method or the newer GUI-based settings and using even newer software that automatically dials a time clock and sets the time for you
- [ ] How to create desktop shortcuts to improve your ease of use
- [ ] All about synchronizing the domain servers
- [ ] How to set up the UPS for your server

Workshop

To wrap up the day, you can review terms and tasks from the chapter, and see the answers to some commonly asked questions.

Terminology Review

administrator—The person responsible for performing daily administration of the server.

Alerter—NT's service that allows a message to be sent indicating abnormal operation of NT.

event—The occurrence of an action taken by a user or an application that is recognized and interpreted by NT as an action.

UPS—The term used for uninterruptible power supply, a device used to provide temporary power to a computer following a power loss.

Task List

The information provided in this chapter showed you how to manage the file server and operate it effectively. You learned to do the following tasks:

- ☐ Start and stop services
- ☐ Add computers to your domain
- ☐ Synchronize the domain database
- ☐ Add RDISK to your Start menu
- ☐ Change a service to log in using a new user account
- ☐ Add a UPS device and configure it

Q&A

Q Should I synchronize the domain database manually or automatically?

A A domain consists of a number of machines with PDCs and BDCs alongside client workstations. Of course, it can also consist of two or three machines. On a very large network, you are likely to occasionally need to perform a manual synchronization due to a network failure or some server that is being pulled off the network for maintenance.

In most instances, you can let the system perform and manage this task. It is usually unnecessary, except in those examples previously listed, to concern yourself with synchronization because it is performed based on your schedule. If you are unsure whether it is being performed often enough, change the frequency as explained earlier.

15

Q Why would I change a service to use a different login user account?

A As you saw earlier in the chapter, at times you might decide to improve control over a particular service. For example, suppose that you want to allow the Backup Operators to run scheduled backups each night using the Schedule Service. The default user account it uses does not allow access to all the files you will back up, so another method is needed. You might create a backup user account and grant it a permanent password and then use this to perform scheduled backups.

Q How important is the virus concern to my NT Server network?

A The answer to this question really depends on how important your network is to your business. It appears that many organizations today are impacted with viruses as users scan the Internet, download files from friends, and pass information between home and work. Using a virus program on a regular, ongoing basis is not only prudent business practice, but necessary.

Chapter 16

Managing the Print Server

Ask any system administrator: Printing is a very difficult resource to share effectively on a network. Network printing is at the same time an extremely useful function of your network and a pain. Printers are essential in any office where employees use computers. Everybody wants to print reports, memos, letters, graphs, and whatnot. These user wants quickly turn into user demands, and they can take over all your time. So it is extremely important that you understand printing concepts. This is why this chapter deals exclusively with printing.

On your first day, in Chapter 2, "What Is Windows NT Server?" you learned that Microsoft heeded the experience of other software vendors when developing Windows NT. Printing is an excellent example of this diligence. Microsoft took a clue from the most oft-heard complaint about Novell NetWare: Network printing is difficult to configure and maintain.

To fully understand printing, you must fully understand printing components and their configuration. In this chapter, you'll learn about these topics:

☐ Printer devices, print queues, and print servers

☐ Creating and fine-tuning network printer queues

☐ Optimizing the printing process

☐ Controlling access to the printer

This chapter looks at these components in depth, including their use and function.

Understanding Printing Basics

Before setting up printers and servers, it is important that you grasp the meaning of printing terminology. So, let's begin our journey.

NT Server uses some special vocabulary when discussing printing:

☐ *network-interface printers:* Whereas other printers connect to the network through a print server connected to the network, network-interface printers connect directly to the cabling without requiring an intermediary. These printing devices have built-in network cards.

☐ *print server:* The computer where the printer is connected and where the drivers are stored.

☐ *printer:* The logical printer as perceived by NT Server. As you'll see in this chapter, the ratio of printers to printing devices is not necessarily one to one. You can have one printer and one printing device, one printer and multiple printing devices, or multiple printers and one printing device, or some combination of these components. Later in the chapter, you will see situations in which you might find these arrangements practical.

☐ *printing device:* The physical printer itself.

☐ *queue:* A group of documents waiting to be printed. In other operating systems, the queue is the primary interface between the application and the printing devices, but in NT Server, the printer takes its place.

To clarify the preceding points, in Windows NT, there are two types of printers: physical printers and logical printers. And there are two types of physical printers: server attached and network attached. You'll read more about printers in a few paragraphs.

Print servers are PCs that are configured to collect user print jobs and send them to the printers as needed.

Generally, a print queue is a shared area on a file server for storing print jobs in the order in which they are received. Print queues are the method that print servers use to store, or queue, user print jobs. The print queue lines up the print jobs and sends them to the printer in an orderly and efficient manner. In turn, the print server directs the print jobs from the queue to the printer. The printer, which is the actual physical device, receives the job and typically outputs it to paper. When a user sends a print job to a print server, the print server stores the print job in the appropriate print queue until the printer is available to accept the print job. You'll learn more about print queues in a few paragraphs.

You can use almost any of the Microsoft line of Windows operating systems as a print server. Most print server PCs share a locally attached printer through one of the following operating systems:

- [ ] Windows NT Server or Workstation
- [ ] Windows 95
- [ ] Windows for Workgroups
- [ ] Windows 3.1 when running the MS Network Client
- [ ] LAN Manager

As you just learned, NT also supports direct network-attached printers that use the HP JetDirect card (with built-in service software) or a similar network attachment device. These direct-attach printers can receive print jobs straight from users. The best way to configure network printers like these, however, is to let an NT server act as the print server, collecting print jobs and sending them to the printer when it is available. This way, no user print jobs are delayed or rejected while the printer is printing another job. These printers have a limited buffer to store print jobs.

Fundamentally, the print server spools print jobs in a print queue until the printer is ready. Using print queues and spooling print files is by far the most efficient use of direct network-attached printers. For an NT server to act as a print server for direct network-attached printers, you must load the Microsoft DLC protocol in your NT server's network setup. NT uses the DLC protocol to talk to network-attached printers.

Using LAN-transparent applications, the users think they are printing directly to the printer down the hall. This illusion, however, is often quite difficult for the system administrator to achieve.

This description doesn't explain the whole story, so a more in-depth review of these components is required. Let's start our discussion by looking at printers.

Printers

Printers are the devices your users are most familiar with, after, of course, their workstation. Network printers are shared devices. You can attach them to a file server, a print server, or a local workstation acting as a remote printer.

Today, you also will find intelligent printers with print service and network interface cards built-in that can attach directly to the network and act like workstations with remote printers attached. Apple's printers have worked this way since about 1986.

Printers get print jobs via print servers. At this time, it is appropriate to refine the definition of a print server. The only thing more critical to the print process than a print user is a printer. As mentioned earlier, there are two types of printers under NT Server and three ways to attach printers to your network. The two types of printers are physical and logical printers. Physical printers are just that: a physical device or printing hardware. Logical printers are an NT creation that enables you to set up a single print definition serviceable by multiple physical printers, or multiple print definitions served by the same physical printers. The three ways to attach printers to your network follow:

☐ *Network-attached (or network printer):* To attach directly to the network, the printer must have a built-in network interface. For instance, high-end laser printers commonly include built-in Ethernet interfaces.

☐ *Server-attached (or server printer):* You simply use a normal printer cable to connect the printer directly to the Windows NT server.

☐ *Workstation-attached (or remote printer):* A normal printer cable attaches the printer to a computer, but this time it's to a workstation attached to the network.

Although all three printers are attached to the network differently, they all share the common characteristic of being controlled by the NT Server that manages them.

For example, let's say you have three identical HP LaserJet 4Si printers in your department. You can define a single logical printer on the NT server. That logical printer can send print jobs to the next available HP LaserJet 4Si printer in your department.

NOTE When you have multiple physical printers served by one logical printer, the physical printers must be the same: the same model, with the same features installed, and with the same amount of RAM.

16

Logical printers serve another purpose. Not only can you assign multiple physical printers to one logical printer, but you also can assign multiple logical printers to one or more physical printers. So you can create different share names for the same physical printer, thus enabling you to assign different access rights, access times, and priority levels to different groups.

Let's say your Customer Service department has two different shifts—first and second. The first shift can use the printer with the share name CSLaser1, whereas the second shift can use the share name CSLaser2 to access the same physical printer. The difference between the two share names is in *when* you can use each share name. This method might allow you to track printer usage properly and to control who can access the printer during the two shifts.

16

Print Queues

Now that you understand the difference between logical and physical printers, let's look at where all those print jobs go to wait for printing: the print queue. The print queue is just that—a queue, or line, of jobs waiting to be printed. In Windows NT, the print queue is transparent to both users and administrators. Therefore, queues are described here mostly for the benefit of those who have used print queues in other network environments, such as you former NetWare administrators—you know who you are.

In Windows NT Server, a print queue is an integral part of a logical printer's definition. When a user sends a print job to a printer that is busy printing, NT Server puts the submitted job in a print queue for that logical printer. When the printer becomes available again, NT sends the next job in the queue to the printer. Under NT, you do not use separate definitions or settings for queues.

What if you don't want your print jobs queued? You certainly have that option too. When you install the printer on the NT Server, on the Scheduling tab of the Printer Properties dialog, you'll see the option Print directly to the printer. If you choose this option, the system passes print jobs directly to the physical printer. There are, of course, some practical reasons for choosing this option. Maybe your print job is confidential and you don't want it available in a queue where someone might read it. The downside of this setting is that when the physical device is busy, your user must wait for the physical printer to become available before continuing.

Imagine staring at the Print dialog box in Word for Windows 95 for several minutes while someone's 25MB spreadsheet prints. This illustration points out exactly why print queues make sense. Enable the Print directly to the printer option in the Printer Properties dialog only when you know that's what you want.

TIP

Printing directly to a printer makes sense when a printer is available for the person's exclusive use. This is a good idea for clients who deal in confidential information, such as a Human Resources clerk.

Print Servers

A print server is software that takes jobs from the print queue and sends them to the printer. A job inserted into the print queue makes its way to the top of the queue, at which time the print server redirects it to the appropriate network printer. When a printer is out of paper, offline, or jammed, the print server can notify the Administrator or print server operator.

Because the server is software, you should think of it more as a process than a device. The print server can be a dedicated device or a process running on another machine. Print servers don't necessarily have to be your main file server, or even computers with NT Server, but there are limitations on who can share a printer with the rest of the network.

Machines running the following operating systems can act as print servers:

- ☐ Windows for Workgroups
- ☐ Windows 95
- ☐ Windows NT Workstation
- ☐ Windows NT Server
- ☐ LAN Manager
- ☐ MS-DOS and Windows 3.1 (when running the MS Workgroup DOS Add On)

Regardless of where the service runs, the print server has the responsibility for controlling and redirecting print jobs from workstations to printers.

So do you want a dedicated or a nondedicated server—that is the question. They both have advantages and disadvantages. You can retrieve your old PC from its current use as a boat anchor or doorstop, because the minimum configuration is an 8088 with a 20MB hard drive and 1MB RAM. On the other hand, using the NT server as a print server really taxes I/O and memory, two resources used extensively by file service.

NT-Specific Printer Sharing Features

The unique printer sharing features that NT Server has can make the process of connecting to a networked print device easier than it is with other operating systems. So let's look at some clients.

NT Workstations Don't Need Printer Drivers

If you're running an NT workstation with your NT Server, not needing printer drivers is likely one of your favorite features, because it makes the connection process a lot easier. When you're connecting the workstation to a printer on the server, you don't have to specify which kind of printer you want to connect to or tell the system where to find the drivers, as you do when connecting a Windows workstation to a networked printing device. Instead, you need only go to the Printers folder or the Add New Printer Wizard (depending on which version of NT you are running, 3.x or 4.x), look to see which printers are shared on the network, and double-click on the one you want. After you've done that, you're connected.

NOTE

> NT's most significant contribution to easy network printing is the concept that an NT Workstation client isn't required to have a print driver installed locally for the network printer in question. NT Server allows an NT Workstation client to route print jobs to a network print queue. From there, the NT Server print driver configures the print job and completes the printing process successfully. Imagine not having to install and configure a copy of the printer driver on every company PC. If you keep the print drivers up-to-date on just one machine, the NT server, every user's print jobs should print perfectly. Printing is simple: Just select File|Print and click OK from your Windows application.

Direct Support of Printers with Network Interfaces

To use a network interface print device (one that connects directly to the network instead of requiring parallel or serial connection to a print server), you only need load the Data Link Control protocol onto the print server. Although network interface print devices can connect directly to the network without an intervening print server, those network interface print devices still work best with a connection to a computer acting as a print server, because they have only one incoming data path. With only one path, after the printer receives one print job, it cannot queue any other print jobs until the job completes. More paths mean more efficient use of printing time, because queuing means that you don't have to keep checking to see whether the printer is done or worry about someone beating you to the printer.

Network interface printers can be useful because, although they still can connect to a print server through the network media, they can be physically distant from it. This works because network interface printers don't get jobs through the parallel or serial port. The network connection also can speed up the process of downloading documents to the printer, because a network connection is faster than a parallel or serial port. The speed difference isn't great, though, because the printer still must access the drivers from the print server.

Setting Up Printing

The Printers window in the Control Panel takes care of all printer maintenance. To connect to, create, fine-tune, or manage a printer, you need only open the Printers window. Basically, you set up printing by carrying out these actions:

- ☐ Adding printers to the network
- ☐ Customizing printers

Adding a Printer to the Network

Adding a printer to your network is fairly easy. To begin with, you physically hook a printer to your server the same way you'd hook any printer to a computer: by using a printer cable and attaching it to a parallel port on the back of the computer. Then, you must logically attach the printer.

For those of you who fondly remember Print Manager, there is some bad news. With Windows NT Server 4.0, Print Manager is no longer a part of the program. Now, now, you'll get over it. The functions previously found in Print Manager are now located in the Printer window.

You can find the Printer window by selecting the Control Panel under the Start menu. For those of you familiar with NetWare and NT 3.51, the process of setting up a shared network printer was called "creating" it. Now, you simply go to the Printer window and click the Add Printer icon. The Add Printer Wizard walks you through the process of setting up a printer.

16

You can find the properties for the printer, give permissions for groups to use the computer, and use all other functions and settings for printers from the Printer window—more specifically, in the Properties dialog box in the File menu. Let's add a printer.

Task 16.1. Adding a printer.

Step 1: Description

The first time you're setting up a printer on the network, you need to add it. To do this, you use the Add Printer Wizard and provide the appropriate information, including the type of printer, its share name, and whether it will be shared with the network. With this task you'll create a printer using the Add Printer Wizard.

NOTE

> You can give one physical printer more than one share name and assign each name to a different group, perhaps with different print privileges. Just repeat the creation process, but assign the printer a different name.

NOTE

> Choose Network printer server to connect your machine to a printer managed by another machine in your domain. Choose My Computer to set up a printer for your server to manage.
>
> You need to set up your own printer (as opposed to connecting to one) when you are
>
> ☐ Physically installing a printer on a computer
>
> ☐ Physically installing a printer that connects directly to the network
>
> ☐ Defining a printer that prints directly to a file (no hard copy)
>
> ☐ Associating multiple printers with diverse properties for the same printing device

Step 2: Action

1. Double-click the Printers icon in the Control Panel folder.
2. Double-click Add Printer. The Add Printer Wizard appears in Figure 16.1.

Figure 16.1.

*The Add Printer
Wizard.*

3. Choose the type of printer you want to install: one physically attached to this server
   or one located across the network somewhere. For this example, let's select My
   Computer. Click Next.

4. Select the port where you will attach this printer, and click Next. If you don't see
   your port listed, click Add Port to see additional choices. You should see a window
   like the one shown in Figure 16.2.

Figure 16.2.

*The Add Printer
Wizard: printer
manufacturers.*

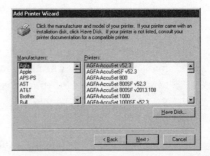

5. In the left scroll window, select the printer manufacturer (for example, HP). In the
   right scroll window, select the printer model (for example, HP LaserJet 4Si). You
   can find printer drivers for most printers on the NT Server CD-ROM. If you don't
   see your printer in this screen, click the Have Disk button and follow the on-screen
   prompts. Be sure to have handy the printer driver from the manufacturer. When
   the driver you selected is already present, the wizard asks whether you want to
   replace it. Click Next to proceed.

6. Choose a name for the printer, and tell Setup whether you want your Windows-
   based programs to use this printer as the default printer. The name can be up to 32
   characters, including spaces. Click Next.

7. Select whether this printer will be shared. If you decide to share it, you have to give it a share name. So type a share name. The share name does not have to be the same as the printer name, but it might be easier to manage the printers when your printer names and share names are the same. Make the share name something meaningful, such as HRLaser for the printer in Human Resources, rather than something obscure, such as Printer1. A share name can be up to 12 characters long, including spaces. You also need to specify what operating systems will use this printer. If you choose one of these operating systems, Setup asks for the pertinent .INF file in a subsequent screen. Click Next.

TIP

> If you want MS-DOS machines to use this printer, you need to make sure that the printer name conforms to DOS's 8+3 naming convention.

8. You are advised to print a test page. Select whether you want to print a test page after the printer is installed. Click Finish. At this point, Setup copies files from your NT Server Installation CD-ROM to your server's hard disk. If you selected an operating system in step 7, Setup asks you where it can find the Windows 95 .INF file.

9. Type the proper path or choose Skip File. Click OK or Skip File to proceed. Setup displays the properties you can set for this printer. You'll see tabs such as General, Ports, Scheduling, Sharing, Security, and Device Settings.

10. To select the port for the printer, select the Ports tab; if the printer is on the LPT1 port, select LPT1 from the list. Go through all the tabs and review the printer's settings. Make appropriate changes or additions. Click OK when you're finished.

Step 3: Review

As you just saw, adding a printer is simple. To add a printer, double-click the Add Printer icon in the Printers window. That is all there is to it—your printer is ready to be used by one and all. Except, of course, you might not want everyone to use the printer. That is where the user permissions come in handy (that topic is covered later in this chapter).

TIP

> RISC and x86 machines use different printer drivers, so you need to install both kinds if you have both kinds of machines on your network.

The task you just completed adds a logical printer. Remember, you can create multiple logical printers that point to a single physical printer. Having different people access the same device from different names allows you to assign different printing priorities to different users, assign different hours during which the printer is available for printing, make one printer for network use and another for local use, and so forth. Having two or more names allows you to fine-tune the network's access to the printer.

The process for adding a second printer to the same print device is the same as that for adding the first one. Select Add Printer from the Printers window and follow the Add Printer Wizard's instructions. Be sure to take the following steps:

1. Select a new name for the printer.
2. Choose the same printer driver for the printer that the other printer on this print device uses, and make sure that all other settings are correct. You don't have to share all printers on the network, even when they're attached to the same printing device.

If you shared the new printer with the network, it is now available for connection.

Printer Pooling

Previously, you read about the inverse situation, in which you assign multiple identical physical printers to a single logical printer. Print jobs migrate to the first available printer with that logical designation. Just because you send a print job to a particular print name doesn't mean that your print job has to print at that one particular printer.

To save time for print jobs, you can use the Properties dialog box to pool several identical printers into one logical printer. When you have more than one identical printer, you can share them under the same printer name to facilitate printing. If you do this, the first available printer handles the job when you send it to that printer name. To the network, it looks as though there is only one printer to connect to, but print jobs automatically go to whatever pooled printer is available first. This process is called *printer pooling*. Printer pooling does not work unless the pooled printers are physically the same, that is, the same make and model and with the same amount of memory.

 TIP

> To set up printer pooling, go to the Ports tab in the Printer Properties dialog box, and click on the ports where you've plugged in the other printers. If the ports you need aren't on the list, you can add them by clicking the Add Port button.

To assign multiple physical printers to one logical printer (that is, to employ printer pooling), select Properties from the Printers pull-down menu, and then select Additional Ports. Indicate the ports for each printer you want to pool under this name. Remember, you can pool a physical printer that also is shared under its own share name. In other words, multiple logical printers can point to the same physical printer or printer pool.

Customizing a Printer's Setup

After you've done the basic work of adding a printer, you can customize it. You don't have to customize your printer when you first set it up; you always can adjust the settings later with the Properties option on the Printer menu.

Using the Printer Properties Dialog Box

Highlight the printer you want, and click the Properties button in the Printers window. From here, you can perform many tasks, including these:

- [ ] List the hours that this printer will print. If you restrict the printing hours, jobs still will spool to the printer during the off-times, but they will not print until the hour indicated.

- [ ] Choose a separator page file to print before each print job. Separator pages are discussed in detail later in this chapter.

- [ ] Choose the ports you want to print to for printer pooling (more on this topic follows).

- [ ] Select the print processor.

- [ ] Determine the printer's priority, if the printer goes by more than one name on the network. For example, if you have the same printer shared under the name HP4-Si and HP4, and you assign a higher priority to the printer name HP4-Si, then print jobs sent to that printer name are printed first. The default priority is 1, which is the lowest priority. You can set the priority from 1 to 99.

Setting the Printer Time-out Number

When the printer you are setting up is connected to a parallel port, you can specify the time lapse before the print server decides that the printer is not responding and notifies the user of an error. Setting the Transmission Retry number higher or lower adjusts the amount of time that the Print Server waits for a printer to prepare itself to accept data.

This setting affects not only the printer you've selected, but also any other local printers that use the same printer driver. To set the number of seconds between the time that you send a print job to the printer and the time that, if the printer doesn't see the job, it informs you of a transmission error, choose the Properties item in the Printer menu, click on the Ports tab, and choose Configure Port in the number of seconds you want for the time-out. To adjust the time-out, just click on the up and down arrows on the right side of the box or type a number.

Separator Pages for Sorting Documents

Separator pages are extra pages printed before the main document. You can use them to identify the owner of the print job, record the print time and date, print a message to users of the printer, and record the job number. Separator pages also are useful for keeping documents sent to the printer separate from each other. When several people are using the same networked printer, you probably want to use separator pages to help them keep their documents apart. Several separator-page files are included with NT Server, and you also can create your own by using Notepad.

Creating a Separator Page

To make your own separator-page file, begin a new document in Notepad. On the first line, type a single character and then press Enter. This character is now the *escape character*, which tells the system that you're performing a function, not entering text. You should use a character that you don't anticipate needing for anything else, such as a dollar sign ($) or pound sign (#).

Now that you've established your escape code, you can customize your separator page with the variables shown in Table 16.1.

Table 16.1. Separator page variables.

Variable	Description
BS	Prints text in single-width block characters until $U is encountered.
$D	Prints the date the job was printed. The representation of the date is the same as the Date Format in the International section in Control Panel.
$E	Ejects a page from the printer. Use this code to start a new separator page or to end the separator-page file. If you get an extra blank separator page when you print, remove this code from your separator-page file.
$F*pathname*	Prints the contents of the file specified by the path, starting on an empty line. The contents of this file are copied directly to the printer without any processing.

16

Variable	Description
$H*nn*	Sets a printer-specific control sequence, in which *nn* is a hexadecimal ASCII code sent directly to the printer. To determine the specific numbers, see your printer manual.
$I	Prints the job number.
$L*xxxx*	Prints all the characters (*xxxx*) following it until another escape code is encountered.
$N	Prints the user name of the person who submitted the job.
$*n*	Skips *n* number of lines (0 through 9). Skipping 0 lines moves printing to the next line.
$T	Prints the time the job was printed. The representation of the time is the same as the Time Format in the International section in Control Panel.
$U	Turns off block character printing.
$W*nn*	Sets the width of the separator page. The default width is 80; the maximum width is 256. Any printable characters beyond this width are truncated.

An example might help at this time. Open Notepad, and enter the following lines:

```
$
$N
$D
$T
$L This is a test separator page
$E
```

When you use this as a separator, your user will get this page:

```
Kelly 18/2/1997 9:15:15 AM This is a test separator page
```

Even though each entry is on a separate line, the output is all on one line, because $*n* wasn't used to tell the separator page to skip lines between entries.

Choosing a Separator Page

To specify a particular separator page, choose the General tab in the Properties dialog box, and then click the Separator Page button.

When no separator file is listed, you can select one by typing the name of the file you want to use or by browsing for the correct file by clicking the Browse button. After you've selected a separator file, the page with that information in it prints before every print job.

To stop using a separator page, just go to the Separator Page dialog box and delete the entry in the text box. There is no <None> setting in a drop-down list as there is in some menus.

When specifying a separator page, you can type a filename (when you're already in the proper path to find the file) or the filename and path (when you're in another path). You must, however, use a file that is physically located on the computer that controls the printer where you're specifying the separator page. You cannot use any file accessible from the network because the computer controlling the printer stores separator-page information in its registry, so it needs to have that information available locally. If you tell the printer to use a separator file that is not located on its hard disk or one that is not in the path you've indicated, you get an error message that says, `Could not set printer: The specified separator file is invalid.`

If you followed everything so far in this chapter, your users could be merrily printing right about now.

Connecting to and Printing from a Shared Printer

How you connect a workstation to a printer connected to a server running NT Server depends on the operating system of the workstation. Windows and Windows for Workgroups machines can connect from the graphical interface, but OS/2 and MS-DOS machines must make connections from the command line. Easiest of all are the Windows NT machines—they don't even require locally loaded printer drivers.

How Do I Connect a Workstation to a Shared Printer?

The process of connecting a workstation to a networked printer varies with the type of operating system that the workstation is using. To connect DOS and OS/2 machines, use the NET USE command from the command prompt. For Windows and Windows for Workgroups, you can use the Printers folder. For Windows NT machines, use the Print Wizard. Printer drivers for each kind of printer must be loaded locally on all kinds of workstations except Windows NT.

Depending on the type of operating system your network users use, printing on an NT network ranges from ridiculously easy to only a little harder than blinking.

16

Printing from MS-DOS

All DOS workstations, whether they are running Windows or not, require locally installed printer drivers to share printers on an NT Server network. From a DOS workstation that is not running Windows or Windows for Workgroups, you need to install the MS-DOS printer driver file for the laser printer and make sure that it is accessible to all your applications. Depending on how your disk is set up, you might have to copy the file to all your application directories.

To set up a printing port from MS-DOS, go to the command prompt and type net use lpt1:*server**sharename*. For *server* and *sharename,* substitute the name of the print server and the name by which the printer is known on the network. Substitute another port name where LPT1 already is in use.

If you want the connection to be made automatically every time you log onto the network, add the /persistent:yes switch to the end of the command. Just typing /persistent won't do anything, but if you leave off the persistent switch, it defaults to whatever you selected the last time you used the NET USE command.

For example, suppose you have an MS-DOS workstation that does not have a locally attached printer on any of its parallel ports. Because some older DOS programs don't really give you the chance to select an output port, you want the network printer HP4Si, which is attached to the server Balliol, to intercept any output for LPT1 and print it on HP4Si. Suppose also that you want this network printer attached every time you log onto the network. This would be the command for that:

```
net use lpt1: \\balliol\hp4Si /persistent:yes
```

 TIP

> When the print server is using NTFS, workstations might not be able to print from MS-DOS if they have only Read and Execute privileges. The print jobs will spool to the print queue, but never print. To resolve this problem, give all users who print from DOS applications or the command prompt full access to the printer.

DOS workstations, whether or not they're running Windows over DOS, use the locally installed printer driver rather than the one stored on the server. Therefore, when you get an updated version of a printer driver, you need to install it at each DOS/Windows workstation individually.

Printing from Windows and Windows for Workgroups

Connecting to an NT Server shared printer from Windows for Workgroups is just like connecting to the same printer on a Windows for Workgroups server. To connect, go first to the Control Panel and select the Printers icon. The window shows you the printer connections you currently have. To connect an existing printer to a new port, click the Connect button.

If you want to connect to a new printer, you need to click the Network button in this dialog box. It shows you which printers are available for connection. Click on the printer you want, and when its name appears in the Path box, click OK. You go back to the previous screen, where you can ensure that the printer is connected to the port you want.

That's how you connect to a networked printer when the drivers for that printer are already loaded. When they're not loaded, you need to use the Add button in the first screen to add the printer driver to the system. Click the Add button and you see a list of printers.

Select the printer you want (for example, the HP LaserJet 4Si), and then click the Install button. You can use the Browse button or type the proper path when the driver is somewhere on the network; otherwise, you need to insert the appropriate disk. After you've installed the correct driver, you're ready to connect to the printer.

Printing from OS/2

Connecting to an NT Server printer from OS/2 is much like doing it from DOS. To set up a printing port, go to the command prompt (reached from the System folder) and type net use lpt1: \\server\ sharename. For server and sharename, substitute the name of the print server and the name by which the printer is known on the network. Substitute another port name if LPT1 is already in use. If you want the connection to be persistent, add the /persistent:yes switch to the end of the command.

When connecting to network printers, OS/2, like DOS and Windows, uses local printer drivers rather than drivers stored on the print server. Thus, you need to load the printer drivers locally for the printer you connect to, and if you update the drivers, you need to install the new ones at each workstation.

Printing from Windows NT

When you're using Windows NT, connecting to a shared printer is easy. Because NT workstations can access the printer drivers located on the print server, you don't need to load them locally.

Therefore, you don't need to define the proper port, find the drivers, or do anything else; all you need to do is go to the Control Panel, select the Printers icon, and double-click on Add Printer. When you do, you see the first Add Printer Wizard dialog.

When you've reached the dialog, choose the Network printer server option button, and then click the Next button. The next dialog shows you the available printers you can connect to.

Double-click on the printer to select it, or click on it once and then click OK. That's it.

NT workstations use the printer drivers stored on the print server, so when you install a newer version of a driver on the print server, the NT workstations automatically will use it. You don't need to install software on the workstation.

Printer Security

Just because you've networked a printer doesn't necessarily mean that you want everyone on its domain to access it. Maybe it's the color laser printer, or you want to reduce the risk of security breaches by limiting the people who can print company secrets. Either way, you want to control access to the printer just as you would to any other network device.

There are several things you can do:

- ☐ Physically protect the printer
- ☐ Hide the printer
- ☐ Set printer permissions
- ☐ Set job priority
- ☐ Set printing hours

Physical Security for Confidentiality

The simplest control over printers and print servers is to ensure that they are provided the amount of protection warranted by the type of printing they are doing. For instance, in the Human Resources department, you would want to ensure that you adequately protect the printer and print server. You should physically protect access to a printer with confidential information being printed.

Printers represent a large exposure to most organizations. Employees can wait by any printer and get access to sensitive information they normally would not have. Also, many printers are strategically placed next to the office photocopier. But why would someone take a risk by photocopying a document, when they could probably just walk off with the original; most users would decide that there must have been a printing problem and would try again. You will need to educate your users about confidentiality!

Hiding a Printer

You can hide the fact that a printer exists but still share it with the network. To do this, attach a dollar sign ($) to the end of the printer share name. This way, the printer name does not show up on the list of networked printers, but when the user types the name, the user can connect to the printer.

Setting Printer Permissions

As you'll recall from elsewhere in this book, you secure an NT Server network by setting user rights for what people can do on the network, and setting user permissions for what people can use. Just as you can with other devices on the network, you can restrict printer use by setting permissions on it.

To set or change printer permissions, first go to the Printer window and select the icon for the printer you want. Next, go to the Properties dialog box in the File menu, choose the Security tab, and select Permissions.

The Printer Permissions dialog box lists groups with some kind of printer access set up. Using this dialog, you can change the access for each group. The access permissions are shown in Table 16.2.

Table 16.2. Printer permissions.

Access	Description
No Access	No member of that user group can do anything with the printer, including print.
Print	Members of that user group can print documents.
Manage Documents	Members can control document settings, as well as pause, resume, restart, and delete documents that are lined up for printing.
Full Access	Members can do anything with the printer: print; control document settings; pause, resume, and delete documents and printers; change the printing order of documents; and change printer properties and permissions.

By default, only Administrators and Power Users have full access to the printer. Only those with full access can pause or resume a printer or set its permissions. Those who just have print access can only administer their own documents.

16

NOTE

When a user is a member of more than one group with different printer permissions, the system always grants the highest-level permission. So if user Janet belongs to one group with Print privileges and another one with Full Access privileges, she always has Full Access privileges. The only time print permissions are not cumulative is when one group that a user belongs to has No Access to the printer. In that case, No Access overrides all higher levels, and the user has no access to the printer.

To change a group's access, highlight the group and then choose the new access type from the Type of Access pull-down box in the lower-right corner of the dialog box. One group must have Full Access or you cannot change printer permissions in the future.

To add a user group or user to the printer permissions list, click the Add button. You see an Add Users and Groups dialog box. To add a group to the printer permissions list, highlight the kind of permission you want to give that group, click on the group you want, click Add, and click OK. To add only a particular person to the printer permissions list, you have two options:

- ☐ You can select a group that the user belongs to and click on Members. This gives you a list of all the users who belong to the group. Highlight the user you want.

- ☐ You can click the Show Users button and scroll down the user groups list until you see the entry for Users. Below this entry is a list of every user on the system. Double-click on the name, just as you would when selecting a user group.

After you've selected the group or user, the name should appear in the Add Names box in the bottom half of the screen. When you're done adding groups or users, click OK.

Removing a group or user from the printer permissions list is simple: Go to the Printer Permissions dialog box, highlight the name of the user or group, and then click Remove.

Setting Print Job Priorities

You can set printer priorities from the Scheduling tab of the Properties dialog box. If you want to share your printer with the network but don't want everyone else's print jobs crowding out your own, you can give it two names: a name you use that has a high priority, and a name with a lower priority that is used by everyone else who connects to the printer.

You can give the print jobs of a person or group priority over another person or group. To do this, create another printer for the same print device. Click on the Scheduling tab in the Properties dialog box, and you see a dialog box where you can set printer priorities. You can set this number from 1 to 99, with 99 being the highest priority. The default priority is 1.

Setting Printing Hours

To adjust print times, just click on the up or down arrow of the Available From and To boxes, or type the available times for the printer. When you send a print job to a printer during its "off hours," it doesn't disappear but sits there until the printer is authorized to print again.

Although you can set user logon hours and printer hours, you can't set printing hours for a particular user or group that are different from those of the others who have access to that printer. For example, you can't restrict users to a particular printer between 9 a.m. and 5 p.m. when Administrators can access it at any time, unless you adjust the users' logon times and configure their accounts so that the system kicks them off when their time is up.

Although you can't make a printer accessible to one group for one set of hours and to another group for a different set, you still can customize printer access hours for different sets of users. Simply add more than one printer (remember, printers are logical entities, distinct from the physical printing devices), set the hours for each printer as you require, and then tell each group which printer to use.

Sharing Local Printers

Not all printers on your NT network are physically connected to your NT server. Your NT server could be the print server for dozens of printers, all connected to other PCs or to the network directly. You also can make your NT server act as a print server for workstation-attached printers shared by your network users.

Users with printers attached to their machines must create a share for their local printer and assign rights to username NT Server and *no one else*. From the NT Server, choose Network Print Server when adding a new printer configuration on the server. Doing this displays a browse of all the available printers on the network for sharing. Next, select that printer from the list of Network print servers. You continue as you did in Task 16.1.

Given all that to think about, that's it for today.

Summary

So that's printing—NT style. Microsoft has made everything as easy as possible by keeping things consistent among all the various Windows versions. By now, you can sit down with any version of Windows and use a server printer share to share a local printer with the network world (if the version of Windows allows it).

The purpose of this chapter was to introduce you to printing. Printing is a very important part of your network. Most users will use network printing, and they will be quick to tell you when it doesn't work. It is amazing how fast you'll lose friends when printing is a problem.

16

In this chapter, you learned how to add and customize printers and add print servers. Completing these steps makes network printing available to your users.

To help you improve network security, you briefly learned about printer permissions and physical security.

Workshop

To wrap up the day, you can review terms and tasks from the chapter, and see the answers to some commonly asked questions.

Terminology Review

interface—The cables, connectors, and electrical circuits allowing communication between computers and printers.

parallel interface—A printer interface that handles data in parallel fashion, eight bits (a byte) at a time.

parity bit—A way of marking the eighth bit in a data byte so that 7-bit ASCII characters between 0 and 127 are sent and received correctly. There are three kinds of parity: odd, even, and none.

print queue—A shared storage area on the file server where the system sends every print job before sending to the print server.

print server—Software that takes jobs from the print queue and sends them to the printer.

serial interface—A printer interface that handles data in serial fashion, one bit at a time.

Task List

The emphasis of this chapter has been to set up network printing. As a system administrator, you need to learn how to add printers, define printers, and assign permissions to groups. You learned how to perform several tasks in this chapter:

- ☐ Adding a printer
- ☐ Customizing printers
- ☐ Pooling printers
- ☐ Setting printer permissions

Q&A

Q How do I set up more than one printer with the same name?

A To have more than one printer handle print jobs sent to the same print name, you must set up printer pooling. To do this, go to the Properties item in the File menu, and click the Ports button. Select the ports that correspond to the ports where you've plugged in the other printers.

On an NT Server machine, you need only one copy of the driver for the type of printer you're pooling, unlike Windows for Workgroups, which requires one copy of the driver for each printer.

Q How do I print directly to ports?

A To send print jobs directly to the port where the printer is connected instead of spooling, go to the Properties item in the File menu of the Printers window, and click the Scheduling button.

DAY

9

Chapter 17

Understanding Windows NT Server Remote Access Services (RAS)

First, the title of this chapter is a little misleading because it refers to RAS. In NT Server 4.0, Microsoft changed the name of RAS to DUN, or Dial-Up Networking, to remain consistent with a term begun in Windows 95. To avoid any additional confusion, we continue using the term RAS throughout this chapter. If you are more comfortable with the term DUN, mentally translate RAS to DUN whenever you encounter it.

NOTE

> The term RAS is still used within NT Server 4.0, although the newer term Dial-Up Networking, or DUN, is becoming more familiar. Either term will do in the general sense of defining remote access unless you really want to get technical. NT Server 4.0 still refers to RAS more than DUN in its Help files.

In this chapter, you'll learn all about RAS, what to use it for, how to set it up, and what to look for when implementing it.

What Is RAS?

What is RAS? Consider it an extension of all your local area network functions using a dial-up modem connection. This means you can read files, update information, print reports, or do almost anything you can do when you connect via your workstation. True, no modem is as fast as a good network connection, but the functionality remains. You get to perform all the functions of your job from a remote location such as your house or the local bar. (Just kidding. We know that you wouldn't work at the local bar; it's far too distracting. This joke, however, works to highlight some of the difficulty with allowing remote access to an organization's mission-critical local area networks or other machines. Do you know where your remote users are?)

You can consider remote access using RAS to be the same as using your serial ports on your laptop as network cards, such as Ethernet or Token Ring. Just as you connect at the office to perform your day-to-day work, you connect through a modem to perform the same work at home or in a satellite office. We use the term *modem* as if it's the only way to connect the machines, but it isn't. RAS also allows connections using the older X.25 packet-switching network, ISDN (Integrated Services Digital Network), and fully digital T1 lines.

In NT Server 4.0, you find RAS in two places. You find the client side by looking in Accessories|Dial-up Networking, and you find the server-side tools in Administrative Tools (Common)|Remote Access Admin. Remember that server side refers to applications that are executed on a server and receive requests from the workstations, whereas client side refers to applications that are executed on a workstation and connect to a server running a companion application—hence the term *client/server*.

Most RAS connections are made using a modem, and that thread is followed throughout this chapter. Starting RAS on your machine makes that machine the RAS server, just as you might be using a file server, application server, or database server. This doesn't mean that you need a separate server to run RAS, however; you can set it up to run on your PDC or BDC as long as the equipment can handle the overall service load.

NOTE

> You need to review some of the basics concerning network protocols before continuing too far because this information is very germane to the remaining discussion. If you are unfamiliar with networking protocols, you might want to skip ahead to this afternoon's chapter on network protocols and review some of the terms used before continuing.

RAS, therefore, acts as a network to the user, allowing remote access to the familiar desktop. It does this in part by managing to *tunnel*, or hide, certain protocols such as TCP/IP and IPX/SPX within others such as the Point-to-Point protocol, or PPP. This allows NT Server to talk to machines that are not running RAS or NT.

RAS does allow for the use of the slower and older SLIP or Serial Line Interface Protocol; however, most sites have moved to PPP, and SLIP is slowly fading into the sunset.

Is RAS the same as using packages such as Carbon Copy and Symantec's Remote Control? It is similar in that both types of access permit you access to the network and allow you to perform functions remotely, but it differs greatly in what each access does and its planned intent. RAS is designed for users to access the network and perform their day-to-day jobs with little difference in the look and feel of their workstations. They are working at home just as they do at work on their desktop. Remote Control and Carbon Copy, however, are designed to allow users to take control of a system and manage it, primarily for support purposes, although they certainly function well in "workstation" mode. The primary difference is in how each functions. Using RAS, users see what they always see, their day-to-day applications. With Remote Control and Carbon Copy, users see the other machine's functions, how it looks and appears, not how their workstations should look. Another way to think of it is that with RAS you see your workstation, whereas with Remote Control and Carbon Copy you see the other machine, in addition to yours.

What Is X.25?

We talked earlier about how RAS allows connections between various protocols and mentioned X.25. What is this protocol and how does it work? X.25 allows you to route information through a packet-switching public data network, such as Datapac. An older technology, it operates at a top speed of 64Kbps, and it was designed for earlier days when telephone networks were less reliable than they are today.

X.25 is in use today primarily because of its widespread availability throughout the world. If you are part of a large multinational corporation, you might still use this technology in parts of your network. It is very dependable and can tolerate poor telephone-line quality, so it offers a reasonable service in countries that use less-reliable telephony. The error-checking capability it offers is still attractive even though this capability slows the connection considerably. Better slow data than no data.

Connecting RAS using an X.25 network requires that you use an X.25 pad, or packet assembler-dissembler. This device takes the data streams from one end of the connection and converts them so that they can travel over the X.25 network. The pad at the other end changes the data packets back to their original message format for the system to use.

Why Use RAS?

What are some of the applications you can perform using RAS? By far, the most common is allowing users remote access to their NT network. Using a Windows 95, DOS, Mac, or Windows for Workgroups workstation, the user signs onto the network from home using his modem. After being connected, the user performs his daily work duties as if he were at the office.

RAS is also used for remote dial-in to non-NT machines, such as those running the TCP/IP or IPX/SPX protocols. Additionally, you use RAS for setting up your NT Server as a gateway, connecting your organization's network to the Internet or to other networks.

Finally, you use RAS to set up your server as a Web, Telnet, and FTP server or even offer complete ISP (Internet Service Provider) services. When you connect to Microsoft's Web page and FTP server, you are talking to an NT Server machine.

Requirements for Using RAS

First, you need not be running NT Server 4.0 to use RAS. As you recall from earlier in the chapter, RAS is available in the Workstation version of NT. They work the same except that in the workstation you are limited to one connection; in NT Server you can maintain 256 concurrent sessions.

Apart from a current version of NT, you also need a minimum of two compatible modems, typically one for the laptop and the other at the server you want to dial. Between these two modems is the telephone line. Note that although you are able to use a cellular telephone connection and travel across the resulting cellular network, this network is not as consistent as local telephone land lines, and as you travel between cells on the cellular network, the connection might be lost.

We recommend that you try to stick to using a standard modem in your network because you'll sometimes encounter difficulties connecting when using different brands of modems on the client and the server. In addition, remember that NT can be picky and might not work with some brands. Use the NT Hardware Compatibility List to determine those modems Microsoft has tested with NT Server. This is especially true with higher-speed modems because small differences can affect the operation, and each manufacturer can use a different method to achieve the high speed. Sticking to Hayes standard modems and V.32 or V.34 bis standards also helps.

You are able to connect using a serial null modem cable and RAS. A small organization might use this for fast and fairly inexpensive access because null modem cables can be purchased for $10 and up, depending on their length. Using a serial cable connection voids any need for network cards or modems. This method, however, is far slower, and the performance of such a connection is not stellar. If you plan to try a serial RAS connection, be sure to study the exact null cable specification in NT because you cannot use just any cable due to the specific pin connections RAS requires.

One really nice addition to NT 4.0 is the potential for pooling your modems and telephone connections and connecting to an NT Server at a far higher speed than possible through one modem alone. NT refers to this capability as *multilink PPP*. We detail how to do this later in this chapter.

What are the major components for using RAS? The various pieces include these:

☐ Two compatible modems

☐ A telephone or cellular line

☐ Windows NT Server or Workstation

To use ISDN, the requirements are similar in concept. You must have two ISDN network cards (or the newer external ISDN modems), a digital-grade copper or fiber-optic cable connecting the two cards, and network termination devices to connect the cable to each card. (The network terminators might be built into your network cards. Most newer cards support this method.) This service is becoming very popular now and can be purchased for home use at a reasonable price, greatly improving your network access speed.

This book focuses on using RAS with modems because this use is more common and we are limited in the page count available for each subject.

Installing RAS

RAS does not install automatically when you first set up NT Server unless you specify that the new server is participating in an existing network. In the book *Windows NT Server Secrets*, Jason Garms, et al, Sams Publishing, 1996, the author states that it is best to wait to install RAS rather than install it when you first install NT. This is because there are a number of things you need that make the installation and implementation of RAS a lot easier if they already exist. Although you might have chosen to add RAS during the initial NT Server install process, we concur with the belief that it's easier to wait and add it later, as you'll see in this section.

Before performing the RAS install, you should install the necessary network protocols such as TCP/IP or IPX. Do not install protocols that are not needed because each protocol takes memory, with TCP/IP being the biggest memory user. Blindly installing everything reduces your system performance. Ensure that your modems and I/O ports are properly installed and configured as suggested earlier, in Chapter 3, "Installing Windows NT Server on the File Server." For normal RAS dial-in, these are the key components. If you plan to use RAS for heavier duty, consider installing the DHCP (Dynamic Host Configuration Protocol) and WINS (Windows Internet Naming Service) servers as well if they are not already running somewhere on your network. This addition helps minimize your problem-solving if something should go wrong when you begin to install RAS. Finally, make sure that your modem and I/O ports are correctly configured and working, to minimize the chance of an error further confusing your install of RAS.

Task 17.1. Installing RAS.

Step 1: Description

In this task, you'll learn to install the Remote Access Services facility.

Step 2: Action

1. Begin by signing on as Administrator. Next, choose NT Control Panel and double-click the Network icon. Select the Services tab. The Network dialog box appears, as shown in Figure 17.1.

Figure 17.1.

The Network dialog box.

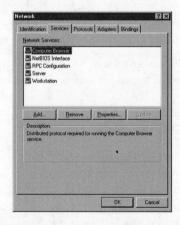

2. To add a service (we want to add RAS), click the Add button. NT lists all the available services in a scroll list. Select Remote Access Service by scrolling down the list and highlighting it. (You can press the R key on the keyboard to get there faster.) Click on the OK button to continue. You see an example in Figure 17.2.

Figure 17.2.

Selecting Remote Access Service to install.

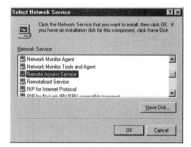

3. NT asks for the installation CD-ROM to gather the information it needs to complete the task. Insert the CD and click OK. It might start by asking for drive A:. Just change this to read E:\I386 (if your CD-ROM is drive E:) and click the Continue button.

4. NT continues with the installation of all the necessary files. When it is ready, the install process stops and asks you to tell it which connection device to use. This is where your earlier work pays off, because the modem or X.25 device will be available for use. If you did not set up the device, you can do so now by clicking the Install Modem or X.25 pad buttons and following the steps provided. You need to set up and properly configure the X.25 devices before RAS can use them. You see an example of the Add RAS Device dialog box in Figure 17.3. RAS occasionally does not recognize a setup device, and you will need to add it manually.

Figure 17.3.

The Add RAS Device dialog box.

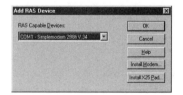

5. Select the appropriate device from the drop-down menu. Click OK to add that device to RAS. You can tell RAS about more than one device at this stage, so add all the devices you want. You can also add devices later, so don't worry if you're not sure how many you need. Figure 17.4 shows this dialog box.

Figure 17.4.

The Remote Access Setup dialog box.

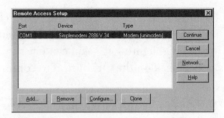

6. As you see, you can add, remove, and reconfigure devices by clicking the appropriate buttons. RAS provides a Clone button to allow you to quickly set up numerous similar modems instead of setting up each modem individually. The Network button allows you to set up the network options for RAS.

7. After adding all the devices you need, you must select each one and click the Configure button to properly set up the type of service you want to permit. Each device can be set to allow dial-in, dial-out, or both, and as you see, NT initially configures the device to be a dial-in port only. Decide on the need for dial-out services and add this option as needed. Do not set up devices as both dial-in and dial-out simply because it's easiest. There can be very good reasons for not allowing staff to dial out of your network. For example, one reason might involve not wanting Internet or other dial-up services made available to your network without a firewall. Configure all your devices and continue to the next step.

8. Click the Network button. NT show you the configuration setup dialog box. This dialog box allows you to set up the protocols, services, and encryption settings. You can see an example in Figure 17.5.

Figure 17.5.

The RAS Network Configuration dialog box.

9. Any area of the dialog box that is grayed out means you cannot select the options in that area. As you see, the first area concerns the protocols that are permitted to be used when dialing out. NT automatically allows all installed protocols. Change this by deselecting any protocol you do not want used.

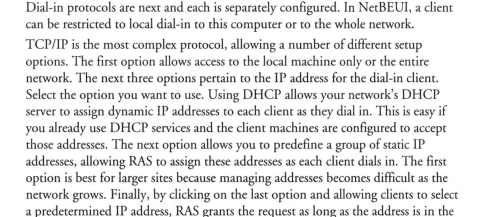

Dial-in protocols are next and each is separately configured. In NetBEUI, a client can be restricted to local dial-in to this computer or to the whole network.

TCP/IP is the most complex protocol, allowing a number of different setup options. The first option allows access to the local machine only or the entire network. The next three options pertain to the IP address for the dial-in client. Select the option you want to use. Using DHCP allows your network's DHCP server to assign dynamic IP addresses to each client as they dial in. This is easy if you already use DHCP services and the client machines are configured to accept those addresses. The next option allows you to predefine a group of static IP addresses, allowing RAS to assign these addresses as each client dials in. The first option is best for larger sites because managing addresses becomes difficult as the network grows. Finally, by clicking on the last option and allowing clients to select a predetermined IP address, RAS grants the request as long as the address is in the DHCP server or static address pool.

10. The RAS install process continues for a short while, reading files from the CD before finally ending. After you reboot the server, RAS services are available. Finally, after installing a new service or hardware component, you need to reinstall any service packs that are currently installed. Service packs are collections of software fixes that Microsoft provides from time to time to fix outstanding problems within NT.

Step 3: Review

This task showed you how to add Remote Access Services and give users the ability to dial in and dial out of NT. You learned about setting up the devices such as modems and configuring the necessary protocols and other necessary elements. You can now permit users to utilize Remote Access Services on your server.

The preceding task allows you to use RAS and connect your dial-up machines to the network. RAS cannot be used as a LAN-to-LAN link, however, because it does not perform packet broadcasts, sending packets from one LAN segment to another.

Administering RAS

After RAS is installed on your server, it's time to administer access and manage the dial-in process. This is accomplished via the Remote Access Admin application found in Start|Programs|Administrative Tools (Common)|Remote Access Admin.

After starting the Remote Access Server, you see a dialog box that shows various options and also a list of all RAS servers currently running in your domain. The open window consists of four fields with the following titles:

- ☐ Server
- ☐ Condition
- ☐ Total Ports
- ☐ Ports In Use

Under the section titled Server, you find a list of any servers in your domain that are running RAS. Although our domain is very small and uses only one RAS server, yours might have multiple servers set up to run RAS and allow dial-in or dial-out. Next, under the Condition title, you see whether a server is active (running) or stopped. The Total Ports section indicates the number of ports configured to provide RAS service, and Ports In Use tells how many of those ports are presently active.

Double-clicking on a server provides additional detail and shows you the actual port addresses that are defined and, if in use, who the user is and when that dial session began. On the side of the dialog box are options that enable you to review the port status of any selected port (highlight the port address you want additional information about, and then click the Port Status button), as well as buttons that allow you to disconnect a user, send a user a message, or send all dial-up users a message.

The Port Status button provides detailed information about that port such as line condition (authenticated user, connected), the speed of the connection, incoming and outgoing number of bytes, error conditions, and the IP or IPX address.

Disconnection of a user with the Disconnect User button takes effect immediately and does not provide the user any warning. On an NT Workstation, the user automatically receives any message sent via the Send Message button. Windows and Windows 95 users must be running NetPopup or other network mail software. To send a message to all users on this RAS server, you use the Send to All button.

Under the Server menu option on the RAS main screen are several options:

- ☐ *Communication Ports:* Shows all ports for the highlighted server.
- ☐ *Start Remote Access Server:* Allows you to start a RAS server.
- ☐ *Stop Remote Access Server:* Allows you to stop a RAS server and automatically disconnect all users.
- ☐ *Pause Remote Access Server:* Temporarily halts the use of RAS but leaves the current users connected.

☐ *Continue Remote Access Server:* Starts RAS again after a pause, allowing new calls to occur.

☐ *Select Domain or Server:* Browses any RAS domain where you have an Administrator account.

The Users menu contains two additional items. These are used to modify security and control how RAS is used and where a user must be to call in to the server.

☐ *Permissions:* Grants or denies RAS permissions to users. By default, all users are denied access to RAS services.

☐ *Call Back:* Sets up RAS callback options. Allows you to set up RAS to call a user back at a predetermined telephone number, providing additional security and limiting the need for users to dial long distance.

The final two menu items are View and Options. These provide the ability to refresh the list of servers, toggle between Low Speed connections, and save the setting you choose. The Low Speed connection option tells RAS to remove the browsing capability it offers and not support browsing. Figure 17.6 shows you the Remote Access Admin window.

Figure 17.6.

The Remote Access Server Administration dialog box.

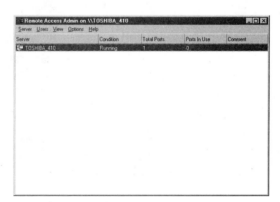

You see that various facilities are used in this window to modify RAS according to your needs.

Installing a New Modem

In the earlier section, we installed the Remote Access Server software. During the install, the process asked for information on which modems you are using. Perhaps you didn't set them all up at that time and have additional modems to add. This task shows how to add a new modem and tell NT Server all about it.

Task 17.2. Installing a new modem.

Step 1: Description

In this task, you'll learn to install new modems and tell NT Server about them.

Step 2: Action

1. Begin by signing onto your server as Administrator. Next, choose NT Control Panel and double-click the Modems icon. If you already have at least one modem installed, the Modems Properties dialog box appears, as shown in Figure 17.7. If no modem is installed, follow the installation prompts.

Figure 17.7.

*The Modems Proper-
ties dialog box.*

2. To add a new modem, click the Add button. NT tries to find your modem by default. We recommend that you choose the Don't Detect option because it is usually faster and more accurate. NT often misses modems and chooses a default setting. You see an example of this dialog option in Figure 17.8.

Figure 17.8.

*Choosing the option to
manually select a
modem.*

3. Click on the small check box to select the manual option. Then click Next to continue.

4. NT continues and provides a list of available modems. Choose your modem from the list by selecting the manufacturer and then the particular type of modem. You see an example of the Install New Modem list dialog box in Figure 17.9.

Figure 17.9.

The Install New Modem dialog box.

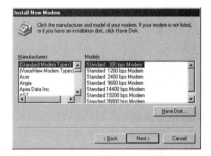

5. Select the appropriate device from the drop-down menu. Click the Next button to add that device. Note that you can also set up a direct serial cable link between machines using this option.

6. After you select the modem, NT asks for the COM ports that the modem will use. Select the port your device is on (usually COM1 or 2) and click the Next button. NT then goes and finds the necessary drivers to install your modem. When it finishes, you get a message telling you to restart the system before the device is made available.

7. Click OK to continue. Don't worry, NT does not restart the system at this time. First you get a successful installation message, and you need to click the Finish button. You see an example of this message in Figure 17.10.

Figure 17.10.

NT's completion of the Modem setup dialog box.

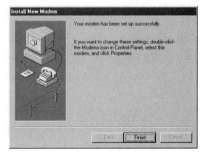

8. Click the Finish button to complete the task. Remember that you need to restart the system before NT recognizes the new modem. You see the modems that are set up for use in NT in the Modems Properties dialog box.

9. You get a message indicating that Dial-Up Networking needs to be configured because the list of modems is changed. NT provides you with the option of making these changes now or later. Click the Yes button to continue setup. NT goes away and verifies the present configuration before returning with a dialog box for RAS. You need to set up RAS to accept the new modem as described earlier in Task 17.1, "Installing RAS," starting at task item number 6.

Step 3: Review

This task showed you how to add new modems to NT Server 4.0. Use this task any time a new modem is installed.

Enabling Multilink PPP Connections

One of the options you can use in NT Server is the capability to allow a connection to occur using more than one modem. For example, you set up two 14.4Kbps modems on the client machine to call NT Server and use the combined speed of each modem as a single connection. Neat! In our example, you end up with a modem speed of 28.8Kbps. Using two of the more common 28.8Kbps modems can give you a throughput of 57.6Kbps!

To use this service, you must be connecting an NT Workstation client to your server. It is not offered for other client software. Let's see how we might set up this service. Finally, both the server and the client must have multilink enabled.

Task 17.3. Installing multilink PPP.

Step 1: Description

In this task, you'll learn to install the Remote Access Services facility that allows you to combine a number of modems into one faster connection. You can connect a workstation using two 28.8Kbps modems and obtain a connection with the server at 57.6Kbps speed.

Step 2: Action

1. Begin by signing onto your server as Administrator. Next, choose Start|Settings|NT Control Panel and double-click the Modems icon. You see a list of modems presently known to your system. This list is shown in Figure 17.11.

Figure 17.11.

The Modems Proper-
ties dialog box.

2. If your modems are not already set up, refer to Task 17.2 for instructions. Now you need to add the multilink PPP option.

3. Double-click the Network icon within Control Panel. Select the Services tab and then select Remote Access Services. Click Properties. NT performs some background searching and displays the Remote Access Setup dialog box.

4. Click the Network button. You see a Network Configuration screen such as the one shown in Figure 17.12.

Figure 17.12.

The Network
Configuration dialog
box.

5. At the bottom of that panel is a check box called Enable Multilink. Click on the small check box to enable this service, and click OK.

6. NT shows the previous setup dialog box. Click the Continue button. NT updates some files and brings you back to the main Network dialog box. Click the Close button to finish setting up the server.

7. After NT finishes updating all its files, it tells you to shut down to enable the settings to take effect. Click the Yes button to do a shutdown and restart of the server.

8. To complete the installation, you need to perform the same function on your NT Workstation. This sets up NT networking to allow multilink PPP access. As mentioned earlier, if you had any service packs installed prior to this, you need to re-install them now.

Step 3: Review

This task showed you how to add multilink PPP access and give users the ability to dial in using the combined speed of two separate modems. This is a neat way of providing additional bandwidth without paying for higher-cost services such as ISDN or dedicated T1 access.

Disconnecting a User

Now that we have connected users in various ways, how can we forcibly disconnect someone? It isn't too hard. Start a DOS command prompt and type the following command:

```
net session \\computername  /delete
```

Put the name of the computer you want to disconnect in place of the word *computername* in the preceding command. Although the wording indicates that it will delete something, it's just Microsoft's little joke. It only disconnects, or ends, the connection. Be careful to specify a computer or NT will disconnect all the currently connected users.

If you prefer, you also can use NT's GUI interface to disconnect someone. Select Start| Programs|Administrative Tools (Common)|Remote Access Admin. You see an example in Figure 17.13.

Figure 17.13.

Disconnecting a user by using the GUI interface.

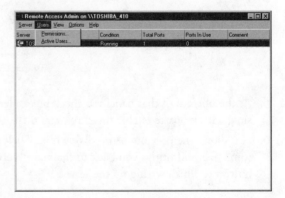

Select Users|Active Users to see a list of all users currently signed onto the server. Select the user you want to disconnect and click the Disconnect User button. That user will be disconnected from the server.

Using Dial-Up Networking

In this section, you'll learn how to use RAS to connect to other services such as the Internet or another computer.

Task 17.4. Connecting to a server using the RAS client.

Step 1: Description

In this task, you'll learn to use the RAS client software to set up your phone books and make client connections. You must have set up at least one NT RAS port for dial-out before starting this task. You also need RAS (or Dial-Up Networking) running on both machines for this task to work.

Step 2: Action

1. Begin by selecting Start|Programs|Accessories|Dial-up Networking. The first time you start Dial-Up Networking, NT tells you it cannot find a phone book entry and indicates that you need to add one. Click OK and NT shows you the New Phonebook Entry Wizard. As mentioned earlier in this book, NT 4.0 offers many of the Windows 95–style Wizards to help guide you through various setup routines. This dialog box is shown in Figure 17.14.

Figure 17.14.

The New Phonebook Entry Wizard.

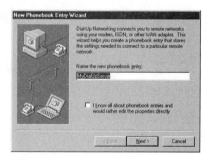

2. Enter a machine name into your phone book if you want, or accept the default name NT provides. Click the Next button to continue.
3. If a phone book entry is already in place, NT shows you the first entry and asks whether this is whom you want to dial. Choose to add a New entry if you want, and set up another machine to dial into. Click the Next button to continue.

4. Check all the options that apply on the screen that shows. Click the Next button to continue.

5. Enter the telephone number of the machine you want to call, and click Next.

6. Click Finish to end the setup. You now have one or more entries in your Dial-Up Networking telephone book and can choose one of these to call. NT shows you the main Dial-Up Networking dialog box with the latest telephone number ready for dialing.

7. To perform more detailed operations such as editing an existing entry or setting up preferences, click the More button to see a dialog box similar to that shown in Figure 17.15.

Figure 17.15.

Additional telephone book options.

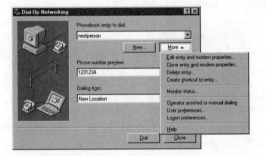

8. As you see in Figure 17.15, various options are available. The first option, Edit entry and modem properties, allows you to customize your entries. As you see in Figure 17.16, there are five tabs that permit a detailed degree of customization.

Figure 17.16.

Customizing telephone book entries.

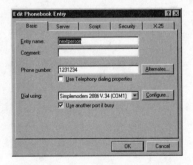

9. Under the Basic tab, you are offered a choice of adding a comment, changing the telephone number or name, or modifying the modem. These are all self-explanatory fields. The Server tab offers you a chance to modify the type of protocol you are using and set up software compression. The available protocols are PPP, SLIP, and Windows NT 3.1 or Windows for Workgroups 3.11.

10. You set up scripts by choosing the Script tab. Scripts tell RAS how to log into the host machine. If you are logging into NT, Windows, or UNIX machines, it's highly unlikely that you will need a script. Typically, the administrator for the machine you are dialing will let you know if there are special requirements. For example, you might use a script to dial into CompuServe.

11. The Security tab offers you the chance to ensure authentication between you and the server you are calling. The first option tells NT not to worry about encryption and allows clear text passwords to be sent. The second option offers an encrypted authentication based on accepted standards, and the third option offers special Microsoft encryption. Using this option allows you to encrypt all the data that flows between machines and is very secure. The option called Use Current Username and Password offers a degree of single sign-on (that is, it limits the number of times you need to enter an account and password to sign onto multiple systems) because RAS will use the account you signed onto as the RAS authentication.

12. The last tab allows you to set up special X.25 pad connections. By clicking on the question mark and moving your cursor to a field, NT Help provides specifics about that field.

Step 3: Review

This task showed you how to add and update telephone book entries for the different machines you might dial up. You use this to set up the specifics about each machine you want to dial. Using Dial-Up Networking then becomes as simple as choosing the name of the machine you are calling.

You might need to connect to your RAS server using a DOS-based client machine. The next task shows you the steps necessary for connecting.

Task 17.5. Connecting to a server using a DOS client.

Step 1: Description

In this task, you'll learn the tasks necessary for setting up your DOS-based machine to connect to the RAS server. You'll find the drivers mentioned in the \clients\ras directory of your NT Server installation CD-ROM. You need to copy them to the DOS machine before starting this task.

Step 2: Action

1. Begin by starting your DOS machine and typing rasload to install the necessary RAS drivers.

2. Next, type rasphone to open the telephone book. Create and save an entry as needed by filling in the blanks as shown.

3. If a phone book entry is already in place, add entries as needed depending on how many machines you intend to dial into.

4. Press Alt+D or use the menu and choose the Connect option. Fill in your password and other data as requested.

5. A dialog box informs you that the DOS machine is attempting a connection. If you entered the wrong number or want to cancel the call, press the Esc key. When the connection is successful, you can use resources you are authorized for as if you were on the network.

Step 3: Review

This task showed you how to set up and use a DOS client for accessing the RAS server. You use this any time you want DOS-based machines to access the server through dial-in.

Finding Out More About Remote Access Server

Microsoft offers an extensive Web site for all its products. The most useful for our purposes is the Knowledge Base, Microsoft's detailed technical support area that is found at www.microsoft.com. Choose the Support option shown. From here, you search by category and word for any available articles.

Performing a search for the category NT Server and the keyword RAS provides a list of topics concerning RAS that can help you correct any problems that occur. Searching for multilink provides a couple of articles relating to this service. For example, in Windows NT Server 4.0, a problem exists with the use of multilink. To use multilink, you need to set the LCP (Link Control Protocol) extensions or multilink does not function.

On our search, we found numerous RAS topics concerning everything from a list of supported modems to logon scripts for Windows for Workgroup clients. The main difficulty with using this service concerns an inability to quickly specify only NT Server 4.0 problems rather than problems associated with earlier versions of NT. Many of the articles apply to NT Server 3.1.

Many of these solutions will provide answers regardless of the version, however, so this is still a good place to look to gather additional problem-solving data.

By using the various Microsoft options on this Web page, you can download new service packs (Windows NT 4.0 Service Pack 2 was available in December when we wrote this book). You also can obtain new drivers or sample files for your applications and equipment.

17

Under the Feature Articles forum, you can find the latest hardware compatibility list and patches. So if you are having difficulty getting a modem to work, look here and see whether the modem is a Microsoft-certified device.

Finally, a Windows NT Server newsgroup forum provides additional details and user experiences. This is also an excellent way to gather information and query others about a problem. The specific RAS and other communication-issues newsgroup is found at the following address:

```
microsoft.public.windowsnt.protocol.ras
```

These Microsoft services are an invaluable aid in determining a problem and possibly finding a solution. As in many situations, it's likely that the problem you are having also occurred elsewhere and that other people have repaired the problem and moved on. They are usually able and willing to share that information with you.

17

Security and RAS

Remote Access Services offer a rich degree of accessibility, but this comes with a price. Installing RAS leaves you somewhat vulnerable to attack from the outside world. So what can you do? Fortunately, there are various things you can do to enhance the level of security over this important service.

First, RAS offers three types of password authentication when dialing into the server. The first option allows the use of standard clear text passwords and is the least secure. Next, NT offers the Require encrypted authentication option, and this supports more robust encryption of the passwords, using algorithms such as SPAP, DES, and CHAP. You choose which algorithm to use. SPAP is used by Shiva LAN Rover devices, DES is the popular encryption technology used by older clients such as Windows for Workgroups (when supporting the RAS client software), and CHAP is a challenge-response authentication offering arguably the best authentication.

The final option, Require Microsoft encryption authentication, uses a special version of CHAP called, funnily enough, MS-CHAP. This version uses an internal algorithm by RSA Data Security Incorporated, offering a very secure level of encryption. Two NT machines will always use the MS-CHAP authentication when talking to one another.

If you use the final option, Microsoft offers additional levels of security by allowing you to fully encrypt the traffic between the machines. This option, though a little slower, provides a strong level of control over outsiders gaining access to data sent over public networks or telephone lines, because all the information is encrypted, not just the passwords.

The RAS service also offers additional ways to protect your system. After it's installed, RAS allows you to control who can use the dial-up service by providing the ability to control dial-in permissions. By default, no one can dial into the NT machine. You need to set up access for each user to whom you want to allow RAS access by using the User Manager dialog box.

Another security mechanism RAS offers is call-back. This mechanism allows you to set up specific numbers for each user so that when the user calls in to access RAS, NT calls the person back at that predefined telephone number. This technique also offers the organization a way of managing long-distance calls because the RAS server, not the user, initiates the final dial-in call.

After you allow dial-in, you can set up additional controls. Perhaps you want users to perform only certain functions from outside the office and not be able to do everything they normally can. By using the network access option, you can restrict users to either the entire network or a particular server. You can find this option in the Network Control Panel dialog box.

These options allow you to customize access and ensure a secure dialog between your client machines and the network. Using the fully encrypted mode and restricting access to a single server offers an excellent level of control. Regardless, we would be remiss if we did not mention that regardless of the level of security added to RAS, if your user community does not select hard-to-guess passwords, your security is still weak. Many system penetrations, we believe, are a result of poor password selection.

Summary

In this chapter, you learned some of the fundamentals of NT's Remote Access Services. The chapter showed you how to set up and manage a RAS connection and how to set up special options that RAS includes, such as encryption and scripts. When combined with the information you'll learn this afternoon and tomorrow about other types of connections and networking fundamentals, you'll become quite proficient in managing Remote Access Services with NT Server 4.0.

Microsoft offers additional technical depth about RAS on its Knowledge Base, and this is a great place to search for additional information. You can find it by going to the Microsoft Web page at www.microsoft.com and going to the Support forum, where you'll find the Knowledge Base search icon.

In this chapter, you discovered a lot about dialing up other machines. You learned the following points:

☐ What RAS is and why you use it.

☐ Why there is some confusion over RAS and Dial-Up Networking and Microsoft's desire to move away from the RAS term, perhaps for consistency with Windows 95 technology.

☐ That RAS does not install automatically when you first install NT 4.0. You need to specifically install this service and set it up to manage your dial-up connections.

☐ How to administer RAS and set up the machines you will call and the protocols you intend to use.

☐ That NT does not automatically find modems like a Windows 95 machine and often picks the wrong one when you tell it to search for the hardware in use. It is often best to manually tell NT which modems are installed and the type and brand of each.

☐ That a really neat option in NT's RAS is the capability of linking more than one modem together and obtaining a single dial-up connection that is twice as fast using the facility called multilink PPP, a facility that you enable on both the server and the client machines.

☐ How to disconnect a user and administer the RAS telephone book.

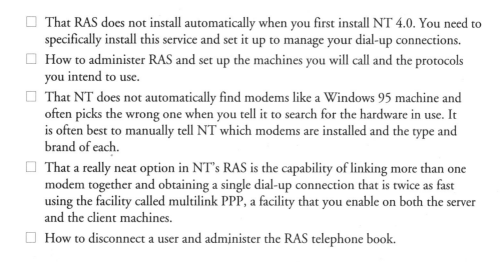

Workshop

To wrap up the day, you can review terms and tasks from the chapter, and see the answers to some commonly asked questions.

Terminology Review

DHCP—The acronym for Dynamic Host Configuration Protocol. This is a tool that allows dynamic IP allocation, simplifying machine configuration in your network.

DUN—The acronym for Dial-Up Networking. Easy to confuse with RAS because it is the newer version of RAS and it performs the same function. It might have been renamed to provide some consistency with Windows 95 terms.

ISDN—Another acronym, this one for Integrated Services Digital Network. ISDN is becoming popular with home users as well as businesses. This type of service is more difficult to set up than other techniques, but it offers up to 128Kbps speed. This is a significant boost over modems that offer 33.6Kbps or even the newer 56Kbps speeds.

ISP—The short term for Internet Service Provider, a firm that offers connections to the Internet for a fee.

NetBEUI—IBM's fast, nonroutable protocol. A simple protocol designed to extend NetBIOS that allows up to 254 sessions.

pad—The short term for packet assembler-dissembler, used in X.25 technologies.

RAS—The acronym for Remote Access Services. This is the NT 3.*x* version of Dial-Up Networking; it is used to connect machines via telephone or other means.

TCP/IP—Transmission Control Protocol/Internet Protocol. This is the protocol suite that drives the Internet. Very basically, TCP handles the message details while IP manages the addressing. It is probably the most widely used network protocol in the world today.

X.25—This protocol allows you to route information through a packet-switching public data network, such as Datapac. An older technology, it operates at a top speed of 64Kbps and was designed for earlier days when telephone networks were less reliable than today.

Task List

The information provided in this chapter showed you how to set up and manage the Remote Access Services of Windows NT Server. You learned to do the following:

☐ Install Remote Access Services

☐ Install a new modem

☐ Install multilink PPP services

☐ Connect to a RAS server using RAS

☐ Connect to a RAS server from a DOS client machine

Q&A

Q Can I connect to the network without using RAS?

A Yes. Remember that RAS lets you connect only through a dial-up modem, but you are always able to connect via the network. In fact, if you are connected through the network, you won't use RAS unless you want to call in from home or while traveling. In addition, there are numerous other ways to dial up and connect. Your organization might use special software such as Citrix or special dial-up modems that offer additional security features.

Q Can I connect more than one or two modems to the system? I have many people who want to dial up the server and work from home, but I see only two ports available on my computer.

A Yes, you can set up a large number of modems. First, NT RAS supports up to 256 connections. Next, you need special hardware called multiport I/O boards to increase the number of modems you can connect to your system. These boards are designed to use one connection on your system and allow a slew of modems on the other side, simplifying your problem. Many modem manufacturers offer special rack-mounted modems, so you don't have to have a couple of hundred standard-type modems cluttering your computer room. Be sure to check the Hardware Compatibility List, though, because not all multiport boards are certified to run with NT 4.0.

Q I heard that you can connect NT to another machine using two modems and combine their speed somehow to get faster access. How is this possible?

A One of the really neat things Microsoft added to the server technology is a service called multilink PPP. Using this service and two NT machines, you can set up two modems on one of the NT machines and connect to the other through them both. Note that both machines need to be running NT. You use either NT Server or NT Workstation to do it, however, because they both offer this capability. What NT does is recognize that you have two modems on the machine and have set an option telling NT to use both when calling another machine. NT then combines the speed of the two modems and connects at the greater speed. The only caveat is this: You must be running only NT machines, and both machines need to have multilink enabled for this to work. We see a number of people inquiring on the NT newsgroups why their particular version doesn't work, and it typically is because only one of the machines is running NT.

17

Chapter 18

Understanding TCP/IP

The term TCP/IP has become the one to know in the 1990s. From relative obscurity, it is fast becoming the most important protocol in the world through its widespread use. Its very strength lies in the capability to handle network traffic in either the LAN or the WAN arena, a feat its brethren—NetBEUI, SNA, and X.25—cannot do.

Yesterday, you learned all about using Remote Access Services and dialing into your server in a secure fashion. Today, you'll learn to use TCP/IP to offer networking services and learn about the way this protocol provides networking services that are robust and efficient.

This chapter begins with an overview of TCP/IP: what it is, how it functions, and why it has become so popular today. The chapter concludes with details on setting up your NT Server to run TCP/IP. You'll also learn about some of the services TCP/IP offers, and you'll learn how to use those services. You'll be introduced to a couple of the most common services of TCP/IP: FTP (File Transfer Protocol) and Telnet.

In this chapter, you'll learn all about RAS, what to use it for, how to set it up, and what to look for when implementing it.

What Is TCP/IP?

What is TCP/IP? It is an acronym for Transmission Control Protocol/Internet Protocol. You can think of it as a collection of tools used originally by the U.S. Department of Defense (DOD) to facilitate communication among the many kinds of computers the DOD had in use.

Now you're probably wondering, what is a protocol? It's simple, really. Think of a protocol as being the set of rules and formalities used by various computers to pass messages to each other, thereby facilitating a dialog that can each understand. One particular protocol might not be sufficient, so you often find various protocols in use, layered on top of each other. TCP/IP, as you can see, actually consists of two protocols: the Transmission Control and the Internet protocols. For ease of use, it is usually referred to as the TCP/IP protocol.

The original goal of TCP/IP consisted of providing solid failure recovery, a capability to handle high error rates, and machine and vendor independence. It was, after all, designed primarily by the military as a defense network.

As discussed earlier, the TCP/IP protocol consists of two separate protocols working in concert to provide communication between disparate computer systems. By looking at how the acronym is created, you can guess that TCP runs on top of the IP protocol, using it for basic networking. Let's look at each protocol in turn and see how each manages its portion of the network. Be warned, however, that the discussion is light and treads only partially into this rather arcane world. For a true understanding of TCP/IP, you need to read and study some of the many books provided on this topic. Here, you'll learn enough to become dangerous and manage the implementation of TCP/IP on your NT Server network.

The Internet Protocol

The Internet Protocol (IP) is the most fundamental part of the Internet network. All data must be packaged in an IP packet to be sent across the network and routed to its destination. In a simple network such as we have in our home office, there is only one segment; therefore, all traffic is sent across the network to all the machines that are connected, and no router is necessary.

In a larger office network, you might have several separate network segments, each connected by some type of router. In a simple network, all machines hear each other. In the more complex network, machines can hear only those machines that are on their segment; they cannot hear any machine that is on another LAN nearby without some device that takes their message and transports it to the other LAN. This device is typically called a router. To perform this routing, the machine needs to know who you are, and this is where your IP address comes into play.

In this hypothetical network, each machine needs to be identified with a particular IP address. This address is then used by routers to identify each machine and to transmit data to and from these machines.

The IP address consists of a 32-bit number assigned by the network administrator for each machine in the network. (You'll learn tomorrow that this isn't necessary anymore if you use the service called Dynamic Host Configuration Protocol, or DHCP.) A bit of math tells you this allows for four billion addresses.

Setting up each machine with this 32-bit number, however, is no easy task. Imagine trying not to make a mistake when typing an address like 11111111 00001000 10101010 00001010 (255 8 170 10). It would be hard to perform without some mistake, and the mistake would be equally hard to find!

To combat this potential problem, the dotted quad or dotted decimal notation was formed. This breaks down the 32 bits into four distinct fields of 8 bits. Each field is then converted to a decimal number that corresponds to the value of the 8 bits it represents. For example, in our earlier example we showed an IP address of 11111111000010001010101000001010. This breaks down into four sections: 11111111 00001000 10101010 00001010. Each of these numbers further breaks down to a decimal value, 255 8 170 10, and this is the number used today to describe an IP address.

Don't worry too much about the need to convert these numbers. Almost no one uses them anymore because you are typically assigned IP addresses using the notation just mentioned. It is helpful, however, to understand how those numbers are generated.

Internally, the IP address contains two parts, the network ID (netid) and the host ID (hostid). Five address classes are available for use: A, B, C, D, and E. Only classes A, B, and C are used for normal company addressing; D and E are reserved for special functions.

The netid portion of the address is what identifies your network as unique. The hostid describes the actual nodes in your network. As you can see in the following list, a class A network has more than 16,777,214 network nodes available to it. Each of the three classes is used to describe a particular type of network. Unfortunately, the developers of this scheme decided to use 8 bits to define each class, severely limiting the real number of addresses available. A class A address uses the first 8 of the 32 bits for its definition. Class B uses the next 8, and class C, the third 8 bits. This leaves the really large networks with huge potential numbers of hosts and leaves class B addresses with up to 65,535 hosts. The lowly class C addresses can have 254 hosts. Here's a rundown of the three classes:

- ☐ *A:* This is used for very large networks. Because only 7 bits are available (one is used to tell how many bits are in the address), there can be only 127 Class A networks. Don't bother trying to get one, no matter how large your company. They are all gone. Each network can have 16,777,214 nodes attached.

- ☐ *B:* The class B addresses allow for up to 16,383 networks, each of which allows for 65,534 nodes. This class is used for medium-to-large types of businesses and is quickly running out of available addresses.

- ☐ *C:* This is the most common IP network. There are 2,097,151 networks available, but each can have only 254 network nodes attached. This number is fine for most small companies.

Even with all these huge numbers of networks, the present IP addressing scheme is running out of room. Although several proposals are in place for expanding the numbering scheme for IP, they are subject to great debate, and no solid plan is yet available.

NOTE

You set up a simple router using a computer with two Ethernet (or Token Ring) cards in it. Network staff call this a multihomed computer. Each Ethernet card is assigned an IP address. Next, one of the cards is attached to one side of the network, and the other card is attached to the second network segment. The machine must be smart enough to transmit data from one card to the other as necessary, making it the router. It does this by knowing what the addresses of each segment consist of and by applying routing logic to send the packets between machines as needed.

Within each of these networks are a few addresses that are reserved for special functions and that cannot be used by one of your machines. Typically, they include the addresses identified in Table 18.1. In the table, the addresses are shown using a convention of A.B.C. to represent the first three levels of the address because, of course, these will differ across organizations.

Table 18.1. Reserved IP addresses.

Name	IP Address	Description
Loopback	127.0.0.1	This is reserved for loopback testing. To test your network, you send a message to this address, and it should be returned to you. A class A address, it's a huge waste of an Internet address space.

Name	IP Address	Description
Subnet mask	A.B.C.1	The first address of your network is typically saved for use as the router address for that subnet. All subnets should have a router address, and by convention this is the address used.
Network number	A.B.C.0	This address is used to tell a router that the entire range of your network is from A.B.C.0 to A.B.C.255.
IP broadcast	A.B.C.255	On a simple C class network, the broadcast address is the last one, or 255.

As the owner of a new class C address, you can add 253 computers because you cannot use some of those addresses. For example, suppose that you have an address of 223.255.100.0. You cannot use that address because it's the one that describes the entire network for you. You cannot use 223.255.100.255 because that is your IP broadcast number, and you don't use 223.255.100.1 because that is used as your router address. This leaves you with all the rest of the numbers to assign to your machines, a total of 253.

IP addresses identify the particular device on a network. IP's primary job is to provide routing, not error checking. In fact, if an IP packet arrives at its destination with an error saying it was damaged in transit, IP just drops the packet and continues to the next one. It doesn't tell anyone, making it not very reliable. So IP does not guarantee that a message will arrive when it is sent. Another protocol is needed to help provide that facility, and that is the job of TCP.

The Transmission Control Protocol

The primary job of the Transmission Control Protocol (TCP) is to provide the orderly transmission of data from one host to another. Its job is to make sure that the data arrives safely. Whereas IP just sends the data and forgets about it, TCP first performs a handshake with the other computer to introduce itself and then sets up the connection between the two machines.

TCP's main job is to provide end-to-end integrity for the messages crossing the Internet on IP. IP packets can arrive in sequence and at any time across the network, leaving TCP to reassemble the packets in order as they reach the receiving host. TCP, then, is in charge of packet sequencing.

NOTE

> An older protocol called UDP, or User Datagram Protocol, works in a similar manner to TCP except that it does not provide the end-to-end integrity that TCP does. Although UDP is still in use, TCP has overtaken it in popularity and effectiveness with its better data integrity features.

TCP also manages flow control, pacing the data being sent so that the receiving host need not worry about sorting each packet. In fact, TCP doesn't send a packet until the receiver is ready for it. Remember that the first task TCP performed is a handshake with the receiving host so that it can coordinate all these functions.

Finally, TCP provides the error detection and correction that IP lacks. TCP manages this task very efficiently, telling the other machine to resend a block if it doesn't hear back quickly enough. Each machine, of course, knows how many blocks it can send and at what speed and knows to expect an acknowledgment when each block is processed. If a block is sent and has an error, the receiver merely drops it and waits for the sender to resend the block after not getting a reply.

Working together, TCP and IP provide a robust error-checking suite of protocols that provides the services for most of the machines using the Internet today.

Installing TCP/IP

So enough about the background already. Let's see what the steps are to install this protocol on your NT Server. In Task 18.1, you'll install TCP/IP.

Task 18.1. Installing TCP/IP.

Step 1: Description

In this task, you'll learn to install the Transmission Control Protocol/Internet Protocol on your NT Server. You can install TCP/IP during the NT installation process. As you recall, we suggested in Chapter 3, "Installing Windows NT Server on the File Server," that you leave out that portion of the installation until later. Now is the time.

Step 2: Action

1. Begin by signing onto your server as Administrator. Next, open the Control Panel and double-click the Network icon. The Network dialog box appears, as shown in Figure 18.1.

18

Figure 18.1.

The Network dialog box.

2. Click on the Protocols tab. Any protocols you already installed show in the list.

3. Click the Add button to add a new protocol. NT builds a list of all the protocols it supports and provides this to you. You see an example in Figure 18.2.

Figure 18.2.

All the network protocols available.

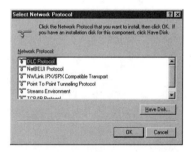

4. Select the TCP/IP protocol from the list, and click the OK button. NT asks whether there is a DHCP server on your network and whether you want to use that server to obtain your addresses. For this example, choose No. You'll learn all about using and configuring a DHCP server tomorrow. Figure 18.3 shows you the DHCP dialog box.

5. You might be asked to provide the address of your installation files. Place the NT install CD-ROM in the drive, and enter its address. Click OK when you are ready. NT copies a bunch of files to the local NT system directory. If RAS is installed, the installation asks whether you want RAS configured to use TCP/IP. Choose an appropriate answer to continue.

Figure 18.3.

Specifying whether to use DHCP.

6. When the install finishes adding TCP/IP to RAS, you should see the TCP/IP protocol displayed in the Protocols tab of your Network Protocols dialog box. You can see an example in Figure 18.4.

Figure 18.4.

TCP/IP appears in the Protocols list.

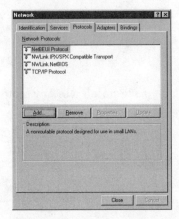

7. Click the Close button. NT goes through various binding processes before displaying the Microsoft TCP/IP dialog box. You see an example in Figure 18.5.

Figure 18.5.

The TCP/IP configuration dialog box.

18

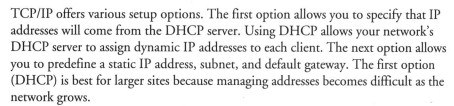

TCP/IP offers various setup options. The first option allows you to specify that IP addresses will come from the DHCP server. Using DHCP allows your network's DHCP server to assign dynamic IP addresses to each client. The next option allows you to predefine a static IP address, subnet, and default gateway. The first option (DHCP) is best for larger sites because managing addresses becomes difficult as the network grows.

8. Enter the necessary IP addresses for your network. Click OK when you are done. NT completes the process and tells you to reboot the server, after which TCP/IP services are available.

Step 3: Review

This task showed you how to add TCP/IP to your network and enable users to use this dynamic protocol suite. You needed to add some IP addresses to complete the task.

The preceding task allows you to connect your machines by using the Transmission Control Protocol/Internet Protocol over the network. But you do not want to use all these IP addresses all the time. Surely there is another method for finding companies across the Internet. In the next section, you'll learn about using the HOSTS and DNS systems for resolving IP addresses to host names.

The Windows HOSTS Naming System

Microsoft provides a simple method for tracking IP addresses and resolving them to a host name. In this method, a file called HOSTS provides a table of IP addresses and host names. It is a simple ASCII text file you create to store these name resolutions. You store the file in the \winnt\system32\drivers\etc directory in an NT system and in the Windows directory on any Windows 95 or Windows client machines. NT then looks at this file when trying to resolve a name you specify.

On each line, you type the host computer's IP address followed by at least one space and the computer's host name. That's not too hard, is it? You create this file and just maintain it as each computer is added to or removed from your network. The file is read each time the system does a name resolution, so you do not need to reboot to make any changes effective.

Unfortunately, using the HOSTS file it isn't quite that easy. You need to create and manage this file on every computer in your network! Every time you make a change, you need to change the file on each workstation manually as well. Aaarghh. There has to be a simpler way to maintain this information. That's where the Domain Name System (DNS) comes into play.

18

Domain Name System

After managing the overview of IP addressing, you probably wonder why you do not use those numbers when communicating across the Internet. (Some of you might use the IP address, but most folks today use another method.) Most of us today use some form of name when we connect to other domain computers. For example, if you want to connect to Microsoft, you do not use the address `207.68.137.62`. You tend to use `www.microsoft.com` instead. This is the Domain Name System (DNS) at work. Note that we are not talking about individual machines here; you use DNS to identify and name *domains*.

NOTE

> DNS has an identity crisis. It is often referred to as the Domain Name Service or the Domain Name Server. It can also be called the Domain Name System. In fact, it isn't terribly important which of these terms you use because most folks will understand what you mean regardless. Technically, however, it seems that the proper name is Domain Name System. This is the name supplied by the original Request For Comments (RFC) papers numbered 1034 and 1035 that first defined DNS. People often use the Domain Name Server term to designate the machine the system runs on.

DNS, then, provides address resolution across the Internet. Instead of trying to remember a bunch of numbers every time you want to connect to another domain, you can use an easier-to-remember name.

DNS is really only a list of IP addresses and an associated name for each address. You might think of it as a table with two entries in the forms of *IP address-name*. For example, you might see an entry like this:

```
207.68.137.62 - www.microsoft.com
```

So who controls all these names and addresses? The central authority for DNS is the InterNIC Registration Services, the people you go to when you first register a domain name. Makes sense, doesn't it? This organization ensures that your name is unique and that a current IP address is associated with it.

You can do the same thing inside your corporate network by creating and maintaining your own DNS server. But that's for another day.

The Domain Name System uses a hierarchy to establish and manage domain names. Remember the com we mentioned earlier as part of `www.microsoft.com`? DNS uses the last portion of the name to differentiate between types of domains. In Table 18.2, you see a few of the names used today.

Table 18.2. DNS domain types.

Type	Description
com	Commercial
edu	Educational
gov	Government
mil	Military
net	Network providers
org	Organizations
ca	Canada
uk	United Kingdom

Many other names now exist, of course, because more and more countries have been added. But you get the idea.

NOTE

By the time this book is published, you will be reading of the plan by the International Ad Hoc Committee (IAHC) to add several new top-level names to the Domain Name Service list. The 11-member International Ad Hoc Committee, chaired by Donald M. Heath, president and CEO of the Internet Society, sets the standards for the Internet. This plan increases the number of domains available, and this is good because most of the popular com names are already taken. These are the new names:

.firm—For businesses or firms

.store—For those offering goods to purchase

.web—For those emphasizing activities related to the WWW

.arts—For those emphasizing cultural and entertainment activities

.rec—For those emphasizing recreation/entertainment activities

.info—For those providing information services

.nom—For individuals or personal nomenclature

In addition, up to 28 new registrars will be established to grant registrations for these new second-level domain names. The new registrars will be selected by lottery from applicants who fulfill specific requirements established by the IAHC.

18

As you can imagine, the DNS servers must be really busy. InterNIC maintains something like nine of these servers across the world to manage all the requests. To recap, on your own network, you use a local name server, and when you need an address outside your own domain, you begin to use the InterNIC Domain Name Servers.

Let's look at configuring your NT system to use an existing DNS server.

Task 18.2. Configuring NT for existing DNS servers.

Step 1: Description

In this task, you'll learn to set the configuration options to let NT use an existing Domain Name Server. You perform this task if your organization has set up internal DNS servers.

Step 2: Action

1. Begin by signing onto your server as Administrator. Next, select the NT Control Panel and double-click the Network icon. Click on the Protocols tab, and then double-click on the TCP/IP protocol. (You can select TCP/IP and then click Properties to get the same effect.)

2. Next, click on the DNS tab. This tab displays the configuration options, as shown in Figure 18.6.

Figure 18.6.

The DNS configura-
tion options dialog
box.

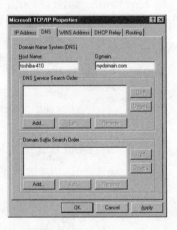

3. Enter the DNS domain name in the box titled Domain. By default, your computer's NT registered name is entered in the Host Name box.

4. Click the Add button to add a DNS server already existing on your network. You can specify three servers and change the order in which they are tried by using the up and down arrows. If the first server fails to resolve a name, NT tries the next and then the third.

18

5. Finally, you assign default domain suffixes in the box called Domain Suffix Search Order by using the Add button shown. NT allows six additional domain suffixes. Again, use the up and down arrows to tell NT in what order they are to be searched.

6. Click OK to finish the setup. Your NT machine is now set to use the internal domain names specified.

Step 3: Review

This task showed you how to configure DNS services on your NT Server. Use this any time new DNS servers are added to your network.

Understanding Winsock

By now you will know that Windows NT and other versions all use and need something called a socket interface or, in the case of Windows, a Winsock. Just what is this thing, and why is it crucial to running the network?

As you can already guess, when one machine wants to talk to another, it must know whom to call (the IP address), what type of call to make (TCP or UDP), and which program to talk to at the receiving computer.

TCP uses the IP address to find your machine, but then it needs to know what program to talk to and where to find that program. This is where *port* numbers come into play. The TCP/IP suite assigns each program that uses it a special number known as the port. You'll find that these port numbers are fairly consistent for most major programs. The following list shows a few of them:

- ☐ 5: Remote Job Entry
- ☐ 7: Echo
- ☐ 20: FTP (data)
- ☐ 21: FTP (control)
- ☐ 23: Telnet
- ☐ 25: SMTP
- ☐ 53: Name server
- ☐ 80: Web servers
- ☐ 110: Post Office Protocol (POP3)

TCP combines the IP address with a port number to produce the socket address. When my computer calls yours, it asks whether you want to talk on such and such a socket number and mentions that it can accept *x* amount of data in its buffers. If your computer is waiting, it says okay, start sending me *y* bytes of data, and the session starts. (The size of the buffer is machine dependent.) It is this exchange that makes TCP so civilized and error free.

After the computers are finished, each machine signs off and hangs up. Your program might then wait for the next connection to begin. The Winsock interface was created some time after various vendors all produced their own versions of a socket program. This led to much confusion because each program needed a particular socket in order to work. The Winsock program helped implement a more consistent approach that all vendors of TCP/IP software could support.

TCP/IP Diagnostic and Connectivity Utilities

NT provides several utilities that are common to UNIX systems. These are all automatically installed when you install TCP/IP. You'll find these services in the \winnt\system32 directory.

hostname

The hostname command simply shows you the name of the host where the command is run. The name is returned using the computer defined in the DNS tab of your TCP/IP configuration window. There are no options for the command. You see an example in Figure 18.7.

Figure 18.7.

A sample hostname *command.*

ipconfig

The ipconfig command provides you with a system's TCP/IP configuration data. It is especially useful if you receive your IP addresses using a DHCP Server. You see an example in Figure 18.8.

Figure 18.8.

Using the ipconfig *command.*

Various options are available when you're using this command. As you see in the figure, using the command without any options returns the default IP address, subnet mask, and default gateway address for any network cards bound with TCP/IP.

Following is the syntax for this command:

```
ipconfig /all ¦ /release adapter ¦ /renew adapter
```

/all: This switch causes the command to return additional IP information for all network adapters running TCP/IP. This includes the host name, all the DNS servers, the node type, the state of IP routing on your system, the NetBIOS scope ID, information as to whether your system is using DNS for NetBIOS name resolution, and the current state of WINS proxy on your system. You also get the physical address of each adapter using TCP/IP, the IP address of the adapter and its subnet mask, any WINS server it is using, and its default gateway.

/release adapter: When used without a specified optional adapter, this switch releases DHCP bindings for all adapters. You can optionally tell the switch which adapter to release from DHCP. This is useful only when you're using DHCP to obtain IP addresses.

/renew adapter: Useful only when you're using a DHCP server, this switch renews the DHCP lease. When used without a specified optional adapter, it renews DHCP bindings for all adapters. You can optionally tell the switch which adapter to renew.

nbtstat

The nbtstat command displays the status of NetBIOS over TCP/IP. You see an example in Figure 18.9.

18

Figure 18.9.

Using the nbtstat *command.*

Various options are available when you're using this command. The syntax consists of

nbtstat *switches*

where *switches* can be any of the following options:

-a *remotename*	Displays the remote computer's NetBIOS name table using the host-name address to find the computer.
-A *IP address*	Displays the remote computer's NetBIOS name table using the IP address to find the computer.
-c	Displays the local computer's NetBIOS name cache with the IP address.
-n	Displays the local computer's NetBIOS names.
-r	Displays names resolved by WINS and broadcast.
-R	Purges and reloads a remote computer's cache name table.
-s	Displays the sessions table using host names from the HOSTS file.
-S	Displays the sessions table with the IP address.
interval	Redisplays the selected statistics using the number of seconds indicated by the *interval* parameter as the intervening pause. Ctrl+C stops the display.

netstat

The netstat command displays the statistics for all TCP, UDP, and IP connections.

Various options are available when you're using this command. The syntax consists of

netstat *switches*

where *switches* can be any of the following options:

18

-a	Displays all current connections and listening ports.
-e	Displays all Ethernet statistics. Can be combined with the -s switch.
-n	Displays addresses and port numbers numerically.
-r	Displays the contents of the routing table.
-p *protocol*	Displays the connections for the protocol specified. The protocol can be TCP, UDP, or IP when used with the -s switch.
-s	Displays all protocol statistics.
interval	Redisplays the selected statistics using the number of seconds indicated by the *interval* parameter as the intervening pause. Ctrl+C stops the display.

ping

The ping command sends small packets to a host to verify whether the host is active. ping is a very common troubleshooting command for dealing with networks.

Various options are available when you're using this command. The syntax consists of

ping *switches*

where *switches* can be any of the following options:

-a	Resolves the IP address to the DNS host name.
-n *number*	Specifies the number of echo requests to send.
-1 *size*	Sends the packet length specified. The default is 64 bytes, and the maximum is 8,192 bytes.
-f	Sets the Do Not Fragment flag.
-i *ttl*	Sets the time-to-live field for the packets. Valid values are between 1 and 255.
-j *host-list*	Sets the loose source route using the entries in *host-list*.
-k *host-list*	Sets the strict source route using the entries in *host-list*.
-r *number*	Records the route of the packets in a Record Route field. Maximum of 9.
-s *number*	Specifies the time stamp for the number of hops specified by *number*.
-v *TOS*	Sets the type of service field to the value specified.
-t	Pings the host until interrupted.

18

In Figure 18.10, you see an example of the ping command at work. In our example, we pinged the Microsoft network because it is more readily recognized. We do not suggest that everyone use this, however, in politeness to Microsoft. Choose any other Web service to do your test.

Figure 18.10.

Using the ping *command.*

route

The route command is used to manipulate local routing tables for the TCP/IP protocol.

Various options are available when you're using this command. The syntax consists of

route *switches*

where *switches* can be any of the following options:

-f	Empties the routing table of all prior gateway entries. When it's used with another switch, the tables are emptied first, and then the other switch is run.
-command	Can be one of four commands:
	PRINT: Prints a route.
	ADD: Adds a route.
	DELETE: Deletes a route.
	CHANGE: Changes an existing route.
destination	Specifies the host to ping.
gateway	Specifies a gateway.
MASK	Specifies that the next parameter is the netmask.
netmask	Specifies the subnet mask value. The default is 255.255.255.255.
METRIC	Specifies the metric/cost for the destination.
-p	When used with ADD, keeps a route persistent across system boots. Used with PRINT, it displays all persistent routes.

Telnet

The Telnet utility is used to connect to any service running a standard Telnet server. Many universities offer Telnet services; one, the University of Michigan, offers a weather service. Most people today use the Web rather than Telnet, but if you come from a UNIX background, you'll still find many uses for Telnet. You see an example of the Telnet window in Figure 18.11.

Figure 18.11.

Using the Telnet utility.

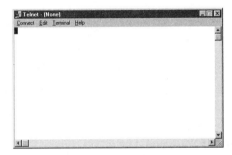

As you see in Figure 18.11, Telnet offers various menu items. NT Server does not offer a built-in Telnet server. If you want to run a Telnet service on your NT system, you will need to obtain a third-party program.

Task 18.3. Running Telnet.

Step 1: Description

In this task, you'll learn to connect to a remote terminal using Telnet. You need to have set up your modem and network parameters before starting this task. For further information, refer to Chapter 17, "Understanding Windows NT Server Remote Access Services (RAS)."

Step 2: Action

1. Begin by signing onto your server. Next, choose Start|Run and type `Telnet`. Click OK when you are ready.

2. You see a window like the one shown in Figure 18.11.

3. Click on the Connect menu and select Remote System. Telnet provides you with a Connect dialog box, as shown in Figure 18.12.

4. In the area called Host Name, type the address of the computer you are connecting with, and click the Connect button. The address can consist of either an IP address or a host name. NT connects you with the specified host.

Figure 18.12.

The Telnet Connect dialog box.

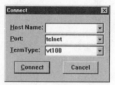

5. When you are ready, disconnect by clicking on the Connect menu and selecting the Disconnect menu option, and then click the Exit button to close Telnet. A shorter way to exit from the Telnet session is to simply type exit at the session prompt.

6. Telnet lets you create a log of your activity. To start logging, select Terminal|Start Logging. You are asked to provide the name and location of the log file. Enter an appropriate name, and Telnet begins to log all activity. You stop the logging by selecting Terminal|Stop Logging.

Step 3: Review

This task showed you how to use Telnet to connect to a remote host. You use this to connect to any server offering Telnet capability.

FTP

FTP, or File Transfer Protocol, is used to connect to other machines and download or upload files. The version that is offered with NT provides a fairly extensive Help file, as you see in Figure 18.13.

Figure 18.13.

The FTP Help utility.

You use the Open command to access a site. Specify the IP address or FTP site address after typing Open, and press Enter. The program goes to the site and provides you with the directory list. After you're connected, you use the commands as necessary to perform the work you need. To end the session and close the FTP window, type BYE or QUIT at the command prompt. If you started the FTP session from the DOS prompt, you need to manually close the FTP window following your BYE or QUIT command.

As you see, FTP is not designed to be user-friendly or even terribly GUI oriented. This is an old service that provided a sound method for exchanging files long before the Internet became as popular as it is today. You navigate through an FTP site by using methods similar to those under DOS and UNIX (after all, DOS was built based on how UNIX worked at that time). Therefore, if you are familiar with either of these operating systems, the file and directory structure appears normal to you.

You can use the version provided with NT because it does work well enough. Several third-party FTP products, however, are far more intuitive and offer a better user interface. One of these is called WS_FTP32, by a company called Ipswitch Inc. You can reach Ipswitch at info@ipswitch.com or by phone at (617) 676-5700. You can see an example of this shareware program in Figure 18.14.

Figure 18.14.

The shareware
WS_FTP32 program.

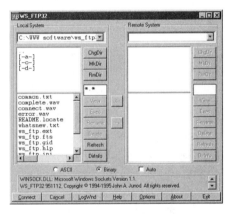

18

We're sure you'll agree that using this program is a lot easier than using the more cryptic FTP commands provided with NT. Finally, if you want to become really fancy and offer your own FTP site for others to access, you can learn to install your own FTP Server in Chapter 26, "Using NT with the Internet Information Server."

Finger

Finger is a command-line utility that is used to gather user information from any system running a finger service. NT 4.0 does not offer this service. You need to find a third-party program if you want to allow others to access your server using this command.

The syntax for the finger utility consists of

```
finger @hostname
finger username@hostname
```

where *hostname* is the computer from which you want to gather user information. Specifying only the host name provides you with a list of all users presently signed onto that computer.

Using a particular username provides the full name, address, or telephone number of the user if present.

Summary

In this chapter, you learned about some of the fundamentals of TCP/IP. The chapter shows you how to set up and manage a TCP/IP connection and how to use some special utilities designed to help you while you're connected to the network.

You learned all about the IP addressing scheme and how TCP uses a program called a socket to get the computers to communicate. Finally, you learned that the FTP program which NT provides can be replaced by better (in our opinion) shareware versions that you obtain from the Internet.

In this chapter, you discovered a lot about TCP/IP. You learned the following points:

☐ What the term TCP/IP means.

☐ What the two parts consist of and why they work together to provide error-free networking.

☐ That DNS is the acronym for Domain Name System and that many other versions of this name are used, including Domain Name Server and Domain Name Services.

☐ How to set up your NT system to use a DNS server on the Internet.

☐ How the IP address is set up and how to convert all those numbers into something more meaningful.

☐ That to talk to another machine, you use a socket program that combines the IP address and the port number to create a socket address. Your computer then uses that socket address to talk to a program on the receiving computer that is associated with that address. For example, on most machines, Telnet is associated with port number 23.

☐ How to run diagnostic utility programs.

Workshop

To wrap up the day, you can review terms and tasks from the chapter, and see the answers to some commonly asked questions.

18

Terminology Review

FTP—An acronym for File Transfer Protocol. A program that enables clients to transfer files between computers.

IP—An acronym for Internet Protocol. Performs the basic routing function to get data from one site to another.

multihomed—A computer that has more than one network card, either physically or logically. Often used as a router for connecting two networks.

router—A complex internetworking device used to send data between separate network segments. Its key benefit is the capability to connect different types of networks together, such as Ethernet and Token Ring. Routers can be set to filter the information passing through them, offering a degree of security and control in the network.

TCP—An acronym for Transmission Control Protocol, the program that handles error checking and message flow control.

Telnet—A program that allows terminal emulation for communicating between machines.

UDP—An acronym for User Datagram Protocol, an older protocol that does not offer good error detection or recovery. It is used by SNMP and TFTP as well as the Network File System (NFS).

18

Task List

The information provided in this chapter shows you how to set up and manage TCP/IP on your Windows NT Server. You learned to perform the following tasks:

- ☐ Install TCP/IP
- ☐ Configure your NT system to use existing DNS servers
- ☐ Run Telnet

Q&A

Q The TCP/IP protocol suite sounds complicated. Can I learn to use it?

A TCP/IP is a very complex set of protocols, but as you see in this chapter, you can learn enough to use the suite even though you might not clearly understand everything about it. TCP/IP books are plentiful and go into various levels of detail. We provide enough of an overview for you to understand the basics and be able to set up your NT Server to use it. To learn more, look for some of the excellent books in your local bookstore.

Q I keep hearing that the Internet will soon run out of IP addresses. Is this true?

A As you saw earlier in the chapter, around 4 billion addresses are available under the present IP address scheme. Unfortunately, the way the addresses have been assigned has sharply reduced that number. There are essentially three classes of address, A through C. Class A is already fully assigned, and no more addresses are available. The B class is filling fast and will likely be the next to go. The problem is how the addresses were split to define each class. The IP address is only 32 bits long, and the first 8 bits are used to determine a class A address, the second 8 bits determine class B addresses, and the third 8 are class C. The problem is that this means there are only 127 class A addresses and 16,384 class B addresses, so you can see how they are quickly used up. There can be about 2,097,152 class C addresses, but each of these allows only at best about 254 hosts. This is fine for small companies with only a couple of hundred machines but is a big problem for anyone using more than that number. A couple of solutions are being looked at, including making the IP address longer and using a newer method for splitting the IP address called CIDR, or Classless Internet Domain Routing.

Q Should I create my own DNS server for my network?

A The answer to this question really depends on how large your network is and whether you want to go through the considerable effort needed to implement and manage a Domain Name Server. A small organization might just use a HOSTS file and manage its network mostly using manual methods. If you are running a large private network, you are likely going to set up your own DNS server to manage that network. The Internet, of course, uses the InterNIC DNS servers.

DAY

10

Chapter 19

Understanding DHCP

Every computer running TCP/IP needs specific information to identify itself uniquely, the network of which it is a member, and the location for packets not bound for computers on the local network. This information is referred to as the IP address, subnet mask, and default gateway, respectively. (If you haven't yet read Chapter 18, "Understanding TCP/IP," do so before reading this chapter.)

Windows NT 4.0 supports several protocols for determining this information. You must make these protocols recognize each other so that they understand the names you give your computers, users, groups, and network resources. TCP/IP parameters are difficult to manage properly and easy to configure incorrectly, and they require a great deal of administrative overhead.

Microsoft provides NT facilities such as the Windows Internet Naming Service (WINS), the traditional IP Domain Name Service (DNS), and the Dynamic Host Configuration Protocol (DHCP) to help.

The Dynamic Host Configuration Protocol, the subject of this chapter, was designed to dynamically configure workstations with IP addresses and related TCP/IP information. This chapter describes how to install DHCP Servers and how to use the DHCP Manager to manage these servers. In this chapter, you'll learn about these topics:

- [ ] Naming components and addressing your network properly
- [ ] Managing dynamic IP addresses with DHCP
- [ ] Implementing DHCP
- [ ] Defining DHCP scopes
- [ ] Configuring DHCP options
- [ ] Administering DHCP Clients
- [ ] Backing up and restoring DHCP database files

Before you embark on these tasks, it is important to spend a little time learning about naming and name resolution.

Name Resolution

On a TCP/IP network, computers use IP addresses to find each other. You know from yesterday that IP addresses are the unique identifiers for every computer and device on the Internet (that is, node). But on the Internet and on a Windows NT Server network, users normally rely on computer names because they are easier to remember.

A computer's Internet address consists of two basic components: a *host* name and a *domain* name. A host name is the name of a computer (usually the name you gave your computer when you set up Windows NT Server). For Internet purposes, a domain name is typically an organization name. The domain name is used, along with the host name, to create a Fully Qualified Domain Name (FQDN) for the computer. The FQDN is the host name followed by a period, followed by the domain name. An example is `sales01.pda.com`, where `sales01` is the host name and `pda.com` is the domain name. Host names are stored in the Internet Domain Name System in a table that maps names to IP addresses.

Resolving Host Names

On Windows NT Server networks, computers typically use WINS and DNS to find the Internet addresses they're looking for.

Using Windows Internet Name Service

A WINS server maintains a database that dynamically maps computer names to IP addresses on a Windows NT Server network. When you enable the WINS service, name resolution takes place automatically. Tables on the WINS server are created, maintained, and updated automatically by the service. This is a built-in service that ships with Windows NT Server;

19

it completely removes the drudgery of manually managing the IP to the host-name mapping table, a formerly tedious IP network-management chore. You'll learn all about WINS this afternoon.

Using Domain Name System

DNS is a standard TCP/IP application used to provide domain and host names to IP address translations on the Internet. DNS can handle two-way translations (from name to address and back again). The key task for DNS is to take host names and convert those names to the IP addresses that the Internet requires for transmission. The information DNS needs to do this is maintained on *domain name servers* that reply to queries for specific name information.

To enable DNS name resolution on a Windows NT Server network, all you need do is specify the DNS options in the DNS Configuration dialog box that comes up when you install TCP/IP services. In most cases, you'll be furnished with a DNS Server address by your ISP, which you'll use to configure your client IP software and your Windows NT Server. For small networks, maintaining your own DNS Server isn't necessary; you should rely on using your ISP's DNS Server. For larger networks, Windows NT Server versions of DNS Servers are available with the Microsoft Internet Information Server.

Configuring TCP/IP

If your organization has absolutely no plans to ever connect to the public Internet, you can assign any IP address you choose. If you later want to connect to the Internet, however, you'll be facing a painful reconfiguration process. If your company does plan an Internet connection, you must allocate the IP addresses that have been assigned to your organization by your ISP.

Whatever plan your business adopts, you have two choices as to how to assign these addresses on your network. As the Windows NT Server network administrator, you can assign IP addresses for an intranet and then individually configure each host and device. Another option is to use the DHCP to assign these addresses automatically.

19

Dynamic Host Configuration Protocol

Using the DHCP service on your Windows NT Server network allows you to dynamically assign IP addresses and other configuration parameters from an available address pool to individual computers and devices on the local network or subnet. You install DHCP as part of the process of installing Microsoft TCP/IP. You must configure the DHCP Server manually, because it cannot dynamically assign an IP address to itself. After you complete this configuration, a pool of available IP addresses is entered into a table on the DHCP Server. When a Windows NT Server TCP/IP workstation starts, the DHCP Server automatically configures it from the predefined pool of IP addresses.

Naming Services

You can execute a simple command such as `net use f:\\pda\apps` to map drive F: to the apps share on the PDA server. When you're using the TCP/IP protocol, however, it doesn't know how to interpret the name PDA as the server. Instead, it understands IP addresses, such as `199.199.199.2`.

If you use the TCP/IP protocol on your network, you need a utility to convert IP addresses into names and vice versa. The next sections discuss naming considerations for your network.

NetBIOS Names

A NetBIOS name often is referred to as a computer name. When you installed your NT network, you gave each workstation and server a unique computer name. Then all your related utilities knew the machine by its name. Each time you issue a command that requires the computer name, NT knows what device you're talking about. Previously, you learned about creating good names. The best naming scheme is one that is meaningful and requires the least amount of maintenance.

TCP/IP Names

TCP/IP uses a scheme for names different from the NetBIOS/NetBEUI naming scheme. TCP/IP uses 32-bit numbers to construct IP addresses (for example, `199.199.199.2`). Each computer, host, or node on a TCP/IP network must have a unique IP address.

IP addresses are not meaningful to most humans and are therefore difficult to remember. Thus, it's helpful to have a way to convert IP addresses into meaningful names. On an NT network, you use computer names (also known as NetBIOS names). The Internet community uses domain names. Translation methods, such as WINS and DNS, maintain databases for converting an IP address to either a computer name (WINS) or a domain name (DNS).

If you've ever used a Web browser on the Internet, you know that you can type a URL (Uniform Resource Locator) such as `http://199.199.199.2/default.htm` or `http://www.pda.com/default.htm` to obtain access to a Web page. That's because the Internet uses DNS to resolve IP addresses to domain names and vice versa. If you type the IP address, your Web browser goes directly to the location. If you type a domain name, your request is routed to a DNS Server that resolves the name to an IP address, and then your Web browser goes to the location.

The naming scheme you can use when you plan to connect to the Internet is limited. That's because the Internet Network Information Center (InterNIC) is in charge of approving and maintaining the database of Internet domain names. You can request any domain name you want, but when someone else is using it or has a legitimate legal claim to a trade or brand name, you can't use it. For example, you probably cannot use coke.com or honda.com; likewise, when the name pda.com is registered to someone else, you can't get that name for your use.

The format of an IP name is *host.domainname*. The domainname is something you can't guarantee, but it typically represents your organization. The host name usually is the name of the computer you attach to when you log onto your network. For example, if your domain name is pda.com and your computer name is oriole, your Fully Qualified Domain Name is oriole.pda.com. To be valid, the FQDN must have a corresponding entry in some DNS Server's database that translates it into a unique IP address; for example, oriole.pda.com might resolve into 199.199.199.2.

As long as you're isolated from the Internet, you can assign any names you like on your network. But if you ever connect your network to the Internet, you'll have to go back and change everything. If your network might ever connect to the Internet, obtain and install valid addresses and domain names now. That way, you'll be ready when you go to connect to the Internet. For more information, ask your ISP for details on obtaining a domain name. They will probably need to install it and its corresponding IP address in their DNS Server, so they're the right source for this information.

To learn more about the process of obtaining a domain name in general, visit InterNIC's Web site. You'll find details on name registration services as well as the directory and database services that support the Internet's distributed collection of DNS Servers.

Protocol Addressing Differences

To summarize, different protocols use different addressing schemes. TCP/IP understands numbers (for example, 199.199.199.2). NetBIOS understands computer names (for example, \\oriole). When you install NT on a server, you give it a computer name. If you're using the IP protocol, you also assign an IP address to the server. So now the server has a computer name and an IP address.

Suppose that you're trying to find your server from a workstation. If you're using a utility such as Windows NT Explorer, you type the server's name rather than its IP address. If you're using a TCP/IP utility such as PING (the Packet Internet Groper), you type the server's IP address.

So how does Windows NT handle the different addresses? Well, that's the subject for this afternoon, but let's look at it quickly.

Using WINS

WINS is a dynamic database that Microsoft designed to resolve NetBIOS-derived computer names to IP addresses (for example, server name to 199.199.199.2). You enter a computer name and out pops the IP address. The database is dynamic, which means that as the network changes and names come and go, the database changes automatically. WINS is something like a French-English dictionary that's constantly updated as new words are added. You give it a French word, and out pops the English word or translation.

WINS Servers

A WINS Server maintains a database that maps IP addresses to their respective computer names. Instead of sending out broadcasts for address information, which consumes excess network bandwidth, a workstation in need of address information makes a request directly to a nearby WINS Server. This lets workstations take advantage of well-defined local service and obtain address information more quickly and efficiently. Also, when workstations log onto the network, they will provide information about themselves to the WINS Server so that any changes in their names or addresses automatically will cause the server's database to change accordingly.

WINS Clients

When configuring workstations on your network, you'll provide the IP addresses for the WINS Servers on your network. When workstations boot, they provide the WINS Server with their computer names and IP addresses. The server handles everything else. If a workstation needs an IP address that corresponds to a computer name, it asks the WINS Server.

The Automated Method

The best way to implement an address translation service is to automate it and remove the possibility of human error. That's exactly what WINS does for a network. The WINS Server handles the mapping between computer names and IP addresses, and it maintains a dynamic database that's updated automatically as computer names or IP addresses change. Systems querying the WINS Server to get the translated information are known as WINS clients.

The Manual Method

If you've spent any time around LAN Manager networks, you might be familiar with a text file called LMHosts in the *SystemRoot*\SYSTEM32\DRIVERS\ETC subdirectory. It too can provide a source of information for translating between NetBIOS names and IP addresses.

If you want to use LMHosts on your network, you must manually establish and then update the mappings between NetBIOS names (or computer names) to IP addresses yourself. That is, if a computer name or IP address changes on the network, you must update this file by hand. In a large organization, this method is impractical. For small networks of 10 addresses or fewer, it's not unworkable, providing that the names on your network don't change too often.

With the LMHosts approach, an oversight or mistake on your part might introduce an addressing error on your network. A duplicate name or address on your network or a mistake in an address assignment can prevent a user from using the network. Perhaps it's better to let Windows NT handle this job automatically.

The DHCP Method

Now that you understand why each node on your network needs a unique address, a question arises: How should you assign IP addresses to your entire network? That is, should you assign these addresses manually, which forces them to be assigned permanently (that is, static addresses)? Or should you let the system make the assignments automatically, which means that the addresses are assigned dynamically?

Until the release of Windows NT 4.0, WINS did not make sense for smaller networks. For them, it was easier to assign static IP addresses, but it was a never-ending task. With Windows NT, however, Microsoft included the Dynamic Host Configuration Protocol, which automates the assignment of IP addresses to clients. No more manually managing addresses. With DHCP, your server handles this task. You simply tell the server that it's a DHCP Server. You can do this during installation, or you can add the service later (DHCP runs as an NT service). After DHCP is installed, you configure it to manage a range (also called pool) of IP addresses, and the DHCP service handles the allocation and assignment of these addresses. DHCP even manages variable checkout intervals for individual addresses so that regular users can obtain permanent assignments, and contractors or short-term users can obtain only limited leases on their IP addresses.

You configure your DHCP Server service with a range of IP addresses, any addresses within that range that shouldn't be used, and one or more subnet masks. If you're not sure what a subnet mask is, ask your ISP to explain it to you. You also tell the server how long each assignment should last (that is, the lease period).

For example, let's assume that you assign the DHCP Server the range 199.199.199.60 through 199.199.199.90 with a subnet mask of 255.255.255.224. Based on that assignment, the server knows that it can assign any unused address within that range (that is, 199.199.199.60,

19

`199.199.199.61`, `199.199.199.62`, and so on through `199.199.199.90`) to a client that needs an IP address. If you told the DHCP Server to exclude certain addresses, it would not assign those addresses under any circumstance.

When a client or workstation boots up with the IP protocol, it sends a message saying, "I need an IP address. Is there a server out there that can give me one?" The DHCP Server responds by sending the workstation an IP address with a lease period. This means that the workstation can use the IP address, but only for a temporary period of time—hence the term *IP lease*. You might have noticed that you can set the term of an IP lease from DHCP; it's one of the settings in Scope|Properties.

The client then knows how long it will have the lease. Even when you reboot or reset your computer, it remembers what lease is active for it and how much longer the lease will be in effect.

NOTE

On a Windows 3.*x* machine, the lease information is kept in DHCP.BIN in the Windows directory.

On a Windows 95 machine, it's in `HKEY_LOCAL_MACHINE\System\` `CurrentControlSet\Services\VxD\DHCP\Dhcp-infoxx`, where *xx* is two digits.

Windows NT DHCP Clients store their leased IP address in the Registry. Each time the system boots and sends a `DHCPDISCOVER` message, it requests the IP address that was stored in the Registry.

So if your PC had a five-day lease on some address and you rebooted two days into its lease, the PC wouldn't just blindly ask for an IP address; instead, it would go back to the DHCP Server that it got its IP address from and request the particular IP address that it had before. If the DHCP Server was still up, it would acknowledge the request, letting the workstation use the IP address. If, on the other hand, the DHCP Server had its lease information wiped out through some disaster, it would do one of two things. It would either give the IP address to the machine (when no one else is using the address) or send a negative acknowledgment, or NACK, to the machine, and the DHCP Server would make a note of that NACK in the Event Log. Your workstation would then be smart enough to start searching for a new DHCP Server.

Like BOOTP, DHCP remembers which IP addresses go with which machine by matching an IP address with a MAC (Media Access Control, that is, the Ethernet address).

DHCP is an easy service to use and very handy. If you use the TCP/IP protocol on your network, install DHCP during the NT installation and use it right away. If your workstations

19

already have IP manually installed, you might need to switch over gradually. If you're planning to connect to the Internet, make sure that the addresses you use are valid IP addresses that you can verify with your Internet Service Provider.

TIP

> If you use DHCP on your network, also use WINS so that you can see the computer names in the WINS database mapping. By itself, DHCP does not tell you anything about NetBIOS computer names.
>
> You'll learn about using WINS this afternoon.

DHCP Overview

DHCP was designed by the Internet Engineering Task Force (IETF) to reduce the amount of configuration required for use of TCP/IP. DHCP is defined in RFCs (Request For Comments) 1533, 1534, 1541, and 1542.

DHCP centralizes TCP/IP configuration and lets you manage the allocation of TCP/IP configuration information by automatically assigning IP addresses to systems configured to use DHCP.

Under Windows NT, DHCP consists of two services: a DHCP Client service and a DHCP Server service.

Configuring DHCP Servers for a network provides two benefits:

☐ The administrator can centrally define global and subnet TCP/IP parameters for the entire internetwork and define parameters for reserved clients.

☐ Client computers do not require manual TCP/IP configuration. When a client computer moves between subnets, it is reconfigured for TCP/IP automatically at system startup time.

How DHCP Works

DHCP was designed as an extension to the Bootstrap Protocol (BOOTP), originally used to boot and configure diskless workstations across the network.

NOTE

> The Bootstrap Protocol was originally defined in RFC 951. The latest BOOTP RFC is RFC 1542, which includes support for DHCP. The major advantage of using the same message format as BOOTP is that

> an existing router can act as an RFC 1542 (BOOTP) relay agent to
> relay DHCP messages between subnets. Therefore, with a router acting
> as an RFC 1542 (BOOTP) relay agent between two subnets, it is
> possible to have a single DHCP Server providing IP addresses and
> configuration information for systems on both subnets.

BOOTP's capability to hand out IP addresses from a central location is terrific, but it's not dynamic. The network administrator must know beforehand the MAC addresses of the Ethernet cards on the network. This isn't impossible information to obtain, but it's not fun (usually typing `ipconfig /all` from a command line yields the data). Furthermore, there's no provision for handing out temporary IP addresses, such as an IP address for a laptop used by a consultant.

DHCP improves on BOOTP because you give it a range of IP addresses that it's allowed to hand out, and it just gives them out—first-come, first-served to whatever computers request them. If, on the other hand, you want to maintain full BOOTP-like behavior, you can; it's possible with DHCP to pre-assign IP addresses to particular MAC addresses, as with BOOTP.

Generally, with DHCP, you have to permanently assign the IP addresses of only a few machines, such as your BOOTP and DHCP Server and your default gateway.

Leasing an IP Address

A DHCP Client gets an IP address from a DHCP Server in four steps:

1. *Initializing State.* A DHCPDISCOVER broadcasts a request to all DHCP Servers, requesting an IP address.
2. *Selecting State.* The servers respond with DHCPOFFER of IP addresses and lease times.
3. *Requesting State.* The client chooses the offer that sounds most appealing and broadcasts back a DHCPREQUEST to confirm the IP address.
4. *Bound State.* The server handing out the IP address finishes the procedure by returning with a DHCPACK, an acknowledgment of the request.

Renewing IP Address Leases

DHCP Clients lease their IP address from a DHCP Server. When the lease expires, they can no longer use the IP address. Hence, DHCP Clients must renew their lease on the IP address, preferably before the lease has expired or is about to expire. Once again, during the process of renewing its lease, a DHCP Client passes through states, as listed here:

☐ *Renewing State.* By default, a DHCP Client first tries to renew its lease when 50 percent of the lease time has expired. To renew its lease, a DHCP Client sends a directed DHCPREQUEST message to the DHCP Server where it obtained the lease.

When permitted, the DHCP Server automatically renews the lease by responding with a DHCPACK message. This DHCPACK message contains the new lease as well as any configuration parameters so that the DHCP Client can update its settings in case the administrator updated any settings on the DHCP Server. After the DHCP Client has renewed its lease, it returns to the bound state.

☐ *Rebinding State.* If a DHCP Client attempts to renew its lease on an IP address and for some reason can't contact a DHCP Server, the DHCP Client displays a message similar to this:

```
The DHCP Client could not renew the lease for the IP Address
199.199.199.10. Your lease is valid until Mon March 31 05:55:55 1997.
DHCP will try to renew the lease before it expires. If you want to see DHCP
messages in the future, choose YES. Otherwise choose NO.
```

When, for some reason, the DHCP Client cannot communicate with the DHCP Server where it obtained its lease, it attempts to contact any available DHCP Server when 87.5 percent of the lease time has expired. The DHCP Client broadcasts DHCPREQUEST messages so that any DHCP Server can renew the lease. Any DHCP Server can respond with a DHCPACK message that renews the lease or a DHCPNACK message that forces the DHCP Client to re-initialize (begin the leasing process anew) and obtain an IP address lease for a new IP address.

Note When a short lease period is being specified, it's critical that the DHCP Server remains available to accommodate clients seeking to renew leases. Backup servers become particularly important with short lease periods.

19

If the lease expires or the DHCP Client receives a DHCPNACK message, the DHCP Client must immediately stop using the expired IP address. The DHCP Client can, however, return to the initializing stage and attempt to obtain another IP address lease.

Implementing DHCP Servers

Before you actually run DHCP Servers, you should take time to plan the installation carefully. To get ready for DHCP installation, you should

☐ Have an IP address ready for your DHCP Server; this is one computer on your network that must have a static address.

☐ Know which IP addresses are available, because you use these available IP addresses to create a pool of IP addresses.

Installing DHCP Servers

Usually, you install the DHCP Server when installing TCP/IP. Before installing a new DHCP Server, check for other DHCP Servers on the network to avoid conflicts.

To install, you must log on as a member of the Administrators group for the computer where you are installing or administering a DHCP Server.

Task 19.1. Installing DHCP Servers.

Step 1: Description

DHCP Servers are the machines that provide IP addresses to machines requesting access to your network. You use the Services tab of the Network applet to install a DHCP Server.

Step 2: Action

1. Double-click the Network icon in the Control Panel. When the Network dialog box appears, click the Services tab and then click Add to display the Select Network Service dialog box, as shown in Figure 19.1.

Figure 19.1.

The Select Network Service dialog box.

2. From the Network Service list, highlight Microsoft DHCP Server, and then click OK.

3. Windows NT Setup displays a message asking for the full path to the Windows NT Server distribution files. Provide the appropriate location and click the Continue button. All necessary files are copied to your hard disk.

4. Complete all the required procedures for manually configuring TCP/IP as described in Chapter 18. All the appropriate TCP/IP and DHCP software is ready for use after you reboot the computer.

Step 3: Review

With this task, you used the Network applet to install a DHCP Server. After you reboot the system, you'll find a new icon in the Administrative Tools (Common) group: the DHCP Manager.

WARNING

Unless your network is small, you should have two or more available DHCP Servers for the network that can provide a DHCP Client with a valid IP address and configuration information. When there is only one DHCP Server and it fails, the client can no longer use TCP/IP on the network when the DHCP Client's lease on the IP address expires. As a result, the DHCP Clients cannot use TCP/IP to communicate on the network. In addition, new users without a lease cannot use TCP/IP on the network.

After it's installed, the DHCP Server service starts automatically during system startup. You should pause the service while configuring scopes for the first time.

To pause the DHCP Server service at any Windows NT computer, follow these steps:

1. In the Control Panel, choose the Services icon. Or in Server Manager, choose Computer|Services.

2. In the Services dialog box, select the Microsoft DHCP Server service.

3. Click the Pause button, and then click the Close button.

You also can start, stop, and pause the DHCP service at the command prompt by using the commands `net start dhcpserver`, `net stop dhcpserver`, or `net pause dhcpserver`.

Understanding DHCP Scopes

For DHCP to give out IP addresses, it must know the range of IP addresses it can give out. How does it find out the addresses? You tell it with a scope. A scope simply is a range of IP addresses or pool of addresses to draw on. You create a scope for each subnet on the network to define parameters for that subnet.

As mentioned, the DHCP Manager icon is added to the Network Administrative Tools group under Programs in the Start menu when you set up a Windows NT Server computer to act as a DHCP Server. You use DHCP Manager to perform these tasks:

☐ Create one or more DHCP scopes to begin providing DHCP services

☐ Define properties for the scope, including the lease duration and IP address ranges for distribution to potential DHCP Clients in the scope

☐ Define default values for options (such as the default gateway, DNS Server, or WINS Server) to be assigned together with an IP address

☐ Add any custom options

19

Each scope has the following properties:

- [ ] A unique subnet mask used to determine the subnet related to a given IP address
- [ ] A scope name assigned by the administrator when the scope is created
- [ ] Lease duration values to be assigned to DHCP Clients with dynamic addresses

To Start DHCP Manager

Double-click the DHCP Manager icon in the Administrative Tools group. Or, at the command prompt, type `start dhcpadmn` and press Enter. The DHCP Manager window appears.

The first time you start DHCP Manager, the DHCP Manager window shows the local computer. Subsequent times, the window shows a list of the DHCP Servers where DHCP Manager has connected, plus their scopes. The status bar reports the current DHCP Manager activities.

When you are working with DHCP Manager, all computer names are DNS host names only, such as `sales01.pda.com`. The NetBIOS computer names used with Windows networking are not allowed.

To connect to a DHCP Server, do the following:

1. Choose Server|Add.
2. In the Add DHCP Server To Server List dialog box, type the IP address for the DHCP Server where you want to connect, and then click OK.

To disconnect from a selected DHCP Server, go to the Server menu and choose Remove, or press Delete.

Creating Scopes

You use DHCP Manager to create, manage, or remove scopes.

Task 19.2. Creating a new DHCP scope.

Step 1: Description
You'll use the DHCP Manager to create a scope for the DHCP Server.

Step 2: Action
1. In the DHCP Servers list in the DHCP Manager window, select the server where you want to create a scope.

2. Choose Scope|Create. The Create Scope dialog box is displayed, as shown in Figure 19.2.

Figure 19.2.

The Create Scope dialog box.

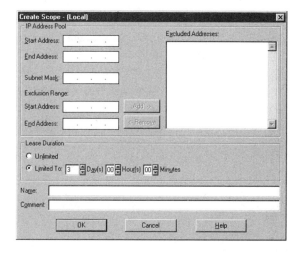

3. To define the available range of IP addresses for this scope, type the beginning and ending IP addresses for the range in the Start Address and End Address boxes. The IP address range includes the Start and End values. You must supply this information in order for the system to activate this scope.

4. In the Subnet Mask box, DHCP Manager proposes a subnet mask, based on the IP address of the Start and End addresses. Accept the proposed value unless you know that a different value is required.

5. To define excluded addresses within the IP address pool range, use the Exclusion Range controls, as detailed here:

☐ Type the first IP address that is part of the excluded range in the Start Address box, and type the last number in the End Address box. Then click the Add button. Continue to define any other excluded ranges in the same way.

☐ To exclude a single IP address, type the number in the Start Address box. Leave the End Address box empty, and click the Add button.

☐ To remove an IP address or range from the excluded range, select it in the Excluded Addresses box, and then click the Remove button.

The excluded ranges should include all IP addresses you assigned manually to other DHCP Servers, non-DHCP Clients, diskless workstations, and RAS and PPP clients.

6. To specify the lease duration for IP addresses in this scope, select Limited To. Then type values defining the number of days, hours, and seconds for the length of the address lease. If you do not want IP address leases in this scope to expire, select the Unlimited option.

7. In the Name box, type a scope name. Use any name that describes this subnet. The name can include any combination of letters, numbers, and hyphens. Blank spaces and underscore characters are also allowed. You cannot use Unicode characters.

8. Optionally, in the Comment box, type any string to describe this scope, and then click OK.

9. When you finish creating a scope, a message reminds you that the scope has not been activated and allows you to choose Yes to activate the scope immediately. You should not activate a new scope, however, until you have defined the DHCP options for this scope.

Step 3: Review

You use the Create Scope dialog box to create a new scope. After you do, you can configure DHCP options. After you have configured the options for this scope, you must activate it so that DHCP Client computers on the related subnet can begin using DHCP for dynamic TCP/IP configuration.

To activate a DHCP scope, choose Scope|Activate. The menu command name changes to Deactivate when the selected scope is currently active.

Changing Scope Properties

The subnet identifiers and address pool make up the properties of scopes. You can change the properties of an existing scope.

Task 19.3. Changing the properties of a DHCP scope.

Step 1: Description

Using the DHCP Manager, you can change the properties of an existing scope.

Step 2: Action

1. In the DHCP Servers list in the DHCP Manager window, select the scope where you want to change properties, and choose Scope|Properties. Or, in the DHCP Servers list, double-click the scope you want to change.

2. In the Scope Properties dialog box, change any values for the IP address pool, lease duration, or name and comment.

3. Click OK to have the changes take effect.

Step 3: Review

You used the DHCP Manager to change the properties of an existing scope.

Removing a Scope

When you are no longer using a subnet or whenever you want to remove an existing scope, you can use DHCP Manager to remove it. If any IP address in the scope is still leased or in use, you must first deactivate the scope until all client leases expire or all client lease extension requests are denied.

Task 19.4. Removing a scope.

Step 1: Description

By using the DHCP Manager, you can remove an existing scope.

Step 2: Action

1. In the DHCP Servers list in the DHCP Manager window, select the scope you want to remove.

2. Select Scope|Deactivate. (This command name changes to Activate when the scope is not active.) The scope must remain deactivated until you are sure that the scope is not in use.

3. Select Scope|Delete. (The Delete command is not available for an active scope.)

Step 3: Review

Just as you did to add or change a scope, you use the DHCP Manager to remove a scope.

Configuring DHCP Options

You use DHCP Manager to define the configuration parameters that a DHCP Server assigns to a client as DHCP options. Most options you want to specify are predefined, based on standard parameters defined in RFC 1542.

When you configure a DHCP scope, you can assign DHCP options to govern all configuration parameters. You also can assign, create, edit, or delete DHCP options. These tasks are described in the following sections.

Assigning DHCP Configuration Options

Besides the IP addressing information, you must configure other DHCP configuration options pertaining to DHCP Clients for each scope. You can define options globally for all scopes on the current server, specifically for a selected scope, or for individual DHCP Clients with reserved addresses. Active global options always apply unless overridden by scope options or DHCP Client settings. Active options for a scope apply to all computers in that scope, unless overridden for an individual DHCP Client.

Task 19.5. Assigning DHCP configuration options.

Step 1: Description
Using the DHCP Manager, you can assign configuration options to a scope.

Step 2: Action

1. In the DHCP Servers list in the DHCP Manager window, select the scope you want to configure.

2. From the DHCP Options menu, choose the Global or Scope command, depending on whether you want to define option settings for all scopes on the currently selected server or the scope currently selected in the DHCP Manager window. The DHCP Options: Scope dialog box appears.

3. In the Unused Options list in the DHCP Options: Scope dialog box, select the name of the DHCP option you want to apply. Then click the Add button to move the name to the Active Options list. This list shows predefined options and any custom options you added. For example, if you want to specify DNS Servers for computers, select the option named DNS Servers in the Unused Options list, and click the Add button. If you want to remove an active DHCP option, select its name in the Active Options box, and then click the Remove button.

4. To define the value for an active option, select its name in the Active Options box and click the Values button. Then click the Edit button and edit the information in the Current Value box, depending on the data type for the option, as described here:

   ☐ For an IP address, type the assigned address for the selected option.

   ☐ For a number, type an appropriate decimal or hexadecimal value for the option.

   ☐ For a string, type an appropriate ASCII string containing letters and numbers for the option.

For example, to specify the DNS name servers for use by DHCP Clients, select DNS Servers in the Active Options list. Then choose the Edit button and type a list of IP addresses for DNS Servers. The list should appear in the order of preference.

> If you are using DHCP to configure WINS Clients, set options #44 (WINS Servers) and #46 (Node Type). These options allow DHCP-configured computers to find and use the WINS Server automatically.

5. When you have completed all the changes, click OK.

Step 3: Review

Besides the IP addressing information, you must configure other DHCP configuration options pertaining to DHCP Clients for each scope. You use DHCP Manager to do this.

Administrating DHCP Clients

The easiest method for installing and configuring a system to use TCP/IP is to enable automatic DHCP configuration on the system. With this enabled, the DHCP Client contacts a DHCP Server during system boot for its configuration information: IP address, subnet mask, and default gateway.

A Windows NT Server set up as a DHCP Server can service the following DHCP Clients:

- [ ] Windows NT Workstation
- [ ] Windows NT Server
- [ ] Windows 95
- [ ] Windows for Workgroups 3.11 (WFW), with the Microsoft 32-bit TCP/IP VxD installed
- [ ] Microsoft Network Client for MS-DOS with real-mode TCP/IP driver (included on the Windows NT Server CD)
- [ ] LAN Manager 2.2c for MS-DOS (included on the Windows NT Server CD)

Tip

> You can use the ipconfig utility to troubleshoot the IP configuration on computers that use DHCP. You also can use ipconfig to troubleshoot on TCP/IP-32 clients on Windows for Workgroups 3.11 computers and on computers running Microsoft Network Client version 2.0 for MS-DOS.

19

Managing Client Leases

The lease for the IP address assigned by a DHCP Server has an expiration date, which the client must renew when it is going to continue to use that address. You can view the lease duration and other information for specific DHCP Clients, and you can add options and change settings for reserved DHCP Clients.

You can edit the name, unique identifier, and comment, or click the Options button in the Client Properties dialog box only for clients with reserved IP addresses.

You can cancel the DHCP configuration information for a DHCP Client that is no longer using an IP address or for all clients in the scope. This has the same effect as if the client's lease had expired: the next time that client computer starts, it must enter the rebinding state and obtain new TCP/IP configuration information from a DHCP Server.

Delete only entries for clients that are no longer using the assigned DHCP configuration. Deleting an active client could result in duplicate IP addresses on the network, because a DHCP Server might assign deleted addresses to new active clients.

You can use `ipconfig /release` at the command prompt to get a DHCP Client computer to delete an active client entry and safely free its IP address for reuse.

To cancel a client's DHCP configuration, follow these steps:

1. Make sure that the client is not using the assigned IP address.
2. In the IP Client list of the Active Leases dialog box, select the client you want to cancel, and then click the Delete button.

Managing the DHCP Database Files

Some key files are used by DHCP. The following list shows the files that are stored in the *SystemRoot*\SYSTEM32\DHCP directory that is created when you set up a DHCP Server:

☐ DHCP.MDB is the DHCP database file.

☐ DHCP.TMP is a temporary file DHCP creates for temporary database information.

☐ JET.LOG and the JET*.LOG files contain logs of all transactions done with the database. These files are used by DHCP to recover data when necessary.

☐ SYSTEM.MDB is used by DHCP for holding information about the structure of its database.

WARNING

19

Do not remove or tamper with the DHCP.TMP, DHCP.MDB, JET.LOG, and SYSTEM.MDB files.

Because the DHCP database contains all the DHCP scopes for the server and the configuration parameters, it is a good idea to implement a backup policy. Normally, the system automatically backs up the DHCP database, and this backup is used if the original is corrupted; however, you should not rely on this as your only backup. Instead, back up the database regularly, and copy the files from the *\SystemRoot*\SYSTEM32\DHCP\ BACKUP\JET directory.

The DHCP database and related Registry entries are backed up automatically at a specific interval (15 minutes by default, according to the Resource Kit), based on the value of Registry parameters. You also can force database backup while working in DHCP Manager.

TIP   You can make DHCP back up the database less or more often with a Registry parameter. In HKEY_LOCAL_MACHINE\System\ CurrentControlSet\services\DHCPServer\Parameters, look for (or create) a value entry called BackupInterval of type REG_DWORD. Enter the value (in hexadecimal of course) in minutes. You can enter any value from 5 to 60 minutes. If you select and enter a binary value, the system automatically converts it to hexadecimal for you.

Working with the DHCP Database

You might find a situation in which you need to back up a DHCP database to another computer.

To move a DHCP database, use the Replicator service to copy the contents of the DHCP backup directory to the new computer.

To ensure that the DHCP services are running:

1. Use the Services option in the Control Panel to verify that the DHCP or WINS services are running. In the Services dialog box for the client computer, Started should appear in the Status column for the DHCP or WINS Client service. For the DHCP or WINS Server itself, Started should appear in the Status column for the DHCP or Windows Internet Name service.

2. If the necessary service is not started on either computer, start the service.

In rare circumstances, the DHCP Server might not boot or a STOP error might occur. If the DHCP Server is down, follow these steps to restart it:

1. Turn off the power to the server, and wait one minute.

19

2. Turn on the power, start Windows NT Server, and log on under an account with Administrator rights.

3. At the command prompt, type net start dhcpserver and press Enter.

Restoring the DHCP Database

In true NT fault-tolerant fashion, DHCP will check itself for internal problems whenever it starts. If it detects a problem, it automatically restores from the backups.

If, however, you determine that the DHCP services are running on both the client and the server computers, but error conditions persist, the DHCP database is not available or is corrupt. If a DHCP Server fails for any reason, you can restore the database from the automatic backup files.

To restore a DHCP database, restart the DHCP Server. When the DHCP database becomes corrupted, it is automatically restored from the DHCP backup directory specified in the Registry.

If you have a corrupted primary database file and this is not detected by the DHCP service, you can force the backup copy to be used by editing the Registry.

To force the restoration of a DHCP database, set the Registry key HKEY_LOCAL_MACHINE\ SYSTEM\CurrentControlSet\Services\DHCPServer\Parameters\RestoreFlag to 1. Then restart the DHCP service by entering net stop dhcpserver followed by net start dhcpserver.

And when all else fails, you can manually restore a DHCP database. When the preceding restore methods do not work, manually copy all DHCP database files from the backup directory to the \DHCP working directory, and then restart the DHCP Server service. Then go into DHCP options and click on Reconcile Database to ensure that the database is internally consistent.

Summary

In this chapter, you learned about naming conventions and naming resolution. Windows NT uses a NetBIOS address that needs to be translated into an IP address for the Internet.

This chapter focused on the Dynamic Host Configuration Protocol (DHCP), used to give out IP addresses dynamically to hosts as they join the LAN. You learned that you can permanently assign IP addresses if you so desire.

DHCP can accomplish the job of giving out unique IP addresses, and that's an important job. But it doesn't handle the big job of relating host names to IP addresses. For that, you need a name service. That service is the Windows Internet Naming Service, or WINS. This afternoon, you'll learn about WINS.

Workshop

To wrap up the day, you can review terms and tasks from the chapter, and see the answers to some commonly asked questions.

Terminology Review

address—A number or group of numbers uniquely identifying a network node within its network (or internetwork).

Boot Protocol (BOOTP)—A protocol used for remotely booting systems on the network.

domain name—A name assigned to a domain.

Domain Name System, or Server (DNS)—A distributed database system that allows TCP/IP applications to resolve a host name into a correct IP address.

Dynamic Host Configuration Protocol (DHCP)—A protocol used by a server to dynamically allocate IP addresses on a network. Designed to allow networked hosts to access configuration information across the network, instead of having to be configured by hand directly.

Fully Qualified Domain Name (FQDN)—The complete host name and domain name of a network host.

gateway—A multihomed host used to route network traffic from one network to another. Also used to pass network traffic from one protocol to another.

host name resolution—The process of determining a network address when presented with a network host name and domain name, usually by consulting the Domain Name System.

IP address—A 32-bit network address that uniquely locates a host or network within its internetwork.

Media Access Control (MAC)—Part of the physical layer of a network that identifies the actual physical link between two nodes.

network address—A unique identifier of an entity on a network, usually represented as a number or series of numbers.

Network Basic Input/Output Operating System (NetBIOS)—A network file-sharing application designed for use with PC-DOS personal computers, usually implemented under TCP/IP at the application layer.

node—A system or device connected to a network.

PING—A network application that uses UDP to verify "reachability" of another host on the internetwork.

19

Request for Comments (RFC)—The official designation of Internet de facto standards document.

subnet—A physical or logical subdivision of a TCP/IP network; usually a separate physical segment that uses a division of the site's IP network address to route traffic within the organizational internetwork.

Windows Internet Naming Service (WINS)—A service that translates Windows computer names (or NetBIOS names) to IP addresses.

Task List

The emphasis of this chapter has been to introduce you to Windows and Internet naming conventions and tools. As a system administrator, you will need to learn how to implement DHCP. You completed seven key tasks in this chapter:

- ☐ Installing DHCP Servers
- ☐ Creating a new DHCP scope
- ☐ Changing the properties of a DHCP scope
- ☐ Removing a scope
- ☐ Assigning DHCP configuration options
- ☐ Managing client leases
- ☐ Restoring the DHCP database

Q&A

Q Can I set a lease to Infinite?

A Well, yes, you can set the leases to Infinite, but don't. This might seem like an easy way to assign fixed IP addresses, but let's look at that. The first time a system logs on, it would get an IP address. However, this presents two problems. First, a minor problem: What if you have to reinstall your DHCP Server but did not back up the Registry, where the DHCP database lives? Then your system would spend lots of resources NACKing PCs. Second, what happens when you want to reconfigure your network? Suppose you have 100 people in two departments on the same subnet. You decide to divide them into two subnets. Fifty users from the old subnet are now on a new subnet, requiring a whole new set of IP addresses. Obviously, you have to create a new scope, but creating the new scope is easy. The problem is, how do you force a new IP address on the people in the new subnet?

19

Their leases never expire, so they never really give the DHCP Server a chance to assign them new addresses. (Well, it will, but only after lots of NACKing and plenty of systems that will randomly refuse to communicate with anything.) Set the lease to a few days, and then you can enforce changes to your subnet structure automatically through the DHCP Servers.

Q How do I get a client to immediately release a lease?

A If you need a DHCP Client to immediately release its IP address on shutdown, the user shutting down the system should first enter `ipconfig /release` from a command prompt. Otherwise, the DHCP Server maintains the IP address as leased and unavailable for 24 hours after the IP address lease time expires.

19

Chapter 20

Understanding WINS

Maintaining a TCP/IP network can place a huge burden on you, the system administrator. In addition to the normal responsibilities that go along with administrating a Windows NT network, TCP/IP introduces another facet of administration: managing computer names and addresses. With LAN Manager and older versions of NT, system administrators manually created and maintained LMHOSTS files to map computer names to IP addresses. But along came DNS (Domain Name Service, or System) and WINS (Windows Internet Name Service) to help administrators. DNS and WINS are distributed databases for registering and querying dynamic computer-name to IP-address mappings.

This morning, you learned about assigning addresses dynamically. Now, this afternoon, you will learn about WINS operation and how to install and configure WINS Servers. Specifically, you will learn about these topics:

- ☐ Configuring WINS Servers
- ☐ Starting and stopping the WINS database
- ☐ Creating static mappings on a WINS Server
- ☐ Backup and restoring a WINS Server

Let's review name resolution before installing and configuring WINS.

Name Resolution for TCP/IP on Windows NT

To communicate over a TCP/IP network, your system has to resolve computer names into IP addresses and vice versa. TCP/IP has no idea how to establish communication with a computer name such as `\\sales01`, but it does know how to communicate with `199.199.199.2`. The process that TCP/IP networks use to discover a computer's IP address from the computer's name is known as *resolution*. Resolving a computer's IP address from its name is not enough; each node on a TCP/IP network must have a unique name and address. To ensure that each Windows NT computer on a TCP/IP network has a unique name and address, the computer registers its name and IP address during startup. This process is called *registration*.

How WINS Works

DHCP made IP addressing simpler but ignored the newly created problem of keeping track of the newly assigned IP numbers and the hosts attached to them (that is, registration). If you sat at a TCP/IP-connected workstation with a host name like, for example, `oriole.pda.com` that had gotten its IP address from a DHCP Server, and if you were to type `ping oriole.pda.com`, then you would get a timed-out message. Your system wouldn't know its own name, because no DNS Server knows what's going on with its dynamic IP address, and no one updated a HOSTS file. So your system needs a dynamic name resolver—recall that *name resolution* is the term for determining that `oriole.pda.com` might really be `199.199.199.2`.

That's where Windows Internet Name Service comes in. Now, whereas DHCP is part of a wider group of BOOTP-related protocols, WINS is a Microsoft proprietary protocol, recognized only by Microsoft client software (NT, Windows for Workgroups, DOS, Windows 3.*x* and 95, and eventually OS/2 clients). WINS is not DNS-compatible and that's a major problem. What WINS is really good for is administering NetBEUI networks over routers.

Basically, this means that the name resolution task can be handled just fine inside your network or internetwork by WINS, but name resolution outside your network—by someone inside your network trying to resolve an Internet address, or someone outside the network trying to resolve a name inside your network—requires a DNS Server.

WINS is, therefore, only half of the answer to the name resolution problem, albeit an important half.

Names in NT

Consider the two following commands, both issued to the same server:

```
ping sales0l.pda.com
```

and

```
net use * \\sales0l\public
```

In the example that uses the `ping` command, the server is referred to as `sales01.pda.com`. In the example that uses NET USE, that same server is called `sales01`. The difference is important.

Why Two Different Names?

The `ping` command is clearly a TCP/IP/Internet command. You can't use `ping` unless you're running TCP/IP. It's a valid command on UNIX, VMS, Macintosh, or MVS machines, because those computers have a TCP/IP protocol stack.

In contrast, NET USE is a Microsoft networking command. You can use NET USE on an NT network no matter what protocol you're running, but the command usually isn't valid on a UNIX, VMS, or Macintosh computer.

The difference is in the network application program interface (API) that the application is built atop. PING was built on top of the TCP/IP sockets interface or, actually, the common PC implementation of TCP/IP sockets, the Winsock interface. Building PING atop sockets was a good idea, because then it's simple to create a PING for any operating system, as long as the computer has a socket interface. In fact, people basically use the same source code to create PING for Windows, UNIX, VMS, or MacOS. The `sales01.pda.com` is a DNS name, so for PING to recognize who `sales01.pda.com` is, you would need a DNS name resolver—or DNS Server—on your network.

In contrast, NET USE was built atop the NetBIOS API, because Microsoft has been selling the software to do NET USE commands since 1985. The `\\sales01` name is a NetBIOS name, rather than a DNS name, meaning that to make NET USE work, you would need a NetBIOS name resolver or a NetBIOS name server. That's exactly what WINS is.

If the `sales01.pda.com` and `\\sales01` distinction still isn't clear, think of the APIs as communications devices. Telephones and the postal service are communications mediums. PING's job is to communicate with some other PC, and NET USE also wants to communicate with some PC. But PING uses Winsock (the telephone), and NET USE uses NetBIOS (the mail). If you use the telephone to call your friend Barry, the friend's name, as far as the phone is concerned, might be something like (416) 555-2121. As far as the mail is concerned, however, the friend's name might be Barry Lewis, 124 Main Street, Anytown, ON, postal code H0H 0H0. Both are perfectly valid names for Barry, but they're different because different communications systems need different name types.

20

NetBIOS atop TCP/IP (NBT)

The NetBIOS API is implemented on the NetBEUI, IPX/SPX, and TCP/IP protocols that Microsoft distributes. That makes Microsoft's TCP/IP a bit different from the TCP/IP you find on UNIX, because the UNIX TCP/IP almost certainly won't have a NetBIOS API on it; it'll probably have only the TCP/IP sockets API on it. (Microsoft's TCP/IP also has sockets in the form of the Winsock API.)

NetBIOS on the Microsoft implementation of TCP/IP is essential, because if the TCP/IP didn't have a NetBIOS API on it, you couldn't use the NET LOGON, NET START, NET STOP, NET USE, NET VIEW, and other commands to allow your PC-based workstation to talk to an NT Server. Microsoft's NetBIOS on TCP/IP even has a name: NBT.

So the server's name, as far as NetBIOS or NBT is concerned, is sales01, and its name so far as Winsock is concerned is sales01.pda.com. (That name type, by the way, is called a Fully Qualified Domain Name, or FQDN.) You can run programs that call on either NBT or Winsock, but you have to be sure to use the correct name.

Name Resolution Issues

After NBT has a NetBIOS name or Winsock has an FQDN, they have the same job: to resolve that name into an IP address. So computers on a Microsoft-based network using TCP/IP need some kind of name resolution.

You could use Domain Name Service. DNS clearly could do the job, so Microsoft could have designed NBT to do its name resolution via DNS. But Microsoft didn't, for a couple of reasons:

☐ First, DNS is not dynamic, so you would have to add the new computer's name and IP address to DNS every time you put a new computer on your network. Then you would have to stop the DNS Server and restart it to get DNS to recognize the new name. A dynamic name server obviously would be more desirable.

☐ Second, Microsoft didn't ship a DNS Server with NT until version 4.0. So a DNS was not the answer.

NetBIOS name resolution over TCP/IP is not simple. Many people realized this fact; hence there are two Internet RFCs (Requests For Comment) dealing with this topic: RFC 1001 and 1002.

20

B Nodes, P Nodes, and M Nodes

The RFCs attacked the problem by offering options:

☐ The first option was simplistic: Just do broadcasts. A computer using broadcasts to resolve NetBIOS names to IP addresses is referred to in the RFCs as a *B node*. To find out who `sales01` is, then, a PC running B node software would just shout out, "Is anybody named sales01?"

Simple, yes, but fatally flawed: Remember what happens to broadcasts when they hit routers. Because routers don't rebroadcast the messages to other subnets, this kind of name resolution would work only on single-subnet networks.

☐ The second option was to create a name server of some kind and to use it. Then, when a computer needs to resolve the name of another computer, all it needs to do is send a point-to-point message to the computer running the name server software. Because point-to-point messages do get retransmitted over routers, this second approach would work fine even on networks with routers. A computer using a name server to resolve NetBIOS names into addresses is said to be a *P node*.

Again, a good idea, but it has all the problems of DNS. The name server for NetBIOS name resolution is, by the way, referred to as a NetBIOS Name Server, or NBNS.

☐ The most complex approach to NetBIOS name resolution over TCP/IP is the *M node*, or mixed node. It uses a combination of broadcasts and point-to-point communications to an NBNS. When the people at Microsoft started out with TCP/IP, they implemented a variant of the M node. It was point-to-point in that you could look up addresses in the HOSTS file, or a file called LMHOSTS, and if you had a DNS Server, then you could always reference that. Other than those options, Microsoft TCP/IP was mainly a B node, which limited you to single-subnet networks. Clearly, some kind of NBNS was needed, and the simpler it was to work with, the better. Because the RFCs were silent on the particulars of an NBNS, vendors could invent anything they wanted, and they did—and none of them can talk to each other.

That's where WINS comes in. Simply, WINS is Microsoft's proprietary NBNS service. Microsoft client software with WINS actually doesn't implement B, P, or M nodes; rather, Microsoft uses what is called an H, or Hybrid, node.

TIP The term *H node* refers to a NetBIOS over TCP/IP mode that defines how NBT identifies and accesses network resources.

You're probably thinking that M node is a hybrid. Well, M nodes and H nodes use both B node and P node, but the implementation is different:

☐ With M node, a computer does name resolution by first broadcasting (B node) and, when that fails, communicating directly with the NBNS (P node).

☐ With H node, a computer tries the NBNS first. If that fails, it tries a broadcast.

So as you can see, the difference merely is in the order of operation.

To resolve the computer name to its IP address, TCP/IP can use various name resolution methods:

☐ A static mapping file (HOSTS)

☐ Broadcast name resolution

☐ Another static mapping file (LMHOSTS)

☐ DNS name resolution

☐ Windows Internet Name Service (WINS)

HOSTS File

HOSTS is a simple ASCII file. Each line within the file contains an IP address, at least one space, and a name. This is a static file that must be constantly updated.

Resolving a host name into an IP address is particularly simple when a HOSTS file is used: The process compares the host name to the host names and aliases provided in the HOSTS file. As you can see in the following sample HOSTS file, a HOSTS file is relatively easy to create but is easy to maintain only in small, static networks.

```
199.199.199.1    router    cisco
199.199.199.2    iserver   www    ftp
199.199.199.3    balliol
199.199.199.4    merton    oxford
```

HOSTS files include the IP address, followed by the host name assigned to the IP address, and an optional alias name.

Broadcasts

Broadcasting on a computer network is similar to taxi dispatch. The dispatcher's voice is put on the air (broadcast) over a channel so that all drivers with radios turned on can hear the message. To contact a particular person, the dispatcher's message customarily includes the name or car number of that person. Every person receiving the broadcast message listens to determine whether it is for him or her, and the person whose name was called in the message responds to the dispatcher.

As with the taxi dispatch system, to make sure that all systems on the network can communicate with each other, all broadcasts are forwarded throughout the network. Depending on the number of name resolutions at any one time, this operation can cause significant network traffic. In addition, every system on the network must examine every broadcast to determine whether the broadcast is meant for that particular system.

By relying on broadcasts to resolve computer names, the network becomes bogged down with additional network traffic. The more computers you have on a given network, the more broadcasts on the network, which can lead to heavy network congestion. Each time a computer tries to make a network connection, it broadcasts one or more times in an effort to resolve the computer name of the system at the other end of the connection to an IP address.

LMHOSTS File

An LMHOSTS file contains a list of computer names mapped to IP addresses. When you use an LMHOSTS file to resolve a computer name to an IP address, you have to maintain that file. As the network administrator, you have to keep track of each workstation's computer name and the IP address used by the workstation. When a workstation changes computer names or IP addresses, you have to update the LMHOSTS file. Because each workstation has its own local copy of the LMHOSTS file, you have to update the file and distribute it to all the other workstations every time a computer name or IP address changes. To decrease this double-duty maintenance, most systems use LMHOSTS files with one of the other two name resolution methods. Typically, most workstations are configured to try broadcasts first and then try the LMHOSTS file.

When the LMHOSTS file is being used for name resolution and the DHCP is being used for IP address assignment, significant overhead is still involved in maintaining the IP-address to host-name mappings. This is because the LMHOSTS file is a static file that must be manually modified each time a DHCP Client receives a new IP address from a DHCP Server. Each DHCP Client requires a copy of the modified LMHOSTS file. For example, workstations that frequently move between subnets receive a new IP address every time they change subnets, which requires you to modify the LMHOSTS file on all workstations.

DNS Server

The DNS Server uses a distributed database with a hierarchical naming system for resolving computer names. The DNS Server naming scheme uses a very structured naming scheme that must be followed closely, such as `sales01.pda.com`, where `sales01` is the computer name and `pda.com` is the domain name.

DNS can provide the IP address matching a particular host name, as well as the host name when it is queried with an IP address.

WINS

Microsoft designed the Windows Internet Name Service to eliminate the need for broadcasts and to provide a dynamic database that maintains computer-name to IP-address mappings.

A network typically has one or more WINS Servers that WINS Clients can contact when they need to resolve a computer name to an IP address. You can set up WINS Servers on a given network so that they replicate all computer names to IP address mappings in their WINS databases to each other. In general, you should implement WINS Servers so that you can accomplish the following goals:

☐ *Reduce broadcast traffic on the network.* Instead of broadcasting to every computer on a network in an attempt to resolve a computer name to an IP address, the workstation sends a message directly to a WINS Server requesting the IP address for a given computer name. Furthermore, a DHCP Server can provide a DHCP Client with IP addresses for WINS Servers.

☐ *Eliminate the need for the LMHOSTS file.* Using WINS eliminates the need for network administrators to maintain the LMHOSTS file. Because administrators do not need to keep track of what computer name maps to what IP address, there is less administrative overhead involved in using TCP/IP.

☐ *Provide dynamic name registration.* WINS complements DHCP on a network. When you use DHCP alone, you still have to maintain the LMHOSTS file. Using WINS with DHCP, however, provides dynamic IP addressing and name resolution without broadcasts or static files.

☐ *Prevent duplicate computer names.* Every time a WINS Client starts, it registers its computer name with a WINS Server. When the WINS Server already has a registration for the requested computer name, it rejects the WINS Client's registration attempt, thereby preventing duplicate computer names.

☐ *Eliminate the need for DNS Servers.* Because WINS uses NetBIOS names, it is more flexible than DNS for name resolution. You can gain some advantages, however, by using DNS Servers with WINS Servers.

How WINS Works

Before WINS, there were two alternatives: Everyone sent a broadcast that could go unanswered, or the administrator had to maintain static files. Now let's look at what happens with WINS.

WINS Needs NT Server

To make WINS work, you must set up an NT Server (it won't run on anything else) to act as the WINS Server. The WINS Server then acts as the NBNS Server, keeping track of who's on the network and handing out name resolution information as needed.

WINS collects name information. When a workstation wants to address name resolution questions to a WINS Server, it first must introduce itself to the WINS Server, and in the process, WINS captures the IP address and NetBIOS name of that workstation, augmenting the WINS database further.

WINS Holds Name Registrations

Basically, when a WINS Client first boots, it goes to the WINS Server and introduces itself. (Remember, Microsoft defines a client as "any PC running a Microsoft enterprise TCP/IP network client software designed to use WINS for NBT name resolution.") It knows the IP address of the WINS Server either because you hard-coded it into the TCP/IP settings for the workstation or because the workstation got a WINS address from DHCP when it obtained an IP lease.

That first communication with the WINS Server is called a *name registration request.* In the process of registering its name with a WINS Server, the workstation can ensure that it has a unique name. When the WINS Server sees that another computer has the same name, it tells the workstation it can't use that name. The name registration request and the acknowledgment are both directed IP messages, so they can cross routers. And when a workstation shuts down, it sends a "name release" request to the WINS Server telling it that the workstation no longer needs the NetBIOS name, enabling the WINS Server to register it with another machine.

During name registration, the WINS Client follows these steps:

1. Checks to see whether it is the local machine name.
2. Checks its cache of remote names. Any name that is resolved is placed in a cache, where it remains for 10 minutes.
3. Tries to contact the WINS Server.
4. Tries broadcasting.
5. Checks the LMHOSTS file, when configured to use it.
6. Checks the HOSTS file and then a DNS, when so configured.

When a workstation can't find the WINS Server as it boots, the workstation simply stops acting as a hybrid NBT node and reverts to its old ways as a "Microsoft modified B node," meaning that it depends largely on broadcasts but also will consult HOSTS and LMHOSTS when they're present.

20

WINS Renewal Intervals

Like DHCP, WINS registers names only for a fixed period of time called a *renewal interval.* By default, this period is four days (96 hours). Forty minutes is the least WINS will accept.

In much the same way that DHCP Clients attempt to renew their leases early, WINS Clients send "name refresh requests" to the WINS Server before their names expire. According to Microsoft documentation, a WINS Client attempts a name refresh after one-eighth of the renewal interval. The WINS Server usually resets the amount of time left before the name must be renewed again (this time is sometimes called the time-to-live, or TTL). After the client has renewed its name once, however, it doesn't renew it again and again every one-eighth of its TTL; instead, it renews its names every one-half of the TTL.

Installing WINS

Installing WINS is much like installing all other Windows NT software. The first step is to plan for your installation.

When you're planning how many WINS Servers you need and where to put them, consider that you need not put a WINS Server on every subnet. It is, however, a good idea to have a second machine running as a secondary WINS Server or a backup. Remember that when a workstation comes up and can't find a WINS Server, it reverts to broadcasting, which limits its name resolution capabilities to just its local subnet and adds traffic to the subnet.

Normally, the client would find the server, but occasionally, the WINS Server might be too busy to respond to the client in a timely fashion, causing the client to give up on the server. That's when a secondary WINS Server is useful. If you have a backup domain controller, put a WINS Server on that machine as well. The WINS software actually does not use a lot of CPU time, so it probably won't affect your server's performance unless you have thousands of users all hammering on one WINS Server. If that's the case, dedicate a computer solely to WINS.

Task 20.1. Installing a WINS Server.

Step 1: Description

To get a WINS Server set up, use the Network applet in the Control Panel.

Step 2: Action

1. Double-click the Network applet icon within the Control Panel under Start.
2. Select the Services tab.

3. Click the Add button.

4. Highlight the Windows Internet Name Service, and click the OK button.

5. Windows NT Setup displays a message asking for the full path to the Windows NT Server distribution files. Provide the appropriate location and click the Continue button. All necessary files are copied to your hard disk.

6. Click Close.

Step 3: Review

Use the Network Applet in the Control Panel to install WINS. Select the Services tab and add the Windows Internet Name Service.

You'll get a message to restart the system; do so. After your server has rebooted, you will find a new icon in the Administrative Tools (Common) group, the WINS Manager. Start it, and it should look as shown in Figure 20.1.

Figure 20.1.

The WINS Manager dialog box.

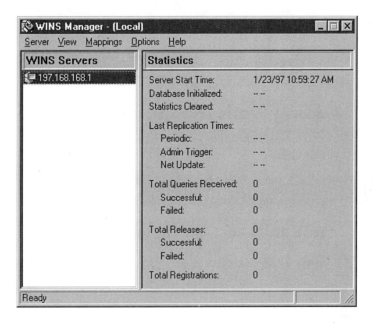

The first thing you should do on your WINS Server is inform it of the machines on your subnet that have hard-coded or static IP addresses. You do that by selecting Mappings|Static Mappings. You then see a dialog box like the one shown in Figure 20.2.

Figure 20.2.

The Static Mappings dialog box.

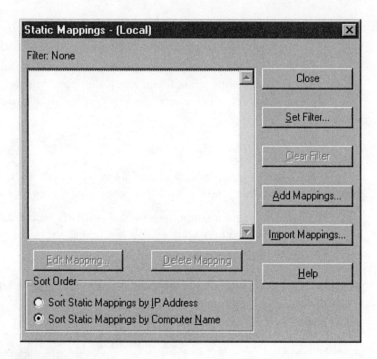

Adding Static Mappings

You can use either of two methods to add static mappings to the WINS database for specific IP addresses:

- ☐ Type static mappings in a dialog box.
- ☐ Import files that contain static mappings.

Task 20.2. Adding static mappings.

Step 1: Description

To add static mappings to the WINS database, use the Static Mappings of the WINS Manager.

Step 2: Action

1. In the Static Mappings dialog box, click the Add Mappings button.

2. In the Name box of the Add Static Mappings dialog box, type the computer name of the system for which you are adding a static mapping. You do not need to type two backslashes because WINS Manager adds them for you.

3. In the IP Address box, type the address for the computer. If Internet Group or Multihomed is selected as the Type option, the dialog box shows additional controls for adding multiple addresses. Use the down-arrow button to move the address you type into the list of addresses for the group. Use the up-arrow button to change the order of a selected address in the list.

4. Select a Type option to indicate whether this entry is a unique name or a group with a special name, as described in Table 20.1.

Table 20.1. Type options for static mappings.

Type Option	Description
Unique	Unique name in the database with one address per name.
Group	Normal group, where addresses of individual members are not stored. The client broadcasts name packets to normal groups.
Internet Group	Groups with NetBIOS names that have 0xlC as the 16th byte. An Internet Group stores a maximum of 25 addresses for members. For registrations after the 25th address, WINS overwrites a replica address, or when none is present, it overwrites the oldest registration.
Multihomed	Unique name that can have more than one address (multihomed computers). The maximum number of addresses is 25. For registrations after the 25th address, WINS overwrites a replica address, or when none is present, it overwrites the oldest registration.

5. Click the Add button. The mapping is immediately added to the database for that entry, and the boxes are cleared so that you can add another entry.

6. Repeat this process for each static mapping you want to add to the database, and then click the Close button.

Step 3: Review

Using the WINS Manager, you can set the Static Mappings. These static mappings are for the machines on your subnet that have hard-coded IP addresses.

NOTE

Because each static mapping is added to the database when you click the Add button, you cannot cancel work in this dialog box. If you make a mistake in entering a name or address for a mapping, you must return to the Static Mappings dialog box and delete the mapping there.

20

Importing Static Mappings

You also can import entries for static mappings for unique and special group names from any file that has the same format as the LMHOSTS file. The WINS database ignores scope names and keywords other than #DOM. However, you can add normal group and multihomed names only by typing entries in the Add Static Mappings dialog box.

To import a file containing static mapping entries, you carry out the following actions:

1. In the Static Mappings dialog box, click the Import Mappings button.

2. In the Select Static Mapping File dialog box, which is similar to the standard Windows NT Open dialog box, specify a filename for a static mappings file by typing its name in the box or by selecting one or more filenames from the list. Then click OK to import the file.

The specified file or files are read, and a static mapping is created for each computer name and address. If the #DOM keyword is included for any record, an Internet group is created (when it is not already present), and the address is added to that group.

Editing Static Mappings

You can change the IP addresses in static mappings owned by the WINS Server you currently are administering.

To edit a static mapping entry, you following these steps:

1. In the Static Mappings dialog box, select the mapping you want to change, and click the Edit Mapping button; or double-click the mapping entry in the list.

   You can view, but not edit, the Computer Name and Mapping Type option for the mapping in the Edit Static Mappings dialog box.

2. In the IP Address box, type a new address for the computer, and then click OK. The change is made in the WINS database immediately.

If you want to change the computer name or group type related to a specific IP address, you must delete the entry and redefine it in the Add Static Mappings dialog box.

Filtering the Range of Mappings

You might want to limit, or filter, the range of IP addresses or computer names displayed in the Static Mappings or Show Database dialog boxes.

You can specify a portion of the computer name or IP address or both when filtering the list of mappings. To filter mappings by address or name, you follow these steps:

20

1. In the dialog box for Static Mappings or Show Database, click the Set Filter button.

2. In the Set Filter dialog box, type portions of the computer name, address, or both in the Computer Name or IP Address boxes. You can use the asterisk (*) wildcard for portions of the name and address or both. For example, you could type \\sales* to filter all computers with names that begin with sales. For the address, however, you can use a wildcard only for a complete octet. That is, you can type 199.199.*.*, but you cannot enter 199.199.1**.1 in these boxes.

3. Click OK. The selected range is displayed in the Static Mappings or Show Database dialog box. The filtered range remains until you clear the filter. A message tells you when no mappings match the range you specified, and the list of mappings is empty. When a filter is in effect for the range of mappings, the Clear Filter button is available for restoring the entire list.

To clear the filtered range of mappings, in the Static Mappings or Show Database dialog box, click the Clear Filter button. The list now shows all mappings found in the database.

Configuring WINS Servers

WINS consists of two components: the WINS Server, which responds to name queries and registrations; and the WINS Client, which queries the server for computer name resolution. After you install the WINS Server on a Windows NT Server Version 4.0 system, the WINS Server is ready to receive name registrations and resolve name requests when you restart the computer. Installation is the only step required to get the WINS Server up and running. After the initial installation, however, you might want to configure the WINS Server to improve the performance of the WINS Server and the network.

You use the WINS Manager (WINSADMN.EXE) utility from the Administrative Tools (Common) group under Programs to configure local and remote WINS Servers. The first step is to connect to a WINS Server in the WINS Manager dialog box.

Whether a computer name or an IP address is specified in the WINS Manager dialog box determines how WINS Manager establishes the connection to the WINS Server. When a computer name is supplied, WINS Manager establishes the connection to the WINS Server via named pipes. When an IP address is supplied, WINS Manager uses TCP/IP to establish the connection.

To configure a WINS Server, you carry out the following steps:

1. Choose Server|Configuration. (The Configuration command is available only when you are logged on as a member of the Administrators group for the WINS Server you want to configure.) The WINS Server Configuration dialog box appears, as shown in Figure 20.3.

20

Figure 20.3.

The WINS Server Configuration (Local) dialog box.

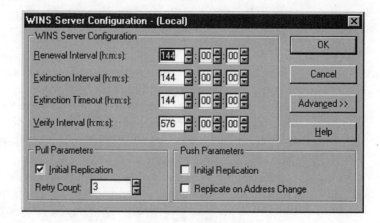

2. To view all the options in the dialog box, click the Advanced button.
3. For the configuration options in the WINS Server Configuration dialog box, specify time intervals using the spin buttons, as described in Table 20.2.

Table 20.2. WINS Server intervals.

Configuration Option	Description
Renewal Interval	Specifies how often a client reregisters its name. The default is five hours.
Extinction Interval	Specifies the interval between when an entry is marked as released and when it is marked as extinct. The default is four times the renewal interval.
Extinction Timeout	Specifies the interval between when an entry is marked extinct and when the entry is finally scavenged from the database. The default is the same as the renewal interval.
Verify Interval	Specifies the interval after which the WINS Server must verify that old names it does not own are still active. The default is 20 times the extinction interval.
Initial Replication (Pull Parameters)	Enables the WINS Server to pull new WINS database entries from its partners (other WINS Servers).
Retry Count	The number of times the WINS Server attempts to contact a partner from which to pull the WINS database entries.

20

Configuration Option	Description
Initial Replication (Push Parameters)	Allows the WINS Server to notify its partners of the status of its WINS database when the system is initialized.
Replicate on Address Change	Allows the WINS Server to notify its partners of its WINS database status when a name registration changes.

4. If you want this WINS Server to pull replicas of new WINS database entries from its partners when the system is initialized or when a replication-related parameter changes, check Initial Replication in the Pull Parameters options, and then type a value for Retry Count.

   The retry count is the number of times the server should attempt to connect (in case of failure) with a partner for pulling replicas. Retries are attempted at the replication interval specified in the Preferences dialog box. If all retries are unsuccessful, WINS waits for a period before starting replication again.

5. To inform partners of the database status when the system is initialized, check Initial Replication in the Push Parameters group.

6. To inform partners of the database status when an address changes in a mapping record, check Replicate on Address Change.

7. As a final step in configuring the WINS Server, you should specify advanced configuration options. Click the Advanced button to expand the WINS Server Configuration dialog box (when advanced options do not already show). Set any Advanced WINS Server Configuration options described in Table 20.3. When you have completed all changes in the WINS Server Configuration dialog box, click OK.

Table 20.3. Advanced WINS Server configurations options.

Configuration Option	Description
Logging Enabled	Specifies whether logging of database changes to JET.LOG should be turned on.
Log Detailed Events	Specifies whether logging events are recorded in detail. This option requires considerable system resources and should be turned off when you are tuning for performance.

continues

20

Table 20.3. continued

Configuration Option	Description
Replicate Only With Partners	Specifies that replication proceeds only with WINS pull or push partners. When this option is not checked, an administrator can ask a WINS Server to pull or push from or to a non-listed WINS Server partner. By default, this option is checked.
Backup On Termination	Specifies that the database backs up automatically when WINS Manager is closed.
Migrate On/Off	Specifies that static unique and multihomed records in the database are treated as dynamic when they conflict with a new registration or replica. This means that when these records are no longer valid, they are overwritten by the new registration or replica. Check this option when you are upgrading non-Windows NT systems to Windows NT. By default, this option is not checked.
Starting Version Count	Specifies the highest version ID number for the database. Usually, you do not need to change this value unless the database becomes corrupted and you need to start fresh. In such an eventuality, set this value to a number higher than the version number counter for this WINS Server on all the remote partners that earlier replicated the local WINS Server's records. This value can be seen in the View Database dialog box in WINS Manager.
Database Backup Path	Specifies the directory where the computer stores WINS database backups. WINS uses this directory to perform an automatic restoration of the database when the database is determined to be corrupted at WINS start up. Do not specify a network directory.

Configuring WINS Clients

When you install TCP/IP on a workstation, you can configure it to use a WINS Server to resolve computer names to IP addresses by supplying the IP addresses of a primary and secondary WINS Server.

20

A Windows NT Server Version 4.0 operating as a WINS Server can support the following operating systems as WINS Clients:

☐ Windows NT Workstation Version 4.0

☐ Windows NT Server Version 4.0

☐ Windows for Workgroups 3.11 (WFW), with the Microsoft 32-bit TCP/IP VxD installed

☐ Microsoft Network Client for MS-DOS with real-mode TCP/IP driver, which is one of the clients included on the Windows NT Server Version 4.0 CD

☐ LAN Manager for MS-DOS 2.2c, which is included on the Windows NT Server Version 4.0 CD

As you saw this morning, if you use a DHCP Server to supply an IP address and other configuration information to DHCP Clients, you also can configure the DHCP Server to supply WINS configuration information. To supply the necessary WINS configuration information to DHCP Clients, the DHCP Server must have the following DHCP Options set:

☐ 044 WINS/NBNS Servers configured with the IP address of one or more WINS Servers

☐ 046 WINS/NBT Node Type set to 0x1 (B node), 0x2 (P node), 0x4 (M node), or 0x8 (H node)

Using WINS Manager

As you saw earlier, when you install a WINS Server, Windows NT adds WINS Manager to the Administrative Tools (Common) group under Programs. You can use WINS Manager to view and change parameters for any WINS Server on the internetwork. To administer a WINS Server remotely, run WINS Manager on a Windows NT Server computer that is not a WINS Server. You must log on as a member of the Administrators group for a WINS Server to configure that server.

To start WINS Manager, double-click the WINS Manager icon in Programs|Administrative Tools (Common). Or, at the command prompt, type net start winsadmn and press Enter. You can include a WINS Server name or IP address with the command.

If the Windows Internet Name Service is running on the local computer, that WINS Server opens automatically for administration. If the Windows Internet Name Service is not running when you start WINS, the Add WINS Server dialog box appears, as described in the following procedure.

If you specify an IP address when connecting to a WINS Server, the system connects using TCP/IP. If you specify a computer name, the system connects over NetBIOS.

20

To connect to a WINS Server to administer it, you perform the following steps:

1. In the WINS Manager window, select a server in the WINS Servers list. This list shows all WINS Servers where you previously connected or have been reported by partners of this WINS Server. Or, if you want to select another server where you have not previously connected, choose Server|Add WINS Server.

2. In the WINS Server box of the Add WINS Server dialog box, type the IP address or computer name of the WINS Server where you want to work, and then click OK. You do not have to include double backslashes before the name. WINS Manager adds these for you.

   The title bar in the WINS Manager window shows the IP address or computer name for the currently selected server, depending on whether you used the address or name to connect to the server. WINS Manager also shows some basic statistics for the selected server, as described in Table 20.4. You can display additional statistics by choosing Server|Detailed Information (see Table 20.5).

Table 20.4. Statistics in WINS Server.

Statistic	Description
Database Initialized	The last time static mappings were imported into the WINS database.
Statistics Cleared	The last time statistics for the WINS Server were cleared with the Clear Statistics command from the View menu.
Last Replication Times	The last time the WINS database was replicated.
Periodic	The last time the WINS database was replicated based on the replication interval specified in the Preferences dialog box.
Admin Trigger	The last time the WINS database was replicated because the administrator clicked the Replicate Now button in the Replication Partners dialog box.
Net Update	The last time the WINS database was replicated as a result of a network request, which is a push notification message that requests propagation.
Total Queries Received	The number of name query request messages received by this WINS Server. Successful indicates how many names were successfully matched in the database, and Failed indicates how many names this WINS Server could not resolve.

20

Statistic	Description
Total Releases	The number of messages received which indicate that a NetBIOS application has shut itself down. Successful indicates how many names were successfully released, and Failed indicates how many names this WINS Server could not release.
Total Registrations	The number of messages received that indicate name registrations for clients.

To see detailed information about the current WINS Server, you do the following things:

1. Choose Server|Detailed Information. The Detailed Information dialog box shows information about the selected WINS Server, as described in Table 20.5.

Table 20.5. Detailed information statistics.

Statistic	Description
Last Address Change	Indicates the time when the last WINS database change was replicated.
Last Scavenging Times	Indicates the last times the database was cleaned for specific types of entries.
Periodic	Indicates when the database was cleaned based on the renewal interval specified in the WINS Server Configuration dialog box.
Admin Trigger	Indicates when the database was last cleaned because the administrator chose the Initiate Scavenging command.
Extinction	Indicates when the database was last cleaned based on the Extinction interval specified in the WINS Server Configuration dialog box.
Verification	Indicates when the database was last cleaned based on the Verify interval specified in the WINS Server Configuration dialog box.
Unique Registrations	Indicates the number of name registration requests that have been accepted by this WINS Server.
Unique Conflicts	Indicates the number of conflicts encountered during registration of unique names owned by this WINS Server.
Unique Renewals	Indicates the number of renewals received for unique names.

continues

20

Table 20.5. continued

Statistic	Description
Group Registrations	Indicates the number of registration requests for groups that have been accepted by this WINS Server.
Group Conflicts	Indicates the number of conflicts encountered during registration of group names.
Group Renewals	Indicates the number of renewals received for group names.

2. To close the Detail Information dialog box, click the Close button.

Setting Preferences for WINS Manager

You can configure several options for the administration of WINS Servers. The commands for controlling preferences are on the Options menu.

Task 20.3. Setting WINS Manager preferences.

Step 1: Description

To set preferences for WINS Manager, select Preferences from the Options menu.

Step 2: Action

1. Select Options|Preferences.

2. To see all the available preferences, click the Partners button in the Preferences dialog box.

3. Select an Address Display option to indicate how you want address information to be displayed throughout WINS Manager: as a computer name, an IP address, or an ordered combination of both.

> **NOTE**
>
> Remember that the kind of address display affects how a connection is made to the WINS Server: for IP addresses, the connection is made via TCP/IP; for computer names, the connection is made via named pipes.

4. Check Auto Refresh if you want the statistics in the WINS Manager window to refresh automatically. Then enter a number in the Interval box to specify the number of seconds between refresh actions. WINS Manager also refreshes the statistical display automatically each time an action is initiated while you are working in WINS Manager.

5. Check the LAN Manager-Compatible check box if you want computer names to adhere to the LAN Manager naming convention. LAN Manager computer names are limited to 15 characters, as opposed to the 16-character NetBIOS names used by some other sources, such as Lotus Notes. In LAN Manager names, the 16th byte is used to indicate whether the device is a server, workstation, messenger, and so on. When this option is checked, WINS adds and imports static mappings with 0, 0x03, and 0x20 as the 16th byte.

All Windows networking, including Windows NT, follows the LAN Manager convention. So check this box unless your network accepts NetBIOS names from other sources.

6. Check Validate Cache Of Known WINS Servers At Startup Time if you want the system to query the list of servers each time the system starts to find out whether every server is available.

7. If you want a warning message to appear every time you delete a static mapping or the cached name of a WINS Server, check the Confirm Deletion of Static Mappings and Cached WINS Servers option.

8. In the Start Time box, specify the default for replication start time for new pull partners. Then specify values for the Replication Interval to indicate how often data replicas are exchanged between the partners. The minimum value for the Replication Interval is 40 minutes.

9. In the Update Count box, specify a default for how many registrations and changes can occur locally before a replication trigger is sent by this server when it is a push partner. The minimum value is 5.

10. When all options are set for your preferences, click OK.

Step 3: Review

Configuring options for the administration of WINS Servers is easy. Just select Preferences from the Options menu.

Managing the WINS Database

Because your WINS Server uses the same database format as the DHCP Server (a modified Access database), it has the same basic issues. So it is important to manage the various files used by WINS.

The system stores the following files in the *SystemRoot*\SYSTEM32\WINS directory created when you set up a WINS Server:

☐ SYSTEM.MDB is used by WINS for holding information about the structure of its database.

20

☐ WINS.MDB is the WINS database file.

☐ WINSTMP.MDB is a temporary file that WINS creates. This file might remain in the \WINS directory after a crash.

☐ JET.LOG is a log of all transactions for the database. This file is used by WINS to recover data when necessary.

You should back up these files when you back up other files on the WINS Server.

The WINS database contains all the address mappings for your WINS Clients. Like any database, it requires a certain amount of maintenance. The following discussion deals with maintenance issues such as purging entries, compacting the database, and backing up and restoring the database.

WARNING

As mentioned in the discussion of DHCP, you never should remove the SYSTEM.MDB, WINS.MDB, WINSTMP.MDB, and JET.LOG files!

As you add and delete records, the database naturally gets larger. Its growth affects the performance of the WINS Server. As with any database, you periodically need to clean up and back up the WINS database of address mappings. As your WINS.MDB database approaches 25 megabytes, you should compact it.

To compact the WINS database, you should carry out the following steps:

1. At the WINS Server, stop the Windows Internet Name Service by using the Control Panel Services option or by typing `net stop wins` at the command prompt.

2. Run COMPACT.EXE (which is found in the *SystemRoot*\SYSTEM32 directory) with the following syntax:

`COMPACT DatabaseName TemporaryDatabaseName`

DatabaseName is the name of the database to compact (or any fully qualified pathname), and *TemporaryDatabaseName* is a name to use as a temporary database. It too can be a fully qualified pathname.

WARNING

Do not compact the SYSTEM.MDB file. This can cause WINS Server service not to start. If you compact it accidentally, restore your configuration from a previous backup.

20

3. Restart the Windows Internet Name Service on the WINS Server.

WARNING

Because there is potential for failure caused by the compact utility or by data corruption on your *SystemRoot* partition, you should back up your WINS databases regularly, and definitely before you compact them. Before you back up or compact the database, you should scavenge (clean) the database to delete old records that are no longer needed.

WARNING

The MDB databases are in Access format. If you have Microsoft Access, resist any temptation to look at these databases. Any accidental modifications would corrupt the database. If you corrupt it accidentally, restore from a previous backup.

Scavenging the WINS Database

You should periodically clean up the local WINS database of released entries and old entries that were registered at another WINS Server but did not get removed from this WINS database for some reason. This process, called *scavenging*, is done automatically over intervals based on the renewal and extinction intervals in the Configuration dialog box. You also can clean the database manually, for example, when you want to verify old replicas immediately instead of waiting for the specified interval.

The WINS Server automatically performs scavenging in the following manner:

1. If a WINS Client does not renew its name registration before the renewal interval expires, its registration is marked as "released."

2. After the extinction interval expires for a "released" entry, it is marked as "extinct" in the WINS database.

3. Finally, after the extinction time-out has expired, the "extinct" entry is removed from the WINS database.

Using the default times for all the intervals and time-outs, a name registration that has not been removed remains in the WINS database for about four hours. If any of the intervals or time-outs have been increased, the entry remains in the database even longer. Therefore, it is possible to use WINS Manager to force the WINS database to be scavenged through the Initiate Scavenging option under the Mappings menu.

20

To scavenge the WINS database, choose Mappings|Initiate Scavenging. WINS Manager cleans the database and displays its results as shown in Table 20.6.

Table 20.6. Scavenging results.

State Before Scavenging	State After Scavenging
Owned active names in which the Renewal interval has expired	Marked released
Owned released names in which the Extinction interval has expired	Marked extinct
Owned extinct names in which the Extinction time-out has expired	Deleted
Replicas of extinct names in which the Extinction time-out has expired	Deleted
Replicas of active names in which the Verify interval has expired	Revalidated
Replicas of extinct or deleted names	Deleted

Backing Up the WINS Database

WINS Manager provides backup tools you can use to back up the WINS database. After you specify a backup directory for the database, WINS performs complete database backups every 24 hours, using the specified directory. Be sure to perform a full backup by disabling the Perform Incremental Backup option if you plan to use this copy to restore your configuration. You also should periodically back up the Registry entries for the WINS Server.

To back up a WINS database, you take these steps:

1. Choose Mappings|Backup Database.
2. In the Select Backup Directory dialog box, specify the location for saving the backup files. Windows NT proposes a subdirectory of the \WINS directory. You can accept this proposed directory. The most secure location, however, is on another hard disk.

TIP

> Do not back up to a network drive, because WINS Manager cannot restore from a network source.

20

3. If you want to back up only the newest version numbers in the database (that is, changes that have occurred since the last backup), check Perform Incremental Backup. You must have performed a complete backup before you can use this option.

4. Click OK.

The three files that went into WINS_BAK are essentially all there is to a WINS database. Just put the files back in *SystemRoot*\SYSTEM32\WINS, and the database is restored. But you can't do that while WINS is running, so go to the Control Panel and stop the Windows Internet Name Service (open Control Panel, double-click Services, click Windows Internet Name Service, click the Stop button, and then click Yes to confirm that you want to stop the service). Then you can copy the files from the backup location to *SystemRoot*\ SYSTEM32\WINS and restart the service by going to the same place in the Control Panel where you stopped the service and clicking the Start button.

If you modified the settings on the WINS Server, such as modifying the renewal interval or specifying a backup directory, then you might want to back those up as well. Your option settings for the WINS Server are stored in the Registry (of course) in the key \HKEY_LOCAL_MACHINE\SYSTEM\CurrentControlSet\Services\WINS. You can save that part of the Registry in this way:

1. Start the Registry Editor, REGEDT32. (Refer to Day 4 if you forget how to use the Registry Editor.)

2. Open the HKEY_LOCAL_MACHINE subtree.

3. Click on the SYSTEM\CurrentControlSet\Services\WINS key.

4. Click Registry and Save Key.

5. In the Save Key dialog box, specify the path where you store backup versions of the WINS database files, and click OK. After the key is saved, close RegEdit.

So, to summarize, to rebuild a WINS Server you should tell the WINS Server where to do backups, and it will do them automatically every day. And when you make changes to WINS settings, save the part of the Registry that holds the settings. Most important, run a secondary WINS Server, and then you won't have to worry about backing up your WINS database, because you will have two machines working in parallel.

20

Restoring a WINS Database

If all else fails, you will need to restore your WINS database from backup.

Task 20.4. Restoring your WINS database.

Step 1: Description

To restore the settings, use the Registry Editor to restore the WINS key.

Step 2: Action

1. Stop the WINS service by entering net stop wins at the command prompt (or follow the procedure given in the preceding section).

2. Start the Registry Editor, REGEDT32.

3. Open the HKEY_LOCAL_MACHINE subtree.

4. Click on the SYSTEM\CurrentControlSet\Services\WINS key.

5. Click Registry, and then Restore.

6. Point the dialog box to wherever you stored the backups, and fill in the name of the backup file; then click OK.

7. Click Yes to confirm that you want to overwrite the old key.

8. Exit the Registry Editor.

9. Restart the WINS service. You do not need to reboot your system for these changes to take effect.

Step 3: Review

Use the Registry Editor to restore the key, and fill in the name of the backup file to overwrite the old key.

WINS Proxy Agents

Using an NBNS (NetBIOS Naming Service) like WINS can cut down on the broadcasts on your network, reduce traffic, and improve throughput. But as you've seen, this method requires that the clients understand WINS. Older network client software just broadcasts as a B node.

WINS can help those older non-WINS Clients with a WINS *proxy agent*. A WINS proxy agent is a network workstation that listens for older B node systems helplessly broadcasting, trying to reach NetBIOS names that (unknown to the B node computers) are on another subnet, and acts on its behalf.

TIP

> WINS proxy agents don't store information obtained from a broadcast in the WINS Server's database. This is one reason why you need a proxy agent on each subnet containing older clients—non-WINS. Also, you require a WINS proxy agent on each subnet because routers don't pass broadcast messages. So the proxy agent needs to be on the same subnet as the older clients to receive the broadcast. Make sure, however, that only one WINS proxy agent per subnet exists. Otherwise, two agents will respond, causing unpredictable results.

Summary

Name resolution is an important part of your network. This morning, you learned about assigning addresses dynamically. This afternoon, you learned about name resolution, the HOSTS file, DNS, the LMHOSTS file, and WINS. Specifically, you learned about these topics:

- ☐ Configuring WINS Servers
- ☐ Starting and stopping the WINS database
- ☐ Creating static mappings on a WINS Server
- ☐ Backing up and restoring a WINS Server

Now you know the ins and outs of installing and configuring the Windows Internet Name Service.

Workshop

To wrap up the day, you can review terms and tasks from the chapter, and see the answers to some commonly asked questions.

Terminology Review

Domain Name System or Server (DNS)—A distributed database system that allows TCP/IP applications to resolve a host name into a correct IP address.

Dynamic Host Configuration Protocol (DHCP)—Protocol used by a server to dynamically allocate IP addresses on a network. Designed to allow networked hosts to access configuration information across the network, instead of having to be configured by hand directly.

20

time-to-live (TTL)—A counter field used in IP datagrams to indicate the length of time (generally represented by how many different gateways have handled it) that the datagram can continue to be forwarded to other gateways before it will be discarded because it has expired.

Windows Internet Name Service (WINS)—A service that translates Windows computer names (or NetBIOS names) to IP addresses.

Task List

The emphasis of this chapter has been to introduce you to name resolution with Windows NT. As a system administrator, you will need to learn how to implement a WINS Server. This chapter included many very complicated tasks:

- [ ] Installing a WINS Server
- [ ] Adding static mappings
- [ ] Importing static mappings
- [ ] Editing static mappings
- [ ] Filtering the range of mappings
- [ ] Configuring WINS Servers
- [ ] Configuring WINS Clients
- [ ] Starting a WINS Manager
- [ ] Connecting to a WINS Server
- [ ] Setting WINS Manager preferences
- [ ] Compacting, backing up, and restoring the WINS database

Q&A

Q How do you provide WINS names through DNS service?

A To provide WINS names through the DNS service, follow these steps:

1. Use any text editor to open the PLACE.DOM file.

2. Find or create the Start of Authority (SOA) record for the domain where you want to use WINS names. The SOA record points to the computer that is the best source of information on computer names in the domain. The record can span more than one line when you enclose it in parentheses so that the program reads it as a single line.

20

3. Create a new line under this line, consisting of the string $WINS. Note that this must be on a line by itself and start in column 1. Do not put the $WINS line in reverse-looking (IN-ADDR.ARPA.) domains.

4. Save the file.

Q How can I get my UNIX client to a computer that has a WINS name and a changing IP address (for example, an address acquired through the DHCP service)?

A Configure the UNIX computer's resolver to use the Windows NT computer running the DNS service, and make sure that the computer running the DNS service has a properly configured WINS Server service. Then decide in what domain the WINS names belong. For example, you might decide that the domain pda.home.dom is the space where all WINS computers are named. You then would expect WINS lookup to handle queries for workstation.pda.home.dom, looking for the Workstation computer.

20

DAY

11

Chapter 21

File Backup and Recovery

Four days ago, you learned all about files and directories in NT and how to find, manage, and manipulate them. You also learned that NT offers the use of more than one type of file system; the older, more accepted FAT system and the new NTFS (New Technology File System). At this point, you will learn about protecting your files from loss and will learn appropriate methods for backing up and restoring lost files. In this chapter, you'll also learn about accepted ways of managing the backup process by using the tools and techniques available to you in an NT Server environment.

When you used the RDISK command in Chapter 6, "Exploring Windows NT Server," you learned some useful backup techniques. That command provided a copy of your current Registry and is used to recover your server should a problem arise.

A successful backup program consists of various elements, the most important being the actual backup program and your diligence in performing it regularly. Too many times data loss occurs primarily because the backup did not get done or did not run successfully, and recovery was therefore impossible.

This chapter introduces you to a backup and recovery process that should become one of the key tasks in your day-to-day administration of your NT Server system. This afternoon, you'll look at fault tolerance for NT, and you'll get your first glimpse of the proper method for setting up and managing a fault-tolerant system, helping reduce the need for file backup and recovery. Let's start by quickly looking at backing up your server.

Server Backups

In the afternoon, you'll look at creating fault tolerance and protecting the system from a hardware failure by using special devices. No matter how well you configure the system for fault tolerance, however, files are accidentally deleted, and even fault-tolerant drives sometimes malfunction, causing data loss.

One of the first tasks is to consider what device to use for providing your backups. Most servers these days have huge data requirements, and therefore some form of tape or optical disk is necessary to manage the amount of data that needs to be backed up.

Next, it might be a good idea to decide the general backup policy you intend to follow. Are backups to be performed each day? What type of retention cycle will you use, and what about recovering individual files that users might have lost? Finally, how do you verify that the backups are working properly and that you can recover the necessary data when needed? We answer these questions and more in the remainder of this chapter.

Choosing a Tape Drive

In Windows NT Server, as always, your first consideration needs to include the Hardware Compatibility List (HCL). You remember from previous days that NT can be very particular about the devices it will use. Limit your problems by using the HCL whenever you add a new device. When considering the purchase of a new device, be sure to use the storage figures offered without using compression, because these are more accurate. NT doesn't always allow software compression, so your device might offer only half the storage you expected if you considered only the fully compressed storage figures.

It is a good idea to try to standardize all your tape drives within the computer room because this technique offers greater ease of use and flexibility. It's a lot easier to grab and use a tape from a central storage area than it is to find a particular brand for a particular type of tape drive, mixed up among many types.

21

You might have a tape drive in each machine or use an autoloader type of device. Using an autoloader becomes useful if you have more than one server to back up or have really extensive amounts of data to be backed up. Individual tape drives require you to be present to load the tapes needed for each backup cycle. This is fine if all your data fits on one tape, but it becomes a problem if you need more than one because someone needs to be onsite when the backup job is run. This work is often done during the night, and your operation might not normally require onsite operations staff during night hours.

An autoloader solves this problem by providing a bay for a number of tapes to fit into, and the autoloader software then uses each tape as necessary. This solution leaves you free to check the backups each morning rather than be onsite. NT, however, does not support autoloaders, so you need special software from the vendor to use these devices.

What type of tapes are available and how do you decide which to use? We see all kinds in use by our clients, indicating that no one type is the be-all or end-all solution. What is right for your environment might be too little or too much for another. The primary types of tape in use consist of 4mm and 8mm formats. These tapes are easily the most available and have been around long enough to be reasonably priced. A standard 4mm tape might hold anywhere from 2 to 9GB of data, and an 8mm tape holds from 4 to 25GB of data.

When purchasing tapes, you need to watch these claims because they usually consist of the maximum amount after compression. If you already use compression, such as NTFS file-level compression, you're unlikely to get any additional compression gain, so the amount of data held on the tape might differ from the suggested specifications. In this case, you might need more tapes than you thought you would.

One of the newer tape formats is called digital linear tape (DLT). It's gaining acceptance as a reliable, fast backup medium for large server backups. DLT uses an extremely fast transfer rate and provides about three times the storage capacity of other tape formats. It uses a unique multipath, serpentine approach for storing data. On each tape are 64 pairs of track; the backup is performed by moving along one track until the end of the tape is reached and then continuing back on the next track to the beginning of the tape. By performing this snakelike back-and-forth movement, DLT stores data in such a manner that access to any particular piece can be very fast because it's not necessary to read through the entire tape.

When purchasing the tape device, be sure to consider the importance of this decision. An inexpensive device might sound like a good deal or a cost-saving measure, but if your backups are lost or the machine readily breaks, is the savings worth it? You need to find a cost/performance balance that you can live with and that protects your important data assets.

Finally, you need to consider the speed of the device and compare it to the amount of data that needs to be backed up. Too slow a device means your backups will need hours or even days to finish, and the chance of completing the backups regularly will be diminished by other priorities.

21

Installing a Tape Backup Device

As you just learned, keeping a backup copy of your data is essential to ensure that the important information on your network is maintained and always accessible. After you decide on a tape drive, you need to add it to your server and tell NT about the device.

Physically adding a tape drive might mean removing the cover of your server and installing the device in one of the many drive bays. Or it might mean adding a device to the serial port of your server. Regardless of how the tape drive is attached, you need to tell NT that it exists, what it is, and where to find it. Perhaps in the next release of NT (currently called Cairo), Plug and Play will be available, and all you will need to do is add the device and let NT find it. But for now, you need to perform a series of steps.

Task 21.1. Adding a new tape drive.

TASK

Step 1: Description

In this task, you learn to tell NT all about a new tape device and set up that device for use by the system. You begin by first physically attaching the device and then following these steps to complete the installation.

Step 2: Action

1. Log onto the system as an Administrator. You need administrator access to add a new device. Open the Control Panel using the Start|Settings|Control Panel option, and double-click the Tape Devices icon. You see the dialog box shown in Figure 21.1.

Figure 21.1.

The Tape Devices dialog box.

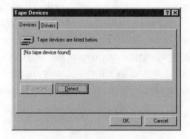

2. Click the Detect button to tell NT to find the attached device. NT might find the particular device you installed or a compatible version.

3. You can manually add the drive if you are not sure that NT chose the correct one by selecting it from the drop-down list provided. You find this list by selecting the Drivers tab and clicking the Add button. This action brings up a window where you can select the tape drive, as shown in Figure 21.2.

Figure 21.2.

Adding a tape device manually.

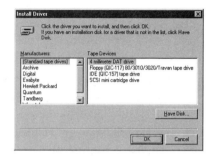

4. After selecting the necessary device or allowing NT to choose it, you might be asked for the NT Server distribution files. Enter the appropriate path, and NT copies the necessary files to operate the new tape drive.

5. Click the OK button when asked whether you want to reboot the system to finish the install process. You must reboot for NT to use the new device.

Step 3: Review

This task showed you how to install a new tape device on your NT Server 4.0 system. Adding this device is the first real step toward providing a sound and effective backup and recovery program.

Your new device is now ready for use. Now you are faced with the task of determining what needs to be backed up and when to perform the backups. You need to develop a strategy that provides you with all the necessary items in case a real disaster occurs and the backup copies become your only source of data.

Creating a Backup Strategy

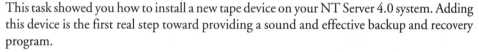

First, it is important to realize that developing a sound, effective strategy is beyond the scope of this book. We provide you with the necessary fundamentals, but each site has different needs. An effective program is developed using input from many different parts of the organization, such as your audit staff and user community. Why do these people need to provide input to your plan? Because without them, you cannot be certain which files need to be backed up and what type of schedule is most effective for that particular data.

You might decide that all data will be backed up on a cycled basis, regardless of its use to the organization. You need to ask yourself, however, whether this means just the data on your servers or all data, including the client machines. Often, this answer depends on whether your site provides a policy for staff that only company data located on the servers is backed up. Users might be told they should not keep data on their local drives for this reason.

21

On the other hand, your site might allow data to be spread out across the network for other reasons, and therefore your backup policy needs to consider all client machines in addition to the servers.

NOTE

Regardless of the method used to back up—either server only or server and workstation files—it is important to ensure that users are well aware of the strategy. This helps prevent data loss from occurring due to a user storing critical data in a location where it is not backed up regularly. Remember that workstations need to be left on overnight for a backup to work, and this is not always the case.

The tapes you use need to be managed well. A rotation cycle needs to be developed that clearly defines the role of each tape in the cycle. For example, a four-week cycle needs four sets of tapes, each labeled according to the week. You might use Week 1, Week 2, Week 3, and Week 4 as your naming convention, or you might use a color scheme with Red, Yellow, Black, and White designating each week.

The cycle needs to include a daily backup and a weekly full backup, using different tapes. If you are concerned about the cost of all these tapes, consider the alternative. How much will it cost to recover your files if they are not backed up? For example, each Saturday you might produce a full backup and produce incremental backups for the rest of the week. This way, you can always recover using the latest weekly full backup and any additional incremental backup tapes you have available.

You might also want to produce a backup tape for each quarter or each month and keep these offsite in the event of a disaster. This way, you can always recover the preceding month's data if you lose everything else in a fire or some other disaster.

The most common method for backups is the grandfather/father/son (GFS) rotation. This method is supported by most backup software, is relatively easy to implement and manage, and is fairly efficient. It is primarily used on small to medium-sized servers. This backup rotation can be implemented using 21 tapes. By increasing the number of daily cycles to protect against excessive tape usage, you can increase the number to 32 or more tapes. In Task 21.2, you'll learn how to set up such a cycle.

Task 21.2. Setting up a grandfather/father/son backup cycle.

Step 1: Description

In this task, you'll learn to set up and use a GFS tape rotation cycle. You can modify the cycle to suit your particular needs.

Step 2: Action

1. Create four tapes and name them Daily Mon., Daily Tues., Daily Wed., and Daily Thurs. These are your daily backups.

2. Create five weekly cycles and call those tapes Weekly One, Weekly Two, Weekly Three, Weekly Four, and Weekly Five. These become the weekly backups.

3. Now create 12 tapes and label them one for each month of the year. These are used as your monthly backups.

4. Use the daily tapes for each week, overwriting the data on each tape on the successive week. For example, the Monday tape is used once per week, on each Monday. For these, you might use an incremental backup.

5. Follow up each Friday with a weekly tape, and perform a full backup. These tapes are overwritten only once every four or five weeks. (The fifth tape is used for months containing an extra Friday.)

6. Finally, use the monthly tapes on each month end, performing a full backup again and providing a further copy of all files. These, of course, get overridden only once per year.

Step 3: Review

This task showed that you can provide a backup program using a straightforward system and only a few tapes. You modify the plan to suit your needs. For example, if archiving is less critical to your organization, substitute the weekly backups with quarterly or semi-annual ones. If it is more important, perform full backups every couple of days or mid-week.

Do not forget to include an offsite rotation for the tapes. Many organizations like to keep the most recent week's backup tapes on hand for quick data recovery of individual files. Users are constantly requiring these, especially, it seems, after they become accustomed to how easily the files are recovered. This retention cycle, however, leaves your site vulnerable to data loss of up to two weeks' worth of information! Carefully consider whether this vulnerability

21

is acceptable, and institute other solutions if you need offsite recovery of less than this time frame. For example, ensure that the full weekly backup is always sent offsite on the following Monday, but retain the incremental tapes for the additional week to allow users to recover files.

One additional method that is very complex is called the Tower of Hanoi method, based on the game of the same name. It is not supported by NTBACKUP and therefore cannot be used without third-party software.

Finally, remember that tapes wear out and that machines sometimes fail in inexplicable ways. Test your backup tapes regularly, such as once per quarter or at least every six months. You do not want to find out the hard way that a tape is no longer any good and the data stored on it is lost.

Your organization's critical data is stored on these tapes, and the tapes are not protected by any form of encryption. If they ever are stolen, everything is accessible and at risk. Lock them up and transport them only using reputable data storage firms. Be sure to institute written procedures to follow for tracking all the tapes during their journeys back and forth between your site and the offsite location to ensure that each is always accounted for and properly tracked.

Various terms are used for backups that you need to understand. NT allows you to select the type of backup based on your understanding of these terms:

☐ *The archive bit:* One way for an operating system to track whether a file is backed up is through the use of a bit that gets set each time a file is created or modified. The bit is called the archive bit. It has been around since the DOS days and has proved to be a reliable method for determining backup status.

☐ *Normal backups:* This backup copies all selected files, regardless of the archive bit setting, and then turns off the archive bit on all those files. This is often referred to as a full backup.

☐ *Copy backups:* This is identical to a normal backup except the archive bit is never changed. This method is normally used to allow you to take an interim backup without affecting the normal backup cycle you are using. Leaving the archive bit alone allows your regular backup cycle to continue unaffected.

☐ *Incremental backups:* This type is used to back up all the files that have been modified or created since the last normal or incremental backup. Typically, you run a normal or full backup, and then instead of running another complete backup of all files, you run an incremental backup, copying only the files changed since the normal backup. You continue running incremental backups after that, copying the files that have changed since the last incremental backup. You do this each day of the week, for example, and run a normal on each Saturday. This technique minimizes the work of the backup program yet ensures that all files are properly backed up.

☐ *Differential backups:* This backup type copies all the selected files with their archive bits set but does not change those archive bits. In this manner, each time you run the backup, the files created or modified since the last full backup are all copied, updating the backup with more and more files each day. Each set contains all the prior sets of files and so keeps growing. Put another way, any one day's worth of differential backups contains all the files up to and including that day. Restoring a damaged disk drive with differential backups means taking the most recent normal backup tape and then the most recent differential tape and using them both to update all the files. Restoring a file is even easier. You look for it on the most recent differential, and if you don't find it, return to the last normal because it will not be on any of the other differentials.

☐ *Daily backups:* This method is used to copy only those files created or modified on a particular day. Again, the option leaves the archive bit unchanged, only this time because it uses the date and does not refer to the archive bit. Using a daily backup type means the copy *must* be run each day or some files do not get backed up. This type of copy also fails to back up modified files if the date stamp is not modified.

These options are used in all backup programs. You might decide to use a normal backup cycle and back up all the files each time. With this option, however, you use a large number of tapes because every file is backed up each time the job runs. In large organizations, this method is far too time-consuming and costly.

You usually end up using a combination of normal, on a weekly basis perhaps, with incremental or differential backups in between the normal jobs. This technique diminishes the number of tapes needed and the time required to perform the backup.

Deciding how your disk drives are used plays a role in the type of backup and how often you might run each one. If you use a single server with one drive, it's no issue. Back it up.

In a multiple-server, multiple-disk-drive environment, the issue gets more complicated. Consider setting up the drives to handle the various types of data involved. For example, place user data and other frequently changed data in one area, and segregate it from less-often-changed data such as system files. This way, you can schedule changes to each type of data and minimize how often each needs to be backed up. An occasional normal backup suffices for system files, but an incremental or differential approach is necessary for files that change more often.

21

The NT Backup Program

NT Server provides a backup program that is more than adequate for the ordinary installation. You might need to use other programs if you install an autoloader, however, because the NT backup program does not recognize these devices. Follow the directions that program provides to manage your backups.

You'll find this free tool rather limiting in its capabilities. Most organizations purchase a higher-end tool that offers improved services such as multiserver capability or the capability to back up multiplatform workstations. In addition, many tools offer the capability to schedule the backups and offer scripting languages for automating your particular backup needs. However, NTBACKUP does provide adequate backup for small sites with modest needs. You'll learn how to set up and run the program in this section.

NTBACKUP handles files residing on either FAT-based or NTFS-based partitions. It also allows you to recover these files onto either system, meaning that a file originally backed up from an NTFS file system can then be restored to a FAT drive, or vice versa. Note that NT does not recognize the new FAT32 partitions that Microsoft is shipping in OEM Windows 95 on all new PCs. NTBACKUP cannot see these partitions and therefore cannot back up from or restore anything to them.

The files and program icons for NTBACKUP are installed by default when you first install NT Server. Before using the program, however, you need to set up the tape drive as you learned to do in Task 21.1. Following this, the other steps you need to consider before actually beginning your first backup are deciding on the tape rotation cycle, labeling and setting up your tapes, and selecting the files and directories for backup. In the next task, you'll learn to run the tape backup program.

Task 21.3. Running tape backup.

Step 1: Description

In this task, you'll learn to tell NTBACKUP which files and directories to back up and you'll complete a backup.

Step 2: Action

1. Log onto the system as an Administrator. You need Administrator or Backup Operator access to ensure that you are authorized to access all the files. Open the program using Start|Programs|Administrative Options (Common)|Backup. You see the window shown in Figure 21.3.

Figure 21.3.

The opening window for NTBACKUP.

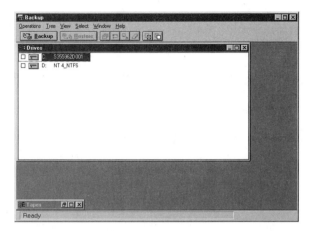

2. Open the Tapes window by clicking the minimized Backup (Tapes) window showing near the bottom of the screen, as you see in Figure 21.3. If a tape is in the device, the program shows the creation date and files in the default window. If the tape is blank, the message Blank Tape shows. Occasionally, NTBACKUP does not recognize a blank tape as correctly formatted. In this case, you need to format the tape.

3. Make sure that the correct tape is mounted in the drive before continuing. Next, choose the Backup (Drives) window. You see the available drives that the program is able to see. Note that the program recognizes a compressed FAT volume, but because NT does not, you are unable to see or back up any files that might exist on the drives. FAT partitions must not be compressed for NT to use. You see a window where you can select the drives, as shown earlier in Figure 21.3.

4. To back up the entire drive, select it by using the check box next to the drive. To selectively back up files, double-click the drive icon. NTBACKUP shows you the files for that drive. You see an example of this in Figure 21.4.

Figure 21.4.

Selecting files in NTBACKUP.

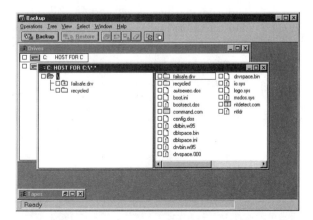

21

5. Single-clicking a file folder shows all the files within the folder. Select folders for backup by clicking the check box next to the file or folder. Do this for all the files you are backing up.

6. Click the Backup button to start the backup process. Before backups begin, NTBACKUP provides some information and presents you with the following options:

☐ *Current Tape:* If the tape you placed in the drive is blank, you see words to that effect. If an existing tape is used, the name you provided is shown.

☐ *Creation Date:* This field remains blank if no data is on the tape, or it provides the date the tape was created.

☐ *Owner:* This field is blank if it's a new tape, or it shows the name of the user who created the tape.

☐ *Tape Name:* You enter a descriptive name for the tape unless you are appending data to an existing tape where NTBACKUP does not let you change the name. Use the information provided earlier to place a name that makes sense to you, such as Cycle Red, Day 2.

☐ *Verify After Backup:* This option allows you to decide whether the program is to verify the data it backed up by reading the data again after it is backed up and comparing it to the originals. This verification provides assurance that the backup is successful but nearly doubles the length of time the backup program needs to complete. If you have the time, using this option provides peace of mind and assurance that when you try to recover a file, the file will be there.

☐ *Restrict Access to Owner or Administrator:* This field lets you control who is able to access the data on the tape. When so marked, only the tape's owner, an Administrator, or a Backup Operator can view its contents. This option is available only during a Replace function.

☐ *Hardware Compression:* If your drive doesn't support hardware compression, the box remains grayed and unavailable. Additionally, some tape drives do not support mixing compression (hardware and the backup program's compression), so if the box is grayed out and your device supports hardware compression, that might be why.

☐ *Operation:* The Append option adds your file backups to any data currently on the tape; Replace overwrites existing data.

21

☐ *Description:* Here you can enter a brief description of the tape or scroll through existing descriptions and choose an appropriate one from the list shown.

☐ *Backup Type:* You select one of five types using this field:

Full (Normal): All selected components are backed up, and their archive bits are cleared.

Copy: All selected components are backed up, but their archive bits are not cleared.

Incremental: All files and folders with their archive bits set are backed up, and the bits are turned off.

Differential: All files and folders with their archive bits set are backed up, but the bits are not turned off.

Daily: All files and folders modified today are backed up, and their archive bits are ignored.

☐ *Log File:* NTBACKUP stores a log file in this location. By default, it is stored in \winnt\backup.log. Consider moving it to a safe location and restricting access because normal staff do not need to see this information. The program supports a few options for managing a log file:

Full Detail: All transaction detail is logged, including the names of all files. Use of this option results in a huge log file, and you need to take care that the log files are well managed and routinely deleted after being backed up.

Summary Only: Only important data is logged, such as start and end time and files that were missed.

Don't Log: The logging operation is disabled.

7. Click OK to start the backup process. The backup process takes a while. When it ends, be sure to remove the tape and place it in a safe location before sending it offsite.

Step 3: Review

This task showed you how to run the tape backup program that comes with your NT Server 4.0 system. Running backups should become part of your everyday administration duties.

You can run NTBACKUP from the command line; this method allows you to schedule the operation so that you need not be present when it runs at, say, 2 a.m. each day. In Chapter 15, "Managing the File Server," you learned to use the AT command and schedule batch jobs.

21

NTBACKUP allows all its options to be run from the command line, so you can place the required setup into a batch file and run the program whenever you want. You'll learn how to do this later, in the section called "Running Backups Using the Command Line."

Restoring Files Using NTBACKUP

Now that your files are safely backed up and you're keeping them on some form of offsite rotation, you need to learn how to recover the files from the backup tapes.

NTBACKUP allows you to restore the backup set to the same drive the files were copied from or to a different drive. Doing so is relatively easy, as you'll see in Task 21.4.

Task 21.4. Restoring files with NTBACKUP.

Step 1: Description

After files are safely backed up, you might occasionally need to restore them. Often, users accidentally delete a file and need it recovered, or in rare instances, a drive failure might necessitate a complete recovery. You'll learn how to perform these recoveries in this task.

Step 2: Action

1. Insert the required tape. You need to review your tape backup list to find the necessary tape. Remember that each day's backups are created using a definite rotation cycle and numbering scheme.

2. Log onto the system as an Administrator or Backup Operator. You need this level of access to restore files. Open the program by using the Start|Programs|Administrative Options (Common)|Backup command.

3. The left pane of the Tapes window shows the name of the inserted tape. Verify that it is correct before proceeding.

4. Double-click on the folder name in the right-hand pane. NTBACKUP loads the tape catalog and displays the file folders available.

5. Select the files and folders you need recovered by clicking the check box associated with each one. When you are ready, click the Restore button to continue.

6. As with the Backup button you saw in Task 21.3, you see a window with various options. In the top third of the dialog box, you see data relating to the tape you inserted. Verify that it is the correct tape to ensure that you do not inadvertently recover a file created on the wrong date.

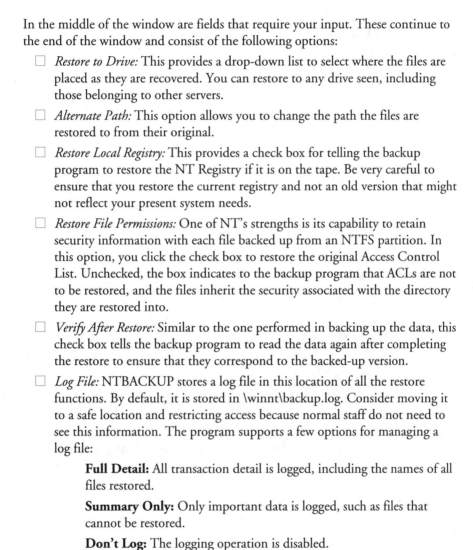

In the middle of the window are fields that require your input. These continue to the end of the window and consist of the following options:

- *Restore to Drive:* This provides a drop-down list to select where the files are placed as they are recovered. You can restore to any drive seen, including those belonging to other servers.

- *Alternate Path:* This option allows you to change the path the files are restored to from their original.

- *Restore Local Registry:* This provides a check box for telling the backup program to restore the NT Registry if it is on the tape. Be very careful to ensure that you restore the current registry and not an old version that might not reflect your present system needs.

- *Restore File Permissions:* One of NT's strengths is its capability to retain security information with each file backed up from an NTFS partition. In this option, you click the check box to restore the original Access Control List. Unchecked, the box indicates to the backup program that ACLs are not to be restored, and the files inherit the security associated with the directory they are restored into.

- *Verify After Restore:* Similar to the one performed in backing up the data, this check box tells the backup program to read the data again after completing the restore to ensure that they correspond to the backed-up version.

- *Log File:* NTBACKUP stores a log file in this location of all the restore functions. By default, it is stored in \winnt\backup.log. Consider moving it to a safe location and restricting access because normal staff do not need to see this information. The program supports a few options for managing a log file:

    Full Detail: All transaction detail is logged, including the names of all files restored.

    Summary Only: Only important data is logged, such as files that cannot be restored.

    Don't Log: The logging operation is disabled.

7. Click OK to start the restore operation. NTBACKUP restores the selected files and folders and performs a compare if requested. Following completion, you need to place the backup tape back in its secure location for safekeeping.

Step 3: Review
This task showed you how to restore files and folders by using the NTBACKUP program that is installed with your NT Server system. You are sure to use this information on numerous occasions as users lose files and occasional accidents occur.

Running Backups Using the Command Line

You learned how to use the GUI interface of NTBACKUP in the earlier parts of this chapter. On occasion, however, you'll need to use the command line to perform these actions. For example, to automate your backups using the AT command, you need to set up a command-line batch file and have the scheduler program execute that batch file.

NTBACKUP provides for this circumstance by allowing you to operate via the command line. Like any other program, it provides a particular syntax and set of parameters for you to follow.

Here is the syntax for running NTBACKUP from a command line:

NTBACKUP *operation path parameters*

Each part of this syntax is explained here:

NTBACKUP: Is the backup program name.

operation: Tells the program whether to run a backup or a restore. Insert the word BACKUP or RESTORE.

path: Tells the program which path or file needs to be backed up or restored. More than one entry is permitted.

parameters: Indicates the specific functions you want the backup program to perform. These are your options:

/a: Tells the program to append data to an existing tape. Not specifying this option tells NTBACKUP to start at the beginning of the tape and replace any existing data. Be careful! It is easy to accidentally replace valuable data by ignoring this field.

/v: Verifies all data after the restore or backup operation. This effectively doubles the amount of time needed yet provides more assurance that your files are safe. Use this option for critical backup and restores.

/r: Enables the restricted access parameter so that only the owner, an Administrator, or a Backup Operator can access the data on the tape.

/d "*text*": Provides a description of the tape using the words specified in the text filed. You might specify words like "Daily Backup of server TOSHIBA_410, Red Cycle" for a description. You need to use the quotation marks in the command.

/b: Tells the backup to include a copy of the local Registry on the tape.

21

/hc:on/off: Tells the backup program to use hardware compression. It is viable only if your tape drive performs this function. It cannot be used with the /a function because NTBACKUP automatically uses whatever compression was originally used on that tape when appending data. Specify the command as /hc:on or /hc:off.

/t *option*: Specifies which type of backup to perform. You specify Normal, Incremental, Differential, Copy, or Daily. Refer to the earlier backup task for explanations of each option.

/l "*filename*": Allows you to specify a different filename for the log file. By default, the program uses \winnt\backup.log.

/e: The default for logging consists of complete log information, and this can become quite extensive in a large backup operation. The /e option tells the program to log only exceptions.

/tape:*x*: NT supports up to 10 tape devices. Use this option to tell the program which device to use. By default, it uses device 0.

As you see from the commands provided, you can specify all the options pertaining to performing a backup or restore directly from the command line. We do not recommend that you use this method for everyday activity unless you plan to automate the process.

If you decide that it would be nice to automate your backups, you need to follow the steps given in the following task.

Task 21.5. Using the command line for backups.

Step 1: Description

In this task, you'll learn to tell NT Server to automate a backup task by using the command-line function and AT scheduler program.

Step 2: Action

1. Log onto the system as an Administrator. Make sure that the scheduler service is running. Open Server Manager; click on Files and then Services. View the drop-down list for Schedule and verify that it is started.

2. In Chapter 15, review the section on using the AT command to refresh your memory. After all, it has been three days.

3. Create a batch script by using Notepad. In the script, place the specific backup commands you want run. For example, you might want to back up the entire drive C: each Saturday morning.

TASK

21

To accomplish this, you might use the following command:

```
ntbackup backup c: /v /d "Full backup of C drive" /b /t Normal /e
```

As you might remember, this command tells backup to perform a backup of drive C:, verify the data it backs up, place a description on the tape, include a copy of the local Registry, perform a normal cycle, and log only exceptions. Use the data gained in Chapter 15 to devise the particular options you need. Save this file as Weekly.bat.

4. Place the file in a directory of your choice, such as c:\users\backups, so that you know where it is and can inform the scheduler program.

5. Tell NT when to run the job. To do this, use the following command from your command prompt:

```
at 02:00 /interactive /every:Saturday "c:\users\backups\weekly.bat"
```

6. NT now schedules your backup job to run each Saturday at 2 a.m. You can check the logs on Monday morning to ensure that the job ran successfully.

Step 3: Review

This task showed you how to run backups in an automated fashion by using the features installed with NT Server. As you see, it is not a GUI-based task, yet it gets the job done. This is often one reason organizations purchase more robust backup programs that offer automation as part of their services.

You see that it is possible to skip those awful 2 a.m. treks into work by applying some of the features NT offers. (You can tell we no longer like the late-hour shifts, can't you? Ah, the joys of getting older.)

Use these principles to set up a backup schedule for your organization. If a task is automated, you have far greater assurance that is being accomplished. Leaving tasks to an administrator to remember leaves you prone to error—daily activities and "fire-fighting" make it likely that backups are occasionally not run, and this leaves you vulnerable to data loss.

Workshop

To wrap up the day, you can review terms and tasks from the chapter, and see the answers to some commonly asked questions.

Terminology Review

archive bit—An attribute stored with each file that is used to determine when a file is created or modified.

autoloader—A machine that acts as a tape loader, automatically adding tapes to a tape device as they are needed.

backup—The process of creating a file copy that serves as a duplicate if the original is lost.

bit—The smallest component of information in a computer. The word *bit* is derived from the words *Binary digIT*. A bit has two states, *on* or *off*, or 1 and 0 within the machine.

DAT—A new tape format using digital technology to enhance the amount of data kept on one tape. An acronym for Digital Audio Tape.

differential—A backup type that copies files for backup purposes and leaves the files archive bits unchanged.

DLT—An even newer tape format called Digital Linear Tape. Fast, robust, and large capacity, it is becoming the tape of choice for larger firms.

incremental—A type of backup that copies files and turns off the associated archive bit for those files.

Task List

The emphasis of this chapter has been to introduce you to file backup and recovery. As a system administrator, you will repeatedly use this process in your daily work. The tasks you should understand from this chapter are listed here:

- ☐ Adding a new tape drive
- ☐ Setting up a grandfather/father/son backup cycle
- ☐ Running tape backup
- ☐ Restoring files by using NTBACKUP
- ☐ Using the command line for backups

Q&A

Q How can I schedule backups in NT Server?

A NT Server offers a service called Schedule that, when running, allows use of the AT command. This command enables an administrator to set up any number of tasks and schedule them for any time of day.

The AT command has various options, which you read about in Chapter 15. In this chapter, you are shown an example of the command used to perform nightly unattended backups.

21

Q Should I use NTBACKUP or buy some third-party product to perform my backups?

A The answer depends on what your backup needs consist of and whether NTBACKUP serves those needs. In a small LAN, the program is likely sufficient for your needs. In a larger LAN, the lack of automation and the incapability to back up multiple workstation operating systems might justify your pursuing alternative tape programs.

Q What is this Tower of Hanoi method, and does NT support its use?

A The Tower of Hanoi method is named after an old game that consisted of three posts and several rings. The object of the game was to relocate the rings, using a minimum number of moves, so that the rings would end up in sequence with the largest ring on the bottom and the smallest on top. By substituting tapes for rings, you can use this same method for backup purposes. The method provides for very even tape wear and a maximum number of saved versions of each file, helping ensure that you can recover from a file loss.

The Tower of Hanoi method is not supported by the present version of NTBACKUP or some other third-party programs. It is a complex method for tape backup, and it needs the benefit of software for it to work because it is not easily performed manually.

Q What is the best tape format to use?

A This is again a tough question to answer directly because the answer depends on the amount of data you back up and the frequency of those backups. Many organizations use the DAT tape format because it offers a reasonable degree of speed, and the amount of data that fits on a tape minimizes the need for multiple tapes.

Larger organizations are moving toward the newer, faster, more robust DLT, or Digital Linear Tape, format. This offers tremendous speed and huge amounts of backup data per tape.

The bottom line is that the best tape is the one you use on a regular basis, verify every so often, and retire before it is worn out.

Q How important is a backup strategy? Can't I just use two tapes and rotate them each day?

A A sound backup strategy allows you to recover files when you need to recover them. Using only two tapes minimizes that possibility because very soon you run out of space and need to remove old files. If these files are only one or two weeks old, you might suffer from data loss.

21

In addition to backing up the files, you need to rotate them offsite to ensure that you can recover in the event of a disaster. This is hard to do with only two tapes.

A proper tape rotation guards against loss by ensuring that files are retained long enough that you are able to recover them if needed. This time frame might be a few weeks or a few months or, in larger organizations, perhaps a year. You need to ask yourself and your users what will happen if a file *xx* days old becomes unavailable. Typically, the user will respond with anguish at the thought that a file might be unrecoverable. Finding a happy medium is hard to do without a complex risk assessment, so most organizations opt to keep files for daily, weekly, and monthly cycles, obviating any problems.

21

Chapter **22**

Configuring Fault-Tolerant Computing Systems

The data stored on your network is the most valuable part of your network. In fact, it might be the most important asset in your company or department. Its value is much higher than the cost of the equipment storing it, and its importance is second only to your users who use the information. This information is, however, at risk.

Nobody wants to face it. It is not a question of whether a disaster will strike, but when it will strike. This axiom definitely applies to networks. Your job as a system and network administrator is to make sure that information is both available to users and protected from corruption or loss. Attacks on your system by hackers, unauthorized users, or viruses can destroy your plans. Just as harmful is a system failure due to natural causes or overburdened systems. A downed system costs you more than frustration: it might cost your business hundreds or thousands of dollars in lost revenue and create a lot of customer dissatisfaction. It also might cost you your job! In this chapter, you'll learn about three topics that directly or indirectly deal with protecting the data on your servers:

- [ ] Providing fault tolerance with disk mirroring and disk striping
- [ ] Providing fault tolerance and data availability by replicating data to other systems
- [ ] Addressing and solving power problems

Fault Tolerance in Windows NT Server

Your organization might use its network for an application in which access to the data and services is extremely important. Your organization might have moved its critical applications off the mainframe, for example, and put them on the network. As a result, redundancy is needed in your local area network. Redundancy provides protection against downtime because of hardware failure.

Fault tolerance refers to the protection of systems against potential hardware failures, disasters, virus infections, hacker attacks, and other risks. You protect data by creating redundant copies, usually in real-time, as well as by backing up your data.

You can use the following methods to protect your data.

- [ ] *Mirrored Disks:* In this configuration, two hard disks (or sets of hard disks) are used, and data is simultaneously written to and read from each disk. When one of the disks fails, the other can provide data to users until the mirrored set is restored.

- [ ] *Stripe Sets with Parity:* In this scheme, data is written evenly over an array of disks rather than to one disk. Parity information also is written to the disks. The parity information is used to rebuild the data if one of the disks in the set fails.

- [ ] *Backup Power:* Windows NT also supports uninterruptible power supplies and includes a program that can detect power failures and provide advance warning before the UPS runs out of backup power.

- [ ] *Backup with Offsite Archiving:* Here data is copied to backup media and carried to safe remote sites for archiving. Backup methods were covered this morning in Chapter 21, "File Backup and Recovery."

Windows NT Server offers several fault-tolerance features you can use alone or in combination to produce a cohesive strategy to ensure that data is protected from potential media problems. Windows NT Server offers fault tolerance (disk mirroring, disk duplexing, striping with parity, and sector sparing [hot fix]), tape backup, Last Known Good Configuration, Emergency Repair disk, and uninterruptible power supply features to help you protect your data.

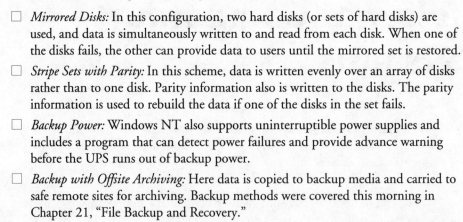

Redundant Array of Inexpensive Disks

The fault-tolerance features listed in the preceding section are actually *strategies*. Fault-tolerance strategies are standardized and categorized by the industry in seven levels, 0 through 6, using the Redundant Array of Inexpensive Disks (RAID) system. The levels offer various combinations of performance, reliability, and cost. Windows NT Server offers RAID levels 0 through 5, as shown in Table 22.1.

Table 22.1. RAID levels.

Level	Description
0	Disk striping
1	Disk mirroring
2	Disk striping with error correction code (ECC)
3	Disk striping with ECC stored as parity
4	Disk striping with large blocks, parity stored on one drive
5	Disk striping with parity distributed across multiple drivers

Level 0: Disk Striping

RAID level 0 provides disk striping to multiple disk partitions. With this method, the system spreads a file across several physical drives. This method can enhance disk performance, particularly when the separate physical drives are on different disk controllers. Because it does not provide redundancy, this method cannot be said to be a true RAID implementation. If any partition in the set fails, you lose all data. Level 0 requires a minimum of 2 and as many as 32 hard disks. It provides the best performance when used with multiple controllers.

Level 1: Disk Mirroring or Duplexing

RAID level 1 provides disk mirroring or duplexing—that is, the maintenance of multiple, identical copies of a physical drive or partition. Disk mirroring takes place at the partition level. You can mirror any partition, including boot or system partitions. This method is the simplest way of protecting a single disk against failure.

Disk mirroring is more expensive than other forms of fault tolerance because disk space utilization is only 50 percent. For peer-to-peer and small server-based LANs, however, disk mirroring usually has a lower entry cost because it requires only two disks. RAID strategies higher than level 3 require three or more disks.

Disk duplexing simply is a mirrored pair with an additional disk controller on the second drive. This method reduces channel traffic and potentially improves performance. Duplexing is intended to protect against controller failures as well as media failure.

Level 2: Disk Striping with Error Correction Code

RAID level 2 introduces bit interleaving and check disks. When a block of data is written, the system breaks up the block and distributes (or interleaves) it across all data drives. At the same time, the system also writes an error correction code (ECC) for the data block, which is spread across all the check disks. In the event of lost data, the system uses the ECC to reconstruct the lost data via a mathematical algorithm.

ECCs require a larger amount of disk space than parity-checking methods. Although this method offers marginal improvement in disk utilization, it compares poorly with current technology.

Level 3: Disk Striping with Error Correction Code Stored as Parity

RAID level 3 is similar to level 2 except that the ECC method is replaced with a parity-checking scheme that requires only one disk to store parity data. Disk space utilization is better than with RAID level 2.

Level 4: Disk Striping Large Blocks with Parity Stored on One Drive

RAID level 4 moves away from data interleaving by writing complete blocks of data to each disk in the array. This process is known as *disk striping*. A separate check disk still is used to store parity information. Each time a write operation occurs, the associated parity information must be read from the check disk and modified. Because of this overhead, the block-interleaving method works better for large block operations than for transaction-based processing.

Level 5: Disk Striping with Parity Distributed Across Multiple Drives

RAID level 5 is the most common strategy for new fault-tolerance designs. It differs from other levels in that it writes the parity information across all the disks in the array. The data and parity information are arranged so that the two are always on different disks. If a single drive fails, enough information is spread across the remaining disks to allow the system to reconstruct the data completely.

Stripe sets with parity offer the best performance for read operations. When disk fails, however, the read performance is degraded by the need to recover the data by using the parity information. Also, all normal write operations require three times more memory because of the parity calculation.

22

Windows NT Server supports from 3 to 32 drives in a stripe set with parity. All partitions except the boot and system partitions can form the stripe set. The system uses the parity stripe block to reconstruct data for a failed physical disk. A parity stripe block exists for each stripe (row) across the disk. RAID level 4 stores the parity stripe block on one physical disk, whereas RAID level 5 distributes parity evenly across all disks. The major benefit of RAID level 5 is a performance gain due to distributed I/O for writes.

NT Server offers you two methods to protect your data's integrity: disk mirroring and disk striping. In the following sections, you look further at these two methods.

Disk Mirroring

Disk mirroring is a continuous backup method. The system writes data to two disks at the same time. Because either disk in the set can continue providing data to users when the other fails, you can avoid the downtime and expense of recovering data from backup sets. Disk duplexing is a disk mirroring technique that also duplicates the hardware channel to avoid downtime caused by the need to replace a disk controller.

Keep in mind that disk mirroring is a hardware backup technique you use to recover from disk failures. You still need to back up data to protect information from corruption. If information is corrupted, it is stored in that corrupted state on both disks, and you need to restore from backup sets.

NOTE

> A mirrored set improves disk read performance because data can read from either disk in the set.

Mirroring is one of the most important features of a successful fault-tolerant system. The overall benefit from mirroring is to provide protection against data loss. It provides fault tolerance to possible hard disk failure by writing the same information to two NTS-partitioned hard disks. In the event of a hard disk failure, the functioning mirrored disk continues to retrieve and store data. The operating system sends a warning message that disk failure has occurred.

With disk mirroring, the hard disk is duplicated, so you can continue if one hard drive fails. You will still be in trouble if the disk channel goes down.

If you have more than one disk, you can *mirror* a partition on one disk onto free space on another. By doing so, you keep an exact copy of one partition on another disk. After you establish this relationship between the two disk areas, called a *mirror set*, every time you write data to disk a duplicate of that data is written to the free space on the other half of the mirror set. Disk mirroring is equivalent to RAID level 1.

With disk mirroring, the system must write data to both drives in the mirror set, but it suffers no performance lag because each disk can do its own writing. In addition, mirrored drives are fast when it comes to reads, as data can be pulled from both halves of the mirror set at once.

Mirroring and Duplexing

If you've heard or read anything about disk mirroring, you've also probably heard a term called *disk duplexing*. Disk duplexing is similar to disk mirroring, except that duplexing generally refers to mirroring information on disks that have their own disk controllers so that the data is not vulnerable to controller failures. In NT Server, disk mirroring means both duplexing and mirroring.

You use the Disk Administrator in the Administrative Tools group to set up disk mirroring. To create a mirrored disk set, you need to have two disks; each must have a free partition roughly the same size as the other one. Excess space on one of the disks is not used. You can mirror any existing partition, including the system and boot partitions, onto an available partition of another disk. The disks can use the same or different controllers. The following task shows you how to build a mirrored disk set.

Task 22.1. Establishing a mirror set.

Step 1: Description

You can mirror a drive's data without affecting that drive's accessibility while you do it. In this task, you use the Disk Administrator to set up a mirror set.

Step 2: Action

1. Log onto the Windows NT Server as Administrator.

2. Choose Start|Programs|Administrative Tools (Common)|Disk Administrator. You should see a Disk Administrator similar to the one in Figure 22.1.

Figure 22.1.

The Disk Administrator.

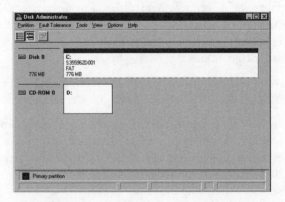

22

3. Click the partition you want to mirror (such as the primary partition).

4. By pressing Ctrl and clicking at the same time, choose the free space on another disk that you want to make the other half of the set. This area must be the same size or greater than the partition or drive you want to mirror. If you select an area of free space that is too small, you get this message: The free space you have chosen is not large enough to mirror the partition you have chosen.

5. Choose Fault Tolerance|Establish Mirror. You have now established the mirror set. The Disk Administrator establishes an equal-sized partition in the free space for the mirror. It also assigns a drive letter to the mirror set. Now, whenever you save a file to that drive letter, the system actually saves two copies of the file.

6. Format the new logical drive. You do so either by choosing Tools|Format or by opening a command prompt and typing

   ```
   format driveletter: /fs:filesystem
   ```

   where *driveletter* is the drive letter of the logical drive and *filesystem* is either FAT or NTFS. To format a newly created drive G: as NTFS, for example, you type

   ```
   format g: /fs:ntfs
   ```

Step 3: Review

In this example, you chose Start|Programs|Administrative Tools (Common)|Disk Administrator to create a mirror drive set. You can create a mirror drive set without affecting its accessibility.

When something unrecoverable—like hardware damage—happens to half of the mirror set, you need to break the mirror set to get to the good data you've backed up. You know when something goes wrong because you'll likely see a message when you try to write to the mirrored drives if one of the disks isn't working. You still can use the drive, but the benefits of mirroring are suspended.

Task 22.2. Breaking a mirror set.

Step 1: Description

If an error occurs on one of the disks in the mirrored set, you need to first break the mirror and then replace the defective disk. While you're replacing the disk, the other disk can handle requests from users. In this task, you use the Disk Administrator to break up a mirror set.

Step 2: Action

1. Log onto the Windows NT Server as Administrator.

2. Choose Start|Programs|Administrative Tools (Common)|Disk Administrator.

3. Select the mirror set you want to break.

4. Choose Fault Tolerance|Break Mirror.

5. Click Yes to break the mirror set.

 TIP   After you create or change any disk configuration, choose Partition|Configuration|Save to save the disk configuration information to a floppy disk.

Step 3: Review

In this example, you broke a mirror set. Breaking a mirror set does not affect the information inside it. Still, as always, before doing anything with the drive holding your data, backing up the drive first is a good idea.

 If you break a mirror set when nothing's wrong with it, each half becomes a primary partition with its own drive letter. The original partition keeps its original drive letter, and the backup partition gets the next available letter.

Recovering Data from a Mirror Set

After you break a mirror set so that you can get to good data, the good half of the mirror set is assigned the drive letter that belonged to the now-defunct mirror set. The half that crashed is now called an *orphan* and is, in effect, set aside by the fault-tolerance driver so that no one will attempt to write to that part of the disk. When you reboot, the crashed disk disappears.

At this point, you can take the good half of the old mirror set and establish a new relationship with another partition, as you did in Task 22.1. When you restart the computer, the system copies the data from the good partition to its new mirror. While the regeneration process is going on, the type on the new half of the mirror set shows in red, but it doesn't take long to regenerate mirrored material. Besides, the process takes place in the background, so you don't have to wait for it to finish if you want to use the computer.

To repair a broken mirror set, do the following:

1. Open the Disk Administrator and select the good half of the mirror set and an area of free space the same size or larger than the area to be mirrored.

2. Choose Fault Tolerance|Establish Mirror. The new mirror set is then displayed in magenta.

Mirroring Considerations

As you're deciding whether to protect your data by mirroring it, keep these points in mind:

☐ Mirroring to drives with the same drive controller does not protect your data from a drive controller failure. If any kind of controller failure occurs, you cannot get to the backup copy of your data unless you mirror (that is, duplex) to a disk with a separate controller.

☐ For higher disk-read performance and greater fault tolerance, use a separate disk controller for each half of a mirror set.

☐ Disk mirroring effectively cuts your available disk space in half. Don't forget that figure as you calculate how much drive space you have on or need for your server.

☐ Disk mirroring has a low initial cost because you must purchase only one extra drive to achieve fault tolerance, but it has a higher long-term cost because of the amount of room your duplicate information takes.

☐ Disk mirroring slows down writes, because the data must be written in two places every time, but speeds up reads, because the I/O controller has two places to read information from.

Disk Striping

Disk striping in Windows NT enables you to spread data over an array of up to 32 disks. The disks appear as a single volume to users. Striping divides the data at the byte level and interleaves the bytes over each disk. The system also writes parity information to each disk partition in the volume to give a level of data protection equivalent to disk mirroring but requiring less disk space and providing faster read performance.

Disk striping provides high performance, especially when users read data more than they write it. Writing to striped sets is slower than writing to mirrored sets, but when you use high-performance servers and drives, you won't notice.

Disk striping with parity for Windows NT Server requires a minimum of three disks to accommodate the way that parity information is striped across the disk set. Disks should be roughly the same size. Any extra space on partitions is not used.

In addition to disk mirroring, NT Server gives you the option of using RAID level 5, also known as *disk striping with parity*. Disk striping with parity differs from regular disk striping in the following ways:

☐ Although data lost from a stripe set without parity is unrecoverable, data from a parity stripe set usually can be recovered. If more than one disk of the 2 to 32 hard disk drives fail, you cannot recover your data.

☐ Regular disk striping improves the speed of data reads and writes. Striping with parity slows down writes but improves access speed.

How Disk Striping Works

Every time you write data to disk, the system writes the data across all the striped disks in the array, just as it does with regular disk striping (RAID level 0). In addition, parity information for your data also is written to disk, always on a separate disk from the one where the data it corresponds to is written. That way, if anything happens to a disk in the array, the data on that disk can be reconstructed from the parity information on the other disks.

RAID level 5 differs from level 4, which also uses parity information to protect data, because the system distributes parity information in RAID level 5 across all the disks in the array. In level 4, a specific disk is dedicated to parity information. RAID level 5 therefore is faster than 4 because it can perform more than one write operation at a time.

Updating the Parity Information

The parity information can be updated in two ways. First, because the parity information is the XOR (exclusive OR) of the data, the system can recalculate the XOR each time data is written to disk. This method requires accessing each disk in the stripe set because the data is distributed across the disks in the array, and that takes time.

What is XOR? Simply, the XOR, or exclusive OR arithmetic, is a function that takes two one-bit inputs and produces a single-bit output. The result is 1 if the two inputs are different, or 0 if the two inputs are the same. More specifically:

```
0 XOR 0 = 0

1 XOR 0 = 1

0 XOR 1 = 1

1 XOR 1 = 0
```

When you use the XOR function on two numbers with more than one bit, just match the bits up and add (XOR) them individually. For example, 1101010 XOR 0101000 equals 1000010. The result you get from this function is the parity information, which the system uses to recalculate the original data.

A more efficient way of recalculating the parity information, and the way NT Server uses, is to read the old data to be overwritten and use the XOR function with the new data to determine the differences. This process produces a bit mask that has a 1 in the position of every bit that has been changed. This bit mask can then be added (XORed) with the old parity information to see where its differences lie, and from this, the new parity information can be calculated. This process seems convoluted, but this second process requires only two reads and two XOR computations rather than one of each for every drive in the array.

As the administrator, you can create a stripe set with parity.

22

22

Task 22.3. Establishing a stripe set with parity.

Step 1: Description

In this task, you use the Disk Administrator to create a stripe set with parity.

Step 2: Action

1. Log onto the Windows NT Server as Administrator.

2. Choose Start|Programs|Administrative Tools (Common)|Disk Administrator.

3. Select three or more areas of free space on from 3 to 32 hard disks. (The exact number is determined by your hardware configuration; NT Server can handle up to 32 separate physical disks, but your hardware setup might not be able to.) To select the free space areas, click the free space on the first hard disk, and then Ctrl+click the others, in the same way you select more than one file using Windows NT Explorer.

NOTE

> The free space you select doesn't have to be equal in size because the Disk Administrator distributes available space evenly and adjusts the size of the stripe set as necessary.

4. Choose Fault Tolerance|Create Stripe Set With Parity. You then see a dialog box that displays the minimum and maximum sizes for the stripe set with parity.

5. Choose the size stripe you want and click OK. The Disk Administrator then equally divides the total size of the stripe you selected among the available disks. Then it assigns a single drive letter to this set.

NOTE

> If you select a size that cannot be divided equally among the number of disks involved in the stripe set, the Disk Administrator rounds down the size to the nearest number evenly divisible by the number of disks in the stripe set.

Step 3: Review

To create a stripe set with parity, you opened the Disk Administrator and selected areas of free space on at least three physical disks. Then you chose Fault Tolerance|Create Stripe Set With Parity and filled in the size you wanted the stripe set to be and clicked OK.

 The system reboots upon your confirmation, and the system initializes the stripe set. As always, you have to format it from the command line.

After you create the stripe set and try to exit the Disk Administrator, you see the usual dialog box that tells you the changes you have made require you to restart your system. Click OK to begin shutdown.

When you restart, rebooting takes a little longer than normal. When you reach the blue screen that tells you what file system the drives on your system are using, the system informs you that the I/O Manager cannot determine the file system type of the stripe set's drive letter—not that the drive is raw, as you've seen before, but that NT System Services can't determine the type. Don't be alarmed; the system has to initialize the stripe set. Wait for activity on the stripe set drives to subside, and then format the new partition. If you don't format the drive first, you get an error message. After you format, everything should be ready to go.

Retrieving Data from a Failed Stripe Set

When an unrecoverable error to part of a striped set with parity occurs, you can regenerate the information stored there from the parity information stored on the rest of the set. You can even regenerate it when one of the member disks has been low-level formatted.

To recover the data, install a new disk and reboot so that the system can see the new disk. Next, go to the Disk Administrator, and select the stripe set you want to fix and free space at least equal in size to the other members of the set. Choose Fault Tolerance|Regenerate, exit the Disk Administrator, and then restart the computer.

When you restart the computer, the fault-tolerance driver collects the information from the stripes on the other member disks and then re-creates it onto the new member of the stripe set. If you open the Disk Administrator while it is performing this job, you see that the text on the part being regenerated is displayed in red. Although the regeneration process might take awhile, you still can use the server. You don't need to keep the Disk Administrator open because the restoration process works in the background, and you can access the information in the stripe set.

After the system fixes the stripe set, you need to reassign it a new drive letter and restart the computer. The failed portion of the original stripe set, called an orphan, is set aside as unusable.

NOTE

When you're regenerating an NTFS stripe set with parity, make sure that you have a new disk in the system. When a disk goes bad, and you try to regenerate its data onto a new one, NT Server does not gray out the Regenerate option even when you don't have a new disk to put the data on. Instead, it tells you that the stripe set with that number has been recovered. When you reboot and check the Disk Administrator, however, you see that the stripe set still is listed as "Recoverable."

22

Task 22.4. Regenerating a failed stripe set.

Step 1: Description

In this task, you use the Disk Administrator to regenerate a failed stripe set.

Step 2: Action

1. Install a new disk and reboot the system.

2. Log onto the Windows NT Server as Administrator.

3. Choose Start|Programs|Administrative Tools (Common)|Disk Administrator.

4. Select both the stripe set you need to fix and an area of free space at least equal in size to the other members of the set.

5. Choose Fault Tolerance|Regenerate. The system shuts down, and the regeneration process takes place in the background after it restarts.

Step 3: Review

To regenerate a failed stripe set here, you chose Start|Programs|Administrative Tools (Common)|Disk Administrator, selected the stripe set you wanted to fix, and then chose Fault Tolerance|Regenerate. The regeneration process doesn't affect your ability to use the computer or access the information being regenerated.

Deleting a Stripe Set

To delete a stripe set, you select the stripe you want to delete from the Disk Administrator, and then choose Partition|Delete. A message then appears advising you that this action will delete all the data and asking you to confirm that you want to take this action. Click Yes to confirm your intention.

WARNING

> Deleting a stripe set destroys the data in it—even the parity information.

Points to Remember About Disk Striping with Parity

Remember these points for disk striping with parity:

☐ When you first set up the stripe set and reboot, the rebooting process takes longer than normal because the system must initialize the stripe set before it can use it.

☐ Striping with parity has a greater initial cost than disk mirroring does because it requires a minimum of three disks rather than two. Nevertheless, you can get more use out of your disk space.

☐ Although you can access the information in a stripe set even after one of the members has failed, you should regenerate the set as quickly as possible. NT Server striping cannot cope with more than one error in the set, so you're in trouble if anything happens to the unregenerated stripe set.

☐ Striping with parity places greater demands on your system than disk mirroring, so you might get better performance from your system if you add 2MB of RAM to the system minimum of 16MB.

☐ When you have fewer than three physical hard disks on your server, you cannot make stripe sets with parity. The option in the Fault Tolerance menu is grayed out.

Which Is Better: Hardware or Software RAID?

In this chapter, you've seen that you can install several drives on your computer and that you can use them as RAID and mirror sets. From a fault-tolerance standpoint, using them this way is a good idea because the probability that you'll actually lose data is considerably reduced. What should you do when drive damage does occur?

Assume that you have a mission-critical system up and running, and one of the four drives in a stripe set with parity goes bad. You take down the server, replace the bad drive with a new good one, and then add the new drive to the stripe set to recover the data.

In practice, this procedure sounds good. But is it practical? First, you have to take down this mission-critical server for several hours while you swap out the old drive, install a new drive, and put the stripe set back together. This downtime most likely is unacceptable for a mission-critical application.

Instead, you can buy a hardware RAID system, a box containing several platters acting as one drive that look to NT as one drive. As with Windows NT Server's fault tolerance, researchers developed disk array systems to prevent loss of data and improve the performance of disk I/O. The most popular disk array is known as RAID, developed by a team of researchers at the University of California at Berkeley.

An external RAID box costs a bit more, but a hardware-based RAID system can rebuild itself faster than can NT's software. Best of all, most hardware-based RAID systems enable you to "hot-swap" the bad drive, that is, to replace the bad drive without taking down the server. So when your application is truly mission critical, think about investing in RAID hardware. Of course, if you can't afford it, NT's solution isn't bad either.

22

Security Through Directory Replication

Directory replication is a fault-tolerant strategy for duplicating data in real-time from a Windows NT Server computer to another computer. You can replicate data for backup purposes or for accessibility at remote locations. In Figure 22.2, the Windows NT Server computer holding the master data is the export server; it replicates data to import computers.

Figure 22.2.

Server replication.

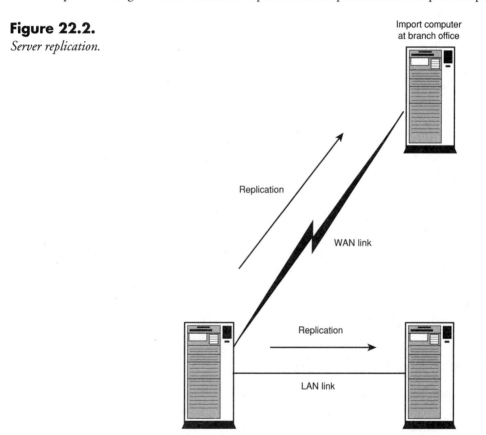

Import computer
at branch office

Replication

WAN link

Replication

LAN link

Export Computer

Import computer
at local site (backup)

In the setup in Figure 22.2, replication is used as follows:

☐ The master data on the export server is on the same local area network (LAN) as administrators or users who update the information. The LAN provides a high-throughput link to the data.

☐ An import server on the local LAN acts as a backup device. It imports the data and stores it at a different location to protect it from local disasters that might take down the export computer.

☐ Import servers also can be located at remote sites and branch offices to provide data to users at those sites. Users can access data locally rather than access the master data over a wide area network (WAN) link.

In the second case, users on the local LAN can access either the computer holding the master data or the import computer holding a copy. This setup provides *load balancing*. In the third case, replicating data to the branch office on a periodic basis uses much less bandwidth than when multiple users access the master database over the wide area network link.

Replication automatically takes place as files are added to the master directory or as information changes. It is necessary to maintain only the master copy of the information. The master copy can be exported to multiple import computers; you can change these exported copies by changing the master. In addition, information can be exported across Windows NT domains.

Keep the following points in mind:

☐ Export servers have a default export path called C:*SystemRoot*\\System32\\REPL\\ EXPORT. Files placed in this directory are automatically exported. You also can attach subdirectories to the path.

☐ Imported files are automatically placed in the Import directory on import servers.

☐ Any number of subdirectories can be replicated, with available memory being the only limit; up to 32 subdirectory levels can exist in the replicated directory.

☐ The Replicator local group on the export server should have Full Control permissions on any directories that are exported.

☐ You can set up any computer running Windows NT Server as an export server. Windows NT Workstation computers cannot export but can import.

Setting Up Replication

The steps for setting up replication services involve creating a special user account, assigning that account to the replicator service, creating the subdirectories you want to export, and designating the directories for export.

Task 22.5. Creating a replication account.

Step 1: Description

You must create a user account that the replicator services can log on with. You create this account by following the steps in this task.

TASK

22

Step 2: Action

1. Start the User Manager for Domains, and create a domain user with a name such as RepAdmin. Make the new user a member of the Domain Users, Backup Operators, and Replicator groups, and do the following:

> Deselect User Must Change Password At Next Logon.
>
> Deselect User Can Not Change Password.
>
> Select Password Never Expires.
>
> Deselect Account Disabled.
>
> Do not define a user profile or logon script.
>
> Allow all hours for logon.

   As you learned in Chapter 12, "Managing User Access," these values are the defaults.

2. Click OK.

3. In the User Manager for Domains, choose Policies|User Rights. The User Rights Policy dialog box then appears, as shown in Figure 22.3.

Figure 22.3.

The User Rights Policy dialog box.

4. Select Show Advanced User Rights. Select Logon as a Service right and click the Add button. You should see a window like the one in Figure 22.4.

Figure 22.4.

The Add Users and Groups dialog box.

5. Scroll down to the Replicator group, select it, and click the Add button.

6. Click OK.

7. Choose Programs|Administrative Tools (Common)|Server Manager and select the server. Then choose Computer|Services. A list of all services running on the server, such as the one in Figure 22.5, then appears.

Figure 22.5.

The Services On dialog box.

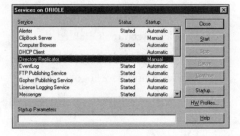

8. Select the Directory Replicator service and choose Startup.

9. Double-click Directory Replicator, and specify the startup type as Automatic in the dialog box shown in Figure 22.6.

Figure 22.6.

Services for Directory Replicator.

10. On the same dialog box, check This Account for Log On As; then type in the name of the user account you create, such as RepAdmin. Also type in the password you specified when creating the account. Click OK to close the dialog box, and then click OK to the information message. If you've set up everything correctly, you see that Directory Replicator now has Automatic for Startup, as shown in Figure 22.7.

Step 3: Review

Using User Manager for Domains, you set up an account for replicator services with all the defaults. In addition, you gave the account the Logon as Service right. Then using Server Manager, you set the Directory Replicator to Automatic startup.

Now that you have a replicator account, you can set up the export computer.

Figure 22.7.
The Services On dialog box, showing Automatic startup.

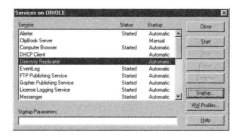

Task 22.6. Setting up master directory replication on an export server.

Step 1: Description

This task describes the steps for setting up master directory replication on an export server.

Step 2: Action

1. Start the Server Manager, and double-click the icon of the computer that will be the replication export server. The Properties dialog box appears for that server.

2. Click the Replication button to open a Directory Replication dialog box similar to the one in Figure 22.8.

Figure 22.8.
The Directory Replication dialog box.

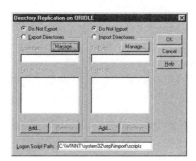

3. Click Export Directories to enable export replication on this server.

4. In the From Path field, use the default path, changing it only if absolutely necessary.

5. Click the Manage button to display the Manage Exported Directories dialog box. You can set the following options in this box:

   Click Add to add a directory. You must have previously created the directory as a subdirectory of *SystemRoot*\System32\REPL\EXPORT. Add does not create directories; it adds them to the list only so that you can set options.

Click Add Lock or Remove Lock to add or remove a lock on the selected subdirectory. (A lock prevents the subdirectory from being replicated, either temporarily or permanently.)

Enable Wait Until Stabilized to prevent replication until at least two minutes after any changes have occurred in a subdirectory or to a file.

Enable Entire Subtree to replicate the entire subtree of the selected directory.

6. Click OK to close the Manage Exported Directories dialog box.

7. Back in the Directory Replication dialog box, click the Add button to add to the To List domains and computers serving as import servers. The To List is initially blank; exported directories are automatically replicated to the local domain. Adding a computer to the To List removes the automatic import status from the local domain.

8. Double-click a domain name to open its list of available computers; then click the name of a computer and click OK.

9. Back at the Directory Replication box, click OK; then click OK again to close the Properties dialog box.

Step 3: Review

The Directory Replicator service is started when the first directory replication is set up on the server. Now you're ready to set up importing on another computer.

You can import files to either Windows NT Server computers or Windows NT Workstation computers. You also can set up importing on a Windows NT Server computer already set up to export. A Windows NT Server computer also can import subdirectories from itself. This importing provides a sort of local backup and set of replicated files that users can access instead of accessing the master files.

Task 22.7. Setting up an import computer.

Step 1: Description

To set up import directories, you don't need to create import subdirectories because they are automatically created the first time the subdirectory is imported. Follow this task to set up importing.

Step 2: Action

1. On the import server, make sure that the Directory Replicator service is assigned to the logon account you created in Task 22.5.

2. In the Server Manager window, double-click the name of the computer that will operate as the import computer. Then click the Replication button in the Properties dialog box that appears. A Directory Replication dialog box appears.

3. Click Import Directories, and then type a new path in the To Path box if necessary. The default path list is appropriate in most cases.

4. To import subdirectories from a domain or computer, choose the Add button under Import Directories. Then complete the information in the Select Domain dialog box that appears. Click OK.

5. Click the Manage button if you need to set a temporary or permanent lock on an import directory to prevent it from importing.

6. The From List is initially blank because the computer imports from the local domain. If you add a computer to the list, it no longer imports from the local domain, but from the computer you listed. After you set up the import computers, replication should begin; any changes to files in the export computer are replicated to the import computer at regular intervals. Click OK to exit the Directory Replication and Properties dialog boxes.

7. Click OK.

Step 3: Review

With this task, you learned how to use the Server Manager program to set up an import computer.

Another recovery tool you have is the use of a backup or redundant power supply. In the next section, you look at using an uninterruptible power supply (UPS) with your server.

Uninterruptible Power Supply

A power outage or interruption can cause considerable damage to your hardware and the data stored on it. Backup power systems provide emergency power in the event of a commercial power outage or interruption. People use the term *UPS* generically to refer to these backup power systems. Most people will tell you that *UPS* stands for *uninterruptible power supply*, but it really stands for *uninterruptible power system*. Another backup power system is a *standby power system*, or *SPS*. The only difference is that a UPS constantly powers your system, whereas an SPS waits to be called into action.

Windows NT can work hand-in-hand with intelligent power systems (IPS) to monitor battery time and recharge times. In coordination with Windows NT, an IPS can orchestrate a fail-safe and shut down the whole network.

Again, this matter is fairly complicated, so you should discuss it with vendors of power supply systems. This topic also is another one to discuss with other administrators. Other system administrators who have gone through the purchase of a UPS or IPS will be happy to share their experiences.

Using Uninterruptible Power Supplies

A basic power and grounding system can be augmented by an uninterruptible power supply. A UPS provides electrical power to computers or other devices during a power outage. Your UPS can come in two forms: standby and online. A standby device kicks in only when the power goes down. It therefore must contain special circuitry that can switch to backup power in less than five milliseconds.

An online device constantly provides the source of power to the computer. As a result, it doesn't need to kick in. When the outside source of power dies, the batteries within the unit continue to supply the computer with power. Although online units are the better choice, they are more expensive than standby units. Because online units supply all the power to a computer, however, that power is always clean and smooth.

When you purchase a battery backup system, be aware of the following:

- The amount of time the UPS battery supplies power
- Whether the UPS provides a warning system to the server when the UPS is operating on standby power
- Whether the UPS includes power-conditioning features that can clip incoming transient noise
- The life span of the battery and how it degrades over time
- Whether the device warns you when the batteries can no longer provide backup power
- Whether the batteries are replaceable

Purchase a UPS that the server can monitor to detect drains. A monitoring cable usually attaches to the serial port. Make sure that the UPS is compatible with Windows NT. To determine compatibility, you should check the Hardware Compatibility List (HCL).

You also need to know the power requirements of the devices you'll hook to the UPS. For a server installation, they might include the CPU, the monitor, external routers, bridges, hubs, concentrators, and wiring centers. You can determine the power requirements of these devices by looking at the backs of the equipment. Labels on the equipment list the power drawn by the units in watts. Simply add the values of all the devices to come up with the requirements you need for the UPS. You need not include the wattage for your laser printers as you cannot hook them up to the UPS.

Attaching a UPS to the File Server

To install a UPS, just attach the device to your computer according to the manufacturer's instructions. You should use a UPS that Windows NT can monitor for power loss. When power loss does occur, Windows can perform an orderly shutdown. An interface between the

22

UPS and Windows NT sends signals about the state of the UPS so that the server knows to warn users that it might be going down.

After installing the UPS, you need to configure how Windows NT will interact with the UPS. Log on as the Administrator, and double-click the UPS utility in the Control Panel. The UPS installation dialog box appears, as shown in Figure 22.9.

Figure 22.9.

The UPS dialog box.

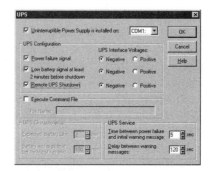

Click the top check box to turn on UPS support; then specify the COM port where your server will communicate with the UPS. Next, fill out the options in the UPS Configuration section based on voltage levels sent by the UPS. Refer to the manual for this information.

In the Execute Command File field, you can specify the name of a program to execute if the power starts to get low. Fill out the lower sections as appropriate for your UPS. You probably should test the UPS yourself to learn its actual battery life and recharge time instead of relying on the information supplied by your vendor.

Sector Sparing (Hot Fixing)

Redundant data storage is used not only for recovering data after a complete disk failure but also for recovering data from a single physical sector that goes bad. Windows NT Server fault-tolerance services add sector-recovery capabilities to the file system during operation.

In a technique called *sector sparing,* FtDisk, the Windows NT driver, uses its redundant data storage to replace lost data dynamically when a disk sector becomes unreadable. The sector-sparing technique exploits a feature of some hard disks, which provide a set of physical sectors reserved as "spares." The file system verifies all sectors when a volume is formatted, and faulty sectors are removed from service. If FtDisk receives a data error from the hard disk, it obtains a spare sector from the disk driver to replace the bad sector that caused the data error. When the system finds bad sectors during disk input and output, the fault-tolerance driver tries to move the data to a good sector and map out the bad sector. When the mapping is successful, the file system is not alerted of the problem.

FtDisk recovers the data that was on the bad sector (by either reading the data from a disk mirror or recalculating the data from a stripe set with parity) and copies it to the spare sector. FtDisk performs sector sparing dynamically, without intervention from the file system or the user, and sector sparing works with most Windows NT–supported file systems on SCSI-based hard disks. Sector sparing is not supported on the high-performance file system (HPFS) of OS/2.

If a bad-sector error occurs, and the hard disk doesn't provide spares, runs out of them, or is a non-SCSI-based disk, FtDisk still can recover the data. It recalculates the unreadable data by accessing a stripe set with parity, or it reads a copy of the data from a disk mirror. FtDisk then passes the data to the file system along with a warning status that only one copy of the data remains in a disk mirror or that one stripe is inaccessible in a stripe set with parity, and that data redundancy is therefore no longer in effect for that sector. The file system must respond to (or ignore) the warning. FtDisk re-recovers the data each time the file system tries to read from the bad sector.

Summary

The purpose of this chapter was to introduce you to one of the most important jobs an administrator has—keeping the network up and running. It is amazing how fast you'll lose users—and maybe your job—when the system is unreliable or unavailable.

To help you with improving network availability, you learned about some of the NTS fault-tolerance features.

Workshop

To wrap up the day, you can review terms and tasks from the chapter, and see the answers to some commonly asked questions.

Terminology Review

back up—To make a spare copy of a disk or of a file on a disk.

backup—A copy of a disk or of a file on a disk.

backup procedures—The provisions made for the recovery of data files and program libraries, and for restart or replacement of equipment after the occurrence of a system failure or of a disaster.

fail-safe—The automatic termination and protection of programs or other processing operations when a hardware or software failure is detected in a system.

FtDisk—The fault-tolerant disk driver.

22

risk—The potential that a given threat has of occurring within a specific period. The potential for realization of unwanted, negative consequences of an event.

Task List

The emphasis of this chapter was to introduce you to fault-tolerance features. As a system administrator, you need to learn how to implement these features. You learned how to perform the following complicated tasks in this chapter:

- [ ] Using Disk Administrator to create and break mirror sets
- [ ] Recovering data from a mirror set
- [ ] Creating a stripe set with parity
- [ ] Regenerating a failed stripe set
- [ ] Deleting a stripe set
- [ ] Creating a replication account
- [ ] Setting up master directory replication on an export server
- [ ] Setting up an import computer
- [ ] Setting up a UPS

Q&A

Q What is the difference between mirroring and duplexing?

A With mirroring, you have two physical drives but one disk controller. With duplexing, you have two physical disk drives and two disk controllers.

Q Does Windows NT Workstation support disk fault tolerance?

A No, it does not. However, it does support RAID 0 or disk striping, which, as you learned, is a non-fault-tolerant RAID level.

Q Does Windows NT Server provide any other automatic fault-tolerance management facilities?

A Yes, Windows NT Server supports symmetrical multiprocessing. The system balances the workload among two or more processors, with the second and subsequent processors providing additional computing power under normal circumstances and full backup in the event of a failure in any processor.

Q Can I do anything else to provide fault tolerance?

A Yes, you can use redundancy in your network for key components. Just as you saw in the previous question, you can have backup processors, and you can have backups for other components. NT Server supports multiple network interface cards in a server, for example, so a network interface card failure doesn't necessarily take down the server.

Day

12

Chapter **23**

Security Monitoring and Audit Trails

Yesterday morning, you learned all about file backup and recovery. You also learned that NT offers more than one method for performing backups, and you learned how to schedule jobs so that the backups occur overnight with little or no operator intervention. Now you'll learn about ensuring that your critical data files and users are properly monitored, and you'll learn to properly audit NT. In this chapter, you'll also learn about C2 level security and its relevance to security in most organizations. Finally, you'll learn which features and functions should be monitored to provide you with a reasonable level of assurance that all is well in your server environment.

A successful audit program consists of various elements, the most important being the decision-making over which elements of the system need monitoring and what actions are taken with the logs. Too many organizations are content to record a few details and let it go at that. As you'll find out, a well-designed audit program can be very useful.

This chapter introduces you to the concepts of an audit program, the specific features NT Server offers, and an approach that provides you with a level of audit logging and reporting that should become one of the key tasks in the daily administration of your NT Server system.

Security and Audit Objectives

An audit program typically is used to define and examine all the necessary elements of a computing environment. From this examination comes an understanding of the elements in use, and the auditor is then in a position to assess the level of control over each element. This assessment forms the basis for continuing improvement in the overall system security and control parameters.

Audit programs have been in existence for many years with the "big iron" mainframes of the last 25 years as the proving ground. But times are certainly changing as LANs, WANs, and client/server architectures begin to flourish and grow like weeds across the corporate landscape.

Your NT Server is, in all likelihood, a critical component of your network and therefore needs a level of control and protection commensurate with that critical nature. It does not, however, operate in a vacuum; it normally forms a part of the overall computing environment. Your computing environment might be small with one server and a few client workstations, or it might be huge with hundreds of servers and thousands of workstations. The audit program needs to consider all these elements and offer a reasonable set of objectives.

Finally, no one set of objectives works for every firm. Organizations differ as greatly as individuals, and their needs and vulnerabilities differ also. We attempt to provide a framework for you to work with in this chapter, but ultimate responsibility for determining the level of monitoring and audit logging must come from within your own organization.

Security in today's environment is far more complex than it was a few years ago. Many organizations were content with their onsite, glass computer room and a well-defined number of dumb terminals. Life was fairly straightforward, and in most of the environments the risks were fairly well known and understood. That is not to say they were managed well, but they were most likely always understood and were managed to the degree each organization felt necessary. If you used this UNIX operating system or that version of IBM's MVS, the exposures were understood and accepted and were dealt with in the manner in which the organization felt was appropriate (or could get away with), and all was well.

Today, however, not only have things changed, but they are continually changing and growth appears to be accelerating. In this chapter, you'll learn to manage that change and help ensure that your NT Server is properly audited and controlled.

So what are some of the objectives and principles to keep in mind as you learn to audit your NT Server? Some issues and descriptions are provided in Table 23.1. Later, you'll learn how to use the tools within NT to help monitor and track events to ensure that these issues are properly managed.

23

Table 23.1. Audit considerations.

Principle/Issue	Description
Availability	Ensuring that data, programs, networks, and systems remain accessible for regular use by authorized persons.
Data confidentiality	Using appropriate security controls and mechanisms to help ensure that only authorized persons can see the data.
Data integrity	Seeing that only properly authorized changes occur to data, files, and programs.
Principle of least privilege	Ensuring that users have access only to the data and files they need in order to perform their day-to-day duties. They should not have excessive levels of access (such as write access to a file if they only intend to read the information within the file), and they should not have any file or system access they do not need.
Accountability	Ensuring that users are held accountable for their actions. This process is helped through the use of individual user accounts and passwords and strict policies against password sharing. Sound auditing policies are put in place to track events at the individual account level.
Separation of duty principle	Allocating responsibilities and privileges in such a way that no one person can control key aspects of a process and cause unnecessary loss. For example, controlling the actions of administrators through the use of authorized procedures and regular audit reports.

Types of Controls

As you learn about controls, you'll realize their place within your NT Server environment. It is one thing to build and maintain a network using NT Server, but it is another thing altogether to manage that network in such a manner that your important assets are not unnecessarily compromised. Judicious use of controls will help you manage this aspect of your network.

Three major types of controls are involved:

- ☐ Preventive
- ☐ Detective
- ☐ Corrective

You'll learn to use each type of control in its proper place within NT and balance their distinctive needs to achieve a sound audit program. Preventive controls are used to stop an event from happening. They are usually in the forefront of technology, and their needs change constantly. An example of this type of control is user authentication, in which a person needs an account and password to be recognized by the system, preventing unauthorized persons from signing on. You apply these controls by using User Manager for Domains to add and change user accounts and modify access rights.

Detective controls record and report on events after they occur. Does this mean they have no useful purpose? After all, we probably know that a person broke in and stole all our data—what good does a detective control do? Well, you are not always aware that unauthorized events are occurring in your system until you read about them in a log of some sort, and that is exactly what a detective control does—it lets you know that something bad happened. These controls are very necessary for tracking and correcting problems.

Finally, corrective controls are put in place after some event to help ensure that the event cannot recur. Corrective action typically might consist of a memo to senior management outlining some system deficiency and requesting that they implement a program to correct that deficiency.

Your audit program needs to consider the use of all these types of controls to help find a balance between operating efficiency and system security.

You have various other controls to consider within your NT environment besides these three high-level types of control. A sound security audit program consists of effective management of the three basics—preventive, detective, and corrective—and also considers the more day-to-day control issues presented in the following discussion.

In any audit program, you need to consider how you intend to manage the issues surrounding each of the following controls:

- ☐ Management controls
- ☐ Logical access controls
- ☐ Physical access controls
- ☐ Operational controls
- ☐ Network controls
- ☐ Application controls

23

This is not intended to be an exhaustive list, rather it represents the crux of audit issues within your NT Server environment. You use management controls each day as you operate your server. How often does the server shut down for maintenance? When will you implement the latest software upgrade, and what steps will you take to protect the present operating system in case things go wrong? Designing and following policies and procedures are all part of management controls.

Logical access controls are very strong within NT, as you learned a few days ago in the chapters on NT security and account management. The manner in which users must have unique accounts and regular password changes all form part of the logical access controls present in your system.

Physical security plays a larger role within the client/server world than it does in the older mainframe environments. In those environments, most of your problems involve locking the computer room and managing the network components. Today, you need to ensure the physical security of your NT server, regardless of where you might place it. We still find mission-critical servers lying on floors or under people's desks. Their very size makes them more vulnerable because you might treat them like desktop machines rather than the complex operating environments they are today.

Operational controls provide you the flexibility needed to monitor and manage your system, yet protect you from inadvertent error by their procedural nature and straightforward structure. Well-designed operational procedures define when, how, and why a task needs to be done, as well as providing the detailed steps taken in performing that task. For example, clearly defining the backup and recovery process for your NT Server and clients helps ensure that the work is accomplished in a consistent manner. This becomes very useful as staff turnover rises and new staff are introduced to manage your servers.

In today's systems, the network has become at least as critical, if not more so, than the operating system it supports. On Days 9 and 10, you learned how to ensure that the proper network controls are used. Today, you'll learn which audit techniques are available to assist in securing the network.

Finally, all the controls over your operating system and network can be for naught if the user application is not sufficiently protected and audited. You need to add the appropriate level of control to each application, ensuring that its users can perform only the tasks they are authorized to perform and that adequate audit trails are produced to determine who did what and when, if necessary. You use NT's extensive rights and permissions to help ensure this level of control.

Many organizations still agonize over informal or formal controls. In most cases, the answer is probably a combination of both. Controls need to be formal enough that you understand what controls are needed and what has to be done to ensure compliance, yet they can be informal enough not to require senior management approval or review. The ideal for most organizations, however, likely lies with the formal approach. Only with the involvement of senior management can effective controls sometimes be implemented because administrators are sometimes more concerned with getting the system up and running than with worrying about all those "security" things. Also, by documenting and publishing the controls, staff are aware of what must be done, and by seeing clearly defined policy and procedures, staff need only heed these processes to ensure their compliance with corporate policy.

Finally, regardless of what tasks you follow today to audit and secure your system, you need to follow the management control cycle: Implement the controls, detect any problems, and correct those problems by implementing new controls. This cycle never ends, so just when you think your NT Server is fully secured and well audited, think again. Something will surely have changed.

NT Server 4.0 and C2 Controls

You read a lot on the newsgroups about NT Server and C2 security. What is this C2 and why do people seem so concerned? To appreciate the meaning, you need to go back to the U.S. Government and its need for a defined level of security that could be applied to the diverse operating systems of the day in a consistent manner. The National Computer Security Center (NCSC) publishes these guidelines and offers them to the general public if they choose to follow them. Only Government departments and agencies must follow the guidelines, but even this compliance is loosely interpreted at present.

What are these guidelines? The Department of Defense published the Trusted Computer System Evaluation Criteria (TCSEC), providing security requirements for Automatic Data Processing (ADP) systems. The book is often called the "orange" book because of its color. You might guess at how long these requirements have been around. Anyway, this old tome set the stage for security requirements throughout the Government and soon became synonymous with good security practices. The networking version of these standards, called the "red" book, offers the same advice from a networking perspective.

While you learn about the criteria in this section of the book, realize that unless your server is within a U.S. Government agency or your firm does work for the Government, the criteria are merely a guideline. In fact, technically speaking, it is highly unlikely that any organization will meet the criteria because they are very rigid and follow strict conventions on precisely which release of the operating system is used, what can be attached, and which processes can run on the machine. Most organizations violate these restrictions as part of their daily use of the system. However, we digress. The standards at least provide a means for evaluating systems and controls.

23

The TCSEC criteria consist of four major classes, with class A being the most secure and class D the least. As you can guess, class C fits somewhere in between these two extremes. Within each class are several levels, designated by a simple number scheme. The different levels and classes are listed in Table 23.2.

Table 23.2. NCSEC evaluation criteria.

Class	Description
D	The minimal level assigned. Provided to any system that fails to achieve a higher class.
C1	Also termed discretionary protection, this level used to be popular in the early 1980s as system security began to become an issue. User-level controls are expected. Users need a unique identity and password.
C2	A popular level today, most systems use this as the minimum basis for their controls. Access to files must be granted or restricted on a user-by-user basis. Users can be held accountable, and audit tracking is performed on a user basis.
B1	The standard that most mainframe software currently achieves. It requires that data be labeled, and the labels must transfer with the data. A user cannot override a given label despite having individual privileges.
B2	Even tighter controls. Requires a formal, structured policy with tighter user authentication. All output needs to be labeled with an appropriate sensitivity description. Requires a guaranteed trusted path for initial login.
B3	Scrutinized and tested security system containing no code not relating to security. Highly resistant to penetration and generally considered tamper-proof.
A1	Security that is the same level as B1 but formally verified and tested.

As you see, there are several levels; explaining each is probably counter-productive because the topic gets very technical and difficult to assess. For your purposes, it is enough to know that software cannot be assigned one of these levels without approval from the Department of Defense. The fact that NT Server 4.0 is assigned a C2 level is enough; getting into long-winded arguments about whether the "red" book version or the "orange" book version is applied is only really beneficial to academics or theoreticians. In fact, Microsoft suggests that Windows NT Server is so secure that certain processes such as identification and authentication, and the capability to separate a user from their functions, meets B2 security requirements. As you can see, the debate can easily rage on, ad infinitum.

Microsoft has offered the C2 level of control for NT 3.5.1 with Service Pack 3. NT Server 4.0 comes C2 equipped out of the box. Does that mean it is C2 compliant when it is installed? No. It merely means it is designed to be a C2 system. How you implement and use it determines whether it can be classified as C2. For example, not requiring your users to enter a password before being signed on invalidates C2 (and any other reasonable expectation of security).

NOTE The C2 rating serves as a guide for certain Government agencies. You use it in other industries only to provide a guide as to whether a particular system meets this minimal level of security and control. It is far more important how you manage the system than whether it is C2 compliant.

Auditing NT Server 4.0

Here, we introduce the concepts and show you some tasks designed to allow you to assess or control the level of audit and control within your NT system. In the next chapter, we show you how to change and manage the specific audit logs and events in order to set up a secure environment.

By default, NT does not initiate any audit logging. This is primarily due to the fact that auditing takes processing time and disk storage and needs to be carefully considered.

As an administrator, you need to consider what you want to record and log and what you will do with those logs after they are created. Following are some of the things you might be interested in knowing:

☐ Is anyone attempting unauthorized access by trying to sign on to one account many times or to different accounts in some form of pattern?

☐ Are all uses of privileges authorized?

☐ Who is logging on after hours?

☐ Are certain sensitive files being accessed too often, or are unauthorized persons trying to access them?

☐ When is the server shut down and started?

☐ How many user accounts remain unused in the system?

Answers to these and other questions provide you with important information about your system and its safety. Only through an effective audit program can you provide these answers and understand their impact.

23

Windows NT Server provides a unified view of auditing through its Event Viewer, enabling you to find out data about the operating system events or application or security events from a single source. You customize the auditing of events to a greater degree than previously possible and do so in an intuitive, GUI-based manner. NT's audit logs are kept secure from casual browsing and snooping, helping ensure that a hacker doesn't wipe out all trace of his activity.

How much activity you need to audit depends to some degree on your organization's data and services that run on the machine. Is the server considered mission critical? Are sensitive files or databases stored within its file system? Does it merely perform as a router service or gateway? It is a safe bet that whatever your needs, the installed level of audit function is insufficient and you need to do something. You begin by reviewing what can be audited, and then you have a baseline to work with in deciding how much of that you need.

NT provides a wide range of events that can be audited and logged. Using them all might have a serious impact on the throughput of your system. You need to test what sort of impact the number of audit features you want to use will have on your server. Try turning on all auditing for a few days and seeing what the impact consists of and whether throughput is affected for your users. Note that this is likely to be an issue only on extremely high-use systems, because NT's auditing normally offers little effect on the system except for the log size, and you set this by using the event log.

The Audit Event Logs

To facilitate the audit function, NT uses three separate types of logs to store events. Each log maintains events that are relevant, enabling you to manage the space requirements of each log on an as-needed basis. For example, your system log might be larger than the security log file if you choose to limit the logging of security events.

For logging to begin, you must activate auditing through the use of various tools. Security auditing is turned on through User Manager for Domains in the Policies|Audit submenu. You set file and directory auditing by using Explorer, right-clicking on a file or directory and selecting Properties, selecting the Security tab, and then clicking the Auditing button.

You turn on printer auditing by entering the Printers icon in the Control Panel and selecting File|Properties. From Print Server properties, you select the Advanced tab and select the events to be logged.

These three logs consist of

- [ ] The System log
- [ ] The Applications log
- [ ] The Security log

The events stored in each log are viewed with the Event Viewer, as shown in Figure 23.1. As you see, you open each log by using the Log drop-down menu and selecting the required log file by name.

Figure 23.1.

The Event Viewer.

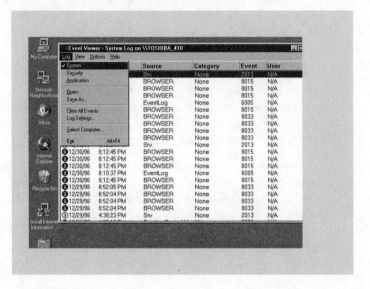

Each log contains events relevant to the type of log. For example, the System log contains a record of events logged by the system components, such as the failure of a driver to start or shut down and startup of the system.

The Security log contains events such as changes to the security system, logon and logoff, user privilege use and security policy changes, and file and directory access events.

The Application log maintains those events logged by your applications. You find database errors and other application-related problems recorded in this file.

Task 23.1. Using the event logs.

Step 1: Description

In this task, you'll learn how to use the event logs to review the present status of your system.

Step 2: Action

1. Log in as system administrator to the server.

2. Open Event Viewer by using Start|Programs|Administrative Tools (Common)|Event Viewer. You see an example of the Event Viewer in Figure 23.2.

Figure 23.2.

The Event Viewer window.

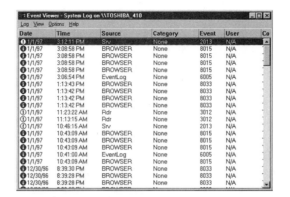

3. As you see, there are several menu items to choose when you're using the Event Viewer. Select the Log menu. The first three options offered are the different logs you can view. You choose one by clicking on it.

   The Open option allows you to open an old log file to view, rather than the current ones. Save As takes the current log you are viewing and saves it elsewhere as a different name. Be careful using the option Clear All Events because this option performs precisely what is asked, wiping out your log file. The option does ask whether you want to save the log before clearing it. You should always select Yes and save it to another file. The Log Settings option provides you the chance to change how large your log files are and how events are managed within those logs. You can view the log files on another machine by selecting the Select Computer option. You must have the necessary privileges on that machine before you can view the logs.

4. Next, select the View menu. This menu provides options for managing the current logs. The default option provides a list of all events. Choose to filter events by using the Filter Events option. As you see in Figure 23.3, the Filter dialog box offers various options for choosing how to see the data presented.

Figure 23.3.

The Event Viewer Filter dialog box.

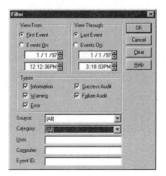

As you see in the figure, NT allows you to filter events by date and time or by all events. The viewer also allows you to set the filter for the types of events, limiting the amount of data you need to look at if you are searching for a particular type of event. For example, you can set the viewer to show only the Error events. Finally, each type of event can be further restricted via the Source and Category fields. In Figure 23.4, you see the Event Viewer with filtering set for a source of Security and a Category of Logon/Logoff. In the background, you see a sample of the output.

Figure 23.4.

Sample filtered log output.

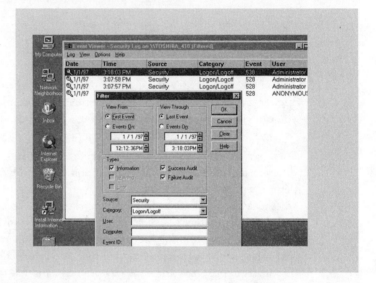

5. Next, you can sort the events using either Newest First or Oldest First, by clicking on the required option under the View menu. Select the Oldest First option to see how the list of events changes. You use these two options to select the events according to your needs.

6. The Event Viewer also offers an extensive Find option. Select it by choosing View|Find. As your logs grow, these options become increasingly useful to you. The options are, for the most part, self-explanatory and similar to those already discussed in the Filter option. You see an example in Figure 23.5.

Figure 23.5.

The Event Viewer Find dialog box.

7. Finally, the View|Detail option provides a list of the presently selected log file entry and provides additional detailed information. Finally, you can refresh the options selected by clicking on the Refresh option. Click the Refresh button to see how the options are refreshed for you. The remaining two menus provide similar functions to those of all the other dialog boxes.

8. When you are finished viewing the logs, select File|Exit or click on the small x in the upper-right corner.

Step 3: Review

In this task, you used the Event Viewer to view all your system logs. You learned to perform filtering and perform extensive find operations. Finally, you learned that the log viewer offers a wide diversity and allows you to manage the logs according to your needs.

In the next task, you're shown how to modify the size of each event log to maximize the use of your disk space and ensure that each log is large enough for your event logging activities.

Task 23.2. Changing the size of the event logs.

Step 1: Description

In this task, you'll decide on the required size for each log and then set each log to operate with that size limit.

Step 2: Action

1. Log in as system administrator to the server.

2. Decide the size for each log file. You can select the default size or choose a larger or smaller size, depending on your needs.

3. Open Event Viewer by using Start|Programs|Administrative Tools (Common)|Event Viewer.

4. Select the Log menu and select Log Settings from the drop-down menu. You see a menu similar to the one shown in Figure 23.6.

Figure 23.6.

The Event Log Settings dialog box.

5. Choose which log to set by using the drop-down list. You change the maximum log size by typing the required number in the scrollbox or by scrolling until the size you want shows.

6. Next, choose how you want the log file to act in the Event Log Wrapping section. You have three options to consider:

☐ Overwrite Events as Needed

☐ Overwrite Events Older than *x* Days

☐ Do Not Override Events (Clear Log Manually)

Each option has its pros and cons. You might consider using the default setting and putting a procedure in place that automatically copies the log file each week to an archive for safekeeping. Regardless, be sure that events are not overwritten and lost forever.

7. Implement the changes by clicking OK when you are finished setting all three log sizes.

Step 3: Review

In this task, you used the Event Viewer to set up the size of your log files and help ensure that events are not lost due to inadequate log size. You performed this action after deciding which events are to be logged in your server and how long you want to maintain those events.

So what functions can you record, and just how detailed do these recordings get? NT offers many kinds of log events for you to choose from as you design your audit system. The handy reference table shown as Table 23.3 details the events available for logging within the various parts of NT. Use the table as a guide. It is designed so that you can check each event and track whether or not it is to be audited. This table then will serve as a handy reference for you.

Table 23.3. NT audit events.

Description	Y - Audit N - No audit	S - Success F - Failure
Logon and logoff		
File and object access		
Use of user rights		
User and group management		
Security policy changes		
Restart, shutdown, and system		
Process tracking		

23

Description	Y - Audit N - No audit	S - Success F - Failure
Printer Access by Group or User		
Print		
Full control		
Delete		
Change permissions		
Take ownership		
File and Directory by Group or User		
Read		
Write		
Delete		
Execute		
Change permissions		
Take ownership		

Each of these events, when selected, records in the associated log file an entry for each occurrence of the event. Log files can become unwieldy and data can be lost, depending on the size and settings chosen. Be sure to back up each log file regularly. The log files are found in the following directory:

```
\winnt\system32\config\*.evt
```

You'll see how to select and update NT to use each of these entries this afternoon in Chapter 24, "Using the Windows NT Server Audit System."

Performing an NT Audit

Finally, you'll learn the steps necessary to perform an audit of your NT server. As you review this section, you will be able to help keep one step ahead of your internal auditors and perform regular audits to ensure that security and control in your server are effective.

This section offers a sample audit list that provides you with the necessary detail to determine whether your basic NT options are set and managed appropriately. As you can imagine, each organization has particular needs, and therefore an audit program is ideally customized for each company. What you'll learn here, however, are the baselines necessary to effect sound security practices. You choose the specific settings depending on your industry needs.

Sample Audit List

☐ *Define the current platform*

Identify all servers, and categorize as server, PDC, or BDC

Identify all workstations, and categorize as NT, Windows, UNIX, and so on

Identify all backup media devices

☐ *Define the software in use*

Identify version, release of NT

Identify current status of service packs

Identify all major applications, databases

☐ *Define the network in use*

Ethernet, Token ring, other

Network protocols

RAS usage

External networks

Internet

Other organizations

Control points

Routers

Bridges

Gateways

☐ *Organization*

Is administration setup centralized or decentralized?

How many administrators?

Is there supervisor review of changes?

Is there a corporate policy statement?

Are there security standards and guidelines?

Do administrators follow written procedures?

☐ *Physical access control*

Are servers in a locked room?

Is access to the room appropriately restricted?

Are cable rooms locked and properly managed?

Is the room adequately fireproof?

23

Are fire extinguishers available?

Are papers kept to minimum?

Is the room clear of clutter?

Are the systems protected with an adequate UPS system?

☐ *Operations*

Are operators adequately trained?

Are there procedures for backup and maintenance?

Are changes to the system scheduled?

Is capacity planning performed?

Is a backup and restore policy in place, and is it followed?

Has a contingency/disaster recovery plan been implemented?

Is fault tolerance in use and adequate for the needs of the server?

Is a virus-protection program in effect, and is it followed?

☐ *Security Administration*

Are procedures documented?

Do users follow a formal change request program to initiate changes?

Who controls the administrator account?

Has the administrator account been renamed?

Is the guest account disabled?

Who is in the Admin group, and is the list reasonable?

Who is in the Backup Operators group?

Who is in the Server Operators group?

Are access permissions that are granted to the Everyone group reasonable?

Are other groups set up in a reasonable manner (both privileged groups such as Print operators, account operators, and so forth, as well as user groups)?

Are user account policies reasonable?

Are passwords changed at least every 30 to 90 days?

Are passwords a minimum of six characters?

Are users forced to change their passwords at next logon?

Are all users assigned a password?

Are old, unused accounts deleted?

Are logs reviewed regularly, and are they adequately protected?

Is the log review done by someone other than an administrator?

23

☐ *Domain and trust relationships*

What type of domain structure is in use?

> Single domain
>
> Master domain
>
> Multiple-master

Is the domain structure that's in use reasonable for the organization?

Are trust relationships in use?

Are the relationships reasonable?

☐ *File and directory protection*

Is NTFS the only file system in use?

Are controls adequate over any FAT-based files?

Are file and directory permissions appropriately set up? (Select a sample of files and directories to verify.)

Is sharing in use?

Are sharing controls adequate?

Are there clear procedures for assigning users access to files and directories?

Is a review of access permissions performed on occasion?

When a new directory is created, NT automatically assigns Full Control to Everyone. Are procedures in place telling administrators to remove this right?

☐ *Application development and change control*

Do users create new applications?

Are all applications properly documented?

Is an application development life cycle followed?

Are revisions tested before being implemented into production?

Is there adequate separation of duty between developers and operations staff?

Are user accounts named consistently, such as last name and initial?

Are formal approvals required for adding new users and assigning privileges?

☐ *Audit logging*

Is logging being performed?

Are the security logging options adequate?

Are the log files being copied for safekeeping on a regular basis?

Have procedures been developed to manage the storage of the logs to ensure that they remain available for a set period?

Have any programs been developed to ease the process of reading the logs and to provide management summary reports?

This brief summary of functions should help you understand the items you need to review when performing an audit of NT. You should take this list and begin to develop a personalized version with the specific settings your organization chooses to use.

Summary

In this chapter, you learned all about auditing your NT Server environment. First, you learned how to set security and audit objectives for your system. Next, you learned a little about the ubiquitous C2 rating for NT Server and what that means to most organizations. Finally, you learned the tasks necessary to perform an audit of your server.

Workshop

To wrap up the day, you can review terms and tasks from the chapter, and see the answers to some commonly asked questions.

Terminology Review

audit—To examine the controls present within a system.

audit trail—The events that are logged from start to finish, providing a trail of what happened on the system.

control—Any manual or automated mechanism that helps ensure the safety and integrity of assets or business processes.

event—An application or system occurrence that requires entry in a log.

least privilege—A principle that users should be assigned only the access needed to perform their business functions.

NCSC— The National Computer Security Center. A Government organization that helps provide information security standards.

TCSEC—The Trusted Computer System Evaluation Criteria. A set of evaluation standards or criteria from the Department of Defense that is used to help define and classify computer systems.

Task List

The emphasis of this chapter has been to introduce you to audit and security of NT. As such, you did not perform too many tasks, but instead learned all about the things you need to do to ensure a reasonable level of control. Many of the tasks covered in this chapter are shown throughout this book and have not been replicated here. Specific audit log operations will be covered this afternoon as you go through the next chapter.

☐ Using the Event Viewer

☐ Changing the size of the event log

Q&A

Q How do I know what an effective audit program consists of?

A Normally, a successful audit program consists of various elements, the most important being the decision-making over which elements of the system need monitoring and what actions are taken with the logs. Too many organizations are content to record a few details and let it go at that. A well-defined audit program not only logs the correct information but also follows up and uses those reports to watch over system activity and take appropriate actions when needed.

Q I don't like to reinvent the wheel. Isn't there a standard audit program that will work for me?

A Unfortunately, no one set of objectives works for every firm. Organizations differ as greatly as individuals, and the needs and vulnerabilities of each organization and industry segment differ also. We attempt to provide a framework for you to work with in this chapter, but ultimate responsibility for determining the detailed level of monitoring and audit logging must come from within your own organization.

Q We keep hearing about this C2 certification. Is it important for us, and do we need to do anything to get it?

A Windows NT Server 4.0 comes certified at the C2 level based on the DND Orange book criteria. Unless you deal with the federal Government in your business or are a government agency, this certification has little if any impact. If you are impacted, the certification criteria sets out specific requirements that must be in place for your site to be properly certified. Contact a specialist in government certification for details.

Q How long should we retain our audit logs?

A This answer depends on various factors. The industry you are in might have legal restrictions on the length of time logs need to be kept, and you'll need to follow these criteria. Apart from legality, you want to ensure that logs are available to help you if an issue arises some time after the event. It's probably a good idea to keep logs at least six months, and one year is even better. This way, you can review actions taken at any time within that period and determine when an event occurred. For example, you might want to track when a terminated employee last logged in and prove that she had not used the account since that time.

Q Where are the audit logs so that I can back them up and copy them to archive files?

A The log files are found in the following directory:

```
\winnt\system32\config\*.evt
```

From here, you should copy them on a regular basis to an archive area and keep track of the logs in some consistent fashion so they are always available for viewing. For example, you might copy them to file names based on the system they are from and the date and time they were originally produced.

23

Chapter **24**

Using the Windows NT Server Audit System

Auditing is critical to maintaining the security of your servers and networks. A network system should collect and maintain information that can be analyzed to detect potential and actual violations of a system security policy. So Microsoft developed an auditing system for NT.

The Windows NT auditing system lets you track events that occur on individual servers related to security policies, system events, and application events. The auditing system produces logs you can view with the Event Viewer. With this system, you can track activities performed by authorized users as well as users who have gained unauthorized access through another user's account.

For auditing to be meaningful, your organization should have system security policies and procedures in place. These guidelines should set the baseline for auditing the client/server environment. A security violation can then be defined as any change to the security of the system and any attempted or actual violation of the systems access control.

Types of Monitoring

Monitoring involves the regular review of system-level attributes which, when not properly controlled, could introduce integrity exposures. Reporting and follow-up in the event of attempted violations is another aspect of monitoring. Auditing verifies compliance with these monitoring procedures as well as the effectiveness of follow-up actions.

Status and event monitoring are two types of security monitoring. Status monitoring looks at the current state of the system or process. Status monitoring is usually performed by the security administrator, but also should be performed at the line level. The hands-on technical person is familiar with the system and can recognize any general deviance from normal operations. The security administrator should monitor all security-related events on an on-going basis.

Event monitoring is based on audit trails. Unlike status monitoring, event monitoring occurs after the fact. Security audit trails, provided by either the operating system or the application, or both, should be reviewed on a timely and regular basis. Any violations in security should be reported and followed up on immediately.

Security Auditing

Security auditing refers to two different activities: day-to-day security monitoring tasks and periodic security audits. The day-to-day monitoring should be part of the administrator's responsibility. Administrators probably will perform these tasks every day, whereas part-time administrators might monitor less frequently.

Periodic reviews and audits can be performed by internal or external auditors annually or less frequently, depending on the size and security needs of an organization.

Built-in audit reporting utilities, such as those provided in Windows NT Server, help the administrator monitor the status of system security in addition to providing audit trails.

Events to audit should include the following events:

- [ ] User identification and authentication
- [ ] Assignment and use of privileges and rights
- [ ] File and object access
- [ ] Account and group authorization
- [ ] Changes in audit status
- [ ] Critical file/utility auditing
- [ ] Changes in trust relationships
- [ ] Changes in system configuration

☐ System initialization

☐ Program installation

☐ Account modification

☐ Transfer of information into or out of the system

Windows NT Server provides facilities to audit all these events.

Auditing Features

Windows NT Server auditing features record events to show this information:

☐ Which users access which object

☐ The type of access attempted

☐ Whether or not the access attempt was successful

For domains, the system writes all auditable events to the Security log on the domain controller and refers to events that occur on the controller and all servers in the domain. For standalone Windows NT workstations, all auditable events are written to the workstation's Security log.

NOTE

> By default, only the administrator has the Manage Auditing and Security Log right.

Managing Security Policies

The User Manager for Domains is part of a quartet of programs that provide network security options in NT Server. Whereas the Explorer/My Computer tandem and the Printer Folder control specific access to files, directories, and printers, User Manager for Domains gives the administrator the capability to assign systemwide rights and to determine the auditing policies of the network.

In User Manager, an administrator can manage the following security policies:

☐ Account, which controls the characteristics of passwords for all user accounts

☐ User Rights, which determines what system rights are assigned to a user or group

☐ Audit, which defines the kinds of security events for logging

☐ Trust Relationships, which establishes how other domains on the network interact with the local domain

Password Characteristics

Under the Account policy, you can set and adjust the password characteristics for all user accounts in the domain. You learned in detail about this topic on the afternoon of Day 6. From the Policies menu of User Manager for Domains, choose Account. You see the Account Policy dialog box, shown in Figure 24.1.

Figure 24.1.

The Account Policy dialog box.

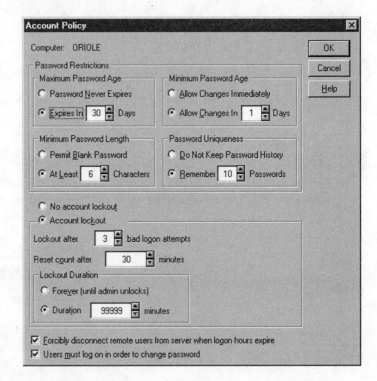

You can set the following options:

- [ ] *Maximum Password Age.* This option sets the maximum time period for a password before the system requires the user to pick a new one.

- [ ] *Minimum Password Age.* This value is the time that a password has to be used before the user is allowed to change it again. If you allow changes to the password to be made immediately, be sure to choose Do Not Keep Password History in the Password Uniqueness box.

- [ ] *Minimum Password Length.* This option defines the fewest number of characters that a user's password can contain.

☐ *Password Uniqueness.* Here you can specify the number of new passwords that must be used before a user can repeat an old password. If you choose a value here, you must specify a password age value under Minimum Password Age.

☐ *Account lockout.* This option prevents anyone from logging onto the account after a certain number of failed attempts:

> **Lockout after *x* bad logon attempts.** This value defines how many times a user can attempt to log on.

> **Reset count after *x* minutes.** This setting defines the time in which the count of bad logon attempts starts over. For example, suppose you have a reset count of two minutes and three logon attempts. If you mistype twice, by waiting two minutes after the second attempt, you'll have three tries again.

☐ *Lockout Duration.* This setting determines whether the administrator must unlock the account manually or can let the user try again after a certain period.

☐ *Forcibly disconnect remote users from server when logon hours expire.* This option is tied into the available logon hours you specified when you created the user account. If this option is selected, the user is disconnected from all connections to any of the domain's servers after the logon hours expire. Not selecting this option enables the user to stay connected after the logon hours expire, but no new connections will be permitted.

☐ *Users must log on in order to change password.* Use of this option requires the user to change her password after demonstrating that she knew it already.

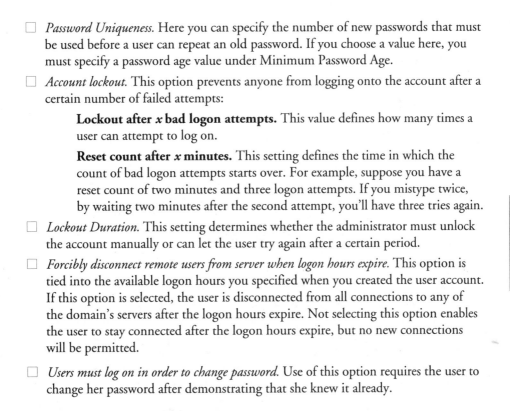

User Rights and Object Permissions

User access to network resources—files, directories, devices—in NT Server is controlled in two ways. The first way is by assigning *rights* to a user that grant or deny access to certain objects (for example, the capability to log onto a server). The second way is by assigning *permissions* to objects that specify who is allowed to use objects and under what conditions (for example, granting read access for a directory to a particular user).

What does this mean? Well, consider the groups Users and Administrators. Administrators can log on right at the server; users can't. Administrators can create users and back up files; users can't. So administrators have rights that users don't have. Remember that what separates one group in NT from another mostly has to do with the rights the groups have. You control who gets what rights via the User Manager for Domains.

Rights generally authorize a user to perform certain system tasks. For example, the ordinary user can't just sit down at an NT Server and log on. This is a right assigned to an administrator. Also, backing up and restoring data or modifying printer options on a shared printer are user rights. You can assign user rights separately to a single user, but for reasons of security organization, it is better to put the user into a group and define the rights granted to the group. You manage user rights in User Manager for Domains.

Permissions, on the other hand, apply to specific objects such as files, directories, and printers. For example, changing files in a directory on a server is an example of a permission. Permissions are set by the creator or owner of an object. Permissions regulate which users have access to the object and in what fashion.

TIP

> You can set permissions only on particular files on an NTFS volume. Directory and file permissions are administered in My Computer and the Explorer, or from the command line; printer permissions are regulated in the Printers folder.

As a rule, user rights take precedence over object permissions. For example, let's look at a user who is a member of the built-in Backup Operators group. By virtue of membership in that group, the user has the right to back up the servers in the user's domain. This requires the ability to see and read all directories and files on the servers, including those whose creators and owners have specifically denied read permission to members of the Backup Operators group; thus the right to perform backups overrides the permissions set on the files and directories.

There are two types of user rights: regular user rights and advanced user rights. NT Server's built-in groups have certain rights already assigned to them; you also can create new groups and assign a custom set of user rights to those groups. As we've said before, security management is much easier when all user rights are assigned through groups instead of being granted to individual users.

To look at or change the rights granted to a user or group, select the domain where the particular user or group resides (when it is not in the local domain), and then choose Policies|User Rights. You see the User Rights Policy dialog box, as shown in Figure 24.2.

Click the down arrow next to the currently displayed user right to see the entire list of regular user rights. By clicking on one of the rights, you can see the groups and users who currently have been granted that particular right. In the figure, you can see that the right "Access this computer from network" has been granted to the Administrators and Everyone group.

Following are the regular rights used in NT Server:

☐ *Access this computer from network.* Allows a user to connect over the network to a computer.

☐ *Add workstations to domain.* Allows you to add a workstation to a domain.

☐ *Back up files and directories.* Allows a user to back up files and directories. As mentioned earlier, this right supersedes file and directory permissions.

☐ *Change the system time.* Grants a user the right to set the time for the internal clock of a computer.

☐ *Force shutdown from a remote system.* Note that, although presented as an option, this right is not currently implemented by NT Server.

☐ *Load and unload device drivers.* Lets a user add or remove drivers from the system.

☐ *Log on locally.* Allows a user to log on locally at the server computer itself.

☐ *Manage auditing and security log.* Gives a user the right to specify which types of events and resource access are to be audited. Also allows viewing and clearing the Security log.

☐ *Restore files and directories.* Allows a user to restore files and directories. This right supersedes file and directory permissions.

☐ *Shut down the system.* Grants a user the right to shut down Windows NT.

☐ *Take ownership of files or other object.* Lets a user take ownership of files, directories, and other objects that are owned by other users.

Figure 24.2.

The User Rights Policy dialog box.

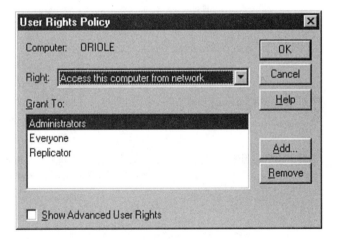

The advanced rights in NT Server are summarized in Table 24.1. These rights are added to the rights list when you click the Show Advanced User Rights option located at the bottom of the User Rights Policy dialog box.

Table 24.1. Advanced user rights.

Advanced User Right	Allows Users To
Act as part of the operating system	Act as a trusted part of the operating system; some subsystems have this privilege granted to them.
Bypass traverse checking	Traverse a directory tree even if the user has no other rights to access that directory; denies access to users in POSIX applications.
Create a pagefile	Just as it says: create a pagefile.
Create a token object	Create access tokens. Only the Local Security Authority can have this privilege.
Create permanent shared objects	Create special permanent objects used in NT.
Debug programs	Debug applications.
Generate security audits	Generate audit-log entries.
Increase quotas	Increase object quotas (each object has a quota assigned to it).
Increase scheduling priority	Boost the scheduling priority of a process.
Load and unload device drivers	Load and unload drivers for devices on the network.
Lock pages in memory	Lock pages in memory to prevent them from being paged out into backing store (such as PAGEFILE.SYS).
Log on as a batch job	Log onto the system as a batch queue facility.
Log on as a service	Perform security services (the user that performs replication logs on as a service).
Modify firmware environment values	Modify system environment variables (but not user environment variables).
Profile single process	Use Windows NT profiling capabilities to observe a process.
Profile system performance	Use Windows NT profiling capabilities to observe the system.
Receive unsolicited device input	Read unsolicited data from a terminal device.
Replace a process level token	Modify a process's access token.

Most of the advanced rights are useful only to programmers who are writing applications to run on Windows NT, and most are not granted to a group or user. However, two of the advanced rights—Bypass traverse checking and Log on as a service—might be useful to some domain administrators. Bypass traverse checking is granted by default to the Everyone group in NT Server. Notice the Increase object quotas right. You might think this option allows you to control how much disk space a user can use—a disk quota. But unfortunately, the quota feature is not in use yet.

Auditing Events

Windows NT provides auditing at the system-event level and at the object level. Any user holding the Manage Auditing and Security Log right can set auditing at the system-event level by using the User Manager. Auditing at the object level for access to files and directories can be defined in File Manager. Auditing changes to the Registry and to printer auditing can be recorded.

System Event Auditing

To turn on auditing, in User Manager or User Manager for Domains, choose Policies|Audit, and select the Audit These Events option. If the Do Not Audit option is highlighted, all Windows NT Server auditing is completely turned off.

 NOTE

> By default, auditing is off. This is not, however, recommended under any circumstance.

When you select Do Not Audit, system-level auditing and file and directory auditing are turned off. When you select Audit These Events, individual events can be selected for auditing. For each event, you can specify whether to audit failed events, successful events, or both.

NT Server maintains three event logs where entries are added in the background: the System log, the Applications log, and the Security log. You can set up security auditing of a number of events on NT Server in User Manger for Domains to help track user access to various parts of the system. To enable security auditing, select Policies|Audit. You then see the dialog box shown in Figure 24.3.

Figure 24.3.

The Audit Policy dialog box.

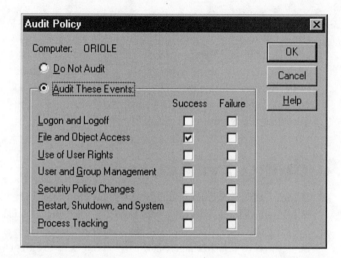

As you can see, the Audit Policy dialog box gives you the option to activate auditing (Audit These Events), followed by a list of the types of security events you can audit. The default setting is Do Not Audit; with this option selected, all the Audit These Events options are grayed out. If you choose to activate auditing, the information about that event is stored as an entry in the computer's Security log. This log, along with the System and Application logs, can then be viewed with the Event Viewer. Table 24.2 describes the auditing options you can select.

Table 24.2. The Security auditing options.

Auditable Events	Description
Logon and Logoff	Tracks user logons and logoffs, as well as the creating and breaking of connections to servers. Provides information on the type of logon and whether it was successful. To minimize unnecessary entries, monitor only failed logon and logoff attempts rather than both successful and failed attempts.
File and Object Access	Tracks access to a directory or file that has been selected for auditing under File Manager; tracks print jobs sent to printers that have been set for auditing under the Printers folder. To minimize unnecessary log entries, as a rule monitor only failed access attempts.

24

Auditable Events	Description
Use of User Rights	Notes when users make use of a user right (except those associated with logons and logoffs). To minimize unnecessary log entries, monitor only failed attempts of Use of User Rights.
User and Group Management	Tracks changes in user accounts or groups (creations, changes, deletions), such as User Created or Group Membership Change; notes when user accounts are renamed, disabled, or enabled; tracks setting or changing passwords.
Security Policy Changes	Tracks changes made to the User Rights, Audit, and Trust Relationship policies, such as granting or revoking user rights to users and groups or establishing and breaking trust relationships with other domains.
Restart, Shutdown, and System	Tracks when the computer is shut down or restarted; tracks the filling up of the audit log and the discarding of audit entries when the audit log already is full.
Process Tracking	Records detailed tracking information for program activation, some types of handle duplication, indirect object accesses, and process exit. Unless necessary, do not enable process tracking because this can generate high numbers of log entries and cause unnecessary system overhead.

24

Because auditing is turned off by default, it is necessary to turn on each necessary audit explicitly. Although it's possible to log each and every user action, event, and process, this activity can generate a tremendous amount of relatively trivial log entries and make it difficult to locate the important entries—those attempts that were unsuccessful. Although the system can record both successes and failures to provide complete audit information, it is important to balance the need to monitor every event against the resources required to do so.

It's important to keep in mind that all the event logs are limited in size. The default size for each of the logs is 512KB, and the default overwrite settings allow events older than seven days to be discarded from the logs as needed. When managing the auditing policy in User Manager for Domains, choose your events to audit carefully. You might find that you get what you ask for, sometimes in great abundance. For example, auditing successful File and

Object Accesses can generate a tremendous number of Security log entries. A reasonably simple process, such as opening an application, opening a single file within that application, editing and saving that file, and exiting the application, can produce more than 60 log events. A couple of users on a system can generate 200 log entries in less than two minutes. Auditing of successful Process Tracking events can produce similar results.

If your network requires you to monitor events that closely, be sure to choose the appropriate log size and overwrite settings. You can change these settings for the Security log (and for the other two logs, for that matter) in the Event Viewer. (See the section "Enabling Event Auditing" later in this chapter.)

File and Directory Auditing

In any network, the administrator sometimes needs to monitor user activity, not just to assess network performance, but for security reasons. NT Server provides administrators the opportunity to audit events that occur on the network.

To record, retrieve, and store log entries of events, the administrator must activate auditing on the server. Not surprisingly, file and directory auditing is activated within the Security tab in the Windows Explorer/My Computer.

Auditing for File and Object Access

With NT Server, an administrator can specify which groups or users, as well as which actions, should be audited for any particular directory or file. The system collects and stores this information in the Security log, which you can view with the Event Viewer.

For directories and files to be audited, you must first set the security audit policy in User Manager for Domains to allow the auditing of file and object access. To do this, open User Manager for Domains and choose Policies|Audit.

An available auditing option in the list is File and Object Access; be sure to select it. As you can see from the dialog box, you can audit both successful and failed accesses.

After activating file and object access auditing, you have to choose which files and/or directories, as well as which groups or users who might use the files and directories, you specifically want audited. To do this, highlight the desired directory or file in the Windows Explorer window. Then, select Security|Auditing.

You can choose a specific set of events to audit for each different group or user in the Name list. Table 24.3 shows the meaning of the file and folder access options.

24

Table 24.3. File and directory audit options.

File Access	Directory Access
Displaying the file's data	Displaying names of files in the directory
Displaying file attributes	Displaying directory attributes
Displaying the file's owner and permissions	Changing directory attributes
Changing the file	Creating subdirectories and files
Deleting the file	Deleting the directory
Changing the file's permissions	Changing directory permissions
Changing the file's ownership	Changing directory ownership
Running the file	Displaying the directory's owner and permissions

By default, auditing settings apply only to the selected directory and its files. To audit all subdirectories, select Replace Auditing on Subdirectories. If Replace Auditing on Existing Files is selected, auditing changes apply to files in subdirectories as well. In general, they both should be selected, unless you have a particular reason to not audit subdirectories.

 NOTE

> To audit files and directories, the File and Object Access option must be selected in the Audit Policy dialog box in User Manager or User Manager for Domains.

To add users and groups to those whose access to the file is being audited, click the Add button and specify the new users and groups in the resulting dialog box. Remove a user or group by selecting it in the current Name list and clicking Remove.

When you are setting up auditing for a directory, you have two additional options to consider: Replace Auditing on Subdirectories and Replace Auditing on Existing Files. The default replace option is Replace Auditing on Existing Files. When this option is selected, changes made to auditing apply to the directory and the files within that directory only, not to any subdirectories in the directory. To apply auditing changes to the directory and its files as well as existing subdirectories within the directory and their files, check both boxes. Clearing both boxes applies the changes in auditing to the directory only, not to any of the files or subdirectories contained within it. Selecting only Replace Auditing on Subdirectories applies audit changes to the directory and subdirectories only, not to existing files in either.

As with file auditing, you can set auditing for each group or user in the list by selecting the name of a group or user in the Name list and specifying which events will be audited for that group or user.

To remove file auditing for a group or user, select that group or user and click Remove. To add groups or users to the audit, use the Add option. When you are satisfied with the auditing options, click OK. The results appear in the Event Viewer. The Viewer isn't the clearest thing in the world, but it gives you the rough information you need in order to track a security violation—provided that you enable auditing. On the other hand, auditing is costly in terms of CPU time and disk space; when you turn on all file audits, you will fill up your event log in no time.

Registry Auditing

The Windows NT Server Registry contains information relevant to security and auditing. You learned all about the Registry on Day 4. As you saw, it contains the default configuration for the event log files, the maximum sizes of those files, and the retention period for data in each file. Registry auditing is set up via the Registry Editor utility. In Registry Editor, you can specify the groups and users whose activities you want to audit for selected Registry keys, and then choose the Auditing command. Registry-related audited events can be viewed in the Security log in Event Viewer.

Task 24.1. Setting up Registry auditing.

Step 1: Description

This task explains how to set auditing for the Registry by using the Registry Editor.

Step 2: Action

1. Select Start|Run.
2. Type C:*SystemRoot*\SYSTEM32\REGEDT32.EXE and click OK.
3. In the Registry Editor, select Security|Auditing. You should see a window like that shown in Figure 24.4.
4. Click the Add button and select a key you want to audit. Table 24.4 explains the Registry audit options.
5. When you have added all the keys for auditing, click OK.

TASK

24

Figure 24.4.

*The Registry Key
Auditing dialog box.*

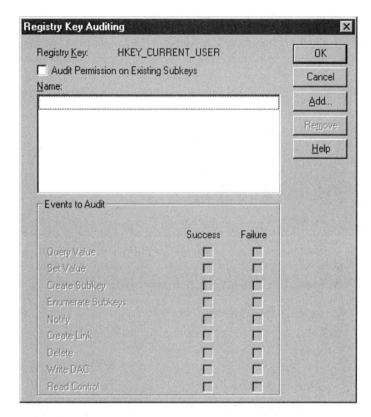

Table 24.4. The Registry audit options.

Audit Option	Events Audited
Query Value	Events that attempt to open a key with Query Value access
Set Value	Events that attempt to open a key with Set Value access
Create Subkey	Events that attempt to open a key with Create Value access
Enumerate Subkeys	Events that attempt to open a key with Enumerate Subkeys access (that is, events that try to find the subkeys of a key)
Notify	Events that attempt to open a key with Notify access
Create Link	Events that attempt to open a key with Create Link access
Delete	Events that attempt to delete the key
Write DAC	Events that attempt to determine who has access to the key
Read Control	Events that attempt to find the owner of a key

Step 3: Review

Registry auditing is turned off by default. To turn on Registry auditing, first turn on File and Object Access auditing in User Manager for Domains. In Registry Editor, choose Security|Auditing and check the items to audit. All keys and subkeys can be audited individually. You should set up Registry auditing on a case-by-case basis, as warranted.

When you want to audit changes to a particular key by a user or an application, you can turn on auditing for that key. Most installations audit only those events that fail. Auditing successful events might produce so many entries that your Security log will quickly fill up.

Printer Auditing

To keep an eye on a printer's usage, it's a good idea to audit it. To set up auditing, first go to the User Manager for Domains and enable File and Object Access auditing. After you've done that, you can set up printer auditing for individuals and groups.

Task 24.2. Setting printer auditing.

Step 1: Description

To configure printer auditing, go to the Printer Properties dialog box and select the Auditing option in the Security tab.

Step 2: Action

1. Click the Printers icon in the Control Panel under Start|Settings.
2. Right-click on the printer you want to audit from the icons in the Printers window.
3. Select Properties from the menu that pops up. You should see a window like the one shown in Figure 24.5.
4. Select the Security tab. When you do, you see the dialog box shown in Figure 24.6.
5. Click the Auditing button. You should see a dialog box like the one shown in Figure 24.7. All the auditing options are grayed out.
6. Before you can audit printer activity, you have to select a group or user to audit. To do this, click the Add button.
7. To select a group for auditing, double-click on it or click on it once and then click Add. When you've selected a user or group, it should show up in the Add Names box in the bottom half of the screen.

Figure 24.5.

The Printer Properties dialog box.

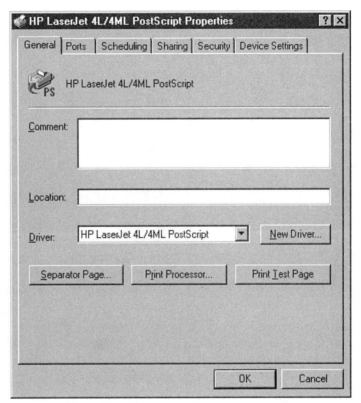

8. When you've chosen all the groups you want to audit, click OK to return to the Printer Auditing screen.

9. For each group or user you've chosen to audit, you can select different items to keep track of by checking the appropriate check boxes. The printer audit options are described in Table 24.5.

10. When you have added all the groups for auditing, click OK. Then click OK on the Printer Properties dialog box.

Figure 24.6.

The Printer Security tab.

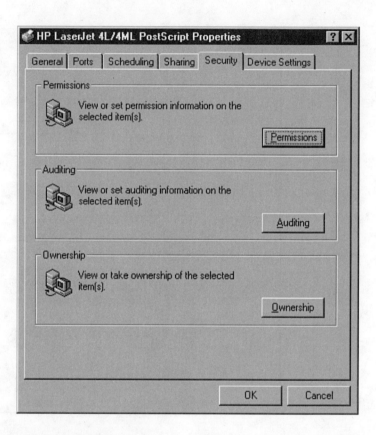

Table 24.5. The printer audit options.

Audit Option	Events Audited
Print	When someone prints a document
Full Control	When someone changes job settings for a document; pauses, restarts, moves, and deletes a document; shares a printer; or changes the printer's priorities
Delete	When someone deletes a printer
Change Permissions	When someone changes printer permissions
Take Ownership	When someone takes ownership of a printer

Figure 24.7.

The Printer Auditing dialog box.

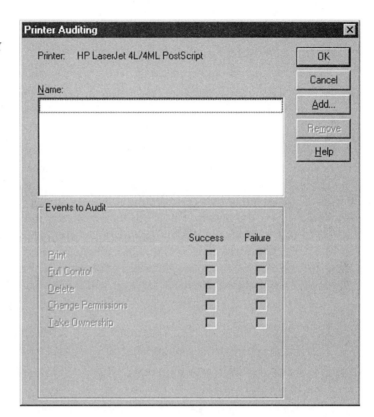

Step 3: Review

To turn on printer auditing, select Properties for the printer under Start|Settings|Printers.

When you highlight a group in the Name box here, you see the auditing items you selected for that particular user or group. No defaults are attached to auditing a particular group, so you have to set them all by hand. To view the audit information, use the Event Viewer in the Administrative Tools program group.

If you want to remove printer auditing for a group or user, follow these steps:

1. In the Auditing dialog box, select the name of the group or user from the list.
2. Click Remove.
3. Click OK.

Dial-Up Networking Auditing

You don't have to rely on intuition and your problem-solving ability when it comes to troubleshooting dial-up networking (DUN). You can either monitor connection attempts as they occur by using the DUN Administrator or check the record of all auditing and error messages stored in the Event Viewer.

Examining Logged Information

If you're having trouble with the connection, note that connection information about each DUN session is saved in a file called DEVICE.LOG in the *SystemRoot*\\SYSTEM32\\RAS directory. DEVICE.LOG contains the strings that are sent to and received from the serial device (that is, the modem or X.25 PAD) that transmits the information between client and server. When looking at this file, be sure to use a text editor that can handle both regular characters and hexadecimal output. You can track the entire progress of a session with this file. It contains the command string sent to the serial device, the echo of the command, the device's response, and, for modems, the rate of transmittal.

Before you can use DEVICE.LOG, you must create it. The process is explained in the following steps:

1. Hang up any remote connections currently in place, and exit DUN.
2. Open the Registry by running REGEDIT32. You can also access the Registry from inside WINMSD.
3. Go to `HKEY_LOCAL_MACHINE` and access the following key:

   `SYSTEM\CurrentControlSet\Services\RasMan\Parameters`
4. Change the value of the logging parameter to 1 so that it looks like this:

   `Logging:REG_DWORD:0x1`

Logging begins whenever you click the Dial-Up Networking icon or restart the service. You don't need to shut down the system or log off and on first. To view the log, open it in WordPad or another text editor. Be sure to use an editor that can handle hexadecimal information, or part of the log ends up unreadable. Also, when looking at this file, you can disregard the hOD and hOA characters at the end of each line, which are, respectively, carriage-return and line-feed bytes. They have no other significance.

WARNING

As always, before editing the Registry, you should make a backup copy of it. Making a mistake with the Registry can affect your system badly so that you need to re-install the operating system. See Day 4 for information on Registry backup and restore.

24

DEVICE.LOG records information about only dial-up connections. If you're having trouble with a direct connection, this file cannot help you.

ClipBook Page Auditing

Use ClipBook page auditing to monitor how specified users or members of groups are using shared ClipBook pages. For a particular ClipBook page, you can audit both successful and failed actions. To set audit parameters, you must be a member of the Administrators group or be assigned Manage Auditing and Security Log rights. Audited events are written to the Security log. Use this feature only when really necessary.

Task 24.3. Setting ClipBook auditing.

Step 1: Description

Auditing ClipBook allows you to track its usage. To audit ClipBook Page usage, open the Clipboard Viewer and select Security to add auditing.

Step 2: Action

1. Select Clipboard Viewer from the Start|Programs|Accessories menu.
2. From the ClipBook Viewer window (shown in Figure 24.8), select the ClipBook page you want to audit.

Figure 24.8.

The ClipBook Viewer window.

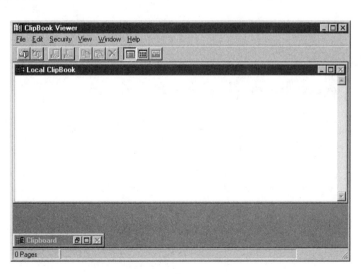

3. Select the name of the group or user you want to track.

4. Select the events you want to audit. You can audit attempts to carry out these actions:

   ☐ Read the page

   ☐ Delete the contents of the page

   ☐ Change permissions

   ☐ Change audit types

5. Click OK and exit the ClipBook Viewer.

Step 3: Review

To audit ClipBook pages, in the ClipBook Viewer window, select the ClipBook page and choose Security|Auditing. Select the name of the group or user and the events to audit.

> **NOTE**   To audit ClipBook pages, you must select the File and Object Access option in the Audit Policy dialog box in User Manager or User Manager for Domains.

If you want to remove ClipBook Page auditing for a group or user, carry out these actions:

1. In the Auditing dialog box, select the name of the group or user from the list.

2. Click Remove.

3. Click OK.

Enabling Event Auditing

As you just saw in this chapter, if you want to determine who might be using shared network resources or abusing their privileges on the network, you need to enable the auditing features provided in Windows NT Server. Auditing is divided into several categories and is not enabled in a single application. To audit system events related to account usage or modification and the programs running on the server, choose Policies Audit in the Server Manager for Domains dialog box.

When you select an event to be audited, it is entered in the Security log, which can be viewed with the Event Viewer. You can select to audit the successful use of a privilege, the failure to obtain access (which indicates a security violation attempt), or both. As you have seen, the following events can be audited:

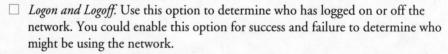

☐ *Logon and Logoff.* Use this option to determine who has logged on or off the network. You could enable this option for success and failure to determine who might be using the network.

24

☐ *File and Object Access.* This option works in conjunction with other applications that have been used to specify auditing. For example, you can use File Manager to enable auditing of a directory and then enable auditing of the success or failure events for the File and Object Access to record access to the audited directory.

☐ *Use of User Rights.* This selection allows you to audit any use of a user right, other than logon and logoff, such as the capability to log on as a service.

☐ *User and Group Management.* This option allows you to track any user account or group. For example, it records when a new user is added, an existing user password is enabled, or a new user is added to a group.

If you have constant problems with a particular user account or group being modified, and you cannot determine who is making these changes, you can enable this option for both success and failure. This step can help you determine who might be making the changes. For example, you might find problems caused by personnel who have administrative privileges but have not been adequately trained. By using this option, you can determine who needs additional training or who should have their administrative privileges revoked.

☐ *Security Policy Changes.* Use this option to help you determine who might be making changes to system audit policies, user right policies, or trust relationships. You could enable this option both for success and failure to determine who might be modifying network policies—particularly when you have several administrators and find that things have been changing without anyone admitting responsibility.

☐ *Restart, Shutdown, and System.* This option enables you to determine who might be shutting down servers or creating any event that affects system security or the Security log.

☐ *Process Tracking.* Use this option to determine which applications are executing on your system. Auditing the success events for Process Tracking can fill up the Security log in a matter of minutes. Enable the previous event for success only when absolutely necessary.

Using the Event Viewer to Monitor Problems

To monitor past problems, you can check the Event Viewer and see what it has to say about a situation. Make sure that auditing is enabled. Three kinds of events are recorded in the Event Viewer:

☐ *Audit.* A normal event recorded for administrative reasons. A normal connection would be recorded as an audit. You can choose to audit only successful events, failed events, or both.

☐ *Warning.* An irregular event that doesn't affect how the system functions.

☐ *Error.* A failed event or network error.

Security Event Logs

Every Windows NT Server system has three logs that record system-, security-, and application-related events:

☐ The System log records errors, warnings, or information generated by the Windows NT Server system.

☐ The Security log records valid and invalid logon attempts and events related to the use of resources such as creating, opening, or deleting files or other objects.

☐ The Application log records errors, warnings, and information generated by application software, such as an electronic mail or database program.

All three logs are kept in the same subdirectory:

`\SystemRoot\SYSTEM32\CONFIG`

Anyone can view the System and Application logs. But only system administrators or users with the Manage Auditing and Security Log right can view the Security log. To view the events in the Security log, open Event Viewer and choose Log|Security.

The Security log is protected by an ACL that restricts access to all but the administrator. The Security log must be secured using NTFS so that the ACL can be used. This is the pathname of the Security log:

`\SystemRoot\SYSTEM32\CONFIG\SECEVENT.EVT`

The Security log contains a header and version number that is placed at the beginning of each log file. This header can be used to ensure that the file being read or written to is a valid log file. The event log service will validate an existing file before writing events to it. It uses the Alert service to inform the administrator when the file is not a valid event log file. When a log file is full, that is, the next record to be overwritten is within the retention period, an alert is sent to the administrator, and the record is not written to the log.

 TIP

You should take care to protect the APPEVENT.EVT, SECEVENT.EVT, and SYSEVENT.EVT audit log files stored in the *\SystemRoot*\SYSTEM32\CONFIG directory. You should then assign access to these files only to the person or persons responsible for auditing in your organization.

24

NOTE   You can use the NET START EVENTLOG command to start the event log, which audits selected events on the network, such as file access, user logons and logoffs, and the starting of programs. You can select which events you want to log, and also whether you want the log to consist of both successful and failed attempts, just failures, or just successes (although recording only successes doesn't sound terribly useful if you're trying to monitor the system). If you're not sure how the NET commands work, review Appendix B, "Windows NT Server Command Reference."

After you've selected the log to display in Event Viewer, the viewer can sort, filter, and search for specific details about events based on fields in the header portion of the Event Detail. When you're viewing the Security log in Event Viewer, double-clicking an event displays a more detailed breakdown of that event for analysis. Figure 24.9 provides a sample of detailed event information.

Figure 24.9.

The Event Detail window.

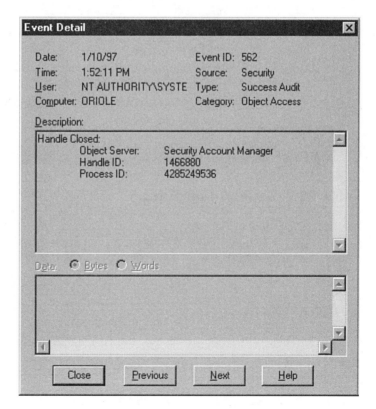

Table 24.6 explains the header information in the Event Detail.

Table 24.6. Detailed event information.

Header Item	Description
Date	The date the event was generated.
Time	The time the event was generated.
User	The account name translation of the SID of the subject that generated the event. This user name is the impersonation ID of the client when the subject is impersonating a client, or it is the user name of the primary ID when not impersonating.
Computer	The computer name for the computer where the event was generated.
Event ID	A unique module-specific ID of the specific event.
Source	The name of the system that submitted the event. For security audits this will always be Security.
Type	Successful or unsuccessful audited security access attempt, depending on whether auditing was set up to audit successful and/or failed events.
Category	A classification of the event by the event source. For example, security categories include Logon and Logoff Policy Change, Privilege Use, System Event, Object Access, Detailed Tracking, and Account Management.

Table 24.7 shows the various categories of events in the Security log and what they mean.

Table 24.7. Security categories.

Category	Description
Account Management (User and Group Management)	These events describe high-level changes to the user accounts database, such as User Created or Group Membership Change. Potentially, a more detailed, object-level audit is also performed (see Object Access events).

24

Category	Description
Detailed Tracking (Process Tracking)	These events provide detailed subject-tracking information. This includes information such as program activation, handle duplication, and indirect object access.
Logon/Logoff (Logon and Logoff)	These events describe a single logon or logoff attempt, whether successful or unsuccessful. Included in each logon description is an indication of what type of logon was requested or performed (interactive, network, or service).
Object Access (File and Object Access)	These events describe both successful and unsuccessful accesses to protected objects.
Policy Change (Security Policy Changes)	These events describe high-level changes to the security policy database, such as assignment of privileges or logon capabilities. Potentially, a more detailed, object-level audit is also performed (see Object Access).
Privilege Use (Use of User Rights)	These events describe both successful and unsuccessful attempts to use privileges. The log also includes information about when some special privileges are assigned. These special privileges are audited only at assignment time, not at time of use.
System Event (Security Policy Changes)	These events indicate that something affecting the security of the entire system or audit log occurred.

24

Using the Log Filter

If you have a busy system, you will have many log records. To make review of the log easier, you might want to filter the log records. You can use the filter to define the date range, type of events, and category of events displayed.

By choosing View|Filter Events, you can specify certain event log parameters for filtering. Figure 24.10 shows the Filter dialog box.

Figure 24.10.

The Filter dialog box.

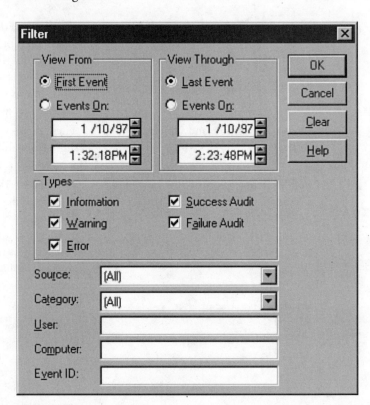

Table 24.8 lists the log filter options.

Table 24.8. The log filter options.

Option	Description
View From	Select either the beginning of the log (First Event) or a particular start date and time. The default is First Event.
View Through	Select either the end of the log (Last Event) or a particular end date and time. The default is Last Event.

Option	Description
Types	Filter according to whether the audited security access attempt was successful or unsuccessful, depending on whether auditing was set up to audit successful and/or failed events. Or filter according to the type of error: information, warning, or error. The default is all types.
Source	Select the name of the system that submitted the event. For security audits, this will always be Security. The default is All.
Category	Select whether you want to include Logon and Logoff Policy Change, Privilege Use, System Event, Object Access, Detailed Tracking, and Account Management records. The default is All.
User	Enter the account name for the SID you want to view.
Computer	Enter the computer name for the computer you want to view.
Event ID	Enter the unique module-specific ID of the event.

Using Event Log Settings

By choosing Log|Log Settings, you can specify certain event log parameters for size and event logging. Figure 24.11 shows the Event Log Settings dialog box.

Figure 24.11.

The Event Log Settings dialog box.

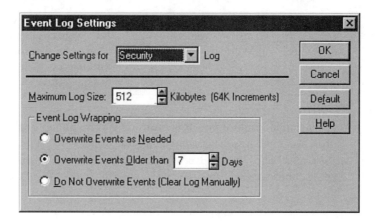

Event logging begins at boot time. When all options in the Audit Policy dialog box (in User Manager), including Process Tracking, are enabled, Windows NT can log a significant amount of activity to the security event log, thereby filling up the log. If the Security log becomes full, the system will halt. Windows NT provides a wrapping facility to ensure that the event log does not become full and cause the system to halt. By default, the maximum size of the log file is 512KB per log. The log capacity can be increased to accommodate system auditing. This number can be set in accordance with disk and memory capacities. An administrator cannot set the log for a smaller size than the current size of the log; the log must be cleared first.

Each organization should outline standard policies for archiving the event log. Archiving, when used in conjunction with one of the three available options for event-log wrapping, can help ensure that all system events are logged and that the log does not become full and halt the system.

Table 24.9 shows the event-log wrapping options available in the Event Log Setting dialog box. You can access the options via the Log Settings menu option in Event Viewer.

Table 24.9. The event log options.

Option	Description
Overwrite Events As Needed	When this option is selected, each new event replaces the oldest event when the event log is full. This is the default setting.
Overwrite Events Older Than x Days	This is the best choice to use in conjunction with a regular archive policy. The default is 7 days.
Do Not Overwrite Events (Clear Log Manually)	This ensures a complete audit log. When it's selected, you must clear the log yourself. Another good choice depending on your archive policy.

You should monitor your system to determine the optimal maximum log size. This is a balance between storage constraints, the amount of auditing being done, and archiving strategies. The Do Not Overwrite Events (Clear Log Manually) option should be selected so that events are not lost.

24

WARNING

To avoid bringing down the system when the log is full or when there is not enough memory to allocate a buffer for the next audit record, set the following Registry flag:

`\Registry\Machine\System\CurrentControlSet\Control\Lsa\`
`CrashOnAuditFail`

When this flag is set and the system cannot for any reason log an audit record (for example, the security event log is full or there is no memory to allocate a buffer for the audit record), the system is brought down. When this flag is not set and the audit log is full, an alert message is displayed to the system administrator.

Summary

Logging and monitoring are key administrative duties. Windows NT provides several facilities to perform monitoring and logging. On Day 14, you'll learn about the Performance Monitor and how it helps fine-tune and troubleshoot your server and network.

You found in this chapter that you can set the following security policies:

- ☐ Account, which controls the characteristics of passwords for all user accounts
- ☐ User Rights, which determines which user or group is assigned particular system rights
- ☐ Audit, in which the kinds of security events to be logged are defined
- ☐ Trust Relationships, which establishes how other domains on the network interact with the local domain

This chapter also showed you how to set up the following items:

- ☐ System event auditing
- ☐ File and directory auditing
- ☐ Registry auditing
- ☐ Printer auditing
- ☐ Dial-up networking (DUN) auditing
- ☐ ClipBook page auditing
- ☐ Event Viewer to monitor problems

Well, that's it for today. Tomorrow, you'll learn about two NT facilities that need monitoring and auditing: BackOffice and Internet Information Server.

Workshop

To wrap up the day, you can review terms and tasks from the chapter, and see the answers to some commonly asked questions.

Terminology Review

audit policy—Defines the type of security events logged for a domain or for an individual computer; determines what NT will do when the Security log becomes full.

auditing—The capability to detect and record security-related events, particularly any attempt to create, access, or delete objects. Windows NT uses security IDs (SIDs) to record which processes performed the action.

event—Any significant occurrence in the system or in an application that requires users to be notified, or an entry to be added to a log.

event log service—Records events in the System, Security, and Application logs.

Local Security Authority (LSA)—An integral subsystem of the Windows NT security system. It manages the local security policy and provides interactive user authentication services. The LSA also controls the generation of audit messages and enters audit messages into the audit log file.

Task List

This chapter introduced you to Windows NT audit features. As a system administrator, you need to learn how to use the System, Application, and Security logs. Several tasks were introduced in this chapter:

- ☐ Setting user rights
- ☐ Setting up file and directory auditing
- ☐ Setting printer auditing
- ☐ Setting up Registry auditing
- ☐ Setting up DUN auditing
- ☐ Setting ClipBook auditing
- ☐ Using the log filter
- ☐ Changing event log settings

24

Q&A

Q How do I set up event auditing for a printer?

A To keep track of printer events, go to the Auditing item in the Printer Properties Security tab. By default, no groups are selected for auditing, so you must select a group. Click the Add button, and a list of possible groups to audit appears. Select a group, click the Add button so that the group name appears in the lower box, and then click OK. After you've selected a group for auditing, you can choose the events you want to audit from the list. For each group you audit, you can set up a special auditing schedule.

24

DAY

13

Chapter **25**

Using NT with BackOffice

So far, you have learned about many of NT Server's different aspects, including file management, auditing, and communication gateways. It has been a busy time for you.

In this morning's session, you'll learn how Microsoft's BackOffice products offer database management, electronic mail, and a host of other services. By now, you might be asking the question What is BackOffice and how does it relate, if at all, to Microsoft Office? You'll find the answer in this chapter.

Microsoft BackOffice is best described as a series of products offering a degree of interaction similar to that of the client software called Microsoft Office. In BackOffice are Exchange Server, which is the electronic mail system; SQL Server, the database product; System Management Server (SMS), a software management and distribution tool; and SNA Server, a mainframe connectivity tool. Various newer products have recently been added. Those are discussed near the end of this document in the section called "The Newer Products." This is primarily because these newer products are more specialized and are less likely to be utilized by most NT customers.

You might think of Microsoft BackOffice as the equivalent product of Microsoft Office, the Word, Excel, and Access suite. Just as these client tools are integrated and use a common interface, BackOffice strives to manage the same feat on the server.

The use of suites of tools, all combining to enable a user to quickly and easily integrate data among products and even using a consistent interface, is becoming ever more popular. Microsoft sees how well the Office suite sells (Office 97 was recently made available) and realizes that a server suite of tools might easily gain the same prominence.

In this chapter, we delve into the use of these tools on an NT Server, where most of them must be run. We discuss how to install and manage each product and offer additional information about using them.

BackOffice Overview

First let's review the basics of this product called BackOffice and see how it helps in the management of a server. At one point early in the creation of client/server systems, the server was a place that ran business applications and little more. As they quickly gained acceptance, they grew to include many additional features designed to help improve their capability to serve the end user and enhance the business cycle.

Today's servers use many kinds of tools, including, as you have seen in previous days, Remote Access Services (RAS), network printing and file sharing, screen savers and sound players, and even telephony support. The NT system is more powerful than ever, and it offers organizations the tools and services they need in a fast-growing world.

Microsoft charges for these additional services, however, so you do not find them installed everywhere. Although Microsoft probably thinks that everyone needs these tools and products, to add them to the base price of the server drives that already-expensive option even higher. (All right, all right. Perhaps it's not that expensive.) With tight integration and excellent services, the BackOffice product becomes a formidable addition to your business system arsenal.

BackOffice offers various products that we alluded to earlier. The following brief review provides you with some idea of what those products are:

☐ *Exchange Server:* This product enables an organization to manage electronic mail across the network. Efficient and effective storage and management of mail means more effective communications and increased ease of data transfer.

☐ *SQL Server:* SQL Server is Microsoft's answer to the Oracle database product. The ease and use of large database systems provide an unparalleled opportunity to quickly gain access to important data. No longer must a user wait for some large "flat" file to sequence completely through its length before providing the answer to a query.

☐ *SMS:* The Systems Management Server provides the capability to monitor, manipulate servers, and distribute client software. No longer is it necessary to sign onto every workstation to upgrade software or add a new application.

☐ *SNA Server:* Many client/server networks still depend on the mainframe for legacy information and storage of large files and databases. While TCP/IP grows in popularity, the main connectivity option is using the IBM network topology called SNA (System Network Architecture).

☐ *MCIS:* MCIS (Microsoft Commercial Internet System) is one of the newer products in the BackOffice family. It provides a full set of Internet services for attracting and retaining customers.

☐ *Merchant Server:* Another newer product in the Office family, Merchant Server allows businesses to create and manage Internet-based stores.

☐ *Proxy Server:* This is a new product that enables you to deliver Internet access to all the desktop machines in your organization in an easy, secure, and cost-effective manner.

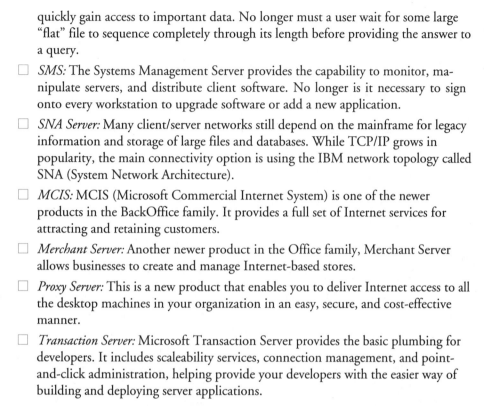

☐ *Transaction Server:* Microsoft Transaction Server provides the basic plumbing for developers. It includes scaleability services, connection management, and point-and-click administration, helping provide your developers with the easier way of building and deploying server applications.

Together these tools provide the basis for the BackOffice family of tools. Working together, NT and BackOffice provide a more or less seamless interface for the user, one that is getting better each year.

Let's look at how well these two products, NT Server and BackOffice, integrate. NT Server manages the overall network needs of the clients, offering network protocol support such as TCP/IP and NetBEUI or IPX. It provides the file and directory management for all the services that run, and it enables the clients to print their reports and share access to their files and databases.

Because the BackOffice products are integrated with NT Server, they share NT's security and access control features. This setup allows for less overhead and administration because user authentication and access control is performed in one place. Finally, most of the BackOffice products use similar tools for viewing events, managing users, and providing disk services. This consistency makes the learning curve for administrators a lot easier.

In the later sections of this chapter, you'll review some of the more common products and learn how to use them. In Task 25.1, you'll learn how to install the products.

Task 25.1. Installing BackOffice products.

Step 1: Description

This task shows you how to install the various components of the BackOffice family. It describes a basic installation methodology for all products instead of reiterating each installation. Each product installs in a similar manner.

Step 2: Action

1. Log onto your system using an administrator account.

2. Insert your BackOffice CD-ROM.

3. Double-click the setup.exe file to start. (Setup might begin automatically if your CD-ROM has an autorun icon.)

4. Follow the instructions as they are presented. For each product, you are provided with choices pertaining to where the product should reside, how much disk space is needed (SQL Server needs around 55 to 75MB, depending on which options you choose), and what name to register under.

5. Setup takes a while, especially if you are installing all the products. Choose Reboot when you're finished, because the products are not available until after the system boots.

Step 3: Review

Setup of most NT products is driven by simple installation steps with options that only you can answer. You can decide whether to install additional items, such as documentation or support for certain protocols, depending on your particular installation needs.

Using and Understanding MS Exchange Server

MS Exchange Server is a reincarnation of the old Microsoft Mail product. MS Mail, designed in earlier days, does not support the large numbers of users common in today's client/server environments. The new Exchange is designed to handle large numbers of users and to use 32-bit processing more effectively.

MS Exchange provides various features for its users, including these:

- ☐ Electronic mail between users
- ☐ File attachments
- ☐ The capability to talk to other mail packages
- ☐ Programming interfaces allowing you to interface with other programs

Microsoft Exchange integrates well with NT as long as you are running a domain. Exchange doesn't run with workgroups, so you need to re-install NT 4.0 if you are not using a domain structure.

NOTE

> Microsoft Exchange must be installed on a PDC or BDC and will not install on a standalone server. You need to re-install your version of NT if you did not choose either of these options in Chapter 3, "Installing Windows NT Server on the File Server." There is no upgrade path from a standalone server to a Primary Domain Controller other than a complete re-install.

MS Exchange offers a robust and scaleable electronic mail system. It does, however, utilize an impressive number of resources, and you need to be sure that the system you choose to run it on is not already busy. Because the mail system is similar to the standard Microsoft Office products, a certain degree of familiarity is already designed into the system. This is helpful in diminishing your learning curve.

MS Exchange allows you to manage your mail by using a preprocessor called the Inbox Assistant. This assistant, which allows you to write certain rules for handling your mail, is a major benefit of the package. By assigning a rules-based scenario to your messages, you are able to delete, forward, move, and copy (among other things) any of the incoming messages you receive. If you get loads of mail each day, using this tool allows you to get rid of the junk and manage the rest.

MS Exchange also integrates its security with NT. You manage your users for NT and Mail all from one place, eliminating overhead and redundancy.

Implementing Exchange takes planning and organization and you can best handle the task by reviewing all the material before you start. You can find numerous white papers concerning this topic on Microsoft's Web page at www.microsoft.com/exchange/plan.htm.

25

You also can find various planning documents and tools in the Migrate directory of your CD-ROM. If you are using a test version of NT Server throughout this book, read the documents before starting, and then do the implementation. You needn't be overly concerned because you will delete it all anyway. If you do not have such a luxury, be careful because after the site and organization and server names are designated, they cannot be changed without a re-install of the product.

You'll use the Microsoft Exchange Administrator to handle most of your tasks when dealing with Exchange. Although various other tools are also on the menu, these mostly deal with optimization and speed issues. Administrator performs the day-to-day tasks.

As mentioned, the install adds some items to your server menu under the name Microsoft Exchange. You can see that they are mostly concerned with managing the performance of the system. Does this mean it is a big issue and you need to be concerned? Perhaps. You certainly need to know that Exchange requires significant memory, depending on how large your user base is and how much it is used. These tools consist of the following items:

- ☐ MS Exchange Administrator
- ☐ MS Exchange Migration Wizard
- ☐ MS Exchange Optimizer
- ☐ MS Exchange Server Health
- ☐ MS Exchange Server History
- ☐ MS Exchange Server IMC Queues
- ☐ MS Exchange Server IMC Statistic
- ☐ MS Exchange Server IMC Traffic
- ☐ MS Exchange Server Load
- ☐ MS Exchange Server Queues
- ☐ MS Exchange Server Users
- ☐ MS Exchange Setup Editor

Exchange offers these tools to help you monitor and address the various components of the system, allowing you to customize how your system reacts. The documentation provided in the Books Online section that you optionally install with the product offers a comprehensive overview of the product. You'll learn most of what you need to know by using these books.

After installing MS Exchange, you are offered a chance to run a program called the Optimizer utility. Running it right away offers the best chance of making sure that your system manages user access in the most efficient fashion. This program determines the best locations for its files and configures memory usage to best advantage, considering other programs and services that might be running alongside the mail program. You run the program every time your user accounts increase significantly or when you change your system configuration.

Task 25.2. Running MS Exchange Optimizer.

Step 1: Description

This task shows you how to use the Optimizer program included with MS Exchange. You run the program whenever changes are made to the system.

Step 2: Action

1. Log onto your system using an administrator account.

2. Start the program using Start|Microsoft Exchange|Microsoft Exchange Optimizer. (If you are still installing Exchange, run the program by selecting Run Optimizer on the Setup box shown.)

3. Specify the number of users, the type of server, and an expected total number of persons in your organization by using the boxes shown. Use the Limit Memory Usage box if other services are in use, and specify the RAM to be used by Exchange. You need 32MB for Exchange to run effectively but, once again, more is better! If you do not limit the memory usage, Exchange will use it all, degrading other services that might be running. Click Next to continue.

4. The program suggests the best locations for its files and allows you to modify those locations in the panel that shows next. Unless you have a need to move the files, leave them where they are installed.

5. If Optimizer recommends moving files, consider the action and be sure that the files are backed up before allowing any movement to occur. Click Finish to complete the job and restart Exchange.

Step 3: Review

Because MS Exchange consumes resources, it is prudent to run this Optimizer program regularly to maximize how it manages the system resources. Running Optimizer each time your system resources change is an effective method of ensuring that MS Exchange runs efficiently.

After your server program is running, you need to update the client workstations to enable them to use Exchange. Installation is necessary regardless of whether your clients are running Messaging or other client mail packages. Installation of the client will update drivers and access to the public folders in Exchange and will set up the machine to use the new features of Exchange Server. You can find the software for this on the Exchange Clients CD-ROM.

TASK

25

After your installation of MS Exchange is completed, you'll find that User Manager for Domains provides you with a new choice called Exchange when you're adding users. This is integration at its best.

Finally, you use the Administrator utility to add new mailboxes and set the properties of all the Exchange Objects. This utility provides for distribution list management and user management. You'll find that it becomes an important aspect of your daily administration of Exchange.

In this brief section, you learned a small piece of the Exchange story. Entire books are available on this topic. Although we have limited space here, we hope that you've learned enough to install and begin to learn the product. And we hope that you'll continue your learning through experience and more product-specific books.

Using SQL Server

SQL Server provides you with a comprehensive relational database management system server. Along with Oracle and DB2, SQL Server adds to the already popular use of relational databases. The acronym SQL comes from Structured Query language, a programming language used for maintaining and managing database information.

A relational database consists of a bunch of tables containing your information. One of the main roles of a relational database is to allow you to manipulate these tables to provide you with access control and a link between each table so that data can be compared and updated.

The SQL Server product adheres to industry standards, using ANSI SQL support, while adding to these standards with such things as declarative referential integrity and server cursor support.

To run SQL Server, you need an Alpha AXP processor, an Intel x86 or Pentium, or a MIPS machine. As with all NT products, it is best to refer to the Hardware Compatibility List to be certain your machine is supported. Microsoft recommends a minimum of 16MB of memory. You might need more, depending on the use of the system. As with most NT software, more is better.

Unlike with Exchange, Microsoft recommends that you not run this product on a PDC or BDC due to the overhead of these services.

When SQL Server is installed, you are provided with various programs. You see that menu in Figure 25.1.

Figure 25.1.

The SQL Server menu.

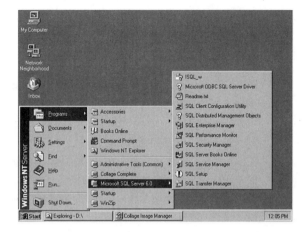

Each of the services provides an aspect of your database management system. In the following list, you see a brief overview of each service and learn a little about which ones you'll use the most.

- [ ] *ISQL_w:* Interactive Structured Query Language for Windows. A graphical utility for querying the SQL database, analyzing plan executions, and viewing statistics.

- [ ] *Microsoft ODBC SQL Server Driver:* A Help file for providing information on SQL Server.

- [ ] *Readme.txt:* A standard readme file providing additional information about installing or upgrading SQL Server.

- [ ] *SQL Client Configuration Utility:* A utility that allows you to modify the settings pertaining to SQL Server Client, providing settings for a default network, and several advanced options.

- [ ] *SQL Distributed Management Objects:* A Help file providing detailed information on what these objects are and providing such data as the properties of each object and how to use them.

- [ ] *SQL Enterprise Manager:* One of the major administrator tools for managing SQL Server. It lets you manage job scheduling, logons, and database management services.

- [ ] *SQL Performance Monitor:* A tool that allows you to monitor server activity and performance, including the number of connections, page writes, and command batches executed.

25

☐ *SQL Security Manager:* The tool for integrating server security with NT. You choose whether a user must have separate accounts and passwords or can use his NT account and password or some mix of the two. It also manages all the grants and revokes that provide database security.

☐ *SQL Server Books Online:* A comprehensive library of information on running and managing the product.

☐ *SQL Service Manager:* A utility that allows you to start and stop the services associated with running a relational database.

☐ *SQL Setup:* The program install routine. Allows you to modify or add selected options.

☐ *SQL Transfer Manager:* A utility that allows you to transfer objects and data from one database server to another.

One of the most helpful aspects of SQL Server is the Books Online documentation. If you are unsure of how to use and manage a database, this is a good place to start. During the database setup, you are offered an opportunity to place this documentation on your hard drive or use the CD-ROM. If space is at a premium, you can run directly from the CD-ROM. When you start the program, you see a window like that shown in Figure 25.2.

Figure 25.2.

The SQL Server Books Online dialog box.

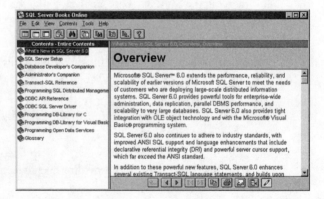

As you see, Books Online is quite extensive in its offerings and provides a great place to start if you are at all unsure.

WARNING

SQL Server is not an easy tool to set up and configure. Anyone setting it up needs to thoroughly read all documentation concerning setup and configuration *before* attempting the install; otherwise, it will not run correctly, if at all.

Starting SQL Server on your system requires you to begin with the SQL Service Manager icon. You start the service by selecting the one you need in the dialog box (the default is MSSQLServer) and double-clicking on the Start/Continue option. This first option starts the databases themselves, allowing interaction to begin. The other option, SQLExecutive, enables you to schedule server tasks. Start it by selecting it and double-clicking on the Start/Continue option as before. You see an example in Figure 25.3.

Figure 25.3.

The SQL Service Manager dialog box.

Close the dialog box when you're finished, or leave it minimized on your desktop. You can select the particular server you want if you have more than one running SQL Server. The database services are now available for you.

Next, you might want to control the database configuration, and for this you need SQL Server Enterprise Manager. After starting the service, you need to register your server. A dialog box appears for you to perform this task. Type the server name you are connecting to, and add your user account and password, making sure that you are authorized for access. By configuring the option in Security Manager, you can set up the database to allow trusted communications so that you do not need to sign in each time.

Type the default user account name of sa where you see Login ID, and click Register. SQL Server automatically supplies this default account for you with no password. At some point, you need to supply a password to protect your database. After processing stops, click the Close button to continue. You should see a window like that shown in Figure 25.4.

Figure 25.4.

The SQL Server Manager window.

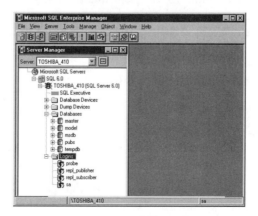

Open each branch as you would open any windows object, by clicking on the small plus sign next to the object. By double-clicking on the object, you obtain an editing dialog that allows you to modify the selected object. You can see an example of the master database we selected in Figure 25.5.

Figure 25.5.

Editing the master database by using Enterprise Manager.

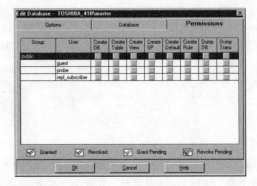

In the figure, you see three tabs: Options, Database, and Permissions. Each of these offers specific fields you can modify. In our example, you see the current permissions that apply. The selected server is indicated by a small icon representing a stoplight. On your server, you see a green color if the server is running. Red or yellow colors indicate a stopped or paused server, respectively.

The expandable menu provides a simple method for managing the server, and as you play with it, you see that it is easy to work with and offers all the flexibility you need.

As mentioned earlier, you can change the password for access to the server. You do so through this window or through the Security Manager. You double-click on the user account you want, and a menu is provided that allows you to modify the account.

You'll learn how to add a new user to SQL Server in Task 25.3.

Task 25.3. Adding a new user to a SQL Server database.

Step 1: Description
This task shows you how to add users to specific databases by using the SQL Enterprise Manager utility.

Step 2: Action
1. Be sure that SQL Server is running by starting the database services using SQL Service Manager.
2. Start SQL Server Enterprise Manager.

3. Sign onto the server using the sa account or an administrator account you have already created.

4. Select Manage|Logins. You see dialog box like that shown in Figure 25.6.

Figure 25.6.

Add a user with Enterprise Manager.

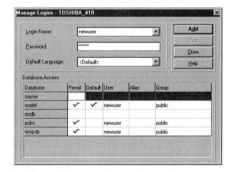

5. Type an account name and password. You change the language by selecting the Default language menu. When you add an account name, the Add button lights.

6. Select the database objects the user is allowed to access by clicking on the Permit field next to the ones you want. In our earlier example, we selected a few default testing databases.

7. Click the Add button when you are ready. You are asked to confirm the password, and the user is added. The Add button becomes the Modify button, allowing you to change the new user if you want. The dialog box does not go away, however, because it thinks you have more accounts to add.

8. Note that you can also select a particular database from the object branch and then select the Manage and Users options. This provides access to only that database because no others are selected. Adding a user here does the same as adding one with the Logins option and specifying the database. For purposes of this task, we chose the greater flexibility of Logins. Click the Close box to finish.

Step 3: Review

This simple task showed you how easy it is to set up new users and access permissions on your database server.

Using the Security Manager you can decide whether access is controlled through NT sign-on or through a separate user account within SQL Server. By default, all NT administrators are provided with the system administrator privilege in SQL Server.

One other tool you use consists of the utility that actually allows you to change and work with the data in your database. When you open the ISQL_w dialog box, you are shown four major tabs. You see these in Figure 25.7.

Figure 25.7.

*The Microsoft ISQL_w
dialog box.*

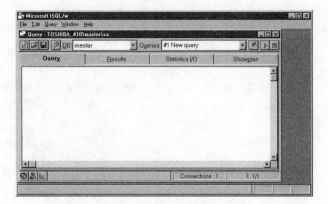

Using this utility, you run queries against your database and view the results. This utility is primarily used by those of you familiar with SQL queries. It allows you to create and run scripts on the fly.

Many organizations use additional products to manage queries, such as the Microsoft Query GUI-based tool. By playing with the options, you can learn how to form simple queries and obtain information. To perform a query, simply type the commands in the Query window, and then click the green forward arrow or select Query|Execute.

Your results are automatically shown in the Results window. Use the extensive Help menu to get more information, or buy one of the many books on SQL Query language.

Finally, you might need to manage your system's performance when running SQL Server. To do that, it is necessary to know how the system is performing, and this is where Performance Monitor is helpful. You see an example of the program in Figure 25.8.

Figure 25.8.

*Using Performance
Monitor.*

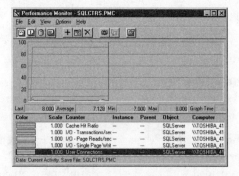

Using this tool is similar to using the NT Performance Monitor that is described tomorrow morning in Chapter 27, "Fine-Tuning Your Windows NT Server." You can read about the details in the morning, when you reach that chapter.

Using a complex database like SQL Server is beyond the scope of this book. You learned some of the simple aspects, but you would need to attend database training classes or read some of the books available to really get a handle on the power of this product. One good book to consider is *Microsoft BackOffice Administrator's Survival Guide*, by Sams Publishing.

Systems Management Server

The Systems Management Server product is probably destined to become far more popular than it currently is, because it addresses a common administration nightmare: software maintenance across a large network.

In the networks of today, managing all the resources becomes difficult. Where once we made do with huge machines and dumb terminals, we now have many smaller (and often just as large) servers with thousands of not-so-dumb machines. User access formerly came through terminals with no software concerns, but now they are usually thought of as workstations and carry all the overhead of a small mainframe.

The SMS program provides various aids to help us manage these increasingly complex networks:

- ☐ The capability to distribute software over the network, helping ease the problem of updating hundreds or thousands of computers
- ☐ The capability to gather a hardware and software inventory, enabling you to better manage your resources
- ☐ A Help desk to gain control of an end-user machine for support and troubleshooting
- ☐ The capability to control application license usage to ensure that you stay within your license agreements

Like all the other products in BackOffice, SMS provides tools and utilities for the purpose of performing all these tasks. The key here is centralized management of your far-flung computing resources. Using the tools in SMS, you gain a new level of control over these resources.

When you open the main menu, called System Management Support, you see a list of items. The list contains the following utilities:

- ☐ *SMS Administrator:* The primary administration tool.
- ☐ *SMS Books Online:* The Help file option that provides you with an extensive amount of detail on using SMS. Nowadays, you get this file rather than printed documentation.

25

- [ ] *SMS Frequently Asked Questions:* A FAQ of common questions. These are popular in Internet newsgroups, and they allow beginners to ensure that a question they have has not already been answered.
- [ ] *SMS Help:* The more normal Help Facility.
- [ ] *SMS MIF Form Generator:* A Management Information Format forms generator to help design reports.
- [ ] *SMS Release Notes:* The latest information about the product that is usually not reflected in the manuals and other documentation.
- [ ] *SMS Security Manager:* The utility for providing access control and user account management.
- [ ] *SMS Service Manager:* The utility that allows you to start and stop the various services that SMS runs.
- [ ] *SMS Setup:* The setup program that allows you to modify your existing setup decisions.

You probably already see a similarity between these offerings and those outlined earlier in the section on SQL Server. This is all part of the BackOffice concept. After you know one product, you more easily can learn the others. It appears that most of the Microsoft product line is heading in this direction of shared GUI interfaces and utilities.

To run SMS on your server requires a minimum of 28MB of RAM, and that is before you run any other services. As usual, consider increasing memory to take better advantage of this and all the NT applications. Do you ever wonder whether Microsoft owns part of Intel or other machine manufacturers? It sometimes appears that way when you see the need for memory increasing all the time, but we guess that's just the price you pay for today's applications.

In addition to the memory you need, you must run a SQL database for SMS to use as its repository. Installing SMS requires about 100MB of disk space, which must reside on an NTFS partition. SMS does not install on a FAT-based partition.

WARNING

> Microsoft recommends that you do not store SMS on a compressed drive because performance suffers. SMS also must be installed on an NTFS partition.

To install SMS, you must first design a site hierarchy to establish how SMS should see your network. Next, you build and configure sites. A site is a logical collection of domains built into an administrative unit and using a central site server for management. Using SMS requires a Site Server, the SQL Server, and the Site Domain Server.

25

A well-designed topology is essential for managing SMS properly and effectively. SMS uses the site concept to distinguish different geographical areas, such as Toronto or New York. You create a Primary Site by establishing an SMS Server in that location. This server is then responsible for maintaining all the information from that site. Any site that doesn't have a SQL Server is a secondary site and is managed by one of the primary sites on the network. Finally, you create one of the SMS Servers as the Central Site for managing all the others.

Designing all this with proper consideration of bandwidth and server capacities is essential. After SMS has been established, it provides for the central collection of all the data from each site, enabling you to quickly gather and report on your inventory information.

SMS Servers use a service called a Sender to communicate with each other. You can use a LAN, RAS, or SNA Sender, depending on your network needs. As indicated by their names, you use the LAN Sender if your servers are on either Ethernet or Token Ring LANs or SNA if you connect to an IBM mainframe. The RAS Sender allows for connectivity through a modem, X.25, or ISDN connection. Many sites use the X.25 connection for international connectivity due to its popularity.

Setting up the SMS Server is not as easy a task as setting up Exchange or SQL Server. It requires up-front thought and planning. We strongly suggest reading the Online Books thoroughly before attempting the initial setup.

The main tool in this package is the SMS Administrator utility. Like most other Office products, it provides a GUI-based view of the maintenance functions available.

Task 25.4. Logging onto the SMS Administrator.

Step 1: Description
This task shows you how to log onto the Administrator tool and be able to use the features it offers.

Step 2: Action
1. Start by selecting Start|Programs|System Management Server|SMS Administrator.
2. SMS displays the Administration Login box. Choose the server and the SQL database if necessary, and type the SQL Server administrator account to sign in. Click OK to continue.
3. You see an Open SMS Administrator dialog box. This might not appear if you previously selected and cleared the Show This Dialog Box option.
4. Select the window Type you want to use. You see a brief description of each window you select. Take a few moments and review this information to familiarize

yourself with the function of each. Click OK when you are ready to continue. You
find a list of each window shown in the following list:

Sites: Displays all the sites in your SMS environment.

Jobs: Allows you to create and administer jobs.

Packages: Manages all the software that SMS inventories or installs.

Alerts: Manages the alerts you enable for informing you of system events.

Machine Groups: Provides the capability to put servers and workstations
into groups for easier administration.

Site Groups: Provides for groups of sites.

Program Groups: Allows for control of shared SMS programs.

Events: Allows for system monitoring of your server.

5. After choosing a window, follow the specific needs of that window.

6. Click the Close button when you finish with SMS Administrator.

Step 3: Review

This simple task showed you how easy it is to use the SMS Administrator tool and manage
your various SMS sites.

In each of the windows outlined previously, double-clicking on a selected item brings you
choices particular to the window you chose. In Sites, you see the properties of the selected
site and gain detailed information about it. The Packages window shows you the elements
necessary for software distribution. You create packages containing the files, configuration
information, and identification data you need for the job and then install it where it is needed.

Three packages are available. The Workstation package provides support for your workstations. Sharing packages allow you to set up data on a network file server for distribution, and
Inventory packages define the rules SMS uses to identify and inventory workstations. After
you create a package, you use the Jobs window to set it up to be delivered and run.

SMS includes a version of Crystal Reports for producing professional reports using the SMS
data it collects about your systems. You can find it on the CD-ROM in the Reports directory.
Included are several preformatted reports that you use as a template. Support is provided by
the Crystal Reports technical staff.

In Remote Control, you are furnished with various useful tools. These include support for
Windows 95 clients and remote chat. This product allows your help desk to communicate
with a remote user via typed text messages that get displayed at the recipient's machine. This
method can sometimes be easier to use than other communication methods. For example,
when the help-desk operator is telling a client what to type, he can show the command instead
of perhaps miscommunicating by voice.

SMS also supports the use of the `ping` command. The administrator can ping the client machine to determine whether it is able to talk on the network.

The SMS package holds great promise for managing the resources of large corporations and for helping to reduce the cost of this management. Organizations spend considerable time and effort upgrading and maintaining desktop computing resources. Budget restrictions and staff reductions pose new challenges for this aspect of system management and control.

Using the Remote Troubleshooting help-desk functions of SMS provides an opportunity for increasing assistance to users while minimizing the associated costs.

The hardware and software inventory controls offer unprecedented opportunity for cost control, compliance checking to corporate standards, and, most important, reduction of the overhead involved in performing all these actions.

Another cost-saving aspect involves using SMS for software distribution. Some of our clients recently performed complete desktop refreshes to install new, consistent software on all their workstations. The task took over one year to perform and involved onsite visits across the organization.

Using SMS solves many issues of cost control, inventory management, and staff reductions. Look for more and more firms to begin using this and similar products.

SNA Server

Unless you are a mainframe bigot, the acronym SNA might be meaningless to you. On the other hand, you might be one of those older folks like us who actually lived through all these cryptic comments about legacy systems, before the golden age of client/server.

SNA, or System Network Architecture, is IBM's protocol for connecting networks. It is definitely an older architecture, but it is still the de facto network for all the "big iron" in use today. So you might need to live with this architecture if an IBM mainframe is in your organization and you are going to connect to it.

Microsoft's SNA Server is one answer to this connectivity dilemma. It seeks to provide a simple (as simple as mainframe connectivity can be, that is) solution for you.

To connect to SNA networks involves attaching to the particular wiring scheme and managing access in products that support this complex network, such as VTAM and Netview.

One other solution is to connect each machine by using terminal emulation cards and the software to run the cards. Each machine then uses both a LAN access and a terminal emulation card and cable for mainframe access. This method provides for duplication of the components; it isn't always the most cost-effective method.

Finally, IBM is announcing even more support for TCP/IP within its large mainframes. This is likely the route to go as these services become more available and more stable. Newer versions of IBM's operating system even offer complete UNIX compatibility. All of this serves only to enhance the prospect of easier connectivity between these older systems and the newer client/server technologies.

Using an SNA network involves various critical network functions and is beyond the scope of this book. Here you learned that connectivity is possible and that with the assistance of your mainframe experts, you connect your NT Server to the mainframe by using SNA Server.

The Newer Products

You learned about the basic BackOffice products in the earlier sections. Here you'll learn a little about some of the newer, more commercially oriented products that have been added to BackOffice in the past year. We recommend that you visit the Microsoft Web site at `www.microsoft.com/backoffice` for more detailed information because these tools are highly specialized.

Microsoft Merchant Server

This product allows customers to build stores and sell products over the Internet. It offers templates of store designs and order-acceptance tools that you can adapt to your own business needs. There is built-in order management that handles inventory, tax, shipping and payment processing, and so forth. It includes a security component that helps ensure that processing orders and getting customer credit information is handled safely and reliably. It uses a secure payment support method called Verifone vPOS, an Internet-based payment-processing software solution.

Vendors might purchase and use this product to begin an Internet-based store and offer goods and services online.

Microsoft Commercial Internet System

This is a product aimed at and sold to Internet Service Providers, public network operators, and Internet Content Providers. It offers a full set of Internet services.

The highly scaleable server components can be fully integrated with the BackOffice family and other Internet standards-based products. These products share a common installation, system administration, and security framework, making them easier to manage.

For commercial service providers, this offering enables them to provide services to their customers. It includes Microsoft Commercial Internet Mail Server, Microsoft Commercial Internet News Server, Microsoft Membership System, Microsoft Content Replication System, Microsoft Personalization System, Microsoft Conference Server, and Microsoft Merchant Server. As you see, it's not for the ordinary organization.

Microsoft Proxy Server

Proxy Server helps prevents unauthorized Internet users from connecting to your organization's private network, integrating tightly with your Windows NT Server user authentication. This enables your system administrator to control who uses the Internet and which services they use.

You can deliver high-performance Internet access to the desktop by using Proxy Server. By sharing a single, secure gateway, the product eliminates the need to share one dedicated machine for the Internet among multiple users, or to run multiple Internet lines into the organization to provide each desktop with a separate connection. This technique helps keep costs down and simplifies Internet administration.

To use Proxy Server, you must install Microsoft Windows NT Server Version 4.0, Microsoft Internet Information Server Version 2.0, which is included with Windows NT Server 4.0, and the latest Windows NT Server 4.0 Service Pack. The Service Pack is provided on the product's CD-ROM.

25

Microsoft Transaction Server

Transaction Server is a product that provides flexibility and low cost with transaction processing features normally found in high-end mainframe systems. It is a system for developing, deploying, and managing Internet and intranet server applications. Transaction Server defines an application programming model for developing distributed, component-based applications. It also provides a runtime infrastructure for deploying and managing these applications.

Microsoft indicates that Transaction Server defines a simpler process for programming and executing distributed, component-based server applications. These applications are developed as though they are for a single user. When they are made to execute within the Transaction Server environment, the server application automatically enables support for many concurrent clients with high performance and reliability.

Summary

You learned the products that BackOffice consists of and how to use them on your server. In addition, you learned how to install each product and manage its use. Finally, you became familiar with the different products and realized their particular benefits.

In this chapter you discovered the following points:

☐ What BackOffice is and what the various components are

☐ How to install the different components

☐ How SQL Server provides database management

☐ Whether SMS needs an NTFS partition or whether it can use a FAT-based system

☐ What SMS Server does and why it is useful

☐ The memory requirements of Microsoft Exchange

☐ That Microsoft Exchange must be installed on either a primary Domain Controller (PDC) or a Backup Domain Controller (BDC), but not on a standalone server

☐ The differences between primary and secondary sites in SMS Server

☐ How to use SNA Server to connect to IBM mainframe computers and their specific network topology

☐ That there are several new BackOffice products designed to enhance your ability to do business over the Internet

Workshop

To wrap up the day, you can review terms and tasks from the chapter, and see the answers to some commonly asked questions.

Terminology Review

ANSI—The acronym for the American National Standards Institute. In Windows NT, it is often used to refer to the character set used in the product.

concurrency—Often used to describe a database management tool's capability to simultaneously handle multiple queries against a database table.

database—A collection of related tables and other objects that are organized into a collection managed by a database application.

packages—A term used in SMS to describe the collection of data for producing change in remote systems.

protocol—A description of the method in which networked computers communicate with each other.

query—A database request for retrieving or manipulating data typically using SQL statements.

SMS—An acronym for Systems Management Server. It provides the capability to monitor, manipulate servers, and distribute client software.

SNA—The IBM mainframe network protocol. An acronym for System Network Architecture.

SQL—Structured Query Language. Usually pronounced like the word *sequel.* A language used as a standard for accessing database information and providing reports and data manipulation.

Task List

The information provided in this chapter showed you how to manage the files and folders within an NT server. You learned to perform the following tasks:

- ☐ Install BackOffice products
- ☐ Run the Microsoft Exchange Optimizer program
- ☐ Add a new user to a SQL Server database
- ☐ Log in to the SMS Administrator

25

Q&A

Q Do the BackOffice products come as part of the NT Server 4.0 software?

A No. Although the Internet Information Server and FrontPage program are being combined with NT Server 4.0, Microsoft sells the BackOffice products as a separate entity. This is becoming a lucrative market for Microsoft, we believe, as interest in using the new electronic mail Exchange Server and the SMS distribution components grows.

Q What products do come with BackOffice, and can I buy them separately?

A BackOffice has four major components. They consist of Microsoft Exchange, an electronic mail server; SQL Server, a relational database management system; System Management Server, or SMS, which provides for distribution of software from a central site and inventory management; and finally, SNA Server, which allows your network to talk with IBM mainframes on their System Network Architecture network. Microsoft does not offer these products for sale individually.

They wouldn't be a suite then, would they? Note that NT Server 4.0 is included in the bundle, so technically you could say it is part of BackOffice, but our intent is to show the additional components, not NT Server, in this chapter. You also find that several new components have been added to the original BackOffice offering. These include Microsoft Merchant Server, Microsoft Commercial Internet System, Microsoft Proxy, and Microsoft Transaction Server. The BackOffice suite is changing rapidly with new products being added regularly. Visit the Microsoft Web page to get the most recent information.

Q My organization uses mainframes and IBM AS/400 machines. Will I be able to connect my network to these machines?

A Microsoft provides a tool called the SNA Server for connecting SNA-based networks with your local area or wide area network. Doing so, however, is an arduous task that must be considered carefully, because typically mainframes are still the primary mission-critical systems and they cannot afford network problems. Be sure to talk with your mainframe folks before attempting to set up and run this service.

Chapter **26**

Using NT with the Internet Information Server

If you want to be a Webmaster, and you want to use Windows NT 4.0 Server as your Internet platform, then this is your chapter.

You would have to be living under a rock if you haven't heard of the Internet and the Web. You hardly can read a newspaper or a news magazine without finding an article or essay on the explosion of the Internet. Why? Because the Internet and the most popular application running on it, the World Wide Web (the Web or WWW), provide many of the basic elements required to connect people globally with the information they seek.

The WWW itself is an information protocol designed specifically for the Internet. Today, the Web has more sites than any other Internet service. Thus, the Web is the most popular and fastest growing part of the Internet, which is itself exploding.

The World Wide Web is built on top of the Internet backbone and uses the Transport Control Protocol/Internet Protocol (TCP/IP) to transport information between Web clients and Web servers. Web servers are not just for the Internet. Web servers also provide a new and unique way to make information available to internal network (intranet) users. With the secure channel and authentication features of Microsoft's Internet Explorer (and other browsers), you can establish secure connections between clients and servers on your network with little trouble. Windows NT includes the Microsoft Internet Information Server (IIS), so your startup costs for implementing Web-based intranet or Internet servers are minimal.

NOTE This chapter covers basic Internet Information Server issues. Security is an important issue for organizations considering the use of the Internet. You'll learn a little about Internet security in this chapter, but it does not explore the incredibly vast issues of security on the Internet. For more information on security issues in general, check with the Computer Emergency Response Team (CERT) (http://www.cert.org) at Carnegie-Mellon University in Pittsburgh, PA.

There's more to the Internet than the Web, a fact recognized by Microsoft, as World Wide Web, Gopher, and FTP servers are included with Windows NT Server. Indeed, you can find other acceptable and desirable alternatives to IIS. For other Internet services such as electronic mail and Usenet news, you need to install non-Microsoft products to meet your users' needs.

If you plan to set up a Web server for internal or external access, the information in this chapter will help you set up the IIS for your Windows NT Server network.

Some Pre-Installation Tasks

Internet Information Server 2.0 requires Windows NT Server 4.0; you can't use it with Windows NT Server 3.5x. You need to be sure that you properly configured the TCP/IP installation on your Windows NT 4.0 Server for the Internet services.

You can run multiple Internet servers on your Windows NT 4.0 Server (such as www.pda1.com and www.pda2.com). Doing so, however, requires that you go to the Advanced TCP/IP Configuration settings and assign multiple IP addresses to your network card connecting to the Internet.

26

NOTE

In general, a single IIS installation can support up to five virtual servers. Using more than five requires you to jump through hoops and delve into the depths of your IIS documentation.

Before installing the Internet Information Server software, you should already have the following items:

☐ *Software:* Microsoft Internet Information Server 2.0 software.

☐ *Network Connection:* To allow your organization to access the server through a Web browser, both the server and the client machines need to install TCP/IP.

During the installation, you need to enter the Internet information from the following list, so you should obtain this information in advance from your Internet service provider (ISP).

☐ The numeric IP address for your Windows NT Server. (If you don't have an Internet connection, obtain this address from your ISP.)

☐ The computer name (the name chosen by whoever performed your installation) of your Windows NT Server (also called the "Web Server" in this chapter).

☐ The e-mail address of the Web server administrator (used to support the users who'll access information on the server).

☐ The numeric IP address for your DNS server (also available from your ISP).

If you're setting up Internet Information Server for internal publishing (on your intranet), you might want to install the Microsoft Windows Internet Name Service (WINS). This step is optional, especially for a smaller system, but this way, users can employ friendly names instead of IP addresses when connecting to your server from your internal network.

26

Installing the Microsoft Internet Information Server

You have the option of installing IIS when you install Windows NT 4.0. If you didn't install IIS at that time, you must install it from the Windows NT 4.0 CD-ROM. You must do so manually, but you can install remotely from a workstation where you're logged on as system administrator. You need the Windows NT 4.0 installation CD-ROM and a connection to the Internet. (If you're installing for an intranet, you need to have WINS or DNS installed and running.)

TIP

As far as security goes, it's best if you install IIS on a Windows NT 4.0 server that's using the NTFS file system. Then you should enable auditing.

NOTE

You can find the documentation for installing the Microsoft Internet Information Server by choosing Start|Microsoft Internet Server (Common)|Product Documentation. The Books Online help system used for most Windows NT 4.0 documentation doesn't contain information about Internet tools.

Notice that the Internet documentation is stored in HTML pages, not in the normal Windows Help format. You also can access these Web pages by pointing your Web browser to

`file:///C¦/WINNT/SYSTEM32/INETSRV/IISADMIN/HTMLDOCS/Inetdocs.htm`

If you haven't installed IIS yet, you can find the Inetdocs.htm in the I386\Inetsrv\Htmldocs directory on the Windows NT Server CD-ROM.

You can set up the Microsoft Internet Information Server in a matter of minutes. It loads as a service and runs in the background after it's installed. In fact, after running the setup procedure, you can start a browser on your own network and access the sample Web documents immediately.

Most of your involvement with the server will be in planning the connections to your intranet or to the Internet, deciding on the structure and content of the Web server, and planning security, which includes figuring out who can access the server and what level of access the users will have. Some tools and techniques for managing the server are covered in the following sections.

Adding Microsoft Internet Information Server is as simple as starting the Setup program on the CD-ROM. If you already have the necessary Internet or intranet connection, you can accept all the default settings during setup. The default setup configurations are suitable for many organizations without any further modifications.

Internet Information Server installs with some helpful sample home pages you can use as a starting point to create your own home pages. After you write your own page, you can replace the sample content and have your own personalized Web server.

26

Task 26.1. Installing Internet Information Server.

Step 1: Description

To install the Internet Information Server services in this task, you must be logged on with Administrator privileges. In addition, to configure the Internet Information Server services by using the Internet Service Manager, your user account must be a member of the Administrators group on the Windows NT Server. At this time, you select the default settings.

Step 2: Action

1. If you need to install IIS, run the file I386\Inetsrv\Inetstp.exe from the Windows NT 4.0 CD-ROM.

2. After you read the copyright information, click OK.

3. Click the Add/Remove button.

> **NOTE**
>
> Click the Help button to get assistance any time you're using a dialog box. When you do so, Setup displays a dialog box explaining the choices you have and the procedures to follow.

4. Specify the location for the installation of the IIS files. You can accept the default if you so choose. Click OK. A second Microsoft Internet Server Setup dialog box appears, displaying the installation options as shown in Figure 26.1.

26

Figure 26.1.

The Microsoft Internet Information Server 2.0 Setup dialog box.

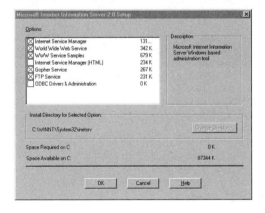

All the following items are selected for installation by default. If you don't want to install a particular item, click the box to clear it.

Internet Service Manager installs the administration program for managing the services.

World Wide Web Service creates a WWW publishing server.

WWW Service Samples installs sample HTML files.

Gopher Service creates a Gopher publishing server.

FTP Service creates a File Transfer Protocol (FTP) publishing server.

The following are options:

> Internet Service Manager (HTML) installs the HTML-based manager's tool.
>
> ODBC Drivers and Administration installs Open Data Base Connectivity (ODBC) drivers. They are required for logging onto ODBC files and for enabling ODBC access from the WWW service.

You can use the Setup program later to add or remove components. You also can use Setup to remove all Microsoft Internet Information Server components.

5. Click OK to accept the default installation directory (C:\INETSRV), or click Change Directory to enter a new directory.

Setup copies the files needed by Microsoft Internet Information Server and creates the Registry entries for all services. If you selected the ODBC Drivers and Administration option box, the Install Drivers dialog box appears.

The installation program then installs the services you've specified. You shouldn't be asked for any input during this process until the program hits the installation procedure for the ODBC drivers. At the time this book was written, the only ODBC driver available was for SQL Server.

6. To install the Microsoft SQL Server driver, select SQL Server Driver from the Available ODBC Drivers list, and then click OK. Setup completes copying files.

Note

If you have SQL Server 6.5 installed with the service pack applied, a dialog box appears, asking whether you want to overwrite a newer SQL Server file with an older one.

Step 3: Review

The preceding task is all you need to do for a simple installation of Microsoft Internet Information Server. You now are ready to publish on the Internet or your intranet. To make

26

configuration changes or to add additional directories, start the Internet Server Manager and view the Help files, if necessary.

After the installation, you see a new group called Microsoft Internet Server (Common) under the Start menu. You go to this group when you want to later install a service (for example, you might not have installed FTP originally, but your users are clamoring for the service). Under this menu, you can select Internet Information Server Setup. Then you are presented with a Microsoft Internet Information Server 2.0 Setup dialog box, where you have three choices:

- ☐ Add/Remove
- ☐ Reinstall
- ☐ Remove All

These choices are pretty straightforward. The Add/Remove button (which you used the first time you installed) enables you to add or remove specific Internet components. The Reinstall choice enables you to reinstall specific Internet components if important files have been deleted or altered beyond recognition; no new components are installed, and the only changes are performed on already-installed components. The Remove All button does exactly as advertised: It deletes all hints of Internet Information Server software from your server, although the content files created for Internet use remain.

Web Protocols and Standards

By now, you should be somewhat familiar with the terms presented here. The World Wide Web Server is an HTTP server that facilitates transactions between a Web browser and a Web server. Gopher is an information publishing protocol that uses menus to access text files. File Transfer Protocol, or FTP, oversees file transfers between Internet software and an FTP server. ODBC drivers are used to connect with ODBC-compliant databases using SQL statements.

Testing Your Microsoft Internet Information Server Installation

After installation, any services you specified for installation should be up and running. You can have an instant Internet or intranet by copying content files in the home directories you agreed to earlier in the installation process. You can copy the World Wide Web pages, for example, to the \wwwroot directory.

26

Testing the Internet Server

IIS places a home page called default.htm in the \iisadmin directory. You can check whether the installation succeeded by opening a connection to the Internet with a Web browser (such as Internet Explorer or Netscape Navigator) and viewing the files in your home directory.

Task 26.2. Testing a server connected to the Internet.

Step 1: Description

In this task, you test your installation by using Internet Explorer or Netscape Navigator to view the files in your home directory.

Step 2: Action

1. Start Internet Explorer (or other Web browser) on a computer that has an active connection to the Internet. This computer can be the server you're testing, although using a different computer is recommended.

2. Type the Uniform Resource Locator (URL) for the home directory of your new server. The URL is `http://` followed by the name of your server, followed by the path of the file you want to view. (Note the forward slashes.) If your server is registered in DNS as `www.pda.com`, for example, and you want to view the file homepage.htm in the root of the home directory, in the Location box you type

   `http://www.pda.com/homepage.htm`

   and then press Enter. The home page should appear on the screen.

Step 3: Review

In this task, you installed IIS on a machine named `pda.com` and viewed the default.htm file, using the following URL: `http://www.pda.com/default.htm`. The default home page then appeared on the screen.

Error Messages

You might receive a few error messages. The most common one appears when your service provider hasn't yet installed your DNS entry and your Web browser can't find your Internet location. This error message should end when your service provider finalizes your Internet installation.

The other common error message occurs when the Web browser successfully finds your Web site but can't find the file. This situation usually occurs when you've misnamed a file (such as default.html rather than default.htm).

Testing the Intranet Server

You use some slightly different procedures to test your intranet server; these changes are mostly due to the different naming conventions used in an intranet.

After making sure that the DNS or WINS services are running, you can fire up your Web browser to connect to the server. Instead of specifying an Internet machine name like www.pda.com, you specify the Windows machine name (such as oriole), followed by the directory (if needed) and the filename you want to view. To view the HTML page named default.htm on the Windows machine named oriole, you use the following URL:

```
http://oriole/default.htm
```

The default home page should appear on the screen.

You might think that a few things are odd about this system (and when compared to the Internet and Windows conventions at large, they are). Even though you're running on a Windows NT system, you still use slashes (/) to specify paths (not the backward slashes used in the DOS/Windows world). Because you're going right to a file, you don't need to tell the Web browser what sort of file (HTML, FTP, Gopher) you're grabbing.

Task 26.3. Testing a server on your intranet.

Step 1: Description

In this task, you test a server on your intranet by using Internet Explorer, Netscape Navigator, or another Web browser to view your home page.

Step 2: Action

1. Ensure that your computer has an active network connection.
2. Start Internet Explorer or your Web browser.
3. Type the URL for the home directory of your new server. The URL is http:// followed by your Windows NT Server name, followed by the path of the file you want to view. (Note the forward slash marks.) When your server is registered with the WINS Server as Admin, for example, and you want to view the file homepage.htm in the root of the home directory, in the Location box you type

   ```
   http://admin/homepage.htm
   ```

   and then press Enter. The home page should appear on the screen.

Step 3: Review

In this task, you used Internet Explorer (or your Web browser) to view the default.htm on your intranet.

TASK

26

Configuring IIS with the Internet Service Manager

Internet Information Service uses the Internet Service Manager to oversee the World Wide Web server and any other Internet services (such as, Gopher or FTP) you have running. The Server Manager is a Windows-based graphical management tool you use to configure the server and its security options. You use it to manage Web services, FTP services, and Gopher services. It is installed automatically on the Web server itself, but you can copy the files to any Windows NT system and manage Internet Information Servers on the network.

To start the Server Manager, choose Start|Programs|Microsoft Internet Server (Common)| Internet Service Manager. You then double-click the server you want to manage and choose one of the property sheets. The options on these property sheets are discussed throughout the remainder of this chapter.

With property sheets, you can manage the following tasks:

- Establishing logon requirements
- Configuring access permissions
- Specifying home directories and other virtual directories
- Creating multiple virtual servers on a single computer
- Setting encryption options
- Configuring event logging options
- Viewing current sessions
- Enabling or disabling server access for specific IP addresses

Working with Properties

From the Internet Service Manager window, you can change properties by double-clicking on a service. Because the WWW service is popular now, the following sections deal with changing the properties of that service.

The WWW Service Properties are governed by their own dialog box. It has four property sheets: Service, Directories, Logging, and Advanced.

The Service Property Sheet

The most important aspects of the configuration options of the Service property sheet govern who can access the WWW service and under what conditions. Each one is covered here.

Connection Time-out

The Connection Time-out setting specifies how long (in seconds) before a connection between the server and an inactive user will be severed. Closing inactive connections is important for a busy Web site; you don't want inactive users to keep valuable connections alive. In addition, the HTTP protocol can contain small errors that do not change a connection when one has been specified by the user.

Anonymous Logon

When you install the Microsoft Internet Information Server, a special anonymous Guest account is created with the name IUSR_*computername,* where *computername* is the name of the server (or the *anonymous user account).* This account can log on locally, so when someone accesses the Web server without providing any sort of logon credentials, that person is granted access to the server as if he or she were logging on locally (at the console). The account is a member of the Guests local group and the Domain Users group.

WARNING

> You don't want to leave this anonymous account online for too long. Intruders know that this account exists and will try to use it to gain access to your system. Change it as soon as possible.

The anonymous user account does not require users to enter usernames or passwords, which makes it easy for users to access your server.

After you create a directory and add it to the Directories property sheet, anonymous users can access a designated directory under three conditions:

- ☐ The Everyone group has at least Read or Execute rights in the directory
- ☐ The IUSR_*computername* account has been specifically granted at least Read or Execute rights in the directory
- ☐ The Guests group (of which IUSR_*computername* is a member) has been specifically granted at least Read or Execute rights in the directory

If you create a directory and want only anonymous users to access the directory, remove the Everyone and Guests groups from the permissions list and add only the IUSR_ *computername* account.

If Everyone or the IUSR_*computername* account does not have permission to access a directory, anonymous users cannot access the directory. By removing these two groups, you restrict a directory to anonymous Web users and require logon access, as described next.

26

Password Authentication

If you want to restrict access to a directory to only users who have accounts on the server, and require those users to log on when they access the Web server, follow these steps:

1. Restrict anonymous user access to directories by removing Everyone, Guests, and IUSR_*computername* accounts from the permission list for the directory.

2. Add the specific user or group you want to access the directory, and assign the appropriate access rights by making a selection in the Type of Access field.

3. In the Internet Service Manager, add the directory to the Directories property sheet if it is not a subdirectory of a directory that is already specified.

4. Enable Basic or Challenge/Response on the Service dialog box. These options are discussed later in this chapter.

The following are the three levels of access for the Web server:

☐ *Allow Anonymous:* This anonymous user option allows Web users to log onto the IUSR_*computername* account. When this option is enabled (the default), users can access directories where Everyone, the Guests group, and/or the IUSR_*computername* accounts have access. If Allow Anonymous is checked and the Basic and Windows NT Challenge/Response check boxes are both cleared, only anonymous users can log on. If you disable this option, you must enable Basic or Windows NT Challenge/Response (then all users must log on by providing usernames and passwords, and those users must have appropriate user accounts on the Web server before any users can log on).

☐ *Basic (Clear Text):* The Basic option requires users to enter usernames and passwords to access a secure folder. This feature is useful when you want to set up a "subscription" service that requires users to log on with a password after they have been "registered" with the service. This option sends passwords in scrambled clear text, a code that's easy for any hacker to break. The password could be compromised, and if it is the same password that users use to log onto more secure accounts, a hacker who captures the password could gain unauthorized access to those accounts. Use this option with care. If you require logon for users who access non-sensitive information, however, perhaps you require passwords as a formality and encryption is not essential.

☐ *Windows NT Challenge/Response:* This option assumes that users have already been authenticated by some other Windows NT (or compatible) computer. When this option is set, the header information in the user's HTTP requests, which contains the user's credentials (username and password), is used to log the user onto the restricted directory. This option is mostly used where the Web server is connected to an internal intranet and users on the network have already been logged on, although you also can use it over the Internet. The Windows NT Challenge/

Response protocol uses an encryption technique that prevents passwords from being transmitted across the network in the clear. At the time of this writing, however, this type of encryption is supported only by Microsoft Internet Explorer browsers.

When the Web server receives a client request that contains credentials, the anonymous logon user account is bypassed, and the credentials are used by the service to log on the user.

Comments

Comments is a text line that appears on the main Internet Server Manager window.

The Directories Property Sheet

The Directories property sheet governs what directories and files are used by the Web.

Directory Listing Box

The Directory Listing box lists which directories are used by the server. It has four columns:

☐ Directory lists the directory path.

☐ Alias is the virtual directories path(s).

☐ Address is the IP address of the directory.

☐ Error lists any errors generated by the system.

By clicking the Add button, you can add directories and virtual servers (complete with their own IP addresses) to this list. You can use the Windows NT tools to browse through directories on the server or on the network. In addition, you can make these directories and virtual servers read-only, so users cannot run programs on them. To make changes with these settings on an existing directory, use the Edit Properties button.

Edit Properties enables you to edit the properties of a path. It's actually the same dialog box you see when you add a directory or virtual server by using the Add button.

The Remove button removes a directory.

After you add a new directory to your server for Web users to access, you add it to the Directories property sheet so that you can set special options. Note that you don't need to add a directory to this list if it is the subdirectory of a directory that is already listed, but if you want to set the special options described here, add it to the list. Click the new directory in the list, and then click the Edit Properties button.

You can specify three types of access for directory permissions:

26

☐ *Read:* With the Read setting, users can view the files in the directory but cannot change the files or add files of their own. This option is the most secure. You enable the Read option on publishing directories and disable it on directories that contain programs, so clients can't download your programs.

☐ *Execute:* With the Execute setting, users can start applications or scripts in the directory. A client request could execute a CGI application or an ISAPI (defined later) application if you type the filename of the application in the URL. You also can use the Web File Extension Mapping feature, which allows your executables and DLLs to be stored somewhere other than the Web publishing tree. You use Web File Extension Mapping to locate a file on the local Web server or another Web server. Refer to the Microsoft Internet Information Server help system for information on the mapping features.

☐ *Require Secure SSL Channel:* When you install Secure Sockets Layer, the Require Secure SSL Channel option is available and allows for the private transmission of information in the directory to the client. When you enable this option, a secure channel with encryption is used between the client and the server.

When you install the Microsoft Internet Information Server, a directory called \SCRIPTS is created. This directory has the Execute permission (not the Read permission) and branches from the root directory of the installation drive. You should store all your Internet Server API (ISAPI) applications and Common Gateway (CGI) scripts in this directory, or create another directory with the same Execute permission for storing scripts.

NOTE

Do not enable the Write permission on directories that hold executable scripts. Intruders or hackers can use the directory to upload and run programs that damage your system.

Enable Default Document

The Enable Default Document setting specifies a default document that users will always see when they log onto your Web server and do not list a specific file. This document is usually called default.htm or index.htm.

Directory Browsing Allowed

If the Directory Browsing Allowed box is selected, users can browse through directory listings sent back by the Web server. If you have a completely secure system and don't mind making all the files visible to a Web browser user, you can select this button. If you're storing files on a server and want to make sure that a user knows exactly what he or she wants when connecting to your Web server, leave this box unchecked.

The Logging Property Sheet

The Logging property sheet tells IIS what to log and when. Logging is an important tool when evaluating your Web server and supported traffic.

Basically, logging tells you who logged onto your Web server (well, the IP addresses of those logging on, anyway), when they logged on, and under what circumstances. This information is valuable as you analyze your server loads and where the hits are coming from. In addition, this information can be passed along to Web analysis tools that perform detailed analyses of your Web traffic.

TIP

IIS uses its own log text format. If you want to convert the log files to European Microsoft Windows Academic Centre (EMWAC) or CERN common log format, you need to use the `convlog.exe` DOS command. For a discussion on how to use this utility, refer to the section "Converting Log Files."

Enable Logging

The Enable Logging check box determines whether logging is turned on. You'll want to enable logging.

NOTE

The logging mechanism you choose here applies only to the specified service, not to the server as a whole. The default is to log everything to the same file. You can log Gopher and FTP requests to one log, however, and your server requests to another.

Log to File

The Log to File option logs information to a text file rather than to an ODBC database. Unless you have some analysis tools that require SQL/ODBC input, you probably will log information to a text file. Because most third-party analysis tools use CERN or EMWAC common log files as input, you need to begin with text-format files to get these files out of IIS.

Automatically Open New Log

The Automatically Open New Log check box tells IIS when to open a new log, as opposed to keeping one huge log. Smaller log files are easier to analyze and manage. The default is to start a new log file daily, although most sites get along fine with new logs weekly. If your Web site isn't really busy, you can probably get by with new logs monthly. You also have the option of opening a new log file when the log file reaches a certain size, a handy option for busy sites.

If you choose to open a log on a daily, weekly, or monthly basis, the system closes existing log files when a new log record is entered after midnight of the last day of the existing log file. If you look at the new log file, you'll see that it includes the first day activity took place.

 NOTE IIS also enforces other log limits. The maximum size of a log-file line is 1,200 bytes, with 150 bytes maximum per field in a log text file and 200 bytes maximum per field in an ODBC log file.

Log File Directory

The Log File Directory field specifies the directory where log files are stored. The default is C:\WINNT\System32\LogFiles. Each log file is stored with similar filenames. If you choose a new log file to be opened at a specific time (daily, weekly, or monthly), the log file begins with IN, followed by the year, month, and date, with a suffix of log. A log file opened on January 1, 1997, therefore, would be named IN970101.log, with an absolute pathname of C:\WINNT\System32\LogFiles\IN970101.log.

If you select the size of the file to determine when a new log is opened, the filename format is S*nnn*.log (where *nnn* is a number that's increased each time a new log file is opened). If you don't choose to open a new log at some interval, the log file is called SLOG.

Log to SQL/ODBC Database

The Log to SQL/ODBC Database option logs information to a database rather than to a log file. This requires that such a database already be set up using the ODBC applet in the Windows NT 4.0 Control Panel. You must enter the following parameters:

- ☐ Datasource
- ☐ Table (not the filename of the table)
- ☐ Username
- ☐ Password

The Advanced Property Sheet

The items in the Advanced property sheet control who can log onto your Web server and the amount of outgoing Internet traffic. These settings have to do with basic system security.

IP Access Control

On the Advanced property sheet, you specify who can access your Web server based on IP addresses. The IP Access Control section of the property sheet controls who can access your Web server. The default is to allow everyone access (as indicated by the Granted Access radio button). You can narrow down this access by specifying IP addresses not allowed access. List IP addresses and subnet masks to be denied access under the Except those listed below: section. You can choose the Add button to specify a particular IP address or a range of IP addresses. You might want to block the IP address of a competitor, for example, to prevent people in that company from accessing your server, or block the IP address of someone who is overrunning your server with requests in a denial-of-service attack.

The two models for specifying IP addresses are Granted Access and Denied Access:

- *Granted Access:* Allows all hosts access to the Web server, except for the IP addresses that are added to the Lower Exception list box.
- *Denied Access:* Denies all hosts access to the Web server, except for the IP addresses added to the Lower Exception list box. You can choose the Add button to specify an IP address or a range of IP addresses. For example, you might choose to limit access to all computers except those using IP addresses controlled by your organization. To do so, you select the Denied Access radio button and add your organization's IP addresses.

You must specify one of the models and then add IP addresses to the Exception list box:

- *Add button:* Click this button to add IP addresses to the exception list.
- *Limit Network Use by all Internet Services on This Computer:* Use this option to control the amount of traffic that the Web server generates. Enabling this option prevents one server from taking up too much of the bandwidth on a shared connection.

Restricting access by IP address is not a foolproof security measure. A hacker or intruder simply can move to a computer with a different IP address or change the IP address. It is, however, an effective way to block known users on your own internal network or users who are flooding your network with unnecessary or intrusive requests.

Limit Network Use

When selected, the Limit Network Use by All Internet Services on This Computer button monitors all outgoing connections from your Internet server and cuts off access when the network traffic reaches a certain point.

26

Managing and Analyzing Log Files

Earlier in this chapter, you learned how to set up the logging capabilities of the Internet Information Server. In the following sections, you'll delve more into the topic.

When someone logs onto your Internet server, that person leaves a trail of what he or she did and when he or she did it. This information is stored in the IIS log files. You learned about log files earlier in this chapter when you followed the steps needed to set them up.

A log file has 14 fields:

- [ ] *Client's IP address:* Lists the Internet Protocol address of the client logging on the server.
- [ ] *Client's username:* Refers to the name of the client when you've chosen mechanisms for which users need to log on.
- [ ] *Date:* Self-explanatory.
- [ ] *Time:* Self-explanatory.
- [ ] *Service:* Refers to the Internet service requests. *W3SVC* refers to the World Wide Web service, *MSFTPSVC* refers to the Microsoft FTP service, and *GopherSvc* refers to the Gopher service.
- [ ] *Computer name:* Refers to the computer name of the server.
- [ ] *IP address of server:* Refers to the IP address of the server.
- [ ] *Processing time:* Specifies the CPU time used by the client.
- [ ] *Bytes received:* Specifies the number of bytes sent from the client to the server, usually in the form of HTTP requests.
- [ ] *Bytes sent:* Specifies the bytes sent from the server to the client.
- [ ] *Service status code:* Refers to a special number that indicates what action was taken.
- [ ] *Windows NT status code:* Specifies a numeral used by the Windows NT Server to indicate what action was taken.
- [ ] *Name of the operation:* Tells what the client asked of the server. For Web servers, the most common operations are GET, HEAD, or POST, whereas other services use their list of operations (for example, the FTP server typically uses file to indicate a file request).
- [ ] *Target of the operation:* Specifies a file on your server, such as index.htm.

NOTE

These fields are separated by commas. Where no information exists for a field, a hyphen (-) is used.

Converting Log Files

The Microsoft IIS uses its own log file format. Microsoft, however, has included a utility called convlog.exe to convert IIS logs to two formats widely used in the Internet world: the EMWAC log file format or the Common Log Format.

To run convlog.exe and see a list of options, open a command prompt and enter the following command lines:

```
C:\> cd \winnt\system32\inetsrv
C:\winnt\system32\inetsrv>convlog
```

The syntax for the convlog.exe is

```
convlog options LogFile
```

where *options* refers to command-line options and *LogFile* refers to the log file being converted.

Table 26.1 lists several useful command-line options.

Table 26.1. Convlog options.

Option	Description
-s[f¦g¦w]	Specifies the services to convert. The default is to convert log entries for all services (you don't need to use -s if this is what you want), but you can specify an individual service (f for FTP, g for Gopher, and w for World Wide Web).
-t[emwac ¦ ncsa[:GMTOffset] ¦ none]	Specifies the format of the new log file. The default is to use the EMWAC format.
-o	Specifies the directory for the output. The default is to use the current directory.
-f	Specifies the temporary file used by Convlog to convert the files. The default is to use the default temporary file as specified in the tmp system variable (usually C:\TEMP).
-n[m[cachesize]¦i]	Converts IP addresses to computer or domain names. The default is not to do so. If you do decide to perform this conversion, use the m command-line option; you use the accompanying *cachesize* to designate how large a cache to use in this operation (the default is 5,000 bytes).

26

Setting Up an ODBC/SQL Database for Log Records

When you set up your server logging mechanisms, you had the choice to set up an ODBC link to an SQL database.

The default in IIS is to send all log entries to a log file. You must tell IIS to send log information to an ODBC driver, where it is sent to the SQL database.

Other Tools and Techniques

The Windows NT Server and the Microsoft Internet Information Server include some additional features, as follow:

- [ ] You can write server programs using the Common Gateway Interface (CGI) or Microsoft's Internet Server API (ISAPI). Of the two, ISAPI is your best bet because it compiles programs into libraries that get loaded into the Internet server's memory and stay there, thus improving performance. Another advantage of ISAPI is achieved by "pluggable" filters, which allow preprocessing of requests and post-processing of responses. This feature permits site-specific handling of HTTP requests and responses. There were some security breaches using CGI in the first version of the Internet Information Server.

- [ ] You can limit the amount of information that can be sent from the server at any one time so that other requests can be serviced with a fair share of time through bandwidth throttling.

- [ ] You can set up several Internet Information Servers on their own network isolated from your internal network but connected to the Internet. You then can manage these servers with the Internet Service Manager running from a Windows NT workstation.

- [ ] The server creates logs that contain information about user activity. You can view logs to see what has been accessed and when. Server logs must initially be configured.

- [ ] The Windows NT Performance Monitor utility can perform real-time measurements of your Web server and provide statistical information you can use to troubleshoot the system, track usage, or justify the need to upgrade equipment.

- [ ] You can use SSL, PCT, or TLS. Microsoft Web clients and servers support the Secure Sockets Layer (SSL) and the Private Communication Technology (PCT) protocols for securing a communication channel. SSL is an older standard, whereas PCT is a more efficient and secure upgrade to the SSL protocol. The Microsoft Internet Security Framework supports SSL versions 2.0 and 3.0 and PCT version 1.0, as well as a new security protocol called Transport Layer Security (TLS).

26

TLS incorporates both SSL and PCT into a single standard that supports both certificates and password-based authentication.

Getting the Word Out That You're Up and Running!

Setting up a Web site on a Windows NT Server can be fun, easy, and rewarding, especially when you're using Microsoft Internet Information Server. After you've set up your site, don't forget to spread the word. You can send a message to the Usenet newsgroup comp.infosystems.www.announce and register your Web site with the "What's New" sections of major search engines, such as Excite, Lycos, and Yahoo!, to let the world know you're online.

You can inform the search engines and lists in several ways. You can submit information to each search engine in turn; not many major search engines are available yet, so submitting information won't take much of your time. You also can go through one of the new announcement Web resources that take your information and submit it to a wide range of search engines and lists. Using these announcement services is simple. You give them information about your Web site (such as the main URL and the content), and they send that information to search engines and lists. Although some commercial announcement services are available, you shouldn't spend money to do something that these announcement services (like the ones listed here) do for free.

Here's a short listing of search engines and lists:

- [ ] AltaVista (http://altavista.digital.com)
- [ ] BizWiz (http://www.bizwiz.com/bizwiz/)
- [ ] Comfind Business Search (http://www.comfind.com/)
- [ ] Excite (http://www.excite.com)
- [ ] Galaxy (http://galaxy.einet.net/)
- [ ] InfoSeek (http://guide.infoseek.com/)
- [ ] Lycos (http://lycos.cs.cmu.edu)
- [ ] Magellan (http://www.mckinley.com)
- [ ] Open Text (http://www.opentext.com)
- [ ] Point (http://www.pointcom.com)
- [ ] Starting Point (http://www.stpt.com/)
- [ ] WebCrawler (http://webcrawler.com)
- [ ] Yahoo! (http://www.yahoo.com)

26

Here's a short list of noncommercial announcement services:

- ☐ Add It! (http://www.liquidimaging.com/submit/)
- ☐ Add Me! (http://www.addme.com)
- ☐ GetNet-Wide (http://www.gonetwide.com/gopublic.html)
- ☐ Submit It! (http://www.submit-it.com/)

Resources on the Internet

As you begin to experiment with Web servers and the Internet, you will discover that the Internet itself is a great resource. Several sites are available for you to use, many offering access to interesting information for a Windows NT system administrator. You might want to visit http://www.microsoft.com, for example, for the latest information on Microsoft and its products. If you need help with a question, the entire Microsoft Knowledge Base for product support is available at http://www.microsoft.com/support. You also can find new information about the Internet Information Server at http://www.microsoft.com/IIS.

Summary

In this chapter, you learned about Internet Information Services. Organizations are using Windows NT more and more as their platform of choice for Internet services for two primary reasons: improved TCP/IP support and the bundled Internet/intranet services.

As you learned on Day 10, Microsoft continues to make TCP/IP more central to its networking capabilities. With Server 4.0, Microsoft has made enhancements to the default network installation and numerous improvements to NT's IP capabilities.

In addition, NT Server 4.0 includes Microsoft's Internet Information Server, a fully functional Web server. Organizations therefore can set up and run Web servers "right out of the box." Windows NT Server 4.0 also includes a Gopher server, plus a management utility that provides a single interface to manage Web, FTP, and Gopher servers from within a single utility.

This chapter also introduced you to the Web server, focusing on the Microsoft Internet Information Server bundled with Windows NT 4.0. Basically, the process of installing and configuring a Web server isn't complicated; servers pretty well install themselves, and because Web servers don't really do a whole lot (basically, they respond to HTTP requests), you don't really need to configure much.

Also, this chapter covered log files and how to use and convert them.

Windows NT's combination of features and functions makes it hard to beat for organizations setting up Internet services. Whether you elect to publish internally or publicly over the Internet, you can find no better platform than Windows NT to address your information publishing needs.

Workshop

To wrap up the day, you can review terms and tasks from the chapter, and see the answers to some commonly asked questions.

Terminology Review

File Transfer Protocol (FTP)—Defined in the TCP/IP protocol suite for transferring files from one host to another.

Gopher—A character-based information publishing protocol using menus to access text files.

World Wide Web (a.k.a. W3, WWW, and the Web)—The global "network" of interconnected systems offering HTTP services to users with appropriate browsing software.

Task List

The emphasis of this chapter was to teach you to install and configure the Internet Information Server. As a system administrator, you might decide to publish documents over the Internet or for your intranet. You learned the following tasks in this chapter:

- ☐ Installing IIS
- ☐ Modifying IIS
- ☐ Testing your Internet or intranet connection

26

Q&A

Q How do I connect to the Internet?

A In most cases, you connect your Web server to the Internet as a standalone system. Your primary concern is then to prevent Internet hackers from attacking the server itself and accessing unauthorized information or corrupting the system.

In other cases, you might have the Web server connected to an internal network outside a firewall or even have a small LAN connected to the Web server for attaching other servers or for attaching the workstations of content developers.

Q Should I use the Guest account for Internet users?

A You should disable the Guest account on any Internet connected systems (use only the IUSR_*computername* account for anonymous logon) and make sure that the Everyone group does not have excess permissions in sensitive directories. Also keep in mind that, by default, the Everyone group gets automatic access to any new directories you create, so you should check permissions after creating new directories.

DAY

14

Chapter 27

Fine-Tuning Your Windows NT Server

In the past two weeks, you learned about installing and exploring NT. You learned about the registry settings and how to manage security and audit the server. By now, you are comfortable using and manipulating the different components of NT Server.

In this morning's session, you'll learn how to fine-tune the server to obtain maximum performance by using the tools and techniques provided by Microsoft. You'll learn how to use the Performance Monitor and the Network Monitor, two of the critical tools that are part of the server software.

Using a systematic approach, you'll find out how to discern any network failures, monitor your network for proficiency, and troubleshoot any problems you might encounter. Because so much depends on the type of server you use and the number of users you connect, and the type of work being performed, it is too hard to provide figures that might give you some idea of how well your particular environment is running. For the most part, NT Server does a fine job of performing with maximum speed and efficiency, and in fact, Microsoft offers few ways for you to manipulate the way in which it manages this function.

Let's start by reviewing some fundamentals and then the main tools—the Performance Monitor and the Network Monitor.

What NT Can and Cannot Do for Performance

For the most part, NT does a good job managing performance. If you are at all unsure, you are better off letting the server manage this aspect of your operation.

There are, however, various things that impact performance that NT can do nothing about; you need to know about these and decide what path you will follow to provide maximum performance. Performance management might be a sound goal for you to achieve, but it is also extremely challenging. You must decide whether the challenge is worth the additional work.

Naturally, performance is excellent if you purchase the largest machine available, have a huge amount of disk space and memory, and provide services for only a hundred or so people who are not demanding in their needs. Unfortunately, we can hear you laughing already. So what else can be done?

Purchasing a high-end computer is an obvious, although sometimes neglected, aspect of performance. Whether you use an Intel 486/66 or a Pentium Pro 200 has an impact that is hard to mitigate any other way. In addition, using 32MB rather than 64MB or even 128MB is a limitation you can easily resolve by adding memory. NT does neither of these things for you. Memory is so inexpensive these days that adding more memory is often a quick solution for speeding up a system.

Does your machine use older IDE technology as opposed to newer SCSI-2 drives, and are you using the latest PCI technology or an older EISA bus type? These factors all conspire to impact the performance your server offers. The newer PCI format offers 32-bit data transfer rather than 16-bit, effectively doubling the speed at which data moves across the bus.

Configuring your data and disk drives offers methods for increasing (or decreasing) performance. By using a file server with only one drive for all data, instead of spreading it across a number of drives, you reduce the server's performance.

Moving applications around can buy you significant processor time. If you are running two heavily used applications on the same server, you can increase the server speed by spreading the applications across multiple servers. Using Microsoft's SMS and SQL Server in addition to IIS can bring your server to its knees if they are all heavily used. Spreading the load across to other servers is more efficient and effective.

27

The type of network cards you use and their respective speeds also conspire to add or detract from system performance. If you think that because your network is an Ethernet 10 or 100Mbps it isn't critical to worry about the particular cards you use, think again. Just as some manufacturers offer faster video cards through more effective design, so do many network card manufacturers. The use of a card primarily designed for a client machine rather than a server might significantly impact service.

In addition, you can slow down your system by loading too many protocols. Adding unnecessary protocols impacts your server's memory and CPU time. Each protocol requires a separate browser list, and these browser lists take services from the master browser, which is often your server.

In addition to all the factors already mentioned, you'll find that as you add BDCs to the network, they can impact your server, especially if they are tuned to update too often. By default, NT uses a five-minute cycle to maintain its BDCs; this might be too often for your network. Raising the limit somewhat can help overall system performance. How often should you perform these updates? It really depends on several factors. The number of users, how busy the system is, and how critical it is to have instant recovery all play a part in setting this value.

Finally, the applications you run can become your largest bottleneck. A poorly designed application offers little opportunity for performance improvement, and you have to live with that. It is important that your developers understand the need for well-designed, fast processes and that they do not rely on the machine for processing power rather than improved application design.

All these things conspire to impact performance and offer NT Server no effective way of improving that performance. You need to manage these items in addition to the things NT lets you manage in order to coax the best out of your server.

Tuning NT Server boils down to managing how NT uses its memory and whether the virtual memory usage is well defined for maximum speed. By far, the single most important change you make to improve performance is to add more memory. If you use a machine with 64MB, adding another 32MB or even another 64MB will do wonders. This is often the fastest and, relatively speaking, least expensive method for speed improvement in NT Server.

27

Managing Server Memory

This is one area where you have a reasonable level of control when tuning your server. Besides the obvious addition of physical memory, you can use various methods to improve memory management over the memory that is presently installed.

Let's review the basics of how NT manages memory. First, you need to know a couple of terms. Later this morning, you'll learn to use Performance Monitor and configure it to provide you with log data for later use. One of the terms used in this tool is *available bytes*. This term applies to how much actual memory NT can acquire at any given time. You need to be aware that if this figure from Performance Monitor falls below about 4 or 5MB, most of the memory is in use, and your system will begin to clog up.

Another term used is *commit bytes*. This term refers to the actual amount of memory that all the applications need at any given moment. As applications start up, they reserve memory but don't actually begin to use it without committing it first. If all the applications running commit to more memory than your server provides, NT begins to thrash the hard drive to page out the applications and continue processing. The more that NT pages data to and from the hard drive, the slower your system becomes.

NT manages disk paging a little different than Windows does. It needs some virtual memory (disk space used as memory) regardless of how much physical memory it has available. NT allows you to manage some aspects of this memory usage.

Task 27.1. Managing virtual memory usage.

Step 1: Description
This task enables you to decide how NT uses memory and set out whether system performance or memory usage is more important to your server. As you recall, virtual memory is the amount of disk space NT uses when there is insufficient physical memory.

Step 2: Action
1. Log onto your system using an administrator account.
2. Open the Control Panel and select the System icon. Click on the Performance tab. You see a screen like that shown in Figure 27.1.

Figure 27.1.

Changing memory usage in the System Properties dialog box.

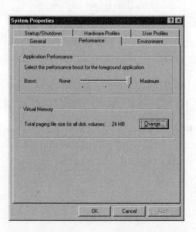

3. By default, the system uses the amount of memory you supply as the figure for disk space. In the Application Performance area, you can modify how NT Server responds to applications running on the server. If you set this bar to None, NT does not provide any special priority to the applications running in foreground.

4. Next, click the Change button in the Virtual Memory field. You get a dialog box like that shown in Figure 27.2.

Figure 27.2.

The Virtual Memory dialog box.

5. Choose the various settings according to your needs. For this task, you change them to see what happens. As you see, various options are available. For the most part, the NT settings are probably fine. If you have trouble, modify them to provide relief. The paging file can grow to 74MB or more, as you can see in Figure 27.2. The administrator will have to examine what he needs to run on the server in order to determine the size of the pagefile needed.

6. You exit by clicking the Close button in the upper-right corner.

Step 3: Review

By specifying different settings, you can provide some measure of performance management. By using the Performance Monitor, shown later, you can monitor the amount of committed bytes over a time frame and note the maximum value reported. This provides you with a guide as to how much memory is needed, and you can set the paging file size accordingly, with a small additional overhead for future growth.

Before you tune anything, however, you need to know that there *is* a problem. You find this out by using the monitoring tools that NT offers.

So what are some of the things NT allows you to monitor? In the following list are some of the tasks and counters available:

☐ Cache

☐ Memory

27

☐ NetBEUI

☐ Objects

☐ Physical disk

☐ Processes

☐ RAS

☐ Server

☐ System

☐ TCP

Now that you understand some of the tasks that NT performs and some of the tasks you need to perform to improve performance, you need to know what the current performance is before deciding whether anything needs to be done. That's the job of the Performance Monitor.

Understanding and Using the Performance Monitor

NT provides new graphical tools for monitoring the system. These are, in our opinion, an improvement over the older designs, because, as someone once said, "a picture is worth a thousand words."

Graphs and charts, however, are only one part of the picture. You need to ensure that the reference is understood to make sense of the numbers. For example, providing a component load figure without providing a frame of reference is useless. Did the load occur over one second or over a month? Figures provided by NT tools usually give you that frame of reference so that you can use them in the proper context.

Finally, using data with little or no long-term frame of reference might not be the most effective method. You need to gather data and try to relate that to a useful trend. For example, you need to review performance over a week or month to see the long-term aspects, yet you also need to review one day compared to another and one part of a day compared to another part to ensure that short-term bottlenecks aren't bringing users to their knees. Part of performance monitoring is in combining these aspects to provide a comprehensive short- and long-term strategy.

The Performance Monitor provides you with several options. In Task 27.2, you'll learn how to start the Performance Monitor.

27

Task 27.2. Starting and running the Performance Monitor.

Step 1: Description

This task shows you how to start the Performance Monitor tools and begin collecting valuable data.

Step 2: Action

1. Log onto your system using an administrator account.
2. Go to Start|Programs|Administrative Tools (Common), and find the tool called Performance Monitor. Click on this option to start the monitor. You see a screen like that shown in Figure 27.3.

Figure 27.3.

Using Performance Monitor.

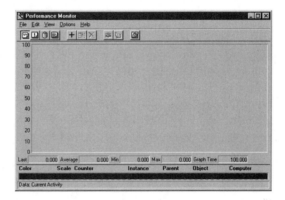

3. By default, the monitor starts in Chart mode. You change the mode by selecting the View menu and choosing another option.
4. Select the View menu. As you see, Performance Monitor uses four types of modes. These include the Default Chart, an Alert Mode, a Log Mode, and a Report Mode.
5. Choose the various modes and experiment with changing them.
6. Exit Performance Monitor by selecting File|Exit.

Step 3: Review

By using Performance Monitor, you see how your system is managing its resources and collect valuable information. This is a significant tool in your performance-management arsenal.

In the following section, you'll learn how to manipulate and use the various parts of Performance Monitor.

Using Performance Monitor

Now that you know how to start Performance Monitor, you need to learn about the various logging and reporting aspects of the tool. Notice that the monitor is not actually doing anything yet. Microsoft does not want to presume that it knows what events you want to use when starting the monitor, so you need to tell it to perform a function. You'll learn to do that a little later in this section. Following is a basic introduction to the components of this tool.

The main menu across the top of the screen shows the typical Windows options of File, Edit, View, Options, and Help. Each of these menu options is further broken down to provide you with additional features.

Under the File menu, you create new charts and save chart settings and workspace. You also use this option to exit the tool. The Edit menu enables you to add to a chart and edit an existing chart. In addition, it offers the option of changing the input time frame for an existing log file or clearing all the lines from a report. Finally, it allows you to delete the selected report.

As mentioned earlier, the View menu allows you to select which type of view you want to use, including Chart, Log, Alert, and Report views. In the Options menu, you can specify various report settings, as well as which toolbar settings you want to see on the window when it opens. This menu also allows you to obtain data from the current activity or from a previous log file. An Update option enables you to set the selected options immediately, and the Bookmark option places a convenient bookmark into the selected output log for later use.

The icons presented just below these menu items offer a quick jump to a few of these options. From left to right, the standard icons consist of the following:

- ☐ View a chart
- ☐ View the alerts
- ☐ View output log file status
- ☐ View report data
- ☐ Add a counter
- ☐ Modify selected counter
- ☐ Delete selected counter
- ☐ Update counter data
- ☐ Place a commented bookmark into the selected log file
- ☐ Options

These icons represent a fast method for performing certain tasks and are useful for you to learn.

Let's begin using the Performance Monitor by adding a counter. Click on the plus sign or select Edit|Add to Chart. You see a dialog box similar to the one shown in Figure 27.4.

Figure 27.4.

*Adding counters to
Performance Monitor.*

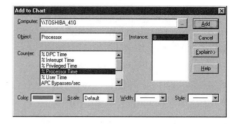

Using this dialog box, you set the options you want. Each option represents a different function, as explained here:

☐ *Computer:* You use this box to select the computer you are going to monitor. You can monitor any machine on the network provided that you have the necessary privileges. Naturally, this applies only to NT Servers and Workstations. As you see in Figure 27.4, you can select the computer by using the small triple-dot button or by typing the computer name preceded by a double-backslash.

☐ *Object:* This is a drop-down list that allows you to select the object you want to monitor. You can monitor almost two dozen different objects, as shown in the following list:

> Browser
> Cache
> LogicalDisk
> Memory
> NBT Connection
> NetBEUI
> NetBEUI Resource
> NWLink IPX
> NWLink NetBIOS
> NWLink SPX
> Objects
> Paging File
> PhysicalDisk
> Process
> Processor
> RAS Port
> RAS Total
> Redirector
> Server
> Server Work Queues
> System
> Telephony
> Thread

27

☐ *Instance:* Most of the objects you monitor have multiple instances, and this option allows you to select one of them for monitoring. An instance relates to the number of items; for example, you might have more than one RAS port, and this information shows in the Instance window.

☐ *Counter:* This scrollable list permits you to select which of the object's associated counters you want to monitor.

☐ *Color, Scale, Width, and Style:* These options allow you to control the look of your chart. You should leave the defaults most of the time, unless you are particular and want to choose different settings.

☐ *Add:* This button lets you add the selected counter to the list for monitoring.

☐ *Cancel:* Click this button to move back to the previous dialog box and not retain the settings specified. After you click the Add button, this option changes to an icon showing the word Done. You click this to return to the previous dialog box.

☐ *Explain:* You can obtain a more detailed explanation of any counter you select by clicking this button. As you see in Figure 27.5, you are shown additional information in a Counter Definition box that appears.

Figure 27.5.

Obtaining additional information in the Add to Chart dialog box.

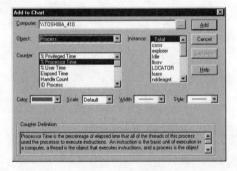

Finally, each time you select a view, this dialog box changes slightly. It is essentially the same for the Report view, but as you see in Figure 27.6, it is slightly different for the Alert view. In Figure 27.7, you see that it is different again for the Log view.

Figure 27.6.

The Alert dialog box.

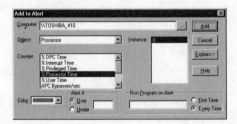

Figure 27.7.

The Log dialog box.

The additional item in the Add to Alert dialog box is an Alert If field, which provides you with an opportunity to set the values for when an alert record is written. The Run Program on Alert area allows you to specify that some special program should be run either the first time or each time the alert condition is met.

The Performance Monitor allows you to monitor more than one machine at a time by selecting the processor objects you want. Using the chart option is fine, but as you see in Figure 27.8, you'll have a problem if you use too many objects. Although the program colors each line differently, you'll find that the lines are difficult to follow.

Figure 27.8.

Lines can become complex in the Performance Monitor.

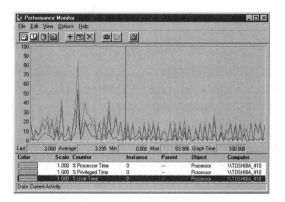

By changing the chart options, you can present the data in a different fashion that is a little easier to read. You do this by selecting Options|Chart. The program shows you a dialog box similar to the one shown in Figure 27.9. This dialog box allows you to control the way data is presented and offers a multitude of settings. By playing with the various controls, you will find a comfortable view for your server.

If you click on the Histogram option, the chart changes to show a chart like the one shown in Figure 27.10. As you see in the picture, the vertical and horizontal grid options are also on, in addition to the vertical labels, which provide a numbering scheme on the left side of the picture. You set the maximum number to use in the Vertical Maximum field. By using the field next to the Periodic Update option, you control how often the information is updated. If you choose, you can set this option to manual and then update it during specific times by manually selecting the Options menu and selecting Update Now.

27

Figure 27.9.

Changing chart options.

Figure 27.10.

Using options to modify the chart.

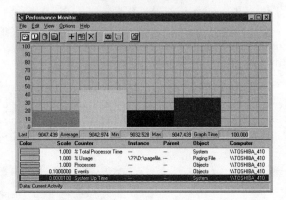

The Legend option shows you the values associated with each chart or line to enable you to tell what each object on your chart represents. Unless your chart is simple, we recommend leaving this option selected.

The Value Bar option provides several counters, including Last, Average, Minimum and Maximum, and Graph Time. You specify whether these should be displayed by clicking on the Value Bar box.

NOTE

You might find yourself with a display that does not contain the File, Edit menu line. This can be disconcerting if you did not actively choose to hide it. You can choose to show this menu bar by double-clicking on the left side of the dialog box, near the vertical labels. A few toggle switches are also available to minimize the data presented. You can use the Ctrl+M key combination to toggle the menu line on or off. Use Ctrl+S to toggle the status line and Ctrl+T to toggle the toolbar. By using these options, you can set up the display to use a minimum amount of your desktop space.

The Alert view in Performance Monitor is useful for keeping an eye on several conditions within your server to detect problems as they occur. Using this view allows you to set various parameters and tell the monitor program to log the events. This way, you can run the monitor over a selected time frame and be able to quickly see only the pertinent data you requested.

Normally, the data that is collected in a Performance Monitor log file is of little use to you or is only selectively useful. Wading through all that data to find out the condition of your server is inefficient. You use the Alert view to select only those critical values that interest you.

For example, you might log the object called Server and select Logons Per Second and Logons Total to see how fast your system grows. These values provide a reasonable indicator of the speed at which your system expands. If the numbers change quickly, your system might be growing fast, and you will need to take care that bottlenecks aren't developing.

In Task 27.3, you'll learn to set up the Performance Monitor to perform in Alert mode and collect only the data that interests you.

Task 27.3. Setting up Performance Monitor to issue alerts.

Step 1: Description

This task focuses on showing you how to set up Performance Monitor to issue alerts concerning conditions you decide.

Step 2: Action

1. Log onto your system using an administrator account.
2. Go to Start|Programs|Administrative Tools (Common)|Performance Monitor.
3. Select the Alert view by clicking the icon showing a log page with an exclamation mark on it or by selecting View|Alert.

    You see the Alert Log screen as shown in Figure 27.11.

Figure 27.11.

Showing the Alert view in Performance Monitor.

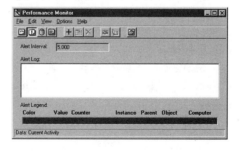

4. Click on the plus sign or select the menu item Edit|Add to Alert.

   You see an Add dialog box similar to the one shown earlier in Figure 27.6.

5. Select the items you want to be alerted about by using the Object and Counter fields, and click the Add button to tell the monitor program which ones you want to use.

6. The key fields in this dialog box are those at the bottom of the screen. Select the Alert If field and enter the out-of-range value to indicate when you want a record written.

7. Select whether the record is written only the first time it occurs or every time, by using the options in the lower-right corner of the screen.

   For example, you might select the PhysicalDisk object and the % Disk Time counter, using an Alert If parameter of 60 to indicate that a record is written every time the disk drive spends more than 60 percent of its time servicing read and writes. For the example shown in Figure 27.12, we set the time for Paging File Usage down to 1 percent merely to indicate some logging.

Figure 27.12.

An example Alert log.

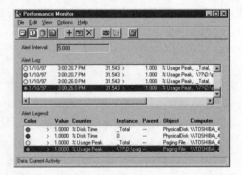

8. After you have set up the logs, minimize the screen to allow it to collect data for a while. When you are finished, select File|Exit to finish.

Step 3: Review

By using the Alert view, you can select the data you want to see and not be inundated with information. Use this view to detect problems or selected parameters on your server.

Task 27.4. Setting up Performance Monitor to alert you about free space.

Step 1: Description

This task shows you how to set up Performance Monitor to issue alerts concerning the amount of free space left on your drives.

Step 2: Action

1. Log onto your system using an administrator account.

2. Go to Start|Programs|Administrative Tools (Common)|Performance Monitor.

3. Select the Alert view by clicking on the icon showing a log page with an exclamation mark on it or by selecting View|Alert.

4. Click on the plus sign or select the menu item Edit|Add to Alert.

   You see the Add dialog box similar to the one shown earlier in Figure 27.6.

5. Select the Object called LogicalDisk and click once. Click on the drive. You can select all drives or individual drives.

6. Select the Counter called Free Megabytes and click once.

7. Select whether the record is written only the first time it occurs or every time, by using the select buttons in the lower-right part of the screen.

8. Decide on the amount of free space you want to be informed about, and enter that number in the Alert If box. Choose whether the figure is to be used as the low or high number by selecting Over or Under. For example, you might select 50 and Under to be informed when the drive has only 50MB of space left on it.

9. Click the Add button to activate the logging. Click Done to complete the action. The Performance Monitor begins logging; it will tell you when the drive has less than 50MB of free space available.

10. Allow the monitor program to run as long as you need. When you are finished, you can select File|Exit.

Step 3: Review

By using the Alert view, you can select specific data to be alerted to and use this to manage your server effectively.

You learn to use the Performance Monitor to your advantage in this section. Setting up and managing the various log activities is not onerous; however, you do need to remember that the act of using this tool might impact some of the figures you log. Like any application, the program uses resources, and if you attempt to log too many objects and counters, overall system performance is affected.

You have other options available to you besides logging the events. You can also tell Performance Monitor to send a message to a user when the event occurs. Select the Options|Alert menu and you see a dialog box that allows you to modify how the program manages data. If you select the Network Alert field and specify a user, Performance Monitor sends that user a message when the event occurs. Naturally, it is important to ensure that the number of messages you send is not excessive, or the user will be inundated with them. You see an example of a message to a user running WinPopUp in Figure 27.13.

Figure 27.13.

Sending a user an alert.

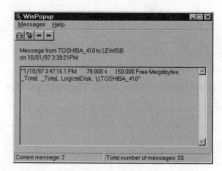

In addition to sending the user a message, the dialog box allows you to log the events in the Application Log and set whether the service updates automatically on a periodic basis or manually.

Finally, collecting the data you need often results in a large amount of information, and the NT Server Tools are poorly equipped to manipulate this data. It is likely you will export the data to a spreadsheet or other program for manipulation. Task 27.5 shows you how to export this data to another application.

Task 27.5. Exporting data by using Performance Monitor.

Step 1: Description

This task shows you how to export the data collected by using Performance Monitor and how to send it to another application for manipulation.

Step 2: Action

1. Log onto your system using an administrator account.
2. Go to Start|Programs|Administrative Tools (Common)|Performance Monitor.

3. You need to log the data first. Select the Log view by selecting the View|Log menu.

4. Click on the plus sign or select the menu item Edit|Add to Log.

5. Select the objects you are collecting data about, and click the Add button. Click Done when you are finished selecting the objects you want.

6. You need to start the actual logging next. Select Options|Log. You are presented with a dialog box asking where you want the log file and under what name. Fill in the boxes as indicated, and click the Start Log button to begin collecting the data.

7. After you have the data you need, select Options|Log. After the screen appears, click Stop Log to complete the logging task. Next, select View|Chart and select Options|Data From.

8. Using the dialog box that appears, select the log file you created by entering the name and location, or by using the small icon to find the file by browsing your directories. Click OK to return to the main screen.

9. Select the menu item Edit|Add To Chart. You see that the Object entry is restricted to those you chose earlier. Select the Counters you want to export, and click the Add button each time. When you finish selecting the Counters, click the Done button. The Performance Monitor Chart shows you the selected data.

10. Select the File|Export Chart option. You are shown a dialog box asking for the location of the export file and its name, as well as the type of file you are creating. Select the file type and name, and click the Save button to produce your export file. The resulting file is ready to export into your application for manipulation.

Step 3: Review

The Performance Monitor allows you to create export files consisting of selected information, ready to be used in your external programs. This provides an effective means for manipulating the data from large files and for providing more detailed and graphical business reports.

Using Event Viewer to Monitor Your Network

In Chapter 24, "Using the Windows NT Server Audit System," you learned how to use the Event Viewer to review and manipulate the log files. You also use this service to monitor events that might impact your system.

This tool records events that have been defined for later use and analysis. These events include server failure, startup and shutdown, and other activities.

You use this tool when Performance Monitor is not running. This doesn't mean there is no data, although it will certainly not be as prolific as when you select data using the monitor program. Nonetheless, there is still useful information for you to peruse.

As you recall from Chapter 24, you start the Event Viewer by selecting Start|Programs|
Administrative Tools (Common)|Event Viewer. The data it collects is always waiting for you
to review, and sometimes you'll find it useful in solving a performance problem.

Looking at the collected data, you can see when staff log on or off the system and view such
activities as privilege use and system events. For example, if a user is unable to sign on, you
can use the event data to see whether a service failed (such as RAS) or whether the user has
the necessary access rights and privileges.

By double-clicking on a particular event, you get a description of what occurred. Figure 27.14
shows the event detail for a system log indicating that the server drive is at or near capacity.

Figure 27.14.

*An event log showing
disk drive capacity
warning.*

As shown in this example, regardless of whether you run Performance Monitor, some data
is available for troubleshooting if you have set up the Event Viewer as shown in Chapter 24.

Using Other NT Tools

As you learned in the previous material, Performance Monitor provides a vast amount of data
for use in detecting and solving performance problems. This, however, is not the only tool
available. NT offers some other tools that, individually, provide you with information.

Using these tools in addition to the main tool offers you an opportunity to gather information
quickly and possibly solve a problem.

Using the Server Applet

This handy little tool enables you to quickly check some of the server settings without needing
the more cumbersome Performance Monitor. You start the program by opening the Control
Panel and double-clicking the Server icon. You see an example in Figure 27.15.

Figure 27.15.

The Server applet running.

The Server applet tool shows you simply and quickly how any users are attached, the number of files that are locked, and a host of other data. The settings include those listed here:

- [ ] *Sessions:* This value shows how many users are connected to the server. You often need to know how many users are on the server to track down a problem.

- [ ] *File Locks:* This number is the number of file locks in use at a given time. Applications lock access to files to improve file integrity; however, if the file is shared by others, they must wait. The user perceives this as a slow or ineffective system if they are continually forced to wait.

- [ ] *Users:* By clicking the Users button, you can get a list of all users connected to the system.

- [ ] *Shares:* A click of this button provides you with the number of shares available and the number of users connected to each share. You see the total number of users connected to a share in addition to a list of user names. You can optionally disconnect a user if you suspect that they might be part of the problem.

- [ ] *In Use:* This button gives you access to a list of the resources currently in use on the server. The dialog box allows you to open or close the resources.

- [ ] *Replication:* You use the dialog box brought up by this button to manage replication properties and specify the path for user logon scripts. A handy reference area for replication problem solving.

- [ ] *Alerts:* This button is a quick way to manage the users and computers that are notified when alerts occur.

The Server applet provides several interesting items that are useful for problem solving.

Using the Services Applet

The Services applet (not to be confused with the Server applet) offers you a quick method for determining which services are running at a given moment. One of your first tasks during a performance crisis might be to see whether any services are running unnecessarily and to shut them down. You use this applet to perform that task.

Start the program by opening Control Panel and double-clicking the Services icon.

27

Using Dr. Watson

Finally, Dr. Watson comes to the rescue by providing a program error-detection utility. Although this is not really a performance tool, we're stretching the point a bit because this utility does provide critical information concerning your applications when they fail, and this failure often impacts the system. If a program is crashing consistently and taking your server response with it, this tool might be useful in helping determine the problem.

The program starts automatically whenever a program crashes. To start the program manually, select Start and type DRWTSN32 in the Run command line, or open a DOS command prompt and type the word there. You see an example in Figure 27.16.

Figure 27.16.

Using Dr. Watson for program problems.

Within this program are options that allow you to set up a log file and maintain a crash dump file for later perusal.

Figuring Out Which Counters to Use

One of the most difficult aspects of monitoring is determining exactly what to monitor and how to set the limits and counters associated with the objects being monitored. Why is this so difficult a task? Because each site has different needs and operational requirements. Additionally, you often have to perform this task along with all your other jobs, and this leaves little time for sifting through all the potential data that is available.

Many of the available counters are extremely specialized and too complex for this book to discuss. Most sites, if they perform monitoring at all, do only what is necessary, and that is what we try to do in this section.

27

By providing a small amount of guidance, we hope to ensure that you are aware of which items you might consider monitoring and how to set the particular counters for each object. Use the suggestions that follow, and consider increasing the settings as needed when a problem occurs.

The best path for you to follow might be to use the available tools and begin monitoring your network to obtain a baseline that fits your needs. In this manner, you ensure that any figures used are germane and reflect how your server is used and its idiosyncrasies. If you have the luxury of time and resources, you might consider performing stress tests and loads on the system to see how it handles the excess.

Following are some of the counters you might use:

- [ ] *Server:Bytes/second:* This counter lets you know how busy your server is at any given time. It tells you how many bytes are transmitted across the network cards per second, allowing you to gauge the activity levels and compare them to your acceptable network load levels.

- [ ] *Server:Logons total:* This counter lets you know how many users are signing onto the server and provides some idea of when the machine is its busiest. It also provides an indication of how big your server is becoming if tracked over time.

- [ ] *PhysicalDisk:Percent Disk Time:* This counter helps you recognize and perhaps mitigate a disk bottleneck. Look for figures that show that the disk is being utilized 80 or 90 percent of the time, and consider ways to reduce the load on the drive.

- [ ] *PhysicalDisk:Disk Queue Length:* This counter also helps you recognize and perhaps mitigate a disk bottleneck. If the queue is greater than 2 or 3 too often, look for ways to reduce the load.

- [ ] *Processor:Processor Time:* If your machine is constantly running near the top of its capacity (80 percent or more) look for ways to reduce the processor load. You might move applications or services to other machines or add additional processors to the existing machine.

- [ ] *Interrupts:Second:* Use this to determine whether too many interrupts are occurring, such as more than about 3000 to 3500 on a Pentium machine. Perhaps the video-board driver is poorly designed or faulty.

- [ ] *Memory:pages/second:* The pages-per-second counter is used to help determine whether the server has a reasonable balance between physical memory and disk space usage. Some paging is normal, but if too much occurs, the system slows. A number is hard to determine because it differs by machine. Watch the counter carefully for a while, and develop a threshold that works for your site. Look for numbers somewhere between 5 or less and no more than 20.

27

Summary

In this chapter, you learned how to monitor and manage performance on your NT Server system. Using various tools, you learned that manipulating and logging performance details is fairly easy.

This chapter offers a challenge to both the writer and the reader in finding the optimal balance between too little and too much information. We certainly have not provided too much information because you can buy entire books concerning NT tuning, and we have but a few pages to offer. We have, though, provided enough data to whet your appetite and offer some direction concerning the tasks available to you as you begin to use NT Server 4.0. If your server is part of an extensive network, you might consider the multitude of more-detailed tuning books available to help increase your knowledge and ability to set up your server in the manner that best serves your interests.

In this chapter you'll discover the following points:

☐ How to start and use the Performance Monitor

☐ Which tasks NT allows you to modify in improving overall system performance

☐ The different tools available for use

☐ How to control the vast amounts of data that Performance Monitor offers

☐ How to export data from Performance Monitor logs into your spreadsheets or word processors

☐ How to set up and manage disk-drive capacity by using the tools available with NT Server

Workshop

To wrap up the day, you can review terms and tasks from the chapter, and see the answers to some commonly asked questions.

Terminology Review

BDC—Backup Domain Controller. A machine that is used to provide a degree of fault tolerance by maintaining a copy of the Security Account Manager (SAM).

commit bytes—This refers to the actual amount of memory that all the applications need at any given moment.

counter—The measurement of activity for a particular object, such as bytes read per second.

27

CPU—The Central Processing Unit, often considered the brains of your server. You can use more than one CPU in an NT Server and increase the overall speed and processing of certain applications.

EISA—Enhanced Industry Standard Architecture. An older data transfer architecture that was designed to manage 8-, 16-, and 32-bit data transfers. Widely used, most expansion cards support this architecture.

IDE—An acronym for Integrated Drive Electronics. The older disk-drive architecture that usually integrates directly with the disk drive instead of using a separate card.

instance—An NT term relating to particular tasks in each object. Objects often have more than one instance, such as the Processor and its %Interrupt Time or %User Time or %Processor Time.

paging—The act of moving data to disk when physical memory is full. A component of virtual memory.

PCI— A 32-bit data-transfer bus used in newer machines that is generally faster than the older EISA bus. Most Intel machines built today support this standard.

PDC—Primary Domain Controller. The machine that provides user authentication for the NT network.

SCSI—The acronym for Small Computer Standard Interface. Originally designed for the UNIX world, it is designed to handle high speeds and multiple devices, such as disk and tape drives.

virtual memory—Combines the physical RAM available in the machine with disk space to simulate an environment where you have more memory than you physically have in RAM. NT tries to assess which parts of memory are least likely to be used, and it pages this information out to the disk area until it is needed.

Task List

The information provided in this chapter showed you how to manage the files and folders within an NT server. You learned to carry out the following tasks:

- [ ] Manage virtual memory usage
- [ ] Set up and run the Performance Monitor tool
- [ ] Set up Performance Monitor to issue alerts
- [ ] Setting up Performance Monitor to alert you about free space
- [ ] Exporting data by using Performance Monitor

27

Q&A

Q **Is there a lot I can do to improve overall performance of my server?**

A NT provides a reasonably well-managed level of performance, but at times you might need to act to improve the performance of your machine. You can do many things to improve performance, such as purchase faster hard drives or increase system memory. The single fastest way to speed up the system is to provide additional physical memory. Adding another 32MB to a machine speeds things up considerably.

Q **Are there ways to monitor what NT is doing at any given time so that I can see where bottlenecks occur?**

A Yes, you run Performance Monitor to see what is happening in the system. This tool provides you with a wealth of information. You need to be careful when using it, however. The addition of the monitoring can impact your system results because the very act of monitoring activity takes resources. Judicious use of this tool provides the administrator with an excellent overview of system bottlenecks.

Q **What type of activity can I monitor in NT?**

A Many objects, counters, and instances are available for monitoring. Using Performance Monitor, you monitor events such as processor times, logical and physical disk activities, paging usage, server work queues, and RAS port activity. Be careful not to monitor too much, however, or you will quickly fill disk space and affect system performance.

Chapter 28

Fine-Tuning and Troubleshooting Your Network

Microsoft designed Windows NT to run smoothly and to connect to just about anything right out of the box. As you saw way back on Day 2, Windows NT provides connectivity to various operating systems and hardware platforms through its native support for NetBEUI, TCP/IP, SPX/IPX, and NWLink transport drivers.

Moreover, Windows NT is a general-purpose operating system. Different organizations use NT for different purposes. So after you install NT, you'll need to fine-tune the operating system.

As the system administrator, you often are caught up in the pursuit of increased performance and greater reliability. You must balance user demands for more resources against your organization's budgetary restraints. So you need to get as much as possible from your investment in computer technology.

In the preceding chapter, you learned to use the Performance Monitor to view some of the elements controlling how Windows NT Server operates. Fine-tuning your server is important, as is fine-tuning your network. You can employ this tool and others to tune and troubleshoot your network. In the remainder of this chapter, you'll consider where to start tuning your system. When you're starting to tune your network, the first place to check is the "Fine-Tuning" section in the Windows NT online facility.

Tuning is important to maximize your existing resources, but it is not as important as keeping your network up. In the network management hierarchy, the cornerstone is reliability. If your network experiences sporadic problems or is not up most of the time, people will find alternatives to your network. So troubleshooting and monitoring your network is a key system administrator responsibility. This chapter discusses client connectivity and the problems you might experience, along with some solutions. Just as with fine-tuning, the first place to check is the "Troubleshooting" section in the Windows NT online Help facility. It appears as a topic in the Topics list (which you get to by clicking the Contents tab in the Help main window).

Specifically, in this chapter you will learn about network bottlenecks and how to overcome them. You will learn about optimizing network parameters. You also will learn about troubleshooting protocols and the tools to use.

When fine-tuning or troubleshooting your network, approach with care. A minor change can quickly leave your system unusable. If you're not sure, don't be shy about asking questions in a user forum or asking someone with more experience.

Having said that, let's get started with the fine-tuning suggestions that provide the biggest benefit to your network—software.

Optimizing Software for Network Bottlenecks

Fine-tuning software, especially application software, provides the biggest bang for the buck. If you have access to the application's source code, you can try to optimize the application itself; otherwise, try optimizing the network parameters as described in the following sections.

Optimizing Windows NT Network Parameters

In Windows NT, it is possible to configure various network parameters for different network transport mechanisms, such as NetBEUI and TCP/IP. Many of these parameters do not appear in the Registry by default, and the system therefore uses a default value. To change the default value, add an entry in the Registry (if it does not appear), and specify a new value.

The NetBEUI parameters are found in the following path:

```
HKEY_LOCAL_MACHINE\SYSTEM\CurrentControlSet\Services\NBF\Parameters
```

Table 28.1 describes the parameters you'll find.

Table 28.1. The NetBEUI parameters.

Parameter	Description
EnableOplocks	Specifies whether the server allows clients to use oplocks on files. Oplocks are a significant performance enhancement but have the potential to cause lost cached data on some networks, particularly wide area networks.
MaxWorkItems	Specifies the maximum number of receive buffers, or work items, the server can allocate. If this limit is reached, the transport must initiate flow control at a significant performance cost.
RawWorkItems	Specifies the number of special work items for raw I/O that the server uses. A larger value can increase performance but costs more memory.

The corresponding TCP/IP parameter is found in this path:

```
HKEY_LOCAL_MACHINE\SYSTEM\CurrentControlSet\Services\Tcpip\Parameters
```

Optimizing Network Traffic

You can increase network throughput in two ways:

- ☐ Provide regular network traffic by submitting load on the network in a periodic pattern; try to avoid output queues. This decreases the number of collisions on the wire and therefore increases the overall network throughput.

- ☐ Submit a few large files rather than many small ones. The optimum is a file size just lower than the expected network media capacity (1.25MB for Ethernet).

Network Performance Issues

Network bottlenecks show up in various ways. Usually, the culprit is the physical LAN infrastructure, the workstation, or software application demands.

28

There are three types of network performance problems, each causing the network protocol to transmit each block of data many times (or to time-out):

☐ *A server overload.* The server is asked to do more than it can, possibly because of another inadequate resource such as memory.

☐ *A network overload.* The amount of data that needs to be transferred is greater than the capacity of the physical medium.

☐ *A data integrity loss.* The network is faulty and intermittently transfers data incorrectly.

For optimal network performance, pay attention to the components you select. This means knowing both hardware and software components: the network medium (for example, 10Base2, 10BaseT, and 10BaseF), the adapter (NIC) type, the NIC driver, the topology (for example, Ethernet, Token Ring, and star), the frame type, and the network speed. For example, selecting Category 5 cabling provides the best results. Careful selection of hardware and software can make a network operate both more quickly and more reliably. Remember that it is a good idea to select hardware from the Hardware Compatibility List (HCL).

You should take the following basic steps before changing performance parameters:

☐ Install a high-performance network adapter card in the server. Network adapters can provide widely varying levels of performance. An adapter's bus type, bus width, and amount of onboard memory affect performance the most. Bus types include ISA, EISA, MCA, and PCI bus architectures. Currently, PCI bus slots on the system board provide the best performance. Bus width translates into the number of pins that connect from the adapter to the bus of the computer where it is installed. When the bus width of the adapter matches (or closely matches) the bus width of the computer, performance tends to be better. Always try to use adapters that match the bus width.

☐ Disable protocols and network cards that you do not use in your environment.

☐ Use multiple network adapter cards, where appropriate. A characteristic of Windows NT Server is its capability to support multiple adapters in the server computer. In the server computer, multiple adapters can be used to connect the server to multiple network segments. This, in effect, increases the total network bandwidth available for accessing the server, because traffic from a given segment does not have to share the network media with traffic from another segment. Also, multiple adapters can be used to connect different network topologies (Ethernet and Token Ring, for example).

☐ Segment the LAN, where appropriate. Think of your city or town. Every time someone builds a new subdivision next to the main thoroughfare (say, Interstate 95), the traffic increases. The more traffic, the higher the likelihood that an accident will occur. The more accidents, the higher the likelihood that the politicians will approve a new highway (say, I-295 and I-495). Then some of the traffic will use the new routes, decreasing the likelihood of an accident on the original highway.

How to Determine a Network Bottleneck

This morning, you saw how to use the Performance Monitor. You can use the Performance Monitor to find bottlenecks. To use Performance Monitor to find a network bottleneck, look for situations which indicate that the demand on network resources is larger than the demand on any other resource in your network.

Network Counters

The Network Interface object type includes those counters that describe the rates at which bytes and packets are sent and received over a network TCP/IP connection. It also describes various error counts for the same connection. Table 28.2 lists the Network object counters.

Table 28.2. The Network object counters.

Counter	Description
Bytes Received/sec	The rate at which bytes are received on the interface, including framing characters.
Bytes Sent/sec	The rate at which bytes are sent on the interface, including framing characters.
Bytes Total/sec	The rate at which bytes are sent and received on the interface, including framing characters.
Current Bandwidth	An estimate of the interface's current bandwidth in bits per second (bps). For interfaces that do not vary in bandwidth or for those for which no accurate estimate can be made, this value is the nominal bandwidth.
Output Queue Length	The length of the output packet queue (in packets). If this is longer than 2, delays are being experienced, and the bottleneck should be found and eliminated where possible. Because the requests are queued by NDIS in this implementation of Windows NT, this value will always be 0.

continues

28

Table 28.2. continued

Counter	Description
Packets Outbound Discarded	The number of outbound packets that were discarded—even though no errors had been detected—to prevent their being transmitted. One possible reason for discarding such a packet could be to free up buffer space.
Packets Outbound Errors	The number of outbound packets that could not be transmitted because of errors.
Packets Received Discarded	The number of inbound packets that were discarded—even though no errors had been detected—to prevent their being delivered to a higher-layer protocol. One possible reason for discarding such a packet could be to free up buffer space.
Packets Received Errors	The number of inbound packets that contained errors, preventing them from being delivered to a higher-layer protocol.
Packets Received Non-Unicast/sec	The rate at which non-unicast (that is, subnet broadcast or subnet multicast) packets are delivered to a higher-layer protocol.
Packets Received Unicast/sec	The rate at which (subnet) unicast packets are delivered to a higher-layer protocol.
Packets Received Unknown	The number of packets received via the interface that were discarded because of an unknown or unsupported protocol.
Packets Received/sec	The rate at which packets are received on the network interface.
Packets Sent/sec	The rate at which packets are sent on the network interface.
Packets Sent Non-Unicast/sec	The rate at which packets are requested to be transmitted non-to-non-unicast (that is, subnet broadcast or subnet multicast) addresses by higher-layer protocols. The rate includes the packets that were discarded or not sent.

28

Counter	Description
Packets Sent Unicast/sec	The rate at which packets are requested to be transmitted to (subnet) unicast addresses by higher-layer protocols. The rate includes the packets that were discarded or not sent.
Packets/sec	The rate at which packets are sent and received on the network interface.

Counters to Watch

Because a network utilization counter is not available, use some of the preceding counters to determine network utilization; that is, compare the total bytes sent and received with the network bandwidth. Find out whether data is waiting on the output queue to the network from the client to the server and from the server to the client.

Compare also the expected network capacity (for Ethernet, 1.25Mbps) with the actual (Bytes Total/sec) and Windows NT's estimate of bandwidth. You most likely will find that Windows NT's estimate of the bandwidth is considerably lower than the expected network capacity. This is due to collisions on the wire that cause the adapter to retry the transmission after a random delay. Urban myth has it that Ethernet networks start to have significant collision at about 67 percent utilization, or 833,375 bytes per second under random load. To obtain higher network throughput, provide a regular traffic pattern on the network where possible.

Use the following counters with the counters just mentioned to determine whether the network, and not the processor, disk, or something else, really is the bottleneck:

- ☐ Processor Time% (Total Processor Time% if more than one processor)
- ☐ Pagefile: %Usage
- ☐ Memory: Available Bytes
- ☐ Memory: Cached Bytes
- ☐ Disk: Bytes Total
- ☐ Interrupt rate

28

General Tips for Configuring Application Software

Whenever you install application software on your Windows NT network, you should think carefully about the implications of the various installation options. Pay particular attention to network traffic, network response time, and resource usage.

When you install network-aware application software, you typically are asked to decide where to store the application's executable data files. You usually have three options:

☐ Place a single, read-only version of the executable files on a share area on the server (where all client users can share them).

☐ Place individual copies of all the executable files on the client's local hard disk.

☐ Use some combination of the first two options (some executables on the server and some on the client's hard disk).

The primary difference in these approaches involves the amount of network traffic each configuration generates, the response time, and the reliability/error recovery implications.

The first option generates the most network traffic. When you store all executables on the server, the system must copy the entire executable over the network to load into client memory. A problem often arises with this option when all the clients load some application programs as part of the boot process. This action can result in large spikes of network activity in the morning when all the PCs are being booted up at the same time. This is the morning traffic jam. In such situations, with very large networks, demand might exceed network bandwidth. This causes performance to suffer. Therefore, it makes better sense to use the third option (a combination of executables stored locally and on the server) when possible.

Another application program issue to consider is the use of overlays. Certain application programs (word processors, in particular) make extensive use of overlays. The system calls these overlays into memory when needed and then returns them to disk when not needed. In a network configuration, these overlays might reside on the server (by default); when they are called, they are loaded over the network. This can cause heavy, unanticipated network traffic, which, when not planned for, can affect overall network performance. It is worthwhile to determine whether any of your applications operate in this manner and, if so, to evaluate how to configure the application to minimize this type of traffic.

Network Response Time

Response time over a network configuration clearly is variable—it can be affected by any number of factors. In general, your goal should be to achieve response times that approximate local resource response times (meaning, for example, that you can load a program over the network in about the same time it takes to load from your local disk). This is how your clients will evaluate response time.

If you experience response time problems, check to see whether they are related to throughput. A simple way to check this is to use the Windows NT Performance Monitor tool. This tool provides the throughput (Kbps read and write) for network drives.

Network Resources

Your application software configuration should make efficient use of network resources. A good rule of thumb is to use only the network resources necessary for the task currently at hand. Often, clients are configured to create multiple links to multiple servers at boot time when, in reality, only two or three of the links are active at any given time. A good solution to such a situation is to use an application launcher product. You can configure these launchers to create the links for an application package when that package is invoked.

Transport Protocol Software

Windows NT supports multiple transport protocols:

- ☐ NetBEUI (NetBIOS Extended User Interface), which is a small, efficient, and fast protocol tuned for small LANs.

- ☐ TCP/IP (Transmission Control Protocol/Internet Protocol), which provides communication across wide area networks (WANs) and routers.

- ☐ NWLink (NetWare Link), which provides a protocol compatible with the Novell NetWare IPX/SPX protocol so that Windows NT computers can interoperate with Novell NetWare servers.

- ☐ DLC (Data Link Control), which provides connectivity between an IBM main-frame and an MS-DOS–based PC. DLC is a transport protocol defined by IBM. Chiefly, it is used to communicate with IBM mainframes and minicomputers, typically model 3270 or AS/400 machines. In addition, Windows NT also uses DLC to communicate with network printers, such as the Hewlett-Packard (HP) LaserJet 4Si. Such printers have a network interface card (NIC) that contains a MAC and a DLC protocol stack.

Tuning TCP/IP Server Transport Protocol

28

The Windows NT Server uses Microsoft's TCP/IP software regardless of the type of TCP/IP software used on the client workstations (Microsoft's, NetManage's Chameleon software, FTP's TCP/IP software, or Wollongong Pathway Access's TCP/IP software).

The TCP/IP parameters most affecting network performance follow:

☐ *TCP/IP window size.* The `TcpWindowSize` parameter determines the maximum amount of data (in bytes) that can be sent or received by the system. By default, it uses 32KB (32,768 bytes) as its window size. Because the default is set for the maximum, increasing your client's window size can often improve the performance of large data transfers. If your typical network client/server operations involve the transfer of large, contiguous files, increasing the default window size on the client to 16KB might improve file transfers.

☐ *TCP/IP segment size.* The `TcpRecvSegmentSize` and `TcpSendSegmentSize` parameters control the minimum amount of data (in bytes) that can be sent or received as a single unit. The two parameters control the maximum amount of data (in bytes) that can be sent or received as a single unit. The default setting for both is 1460 bytes. It is difficult to suggest how to change these values without knowing the specific traffic patterns for a given network. Setting the segment size very small results in the network bandwidth being underutilized. Setting the segment size larger than the maximum packet size of the network requires the IP engine to fragment the data and then reassemble it at the other end.

☐ *TCP keep alive timer(s).* The `TcpKeepCnt` and `TcpKeepTries` parameters control the time that a TCP connection remains active without network activity. In certain cases—typically when users don't log off but instead power off their workstation— you can reduce this timer so that sessions will be properly terminated at the transport protocol level. By default, the TCP/IP transport protocol keeps a non-responsive client connection alive for 40 minutes.

Troubleshooting Network Problems

Network problems can be the toughest to troubleshoot because there are many different components, and the path causing the problem might not be active when you begin troubleshooting.

When troubleshooting network problems, start by verifying the network's operating status before and during the error condition. To evaluate the network problem, check these factors:

☐ *Loose adapter cable.* The first rule of troubleshooting network problems is to make sure that the network is plugged into the network interface card. It sounds silly, but it is always worth checking.

☐ *Network adapter failure.* Check the event log for system errors related to the network adapter, the workstation, and the server components. Use PING or NBPING to determine whether the machine is getting out on the wire and how far. When PING cannot talk to its closest neighbor, you might want to enlist the help of a LAN protocol analyzer to determine whether packets are getting onto the network. If not, work forward from the network control card to isolate the faulty component. When the machine is getting to the wire but not its nearest neighbor, use the analyzer to look for congestion, jitter (Token Ring), and broadcast storms.

☐ *IRQ conflict with new adapter.* If you suspect an IRQ conflict, disable the mouse in the Registry by setting the start value to 0x4. You also might want to disable the serial ports. A little later, you'll see how to use WINMSD to check out the assigned IRQs.

☐ *Protocol mismatch.* When two machines are active on the same network but still cannot communicate, it might be because they are using different protocols. To communicate successfully, both machines must use the same protocol. If machine A is speaking only NetBEUI, and machine B is speaking only TCP/IP, the two machines cannot establish a successful connection. Use the Network applet in the Control Panel to determine supported protocols.

☐ *External network problems.* If the hardware on the local machine checks out, there might be an external network error. Use PING or NBPING to isolate the problem. Attempt to ping the closest neighbor (moving out) until a problem is seen. Also, use a LAN protocol analyzer to help locate jitter (Token Ring only), congestion, and broadcast storms.

Isolating Hardware Problems

Isolating configuration errors from hardware errors is often the easiest way to pinpoint the source of a problem. Hardware problems might originate from a defective network adapter or an incompatible network adapter driver. This is why you always should install Microsoft's Loopback adapter when you install Windows NT Server. This way, you can log onto the system even when the network adapter completely fails.

On a Windows NT Workstation or a Windows NT Server operating in server mode, you always can log on using the local (that is, Workgroup) account database. You log on locally by selecting the computer name rather than the domain name in the logon dialog box's From field. You then can use the Administrator account you created when you installed Windows NT Workstation—that is, if you remember the Administrator password. If you do not know the password and you have no cached authentication information to use, the only recourse is to solve the problem in a blind fashion, as detailed here:

1. Replace the network card.
2. Try the repair process.
3. Copy the system event log to a disk where the file system is a FAT partition.
4. Read the log using another Windows NT computer to try to discover the cause of the failure.

If this process does not work, you have to delete and reinstall Windows NT.

28

Standalone Card Tests

It's a good idea to test the card and the LAN cable before going any further. The four kinds of tests you do on most networks include these:

- ☐ On-board diagnostic
- ☐ Local loopback test
- ☐ "Network live" loopback test
- ☐ Sender/responder test

The first three tests usually come on a diagnostics disk that you get with the LAN board. The first test is a simple test of the circuitry on the board. Many boards have a "reset and check out" feature, so this program just wakes up that feature. If the chips check out okay, this step is successfully completed.

The first test can be a useful check of whether you've set the IRQ to a conflicting level, or perhaps placed any on-board RAM overlapping other RAM.

The second test is one wherein you put a loopback connector (exactly what a loopback connector is varies with LAN variety) on your network board. The loopback connector causes any outgoing transmissions from the LAN board to be "looped back" to the LAN board. The loopback test then sends some data out from the LAN card and listens for the same data to be received by the LAN card. If that data isn't received by the LAN card, something is wrong with the transmitter or the receiver logic of the network card.

Notice that for the first two tests, you haven't even connected your system to the network yet. In the third test, you do the loopback test again, but this time while connected to the network. The board should pass again.

The final test involves two computers, a sender and a responder. The responder's job is to echo back anything it receives. For example, if Barry's machine is the responder and Peter's is the sender, any messages that Peter's machine sends to Barry's machine should cause Barry's machine to send the same message back to Peter's machine.

To make a computer a responder (and any computer can be a responder; you don't have to use a server), you have to run a program that turns it into a responder. But that's where the problem arises. The responder software is packaged on the same disk as the diagnostic software that comes with the network board, and, unfortunately, the responder software usually runs only on network boards made by the company that wrote the diagnostic software. So, for example, if you have an Ethernet network that is a mixture of 3Com, Intel, and SMC boards, and you want to test a computer with a new 3Com Ethernet board, you have to search for another computer that has a 3Com board so that you can run the responder software on that computer.

28

Isolating Resource Conflicts

Resource conflicts generally fall into four categories: an interrupt conflict, an I/O (input/output) port conflict, a DMA (Direct Memory Access) conflict, or a memory conflict. Following are some ways to isolate the conflict.

Interrupt conflicts are the most common problems, particularly because there are only 16 interrupts and not all of them are available for use. If the network adapter is using one of the reserved interrupts or one that is rarely available, that might be the problem. If this is not the case, you might have an I/O conflict, which is generally more difficult to diagnose. If your Windows NT computer is still working, you can try to use WINMSD.EXE (the Windows NT Diagnostics located in the Administrators Tools [Common] group) to help you solve the problem.

Start WINMSD and click the IRQ/Port Status button. The Resources tab box, as shown in Figure 28.1, appears.

Figure 28.1.

The Windows NT Diagnostics Resources tab.

WINMSD does not, however, list every interrupt or I/O port used by the system—only those in use by installable device drivers. Just keep in mind that most manufacturers' I/O port summaries include only a starting I/O address; they rarely include the complete I/O range. It is possible to have I/O overlap, in which one I/O port range starts inside an existing I/O range.

 TIP

> If you have a Plug and Play BIOS, such as those commonly used in computers on a PCI expansion bus, take a look at the BIOS settings. Some PCI components can have their interrupt assigned by the BIOS. This can override the Plug and Play capability to assign an interrupt dynamically. It also can cause problems with Windows NT's capability to detect or change an interrupt assignment for a network adapter.

Supporting Windows NT Clients

Connecting a Windows NT workstation to another computer running Windows NT Server or Windows NT Workstation is the easiest connection you can make. Most of the problems you might experience with Windows NT clients have to do with authentication, provided that the hardware is functioning properly.

Troubleshooting Authentication Problems

You can attribute many network troubles to a failing or improperly configured network card or incorrect network transport drivers. The symptoms caused by a bad network card or an incorrect driver show up in one of two ways:

☐ *Authentication problem.* The client workstation cannot find the domain controller and, therefore, cannot gain access to the network.

☐ *Connectivity problem.* Users on a client workstation cannot access a particular shared resource.

The first indication that you have a hardware-related network problem is a message stating that the initial authentication process failed and that Windows NT has used cached information for authentication and to log you onto the system.

 NOTE

> You can log on using cached information only when you have previously logged on successfully.

28

If Windows NT cannot complete authentication, you cannot log onto the system to solve the problem. On a Windows NT Server domain controller, the incapability to be authenticated is a serious problem. If you encounter an authentication problem just after system installation during the initial logon, it's difficult to correct the problem.

Authentication problems fall into two basic groups. The domain controller might fail to authenticate you during the logon sequence or while attempting to access a shared resource on the domain.

Authentication failures that are not caused by a failed network adapter, as discussed in the preceding section, are often caused by one of the following problems:

- *No computer account.* If a Windows NT client is a member of the domain but has no computer account on the domain controller, there is no trusted connection between the Windows NT client and the domain controller. This means that the domain controller cannot authenticate you or log you onto the system.

  A similar problem can occur when a Windows NT client changes from a domain to a workgroup and then attempts to rejoin the domain. Even though a computer account still exists on the domain controller, the client cannot reuse the account. Instead, you must create a new computer account, although it can have the same name. This is because computer accounts are like user or group accounts in that they have an assigned security identifier (SID). The system stores the SID in the computer account on the domain controller and in the Registry of the Windows NT client. When a user changes from a domain to a workgroup or from one domain to another, however, the system reassigns the SID based on the new configuration.

- *No user account.* Generally, this problem occurs when the user attempting to log on does not have a user account on the domain controller or the user mistypes the user account name or password. You can experience similar problems when you have set up the user account so that the user must enter a new password at the next logon, or when the account has been locked out due to repeated attempts to log onto the system with an invalid password.

- *A trust relationship.* When a Windows NT client is a member of a workgroup, make sure that you do not have any two-way trust relationships established on the domain where that client needs access. In this situation, Windows NT clients cannot establish a trusted connection to the domain, even though the user has a valid user account. It is quite similar to the "no computer account" situation mentioned previously. In a domain without trust relationships or a one-way trust relationship, a workgroup computer can access the domain resources by mapping its local user account to a user account on the domain. When two-way trust relationships exist, user account mapping does not take place.

28

Authentication problems related to accessing shared resources usually have to do with a user's specific permissions or rights. The same problem can occur for printer access or named pipe access. To solve these authentication problems, check the client permissions in the following order:

- ☐ *Group membership.* Make sure that the user account is a member of the group that has permission to access the shared resource.

- ☐ *Share permissions.* Check the shared resource to ensure that the group has the appropriate permission to access the sharepoint. Also, make sure that the user is not a member of any group for which you have assigned the No Access permission. As you saw earlier, the No Access permission assignment overrides any other group permission level for the user. For example, if you have a printer called HP_Laser and you assign a user to the LaserPrinter group that has Print permission for that printer, and you also assign the user to the ColorPrinter group that has the No Access permission assigned for the printer, the user cannot print to the HP_Laser print queue.

- ☐ *Directory and file permissions.* If the user can access the sharepoint but cannot access directories and files, the user account probably is not a member of the appropriate group. The user also can be a member of a group that has the No Access permission assigned.

- ☐ *Cached account information.* Windows NT also caches group account information when accessing a shared resource. If you add a logged-on user to a group that has the appropriate permissions to access the shared resource, the user still cannot access the shared resource. The user must log off and then log back on again to flush the cache. When the user attempts to access the resource again, the system permits access.

NOTE

To flush an internal cache, sometimes you have to shut down and restart the computer instead of just logging off and then back on again.

Solving Physical Network Problems

The most effective way of monitoring the status of your physical network is by the ongoing use of intelligent network hardware, which might support, for instance, the Simple Network Management Protocol (SNMP). These devices collect and store status information that you can use to evaluate the health of your physical network.

If your network does not use such devices, use a network protocol analyzer (such as the Network Monitor tool) to assess the health of your network. You can use these analyzers to capture samples of network traffic and then analyze the captured data for any of the indicators of physical network problems.

If you have the opportunity to analyze network traffic, it usually is worthwhile to identify the longest (in terms of bit delay, not necessarily in terms of physical distance) client-to-server path through the network and use that path to generate network traffic for your data capture (for example, copy large files to and from the server over this path).

TCP/IP Troubleshooting Tools and Strategies

Your approach to troubleshooting TCP/IP should be no different from troubleshooting any other computer problem. Ask yourself the following questions:

- [ ] What works? What doesn't work? When did it last work?
- [ ] Is there any relationship between the things that do and don't work?
- [ ] Did the component or service ever work on this computer or network?
- [ ] If yes, what has changed since it last worked?

With those questions answered, you're ready to proceed with the troubleshooting process. As you work on and solve network problems, you should develop a troubleshooting flowchart. In addition, you should document all problems and their resolutions. This documentation serves two purposes. One, it provides a series of steps for less-experienced staff to follow. Two, it minimizes the amount of time you spend on problem-solving in the future. You can learn from your mistakes.

The following section describes the tools you'll use to troubleshoot TCP/IP problems.

TCP/IP Commands: Network Utilities

If you do not have access to network analyzers or intelligent hubs, you can use some software-only network statistics programs provided with Windows NT to gauge the relative health of the network. You can use these tools to monitor, troubleshoot, and maintain TCP/IP networks.

In most cases, the following tools are designed for internal networks, but you can use some of them over the Internet:

28

☐ *ARP (Address Resolution Protocol):* Lets you view and manage the mapping between IP addresses and physical network addresses.

☐ *IPCONFIG:* Displays diagnostic information about TCP/IP networks and current TCP/IP network configuration values.

☐ *NBTSTAT:* Reports information about NetBIOS over TCP/IP connections.

☐ *NETSTAT:* Displays current TCP/IP connections and protocol statistics.

☐ *PING:* Tests connections on TCP/IP networks.

☐ *ROUTE:* Displays or modifies the route table.

☐ *TRACERT:* Traces how packets hop around your network or the Internet.

Using ARP

The ARP command is useful for viewing the ARP cache. When two hosts on the same subnet cannot PING each other successfully, try running the ARP -a command on each computer to see whether they have the correct MAC (hardware) addresses listed for each other. You can determine a host's MAC address using IPCONFIG. When another host with a duplicate IP address exists on the network, the ARP cache might have had the MAC address for the other computer placed in it. You can use ARP -d to delete an entry that might be incorrect. And you can add an entry by using ARP -s.

Using IPCONFIG

IPCONFIG is a command-line utility that prints out the TCP/IP-related configuration of a host. When used with the /ALL switch, it produces a detailed configuration report for all interfaces, including any configured serial ports (for example, RAS). This is especially useful when you're using RAS and connecting to the Internet. Sometimes RAS is assigned one IP number that's no good, and you can track it down this way. IPCONFIG provides information such as the IP address for each interface device and subnet masks.

Output from this report can be redirected to a file and pasted into other documents.

Using NBTSTAT

The NBTSTAT command displays information and statistics about the current TCP/IP connections using NetBIOS over TCP/IP (that is, NBT). It provides network statistics for active and pending NetBIOS connections. This diagnostic command displays protocol statistics and current TCP/IP connections using NetBIOS over TCP/IP.

You can type the remote name or IP address of another system on a network to get information about it, such as local user names. Use the following syntax:

```
NBTSTAT [-a remotename] [-A Ipaddress] [-c] [-n] [-R] [-r] [-S] [-s] [interval] [-?]
```

Table 28.3 describes the parameters used in the preceding syntax.

Table 28.3. NBTSTAT **parameters.**

Parameter	Description
-a *remotename*	Lists the remote computer's name table using the computer's name.
-A *Ipaddress*	Lists the remote computer's name table using the computer's IP address.
-c	Lists the contents of the NetBIOS name cache, giving the IP address for each name.
-n	Lists local NetBIOS names.
-R	Reloads the LMHOSTS file after purging all names from the NetBIOS name cache.
-r	Lists name resolution statistics for Windows networking. On a Windows NT computer configured to use WINS, this option returns the number of names resolved and registered via broadcast or via WINS.
-S	Displays both workstation and server sessions, listing the remote hosts by IP address only.
-s	Displays both workstation and server sessions. This option attempts to convert the remote host IP address to a name using the HOSTS file.
interval	Redisplays selected statistics, pausing interval seconds between each display. Press Ctrl+C to stop redisplaying statistics. When you omit this parameter, NBTSTAT prints the current configuration information once.
-?	Displays help information.

WARNING

Microsoft recommends that you change the name of the administrator when you install. This is a good policy; however, using the command NBTSTAT -A *Ipaddress* provides the administrator's name.

28

The column headings that are generated by the NBTSTAT utility have the meaning shown in Table 28.4.

Table 28.4. NBTSTAT output.

Heading	Description
Input	The bytes received.
Output	The bytes sent.
In/Out	Whether the connection is from the computer (outbound) or from another system to the local computer (inbound).
Life	The remaining time that a name table cache entry will live before it is purged.
Local Name	The local NetBIOS name associated with the connection.
Remote Host	The name or IP address associated with the remote host.
Type	The type of name. A name can be either a unique name or a group name.
<03>	Each NetBIOS name is 16 characters long. The last byte often has special significance, because the same name can be present several times on a computer. This notation is simply the last byte converted to hexadecimal. For example, <20> is a space in ASCII.
State	The state of NetBIOS connections. The possible states are shown in Table 28.5.

Table 28.5. Possible states for NetBIOS connections.

State	Description
Accepting	An inbound session is currently being accepted and will be connected shortly.
Associated	A connection endpoint has been created and associated with an IP address.
Connected	The session has been established.
Connecting	The session is in the connecting phase where the name-to-IP address mapping of the destination is being resolved.
Disconnected	The local computer has issued a disconnect, and it is waiting for confirmation from the remote system.
Disconnecting	A session is in the process of disconnecting.

28

State	Description
Idle	This endpoint has been opened but cannot receive connections.
Inbound	An inbound session is in the connecting phase.
Listening	This endpoint is available for an inbound connection.
Outbound	A session is in the connecting phase where the TCP connection is currently being created.
Reconnecting	A session is trying to reconnect if it failed to connect on the first attempt.

So NBTSTAT is a useful tool for troubleshooting NetBIOS name resolution problems. NBTSTAT -n displays the names that were registered locally on the system by applications, such as the server and redirector. NBTSTAT -c shows the NetBIOS name cache with its name-to-address mappings for other computers. NBTSTAT -r purges the name cache and reloads it from the LMHOSTS file. NBTSTAT -a *<remotename>* performs a NetBIOS adapter status command against the computer specified by *remotename*. The adapter status command returns the local NetBIOS name table for that computer plus the MAC address of the adapter card. The command NBTSTAT -s lists the current NetBIOS sessions and their statuses, including statistics.

Using NETSTAT

The NETSTAT tool gathers statistics from the network adapter of the local computer or a specified remote computer, as well as some transport layer protocol driver data. You can use the statistics to determine the relative health of that machine's network connection based on the incidence of errors recorded.

The NETSTAT utility provides statistics in the TCP/IP world. If you're running a TCP/IP application on another host, it gives you statistics on the IP address and port number of local and remote computers. Typing NETSTAT *host* produces the statistics information.

Table 28.6 lists the statistics provided by the NETSTAT utility.

Table 28.6. NETSTAT statistics.

Statistic	Description
Foreign Address	The IP address and port number of the remote computer where the socket is connected. The name corresponding to the IP address is shown rather than the number if the HOSTS file contains an entry for the IP address. When the port is not yet established, the port number is shown as an asterisk (*).

28

continues

Table 28.6. continued

Statistic	Description
Local Address	The IP address of the local computer, as well as the port number that the connection is using. The name corresponding to the IP address is shown rather than the number if the HOSTS file contains an entry for the IP address. When the port is not yet established, the port number is shown as an asterisk (*).
Proto	The name of the protocol used by the connection.
(state)	The state of TCP connections only.

To use NETSTAT to display protocol statistics and current TCP/IP network connections, use the following syntax:

```
NETSTAT [-a] [-e][n][s] [-p protocol] [-r] [interval]
```

Table 28.7 describes the parameters used in the preceding syntax.

Table 28.7. NETSTAT **parameters.**

Parameter	Description
-a	Displays all connections and listening ports; server connections usually are not shown.
-e	Displays Ethernet statistics. This can be combined with the -s option.
-n	Displays addresses and port numbers in dotted decimal format (instead of attempting name lookups).
-p protocol	Displays connections for the protocol specified by protocol; protocol can be TCP or UDP. If used with the -s option to display per-protocol statistics, protocol can be TCP, UDP, or IP.
-r	Displays the contents of the routing table.
-s	Displays per-protocol statistics. By default, statistics are shown for TCP, UDP, and IP. The -p option can be used to specify a subset of the default.
interval	Redisplays selected statistics, pausing interval seconds between each display. Press Ctrl+C to stop redisplaying statistics. When this parameter is omitted, NETSTAT prints the current configuration information once.

NETSTAT displays protocol statistics and current TCP/IP connections. NETSTAT -a displays all connections, and NETSTAT -r displays the route table, plus active connections. The -n switch tells NETSTAT not to convert addresses and port numbers to names.

Using PING

PING, or Packet Internet Groper, is a TCP/IP utility. The utility sends a message and looks for a reply. If you get a reply, you know that the system is there, and you can talk with it. If you don't get a response, you know there's a problem, and you won't be able to communicate.

PING uses Windows socket-style name resolution to resolve the name to an address, so if pinging by address succeeds but pinging by name fails, the problem lies in address resolution, not network connectivity.

From your workstation, you can ping another host and wait for a response. The syntax is `PING Ipaddress` or `PING host` (for example, `PING 199.199.199.2` or `PING microsoft.com`). Type `PING -?` to see which command-line options are available. For example, PING allows you to specify the size of packets to use, how many to send, whether to record the route used, which TTL value to use, and whether to set the `don't fragment` flag.

PING is a tool that helps verify IP connectivity. When troubleshooting, you use the `PING` command to send an ICMP echo request to a target name or IP address. First try pinging the IP address of the target host to see whether it responds, because this is the simplest case. If that succeeds, try pinging the name.

Using ROUTE

Use `ROUTE` to view or modify the route table. `ROUTE PRINT` displays a list of current routes known by IP for the host. Use `ROUTE ADD` to add routes to the table, and use `ROUTE DELETE` to delete routes from the table. Note that routes added to the table are not made permanent unless you specify the `-p` switch. Nonpersistent routes last only until someone reboots the computer.

For two hosts to exchange IP datagrams, they must both have a route to each other or use default gateways that know of a route. Normally, routers exchange information with each other by using a protocol such as the Routing Information Protocol (RIP) or the Open Shortest Path First (OSPF). Windows NT did not include support for either of these routing protocols; therefore, when these computers are used as routers, it is often necessary to add routes manually. Microsoft is working on RIP and OSPF support for Windows NT.

Using TRACERT

If you're experiencing problems connecting machine A to machine B on the Internet, you can use TRACERT to trace the routes a packet takes as it traverses the wires. You'll see a screen dump of all the routers the packet travels through, the routers' names, and the time it takes to reach those routers.

TRACERT is a route-tracing utility that uses the IP TTL field and ICMP error messages to determine the route from one host to another through a network.

28

Sometimes TRACERT is useful when you're selecting an ISP, because you can trace the route between the ISP's router and another point to see how many hops are in between and how long it takes to send a transmission between the two. If the ISP routes your packets all over the world before reaching its destination, you'll want to avoid that ISP. Accessing this utility is as simple as typing TRACERT host (for example, TRACERT pda.com) or TRACERT 199.199.199.2 from the command prompt.

You've now seen how the ARP, IPCONFIG, NETSTAT, NBTSTAT, PING, ROUTE, and TRACERT utilities can provide useful information when you are trying to determine the cause of TCP/IP networking problems. Windows NT provides other troubleshooting tools such as the Performance Monitor and the Network Monitor.

Monitoring Activities with the Performance Monitor

The Performance Monitor is a graphical charting and statistics-gathering tool you can use to display performance information about your servers and network. You can have it alert you when certain events occur. Alerts are based on preset values that exceed or fall below a critical limit. You can use the monitoring, charting, and logging features of the Performance Monitor to help with initial performance troubleshooting and capacity planning for the local server or for other servers on the network.

You can start the Performance Monitor by selecting it from the Administrative Tools (Common) group. You can choose what to track and then store the collected information in files for later analysis. Here is a partial list of what you can do with the Performance Monitor:

☐ Set alerts to warn you about intruder activities or attempted unauthorized access to files.

☐ View information about multiple computers at the same time. You can open multiple copies of the Performance Monitor and track multiple events on each copy.

☐ Collect information in the form of charts, logs, alert logs, and reports.

☐ View the charts and dynamically change settings to fit your needs.

☐ Export the information you collect to spreadsheet or database programs for further analysis and printing.

☐ Set up alerts to track and compare counter values against preset thresholds.

☐ Create long-term archives by appending information to log files. Save current settings and values for future charting sessions.

28

This morning, you learned about the use of the Performance Monitor. Like most network management systems, the Performance Monitor tracks *objects*, or processes and services running in Windows NT Server computers. Every object has counters that keep track of specific events or activities. Here's a partial list of the objects you can monitor:

- ☐ Browser
- ☐ Cache
- ☐ FTP (File Transfer Protocol) service
- ☐ Gopher service
- ☐ HTTP service
- ☐ Memory
- ☐ NetBEUI and NetBEUI resource
- ☐ Network interface and segment
- ☐ NWLink IPX, NWLink NetBIOS, and NWLink SPX
- ☐ Physical disk
- ☐ Processor
- ☐ Remote Access Services
- ☐ Server
- ☐ System
- ☐ TCP/IP

The counters for objects are tracked and charted in the Performance Monitor window. You can view a complete list of objects to track and get a description of what they are by clicking the Explain button. The explanation window then opens at the bottom of the dialog box.

You can choose among four different viewing windows in the Performance Monitor. From the View menu, choose Chart, Alert, Log, or Report. Each window is quite different from the others, although all the windows share the menu bar, status bar, and toolbar of the Performance Monitor main window. The basic activities for the Performance Monitor are described here with reference to charting only. Alerts, logs, and reports are set up with similar procedures. For a complete description of how to use this utility, refer to Help.

Using the Network Monitor

NETMON, for Network Monitor, is a network diagnostic tool that monitors local area networks and provides a graphical display of network statistics. Network administrators can use these statistics to perform routine troubleshooting tasks, such as locating a server that is down or that is receiving a disproportionate number of work requests. NETMON is available as a part of Microsoft's Systems Management Server product.

28

Microsoft shipped the Network Monitor, a *sniffer* application, as part of the Systems Management Server (SMS) for the past few years. But SMS is expensive and it really should have been part of NT Server from the start. In NT Server Version 4, Microsoft provides a slightly crippled version of the Network Monitor in NT Server.

The version of Network Monitor shipping with NT Server records only network frames that either originate with or are destined for the particular server where it is running. So if you want to use Network Monitor to examine traffic from your server to machine A, and from machine A to your server, then you can use the version that ships with NT Server. On the other hand, if you want to use Network Monitor to examine traffic moving between machine A and machine B, you can't do that from your server (assuming that your server is neither machine A nor B).

Network Monitor captures packets as they travel across the wire. You then can analyze those packets to troubleshoot hardware and software problems (such as tracking down a faulty NIC). If you can't figure out the problem, you can send a captured trace someplace where it can be read.

The Network Monitor is a diagnostic tool for monitoring local area networks, locating a downed server, or locating bottlenecks on the network. It provides a graphical display of network statistics.

Installing the Network Monitor Agent

You can use Network Monitor Agent services on other Windows NT computers to capture statistics on those computers and have them sent to your Network Monitor computer.

Task 28.1. Installing the Network Monitor Agent.

Step 1: Description

You can install the Network Monitor Agent by opening the Networks utility in the Control Panel and selecting the Services tab. This task will show you how to install the Network Monitor Agent on a Windows NT computer.

Step 2: Action

1. From the Control Panel, double-click on the Network icon.
2. Select the Services tab, and then click Add.
3. From the Select Network Service window, highlight Network Monitor Agent, and then click OK.

28

4. Follow the instructions on-screen for providing a path to the Windows NT distribution files and completing Setup. After installation, you should see a window like the one shown in Figure 28.2, in which the Network Monitor Agent has been added.

Figure 28.2.

The Network dialog box with the Network Monitor Agent added.

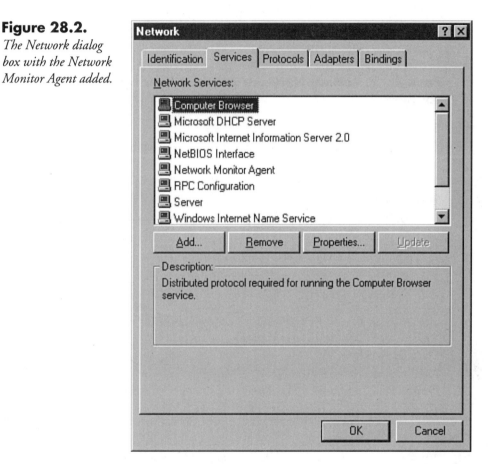

5. Click Close.

6. Restart your computer when prompted.

Step 3: Review

You can install the Network Monitor Agent by opening the Networks utility in the Control Panel and selecting the Services tab.

28

NOTE

> The Network Monitor Agent collects statistics from the computer's network adapter card by putting it in promiscuous mode. A NIC is *promiscuous* when it copies all data into memory rather than only the data intended for the node. You can view the statistics by using Performance Monitor.

Task 28.2. Adding Network Monitor Agent performance counters.

Step 1: Description

To add performance counters, configure the Network Monitor Agent under the Administrative Tools (Common).

Step 2: Action

1. Under Start|Programs|Administrative Tools (Common), select the Network Monitor Agent.
2. On the Edit menu, select Add To Chart.
3. Under Object in the Add To Chart dialog box, click Network Segment.
4. In Counter, select the counters you want to chart.
5. If necessary, you can select other options now, before you click Done.

Step 3: Review

After you have installed the Network Monitor Agent by using the Network icon in the Control Panel, you must add performance counters for the Network Monitor Agent.

NOTE

> The Network Segment object and associated counters are available only when you install the Network Monitor Agent.

The Network Monitor's Help system provides more information on setting up and using its information-gathering tools. With proper use, you can monitor the traffic of users.

The layout of the Network Monitor might look confusing, but notice that it contains four separate windows, each holding information:

- ☐ Information about the host that sent a frame onto the network
- ☐ Information about the host that received the frame

☐ The protocols used to send the frame

☐ The data, or a portion of the message, being sent

The address is a unique hexadecimal (or base-16) number that identifies a computer on the network; it's the hardware address assigned to every network interface card. To discover the hexadecimal address of a system, type one of the commands shown next, replacing *Ipaddress* with the IP address of the computer in question, or *computername* with the NetBIOS name of the computer.

```
NBTSTAT -A Ipaddress
NBTSTAT -a computername
```

The Network Monitor uses a "capture" process to gather information about the network for a certain time period. During this period, information about all the frames transmitted over the network is recorded and made available in the Network Monitor display. You can view information in the graphical display as it occurs, and you can save the captured information to files for later viewing.

When capturing information, you can set filters to view only the information that is essential for detecting intrusions or other problems. For example, you can filter by protocol to view frames related to a particular command that a user might be using. You also can filter by network address to capture frames from specific computers on your network. That lets you track the activities of a particular client. Up to four specific address pairs can be monitored. An address pair includes the addresses of two computers communicating with one another. You also can filter by data patterns, which lets you capture only frames that have a specific pattern of ASCII or hexadecimal data. You also can specify how many bytes of data into the frame that the pattern must occur.

You also can set *triggers*, or conditions that must be met before an action occurs. For example, you can set a trigger that starts capturing when a pattern (such as a code or sequence used by a client) is found, or you can set a trigger to stop the capture of data.

Note that display filters also are available. You can use them to view information that has already been captured.

Because the Network Monitor captures a large amount of information you might not need, you can create filters that prevent it from capturing specific types of frames. You also can set triggers that start a predesignated action when an event occurs on the network, such as when the buffer space is close to being full or when frames might be corrupted.

The Network Monitor requires a network adapter that supports what is usually called promiscuous mode. In this mode, a network adapter passes all the frames it detects on the network to the network software, regardless of the frame's destination address.

28

Securing the Network Monitor

As you just read, the Windows NT Network Monitor captures only frames sent to or from the computer where you are running the utility. It also displays statistics for the network segment that the computer is attached to, such as broadcast frames, network utilization, and total bytes received.

To protect a network from unauthorized use of Network Monitor installation, the Network Monitor provides password protections and the capability to detect other copies of Network Monitor on the local segment of the network. The passwords can prevent someone at a Windows NT Server computer that is running System Management Server from connecting with the computer and running the Network Monitor on that computer.

You use the Monitoring Agent icon in the Control Panel to change the passwords for the Network Monitor or Network Monitor Agent.

If other users run a copy of Network Monitor on their computers, they could use it to watch packets on the network and capture valuable information. Network Monitor detects other Network Monitor installations and displays the information about them, such as the name of the computer, the user, and the adapter address, and whether the utility is running, capturing, or transmitting information.

NOTE   Unfortunately, Network Monitor can only detect the existence of another version of Network Monitor. It cannot detect third-party monitoring software and hardware.

Configuring Alerts

When NETMON starts monitoring unusual activity, you might want the system to send someone a warning message, that is, an alert. Alerts are used to notify a domain administrator of a serious problem that has occurred on a Windows NT computer. You can send an alert to a particular domain user or a specific computer that is monitored by several administrators or support personnel. You can determine which users and computers are notified when administrative alerts occur at a selected computer.

The system generates administrative alerts relating to server and resource use. They warn about security and access problems, user session problems, server shutdown because of power loss when the UPS service is available, and printer problems.

If you want to guarantee that the alerts are sent, you should also modify the client workstation to start the Alert and Messenger services at system startup. This makes sure that the services are functioning and available to send administrative alerts. If the services are left in their default startup setting of manual, the services attempt to send the alert but might fail due to unforeseen circumstances. If the services fail, the alert cannot be sent. Also, to receive an administrative alert, the Messenger service must be running.

Task 28.3. Configuring the Alerter service.

Step 1: Description

To configure the Alerter service, select the Server icon from the Control Panel.

Step 2: Action

1. From the Start menu, select Control Panel.

2. Double-click the Server icon. You should see a dialog box like the one shown in Figure 28.3.

Figure 28.3.

The Server dialog box.

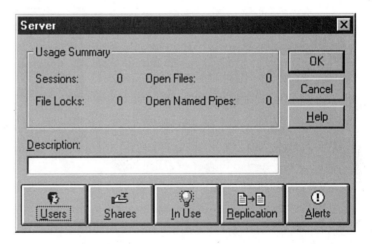

3. Click the Alerts button in the Server dialog box. The Alerts dialog box, shown in Figure 28.4, appears.

4. To add a new computer or user to be notified, enter the computer or user name in the New Computer or Username field, and then click the Add button. The computer or user name is then moved to the Send Administrative Alerts To field.

28

Figure 28.4.

The Alerts dialog box.

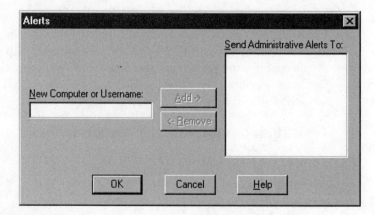

5. To remove a computer or user, select the computer or user name in the Send Administrative Alerts To field, and click the Remove button. This moves the computer or user name to the New Computer or Username field.

 NOTE

> You do not have to include the double backslashes (\\) for a computer name as you do for just about every other usage involving a computer name. If you do include them, the double backslashes are dropped when the name is moved.

6. To add or remove additional computers or users, repeat step 4 or 5.
7. When you have finished entering or removing computer and user names, click OK to return to the Server dialog box.

Step 3: Review

 Using the Server dialog box found in the Control Panel, you can set administrative alerts.

Looking for More Help?

The information in this chapter is somewhat limited. You can purchase other books that focus on fine-tuning or troubleshooting your network. So this section provides some online resources for administering your server and network.

28

First, you can check out the online users forum on CompuServe. Type `GO WINNT` to find the NT forum. While you're there, check the Support Tools (4) library, where you'll find the *NT 4.0 SetUp Troubleshooting Guide.* In addition, one library (3) in the NT forum contains fixes.

If you want to find more fixes, check out `http://ftp.microsoft.com/bussys/winnt/winnt-public/fixes/`. The Internet obviously provides a wealth of information for the Windows NT administrator. For instance, you can find the Windows NT Administration FAQ (Frequently Asked Questions) at `http://www.itech.com/oltc/admin/admin.stm`. You also might want to check the `comp.os.ms-windows.nt.admin.misc` or the `comp.os.ms-windows.nt.admin.networking` Usenet newsgroups.

Furthermore, there is a database of well-known errors out there. You can find a list of possible causes and corrections on the Microsoft Web site (`http://www.microsoft.com`) or on the WINNT forum on CompuServe. Check these areas for hints or try contacting Microsoft support at 206-637-7098. Another good source is Microsoft's TechNet CD, a useful compendium of NT-related information. The subscription costs $395 USD per annum.

Summary

The goal in tuning Windows NT is to determine which hardware resource is experiencing the greatest demand (bottleneck) and then adjust the operation to relieve that demand and maximize total throughput. A system should be structured so that its resources are used efficiently and distributed fairly among the users. The concepts presented in this chapter should be used as guidelines and not as absolutes. Each Windows NT Server environment is unique and requires experimentation and tuning appropriate to its conditions and requirements.

This chapter also looked at some networking tools available with Windows NT that you can use to problem-solve.

Well, you made it through 14 tough, grueling days. We wish you success in administering your server and network. Maybe someday we'll be surfing the Net and we'll visit your site. Good luck.

Workshop

To wrap up the day, you can review terms and tasks from the chapter, and see the answers to some commonly asked questions.

28

Terminology Review

alert—An audible or visual alarm that signals an error or serves as a warning of some sort.

ICMP (Internet Control Message Protocol)—A protocol used to exchange routing and reachability information between hosts and routers on the same network.

sniffer—A trade name of a hardware network analyzer. Now, used generically to specify any hardware or software protocol analyzer.

triggers—Conditions that must be met before an action occurs.

Task List

The emphasis of this chapter has been to introduce you to network fine-tuning and troubleshooting. As a system administrator, you will need to learn how to tune your scarce resources. Moreover, you will need to fix problems occasionally. You learned three simple tasks in this chapter:

☐ Installing the Network Monitor Agent
☐ Adding Network Monitor Agent performance counters
☐ Configuring the Alerter service

Q&A

Q Is there another way to configure and start the Alerter service?

A Yes, you can use the command NET START ALERTER at the command prompt. The Alerter service sends messages about the network to users. You select which events you want to trigger alerts in the Performance Monitor. For these alerts to be sent, both the Alerter and the Messenger services must be running on the computer originating the alerts, and the Messenger service must be running on the computer receiving them.

Q How can you determine whether TCP/IP is installed correctly on a Windows NT system?

A Try using ping on the local system by typing the IP loopback address (127.0.0.1) from the command line, like so: PING 127.0.0.1. The system should respond immediately. If ping is not found or the command fails, check the event log with Event Viewer and look for problems reported by Setup or the TCP/IP service. You also should attempt to ping the IP addresses of your local interface(s) to determine whether you configured IP properly. Successful use of ping indicates that the IP layer on the target system is probably functional.

Q **I cannot get an NT machine to connect to the network. Other machines on the network work fine. What can I do?**

A Well, in typical Microsoft troubleshooting fashion, you should start over. Often you change so many parameters that it just isn't easy to get things set up.

So make sure that there isn't a cabling problem by substituting a working NT machine in place of the one having the problem. Also, confirm that the network adapter is working by trying it in a different machine. Then go into the problem machine, open the Network applet in the Control Panel, and remove everything, including the device drivers for the network adapter. Then reboot the machine. Now, when you go back into the Network applet, it asks whether you want to install the network drivers. Do so, but install only the NetBEUI protocol. This is the simplest protocol, so it has the highest chance of a successful implementation. See whether that protocol can see the rest of the network by trying to connect to something using the Explorer. That almost will certainly work unless there are hardware problems. Now add in the other pieces incrementally, and you are set.

28

APPENDIXES

APPENDIX

A

Microsoft Windows NT Server Certification Programs

In the previous two weeks, you learned about installing, exploring, and managing your NT Server. Now you can learn how to become a certified user of NT.

Microsoft (MS) offers certification programs designed around its product line:

- ☐ Microsoft Certified System Engineer (MCSE)
- ☐ Microsoft Certified Product Specialist (MCPS)
- ☐ Microsoft Certified Solution Developer (MCSD)
- ☐ Microsoft Certified Trainer (MCT)

MCSE graduates are those who achieved the ability to plan, develop, implement, and maintain a wide range of computing platforms and information systems using Microsoft NT Server and the Microsoft BackOffice family of products.

Those with the MCPS designation demonstrated their expertise in particular MS products. To obtain the designation, you must have an in-depth knowledge of at least one MS operating system, such as Windows NT Server or Windows 3.1 and Windows 95.

Obtaining an MCSD requires that you are qualified to design, develop, and create business applications by using MS tools and platforms such as BackOffice and Windows NT.

Finally, an MCT has passed the qualifications and testing necessary to instruct others on official MS curriculum for the various Microsoft Authorized Technical Education Centers.

Why is certification offered, and how does it benefit you? As with any field of endeavor, in the computing field it is often hard to ascertain a person's credentials without some form of assistance. Certification helps fill that gap by providing a base level of expected competence and the assurance that those who are certified pass reasonable examinations and have the anticipated level of knowledge.

Training and certification through this process is time-consuming and expensive. Obtaining the certification for MCSE by taking the needed courses and the exams costs several thousands of dollars. You need to decide whether the cost in time and money is worth the gain. If you plan to work in this field for any length of time, these certification programs might give you the prestige necessary to get that new job or prove to management your dedication and qualifications.

In the remaining section, we discuss each qualification according to Microsoft criteria, and you'll learn more about what is needed to become certified.

Why Obtain Certification?

You might want to become certified for many reasons. Company leaders realize that they must invest in qualified computer professionals who have clearly demonstrated knowledge

of how to design, develop, and support the wide variety of mission-critical solutions that are often utilizing the latest technologies and platforms.

Company leaders also realize that they must upgrade the skills of their existing workforce to remain competitive in an ever-changing marketplace. Certification becomes a cost-effective and useful tool for providing objective methods of measuring competence and ensuring the qualifications of technical professionals, thus helping companies in their quest for excellence.

Finally, information systems are shifting to smaller and smaller groups, and knowledgeable staff are becoming more important. Companies need technical professionals who can implement and maintain the enterprise systems, develop new solutions, and provide technical support—and they need to be sure that the staff they have are able to perform these functions well. Certification helps provide those assurances.

Microsoft offers detailed information concerning the benefits of certification, including several studies that show the improvements in customer satisfaction and cost reduction through the use of certified individuals. Visit Microsoft's Web site for additional information. Look for the document called Mcpback.doc, which clearly outlines these advantages.

You can also obtain a Microsoft Windows–based application that allows you to quickly create a personal training and certification plan. This application, called the Microsoft Roadmap to Education and Certification, is available electronically from the following locations:

Internet: `ftp://ftp.microsoft.com/Services/MSEdCert/E&CMAP.ZIP`

MSN: `Go To MOLI`, Advising Building, E&C Roadmap

CompuServe: `GO MECFORUM`, Library #2, E&CMAP.ZIP

Microsoft TechNet: Search for "Roadmap"

Certification remains a viable and effective method for individuals and corporations to ensure a useful measurement of skills and competence.

Obtaining Certification

You have several steps to take to obtain your certification. First, you need to decide which program best serves your background and interests. Study the four programs and determine which one is best for you.

After deciding on a particular program, consider studying the exam Preparation and Study Guides that Microsoft offers to find out a bit about the exam you will take and what is expected. This effort will give you an idea of how the exam is created, what types of questions are asked, and how the questions are scored. In addition, you can find information about preparing for the exam and topics that you might be tested on.

Now you need to decide whether your qualifications are sufficient to pass the exam or whether you need additional preparation and training. Our book provides you with a sound base for dealing with the MCSE or MCPS designations, but you must decide for yourself whether you have learned enough to pass these exams. Our book is not designed to be the only studying you perform, and you should consider additional training or help before becoming certified.

Microsoft offers instructor-led seminars, as well as self-paced training. The self-paced option offers you ample opportunity to take a course even if your job requires travel or time is hard for you to schedule. Using a self-paced method is fine as long as you are disciplined enough to continue the course with nobody pressuring you. (You might decide to use the self-paced training and have your spouse provide support. Of course, this might introduce too much stress, depending on your personal habits.)

Before taking any of the courses, finish this book and gain additional experience with the product so that you are completely familiar with each function. Then you will be ready to take a self-assessment exam to see how you might fare. You can find these exams on the Microsoft Web site mentioned later, in the section called "Where Can I Find Out More?" This exercise provides you with a good idea of whether your present skill level is adequate or whether you need additional work before taking the official exam. Note that passing an assessment exam doesn't necessarily mean that you'll pass the official exam. Make sure that you're comfortable with your proficiency before spending the time and money on certification.

Finally, Microsoft has an arrangement with a company called Sylvan Prometric for exam sessions. This company has offices across North America and offers exams on a regular schedule. Contact Microsoft for details, or call Sylvan Prometric at 1-800-755-EXAM to register in Canada and the United States. If you are at all in doubt, or if you are in another country, Microsoft suggests that you call the local Microsoft office for details.

The Microsoft Certified System Engineer

Obtaining the MCSE certification shows that you are proficient in the planning, implementation, and maintenance of Microsoft Windows NT and Microsoft BackOffice. It provides you with industry recognition and offers a chance to be one step ahead of an uncertified person, providing that all other things are equal. The I.T. world is fast becoming dependent on such qualifications, much like a university degree, to try to gain an edge in managing the differing levels of expertise available.

Although we believe that this certification is a valuable tool in your business arsenal, we do not believe that it is the be-all and end-all. You still need all other quantifiable aspects of

A

business, including experience. Getting a designation at the expense of obtaining bona fide experience in industry is never a sound decision.

Microsoft offers you various benefits if you obtain the MCSE. The organization provides access to technical information through a subscription to one of its magazines, called *Microsoft TechNet*. It also offers discounts on product support and provides a free ten-pack of priority support calls.

You also become a member of Microsoft's beta program, allowing you to participate in future product development and see the new products before their release. Another magazine, called *Microsoft Certified Professional* magazine, is developed especially for certified folks, and you also get this for some time, along with an Update letter that keeps you informed of what is happening in the certification program.

Finally, Microsoft provides you with a forum on its MSN network to communicate with other certified professionals and with Microsoft.

So what is necessary for you to become a certified system engineer? We provide an answer but strongly suggest contacting Microsoft for details because these programs change without notice, and this material can quickly become dated.

An MCSE needs to pass four operating-system exams and two elective exams to qualify for the designation. The operating-system component includes exams concerning NT 3.51 or 4.0, Windows for Workgroups, or Windows 95. The electives are chosen from such areas as Microsoft SQL Server, SMS, and Microsoft Exchange.

Is certification for you? That's a question you'll have to answer. In our opinion, it is one additional qualification, and that is rarely a bad thing in these competitive days.

Microsoft Certified Product Specialist

The MCPS designation is for persons demonstrating competence with a particular Microsoft product. So what is necessary for you to become a certified product specialist? We provide an answer but again strongly suggest contacting Microsoft for details because these programs change without notice and this material can quickly become dated.

You need knowledge of at least one operating system, and you can take additional exams to further qualify your skills with such products as BackOffice and Windows 3.1.

For our purposes, you are on your way to qualifying for this particular designation upon completion of this book. You would take the Microsoft NT Server 4.0 exam.

Microsoft offers you various benefits if you obtain the MCPS. You're given access to technical information through a free copy of *Microsoft TechNet CD* and a 50 percent discount on the

TechNet Information Network service, which provides information through issuance of monthly CDs.

You also get another magazine developed especially for certified folks, called *Microsoft Certified Professional* magazine, for one year. And you get an Update letter that keeps you informed of what is happening in the certification program.

Finally, Microsoft gives you a forum on its MSN network to communicate with other certified professionals and with Microsoft.

Microsoft Certified Trainer

This final program, MCT, offers something for persons who plan to provide training on Microsoft products. It shows that you are qualified and certified to teach Microsoft's official curriculum. It is available only to trainers who will deliver courses at Microsoft Authorized Technical Education Centers and so is somewhat limited in its use.

To qualify, you go through various steps that Microsoft suggests. First, you need to complete Microsoft's special application form and present your qualifications to Microsoft. Next, you need to prepare and be ready to present the particular course you are being certified to lead. You need to pass the relevant exams for the product you are teaching. And, finally, you must attend one of the courses you plan to teach so that you can see how it is managed and understand any labs that might be involved. For some courses, you might be able to attend a special trainer prep course instead, although you do not get any normal course credit for attending the special class. After these steps are completed to Microsoft's satisfaction, you are licensed to be an MCT.

Obtaining Files and Sample Tests

Microsoft offers additional information for you and provides various files and test samples that you download from Microsoft's Web page. Included in this download page are exam preparation guides, assessment exams that test your current knowledge, allowing you to determine whether you are ready to take the exam and obtain certification.

You also can obtain additional certification guides and updates providing the latest information and changes to these programs. A particularly interesting paper is one called "The Value of Certification for Solution Developers White Paper." In this paper is an authoritative paper from Southern Illinois University at Carbondale that provides an immensely detailed discussion on the value of obtaining this certification. If you are looking at the MCSD designation and need additional data to convince your boss of its value, we strongly suggest downloading this file and using the material to help your cause.

The paper describes in detail the needs and responsibilities of a developer and uses extensive analysis and survey techniques to provide you with a solid answer to the program's effectiveness. We do not intend to give away the answer here, but we again recommend that you find and read the paper for yourself if you have any expectation of obtaining the MCSD designation.

In addition to this guide, you can obtain assessment tests, to provide you with some degree of comfort about your present skill levels, and several certification updates.

Finally, there is a Windows NT 4.0 self-administered assessment file (around 585KB in size) that offers you some assessment of how you are doing now that you are finished with this book. By taking this assessment, you can discover which areas you might need to review and know for certain where your strength lies.

You can find all of these materials by using the following address:

`www.microsoft.com/train_cert/download.htm`

Where Can I Find Out More?

If you have finished reading the information in this appendix, you are ready to obtain more detailed information on when and where testing takes place and how to sign up for the courses.

Microsoft offers detailed information on its Web page, and that is a good place to start. You can find this page at

`http://www.microsoft.com/train_cert/default.htm`

Microsoft also offers you a way to download the entire site and view it offline. Although this is a good idea, you need an extensive network connection and about 4MB of hard drive space to take advantage of the option.

If you are a dial-up user, however, this method might save you time because the site is fairly extensive. Traveling through it all takes a fair amount of time, especially if you choose to study each section in any detail. To download the certification data, go to the site using the following URL:

`http://www.microsoft.com/train_cert/new/offline.htm`

APPENDIX

B

Windows NT Server Command Reference

Because you might occasionally need to use the command prompt, this appendix serves as a useful reference of Windows NT NET commands. You can do just about anything from the command prompt that you can do in a normal session, but typing a command correctly is a bit more awkward than pointing and clicking.

An advantage to using the command prompt over the graphical interface is that you don't have to remember where anything is. When you remember the command name, you can do everything from the same place.

In general, the people who need to use the command prompt to connect are the network's OS/2 and DOS clients. If you're administering the server, you probably don't have much occasion to use the command prompt, except when making adjustments to DOS and OS/2 workstations.

The information for each command can include some or all of the following elements:

- [ ] The name of the command
- [ ] A description of the command
- [ ] The command syntax
- [ ] Command parameters
- [ ] The procedure for using the command
- [ ] Notes about the usage of the command, if appropriate

NET ACCOUNTS

To make individual adjustments to user accounts, you use the NET USER command (discussed later in this appendix). To make adjustments concerning such things as forcible logoff and password age to the entire user account database, you use the NET ACCOUNTS command. When used without switches, NET ACCOUNTS displays the current account information.

Syntax

```
net accounts [/option] [/domain]
```

Parameters

Option	Description
/FORCELOGOFF:{*number* ¦ NO}	Sets the number of minutes a user has between the time that his account expires or logon period ends and the time that the server forcibly disconnects the user. The default is NO.
/MINPWLEN:{*number*}	Specifies the minimum number of characters that a user's password account must have, from 0 to 14. The default is 6.
/MAXPWAGE:{*number* ¦ UNLIMITED}	Specifies the maximum number of days that must pass before the user modifies her password. The possible range for /maxpwage is 0 to 49,710 days (a little more than 136 years, which makes you wonder how Microsoft decided on that maximum value), with a default value of 90 days. You also can set the value to UNLIMITED if you want the password to never expire.
/MINPWAGE:{*number*}	Specifies the minimum number of days that must pass before the user modifies his password. You can set the /minpwage from 0 to 49,710 days, but its default value is 0 days, meaning that the user can change the password whenever desired, even more than once a day.
/SYNC	Updates the user accounts database.
/UNIQUEPW:{*number*}	Determines the number of unique passwords a user must cycle through before repeating one. The highest value you can assign to this variable is 24.

Procedure

1. Select Start|Programs|Command Prompt.
2. Type the command at the DOS prompt.

Usage

When you're performing this operation on a workstation that does not have NT Server loaded, add the switch /domain to the end of the command to make the command apply to the domain controller of the domain you're in. If the machine has NT Server on board, the information automatically passes to the domain controller.

NET COMPUTER

The NET COMPUTER command adds or deletes computers (not users) from a domain.

Syntax

```
net computer \\computername\ {/add ¦ /delete}
```

Procedure

1. Select Start|Programs|Command Prompt.
2. Type the command at the DOS prompt.

Usage

The computername is the name of the computer to be added to or deleted from the local domain. This command works only on computers running NT Server.

Note, by the way, that NET COMPUTER applies to computers, not to users. Users are not members of domains, only computers are.

NET CONFIG

You can use the NET CONFIG command to see how a machine is configured to behave on the network and, to a limited extent, change that configuration.

Syntax

```
net config {server [/option1] ¦ workstation [/option2]}
```

Parameters

Option1 applies to server.

Option	Description
/AUTODISCONNECT:*time*	Sets the number of minutes a user's session with that computer can be inactive before it's disconnected. If you specify -1, the session never disconnects. The upper limit is 65,535 minutes, a little more than 45 hours. The default is 15 minutes.
/SRVCOMMENT:"*text*"	Adds a comment to a server (here, that means any machine that's sharing resources with the network) that people can see when they view network resources with NET VIEW. Your comment, which can be up to 48 characters long including spaces, should be enclosed in quotation marks.
/HIDDEN:{YES ¦ NO}	Allows you the option of not displaying that server on the list of network resources. Hiding a server doesn't change people's ability to access it, but only keeps people who don't need to know about it from accessing it. The default is NO.

Option2 applies to workstation.

Option	Description
/CHARCOUNT:*bytes*	Specifies the amount of data that NT collects before sending the data to a communication device. The range is 0 to 65,535 bytes; the default is 16.
/CHARTIME:*msec*	Specifies the amount of time during which the machine collects data for transmittal before forwarding it to the communication device. If the /charcount:*bytes* option also is used, the specification satisfied first will be the one that NT acts on. You can set the *msec* value from 0 to 655,350,000; the default is 250 milliseconds.
/CHARWAIT:*sec*	Specifies the number of seconds that NT waits for a communication device to become available. The range is 0 to 65,535 seconds; the default is 3600.

B

Procedure

1. Select Start|Programs|Command Prompt.
2. Type the command at the DOS prompt.

Usage

Used without switches, NET CONFIG names the configurable services (namely, the server and the workstation). If you include one of the configurable services in the command, for example, if you type NET CONFIG SERVER, you will see the following items of information:

- ☐ The name of the computer
- ☐ The software version
- ☐ The network card's name and address
- ☐ That the server is visible to the network
- ☐ The limit to the number of users who can log on
- ☐ The maximum number of files that can be open per session with another computer
- ☐ The idle session time

The NET CONFIG WORKSTATION command displays information about the configuration of the workstation service.

NET CONTINUE

To restart a paused service, you use the NET CONTINUE command.

Syntax

```
net continue service
```

Procedure

Type the command at the DOS prompt.

Usage

The NET CONTINUE command affects the following default services:

- [ ] NET LOGON
- [ ] NETWORK DDE
- [ ] NETWORK DDE DSDM
- [ ] SCHEDULE
- [ ] SERVER
- [ ] WORKSTATION

NET FILE

You can use NET FILE to find out what is open and who is using it.

Syntax

```
net file [file ID] [¦close]
```

Procedure

1. Select Start|Programs|Command Prompt.
2. Type net start workstation.
3. Type the command at the DOS prompt.

Usage

Without switches, you can use the NET FILE command to display the open files. The output lets you know what's open and who (users, not computers) is using it. When you add the switches, you can identify that file to the server and shut it down, removing all file locks.

NET GROUP

The NET GROUP command provides you with information on global groups on a server and enables you to modify this information.

Syntax

```
net group [groupname] [/comment:"text"] [/domain]
net group groupname {/add [/comment:"text"] ¦ /delete} [/domain]
net group groupname username [...] {/add ¦ /delete} [/domain]
```

Parameters

Option	Description
/ADD	Adds a new global group to the domain.
/COMMENT:{"text"}	Adds a descriptive comment to a new or an existing group.
/DELETE	Deletes a new global group to the domain.

Procedure

1. Select Start|Programs|Command Prompt.
2. Type the command at the DOS prompt.

Usage

Typed without parameters, NET GROUP just lists the global groups on your server, but you can use the options to modify the membership of global groups, check on their membership, add comments to the group names, or add or delete global groups on the server.

Use the *username* option when you want to add or delete a user to the group.

When you are executing the NET GROUP command from a workstation on which NT Server is not installed, add the /domain switch to the end of the statement to make the command apply to the domain controller. Otherwise, you perform the requested action only at the workstation you are working from. If you're working on a server with NT Server installed, the /domain switch isn't necessary.

NET HELP

You can use the NET HELP command to get information attached to a command. The command's Help file is displayed.

Syntax

```
net help [command] ¦ more
```

Procedure

1. Select Start|Programs|Command Prompt.
2. Type the command at the DOS prompt.

Usage

The ¦ more switch is necessary for commands with more than one screen of information.

Optionally, you can get the same information by typing this:

```
net print /help or net print /?
```

Typing net print /? doesn't net you much information under NT Server—it merely gives you the proper syntax for the command. To view an explanation of all the command syntax symbols, just type this:

```
net help syntax
```

NET HELPMSG

NET HELPMSG works as a decoder for the NT error, warning, and alert messages. When you see an error message with a number attached, use this command to see the Help file attached to that error message.

Syntax

```
net helpmsg number
```

Procedure

1. Select Start|Programs|Command Prompt.
2. Type the command at the DOS prompt.

B

Usage

The *number* is the four-digit error message number.

NET LOCALGROUP

The NET LOCALGROUP refers to local user groups, and NET GROUP refers to global, or domain-wide, ones. Unlike NET GROUP, this command can be used on NT workstations as well as NT Server servers.

Syntax

```
net localgroup [groupname] [/comment:"text"] [/domain]
net localgroup groupname {/add [/comment:"text"] ¦ /delete} [/domain]
net localgroup groupname username [...] {/add ¦ /delete} [/domain]
```

Parameters

Option	Description
/ADD	Adds a new local group to the domain.
/COMMENT:{"text"}	Adds a descriptive comment to a new or an existing group.
/DELETE	Deletes a new local group to the domain.

Procedure

1. Select Start|Programs|Command Prompt.
2. Type the command at the DOS prompt.

Usage

Typed without parameters, NET LOCALGROUP just lists the local groups on your server, but you can use the options to modify the membership of local groups, check on their membership, add comments to the group names, or add or delete global groups on the server.

NET NAME

You're not dependent on e-mail to send messages across the network. From the command prompt, you can send messages and arrange to have your own forwarded so that they catch up with you wherever you are. As long as your computer and the computer where you direct the messages are running the message service, you can reach anywhere on the network.

Syntax

```
net name username [/option]
```

Procedure

1. Select Start|Programs|Command Prompt.
2. Type the command at the DOS prompt.

Usage

The NET NAME command adds or deletes a *messaging name* (also known as an *alias)* at a workstation. The messaging name is the name that receives messages at that station; any messages sent over the network go to where the messaging name is. Although this command comes with two switches, /add and /delete, the /add switch is not necessary to add a messaging name to a workstation; instead, you would need only type NET NAME *username*.

NET PAUSE

If you need to halt a service temporarily, you can use the NET PAUSE command to do it.

Syntax

```
net pause service
```

Procedure

1. Select Start|Programs|Command Prompt.
2. Type the command at the DOS prompt.

Usage

The NET PAUSE command affects the following default services:

- ☐ NET LOGON
- ☐ NETWORK DDE
- ☐ NETWORK DDE DSDM
- ☐ SCHEDULE
- ☐ SERVER
- ☐ WORKSTATION

NET PRINT

With the NET PRINT command, you can control print jobs, just as you can with the Print Manager.

Syntax

```
net print \\computername\sharename
net print [\\computername] job# [/delete ¦ /release ¦ /hold]
```

Procedure

1. Select Start|Programs|Command Prompt.
2. Type the command at the DOS prompt.

Usage

You can get a list of all the jobs currently printing or waiting on that printer by specifying *sharename*, or the name of the printer as it is shared on the network.

You can delete a print job by referring to that number and using the /delete switch. If you want to hold a print job (keep it in the print queue but let other jobs print ahead of it) or release it (free a held job to print), substitute the /hold or /release switch for /delete.

NET SEND

NET SEND is a messaging service for sending a message to one person, to all the people in your group, to all the people in your domain, to all the people on the network, or to all the users connected to the server. NET SEND does not work without its parameters, because you need to tell it what to send and where to send it.

Syntax

```
net send {name ¦ * ¦ /domain[:domainname] ¦ /users ¦ /broadcast} "message text"
```

Parameters

Option	Description
/DOMAIN	Sends the message to everyone in your domain. Just substitute your domain's name for the word *domain*. If you include a name of a domain or workgroup like domain: *domainname* where *domainname* is the name of the domain or workgroup that you want to receive the message, then the message is sent to all users in the domain or workgroup. When you don't include a name with this switch, the message is sent to the local domain.
/USERS	Sends the message to all users connected to the server.
/BROADCAST	Sends the message to all users on the network.

Procedure

1. Select Start|Programs|Command Prompt.
2. Type the command at the DOS prompt.

Usage

To send a message that says "This is a test message" to Barry, who is part of your domain, you type this:

```
net send barry This is a test message
```

If Barry is in another domain, say Balliol, you would type this:

```
net send barry \balliol This is a test message
```

If you want to send a message that says "This is a test message" to everyone in your domain, type this:

```
net send * This is a test message
```

NET SESSION

Used on servers, this command displays information about sessions between the server and other computers on the network.

Syntax

```
net session [\\computername\] [/delete]
```

Procedure

1. Select Start|Programs|Command Prompt.
2. Type the command at the DOS prompt.

Usage

When you type the command without switches, you get a screen showing all the computers that are logged onto that server. When you include NET SESSION switches, you can get more detailed information about a session with a particular computer, or delete a session (that is, disconnect a computer from the server).

WARNING

Be careful when using the /delete switch. If you neglect to include the computer name in the command, you end all current sessions, and everyone has to reconnect to the server.

NET SHARE

The NET SHARE command applies to resources that the server is sharing with the network. The command provides you with information about that particular shared resource.

Syntax

```
net share sharename
net share sharename=drive:path [/users:number ¦ /unlimited] [/remark:"comment"]
net share [/users:number ¦ /unlimited] [/remark:"comment"]
net share {sharename ¦ devicename ¦ drive:path} [/delete]
```

Parameters

Option	Description
/USERS:number	Sets the maximum number of users who can simultaneously access the shared resource.
/UNLIMITED	Specifies an unlimited number of users who can simultaneously access the shared resource.
/REMARK:"comment"	Adds a descriptive comment for the shared resource.
/DELETE	Stops sharing the resource.

Procedure

1. Select Start|Programs|Command Prompt.

2. Type net start workstation.

3. Type the command at the DOS prompt.

Usage

Used alone, this command lists all resources currently being shared with the network. With its switches, you can create and delete shared resources.

NET SHARE is a useful command not only for viewing the setup of existing shared devices, but also for creating new ones and configuring existing shares. You must be using an account with administrative rights to use this command; ordinary user accounts can't use it.

To stop sharing a device, type NET SHARE, the share name, device name, or drive and path, and then add the /delete switch.

NOTE

When using the NET SHARE command, keep in mind that when you enable the guest account, any devices you share with the network are automatically available to the entire network; you can't set individual or group permissions with this command. If you want to restrict access to devices or drives, you must set the permissions on the pertinent device or drive from the File Manager or Print Manager.

NET START

The NET START command encompasses a long list of network services that can be started. The command cannot start all the services available from the Services icon in the Control Panel, but only the network-related ones. On its own, it doesn't do anything except list the services that have already been started. The list you see when you type NET START is not a complete list of all the network services available.

Syntax

```
net start [servicename]
```

Parameters

The default services in Windows NT are shown here.

Service	Description
ALERTER	Sends messages about the network to users. You select which events that you want to trigger alerts in the Performance Monitor. For these alerts to be sent, both the Alerter and Messenger services must be running on the computer originating the alerts, and the Messenger service must be running on the computer receiving them.
CLIPBOOK SERVER	Allows you to start a temporary or permanent storage place for text or graphics that you want to cut and paste between applications. You see a message that the service has been started, or if you've already started it from NT Server, you see a message that the service was already started.
COMPUTER BROWSER	Allows your computer to browse and be browsed on the network. When you start it from the command prompt, however, you get no further information than the fact that the service has started.

Service	Description
DIRECTORY REPLICATOR	Allows you to dynamically update files between servers. You must have replication rights to use this command, which means you have to set up a user account with replication rights before you start this service.
EVENTLOG	Begins the event log, which audits selected events on the network, such as file access, user logons and logoffs, and the starting of programs. You can select which events you want to log, and also whether you want the log to consist of both successful and failed attempts, just failures, or just successes (although just recording successes doesn't sound terribly useful if you're trying to monitor the system).
MESSENGER	Starts the messenger service, which must be running on both the machine sending the message and the receiving one(s) for NET SEND and the Alerter service.
NET LOGON	Starts the net logon service, which verifies logon requests and controls replication of the user accounts database.
NETWORK DDE	Provides a network transport for dynamic data exchange (DDE) conversations and provides security for them.
NETWORK DDE DSDM	Used by the DDE service described earlier, the DDE share database manager (DSDM) manages the DDE conversations.
NT LM SECURITY SUPPORT PROVIDER	Provides Windows NT security to RPC applications that use transports other than LAN Manager named pipes.

continues

B

Service	Description
REMOTE PROCEDURE CALL (RPC) SERVICE	Enables programmers to develop distributed applications more easily by providing pointers to direct the applications. The default name service is the Windows NT Locator.
REMOTE PROCEDURE CALL (RPC) LOCATOR	Allows distributed applications to use the RPC-provided pointer by directing the applications to those pointers. This service manages the RPC NSI database.
SCHEDULE	Starts the scheduling service, which must be running to use the AT command. The AT command can be used to schedule commands and programs (like the backup program, for instance) to run on a certain computer at a specific time and date.
SERVER	Controls access to network resources from the command line. This service must be running before you can perform named pipe, directory and printer sharing, and RPC access.
SPOOLER	Provides print spooler capabilities.
UPS	Starts the uninterruptible power system.
WORKSTATION	Enables workstations to connect to and use shared network resources. After you start this service, you can see what's on the network and connect to it.

Procedure

1. Select Start|Programs|Command Prompt.
2. Type the command at the DOS prompt.

Usage

All two-word commands, such as "clipbook server" and "computer browser" must be enclosed within quotation marks for the NET START commands to work.

In addition to the default Windows NT Server services, you can start the following special services:

- ☐ Client Server for NetWare
- ☐ DHCP Client
- ☐ File Server for Macintosh
- ☐ FTP Server
- ☐ Gateway Service for NetWare
- ☐ LPDSVC
- ☐ Microsoft DHCP Server
- ☐ Network Monitoring Agent
- ☐ OLE
- ☐ Print Server for Macintosh
- ☐ Remote Access Connection Manager
- ☐ Remote Access ISNSAP Service
- ☐ Remote Access Server
- ☐ Remoteboot
- ☐ Simple TCP/IP Services
- ☐ SNMP
- ☐ TCP/IP NETBIOS Helper
- ☐ Windows Internet Name Service

NET STATISTICS

The NET STATISTICS command gives you a report on the computer where you run it.

Syntax

```
net statistics [server ¦ workstation]
```

Procedure

1. Select Start|Programs|Command Prompt.
2. Type the command at the DOS prompt.

Usage

If you use STATISTICS without a switch, you get a list of the services for which statistics are available (server and/or workstation, depending on whether you use the command on an NT or NT Server machine).

You can use either NET STATISTICS SERVER or NET STATISTICS WORKSTATION from any NT or NT Server machine, but the command can give you information only about the machine where you run it.

NET STOP

NET STOP works in the same way that NET START does. On its own, it can't do anything, but when you add the name of a service that you want to stop, this command stops it. See the "NET START" section, earlier in the appendix, for details on what each of the services does.

WARNING

Be careful when stopping a service! Some services are dependent on others (such as NET START, NET LOGON, and NET START WORKSTATION), so when you shut down one, you might shut down another without meaning to. If you just need to stop a service temporarily, use NET PAUSE instead. You need administrative rights to stop a service.

Syntax

```
net stop servicename
```

Procedure

1. Select Start|Programs|Command Prompt.
2. Type the command at the DOS prompt.

NET TIME

Some services, such as directory replication, depend on the server's and the workstations' clocks being set to the same time. To automate this process, you can use the NET TIME command.

Syntax

```
net time [\\computername ¦ /domain:[domainname]] [¦set]
```

Procedure

1. Select Start|Programs|Command Prompt.
2. Type the command at the DOS prompt.

Usage

The NET TIME command works differently when you execute it from a server than when you execute it from a workstation. When you run it from a server, it displays the current time; when you run it from a workstation, you can synchronize your computer's clock with that of the time server, even selecting a server from another domain where there is a trusted relationship between your domain and the other one. Ordinary users cannot set the server time from a workstation; only members of the Administrators or Server Manager groups, logged onto the server (logically, if not physically), can set the system time.

NET USE

After you've browsed the network with NET VIEW, you can connect to all the available goodies (or disconnect from those you don't want) with the NET USE command. Use this command to connect to drives D through Z and printer ports LPT1 through LPT9.

Syntax

```
net use [devicename ¦ *] [\\computername\sharename[\volume] [password ¦ *]
➥[/user:[domainname\]username]
net use [devicename ¦ *] [password ¦ *]] [/home]
net use [/persistent:{YES ¦ NO}]
```

Parameters

Option	Description
/HOME	To connect to your home directory (the directory on the server that has been assigned to you, assuming that there is one).
/PERSISTENT:{YES ¦ NO}	No matter what kind of connection you make, you can make it persistent (that is, remake it every time you connect to the network) by adding the switch /persistent:YES to the end of the line. If you don't want it to be persistent, type /persistent:NO instead. The default is whatever you chose last.
/DELETE	Use this to disconnect from a resource.

Procedure

1. Select Start|Programs|Command Prompt.

2. Type net start workstation.

3. Type the command at the DOS prompt.

Usage

To get information about the workstation's current connections, use the command without options. To actually make connections, use the command's switches.

Also, you use this command to connect to a shared resource such as a printer. You get to specify the port name or drive letter that you want to connect a resource to, but you're restricted to drive letters D through Z and ports LPT1 through LPT9. Also, when the computer that you're getting the resource from has a blank character in its name (that is, has two words in it), you must put the name in quotation marks.

When a password is attached to the resource that you're trying to connect to, you need to include that password in your connection command. Or if you want the computer to prompt you for the password so that it isn't displayed on-screen, append an asterisk. Passwords go before the user's name in the statement.

NOTE

> If you get help on this command, you'll notice that it claims that you can use only printer ports LPT1 through LPT3. Technically, this isn't true, but the Help file probably puts it this way because some MS-DOS applications are not able to access printer ports with numbers higher than 3.

NET USER

You can use the NET USER command from the server to control user accounts—to add them, delete them, and change them. If you type this command without parameters, you get a list of the user accounts for that server. You can use switches and parameters to manipulate accounts.

Syntax

```
net user [username [password ¦ *] [/options]] [/domain]
net user username {password ¦ *} /add [options] [/domain]
net user username [/delete] [/domain]
```

Parameters

Option	Description
asterisk (*)	Placing an asterisk after the user's name prompts you to enter and confirm a new password for the user account.
/ACTIVE:{YES ¦ NO}	This option determines whether the account is active or inactive. If it's inactive, the user cannot log onto this account. Deactivating an account is not the same thing as deleting it: A deactivated account can be reinstated if it's simply reactivated, but a deleted account is dead. A deleted account's parameters are lost, and even when

continues

Option	Description
	you create a new account with the same name and password, you need to rebuild the user rights and other account information. The default is YES.
/COMMENT:"*text*"	Enclose the comment text (no more than 48 characters, including spaces) in quotation marks. You don't have to put a comment on an account.
/COUNTRYCODE:*nnn*	This option selects the operating system's country code so that the operating system knows what language to use for help and error messages. The default for this option is 0.
/EXPIRES:{*date* ¦ NEVER}	If you enter a date after the colon, the account will expire on that date; NEVER sets no time limit on the account. Depending on the country code, type the expiration date as *mm,dd,yy* or *dd,mm,yy* (the format in the U.S. is *mm,dd,yy*). You can enter the year with either four characters or two, and months as a number, spelled out, or abbreviated to two letters. Use commas or front slashes (/), not spaces, to separate the parts of the date.
/FULLNAME:"*name*"	This is the user's full name, as opposed to the username. Enclose the name in quotation marks.
/HOMEDIR:*pathname*	If you've set up a home directory for the user, this is where you include the pointers to that directory. You have to set up the home directory before you set up this part of the account.
/HOMEDIRREQ:{YES ¦ NO}	If the user is required to use a home directory, select YES. You must have already created the directory and used the /HOMEDIR switch to specify where the directory is.

Option	*Description*
/PASSWORDCHG:{YES ¦ NO}	This option specifies whether the user can change the password. The default is YES.
/PASSWORDREQ:{YES ¦ NO}	This option specifies whether a password is required on the user account. The default is YES.
/PROFILEPATH:*path*	This option specifies a path for the user's logon profile, when there is one for the account.
/SCRIPTPATH:*pathname*	This option specifies where the user's logon script is located.
/TIMES:{*times* ¦ ALL}	This option specifies the user's logon hours. Unless you specify ALL, you must spell out the permitted logon times for every day of the week. Days can be spelled out or abbreviated to three letters; hours can be indicated with either 12- or 24-hour notation. Separate day and time entries with a comma, and days with a semicolon. Don't leave this option blank; if you do, the user will never be able to log on.
/USERCOMMENT:"*text*"	With this option, you can add or change the user comment for the account.
/WORKSTATIONS:{*computername*{,...¦ *}	This option lists up to eight computers where a user can log onto the network. If no list exists or the list is *, the user can log on from any computer.

Procedure

1. Select Start|Programs|Command Prompt.
2. Type the command at the DOS prompt.

Usage

When you're performing this operation on a workstation that does not have NT Server loaded, add the switch /domain to the end of the command to make the command apply to the domain controller of the domain you're in.

NET VIEW

You can use this command to see what's available on the network, how to connect to it, and who's using it. You can't change anything with the NET VIEW command; you only can use it to see the resources being shared on the servers and domains on the network.

Syntax

```
net view [\\computername ¦ ¦domain[:domainname]]
net view /network:nw [\\computername]
```

Procedure

1. Select Start|Programs|Command Prompt.
2. Type the command at the DOS prompt.

Usage

When you type the command on its own, you get a list of the local servers on the domain. When you want to see a list of the resources that the server is sharing with the network, you can append the name of the server that you want to look at to the command. For example, if the server is named Balliol, you would type this:

```
net view \\balliol
```

If you omit the domain name from the command, you see a list of all domains on the network.

APPENDIX C

Migrating to NT from Novell

In the previous two weeks, you learned about installing, exploring, and managing your NT Server. You might now be reading this appendix with trepidation because you've been assigned the odious duty of moving all those die-hard Novell users onto NT, and now you are wishing you had never heard of NT Server.

Novell commands a huge market, and you are in the enviable position of being an administrator for the upstart, NT Server. Over the next few years, we predict that this section of the book will gain popularity as more and more organizations convert to NT. Are we biased? Perhaps. After all, we are writing this book on NT Server. Remember, however, that one of us also wrote the book *Teach Yourself NetWare in 14 Days* for Sams Publishing, so we are not totally biased.

But getting into a flame war over which system is better or which will gain or lose market share is of no benefit right now. If you are reading this appendix, you are likely in the position of needing to move users from NetWare to NT, and that is what we concentrate on for the remainder of the section.

Migrating or Integrating

First you need to decide whether your interest lies in actually moving all NetWare users over to NT and removing NetWare, or whether you are interested in being able to let users access both an NT and a NetWare server. This section relates primarily to moving users from their NetWare system and placing them entirely onto an NT Server with no access to NetWare. First, however, some discussion about mixing the two environments might be appropriate.

NT workstations are able to connect to a NetWare server through the use of the Client Service for NetWare software that comes with NT. This software allows you to set up your NT workstations and let them use both systems as their needs dictate. This is probably the more common scenario, the sharing of both NT and NetWare on the same network.

Using this client software, however, applies only to attaching the workstation to NetWare, leaving users with multiple connections on their desktop machines if they also connect to NT. This setup is fairly easy to achieve, and it allows the user flexibility in deciding which system to access. You can, of course, also use the Novell NT NetWare client software for this purpose. Running dual versions of client software, however, presents problems in maintenance and memory usage and offers no real integration between the two systems.

NT offers another solution, called the Gateway Service, that makes all the NetWare resources become NT Server resources. Using this service, you access NetWare through the NT Server.

Gateway Service

Gateway Service is Microsoft's answer to the dilemma posed by organizations that want to continue using NetWare while also using NT Server. The positive aspects of using this service include the fact that you need supply only one set of client software on each workstation, security can be integrated, and remote access and backup types of services are more integrated.

Microsoft first offered this service around June of 1994, releasing both a Client Service and a Gateway Service for NetWare. The Client Service offers full 32-bit NT software that acts as a NetWare Redirector, allowing the user to remain with an NT workstation and be able to use all the NetWare services and resources available to them. All you need is the client software installed on your NT workstation and a valid NetWare account.

Using the NetWare Gateway Service on your NT Server enables all the NT users to see all of NetWare's resources as NT Server becomes the gateway for accessing NetWare. With this service in place, you are provided with shared remote access and backup services, as well as a more integrated user account, because your users remain NT accounts and the Gateway provides access to NetWare.

The only caveat is that because all your users actually use the same NetWare account, it is difficult to segregate their access permissions. What this means is that any user of the Gateway Service is provided with access rights identical to those of any other user. So this solution might be okay for public access, but it is not acceptable for files or services that require more specialized access levels.

Installing the Gateway Service is fairly straightforward and involves following a few basic steps. First, open the Control Panel on your NT Server, and then open the Network icon. Select the Services tab and then click the Add button. Choose Gateway from the services shown, and provide your installation CD when asked.

On your NetWare server, create a user account for the gateway machine and place it in a special group. Perhaps the group name might be NTGATE. Assign this account the same password that your NT Server account uses so each machine has a similar user account and password.

Next, you'll need to tell the service which server to connect to in the NetWare network if you have more than one server. You can leave this field blank by clicking Cancel and then running the command icon called GSNW (for Gateway Server NetWare, of course). This way, you can select a Preferred Server and Default Tree or Context, depending on whether you are connecting to a 3.x or 4.x NetWare machine. This action allows your server to connect to the NetWare machine and see its resources. Now you need to add the client portion.

Open the GSNW icon again and choose the Gateway option. You need to enable the gateway by choosing that option from the resulting window. Enter the user account and password you created earlier on NetWare. Remember that the password needs to be the same on both NT and NetWare.

After accomplishing this task, add the shares you need by clicking the Add button to bring up a share dialog box. Enter those directories and share names you need, along with their respective locations and comments, and click the OK button to finish. At this point, your NT users are able to connect to NetWare and use the shares you set up for them.

As mentioned earlier, your users obtain access using share-level access, and that means they all use the same level of permissions. Be careful how you set this up and what data becomes available.

When connected, authorized users can run various NetWare commands, including these:

- [ ] `syscon`
- [ ] `slist`
- [ ] `setpass`
- [ ] `rights`
- [ ] `fconsole`
- [ ] `grant`
- [ ] `help`
- [ ] `send`
- [ ] `userlist`
- [ ] `volinfo`
- [ ] `whoami`

Although these commands are not in any particular order and represent only a few of the commands available, they offer a glimpse of some of the more important commands that can be run from your NT machine.

Using this service allows you to utilize the services of both NT and NetWare, in addition to allowing you to migrate users slowly from one system to the other. NT does provide a way for you to eliminate NetWare users and migrate them entirely over to NT. We discuss that tool next.

Using the Migration Tool

Microsoft created the Migration tool to help move user accounts completely off NetWare and onto NT. Unfortunately, it isn't the best solution unless you plan to do a mass migration one weekend and eliminate NetWare. It is, however, the only option at this time, so let's see what it does.

Using the Gateway tool, you can slowly move users from one system to the other. You can manage the move in a couple of ways. First, all new users are placed only on NT so that you end any growth of the problem. To do that, however, you need to ensure that access to the applications and services those users need exists in the NT Server environment, or you'll end up needing to provide access to NetWare if certain applications or services are available only on that machine. This is where the Gateway comes into play.

But suppose you have migrated applications and services, or plan to, and you need to migrate all the users. The migration aid is the only tool available from Microsoft to perform this task.

The Migration tool moves all users and groups onto NT by default. You can modify this setting by selecting the necessary options when running Migration Tool for NetWare. The tool allows you to set up a specific mapping of users so that you can control precisely what happens during the conversion. Needless to say, this process requires a well-defined plan. Alternatively, you can set various options, telling the tool what to do in each conflict.

When you migrate a user account, the user name, password, time restrictions, account and password expiration fields, disabled status, and the user's authorization to change his password (if applicable) are all migrated to the new NT system.

Start Migration Tool for NetWare by choosing the tool in the Administrative Tools Menu in NT Server. You see a window like the one shown in Figure C.1.

Figure C.1.

The opening screen of Migration Tool for NetWare.

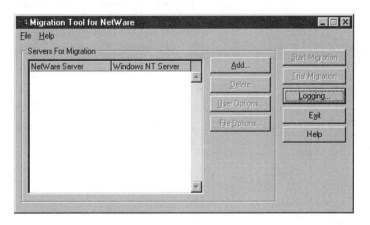

Next, you choose which servers you are going to migrate users from and where you will put those users. The Add button on the Migration tool provides you the option of selecting the two sites, as shown in Figure C.2.

Figure C.2.

Selecting the servers in Migration Tool for NetWare.

Select Servers For Migration   ☒

From NetWare Server: [   ] [...]   [OK]

To Windows NT Server: [   ] [...]   [Cancel]

                                                           [Help]

After you select the servers, the tool shows you the following options:

☐ *Add:* Use this option to select the servers you are moving users to and from as you decide to convert them.

☐ *Delete:* The Delete button allows you to change your mind and remove the previous servers and add different ones.

☐ *Exit:* You leave the program via this option.

☐ *Help:* This button gives you access to the tool's help facility, shown in Figure C.3.

Figure C.3.

The Migration Tool for NetWare Help screen.

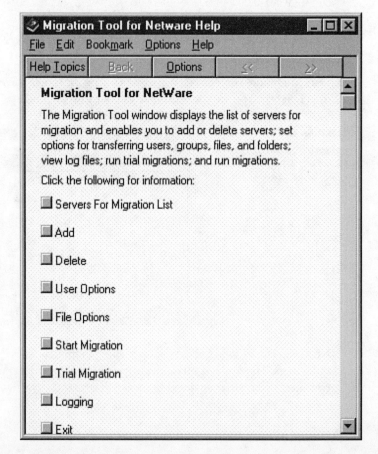

Migration Tool for Netware Help   _ ☐ ☒

File   Edit   Bookmark   Options   Help

[Help Topics] [Back] [Options] [<<] [>>]

Migration Tool for NetWare

The Migration Tool window displays the list of servers for migration and enables you to add or delete servers; set options for transferring users, groups, files, and folders; view log files; run trial migrations; and run migrations.

Click the following for information:

▪ Servers For Migration List

▪ Add

▪ Delete

▪ User Options

▪ File Options

▪ Start Migration

▪ Trial Migration

▪ Logging

▪ Exit

☐ *User Options:* This controls how the migration performs. When selected, it provides several options. First, it lets you decide what Password to assign the new users. Because NetWare will not tell you the current password of a user, you need to assign a new one. Here you decide whether to forego the use of a password, assign one the same as for the user account, or provide a fixed password for all the users.

Next, the Usernames option allows you to set up different options if the Migration tool finds an existing user on the new server that has the same name as one it wants to convert. The tool lets you either log and ignore the fact there is an existing user, overwrite the existing one, or prefix it with a special character string. Choose the option you are comfortable with using. We suggest you consider either logging the fact and dealing with it later or prefixing these users with a special character to identify the accounts and manually resolve them. Either of these choices allows you to deal with the problem after finishing with most of the users.

The Groups option allows you to set up different options if the Migration tool finds an existing group on the new server that has the same name as one it wants to convert. Like the user option, the tool lets you either log and ignore the duplicate entry, overwrite the existing one, or prefix the existing one with a special character string. Choose the option you are comfortable with using. We suggest you consider either logging the duplicate entry and dealing with it later or prefixing those entries with a special character. Either of these choices allows you to deal with the problem after finishing with most of the groups.

Finally, the Defaults option allows you to set up how your account policies are to be handled. These include things such as password expiry, password minimum and maximum lengths, and supervisor privileges. The screen allows you to assign supervisors to the Administrator group if you choose.

☐ *File Options:* This button lets you perform a mass file copy from one server to the new one and lets you decide which files to copy.

☐ *Start Migration:* This is the big one, the whole enchilada, the finale. It starts the process and commits you to the change. Before using this button, consider the Trial button.

☐ *Trial Migration:* This button lets you test what is going to happen with the options that are currently set. You can consider it a dry run or the pilot test. It takes a while to run. The trial run doesn't actually perform the changes, it just informs you of what would have happened. A nice thing about using this is that it gives you a chance to see all the conflicts that will occur and lets you decide whether to take some action before committing to the change.

☐ *Logging:* The Logging button is used to select how the tool should operate.

The first option, Popup On Error, stops the tool each time an error occurs. It's probably not a good idea, because you are likely to have numerous conflicts and this process becomes very time-consuming. A second option, called Verbose User/ Group Logging, lets you record any problems that occur. It's a good idea to set and use this option. The final option is called Verbose File Logging, and it logs each file you copy. Plan to use some sort of additional program to reduce the data provided and find errors or special filenames if you use this option because the amount of data gathered can be extensive.

Using these options and committing the change migrates your users totally of the NetWare machine and onto an NT Server. It is definitely an off-hours or weekend task because most organizations cannot afford to lose access to the server while changes are being made. In addition, each user needs to be trained on the new NT software, and this training needs to be part of the plan you create when deciding to migrate.

Migrating users is a complex and time-consuming project, and care needs to be taken to ensure that users are properly trained, applications are tested and vetted on the new servers, and administrators are aware of the new process for adding and modifying the user accounts and privileges.

Using Directory Service Manager for NetWare

One final note. You might end up running both NetWare and NT Servers on your network temporarily. This dual use is becoming very common also because each server has its pros and cons. How can you manage all the user accounts in such a scenario without the tedious task of logging onto each server and manually trying to manage it? One way is to use Microsoft's tool called Directory Service Manager for NetWare (DSM).

This tool lets you synchronize accounts between the two servers. To use it, you must be running the Gateway services described earlier. You install this service by using Control Panel and opening the Network icon. There, choose Services and click Add. When all the services show, select DSM.

NT creates an account called SyncAgentAccount for DSM to use to log onto the NT Server machine. As with any account, you need to assign a password. Next, you specify the NetWare server you want to synchronize NT with, and then DSM asks you to log onto that server using an administrator account. After you are logged in, you set certain data for DSM to use in managing the synchronization.

The options allow you to force users to change their password the first time they log onto NT and places supervisors into the Administrator Group during conversion. You also set whether file server operators are moved into the NT Console Operators group.

Finally, you set an option that allows you to state which NetWare accounts you want to automatically synchronize with NT. Each time a user changes a password in NT, NT forces a password change for the same account in NetWare. Don't forget to back up the Bindery when asked. Why take a chance that it might get corrupted accidentally? Running DSM then keeps both your NT and your NetWare user account passwords perfectly synchronized.

C

GLOSSARY

access   The ability and the means necessary to approach, to store in or retrieve data from, to communicate with, and to make use of any resource of a computer system.

access category   One of the classes to which a user, a program, or a process in a system can be assigned because of the resources or groups of resources that each user, program, or process is authorized to use.

access control entry (ACE)   An entry in an access control list (ACL). The entry contains a security ID (SID) and a set of access rights. A process with a matching security ID is allowed access rights, denied rights, or allowed rights with auditing.

access control list (ACL)   The part of a security descriptor that enumerates the protection (that is, permission) given to an object.

access control mechanisms   Hardware or software features, operating procedures, management procedures, and various combinations of these designed to detect and prevent unauthorized access and to permit authorized access to a system.

access guidelines   Used here in the sense of guidelines for the modification of specific access rights. A general framework drawn up by the owner or custodian to instruct the data set security administrator on the degree of latitude that exists for the modification of rights of access to a file without the specific authority of the owner or custodian.

access list   A catalog of users, programs, or processes and the specifications of access categories to which each is assigned.

access period   A segment of time, generally expressed daily or weekly, when access rights prevail.

access right   A permission granted to a process to manipulate a particular object in a particular manner (for example, calling a service). Different object types support different access rights, which are stored in the object's access control list (ACL).

access token   An object uniquely identifying a user who has logged on. An access token is attached to all the user's processes and contains the user's security ID (SID), the names of any groups to which the user belongs, any privileges the user owns, the default owner of any objects the user's processes create, and the default access control list (ACL) to be applied to any objects the user's processes create.

access type   An access right to a particular device, program, or file; for example, read, write, execute, append, allocate, modify, delete, create.

access validation   Checking a user's account information to determine when the subject should be granted the right to perform the requested operation.

accessibility   The ease with which information can be obtained.

accidental   Outcome from the lack of care or any situation where the result is negatively different from that intended; for example, poor program design is a result of poor planning.

accountability   The quality or state that enables violations or attempted violations of a system security to be traced to individuals who can then be held responsible.

ACE   The acronym for Access Control Entry. This contains a SID and the associated set of access control permissions for each object.

ACL   The acronym for Access Control List. This is the place where object permissions are kept. ACLs consist of access control entries.

address   A number or group of numbers uniquely identifying a network node within its network (or internetwork).

administrator   The administrator is the person responsible for the operation of the network. The administrator maintains the network, reconfiguring and updating it as the need arises.

alert (1) An audible or visual alarm that signals an error or serves as a warning of some sort. (2) An asynchronous notification that one thread sends to another.

algorithm A step-by-step procedure, usually mathematical, for doing a specific function, for example, a PIN verification algorithm or an encryption algorithm.

American Wire Gauge (AWG) The adopted standard wire sizes, such as No. 12 wire and No. 14 wire. The larger the gauge number of the wire, the smaller the wire; therefore, a No. 14 wire is smaller than a No. 12 wire.

analog A system based on a continuous ratio, such as voltage or current values.

analog transmission A communications scheme using a continuous signal, varied by amplification. Broadband networks use analog transmissions.

analytical attack An attempt to break a code or cipher key by discovering flaws in its encryption algorithm.

ANSI The acronym for American National Standards Institute, which sets standards for many technical fields.

AppleTalk Macintosh native protocol.

application The user's communication with the installation. A software program or program package enabling a user to perform a specific job, such as word processing or electronic mail.

application program/software A program written for or by a user that applies to the user's work.

application programming interface (API) A set of routines that an application program uses to request and carry out lower-level services performed by the operating system.

application system A collection of programs and documentation used for an application.

architecture The general design of hardware or software, including how they fit together.

ARCnet (Attached Resource Computer Network) A local area network scheme developed by Datapoint.

ASCII The acronym for American Standard Code for Information Interchange pronounced "ASK-ee."

assembler A language translator that converts a program written in assembly language into an equivalent program in machine language. The opposite of a disassembler.

assembly language A low-level programming language in which individual machine-language instructions are written in a symbolic form that is easier to understand than machine language itself.

asynchronous   A method of data communications in which transmissions are not synchronized with a signal. Local area networks transmit asynchronously.

attach   To log a workstation into a server. Also, to log a workstation into another file server while the workstation remains logged into the first.

attacks   The method used to commit security violations, such as masquerading and modification.

audit policy   Defines the type of security events logged for a domain or for an individual computer; determines what NT will do when the security log becomes full.

audit trail   A chronological record of system activities sufficient to enable the reconstruction, review, and examination of the sequence of environments and activities surrounding or leading to each event in the path of a transaction from its inception to the output of results.

auditability   The physical or mental power to perform an examination or verification of financial records or accounts.

auditing   The ability to detect and record security-related events, particularly any attempt to create, access, or delete objects. Windows NT uses security IDs (SIDs) to record which processes performed the action.

authenticate   (1) To confirm that the object is what it purports to be. To verify the identity of a person (or other agent external to the protection system) making a request. (2) To identify or verify the eligibility of a station, an originator, or an individual to access specific categories of information.

authentication   The act of identifying or verifying the eligibility of a station, originator, or individual to access specific categories of information.

authorization   The process that grants the necessary and sufficient permissions for the intended purpose.

authorize   To grant the necessary and sufficient permissions for the intended purpose.

automated security monitoring   The use of automated procedures to ensure that the security controls implemented within a system are not circumvented.

back up   To make a spare copy of a disk or of a file on a disk.

backbone   Connection points in a network carrying messages between distributed LANs.

background   A background task or program runs while the user is doing something else. The most common example is a print spooler program. Used in contrast to foreground.

background processing   The action of completing tasks in the background.

backup   A copy of a disk or of a file on a disk.

backup domain controller   For Windows NT Server domains, refers to a computer that receives a copy of the domain's security policy and domain database and authenticates network logons.

backup procedures   The provisions made for the recovery of data files and program libraries, and for restart or replacement of equipment after the occurrence of a system failure or disaster.

bandwidth   The range of frequencies available for signaling; the difference expressed in Hertz between the lowest and highest frequencies of a band.

BASIC (Beginner's All-purpose Symbolic Instruction Code)   A high-level programming language that is easy to use. It is used mainly for microcomputers.

batch   The processing of a group of related transactions or other items at planned intervals.

baud   A unit of signaling speed. The speed in baud is the number of discrete conditions or events per second.

BDC   Backup Domain Controller. A machine that is used to provide a degree of fault tolerance by maintaining a copy of the SAM.

bit   A contraction of the words *binary digit*. The smallest unit of information a computer can hold. The value of a bit (1 or 0) represents a simple two-way choice, such as yes or no, on or off, positive or negative, something or nothing.

board   Chiefly, a term used for the flat circuit board that holds chip sets and other electronic components, and printed conductive paths between the components.

boot   (v) To start by loading the operating system into the computer. Starting is often accomplished by first loading a small program, which then reads a larger program into memory. The program is said to "pull itself up by its own bootstraps"—hence the term "bootstrapping," or "booting." Also means to start a computer or initial program load. (n) The process of starting or resetting a computer.

Boot Protocol (BOOTP)   A protocol used for remotely booting systems on the network.

bps (bits per second)   A unit of data transmission rate.

breach   A break in the system security that results in admittance of a person or program to an object.

bridge   A device used to connect LANs by forwarding packets addressed to other similar networks across connections at the Media Access Control data link level. Routers, which operate at the protocol level, are also called bridges.

broadband   A transmission system in which signals are encoded and modulated into different frequencies and then transmitted simultaneously with other signals.

broadcast   A LAN data transmission scheme in which data packets are heard by all stations on the network.

brute-force attack   A computerized trial-and-error attempt to decode a cipher or password by trying every possible combination. Also known as an *exhaustive attack*.

buffer   A temporary holding area of the computer's memory where information can be stored by one program or device and then read at a different rate by another, for example, a print buffer. Also, the printer's random access memory (RAM), measured in kilobytes. Because computer chips can transfer data much faster than mechanical printer mechanisms can reproduce it, small buffers are generally inserted between the two, to keep the data flow in check.

bug   An error in a program that prevents its working as intended. The expression reportedly comes from the early days of computing when an itinerant moth shorted a connection and caused a breakdown in a room-sized computer.

bulletin board system (BBS)   An electronic system that supports communication via modem among computers. Typically, a bulletin board system supports public and private electronic mail, uploading and downloading of public-domain files, and access to online databases. Large, commercial bulletin board systems, such as AOL, CompuServe, and Prodigy, can support many users simultaneously; smaller, local boards permit only one caller at a time.

bus   A common connection. Networks that broadcast signals to all stations, such as Ethernet and ARCnet, are considered bus networks.

byte   A unit of information having eight bits.

cabling system   The wiring used to connect networked computers together.

CACLS   A command-line program that allows you to modify user permissions by using the DOS command prompt or by placing them within a file and running that file. A handy utility to manage large numbers of changes.

card   Another name for board.

catalog   A list of files stored on a disk or tape. Sometimes called a directory.

CDFS   CD-ROM file system.

central processing unit (CPU)   The "brain" of the computer; the microprocessor performing the actual computations in machine language.

certification   The technical evaluation, made as part of and in support of the accreditation process, establishing the extent that a particular computer system or network design and implementation meet a specified set of security requirements.

channel   An information transfer path within a system. Can also refer to the mechanism by which the path is effected.

character   Letter, numerical, punctuation, or any other symbol contained in a message.

chip   Slang for a silicon wafer imprinted with integrated circuits.

choose   As used in this book, to select or pick an item that begins an action in Windows NT. For example, you often choose a command on a menu to perform a task.

CISC   Complex Instruction Set Computer.

classified   Subject to prescribed asset protection controls, including controls associated with classifications.

classify   To assign a level of sensitivity and priority and, hence, security control to data.

clear text   Information that is in its readable state (before encryption and after decryption).

click   As used in this book, to quickly press and release the mouse button. For example, you often click an icon to start an application.

client   A computer that accesses shared network resources provided by another computer (a server). In a client/server database system, this is the computer (usually a workstation) that makes service requests.

client/server   A network system design in which a processor or computer designated as a server (file server, database server, and so on) provides services to other client processors or computers.

coax   Also known as coaxial, this is a cable that consists of two wires running inside a plastic sheath, insulated from each other.

collision   A garbled transmission resulting from simultaneous transmissions by two or more workstations on the same network cable.

command prompt   The window in NT that provides DOS-like capabilities, letting you enter commands that execute within that window.

commit bytes   The actual amount of memory that all the applications need at any given moment.

communication link   An electrical and logical connection between two devices. On a local area network, a communication link is the point-to-point path between sender and recipient.

communication program   A program that enables the computer to transmit data to and receive data from distant computers through the telephone system.

compartmentalization   The breaking down of sensitive data into small, isolated blocks for reducing the risk to the data.

compiler   A language translator that converts a program written in a high-level programming language (source code) into an equivalent program in some lower-level language, such as machine language (object code) for later execution.

completeness   Having all or necessary parts.

compromise   The loss, misuse, or unauthorized disclosure of a data asset.

computer name   A unique name of up to 15 uppercase characters identifying a computer to the network. The name cannot be the same as any other computer or domain name in the network, and it cannot contain spaces.

condition   An operating situation when a threat arises. The condition is necessary and desirable for operations.

confidential   A protection classification. Loss, misuse, or unauthorized disclosure of data with this protection classification could at most have a major negative impact. Such an incident would be harmful to the organization.

confidentiality   A parameter showing the privacy of the information (used particularly in costing functions involving information that has a security classification or is considered proprietary or sensitive).

configuration   (1) The total combination of hardware components—central processing unit, video display device, keyboard, and peripheral devices—forming a computer system. (2) The software settings allowing various hardware components of a computer system to communicate with each other.

configuration registry   A database repository for information about a computer's configuration, for example, the computer hardware, the software installed on the system, and environment settings and other information entered by persons using the system.

connect time   The amount of time a user connects to the file server.

console   In Windows NT, a text-based window managed by the Win32 subsystem. Environment subsystems direct the output of character-mode applications to consoles.

control codes   Nonprinting computer instructions such as carriage return and line feed.

control program   A program designed to schedule and supervise the performance of data processing work by a computing system.

control set   A complete set of parameters for devices and services in the HKEY_LOCAL_ MACHINE\SYSTEM key in the Registry.

controlled sharing The scope or domain where authorization can be reduced to an arbitrarily small set or sphere of activity.

counter The measurement of activity for a particular object, such as bytes read per second.

crash (n) A malfunction caused by hardware failure or an error in the program. (v) To fail suddenly.

critical Data with this preservation classification is essential to the organization's continued existence. The loss of such data would cause a serious disruption of the organization's operation.

criticality A parameter indicating dependence of the organization on the information.

crosstalk The unwanted transmission of a signal on a channel that interfaces with another adjacent channel. Signal interference created by emissions passing from one cable element to another.

cryptoanalysis The steps and operations performed in converting messages (cipher) into plain text (clear) without initial knowledge of the key employed in the encryption algorithm.

cryptographic system The documents, devices, equipment, and associated techniques that are used as a unit to provide a single means of encryption (enciphering or encoding).

cryptography The transformation of plain text into coded form (encryption) or from coded form into plain text (decryption).

cryptology The field that includes both cryptoanalysis and cryptography.

customer related Identifying or relating specifically to a customer of the organization.

damage Impairment of the worth or usefulness of the information.

data Processable information with the associated documentation. The input that a program and its instructions perform on and that determines the results of processing.

data contamination A deliberate or accidental process or act that results in a change in the integrity of the original data.

data-dependent protection Protection of data at a level commensurate with the sensitivity level of the individual data elements, rather than with the sensitivity of the entire file that includes the data elements.

data diddling Unauthorized alteration of data as it is entered or stored in a computer.

data integrity Verified correspondence between the computer representation of information and the real-world events that the information represents. The condition of being whole, complete, accurate, and timely.

G

data leakage   The theft of data or software.

Data Link Control (DLC)   A printer and host access protocol primarily used by PCs to communicate with IBM minicomputers and mainframes.

data protection   Measures to safeguard data from undesired occurrences that intentionally or unintentionally lead to modification, destruction, or disclosure of data.

data security   The result achieved through implementing measures to protect data against unauthorized events leading to unintentional or intentional modification, destruction, or disclosure of data.

data storage   The preservation of data in various data media for direct use by the system.

database   A collection of information organized in a form that can be readily manipulated and sorted by a computer user.

database management system   A software system for organizing, storing, retrieving, analyzing, and modifying information in a database.

database server   The "back end" processor that manages the database and fulfills database requests in a client/server database system.

debug   A colloquial term that means to find and correct an error or the cause of a problem or malfunction in a computer program. Usually synonymous with troubleshoot.

debugger   A utility program that allows a programmer to see what is happening in the microprocessor and in memory while another program is running.

decipher   To convert, by use of the appropriate key, cipher text (encoded, encrypted) into its equivalent plain text (clear).

dedicated file server   A file server that cannot be used as a user's workstation.

deliberate   Intended to harm. The results of deliberate actions might well be different from those expected by perpetrators or victims, for example, arson and vandalism.

destruction   The act of rendering an asset ineffective or useless. It is a recognizable loss in which the file must be recovered from backup or reconstituted.

device   A generic term for a computer subsystem, such as a printer, serial port, or disk drive. A device frequently requires its own controlling software, called a device driver.

device driver   A software component that enables a computer system to communicate with a device. For example, a printer driver is a device driver that translates computer data into a form understood by the intended printer. In most cases, the driver also manipulates the hardware to transmit the data to the device.

DHCP   The acronym for Dynamic Host Configuration Protocol. This is a tool that allows dynamic IP allocation, simplifying machine configuration in your network.

digital   A system based on discrete states, typically the binary conditions of on or off.

digital transmission   A communications system that passes information encoded as pulses. Baseband networks use digital transmissions, as do microcomputers.

directory   Pictorial, alphabetical, or chronological representation of the contents of a disk. A directory is sometimes called a catalog. The operating system uses it to keep track of the contents of the disk.

disclosure   The act or an instance of revelation or exposure. A disclosure can be obvious, such as the removal of a tape from a library, or it can be concealed, such as the retrieval of a discarded report by an outsider or a disgruntled employee.

discretionary access control (DAC)   The protection that the owner of an object applies to the object by assigning various access rights to various users or groups of users.

disk   A data storage device on which data is recorded on concentric circular tracks on a magnetic medium.

disk drive   An electromechanical device that reads from and writes to disks. Two types of disk drives are in common use: floppy disk drives and hard disk drives.

disk mirroring   The procedure of duplicating a disk partition on two or more disks, preferably on disks attached to separate disk controllers so that data remains accessible when either a disk or a disk controller fails.

disk partition   A logical compartment on a physical disk drive. A single disk might have two or more logical disk partitions, each of which would be referenced with a different disk drive name.

disk striping   The procedure of combining a set of same-sized disk partitions residing on separate disks into a single volume, forming a virtual "stripe" across the disks. This fault-tolerance technique enables multiple I/O operations in the same volume to proceed concurrently.

documentation   A complete and accurate description and authorization of a transaction and each operation a transaction passes through. The written (can be automated) description of a system or program and how it operates.

domain   A collection of computers that share a common domain database and security policy. Each domain has a unique name.

domain controller   The server that authenticates domain logons and maintains the security policy and the master database for a domain.

domain name   A name assigned to a domain.

Domain Name System, or Server (DNS)   A distributed database system that allows TCP/IP applications to resolve a host name into a correct IP address.

double-click   As used in this book, to quickly press and release the mouse button twice without moving the mouse. Double-clicking is a means of rapidly selecting and activating a program or program feature.

download   To transfer a file from a large computer or BBS to a personal computer. To upload is to perform the opposite operation.

driver   A hardware device or a program that controls or regulates another device.

DUN   The acronym for Dial-Up Networking. Easy to confuse with RAS because it is the newer version of RAS and it performs the same function. We think it was renamed to provide some consistency with Windows 95 terms.

duplexing   The concept of using two disk drives and two disk controllers to store data, one serving as primary and the other for backup purposes.

Dynamic Host Configuration Protocol (DHCP)   The protocol used by a server to dynamically allocate IP addresses on a network. Designed to allow networked hosts to access configuration information across the network, instead of having to be configured by hand directly.

eavesdropping   Unauthorized interception of data transmissions.

EISA   Enhanced Industry Standard Architecture. An older system data transfer bus architecture that was designed to manage 8-, 16- and 32-bit data transfers. Widely used; most expansion cards support this architecture.

embarrassment   A parameter indicating the sensitivity of an organization to public knowledge of the information.

employee related   Identifying or relating specifically to an employee of the organization.

emulation   The imitation of a computer system, performed by a combination of hardware and software, that allows programs to run between incompatible systems.

encipher   To convert plain text (clear) into unintelligible form by a cipher system.

enterprise-network   A network bringing all sites together through a communications medium.

error log   An audit trail of system warning messages displayed for the file server.

Ethernet   A local area network protocol developed by Xerox.

event   Any significant occurrence in the system or in an application that requires users to be notified, or an entry to be added to a log.

event log service   A service that records events in the system, security, and application logs.

expected lifetime   A parameter indicating the length of time the information is operative or has value to its owners.

exposure   A quantitative rating (in dollars per year) expressing the organization's vulnerability to a given risk.

extended partition   Free space on a hard disk that is used to allow the disk to be further partitioned into logical partitions or drives.

fail safe   The automatic termination and protection of programs or other processing operations when a hardware or software failure is detected in a system.

fail soft   The selective termination of affected non-essential processing when a hardware or software failure is detected in a system.

FAT   The name given to the DOS file system. FAT stands for file allocation table and refers to the method of managing the files and directories on the DOS system.

fault tolerance   A computer and operating system's capability to respond gracefully to catastrophic events, such as a power outage or hardware failure. Usually, fault tolerance implies the capability either to continue the system's operation without loss of data or to shut down the system and restart it, recovering all processing in progress when the fault occurred.

fiber-optic cable   A cable constructed using a thin glass core that conducts light rather than electrical signals.

field   A particular type or category of information in a database management program, for example, a variable. A location in a record where a particular type of data is stored.

file   A single, named collection of related information stored on a magnetic medium.

file allocation table (FAT)   A table or list maintained by some operating systems, such as MS-DOS, to keep track of the status of various segments of disk space used for file storage.

file attribute   A restrictive label attached to a file that describes and regulates its use, for example, archive, hidden, read-only, and system.

file server   A computer that shares files with other computers. Also, a computer that provides network stations with controlled access to shareable resources.

file size   The length of a file, typically given in bytes.

file system   In an operating system, the overall structure by which files are named, stored, and organized.

format   The process of setting up a drive space to allow an operating system to use the space. Each operating system, such as MAC, DOS, and NT, uses distinct file system formats, and a drive must be formatted in order for the system to be able to use it.

FTP   File transfer protocol. A program that enables clients to transfer files between computers.

Fully Qualified Domain Name (FQDN)   The complete host name and domain name of a network host.

gateway   A device that provides routing and protocol conversion among physically dissimilar networks and computers, for example, LAN to host, LAN to LAN, X.25, and SNA gateways. That is, a multihomed host used to route network traffic from one network to another. Also used to pass network traffic from one protocol to another.

grant   To authorize.

GUI   Graphical user interface.

hacker   A computer enthusiast; also, one who seeks to gain unauthorized access to computer systems.

handshaking   A dialog between a user and a computer, a computer and another computer, a program and another program for identifying a user and authenticating his identity, through a sequence of questions and answers based on information either previously stored in the computer or supplied to the computer by the initiator of the dialog. Also, when used in context, it refers to the controlled movement of bits between a computer and a printer.

hardware   In computer terminology, the machinery that forms a computer system.

hardware abstraction layer (HAL)   A dynamic link library that encapsulates platform-dependent code.

HCL   Microsoft's Hardware Compatibility List. This is a list of all hardware that is certified to run with NT. You can find the list on the Internet at the following address:

```
http://www.microsoft.com/ntserver/hcl/hclintro.htm
```

hertz (Hz)   A measure of frequency or bandwidth. The same as cycles per second.

hierarchical database   A database organized in a treelike structure.

High Performance File System (HPFS)   The file system designed for OS/2 Version 1.2.

host computer   The computer that receives information from and sends data to terminals over telecommunication lines. It is also the computer that is in control in a data communication network. The host computer can be a mainframe computer, minicomputer, or microcomputer.

host name resolution   The process of determining a network address when presented with a network host name and domain name, usually by consulting the Domain Name System.

HPFS   The acronym for High Performance File System, provided by OS/2 operating systems. Files in this format can be read by NT.

hub   (1) A device used on certain network topologies that modifies transmission signals, allowing the network to be lengthened or expanded with additional workstations. The hub is the central device in a star topology. (2) A computer that receives messages from other computers, stores them, and routes them to other computer destinations.

I/O device (input/output device)   A device that transfers information into or out of a computer.

icon   In graphical environments, a small graphics image displayed on-screen to represent an object that can be manipulated by the user; for example, a recycle bin can represent a command for deleting unwanted text or files.

IDE   The acronym for Integrated Drive Electronics, the older disk drive architecture that usually integrates directly with the disk drive instead of using a separate card.

identification   The process that enables, generally using unique machine-readable names, recognition of users or resources as identical with those previously described to a system.

IEEE (Institute of Electrical and Electronic Engineers)   One of several groups whose members are drawn from industry and who attempt to establish industry standards. The IEEE 802 committee has published numerous definitive documents on local area network standards.

information   Includes input, output, software, data, and all related documentation.

information pool   Consists of data designated as accessible by authorized individuals.

initialize   (1) To set to an initial state or value in preparation for some computation. (2) To prepare a blank disk to receive information by organizing its surface into tracks and sectors; same as format.

input/output (I/O)   The process by which information is transferred between the computer's memory and its keyboard or peripheral devices.

instance   An NT term relating to particular tasks in each object. Objects often have more than one instance, such as the Processor and its %Interrupt Time or %User Time or %Processor Time.

integrity   Freedom from errors.

G

interface   A device or program that allows two systems or devices to communicate with each other. An interface provides a common boundary between the two systems, devices, or programs. Also, the cables, connectors, and electrical circuits allowing communication between computers and printers.

interrupt request lines (IRQ)   Hardware lines over which devices can send signals to get the attention of the processor when the device is ready to accept or send information. Typically, each device connected to the computer uses a separate IRQ.

intruder   A user or another agent attempting to gain unauthorized access to the file server.

IP address   A 32-bit network address that uniquely locates a host or network within its internetwork.

ISDN   Another acronym. This one stands for Integrated Services Digital Network, which is becoming popular with home users as well as business. This type of service is more difficult to set up than other techniques, but it offers up to 128Kbps speed. This is a significant boost over modems that offer 33.6Kbps or even the newer 56Kbps speeds.

ISP   The acronym for Internet Service Provider, a firm that offers connections to the Internet for a fee.

job   A combined run of one or more application programs that are automatically processed in sequence in the computer.

kernel   The core of an operating system. The portion of the system that manages memory, files, and peripheral devices; maintains the time and date; launches applications; and allocates system resources.

key   In the Registry, one of five subtrees. Each key can contain value entries and additional subkeys. A key is analogous to a directory, and a value entry is analogous to a file. In cryptography, a sequence of symbols that controls the operations of encryption and decryption.

least privilege   A principle that users should be assigned only the access needed to perform their business functions.

local area network (LAN)   A communications system using directly connected computers, printers, and hard disks, allowing shared access to all resources on the network.

Local Security Authority (LSA)   An integral subsystem of the Windows NT security system. The LSA manages the local security policy and provides interactive user authentication services. It also controls the generation of audit messages and enters audit messages into the audit log file. Creates a security access token for each user accessing the system.

logic bomb   Malicious action, initiated by software, that inhibits the normal system functions; a logic bomb takes effect only when specified conditions occur.

logical access   Access to the information content of a record or field.

logical file   Refers to the data that a file contains.

logical partition   A subpartition of an extended partition on a drive, commonly called a logical drive. See *extended partition*.

login   The process of accessing a file server or computer after physical connection has been established.

logon   The process of identifying oneself to a computer after connecting to it over a communications line. During a logon procedure, the computer usually requests the user's name and a password. Also called login.

mainframe   The term used for very large computers that support thousands of users and huge databases.

map   (1) To assign a workstation drive letter to a server directory. (2) To translate a virtual address into a physical address.

Media Access Control (MAC)   Part of the physical layer of a network that identifies the actual physical link between two nodes.

menu   A list of options from which users select.

menu option   An option on a menu that performs some action, prompts the user for additional information, or leads to another menu.

microcomputer   A general term referring to a small computer having a microprocessor.

mirroring   A method of ensuring data replication using two hard drives that are connected to the same disk controller. Less robust than duplexing because of the shared controller. Otherwise, duplexing and mirroring can be considered to be essentially the same thing.

modem   A modulator-demodulator. A device that lets computers communicate over telephone lines by converting digital signals into the phone system's analog signals and vice versa.

modification   The partial alteration of an asset such that the form or quality of it has been changed somewhat. A file can appear intact and can be perfectly usable, but it can contain erroneous information.

monitoring   The use of automated procedures to ensure that the controls implemented within a system are not circumvented.

multihomed   A computer that has more than one network card, either physically or logically. Often used as a router for connecting two networks.

G

need-to-know   The necessity for access to, knowledge of, or possession of sensitive information to fulfill official duties. Responsibility for determining whether a person's duties require that he have access to certain information, and whether he is authorized to receive it, rests on the owner of the information involved and not on the prospective recipient.

NetBIOS Extended User Interface (NetBEUI)   A small, fast protocol that requires little memory but is not routable.

network   A collection of inter-connected, individually controlled computers, printers, and hard disks, with the hardware and software used to connect them.

network adapter   A circuit board that plugs into a slot in a PC and has one or more sockets to which you attach cables. Provides the physical link between the PC and the network cable. Also called network adapter card, network card, and network interface card (NIC).

network address   A unique identifier of an entity on a network, usually represented as a number or series of numbers.

Network Basic Input/Output Operating System (NetBIOS)   A network file-sharing application designed for use with PC DOS personal computers, usually implemented under TCP/IP at the application layer.

network drive   An online storage device available to network users.

network interface card   See *network adapter*.

network operating system   An operating system installed on a server in a local area network that coordinates the activities of providing services to the computers and other devices attached to the network.

network station   Any PC or other device connected to a network by means of a network interface board and some communications medium. A network station can be a workstation, bridge, or server.

node   A point of interconnection to a network. Normally, a point at which a number of terminals are located.

nonce   A 16-byte challenge issued by the authentication service.

NT File System (NTFS)   A file system designed for use with Windows NT. NTFS supports file system recovery and extremely large storage media.

NTFS   An NT file system acronym for New Technology File System. The particular way data is stored on an NT system if chosen over the FAT or HPFS file systems.

object   (1) A single runtime instance of a Windows NT defined object type containing data that can be manipulated only by use of a set of services provided for objects of its type. (2) Any piece of information, created by a Windows-based application with object linking and embedding capabilities, that can be linked or embedded into another document. (3) A passive entity that contains or receives data. Access to an object potentially implies access to the information it contains.

object handle   Includes access control information and a pointer to the object itself. Before a process can manipulate a Windows NT object, it first must acquire a handle to the object through the Object Manager.

object linking and embedding (OLE)   A way to transfer and share information between applications.

offline   State in which the printer is not ready to receive data.

operating system   Software that controls the internal operations (housekeeping chores) of a computer system. Operating systems are specific to the type of computer used.

owner   An employee or agent of the client who is assigned responsibility for making and communicating certain judgments and decisions regarding business control and selective protection of assets, and for monitoring compliance with specified controls.

package   A generic term referring to any group of detailed computer programs necessary to achieve a general objective. For example, an accounts receivable package would include all programs necessary to record transactions in customer accounts, produce customer statements, and so forth.

packet   A group of bits transmitted as a whole on a network.

pad   The short term for packet assembler-dissembler used in X.25 technologies.

paging   The act of moving data to disk when physical memory is full. A component of virtual memory.

parallel interface   A printer interface that handles data in parallel fashion, eight bits (one byte) at a time.

parity bit   A way of marking the eighth bit in a data byte so that 7-bit ASCII characters between 0 and 127 are sent and received correctly. There are three kinds of parity: odd, even, and none.

partition   A portion of a physical disk that functions as though it were a separate unit.

password   Privileged information given to, or created by, the user, which is entered into a system for authentication purposes. A protected word or secret character string used to authenticate the claimed identity of an individual, a resource, or an access type.

PCI   A 32-bit data transfer bus used in newer machines and generally faster than the older EISA bus. Most Intel machines built today support this standard.

PDC   Primary Domain Controller. The machine that provides user authentication for the NT network.

penetration   A successful unauthorized access to a system.

peripheral   Any device used for input/output operations with the computer's central processing unit (CPU). Peripheral devices are typically connected to the microcomputer with special cabling and include such devices as modems and printers.

permission   (1) A particular form of allowed access, for example, permission to read as contrasted with permission to write. (2) A rule associated with an object (usually a directory, file, or printer) to regulate which users can access the object and in what manner.

physical drive   The actual hardware that is set in the computer and used to store information. Often called the hard drive, C drive, or D drive after the letter assigned to it by the system.

physical security   Physical protection of assets achieved through implementing security measures.

PING   A network application that uses UDP to verify reachability of another host on any internetwork.

plain text   Intelligible text or signals that have meaning and that can be read or acted on without the application of any decryption.

polling   A means of controlling devices on a line.

port   (1) A connection or socket used to connect a device to a computer, such as a printer, monitor, or modem. Information is sent from the computer to the device through a cable. (2) A communications channel through which a client process communicates with a protected subsystem. Ports are implemented as Windows NT objects.

primary domain controller   For Windows NT Server domains, the server that authenticates domain logons and maintains the security policy and the master domain database.

principal   The entity in a computer system to which authorizations are granted; thus, the unit of accountability in a computer system.

print queue   A shared storage area on the file server where the system sends every print job before sending to the print server.

print server   Software that takes jobs from the print queue and sends them to the printer.

privileges   A means of protecting the use of certain system functions that can affect system resources and integrity. System managers grant privileges according to the user's needs and deny them to restrict the user's access to the system. See *need-to-know*.

processing A systematic sequence of operations performed on data.

protocol A set of characters at the beginning and end of a message that enables two computers to communicate with each other.

queue A first-in/first-out data structure, used for managing requests to process data; for example, files to be printed.

RAS The acronym for Remote Access Services. This is the NT 3.*x* version of Dial-Up Networking; it is used to connect machines together via telephone or other means.

read A fundamental operation that results only in the flow of information from an object to a subject.

read access Permission to read data.

read-only A term used to describe information stored in such a way that it can be played back (read) but not changed (written).

record A collection of related information that is treated as one unit within a file.

redirector Networking software that accepts I/O requests for remote files, named pipes, or mail slots and then sends (redirects) them to a network server on another machine. Redirectors are implemented as file system drivers in Windows NT.

Registry As used here, the database repository for information about the computer's configuration, including the hardware, installed software, environment settings, and other information.

Registry Editor An application provided with Windows NT that allows users to view and edit entries in the Registry.

remote administration Administration of one computer by an administrator located at another computer and connected to the first computer across the network.

repeater A device that extends the range of a network cable segment.

Request for Comments (RFC) The official designation of the Internet standards documents.

resource In a system, any function, device, or data collection that can be allocated to users or programs.

resource sharing The concurrent use of a resource by more than one user, job, or program.

revoke To take away previously authorized access from some principal.

rights User capabilities given for accessing files and directories on a file server.

ring A network topology that connects each workstation in a circular fashion and sends the network signal in a unidirectional manner through the circle.

RISC Reduced Instruction Set Computer.

risk The potential that a given threat has of occurring within a specific period. The potential for realization of unwanted, negative consequences of an event.

risk analysis An analysis of system assets and vulnerabilities to establish an expected loss from certain events based on estimated probabilities of the occurrence of those events.

router A Layer 3 device that connects two or more networks together.

scavenging Randomly searching for valuable data in a computer's memory or in discarded or incompletely erased magnetic media.

SCSI The acronym for Small Computer Standard Interface. Originally designed for the UNIX world, it is designed to handle high speeds and multiple devices, such as disk and tape drives.

security Protection of all those resources that the client uses to complete its mission.

Security Account Manager (SAM) A Windows NT protected subsystem that maintains the SAM database and provides an application programming interface (API) for accessing the database.

security descriptor A data structure attached to an object that protects the object from unauthorized access. It contains an access control list (ACL) and controls auditing on the object.

Security ID (SID) A unique name that identifies a logged-on user to the security system. Security IDs can identify one user or a group of users.

security policy The set of laws, rules, and practices that regulate how an organization manages, protects, and distributes sensitive information. For Windows NT, the security policies consist of the Account, User Rights, and Audit Policies, and they are managed using User Manager for Domains.

Security Reference Manager (SRM) A Windows NT Server security subsystem that authenticates user logons and protects system resources.

sensitive A data classification category. Loss, misuse, or unauthorized disclosure of data with this protection classification would have a serious negative impact. Such an incident would be very harmful to the organization.

sensitive program An application program whose misuse through unauthorized activity could lead to serious misappropriation or loss of assets.

sensitivity   The characteristic of a resource that implies its value or importance and can include its vulnerability.

serial interface   A printer interface that handles data in serial fashion, one bit at a time.

server   A computer that shares its resources, such as files and printers, with other computers on a network.

Server Manager   An application used to view and administer domains, workgroups, and computers.

share name   The name of a shared resource.

shared directory   A directory where network users can connect.

shielding   Protective covering that eliminates electromagnetic and radio frequency interference.

SID   A unique identifier maintained internally by NT that identifies a user or group of users to the system.

small computer system interface (SCSI)   A standard used for connecting microcomputers to peripheral devices, such as hard disks and printers, and to other computers and local area networks.

sneaker   A computer professional who seeks to test security by attempting to gain unauthorized access to computer systems.

software   Programs and routines to be loaded temporarily into a computer system, for example, compilers, utilities, and operating system and application programs.

stack   As used in this book, a synonym for protocol.

star   A topology in which each node is connected to a central hub.

subject   The combination of the user's access token and the program acting on the user's behalf. Windows NT uses subjects to track and manage permissions for the programs each user runs.

submenu   A menu below the main menu.

subnet   A physical or logical subdivision of a TCP/IP network; usually a separate physical segment that uses a division of the site's IP network address to route traffic within the organizational internetwork.

TCP/IP   Transmission Control Protocol/Internet Protocol. This is the protocol suite that drives the Internet. Very basically, TCP handles the message details and IP manages the addressing. It is probably the most widely used network protocol in the world today.

TCSEC   The Trusted Computer System Evaluation Criteria.

telecommunication   The electronic transfer of information via telephone lines from computer to computer. See *bulletin board system, modem.*

telnet   A program that allows terminal emulation for communicating between machines.

TFTP   A simpler version of the FTP program that operates using UDP/IP services.

threat   One or more events that can lead to either intentional or unintentional modification, destruction, or disclosure of data. If this eventuality were to occur, it would lead to an undesirable effect on the environment.

Token Ring   A network topology regulated by the passing of a token that governs the right to transmit.

topology   The physical layout of the network cabling.

transaction   A set of operations that completes a unified task.

transient   An abrupt change in voltage, of short duration.

transmission-on/transmission-off (X-ON/X-OFF)   A type of software handshaking.

trapdoor   A set of special instructions, originally created for testing and troubleshooting, that bypasses security procedures and allows direct access to a computer's operating system or to other software.

Trojan Horse   A program, purporting to do useful work, that conceals instructions to breach security whenever the software is invoked.

trust relationship   Links between domains that enable passthrough authentication, in which a user only has one user account in one domain yet can access the entire network. A trusting domain honors the logon authentications of a trusted domain.

twisted pair   A common type of wiring that uses two wires twisted together yet insulated from each other. Can be purchased shielded or unshielded.

UDP   The User Datagram Protocol, an older protocol that does not offer good error detection or recovery. It is used by SNMP and TFTP, as well as the Network File System (NFS).

unbounded media   Media that use radio frequencies, microwaves, or other media to transmit data.

Unicode   A fixed-width, 16-bit character encoding standard that is capable of representing all the world's scripts.

user Used imprecisely to refer to the individual who is accountable for some identifiable set of activities in a computer system.

user group A computer club in which computer users exchange tips and information, publish a newsletter, support a local BBS, and listen to sales pitches from vendors at meetings. A meeting of like-minded individuals who practice information sharing, for example, GUIDE, SHARE, DECUS, ISSA, and EDPAA.

User Manager A Windows NT Workstation tool used to manage the security for a computer. Administers user accounts, groups, and security policies.

User Manager for Domains A Windows NT Workstation tool used to manage the security for a domain or an individual computer. Administers user accounts, groups, and security policies.

User Rights policy Manages the assignment of rights to groups and user accounts.

utilities Useful programs with which you can rename, copy, format, delete, and otherwise manipulate files and volumes.

verification Confirmation that the object is what it purports to be. Also, confirmation of the identity of a person (or other agent external to the protection system) making a request.

virtual memory Combines the physical RAM available in the machine with disk space to simulate an environment in which you have more memory than you physically have in RAM. NT tries to assess what parts of memory are least likely to be used and pages this information out to the disk area until it is needed.

virus A program, usually a Trojan Horse, that copies itself into new databases and computers whenever the infected parent program is invoked.

volume A storage device, such as a disk pack, mass storage system cartridge, or magnetic tape. For our purposes, diskettes, cassettes, mag cards, and the like are treated as volumes.

volume set A collection of partitions possibly spread over several disk drives that has been formatted for use as if it were a single drive.

vulnerability The cost that an organization would incur if an event were to happen.

wideband A communications channel that has greater bandwidth than voice-grade lines.

Windows Internet Naming Service (WINS) A service that translates Windows computer names (or NetBIOS names) to IP addresses.

wiretapping Monitoring or recording data as it moves across a communications link; also known as traffic analysis.

G

workstation   In general, a powerful computer having considerable calculating and graphics capability. For Windows NT, computers running the Windows NT Workstation operating system are called workstations, as distinguished from computers running Windows NT Server, which are called servers.

worm   A program that deletes data from a computer's memory.

WOW   Windows on Win32.

write   A fundamental operation that results only in the flow of data from a subject to an object.

write access   Permission to write an object.

X.25   A protocol that allows you to route information through a packet-switching public data network, such as Datapac. An older technology, it operates at a top speed of 64Kbps, and it was designed for earlier days when telephone networks were less reliable than today.

INDEX

A

MACMILLAN COMPUTER PUBLISHING USA

A VIACOM COMPANY

Technical Support:

If you need assistance with the information in this book, please access the Knowledge Base on our Web site at **http://www.superlibrary.com/general/support**. Our most Frequently Asked Questions are answered there. If you do not find the answer to your questions on our Web site, you may contact Macmillan Technical Support **(317) 581-3833** or e-mail us at **support@mcp.com**.

Robert Cowart's Windows NT 4 Unleashed, Professional Reference Edition

Robert Cowart

This is the only reference Windows NT administrators need to learn how to configure their NT systems for maximum performance, security, and reliability. This comprehensive reference explains how to install, maintain, and configure an individual workstation, as well as connect computers to the peer-to-peer networking. Includes comprehensive advice for setting up and administering an NT Server network, and focuses on the new and improved administration and connectivity features of version 4.0.

CD-ROM includes source code, utilities, and sample applications from the book.

Covers Windows NT 4 Server and Workstation.

Operating Systems

$59.99 USA/$84.95 CDN *1,400 pp.* *Intermediate–Expert*
0-672-31001-5 *7 3/8×9 1/8* *03/01/97*

Windows NT 4 Server Unleashed

Jason Garms, et al.

Windows NT Server has been gaining tremendous market share over Novell NetWare, and the new upgrade—which includes a Windows 95 interface—is sure to add momentum to its market drive. *Windows NT 4 Server Unleashed* is written to meet that growing market. It provides information on disk and file management, integrated networking, BackOffice integration, and TCP/IP protocols.

CD-ROM includes source code from the book and valuable utilities.

Focuses on using Windows NT as an Internet server.

Covers security issues and Macintosh support.

Networking

$59.99 USA/$84.95 CDN *1,100 pp.* *Accomplished–Expert*
0-672-30933-5 *7 3/8×9 1/8* *08/01/96*

Windows NT 4 Workstation Unleashed

Sean Mathias, et al.

NT Workstation is expected to become the platform of choice for corporate America! This new edition focuses on NT Workstation's new and improved features as a high-end graphics workstation and scaleable development platform. Provides in-depth advice on installing, configuring, and managing Windows NT Workstation.

Features comprehensive, detailed advice for NT.

CD-ROM includes Windows NT utilities, demos, and more.

Covers Windows NT 4 Workstation.

Operating Systems

$39.99 USA/$56.95 CDN *696 pp.* *Accomplished–Expert*
0-672-30972-6 *7 3/8×9 1/8* *11/01/96*

Peter Norton's Complete Guide to Windows NT 4 Workstation

Peter Norton & John Paul Mueller

Readers will explore everything from interface issues to advanced topics, such as client/server networking, building their own Internet server, and OLE.

Readers will master complex memory management techniques.

Teaches how to build an Internet server.

Explores peer-to-peer networking.

Operating Systems

$39.99 USA/$56.95 CDN *936 pp.* *Casual–Accomplished*
0-672-30901-7 *7 3/8×9 1/8* *07/01/96*

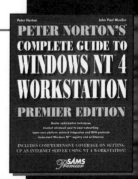

Programming Windows NT 4 Unleashed

David Hamilton, Mickey Williams, & Griffith Kadnier

Readers get a clear understanding of the modes of operation and architecture for Windows NT. Everything—including execution models, processes, threads, DLLs, memory, controls, security, and more—is covered with precise detail.

CD-ROM contains source code and completed sample programs from the book.

Teaches OLE, DDE, drag and drop, OCX development, and the component gallery.

Explores Microsoft BackOffice programming. *Programming*

$59.99 USA/$84.95 CDN	*1,200 pp.*	*Accomplished–Expert*
0-672-30905-X	*7 3/8×9 1/8*	*08/01/96*

Building an Intranet with Windows NT 4

Scott Zimmerman

This hands-on guide teaches readers how to set up and maintain an efficient intranet with Windows NT. It comes complete with a selection of the best software for setting up a server, creating content, and developing intranet applications.

CD-ROM includes a complete Windows NT intranet toolkit with a full-featured Web server, Web content development tools, and ready-to-use intranet applications.

Includes complete specifications for several of the most popular intranet applications—group scheduling, discussions, database access, and more.

Covers Windows NT 4.0. *Internet—Intranets*

$49.99 USA/$70.95 CDN	*600 pp.*	*Casual–Accomplished*
1-57521-137-8	*7 3/8×9 1/8*	*08/01/96*

Windows NT 4 Web Development

Sanjaya Hettihewa

Windows NT and Microsoft's newly developed Internet Information Server are making it easier and more cost-effective to set up, manage, and administer a good Web site. Because the Windows NT environment is relatively new, there are few books on the market that adequately discuss its full potential. *Windows NT 4 Web Development* addresses that potential by providing information on all key aspects of server setup, maintenance, design, and implementation.

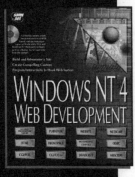

CD-ROM contains valuable source code and powerful utilities.

Teaches how to incorporate new technologies into your Web site.

Covers Java, JavaScript, Internet Studio, and VBScript.

Covers Windows NT. *Internet—Programming*

$59.99 USA/$84.95 CDN	*744 pp.*	*Accomplished–Expert*
1-57521-089-4	*7 3/8×9 1/8*	*07/01/96*

Peter Norton's Guide to Windows 95/NT 4 Programming with MFC

Peter Norton & Rob McGregor

Following in the wake of the best-selling *Peter Norton* series, this book gives the reader a "rapid tour-guide" approach to programming Windows 95 applications. The reader will learn to use, change, and augment the functions of the MFC library.

Readers will use the Microsoft Foundation Class libraries to get the information they need to begin programming immediately.

Covers latest version of MFC for Windows 95/NT 4. *Programming*

$49.99 USA/$70.95 CDN	*1,200 pp.*	*New–Casual*
0-672-30900-9	*7 3/8×9 1/8*	*10/01/96*

Add to Your Sams Library Today with the Best Books for Programming, Operating Systems, and New Technologies

The easiest way to order is to pick up the phone and call

1-800-428-5331

between 9:00 a.m. and 5:00 p.m. EST.
For faster service please have your credit card available.

ISBN	Quantity	Description of Item	Unit Cost	Total Cost
0-672-31001-5		Robert Cowart's Windows NT Unleashed, Professional Reference Edition (Book/CD-ROM)	$59.99	
0-672-30933-5		Windows NT 4 Server Unleashed (Book/CD-ROM)	$59.99	
0-672-30972-6		Windows NT 4 Workstation Unleashed (Book/CD-ROM)	$39.99	
0-672-30901-7		Peter Norton's Complete Guide to Windows NT 4 Workstation	$39.99	
0-672-30905-X		Programming Windows NT 4 Unleashed (Book/CD-ROM)	$59.99	
1-57521-137-8		Building an Intranet with Windows NT 4 (Book/CD-ROM)	$49.99	
1-57521-089-4		Windows NT 4 Web Development (Book/CD-ROM)	$59.99	
0-672-30900-9		Peter Norton's Guide to Windows 95/NT 4 Programming with MFC (Book/CD-ROM)	$49.99	
		Shipping and Handling: See information below.		
		TOTAL		

❑ 3½" Disk

❑ 5¼" Disk

Shipping and Handling: $4.00 for the first book, and $1.75 for each additional book. Floppy disk: Add $1.75 for shipping and handling. If you need to have it NOW, we can ship the product to you in 24 hours for an additional charge of approximately $18.00, and you will receive your item overnight or in two days. Overseas shipping and handling adds $2.00 per book and $8.00 for up to three disks. Prices subject to change. Call for availability and pricing information on latest editions.

201 W. 103rd Street, Indianapolis, Indiana 46290

1-800-428-5331 — Orders   1-800-835-3202 — Fax   1-800-858-7674 — Customer Service

More Than 100 Things to Do with NT Server 4.0